ON THE
# WARPATH
IN THE
# PACIFIC

Jocko Clark on the flag bridge of the *Hornet* surveying his sprawling carrier task group during the Pacific war. The ships are so spread out that only one is seen in the picture. *U.S. Navy photo*

# ON THE
# WARPATH
# IN THE
# PACIFIC

ADMIRAL **JOCKO CLARK**
AND THE FAST CARRIERS

# CLARK G. REYNOLDS

Naval Institute Press
Annapolis, Maryland

Naval Institute Press
291 Wood Road
Annapolis, MD 21402

Library of Congress Cataloging-in-Publication Data

Reynolds, Clark G.
   On the warpath in the Pacific : Admiral Jocko Clark and the fast carriers / Clark G. Reynolds.
      p. cm.
   Includes bibliographical references and index.
   ISBN 1-59114-716-6 (alk. paper)
   1. Clark, Joseph James, 1893–1971.   2. Admirals—United States—Biography.
3. United States. Navy—Biography.   4. World War, 1939–1945—Naval operations, American.   5. World War, 1939–1945—Pacific Area.   6. Aircraft carriers—Pacific Area—History—20th century.   7. World War, 1939–1945—Aerial operations.
8. United States. Navy—Aviation—History—20th century.   I. Title.
   E746.C55R49 2005
   940.54'5973'092—dc22

                                                                                    2005010431

Unless otherwise noted, all photographs are official U.S. Navy photos or snapshots provided by the Clark family.

Cherokee Indian basket design courtesy of the National Museum of the American Indian, Washington, D.C.

Printed in the United States of America on acid-free paper ∞
12  11  10  09  08  07  06  05     9  8  7  6  5  4  3  2
First printing

For *Connie*
Superb and patient typist,
proofreader, and copyeditor
as well as
wonderful wife and excellent mother
of our three fine children

# Contents

# A NOTE ON CITATIONS

ALL DIRECT QUOTATIONS OF ADMIRAL CLARK, UNLESS OTH-erwise noted, are from his recorded interviews by the Naval Photographic Center (some of which are on the CD accompanying this book), the Columbia University Oral History Program, and interviews that I conducted during the 1960s. Some of them were previously published in his 1967 autobiography, *Carrier Admiral* (on which I was his collaborator/ghostwriter).

Chapters 1 through 4 are based on these interviews, as well as on genealogical records provided by his family (both listed in the bibliography). Endnote citations of specific sources do not begin until chapter 3. All cited publications appear in abbreviated form (author, short title, page number) at the end of sentences within the text. Each source is listed in complete form in the bibliography.

Quoted remarks and observations by all other persons—unless otherwise noted in the text—are taken verbatim from tape-recorded interviews of the individual quoted; all interviews are listed in the bibliography. Those conducted by the U.S. Naval Institute have been transcribed and given page numbers. Those conducted by the author were not given page numbers.

No directly quoted statements have been fabricated by the author.

# PREFACE

JOSEPH JAMES "JOCKO" CLARK WAS THE FIRST PERSON OF AMERICAN Indian descent to attain the four-star rank of full admiral in the U.S. Navy. His Cherokee roots helped shape his character as one of the most respected, even beloved, fighting skippers and admirals in the Pacific war against Japan.

My first memory of him was his toiling away in a large backyard vegetable garden in San Diego, in much the same manner as he had done as a boy in the Indian Territory (later Oklahoma). The year was 1951, and I was visiting Clark's home with my uncle Bob. The Korean War raged, and Clark, as rear admiral, commanded the Navy's air bases along the West Coast. At 57 he looked every bit as much the Indian warrior as his ancestors. I was all of 11 years old. (By happenstance, my first name, Clark, was my mother's maiden name, and I also am part American Indian, likely Miami Nation, three generations back.)

My "Uncle Bob"—Frank Robert Reynolds—had been recalled from teaching high school in Los Angeles to active duty, resuming his World War II role as the admiral's personal aide and flag lieutenant. They had been comrades-in-arms in the Pacific on board Jocko's ship, the second aircraft carrier to be named *Yorktown* (CV-10)—the famous "Fighting Lady"—and on his flagship, the second *Hornet* (CV-12), of Fast Carrier Task Group 58.1. Now, the admiral was earmarked for command of the Seventh Fleet fighting the Communist North Koreans and Chinese.

All of this I learned much later, of course, but our meeting helped ignite my fascination with history, naval history in particular. The evening after our encounter in the garden, Admiral Clark hosted a dinner for my family at San Diego's U. S. Grant Hotel. My only memory of this occasion was the waiter taking our orders: when he offered rice as a side-dish choice, both the admiral and my uncle started laughing and cursing it. They had grown quite sick of eating rice in the war-torn Pacific!

From that time on I paid close attention to my uncle's war stories. An exuberant, happy-go-lucky guy who loved people—and knew how to handle them, Uncle Bob tended to exaggerate when he reminisced. I learned to discern the essence of his stories when, as a teenager, I read everything published about the Navy in the Pacific war (which really wasn't much in the 1950s). Bob and I even spent an overnight cruise together out of Long Beach, California, on board the *Yorktown* in the spring of 1957 as part of a Navy public relations campaign for high school journalists.

Not coincidentally, many years later (from 1978 to 1987), I was employed as the first historian-curator of that very ship after its arrival in Charleston Harbor, South Carolina. There it became the centerpiece of the Patriots Point Naval and Maritime Museum, where Jocko's memory is enshrined.

During my undergraduate years at the University of California at Santa Barbara (1957–61) my interest in the Pacific war and history in general deepened to the point where I decided to become a historian. I even planned to write my doctoral dissertation on the wartime Fast Carrier Task Force to which Jocko Clark and the new *Yorktown* had belonged. The revised and expanded dissertation was first published in 1968 as *The Fast Carriers: The Forging of an Air Navy* and has remained in print almost continuously ever since.

One day in 1959, however, my uncle told me that the admiral was trying to write his autobiography and that he needed a professional writer or historian as his "collaborator" (ghostwriter). Impetuously, I (at age 19, in between my sophomore and junior years in college) suggested that I be that person. Whereupon Uncle Bob telephoned his old boss—with whom he had had a recent falling out over a joint business venture—and told him of my interest. Then Uncle Bob handed *me* the phone.

Admiral Clark was polite, considering my relative youth and inexperience, and I informed him that I could not help him until I finished graduate school—which I had not yet even started. My parents even let me fly to New York that summer to discuss it with him as his houseguest. We left the possibility of future collaboration open, although I drew on his knowledge when I wrote my carrier study. I repeated my promise in person and in letters during my graduate years at Duke University (1961–64), and as soon as I received my PhD, the admiral and I got to work on his memoir. We signed a contract with the David McKay publishing house to produce it as a trade book.

"Jocko"—as I addressed him, a familiarity he initially only tolerated—turned out to have almost total recall of the important events of his life. He repeated them often to me, answering my questions with unfailing consistency. (The selected portions of his interviews for the Naval Photographic Center—on the CD that accompanies this book—are samples of his keen memory.) The admiral proved to be gruff, even difficult, but also patient with me. We made steady progress, thanks also to the sage counsel of McKay's executive editor, Howard S. Cady. The result was *Carrier Admiral,* published at the end of 1967.

Clark's transcribed reminiscences in his oral history interviews at Columbia University during 1962 provided the core of that book. Our conversations and correspondence were supplemented by official Navy records, interviews with many of his former shipmates, and wartime and postwar publications. No family members were consulted, and his personal life was not addressed (although he told me plenty about it), inasmuch as the project took place in the midst of an unhappy marital situation.

Worse, the early chapters were stricken from the final draft by the publisher: Jocko's Cherokee heritage, boyhood antics, Naval Academy high jinks, World War I convoy duty, and postwar excitement in occupied Germany; the conflict between Turkey and Greece; and the Russian civil war. The head of the publishing company preferred to focus on Clark's distinguished career in naval aviation, which began in 1924.

These omissions are part of the reason for the present work. J. J. Clark deserves a balanced treatment of his early life and road to success as one of the key figures in the development of American naval aviation, in the war in the Pacific, and in naval operations in the Korean conflict. I never doubted his importance during the course of our collaboration, nor have I in the years since.

A combat leader, rough and tough, Jocko Clark was the genuine article. In his private life he had serious shortcomings. They were never great enough, however, to interfere with his finishing the job and "meeting every schedule"—to use his own words—for the Navy and his country.

CLARK G. REYNOLDS

ON THE
**WARPATH**
IN THE
**PACIFIC**

# ONE

## Cherokee Kid, 1893–1913

"THE RIGHT REVEREND J. JONATHAN JOCKEY CLARK!" SHOUTED a burly plebe in the rear ranks at Annapolis one summer day in 1913. The object of this nonsensical jibe was a Naval Academy classmate of medium build from Oklahoma—Joseph James Clark.

Part of the Academy's unwritten initiation rites into the officer fraternity was to provide a nickname created by the plebe's new comrades and meant to last an entire career—in spite of unwelcome or inappropriate connotations (World War II Admirals Ernest J. King and Harold R. Stark, classes of 1901 and 1903, were labeled respectively "Dolly" and "Betty").

"Mr. Clark"—perhaps because he displayed an earthiness far removed from piety—might have been thereafter dubbed "Reverend" or even "Holy Joe" from the incident. Instead, his peers seized on the horse-racing epithet and started addressing him as "Jock." To family and boyhood friends, however, he remained simply "Joe." An "o" was added to "Jock" during World War II: "Jocko."

Clark's skills in the saddle had been learned as a kid in Cherokee country and befitted his looks. One of his classmates recalled that he had "everything but the feathers on him" when he arrived at Annapolis, and a later report (in a 1944 *Honolulu Star-Bulletin* article) described him as having "the deep tan and high cheek bones of an Indian."

The next year, a *Life* magazine war correspondent remarked on his "hump-bridged nose and short-clipped, sparse hair which resembles a scalp lock and waves like prairie grass" on the western plains. Yet another newsman described his brown hair as stiff and "roached"—cut short enough to stand upright. His brown eyes matched his hair.

Simply put, Clark resembled the stereotype of an Indian warrior. This was no accident. He was born into a Cherokee tribe in Indian Territory (later Oklahoma) 19 years before entering the Academy. The Cherokee, one of the five so-called civilized Native American tribes, had originally been concentrated in a confederacy of towns in the western Carolinas and Tennessee. By the time the United States became an independent nation in the 1780s the Cherokee were rapidly assimilating into white culture. Intermarriage became so common that half-breeds—the term commonly used before 1900—quickly outnumbered the full-blooded minority, a disparity that grew as Joe Clark's forebears multiplied. The Cherokee came to regard any individual having some of their blood as Cherokee.

Tenacious fighters, the Cherokee regarded warfare as so vital that the tribal elders designated each town to be either war-oriented or devoted to peaceful pursuits. Part of their heritage was fighting many foes: other tribes; the British; the colonists rebelling against Britain; white coastal settlers threatening their lands in the southern Appalachians; and even among themselves over the issue of assimilation.

But the latter practice could not be reversed, as seen in Jock Clark's ancestors. Five generations before him, Bryan Ward (1720–1815) left wife Ann and several children at home in Ireland, probably to escape harsh British rule there, to go to frontier America to trade with the Indians. In western Georgia he "took up" with full-blooded Cherokee Nancy, widowed wife of the warrior Kingfisher and mother of Five Killer. Bryan and Nancy fought the British during the American Revolution (1775–83) and produced a daughter (who married a U.S. Army officer). Bryan left Nancy after his family arrived from the old country.

Bryan's son John Ward (1741–ca. 1838) married Catherine McDaniel (1757–ca. 1838), a half-Cherokee whose mother was Sookie, the daughter of Cherokee chief Old Hop (1690–1760), and whose father was Anglo-Scottish Indian trader David McDaniel. John and Catherine's son George Ward, one-fourth Cherokee (1787–1863), was Jock Clark's great-grandfather. In 1805 George Ward married a white woman, Lucy Mayes (1789–1867), whose brother wed a part Cherokee who parented two principal chiefs. George and Lucy had 11 children. The seventh, Jock's grandmother, was one-eighth Cherokee Mary Ward, who was born in 1823 and nicknamed "Polly."

The insatiable hunger of American whites for Indian lands led the U.S. government—by treaty and coercion—to force the Cherokee and other tribes to give up their ancestral lands and relocate west of the Mississippi River. The final removal was forced, although several hundred Cherokee escaped into the Great Smoky Mountains. During 1838–39 some of the 13,000 went by river steamer, but the U.S. Army escorted most of the Cherokee westward over a route they labeled the "Trail of Tears." Polly

Ward and her parents, George and Lucy, survived the ordeal, but over 4,000 others did not, victims of sickness and exposure. This likely included her grandparents John and Catherine Ward, who were known to have died about 1838.

The Cherokee settled in the northeastern part of the Indian Territory, a region shared with other relocated tribes as well as white pioneers participating in the general westward movement. They were given the very corner of the territory, designated the Cherokee Nation (eventually arranged into 14 counties). One of the migrant whites was Joseph Henry Clark, a young wagon master of English descent born in 1822, likely in Massachusetts. He soon met, courted, and married Polly Ward, one year younger, about 1840 and settled down to a farming life near Tahlequah, the Cherokee capital. In 1843 their union produced the first of eight children. Their last child became Jock's father.

William Andrew Clark, one-sixteenth Cherokee, entered the world at the Tsa-La-Gi (an ancient name for the Cherokee) site at Park Hill four miles south of Tahlequah on 2 June 1861. But mother Polly contracted pneumonia and died ten days later, at 38. Baby "Willie" was rescued and raised by family friends George Wilkerson, a full-blooded Cherokee, and his wife, Susan (whom Jock remembered affectionately as "Aunt Susan").

The Civil War had just broken out, and food shortages forced Susan to milk a mare to keep the infant alive. He was luckier than a brother and sister who died of privation. Because the Wilkersons spoke Cherokee around the home, young Willie learned to speak it fluently and indeed went on to study and preserve Cherokee culture throughout his adult life.

The Cherokee initially sided with the Confederacy, and widower Joseph Clark farmed and traded, using several black slaves, and hauled provisions to Confederate Indian forces in the embattled territory. Late in 1862, learning that Union President Abraham Lincoln was about to emancipate the slaves, Joseph sold his own for $5,000 in gold, which he reputedly buried on his property. Treasure hunters searched for it for over half a century, apparently in vain.

In 1863 most of the Cherokee switched their loyalty back to the Union, but Clark was among those who elected to remain with the South and with Colonel Stand Watie (three-fourths Cherokee and a chief), who was promoted to brigadier general in the Confederate army in 1864. For a time Clark served as a soldier in Company A, 2nd Cherokee Mounted Volunteer Regiment, one of several units raised by Watie. His two oldest sons, George, 18, and James, 16, also served under Watie; James died in battle. One day in November 1864, farmer Clark—who was deaf—was hauling a wagonload of flour for the army from Fort Gibson (near Muskogee) to Park

Hill when bushwhackers from the rebel army called out to him to stop. He failed to hear the order, however, and kept on going, so the soldiers opened fire. They killed their own man.

This tragedy made orphans of Joseph's children which was compounded when the renegades ransacked the family home in search of gold. Finding none, they burned it down, turning out his four other children into the cold. Teenagers Lucy and Louisa were saved by a neighbor woman, who wrapped their feet in rags and employed them carrying wood in the snow in order to earn a living. Another family took in the remaining child.

Willie, not yet four, remained with the Wilkersons, who soon after the war sent him to "Jack Cookson's school," located in the nearby White Oak Hills (also a regional refuge for outlaws). He also briefly attended the Woodhall School. In 1871, at the age of ten, he became the first of the original 54 students to be enrolled at the new Cherokee Orphans Asylum, built by the federal government for boys orphaned by the war. First located at Tahlequah, it was later moved to nearby Salina.

Jock's father yearned to become a cowboy, however, and ran away from the home "as many times as I have fingers and toes," he recalled. In 1877 he matriculated at Cherokee Male Seminary for one year.

Finally, in 1878, Willie Clark, wiry and lean, realized his dream. Seventeen years old, he signed on as a cowboy in the employ of second cousin Cherokee chief Sam Houston Mayes and W. T. Halsell of Vinita. Texas cattle were being driven overland on the open range to the lush bluestem grass of the Indian Territory for fattening. Willie joined his fellow Cherokee in their rough-and-ready life of herding the beef over the trail named for Cherokee guide Jesse Chisholm.

They drove the herds north to the railhead at Dodge City, Kansas, or south to the new one at Abilene, Texas, for shipment to Kansas City, St. Louis, and Chicago. Cowpuncher Clark accompanied the critters on their final trip by rail and grew a mustache that lasted a lifetime.

The westward movement of European-descended Americans brought Willie Clark a wife. The German family of Jacob Fredrich Lachenouer (Anglicized to Lockenour) had migrated to colonial Maine around 1753, when Jacob was but a child of two, and thence to Moravian western North Carolina (near Charlotte). There he fought in a Revolutionary War regiment against the British, for which the federal government eventually rewarded him with a grant of land. After 1800 he migrated to southern Indiana, raising two generations on a farm near Salem. There Jane Lockenour was born in 1849. She met and, at age 15 in March 1865, married 27-year-old Joseph Manning Berry. They became Jock Clark's maternal grandparents.

Joseph Berry's family had also been in western North Carolina since before the American Revolution and lived in tiny Asheville at the time of his birth in 1837. Joseph Berry eventually left the region and his Baptist family, who, Jocko Clark recalled, later sold some of its land to George Vanderbilt for his opulent Biltmore estate. Joseph moved to Salem, Indiana, as an itinerant minister (the only "reverend" in Jock's lineage). He belonged to the "Christian Church," the name by which the frontier-spawned Disciples of Christ was known. Usually traveling the Indiana-Tennessee circuit preaching the gospel, he left Jane at home to raise a constantly growing family, which eventually numbered ten children.

On 29 October 1872 she gave birth to Lillie Belle Berry in the southeast Tennessee foothill town of Athens. Berry later moved his family by covered wagon to Arkansas, which enabled him to preach there and in the neighboring Indian Territory. Lillie Belle attended Little Rock schools and grew up wanting to be a teacher, although she only completed the eighth grade.

In 1890 Berry again moved his family, this time to Chouteau near Pryor's Creek (later Pryor) in the Cherokee Nation; there 17-year-old Lillie was able to realize her ambition because good teachers were scarce. She was hired by a close friend of the family, her "Uncle" Web Vann at Vann's Chapel, a "subscription" school (the tuition was paid by parents) in a log cabin six miles west of Pryor's Creek. Lillie almost immediately met cowboy Willie Clark there. He was ten years older and a Methodist; like most Cherokee he was associated with the Southern wing of that divided church.

Willie and Lillie struck up a whirlwind courtship, although he took a dim view of father Berry's wandering ways, an assessment that deepened through the years. She nevertheless accepted Willie's marriage proposal.

When the appointed day arrived, 17 June 1891—two weeks after Willie's 30th birthday—he had to borrow one of the few horse buggies in the area to drive his 19-year-old bride to the Presbyterian manse in Pryor's Creek. There they were married under Cherokee tribal laws. Lillie remained loyal to her father's church yet agreed with Willie to raise all their children as Methodists. But Willie adamantly refused to sign the church book deemed essential for final salvation. He never said why; perhaps it only reflected his independent cowboy spirit.

The newlyweds set up house in a white one-room building on a 40-acre tract of prairie near Vann's. It belonged to the small community of Alluwe, between Chelsea and Nowata. Lillie continued to teach at Vann's, while Willie rode herd for Sam Mayes. He often worked 17 hours a day for $25 per month, except for the lean summer months, when the salary was $10 a month. Fortunately, Mayes usually paid Willie in cattle, enabling him to raise his own beef. Willie also trapped and hunted, selling the pelts for additional income. In March 1892, nine months after the wedding, their first child, Frank Earl, arrived but died at birth.

Undeterred, they tried again, and on 12 November 1893 Joseph James Clark was born in their little home. He was named for both his grandfathers (Joseph Henry Clark and Joseph Manning Berry) and for the uncle killed in the Civil War (James Clark). Through his father, little Joe Clark was one-thirty-second Cherokee and immersed in that culture. The Cherokee eventually gave him the tribal name Thunderbird.

Early on, Joe assumed a leadership role as the eldest of the eight siblings who followed, especially as the only boy for his first ten years. Will and Lillie, anticipating a large family, moved up on Dog Creek into a spacious three-room house where their first three daughters were born: Lucy Jane in 1895, Mary Louise in 1897, and Stella Clarinda in 1900. As was the custom, to help raise the kids, the family employed a black nanny. The children called her "Mammy" and addressed their parents as "Mama" and "Papa."

Cherokee fortunes were being generally improved when Joe Clark arrived. In 1887 the Dawes General Allotment Act enabled the government to close down the open range and cattle drives in favor of extended rail connections and privatizing the land. This included breaking up tribal holdings and—under the Curtis Act of 1898—making Indians into farmers by allocating each one a plot of 80 acres of top-grade farmland. These allotments ended in May 1906, the year before the Indian Territory achieved statehood as part of Oklahoma.

In 1898 Papa Will took young Joe to Muskogee to be registered for his eventual allotment of land. Because precise family records were unavailable, and likely also for convenience sake, Will registered himself as one-fourth (instead of the correct one-sixteenth) Cherokee and each of his children as one-eighth (rather than the actual one-thirty-second). Throughout his life Jock saw no reason to change his official designation, which he most likely believed to be correct (only recent genealogical "digging" has proven otherwise). Most Native Americans became citizens in 1901 (the rest in 1924) as federal laws replaced those of the tribes.

One day in 1899 Will mounted his horse to look for a better farm under the allotment and soon found a nice existing farmstead in Nowata County seven miles northwest of Chelsea, near Alluwe. The non-Indian owner, who tried to retain title as a "white adopted Indian," had improved it, but the government forced him to sell it. Will, having no extra money, borrowed $3,000 from a Pryor entrepreneur to purchase it and also to lease adjacent land on which to graze his cattle.

On 1 September 1902 the family moved in, dazzled by the story-and-a-half, four-bedroom white house, plus two barns and two large granaries.

*Inset:* Joseph James Clark, about 11, ca. 1904–5. *Clark family photo*
Will Clark family members in front of their farmhouse near Alluwe, Indian Territory, in 1906. *Left to right:* Joe, 12, with dogs; "Papa" Will, 45; Mary, 8; Stella, 6; "Mama" Lillie Belle, 33, holding 3-year-old twins Bill Jr. and Dollie; and Lucy, 11. Live-in maid "Mammy" holds newborn John in upstairs window above Papa. *Clark family photo*

The total allotment of 80 acres per person (two adults, four children) came to 480 acres, increased by another 160 the next year when Lillie gave birth to twins—"juniors" named after both parents and nicknamed Bill and Dollie. Will had to hire farmhands, and Lillie had to cook for them as well as for her growing family.

No sooner had the family moved in than a family friend, Douglas W. Franchot, discovered oil on sister Mary's acreage. It produced handsome dividends as the nation gradually shifted from coal to oil for its energy needs. But the relatively sudden economic shift from herding to farming and even oil production proved difficult for some Cherokee accustomed to the old ways.

Jock recalled from his boyhood that a certain farmer living along the Verdigris River—nearly dry in summer but overflowing during spring floods—tried to sell his weather-tortured land. A real estate agent from Kansas City looked it over and asked, "Does the river flow here?"

"No," replied the farmer, "the river never gets up here."

"Well," said the agent, "what were those oil marks I saw on the trees about eight feet above the ground?"

"That's where my hogs rub their backs" came the quick answer.

"Mister," announced the savvy realtor, "I don't want to buy any of your land. But you can ship me a couple carloads of your hogs!"

All the Clark family members soon leased their allotted properties to oil operators, and their wells delivered small but steady quantities of oil through the years. Joe and several of his siblings eventually sold their holdings. Will soon earned enough oil money to pay off the loan on his farm. Unfortunately, the last three children were born after the 1906 deadline for allotments and received no acreage: John Daniel in 1907, George Washington in 1913, and Virginia Elizabeth in 1917. (The two boys were bequeathed their parents' two allotments, and Virginia was given the final family home in Chelsea.)

Growing up on a farm was "pleasant enough," the future admiral recalled, except for one of his earliest memories from about age four: out playing in the yard he was suddenly visited by two rattlesnakes. His black nanny swiftly decapitated them with a hoe, leaving an odor so sickening that he never forgot it—or the fact that Mammy had saved his life.

On another occasion he ran a rusty nail clear through his foot. Mama Lillie set him down, pulled it out, placed the foot in a pan of coal oil, then applied turpentine and sugar to the wound—and it healed. Although her brother Virgil Berry was at that time a prominent physician in the territory, he lived in distant Wetumka, and a dearth of local doctors forced farm folk to improvise.

Lillie had a midwife attending at all her home births except for the last two (when she had a doctor), and she developed a medicine table of home-spun cures: turpentine and sugar for a cut, honey and whiskey for a cough, a mustard plaster for a chest cold, castor oil for almost everything. But Lillie, pregnant with John, could do nothing after Will brought home a sickly stray cat in late 1906. Suddenly, both her twins contracted an illness that was not diagnosed as diphtheria until Dollie died. A doctor from Vinita then gave the entire family an antitoxin, but surviving twin, Bill, did not recover fully until he was almost an adult.

Will and Lillie were good and generous parents, though firm, God-fearing, and insistent on discipline. Mama did not tolerate the drinking of alcohol, card playing, or other frivolous behavior. She did all the cooking, laundry, and housekeeping for the family and hired hands. She raised the vegetables, canned the fruit, and read nightly to the children by candlelight—poetry, the Scriptures, and novels ranging from *Black Beauty* to *David Copperfield*. And she took in relatives in subsequent years. Will, who had been an orphan, welcomed the larger family.

In June 1907 Lillie's sister Laura Berry Parker died in her prairie dugout dwelling near Shattuck on the Texas border 300 miles to the west, leaving her husband with five children ages six months to seven years. Perceiving his dilemma, Lillie loaded her older children onto the train for the long trip there. Her sister Emma took the baby boy, and Lillie had to travel to Guyman in the Oklahoma panhandle to deliver the other two boys to her mother, Jane, and sister Josie. This required a 500-mile round-trip detour via Amarillo, Texas, an ordeal she handled with great aplomb.

Lillie brought seven-year-old Ava and two-year-old Ruth home to raise as her own (the father reclaimed them only briefly a few years later). They fit in well at the bustling Clark farm, learning right away that Papa Will "knew how to make kids work"—as Ruth recalled in 2002 (at the brisk age of 97). The girls remained in the Clark household until they completed high school, at which time Lillie obtained scholarships for Ava and a brother to Phillips University in Enid, Oklahoma.

Lillie later took in the four children of a deceased cousin, then Grandma Jane, and finally Aunt Josie for 25 years. Three meals a day for a table setting of 14 to 16 people became common during Joe's teenage years, and they were much larger during homecomings throughout his 40-year naval career. Both parents lived that long—hardly surprising, however, for the Cherokee part of Oklahoma. It was a place, recalled the admiral, "where everybody lives forever, and nobody ever thinks about dying until he gets to be about 80." The death of Grandpa Berry at 74 in 1917 led folks to say he died "in his prime" (but he had left Oklahoma and moved back to Indiana).

To Papa Will the family "meant everything," remembered daughter Virginia in 2001 (at age 84), a feeling he instilled in all its members. His June 2nd birthday was regularly celebrated by a huge gathering of family who "came from near and far." The birthday feast was highlighted by hand-cranked ice cream and "a ton" of Aunt Josie's yeast rolls. "The kids stood around," in the words of oldest daughter, Lucy, in 1983 (at age 87), "and drooled over them" while they baked.

Grandpa Berry often visited, sitting in a rocking chair singing and composing songs. Papa Will used the same chair often and sang the old ballads, cowboy songs, and "made up some as he went," according to Joe Clark's niece Betty Joe (so named for her uncle). The problem was that Will also "chewed Red Man Tobacco and spit in old coffee cans. And we would absolutely die or cry when we had to kiss him goodnight because of that old tobacco juice and smell. Ugh!"

Eldest child, Joe, provided the second echelon of leadership in the family and was regarded by his siblings as "a protector," according to Lucy in 1972. When Joe was four years old (1897) Lucy fell into the rock-lined family well while trying to collect a bird's nest. Joe grabbed hold of her dress and yelled for some time until he was heard and Uncle Homer Berry, who was plowing in the field, rescued Lucy. Joe, Lucy, and Mary joined Lillie in an all-night search in 1902 for two-year-old Stella, who had wandered half a mile from home before a hired hand on horseback found her on a hilltop.

Navy-destined Joe learned about both leadership and teamwork from his life on the farm. When he was old enough to ride a horse, Papa Will presented him with a pony of his very own, which he used for herding the family's Hereford cattle and for hunting forays. His dad bought and sold cattle and occasionally took him on the train when delivering them to the cities. The family also raised hogs and grew wheat, oats, and corn. Joe had to "turn out" at 4:30 every morning to chop corn to feed to the livestock (a predawn hour that prepared him for life at sea and in naval aviation).

He was also up at 4:30 for quail-hunting expeditions with his father and Douglas Franchot. Because wild turkey, deer, and coyotes were also prevalent, Will kept a pack of hounds busy retrieving their carcasses; he once impressed his son by killing two turkeys with one shot. At this rate, however, turkey and deer were soon depleted, forcing the closure of the hunting seasons on them. Will kept one good bird dog, however, to help him hunt or trap bobwhite quail, duck, opossum, skunk, and raccoon.

Joe Clark became a marksman with the rifle and made spending money by selling hides over the winter. Skills with hand weapons stayed with him throughout his life. As an adult he earned the Navy Expert Pistol Shot Medal.

Farm life was rough-and-ready, full of fun and "rascality," as he put it, but it also required obedience to develop good character. Whenever Joe and his siblings got into fights, for example, they got "whipped" (spanked) by their Papa. By the same token, however, neighborliness was crucial to survival, and Joe learned about human relationships through hard lessons on the prairie.

During the fall harvest, for example, a threshing machine made the rounds from farm to farm, followed by the neighbors as they "traded labor." Joe carried water to these visiting farmhands. Of one such occasion, he remembered:

> At our place a new neighbor was helping with others. His wagon was purposely loaded light in deference to his team [of smaller horses]. Press Thompson, another of our neighbors who lived close by, began making snide remarks about the light loads. After this ridicule had

gone on for some time the new man, exasperated beyond endurance, ran out of patience. Grabbing the pitchfork, he rammed it through Thompson on the spot. Thompson died right then and there.

The man quickly unloaded his wagon and drove off. Nobody said anything to him or tried to stop him. We had no town marshal. He simply went away, leaving that part of the country for good. My father said it served Press Thompson right. That was a lesson I never forgot; humor should have no barb. Fun is fun, but when people are embarrassed it hurts.

Clark was influenced in a more positive way about humor by another Cherokee neighbor, Will Rogers. The most famous humorist of his day, this rope-twirling cowboy wit had been born 14 years before Joe (in 1879) in nearby Oologah, a railroad switching station near the Verdigris River. He was one-sixteenth Cherokee and descended from the Vann family. When Rogers's family went "to town" it was Claremore, ten miles away and usually listed as his hometown. In actuality, his hometown was Chelsea, 15 miles from Claremore by rail. In Chelsea Rogers's three older sisters married, lived, and died. "We used to say," recalled Jock, "that when Will Rogers went home"—from his Wild West and Broadway shows and Hollywood movies—"he went to Claremore, but when he came to see his folks he went to Chelsea."

Younger Joe Clark remembered a particular Sunday picnic near the river about 1910 with the Clark family and the families of Rogers's sisters, including kids around his age. Will Rogers—now 30 and a successful vaudeville performer—"kept everybody in stitches for about four hours, telling stories and anecdotes. At once I was impressed with him. I realized he was no ordinary person." Four years later Rogers joined the Ziegfeld Follies and Midnight Frolic as a headline act. His humor did get pointed from then on but was usually aimed—deservedly so—at politicians.

Great good humor was only one facet of the home life that molded the character of Jock Clark. His family had a reputation, wherever it lived, for its hospitality as well as its religious convictions. Lillie's minister father imbued her with a strong faith as revealed by her nightly Bible readings to the children and faithful attendance at Methodist services. Often they were held at an old Baptist church located near Alluwe and founded by Cherokee Chief Journeycake. Lillie taught Sunday school and insisted at home that Joe "read the Bible from cover to cover in the hope that I would enter the ministry," he recalled, "but I never felt the call for it."

This understatement could have been partly attributable to what Jocko later called his "farm-life freedom, conducive to rascality." The family later attended services at Rigg's Chapel near Chelsea, the town's meetinghouse during weekdays, driving there in the family surrey, "fringe and all." Joe, however, rode his horse. One Sunday when he was nine years old, after Sunday school, he wandered out back of the chapel where other youngsters were "swapping yarns while they waited for their elders to complete their worship."

> A stray dog appeared, and someone dared my friend Burr Sharp and me to tie a tin can to this dog's tail. At the age of nine a dare was a must. The moment we released the dog I had a premonition. I said to Burr, "Let's get the hell out of here." We jumped on our horses and galloped away.
>
> The dog ran into the church right under the seats. Finally he stopped alongside the minister who at the moment was engaged in prayer. Pounding his tail against the altar and banging the tin can he yelped frantically. The congregation howled with laughter, and church services were terminated forthwith.
>
> When questioned later by my mother I denied any part in the episode. That is the only time I can recall telling a falsehood.

Joe's moral upbringing came from his parents, although he did not adhere to one denomination. As an adult, he listed his religion as Episcopalian. Both parents wanted their children to have a better education than their own—Willie's in the orphanage, Lillie's only to the eighth grade. She taught her children to read, and Joe became an avid reader of anything he could find. Mama also corrected her children's speech, giving them an advantage over most of their peers.

But the only primary schools were small private log houses with clapboard benches and mediocre teachers—usually unmarried women. These schools often "played out" due to financial or staffing problems, as was the case in the first one he attended—Vann's. This forced Lillie to hire a governess for the home schooling of both Joe and Lucy.

The problem of distance to a small public school was solved when Joe and his sisters were old enough to walk there—three and a half miles each way to the Dogtown School (no town, just a small frame schoolhouse). Their teacher was Isis Justise, whom Lucy remembered as "great" and Joe regarded as "a redhead who indeed lived up to her name by dispensing justice."

When Joe got into a fight with an older boy just before Christmas, Miss Justise "caught us by the napes of our necks and dragged us inside the school." She sent other boys outdoors to fetch a switch with which to administer the prescribed punishment of 30 "licks" to both scrappers. But the searchers selected a hollow tree branch into which, using penknives, they cut rings about every inch to weaken it. "As Miss Justise whacked me across the backside with the first lick, the stick flew apart into many pieces. Everybody burst into laughter. Undaunted, she went out, got her own switch, and gave us our 30 licks in earnest. Ordinarily I would have been in line for another switching at home, but when my sisters gave my parents their account of the affair, it seemed so funny that no further justice was ordered."

Then Miss Justise got married, and the school folded. As a result, the Clark kids enrolled at Alliance Hall on Lightning Creek, with Cassie Iliff as their teacher. This was also a three-mile walk, in company with the three children of Turner Milam. One day en route Joe got into a fracas with Walter Milam. When they arrived at school, recalled Lucy, "Cassie Iliff whipped both, and Joe got another whipping when we got home. That was the policy of the family."

Mrs. Milam, now fearing for her children's safety, accompanied them to school with the "savage Indian" Clarks, in Lucy's words, but "soon got tired of it and let us walk in peace."

Then came statehood in 1907 with formal school districts and a short-lived one-room affair over a store. Joe's parents moved his sisters to a two-room school in Alluwe and sent their precocious 14-year-old son to Willie Halsell College at Vinita (which Will Rogers had attended in the early 1890s)—in reality a high school that soon closed for lack of sufficient students.

Mama Lillie, concerned for her son's future, convinced him to return to grammar school and thus repeat the eighth grade. Joe was filling out physically to a height of 5 feet 11 inches with a slight but hardened build that would reach a weight of 140 pounds by the time he entered the Naval Academy. He objected to the setback but agreed when informed he would be enrolled in a better school at Chelsea—and that he could ride his black pony the seven miles each way to school. Jock later acknowledged his mother's wisdom; the repeated year gave him a solid foundation from which "I constantly profited."

But he had another awakening that provided additional impetus. "My faith in the blessings of life on a farm," he reminisced, "was badly shaken one foggy rainy Sunday morning. The hogs got out, and I had to round them up. Barefooted and barelegged I chased them through the smartweeds and blackberry briars. Every scratch itched and burned. Right then I came to the conclusion that there must be some better way to make a living."

In 1909, on the eve of his 16th birthday, Joe Clark gained admission to Oklahoma Agricultural & Mechanical College (now Oklahoma State

University) at Stillwater. The first two years there followed a prep school curriculum equivalent to four years of high school. The final three years at A&M amounted to a normal four years of college and led to a bachelor's degree.

No sooner had he left home than Lillie and Will Clark decided to move to a big house in Chelsea so their other children and two adopted daughters (nieces) could obtain decent high school educations. They made the move to the little country town in 1910. The high school and its teachers lived up to their expectations, and the remaining children eventually followed Joe to other colleges in the Midwest.

Thus, at 49, Will gave up the farm to his children per their allotments (because perhaps now *he* had to chase the loose hogs!?) and became a founder and initial director of the First National Bank in Chelsea. Lillie Belle, only 38, became active in both the Southern Methodist and First Christian churches and in sundry community activities.

Joe advanced easily from his college prep program into the higher curriculum in 1911 with a declared major in electrical engineering. Family friend Douglas Franchot, owner of an oil company, promised him a job in the lucrative business upon graduation in 1914.

Joe was also attracted to the state's voluntary military program, so he joined up, was appointed corporal, and advanced to sergeant in the first year. To improve their marksmanship, Joe and a classmate hoarded 5,000 rounds of rifle ammunition so they could hold additional target practice on their own out in the countryside. One day, their instructor, a U.S. Army captain, caught them and demanded an explanation. When they answered that they were practicing to become better shots, he remarked, "That's the only way you can ever become a good soldier," and much to their surprise let them continue.

By the end of his third year at A&M, in the spring of 1912, Joe made the momentous decision to switch to a military career. This meant gaining admission to the U.S. Military Academy at West Point, New York. Once home, Joe so informed Papa Will, who took him to see their congressman, James S. Davenport. The two were old friends who had "split rails together," remarked the representative from Oklahoma's Third Congressional District.

But when he heard of Joe's desire to become an Army officer, Davenport, a large man, put his arm around Joe and said, "My boy, I will send you to West Point, but I want you to go to the Naval Academy. The Navy is a better life. The Navy offers you a chance to see the world!" At least that was his impression from a cruise he had taken with his family on a Navy transport.

The one-sided American naval victories in the 1898 war with Spain were well known, as was the global voyage by Teddy Roosevelt's "Great White Fleet" from 1906 to 1908. Indeed, the U.S. fleet was the third largest in the world—behind only Great Britain's and Germany's.

Farm boy Joe Clark knew little of these things, but the Oklahoma legislator painted such a rosy picture that Joe replied, "All right, I'll go in the Navy." Yet he had no knowledge of where it got its officers. The only thing he knew about the Naval Academy at Annapolis, Maryland, was a pennant hanging on Davenport's wall with the picture of the mascot goat and the name "Annapolis" on it.

Davenport gave Clark an appointment to the Academy. Each congressman was allowed a quota of two midshipmen attending the Academy at one time. But naval officers from the new state of Oklahoma were rare, and appointments often went begging. As luck would have it, one of Davenport's slots would become vacant the following June when Midshipman John M. Kates from Claremore was scheduled to graduate with the class of 1913 (he would attain the rank of lieutenant commander and die on active duty at Annapolis in 1918).

So Davenport nominated Joe, who soon learned that he first had to pass an entrance examination. Will and Lillie insisted that their son continue his work at Oklahoma A&M in the intervening year. But during the fall semester there, Joe realized that the only way an aspirant could expect to pass the exam was by first attending a special preparatory school for it in the East. He pleaded with his father that he could not both attend school and prepare, and he finally convinced Will after Christmas 1912 to let him withdraw from A&M in order to attend an Academy prep school.

En route home from Stillwater, Joe stopped off near Tulsa to see Douglas Franchot to inform him that he had selected a naval career instead of one in Franchot's oil company. They visited the recently discovered huge Glenn Pool oil field at Kiefer where Franchot introduced Joe to several prominent oilmen and a distinguished visitor, the famous historian and British ambassador to the United States, James Bryce.

Franchot not only endorsed Joe's decision for a naval career but also gave the 19 year old "much valuable advice" and wrote letters of introduction to several friends in Washington and Annapolis. Although a Yale graduate, Franchot knew many naval officers, to whom he sent letters. Among them were Spanish-American War hero and Alabama Congressman Richmond P. Hobson, a champion of minorities (including Indians) for the service academies, and Commander Louis M. Nulton. Both men were alumni of the class of 1889; Hobson was top man, Nulton was ninth and was then on the Academy faculty.

Franchot's encouragement only deepened Clark's determination to enter the Navy, despite the likelihood that, had he remained with Franchot, "I would have made millions of dollars in oil, as he eventually did," Clark remembered. "But from the moment I left him my life was guided by one aim: to become the best possible naval officer and to do the best job I could in the Naval Service of the United States."

Joseph James Clark underwent a physical examination at Stillwater to ensure he met the Navy's rigorous requirements for fitness. Then, on a cold day early in 1913, most of the family "chaperoned" him to the station in Chelsea—as adopted sister Ruth, then eight, recalled 89 years later—and put him on the train to St. Louis. There a change of trains sped him to Washington, D.C., Annapolis, and the future. He never looked back.

# TWO

# Academy High Jinks, 1913–1917

"GREENER YOUNG MEN MAY HAVE GONE TO ANNAPOLIS," CLARK reflected half a century later, "but I doubt it." When the train brought him to Washington on a wintry day in 1913 he sought out Congressman Davenport, who took him along with Franchot's letter of recommendation to see Congressman Hobson. From a list of Academy prep schools both legislators strongly recommended the Werntz Naval Academy Preparatory School in Annapolis—known to its students as "Bobby Werntz's War College." This was a tongue-in-cheek allusion to the no-nonsense owner and his teaching style.

So, late on a wet Saturday afternoon, the 19-year-old Oklahoman boarded the electric-powered train of the Washington, Baltimore and Annapolis Railroad, or "W. B. & A," nicknamed by midshipmen the "Witch, Bitch, and Itch." The 30-mile run terminated after dark on Church Circle near the state capitol building. Seeing a "Maryland Hotel" sign from the train window, Joe Clark figured it ought to be of "Grade A" quality.

But as soon as he registered there "the image vanished," Clark recalled. "The beds were beat-up cast iron with straw-thick mattresses, and the plumbing was conspicuous by its absence. The hotel was pretty much a rat trap, even by Oklahoma standards." The food was good, but expensive.

After breakfast next morning Joe beckoned the hefty black headwaiter named Ollie and asked confidentially, "Where is the ocean?" The man's eyes widened, "Boss, tain't no ocean around hyah!" Nonplussed, Clark took a walk around the small downtown waterfront. The water belonged to the Severn River, and the low-lying morning fog obscured the Chesapeake Bay beyond, leading him to conclude that the headwaiter had been "spoofing him." Surely, an academy for training naval officers *had* to be located on an oceanfront.

On learning the truth, Clark "decided then and there never to ask any question that could possibly be avoided. I made that a lifelong rule. If you ask a needless question you only display your ignorance."

The afternoon was spent strolling around the grounds of the Naval Academy, admiring the buildings, which he called "the most beautiful I had ever seen." Most impressive was the chapel and beneath it the crypt of Revolutionary War hero John Paul Jones. Moved by it, Joe Clark silently rededicated his life to the Naval Service.

Rising early Monday—in Oklahoma "we always started the day with the chickens"—he decided to visit Bobby Werntz at his home. The black maid answered the door and let him wait until Werntz eventually appeared, unshaven and in a dressing gown. Clark explained his "lofty aspirations," whereupon Werntz retorted, "Young man, if you do your part, we'll get you in that Naval Academy!"

> Period. End of conversation. The maid opened the door and ushered me out. I was abjectly disappointed until I realized that he had put the issue squarely up to me. I accepted his challenge and forgot about looking up any other prep schools.

Robert Lincoln Werntz had graduated from the Naval Academy in 1884 but soon resigned his naval engineer's commission in order to open the prep school with his brother Jimmy, a former locomotive engineer. The tuition was high, but their system worked—a "racket" so successful "rumor had it that Bobby owned nearly all of Annapolis."

Werntz's "war college" was located two blocks from the main gate of the Academy on a dingy third floor over a grocery store—not unlike some of Clark's earliest schools in the Indian Territory. Discipline and rules were nonexistent, and attendance was not required. Responsibility for learning lay with the individual. The instructors knew their lessons by heart and how to drill into the students' memories the virtually unchanging Academy entrance exam questions and answers. To succeed, the prospective midshipman needed a virtually photographic memory.

The atmosphere—literally and figuratively—was not particularly conducive to learning. Before class began, the air was often blue with smoke from the calabash pipes then in vogue—"the bigger the pipe the more the distinction of the owner." Some of the 30 or so students might be having a crap game before the bell rang. But when it sounded everything was strictly business.

Joe Clark wisely engaged the best teacher at the school to tutor him privately—"Professor" Roland M. Teel. Teel's methods were so superior to those of Werntz that he later founded the Severn School, which ultimately surpassed Werntz's in quality. Throughout his life Clark credited his passage of the entrance exam to Teel's teaching.

Werntz himself was something of an eccentric who talked in a "whiny squeaky voice." He nursed a permanent sore in the palm of one hand with Vaseline from a small jar, especially when chalk dust got on the sore. One day someone put red-hot cayenne pepper in the jar, with obvious effect. He dealt with the pain "manfully" but said to his class, "Gentlemen, there are two kinds of sons-of-bitches in this world. One is the common ordinary son-of-a-bitch, and then there is the low down dirty son-of-a-bitch, and that's the son-of-a-bitch that put cayenne pepper in my Vaseline."

As the 4 March 1913 inauguration day for President Woodrow Wilson approached, Werntz encouraged his young charges to take the day off to attend the ceremonies in Washington. Clark and about ten others said they preferred to stay at school and study, so Werntz had to hold class. But when only Clark and two others showed up on the 4th their professor took them himself by the next train to Washington. They arrived at the Capitol in time for Clark to see Wilson on Pennsylvania Avenue and follow his automobile to the White House.

In Annapolis Joe lodged in a boarding house run by a family named Feldmeyer next to the Carvel Hall hotel. Midshipmen dropped in on Saturdays and holidays, and on one occasion Clark met his first "mid"—a plebe (freshman). He was Robert B. "Mick" Carney, who with several classmates convinced Joe to smuggle a quart of whiskey into the Academy grounds on Saturday night—about the only free recreational evening the mids had.

He got past the "jimmy legs" (yard police) at the main gate after dark with the bottle in his overcoat pocket. His "new friends" met him on the lacrosse field, and they proceeded to some open bleachers with possible escape routes in every direction should the jimmy legs approach. Each had a few nips but not enough to finish the bottle. So they hid it in a small opening in the brick foundation of a nearby bandstand. Such was the first of a series of Saturday night social events that lasted all of Clark's four years at the Academy. That the merrymakers were never caught was fortunate, especially for Carney, who defied the system by drinking, smoking, and hazing another year before knuckling down to study; he eventually rose to become Chief of Naval Operations.

Clark passed his physical exam easily, but his roommate at Feldmeyers, a youth named Fred Wilson, did not because of an ear defect of which he had been completely ignorant. That scotched Wilson's chances for admission, something Joe, who had wanted to room with him, regretted. Joe journeyed to Washington in early April to take his mental examinations, administered by the Civil Service Commission. A few days later, Congressman Davenport gave him advance information that he had passed.

Jubilant, Clark went straight to the Naval Academy where he apprised the admissions officers of his immediate availability. They told him to come back in May, enabling him to celebrate with a month-long holiday back in Oklahoma.

On his return to Annapolis, he and about 15 others reported for swearing in as midshipmen on 22 May 1913. Unfortunately, they were informed that because the 1912–13 academic year had not yet ended they could not be added to the existing plebe class, about to be advanced to "youngster" (sophomore) status. The newcomers were allowed to take the oath that day (the formal appointment was issued 6 October), but they were to be called "functions" instead of midshipmen. So, recalled Clark, "I became the lowest rank the Navy ever had—'function for midshipmen.'"

Worse, no rooms were available for these "functions" in the sprawling dormitory, Bancroft Hall, and they had to be quartered aboard the ex-Spanish warship *Reina Mercedes,* which was permanently docked at the Academy ship basin. Captured in Cuba during the 1898 war, it served as station ship as well as prison ship for misbehaving midshipmen and sailors. Joe and his peers lived aboard as regular sailors, sleeping in hammocks and eating in the general mess.

The first night, however, several functions decided to smoke cigarettes, which was strictly forbidden, only to be caught by the midshipman officer, Karl Shears, a second classman (junior). He gathered the newcomers around him for a lecture: "Now you young men are just starting your careers in the Navy. I don't want to see you have a black mark on your record the very first day. So I'm going to let you off this time in the hope that you will do better in the future." "We kept right on smoking," Clark admitted, "but after that we were more careful by posting our 'anchor watch' to keep an eye out in all directions."

Next day he and his mates plunged into an intense training program of rowing, swimming, workouts, and sailing. Sailing ship exercises were conducted on the training brig *Boxer* without actually setting sail, which Clark found most interesting. They went through spreading and furling both the square and fore-and-aft sails (hence its rating as a "hermaphrodite" brig). High atop both of its masts was an iron spike, onto which each man had to "spike" his hat after the difficult climb aloft. Such a holed hat was non-regulation but highly prized as a souvenir. The Oklahoman spiked his and kept it for many years.

As the days got warmer, the trainees quenched their thirst from a large wooden scuttlebutt (water cask) with a big keg of ice in it on the well deck of the *Boxer*. They used a half-gallon dipper, and after a couple of swigs tossed the remaining water over the side. Joe did just this on one particular occasion when he saw the oars of a cutter coming alongside the gangway being brought vertical ("toss oars"). He then peered over the side and to his horror beheld the soaking wet chest of a lieutenant junior grade (jg) standing in its stern.

The officer had not seen the culprit, "but I was nearly scared out of my wits." Revering any officer "as almost being up with the angels," and therefore seeing his career already in jeopardy, Clark returned to the side and called down, "Sir, I am sorry I threw that water on you." The officer, John S. Barleon, replied, "That's all right, you didn't mean to do it."

The truth paid off, and Clark did not encounter Barleon again for 25 years, at which time the officer was captain of a cruiser, and Clark "offered my apologies again with better grace." (Five months after the incident Barleon's wife gave birth to a son, who went on to graduate from the Academy in 1935 and followed a career in naval aviation.)

On 6 June the class of '13 graduated, and the functions became midshipmen plebes of the new fourth class ('17). They moved to Bancroft Hall to begin plebe summer with the more recent arrivals—266 in all.

Soon the acquiring of nicknames began. Although some plebes tried to call him by his initials, "J. J.," the name "Jock" stuck after Bruce L. Sizer called him that during a formation that summer. Sizer was nicknamed "Bull" for being the class "strongman." Giving Joe Clark a moniker was apparently Sizer's only notable achievement at the Academy; he did not complete the plebe year.

Jock Clark's roommate, Floyd W. Bennett (no connection with the later aviator of that name), hailed from Pennsylvania and was also 19 years old. He was talking in ranks one day, whereupon another classmate in the role of temporary company commander shook his fist at Bennett, "Knock that off, or I'll knock your block off!"

Clark thought his manner inappropriate and later went to this temporary leader's room. Even though the classmate was about 50 pounds heavier than he was, Jock remarked, "I did not like the way you spoke to my roommate."

"You don't?" he growled. "What are you going to do about it?"

"If it happens again there is going to be a fight."

"No time like the present," said the big man, whereupon Clark grabbed him by the collar and socked him.

Another classmate, William K. "Sol" Phillips from Georgia, happened to be passing the open door, got between the two "just as I was about to be clobbered," remembered Clark, and stopped the fight.

When Clark and Phillips got outside the room Phillips said loud enough for the temporary commander to hear, "I figured the son-of-a-bitch could not lick both of us." Thereafter he treated Jock and Sol with more respect, although Clark had come close not only to a beating but a court-martial and expulsion for fighting.

The original object of this fracas, Jock's roommate Bennett, did not last beyond the plebe year, though he likely could have handled himself well enough in any scrape. Bennett later joined the U.S. Marine Corps and rose to the rank of colonel in World War II.

By the beginning of the academic year in September 1913 Jock and his fellow plebes were well established "living by the bugle." The kid from Indian country had little difficulty academically, given his excellent education at Oklahoma A&M. All that a "mid" had to do was complete daily homework assignments and be prepared to demonstrate it in class via the "slip" system. Each student drew a slip of paper with questions on it to be answered at the blackboard or on a paper handed in to the instructor (about half the faculty were civilian professors, the rest naval officers).

The students knew they were competing with one another and rarely asked questions, because they needed the time to provide complete answers. Clark admired the slip system for forcing a student to discipline himself to do his homework and thereby teaching him self-reliance: "I came to believe that too much mollycoddling of a student is harmful; what counts most and what the student remembers best is what he gets done himself."

The final reckoning came at the end of the four years when a man was ranked in his graduating class (1917 in Clark's case) in order of academic and "professional" performance. The latter included midshipman brigade duties, athletics, other extracurricular activities, and personal behavior— meaning a minimum of demerits (too many, such as for fighting, led to dismissal from the Academy).

Among the favorite teachers was Commander Paul J. Dashiell, professor of mathematics, the commander rank then being phased out in preference for simple civilian status. The midshipmen nicknamed him "Skinny Paul," and because he doubled as a football coach they devised a yell in his honor: "Highball, lowball, Skinny Paul, our Paul, old Paul, Paul Dashiell."

He also taught electricity and one day in class asked his students if they knew their lesson. A bright mid spoke up, "Yes, sir!" Skinny Paul said, "Then please press that switch and get some light in here."

One foreign language "prof" was M. A. Colton, a bachelor with a long drooping mustache who was nicknamed "the Walrus." When somebody suggested Colton ought to get married, Sol Phillips contrived an anonymous advertisement that he, Jock, and others placed in a matrimonial magazine, *Cupid's Columns:* "Handsome young college professor is making his annual cruise to Europe this summer and desires matrimony before the voyage. Strike while the iron is hot, girls!"

The mids all had a great laugh, remembered Clark, "but Colton evidently had the last laugh for he got married soon afterwards. We never knew whether our ad was the cause."

Among the "duty" officers in the Executive Department was Lieutenant William F. Halsey Jr., "strict but fair to midshipmen" and promoted to lieutenant commander while on the faculty. After the midday meal the first classmen (seniors) could retire to Smoke Hall adjacent to the mess hall. Lower classman Clark and his chums, not yet permitted to smoke, repaired to an adjoining arcade for a few puffs but grew lax by not always posting an "anchor watch" as lookout. One day, just as Jock was rolling his own Bull Durham cigarette, Halsey suddenly appeared and immediately had his midshipman assistant take down names. When Clark's turn came, he said,

> "Sir, I have not smoked." Halsey said, "That's all right, you've got your cigarette in your hand!" Possession of tobacco was the same as smoking, so I was hooked. But we never felt any animosity. The officers were doing their duty. Many years later I recounted the episode to Admiral Halsey, and we laughed over it.

A few demerits were the result, but "our Saturday social with our bottle of rye at the bandstand was never disturbed." One of Jock's classmates, William C. Luth, had been nicknamed "Whiskey" after having given a speech in favor of prohibition as a course requirement in high school. At the Academy Bill Luth was popular and a good football player, but he was not much of a student.

Faced with the necessity of getting at least a 2.0 grade on his final exam in mathematics in January 1916 in order to pass the course at 2.5, Luth decided that a big swig of whiskey just before the test would assure him of passing it. The preceding night he ordered a "mess moke"—one of the mids' black mess boys—to bring him a pint of whiskey after breakfast. Minutes after that happened Jock grabbed the bottle from Luth, but he had already drunk about half the contents.

Once in the exam room Luth worked the first problem correctly; "after that he could not see." He made 1.0 on the test, and that was the end of his naval career. But he joined the Army during World War I, was wounded twice, decorated several times, and emerged from the fighting as a captain.

Athletics, especially football, was the main diversion from academic studies, although at 140 pounds Clark was too light to try out for the football team. The 1913 Navy team had seven All-American players and won a string of victories. But the Army game meant everything, and the West Pointers were upset late in the season by Notre Dame's star end Knute Rockne, who in that game initiated the Army (and the entire world of football) into the virtues of the little-used forward pass.

Because the Army-Navy game was to be played in New York, the Brigade of Midshipmen went there by train. It was Clark's first visit to that metropolis. The mids all put their money on their team with confidence. Navy won the coin toss to receive the opening kickoff, then marched down-field and kicked a dropkick for a field goal.

> After that we never saw the ball again. Army took to the air and defeated us soundly, 16-3. It was the same my next three years at the Naval Academy; we always lost. But many years later I got my money back from the Army, and with interest, on baseball in Honolulu.

The 140-pound Clark found lacrosse especially to his liking. Origi-nated by Iroquois tribes near the easternmost Great Lakes, the hockey-like sport had been developed by the Cherokee as "the little brother of war." Its late-nineteenth-century American popularity had been centered in Mary-land and the Naval Academy in particular. So Clark had double exposure to it as "the right game for me." It developed lung power and stamina. He played class (of '17) soccer and occasionally Sunday afternoon interclass baseball as well.

Clark believed that athletics not only builds up one's physique but teaches teamwork and the "all-important will to win." Throughout his naval career he organized and led baseball teams on ships on which he served, and he followed major league baseball to the end of his life.

Another physical activity required at the Academy was social dancing, which in the decade of the 1910s was becoming a nationwide passion. To perfect their "society graces" the mids had to take, and pay for, dance lessons from an instructor known as Professor Bell.

> Since no ladies were available we practiced with each other. The "pro-fessor" would call time for us to the piano music played by his accom-panist, "Bang-drip-drip! Bang-drip-drip!" [waltz time], and if he wanted to correct us it would be "Bang-drip-drip-Out!"
>
> One of Professor Bell's favorite gems of social advice was, "I would rather see a man spit tobacco juice in the middle of a ballroom floor than bow to a lady with his feet apart." His fees were exorbitant, and we thought he was a prime racketeer, but he certainly taught us to dance.

Eight months of "vigorous studies" ended in June 1914 with the class of 1917 being advanced from plebe to youngster status and embarking on its first summer cruise—to Europe at that. Clark was assigned to the 13,000-ton "reserve" battleship *Idaho*, which was being sold to Greece to make way for more modern capital ships. This 1905 vessel displayed the Battle Efficiency Pennant, or "Meat Ball"—a red pennant with black ball in the center—used to encourage fair competition in the fleet. The 17-knot vessel lumbered across the Atlantic throughout June.

Clark was assigned as midshipman orderly to the *Idaho's* executive officer, Lieutenant Commander Hugo W. Osterhaus, a strict disciplinarian. One morning while making the rounds they encountered a young sailor with long blond bangs sticking out from under his cap. The exec ordered him to get a haircut, but next day the bangs were still there. Hugo proclaimed, "Now you'll have your head shaved!" He enforced the order, making him unpopular to many in the crew. But he was always good to Jock.

The least favorite individual in the naval hierarchy in the eyes of the midshipmen, however, was Secretary of the Navy Josephus Daniels. A staunch prohibitionist, Daniels had decreed the elimination of alcoholic beverages aboard all naval vessels, thereby abolishing an age-old custom. Daniels's infamous General Order 99 went into effect at midnight 30 June 1914. In the late hours preceding that moment the officers of the *Idaho* closed the wine mess by drinking its stores dry "with great ceremony, conviviality, even hilarity. As midshipmen we watched through the skylight with a sense of longing as we agreed that the Navy was going to hell. Events proved, however, that it was a sound policy, and I never ever heard a senior officer who wanted the wine messes returned. Still, it marked the end of an era."

The *Idaho* fell in with sister ship *Mississippi*, also purchased by Greece, as they approached the Strait of Gibraltar. Both were on their way to Naples for a ten-day visit. The midshipmen were granted leave to take the train to Rome, where they were granted an audience with Pope Pius X at St. Peter's Cathedral (one month before his death). Jock and his pals discovered a golden stairway with many steps that "everyone supposed would bring forgiveness for a certain number of sins. One of my classmates wanted to run up and down these stairs a few times, but we persuaded him that besides being sacrilegious it would not serve his purpose."

Reembarking on the *Idaho*, the mids slaved away to make their proud ship presentable to the Greeks—shining the bright work, holystoning the decks—on a short voyage to the beautiful little harbor of Villefranche near Nice on the French Riviera. There on 17 July the *Idaho* anchored next to the 1902 battleship *Maine*, built to replace her namesake sunk off Havana, Cuba, in 1898. Greek crewmen came on board, relieving the Americans, who transferred to the *Maine*, which had brought only a skeleton crew in order to have room for the midshipmen.

Unfortunately, *Maine* was very dirty, forcing the mids to "turn out" and clean her up too. Worse, next day, "we visited our old home *Idaho*, and the filth accumulated in one day appalled us. The Greeks had pigs roaming the decks, and a cow resided in the midshipmen head which we had so carefully scrubbed!" Jock was "disgusted with their idea of cleanliness." (The former *Idaho* and *Mississippi* served as Greek coastal defense ships until sunk by German planes in Salamis Bay early in World War II.)

The midshipmen were rewarded for their labors, however, one month and several port calls later with a visit to nearby Monte Carlo and its famous casino and "jockey club." They had to rent civilian coats, shirts, and neckties to be allowed to enter and gamble. The mother of Joe Lawton, one of Clark's classmates, happened to be present and coached Jock in the art of playing roulette, which he had never seen before. He made money "hand over fist" until she turned to help others. Then he started to lose, as everyone else did, except that he alone stopped with $20 still in his pocket.

Reclaiming their uniforms, the merrymakers joined a large crowd of excited French soldiers and citizens gathering in the street. The American boys, who had heard rumblings of war, turned to the classmate most proficient in French, George F. Mentz—called "the Egg" because he was prematurely bald. He learned that France had just ordered mobilization of its army. A French flag was unfurled, and the American midshipmen rendered a salute to it. At this, "the French soldiers gave us an enthusiastic cheer." World War I was beginning in Europe.

Returning to Nice that evening Clark had to use his earnings to buy dinner for his friends. Most of them happened to be from the South and became indignant when a black enlisted crewman from the *Maine* came into the restaurant and sat down at a nearby table. The midshipmen held what Clark remembered as "an indignation meeting, and I appointed myself as a committee of one to go to the Negro's table to tell him to leave. He was most courteous," not having noticed the white midshipmen until after having been seated. So he promptly left.

> The next week I was assigned to the engine room, where I found that this Negro, whose name was Johnson, was rated machinist's mate, first class. His rating was most unusual at that time as nearly all Negroes were stewards or mess attendants. Johnson knew more about the engine room than anybody else and, unfailingly polite, never showed any resentment to me for my previous action. From him I learned a great

deal about the ship's engines. But more than that he taught me that color is no measure of a man.

The *Maine* proceeded to the British base at Gibraltar en route home, and when the midshipmen went ashore at "the Rock" Jock decided to try out the Spanish he had been attempting to learn at the Academy. He always addressed any likely Spaniard with "¿Habla usted español?" If the reply was encouraging, he would begin a discourse, "although I could hardly speak the language." At Gibraltar he put the question to a Spanish-looking gentleman, who replied, "No, but I speak pretty damned good English!" "That," recalled Clark, "dampened my ardor for Spanish, and I took up French for the rest of my stay at the Academy."

After the *Maine* returned home, Jock visited his family in Oklahoma for his summer leave. A major addition to the family was Papa Will's first automobile purchase, a Buick. It was a challenging contraption for small Chelsea, given the town's lack of paved roads, and it was equipped with a shovel for mud and ruts. Ex-cowboy Will Clark "never really learned to drive a car correctly," remembered daughter Lucy, "he just herded it." Neither did Joe, who eventually had someone to drive for him in the Navy.

The family owned most of the other lots on the street dominated by the Clark house; on them it kept livestock and raised vegetables and fruits in enormous gardens. After being harvested, the produce was wrapped in paper by the children and stored in the cellar through the winter. With the birth of their last child, Virginia, in 1917, however, the family needed more room. So two years later Will had the house torn down and a new, bigger one erected in its place. Joe attended the annual family reunions and visited whenever he could throughout his career.

He returned to Annapolis in September 1914 as a full-fledged third classman or youngster and lost no time in "running" (hazing) the new plebes of '18 as part of their indoctrination. This fraternal ritual had been outlawed by Congress in 1906 and was anathema to reform-minded Navy Secretary Daniels. A more serious crime was cheating on examinations—a violation of the honor code—as was the failure to report knowledge of it. Jock "coasted along" with good marks. He—and his friends—knew about "the gouge" (solutions to the exams) and did not engage in "gouging" (cheating on exams) by being given advance "dope" (information) about forthcoming tests. In addition, they turned a deaf ear to "scuttlebutt" (rumors) of such gouging.

As the 1914–15 academic year neared its end in May Secretary Daniels and his wife dined with the superintendent, Rear Admiral William F. Fullam, at the first class's after-dinner speaking program: to sharpen one's social skills each graduating "firstie" at the table spoke extemporaneously for a few minutes. Days later, scuttlebutt spread of widespread "gouging" on the final exam in "dago" (Spanish), leading to a tribunal and the recommended dismissal of several mids, including Jock's good friend and classmate Donald B. "Wu" Duncan.

The beginning of June 1915 brought three 12,000-ton reserve battleships to the Academy for the annual summer training cruise of the makeshift "Crab Fleet," which was to visit the San Francisco Panama-Pacific International Exposition via the newly completed Panama Canal. Jock boarded the *Wisconsin* (or "Wisky" to the mids). Secretary Daniels gave the graduation speech for the class of '15 on the 4th but held up handing out the officer commissions and the ensigns' pay that went with it until all cheating violations were investigated. Accused midshipmen were moved to the *Reina Mercedes* prison ship, and the departure of the three battleships was postponed.

Admiral Fullam convened a court of inquiry, which drew congressmen to Annapolis to defend their indicted appointees. The hearings lasted for weeks until Clark's classmate John Baptist Heffernan put the "finger of guilt" on Charles M. Reagel, another classmate whom Jock hardly knew. Testimony revealed that Reagel had used keys or burglar tools to break into departmental offices where he stole or photographed copies of the exams. He had then taken them to Ralph M. ("Savvy" for being very bright) Nelson Jr., who worked out the answers and gave them to friends in need of academic assistance. In the process Nelson had garnered a 4.0 grade point average to rank as third man in the graduating class of '15.

Reagel confessed on 22 June and three days later elaborated that as a plebe he had been forced by upper classmen to gouge as a form of hazing. Furthermore, Reagel exposed and defended hazing as common practice because it "took the conceit out of a man." This deliberate parting shot further dampened the Academy's image, and an enraged Admiral Fullam now ordered boards of investigation convened on board the three waiting battleships to quiz every midshipman. The immediate result was the arrest of seven of them for hazing, sufficiently shocking to make the front page of the *New York Times* on 1 July.

Jock Clark took the Fifth Amendment, refusing to answer on the grounds of self-incrimination. He and about 30 others were moved ashore to Bancroft Hall where they were formed into a special Company A for a new investigation. The summer cruise ships then sailed for the West Coast without them.

The 1906 law forbade any mid from forcing another "to suffer any casualty, indignity, humiliation, hardship or oppression." And every faculty member or midshipman was honor bound to report any act of hazing. Typical physical hazing offenses were forced pushups, "sitting on infinity" without a chair, or "landing the *Emma Giles*" (simulating the old Chesapeake Bay paddle wheel steamer of that name by sitting in a half-filled tub of water and scooting across the room without limbs touching the floor).

More than one act of physical hazing meant expulsion from the Academy. A lesser penalty could be assigned for requiring a plebe to announce recent baseball scores, recite poetry, or tell a story.

Clark's own plebe experience in the old Fourth Company was "all done in high good humor" including sitting at a mess table, and, if the dessert was good, having to reject it by saying "dessert is for the first class," who then ate it all up. As a youngster, Jock hazed along with his mates as tradition demanded but without malice.

"Unfortunately, I was given credit for a lot of hazing I never did," Clark recalled, because his top-floor room in Bancroft Hall earned the sobriquet "Plebe Hell." Plebes were hazed there because of its clear view of any approaching authorities. Still, by hosting such shenanigans, he was able to exercise a modicum of control. On one occasion, for example, "one of my friends had a plebe stand on his head and threatened to pour ink down his nose. I put an immediate stop to this nonsense."

On Saturday, 26 June, during the cheating hearings, Clark and his pals were returning to the *Wisconsin* from liberty in town when they noticed the new plebe baseball team coming in from practice:

> We lined them up against the wall inside the gymnasium and made them tell funny stories. One plebe burst out laughing at another of his classmates' efforts. I said, "You shouldn't laugh at your classmate. You better stand on your head." He took his punishment in fun and did not seem to mind.

But the timing was bad, for now Clark was brought before a new three-man board established to investigate the hazing. It was chaired by Commander Henry B. Price, head of the Academy's "steam" department (Marine Engineering and Naval Construction). The steam boiler appellation and the man's fiery red beard had led the mids to refer to him as "High Pressure Price." The other members were also commanders: John F. Hines, Clark's former skipper on the *Idaho,* and James J. Raby. Congressman Davenport came all the way from Oklahoma to act as Jock's legal counsel.

Each midshipman was given his rights as an "interested party" and not required to testify. The usual witnesses were plebes asked only to identify any of the 30 suspected hazers seated at a large table and tell what manner of hazing they had been put through. The august hearings proceeded calmly until one plebe said, "Sir, they made me recite poetry that was a little bit off color."

"What was the nature of this poetry?" asked a board member.

"It is called 'Change the Name of Arkansas,'" answered the plebe, referring to a notoriously ribald poem based on an old dispute over the two different pronunciations of the state name, a dispute that occurred even on the floor of the U.S. Senate. Of the state's two senators, one was always introduced as hailing from Ar-KAN-sas, the other from AR-kan-SAW. After a heated debate in 1881 the state legislature had finally ruled in favor of the latter pronunciation. Naval Academy upper classmen required their plebes to know the quite fictional poetic compendium of obscenities against Ar-KAN-sas but apparently not before the early 1890s when the three members of the 1915 hazing board, who had never heard of it, had been midshipmen.

The board asked the young man to recite the poem. He did an extemporaneous job of paraphrasing it, keeping the sense and rhythm but eliminating the obscene words. High Pressure Price said, "There is nothing very bad in that," and he excused the witness.

Several days later the board asked the same question of another plebe and got the same answer. Commander Price stroked his red beard and said, "We had that last week. We didn't see anything very smutty in that."

This plebe insisted, "Sir, I don't know what *you* call smutty, but I call *that* smutty."

"Suppose," one investigator suggested, "you give us your version."

The plebe cut loose with the unabridged version of the nonsensical poem. In it a representative from Johnson County, Arkansas, one Hiram D. Johnson, is identified as having made such a speech to the state legislature opposing a change to Ar-KAN-sas because it would create a comparison with the state of Kansas. Whether such a politician existed is hardly relevant, although the well-known reform governor of California from 1911 to 1917 was Hiram W. Johnson. Johnson County is bordered on the south by the Arkansas River. (Although Jock Clark probably did not realize it, Johnson County lies only about 120 miles from his childhood homes in and around Chelsea, Oklahoma, with the county's seat at Clarksville.)

Such geographic matters immediately proved inconsequential as the air got bluer and bluer from the filthy language. The point of its preservation here is merely to demonstrate plainly that great leaders are not necessarily honed only by antiseptic educational experiences. An added humorous aspect is that, when recited aloud, parts of this perambulating piece pertaining to a "Peruvian prince" make it a disgustingly difficult and downright dirty tongue twister.

### "Change the Name of Arkansas"

Mr. Speaker! Mr. Speaker! Goddam your ornery soul to hell!
I've been trying to get your bastardly attention for the
    past fifteen minutes,
And every time my eye catches your eye,
You squirm like a bitch dog with a cunt full of fleas.

My name is Johnson, Hiram D. Johnson, from Johnson County, Arkansas.
Somebody in this body has the audacity to suggest that the
    Name of AR-kan-SAW be changed to Ar-KAN-sas.
Why, Arkansas is a place so rough and so tough
That a young girl at the tender age of twelve can flip her left tit
Over her right shoulder and squirt buttermilk up her ass.

It's a place so rough and so tough that a body can't even
Stick his own ass out of his window at 11:00 o'clock at night
Without getting it shot full of buckshot.

I got my first pair of shoes when I was twelve,
And walked backwards in the sand for five miles just to see the tracks.
When I was fourteen I had a cock as big as a corncob
And could piss halfway across the Arkansas River.

Why, comparing Kansas to Arkansas is like
Comparing the gentle oscillations of a little June bride to
    the frantic clutches of a Klondike whore;
Like comparing the pretty pink prick of a Peruvian prince
    to the dirty dangling dick of a Detroit dog.

Why, change the name of AR-kan-SAW to Ar-KAN-sas?
    No! Never! Not until the Statue of Liberty turns on her pedestal
    And pisses on the island of Manhattan!

At this point High Pressure Price banged his fist on the table and exclaimed, "Young man, we'll have no more of that! That's *treason!*" But that was the end of the infamous poem.

Eventually, the plebe that Jock Clark had made to stand on his head in the gymnasium appeared as a witness but could not identify his hazer. He even remarked that he had enjoyed the incident as having been done in good spirit. Lacking evidence against Clark, Commander Hines then assured Congressman Davenport that Clark had nothing to worry about, so Davenport went back to Oklahoma. Jock relaxed, mistakenly expecting only to have to write a letter of apology or suffer some similar minor punishment. The court completed its investigation on 24 July. Lacking proof, it could only claim a moral certainty of Clark having hazed someone.

However, Jock had the ignominious distinction of getting his name in the *New York Times* on 2 October 1915 as one on the list of midshipmen being punished. The cheating scandal resulted in only two dismissals, Reagel and Nelson, plus lesser penalties to several others. Secretary Daniels was tougher on hazing, which he linked to the apparent snobbery of the officer elite: 6 midshipmen were dismissed; 15 were turned back one year, including Clark; and 4 were suspended a year without pay. Wu Duncan and Arthur "Rip" Struble, both future four-star admirals, were cleared.

At least Clark was in the high company of two other classmates being forced to repeat their youngster years: the sons of the governor of North Carolina and of the Chief of Naval Operations, Admiral William S. Benson, although Benson's son was soon reinstated in the class of '17. Most of those punished in both scandals had abbreviated naval careers, with only two attaining the two-star rank of rear admiral, and Clark the only one to attain four-star. Several of them later enlisted in the Army to fight in World War I, notably Alexander R. Bolling '18, who finished his career as a lieutenant general commanding the Third Army in the 1950s.

So Jock Clark now left his class of '17 classmates to become an elder member of '18 in November 1915. He was 22 years old and had three more years ahead of him at the Naval Academy. He regarded his penalty as harsh, "but it cured my interest in hazing, and I learned to respect the law."

And, he turned adversity into advantage academically. Only coasting along in the class of '17, he later reckoned that he probably would have graduated in the middle of its 182 graduates. Among them were five future four-star admirals, including Oklahoman Albert G. Noble and aviators Duncan and Felix B. Stump. Now he dug into his studies to eventually graduate in the top quarter of '18—47th out of 199. But he might have stood even higher "had I not collected some demerits for indulging in too much visiting in the dormitory." He was always a social fellow.

Fortuitously, Clark's new class included future important naval aviators like himself—Forrest Sherman, John Ballentine, Thomas and Clifton Sprague, and Miles Browning. Clark and the first three made up most of the

Class of 1918 *Lucky Bag*
photo of graduating
Midshipman Jock Clark: "a
he-boy . . . in a fight or a
frolic" with "no limit to what
he will do for his friends."
*U.S. Naval Academy*

seven full admirals to come out of '18. The others included Jerauld Wright, the Supreme Allied Commander in the Atlantic during the late 1950s, and Jock's old pal Sol Phillips. He also was turned back to '18, likely for academic reasons; even with the extra year he still finished eighth from the bottom.

Clark had no difficulty repeating the same third class courses and even—déjà vu—boarding the reserve battleship *Wisconsin* again in 1916 for the cruise he had missed the previous summer. Instead of the West Coast, the destination of his second training cruise was the Caribbean. The ships called at the Navy's base at Guantanamo Bay in Cuba and at St. Thomas in the Virgin Islands, then being purchased by the United States from Denmark. The squadron cruised on to Boston and Cape Cod.

The midshipmen on the *Wisconsin* attributed the pleasantness of the voyage largely to their captain, the popular Academy teacher and speaker Commander Wat T. Cluverius Jr. The class of '18 later dedicated its *Lucky Bag* yearbook to him: "To know 'Clu' is to add something vital to your life."

One day, emerging from a compartment aboard ship, Jock Clark bumped smack into a classmate and fellow hazing turnback, Thomas G. "Bubbles" Fisher. They knew each other only casually, though Jock was aware of Bubbles's athletic renown: he eventually became captain of the Academy football and baseball teams and the Academy light heavyweight boxing champion. Nevertheless, "without further provocation or a word being spoken between us, we started slugging away at each other. Fortunately, my friend Sol Phillips was on the spot and separated us. Bubbles and I shook hands and became fast friends thereafter. Sol Phillips had saved me again." And like Clark, Fisher would become a naval aviator.

The fall of 1916 semester of Clark's second class year was dominated by the growing likelihood of America's entry into World War I on the side of the Allies against Germany. When the German navy initiated unrestricted submarine warfare against neutral U.S. merchant ships early in 1917 midshipmen began to resign in order to join the Army or Navy before the United States entered the fighting, thereby depleting all four classes.

President Wilson authorized the class of '17 to be graduated nine weeks early—on 29 March 1917. This accelerated the class of '18 to advance to first class status at the same time. But a week after this happened, on 6 April, Congress declared war on the Central Powers. Graduation for Jock's class of '18 was immediately moved up to 28 June 1917—almost one full year ahead of schedule. Jock's earlier having been turned back a year was thereby nullified.

Coursework was so greatly condensed that only the bare essentials could be learned. Both second and first class courses were completed in just three months, with final examinations taken in late June.

> To celebrate, my close friends and I hid a new quart of whiskey in our favorite hiding place, the bandstand on the lacrosse field. Saturday night after the last exam we gathered but, alas, the quart was gone! For four years the custom had been foolproof but failed at the last moment of our academic life! We never knew who got the bottle.

Papa Will and sister Lucy took the train from Oklahoma to attend Joe's graduation. Mama Lillie Belle could not come because she had to care for five-month-old Virginia, her tenth and last child (whose own fourth and last child in 1951 would be named Joseph James, after Virginia's oldest brother). One of Will's cousins, Bill Hastings, was a congressman; he drove the family visitors around Washington in his Cadillac.

The graduating midshipmen, knowing that they were going to have a chance to get into the fighting, were relieved to get their commissions as ensigns. So when they received them on the 28th and threw their midshipman caps into the air, they "did so with great glee." Wartime promotions would come swiftly as new ships swelled the fleet. Clark became lieutenant (junior grade) in less than three months and full lieutenant six months after that.

The last impression each graduate left at the Academy was a partly comical profile written by his peers in the *Lucky Bag*. Someone told a tall tale about J. J. Clark buying stock while briefly bedridden in the Naval Hospital during his first youngster year. "Jock . . . has been paying for it ever since," the account ran. "He has it all doped [figured] out that by the time he is a rear-admiral he will have it paid for."

This passage was likely an early allusion to Clark's lack of success in budgeting money—an unfortunate trait throughout his life. That jibe aside, he regarded the concluding description of him as a high compliment:

> As a fusser [partygoer], dancing man [with the ladies], and general tea-lapper [drinker of liquor], we are forced to admit that Joe gets the cheese [the cake, nowadays]. But when you want a he-boy alongside of you in a fight or a frolic I guess old Joe could just about fill the bill. There is no limit to what he will do for his friends.

# THREE

# Germans, Destroyers, and Aviators, 1917–1921

ENSIGN CLARK INSPECTED ONE OF MANY NEW WARTIME DESTROYERS, the *Manley*, when it tied up at the Naval Academy dock just before his departure in June 1917. The pristine vessel impressed him so much that command of just such a ship immediately became his highest ambition. He could not have imagined that this goal would be achieved in less than five years. In that time he fought the Germans, policed the troubled postwar waters of Europe and the Middle East, and became intimately associated with the Navy's fledgling air arm and its earliest pilots.

Clark and four classmates reported on 3 July to the 14,500-ton armored cruiser *North Carolina* anchored with the fleet in the York River off Yorktown, Virginia. The ship's 10- and 6-inch guns came as no surprise, but several crude 3-inch antiaircraft guns affixed to the upper superstructure did. The 1908 cruiser had been converted into the Navy's first experimental aviation ship, equipped with a unique but untrustworthy shipboard catapult and two Curtiss AB "hydroaeroplanes" (seaplanes)—single-seat aircraft fitted with pontoons for taking off and landing on the water. In addition, a wire-tethered balloon could carry an observer aloft to look for German U-boats (submarines).

Captain Mark L. Bristol had been assigned command of the *North Carolina* because of his role in her conversion while he was second director of naval aeronautics in 1913–16. Already a recognized expert in both gunnery and torpedoes—unusual for a single individual—he had seen the future of aviation, though he was himself (45 in 1913) too old to fly the primitive and accident-prone "aeroplanes" of the day. That Bristol had a rugged physique, however, became evident to Clark during one harsh winter crossing of the North Atlantic when the skipper stood on the bridge, exposed to the elements, continuously, for 48 hours:

This feat, as well as Bristol's kindliness and consideration, led me to form an immediate admiration for him. A long-standing naval custom has been that each young officer try to pattern his life after some senior officer whom he admires. Bristol was my choice. Throughout my naval career he stood out as one of the truly great naval officers I ever met or served with.

Although Jock's future was in naval aviation, his initial assignment was to the *North Carolina's* Fourth Division, the starboard broadside 6-inch battery. It was headed by a pioneer flyer (Naval Aviator No. 23), Lieutenant William M. Corry Jr. Because Corry's primary and demanding duty was ship's senior aviation officer, he let the new ensign run the division. This delegation of responsibility increased Clark's self-confidence, and the two men became friends.

Corry taught Jock something about leadership, triggered by the latter's naïve notion of never asking any of his men to do anything he would not do himself. This included the particularly dirty task of shoveling coal into bags inside barges for hoisting aboard the coal-burning *North Carolina*. One day Corry took him aside and suggested he stop it: "You're getting paid for something else."

"Oh, but I like the work," replied Clark. "The exercise is good for me."

Corry smiled, saying that was Clark's choice, but he repeated the admonition. Then one day Jock was shoveling away in stifling heat within the virtually airless hold of a coal lighter off Norfolk:

> My back was about to break, when, out of the corner of my eye, I noticed this coxswain leaning on a stanchion laughing at me. I said nothing and just passed the shovel to him. I learned an important lesson in leadership, and I've been passing the shovel ever since!

Through Corry, Clark became acquainted with the other two pilots on board, Lieutenant Harold T. Bartlett (Naval Aviator No. 21) and Marine Corps Captain Roy S. Geiger (No. 49). He quickly developed an interest in the fledgling air unit, nicknamed the "Eyes of the Fleet"—a title later adopted for naval aviation in general. But the two pontoon-equipped aircraft were too frail ever to be lowered over the side and launched, much less recovered at sea—only in smooth harbor waters.

When the ship was anchored in New York City's North River (the Hudson), Corry allowed Clark to make an ascent in the balloon with its pilot Roy Geiger. The weather was cold and blustery, and the wind sweeping down over the New Jersey Palisades began to buffet the balloon. The basket swayed back and forth, at times becoming horizontal to the earth below. When Jock looked down "I was not alarmed, but when I looked up at the gasbag I fully expected the basket to turn upside down. I had never been so scared in my life!"

As soon as the two men were reeled back down to the ship, Clark concluded that if he did go into aviation "it would not be in lighter-than-air gasbags but in heavier-than-air planes." Geiger reached the same conclusion and went on to direct Marine Corps aviation as a major in the early 1930s and again as a major general in wartime 1943.

Jock Clark had seen enough of the seaplanes and their pilots, however, to whet his appetite to want to join their ranks. He sought Bill Corry's advice and help in composing a letter to the Bureau of Navigation (later renamed the Bureau of Naval Personnel) applying for transfer to flight training at Pensacola. When the letter reached Captain Bristol he sent for Clark.

"Young man," he said with his piercing black eyes, "we're in a war. You have an important job in this ship. And you will get increasingly important jobs as the war goes on. What you need is sea service in a seagoing ship."

He advised Clark to wait until after the war when he would have plenty of time to apply. "Bristol made sense," recalled Jock, "so I tore up my request and did not submit another for seven years. I thus passed up the chance to be one of the early naval aviators."

It may have been a blessing in disguise, given the risks of flying the early planes. Bill Corry, for example, was transferred off the ship with its two seaplanes and catapult in October 1917 and established the first American seaplane patrol station in France. But three years later, after the war, the plane he was flying crashed; he crawled back into the burning wreckage to rescue his mechanic, only to be consumed by the flames.

Clark made four wartime round-trip crossings of the North Atlantic aboard the *North Carolina* escorting troop convoys of five to 20 merchant ships. Accompanying destroyers guarded against attacks by U-boats. The cruiser occasionally sent up the balloon to look for the subs but never sighted any. Its main mission was to use its guns against German surface raiders, though none were ever encountered. The speed of each convoy was determined by that of the slowest ship; *Arethusa* kept one convoy at nine knots, but most merchantmen averaged 16. When a convoy reached a point 200 miles off Brest, France, Allied warships relieved *North Carolina* and the escorting destroyers, enabling them to return to New York to pick up another convoy.

As a lowly ensign, Clark stood continuous "watch-and-watch" duty, always looking for enemy submarines on each trip, the longest of which lasted 26 days. But Captain Bristol recalled that "in the old days" he had served on a sailing ship without sighting land for 85 days. In order for Clark and his peers to stay awake on the long watch-and-watch vigil, they "were served the strongest coffee I had ever tasted. It must have been made from bilge water and boiler compound. I drank, on that occasion," he remembered, "all the coffee I *ever* needed." From then on, he was one of the Navy's few officers who never drank coffee. "But we kept a sharp lookout" on that last occasion when he did.

In the fall of 1917 Clark was promoted to lieutenant (junior grade) and given command of the upper deck's Sixth Division, which included the antiaircraft guns. As such, he stood watches as officer of the deck (OOD), an unheard-of responsibility for a "jg" before the United States had entered the war. He was sufficiently successful, however, that promotion to senior grade lieutenant soon followed in January 1918. Initially lacking in forcefulness, by that spring Clark had impressed Bristol enough to believe he would "make a very good officer if he keeps it up." (1917–18 fitness reports)

The enhanced responsibilities increased the risks as well, as Clark discovered one day in February when the ship was anchored in Hampton Roads, Virginia. It was held fast by eight inches of ice that covered the Chesapeake Bay but threatened to break up into large ice floes that could endanger the ship. When Clark took over as OOD on the quarterdeck—the custom when in port—Captain Bristol had the steam raised in the engines and an anchor watch set to get the ship under way should it become endangered by the sudden movement of ice.

But the navigator, Lieutenant Commander Herbert F. Emerson, ordered the OOD watch shifted to the bridge. As the two men made their way up to the bridge Emerson remarked to Clark, "If the ice comes down on you, there is nothing you can do about it. We are merely putting you there for court-martial purposes." Damage to a ship could mean the end of a career for an OOD, the navigator, and/or the captain. So Clark was happy that the ice caused no trouble.

Given collateral duty as the *North Carolina*'s athletic officer soon after reporting aboard, Jock inherited the crew's excellent baseball team. The experience so strengthened his interest in sports that for the next 20 years, until he reached the rank of commander, he was athletic officer on board every ship in which he served. When, during the warmer months of 1917 and 1918, the ship was in its home port of New York, the teams practiced ashore.

In New York Clark took shore liberty every day to play tennis with classmate (and future vice admiral) Jack H. Duncan. Afterward, they repaired to a bar near the ship's landing at 96th Street to enjoy a drink. They did so in their tennis garb, inasmuch as liberty otherwise had to be spent in uniform, and the Navy forbade drinking while in uniform.

The subterfuge worked, except that it enticed the ship's paymaster, Lieutenant Commander John L. Chatterton, to join them. "A jolly old drinker who must have weighed 300 pounds," Chatterton bought fancy tennis attire but always stayed in the bar while Jock and Duncan were playing. Unfortunately, "he made the mistake of telling sea stories of his trips to the war zone in a 16,000-ton cruiser to two secret service men." For revealing this officially secret but unofficially useless information, "Pay" Chatterton was court-martialed. Clark "thought the court was a bit harsh on the old boy, but war is war, and the divulging of military secrets cannot be condoned."

In New York Jock renewed his acquaintance with fellow Oklahoman Will Rogers, now a Ziegfeld Follies headliner. Rogers gave his old friend Joe Clark a ticket to the show. Afterward they had dinner together, "talked Oklahoma," and the famous comedian invited Clark to his Long Island home in Hempstead. Jock subsequently spent weekends there with Will and his family, often discussing aviation, in which Rogers had developed a deep interest. Soon after one of Jock's early visits with him, Will included his old friend in his daily newspaper column:

### "The Worst Story I Ever Heard"

My friend, Ensign Joe Clark of the battleship *North Carolina*, was holding bag inspection the other day. His men had their belongings neatly laid out on the deck. As he inspected one seaman's gear, he asked, "Young man, where is your toothbrush?"

The sailor picked up a large brush, called a 'Kiyi,' which is used to scrub decks, saying, "Here it is, sir."

Ensign Clark exclaimed, "Do you mean to tell me that you can get that thing in your mouth?"

"No, sir," the sailor replied, "but I can take my teeth out!"

The yarn was pure Will Rogers: it was the first time Clark had ever heard the story. Also, the *North Carolina* was only a cruiser, not a battleship, "but he always raised everybody a notch."

In March 1918 Captain William D. MacDougall relieved Bristol and took out the *North Carolina* on another convoy. It was a fairly routine crossing until the afternoon of 28 May when Clark as OOD signaled an incorrect course change to the convoy and failed to report his mistake promptly. The captain put him "under hack" (suspended from duty) for two days. (MacDougall to Clark, 1 July 1918)

Jock learned from his mistake and in July proceeded with the ship to Portsmouth Navy Yard, New Hampshire, en route to pick up another transatlantic convoy at Halifax, Nova Scotia. As the *North Carolina* headed into the Portsmouth dock on the 18th, Clark's division reported to the forecastle to ready a big steamer chain for tying up the ship to the dock. His men pulled smartly on the hook rope that ran out the end of the chain through a chock (metal wedge) to line handlers on the dock. A second hook rope was hooked into an outboard link of the chain to help steady it.

Suddenly, as the chain ran over the side, this second hook slipped out of the link, and the chain ran out free by its own weight.

Clark instinctively yelled for his men to get clear of the chain and even tried to stop it with his right foot—an impossible and life-threatening act. As he then raised his foot away from the chock, the approaching bitter end of the chain skewed around and struck his right ankle and broke his leg. Had his foot not been raised in the air, it would likely have been knocked off.

Doctors at the Portsmouth Naval Hospital found four breaks, two at the ankle and two at bones about halfway to the knee. The leg was badly bruised by the blow, with infection setting in. They considered amputating the leg, but Clark pleaded with them not to do it. The commanding medical officer of the hospital was Captain F. W. F. Wieber, who happened to know of Clark through his son, Jock's classmate (and future naval aviator) Carlos W. "Buddy" Wieber.

After listening to Clark's pleas the German-born Dr. Wieber said, "Young man, you're in good health. I think maybe 've' can save your leg." He put a cast on the leg, with a well cut into it for periodic redressing of the infected bruise. This weakened the cast, requiring it to be changed often, "a very painful process in its early stages. I finished out the war in this condition."

Jock's four months in the hospital enabled him to read a book a day on average but especially to appreciate Wieber, not only for saving his leg but for his daily kindness to all patients. One of them, a warrant machinist in the next room afflicted with stomach ulcers, complained chronically, especially about the food—a view Clark did not share.

The man told Jock he was going to complain to the doctor, and one morning when Wieber walked from Clark's room to the adjoining machinist's room Wieber said, "Vell, how's de appetite?" The man started in, "Oh, doctor, I can like eat like a horse—," whereupon Wieber, who was accustomed to his griping, cut him off: "Fine, ve vill get you some oats!" and walked out, leaving the man speechless.

In early November, just days before the war ended, Jock took sick leave and went home on crutches to visit his parents. They all celebrated the Allied victory, although many of Jock's boyhood friends had been wounded or were buried in France. Clark was more fortunate. Back at the hospital in

January 1919, he was walking but with a cane because of his still stiff ankle. A board of medical survey offered him retirement, but he protested, asking instead for active duty.

The compromise was six months' light shore duty putting new destroyers into commission while seeing whether ankle and leg improved. Reporting in February, he impressed Navy personnel there with his "remarkable persistence" in spite of the partially healed injury. (1919 fitness report by Commander E. H. DeLany) The first ship was the *Aaron Ward*, nearing completion at Bath Iron Works in Maine. Her skipper was Lieutenant Commander Raymond A. Spruance, whom Clark liked immediately and wanted to accompany to sea. When the day of commissioning came in April 1919, "nobody said anything, and I just slipped out to sea with the ship." Spruance assigned him as gunnery officer and first lieutenant.

*Aaron Ward* took station 200 miles off Newfoundland as one of many rescue ships along the flight path of the three four-engine Navy NC flying boats attempting the historic first transatlantic flight. Half an hour before midnight on 19 May the *Aaron Ward*'s antiaircraft guns fired star shells to assist the NCs' navigation, and the crew cheered as they flew over. Only the NC-4 completed the epic flight without mishap (making one stop in the Azores), and Clark's appreciation of the "eyes of the fleet" deepened.

Given the two men's relationship in the coming Pacific war, Spruance's evaluation of Clark as "an excellent officer" during their one month as shipmates is revealing about both future admirals. Spruance found Jock "somewhat quick-tempered, active, and conscientious." Overall, however, as first lieutenant he kept the ship "very clean with [the] new crew." (April–May 1919 fitness report)

A month passed before the Navy discovered Clark's whereabouts and ordered him "to return to the beach." This was the Bethlehem Shipbuilding Company in Quincy, Massachusetts, where he became the plank-owning gunnery officer of the new destroyer *Aulick* under Lieutenant Commander Lee P. Johnson. Jock used the occasion to have the doctors look at his injured ankle, which was still stiff. So in July—one year after the injury—a specialist at the naval hospital at nearby Chelsea cut out a small piece of anklebone in a minor operation to increase movement. This left Clark with only a slight limp, which remained with him the rest of his life. But several months later he was back on the tennis court. In addition, he soon became athletic officer for the ship and a year later for Destroyer Division 29.

The *Aulick*, commissioned in July, needed a crew, leading Captain Johnson to send Clark to New York City in the second half of September to recruit and assemble one. He was so successful in this and his other duties that Johnson praised him as "unusually invaluable to a ship"—"thoroughly reliable," "enthusiastic," "particularly energetic," and possessing "excellent" judgment. Jock channeled some of his energies into receiving instruction to qualify as an engineering officer during the second half of his tour on the ship. (1919–20 fitness reports)

Following shakedown, the *Aulick* transited the Panama Canal to join the Pacific Fleet at San Diego. From there it departed with the fleet for Hawaii in January 1920 to help celebrate the centennial of the native Hawaiians openly accepting the Western world and Christianizing. The ship was assigned to the destroyer squadron commanded by Captain Franck Taylor Evans, as colorful a character as his legendary father, Admiral Robley D. "Fighting Bob" Evans. It steamed abreast of Spruance's *Aaron Ward*, which Clark one day watched ram into the stern of the brand-new destroyer *Chauncey*, skippered by Lieutenant Commander William F. Halsey Jr.

No one was injured, but the bow of the *Aaron Ward* chopped a ten-foot gash in the stern of Halsey's ship. After the commotion—so the story went around—*Aaron Ward*'s OOD, an Ensign Opp, was relieved by another officer, and when Spruance returned to the wardroom where he had been eating lunch, the guilty ensign was at the table. Spruance said quietly, with no sign of rancor, "Well, Opp, I guess you'll get a one-gun salute," traditionally fired to announce a court-martial. Clark thought that Spruance showed "remarkable restraint." Later in battle he became noted for his calm and unruffled demeanor. Fortunately, like Spruance, Halsey also survived the accident, both to become major leaders in World War II.

In Hawaii Clark met many British naval officers, notably Prince Edward, who was Clark's age, 26, and destined to become King Edward VIII of England. He had come to the islands on a cruiser to represent his government in the ceremonies.

Soon after the squadron's return to San Diego, Captain Evans caused a calamity that shortened his career. At the end of one day's maneuvers he headed the squadron back toward the bay in a formation of triple line abreast, six ships to a column. They were moving at the standard speed for naval exercises of 25 knots. But as the destroyers approached the entrance buoy off Point Loma, Clark, watching from lower deck of the *Aulick*, realized they were not slowing down to get sufficient sea room to make the necessary 90 degree turn at the buoy. Evans "liked to operate the squadron at high speed because, he said, it was good training for the officers, making them alert and responsive to emergencies."

Clark went up to the bridge to witness "what I feared would be a certain debacle." Sure enough, he watched in horror as the *Buchanan* and the *Wickes* collided on the port hand. Immediately after that the *Stansbury* "slammed against our port side, crushing our whale boat to splinters and interlocking her port propeller with our starboard propeller." Then it bounced clear, but each ship had but one usable engine. Now all the "tin cans," as the destroyers were called, slowed down, the crippled ones limping into port. Captain Evans manfully and correctly took full responsibility for all the damage. He never made admiral.

The final blow to the *Aulick,* moored to a buoy in the harbor, occurred two days later when destroyer *Welles* backed away from the *Aulick*'s port side, overlapping and knocking out the *Aulick*'s remaining good propeller. Only able to make three knots, the *Aulick* was ordered into reserve commission, like a great many ships built for the war but no longer needed.

On the other hand, Clark learned that the new destroyer *Brooks* needed a chief engineering officer before departing for European waters. Since he had qualified for engineering aboard *Aulick,* he hastened to the Bureau of Navigation in Washington where he "pulled the necessary strings" with friends there to get the job.

After Clark's experiences with pioneer aviation enthusiasts Mark Bristol, Bill Corry, and Roy Geiger aboard the *North Carolina,* his new skipper on the *Brooks* turned out to be Commander Theodore G. "Spuds" Ellyson, Naval Aviator No. One. Ellyson had earned his "wings" as the Navy's very first flyer in 1911, and although he had since left aviation he still talked about it sufficiently to maintain Jock's interest—and was soon to return to flying. The executive officer, Lieutenant Henry M. Mullinix, top man in the class of '16, was also destined to become an aviator of distinction.

In August 1920 Lieutenant Clark joined the *Brooks* in New York and immediately crossed the Atlantic in company with the destroyer *Gilmer.* The voyage was made eventful for Clark, an excellent poker player, only because he lost at high stakes play to a Naval Reserve lieutenant commander. As a naval officer, however, this worthy "left something to be desired. Piloting the ship into Lisbon, he ran us into a sandbar. Fortunately, we could back off." Wardroom gambling activities had been initiated by turning a blind eye to Navy Regulations "at the insistence of the skipper," Ellyson, who invariably lost at cards.

The two ships, bound for Italy and the Adriatic Sea, were ordered to change course to Lisbon, Portugal, and then head north to the Baltic Sea. Officers and crew hastened ashore in Lisbon to celebrate their escape from "dry" America, where national prohibition had been initiated several months before. All hands drank heavily, notably Ellyson who landed in jail. After his quick release, he joined Clark and the other officers returning to the dock. When they got there, recalled Clark, the crews of the two destroyers were engaged in a general free-for-all fist fight. We started to part them and restore order. I was assisted by a big Irish water tender named Coakley. Ellyson was trying to help also, when suddenly he swung on Coakley but missed and hit the wrong man. Finally we managed to separate the crews of both ships and send them back to their vessels in the two motor launches. They were a sorry sight, with blood smeared all over their formerly spotless white uniforms.

In fact, the crew of the *Brooks* proved to be the most unruly bunch of swabbies Ellyson had ever encountered, but his own antics worked against maintaining discipline.

*Brooks* and *Gilmer* left Lisbon, bound for the Baltic with port calls en route. Next morning Ellyson, Mullinix, and Clark relaxed in the wardroom, oblivious to the deep steady roar of the fire room blowers maintaining air pressure there. Without warning, the blowers' rings shrieked up to high pitch. Instinctively, Clark—fearing an explosion—bolted from the wardroom to a ladder.

The boiler in one of the two fire rooms then did explode, filling the space with smoke and steam, forcing Jock's firemen to shut it down. The *Brooks* lost engine power and began to drift. Under Clark's direction, however, the crew—minus one badly injured fireman—got a generator working in the undamaged fire room. By radio, Ellyson received permission to put into Plymouth for repairs instead of Southampton as had been planned. He also had to avoid Brest, France—the planned refueling stop—due to heavy seas, so the British at Plymouth provided the oil.

At Plymouth the *Brooks* and *Gilmer* received orders to proceed forthwith without delay to Copenhagen, bypassing two other planned ports of call. Rear Admiral Harry M. P. Huse, senior officer in the Baltic, needed them immediately to patrol the lawless coasts of a defeated Germany and civil war–racked Russia. The British had them on their way by the end of the day, 19 September 1920.

*Brooks* took ten hours to pass through the Kiel Canal en route to Copenhagen, only to receive orders to return to the port of Kiel to rendezvous with Admiral Huse in the cruiser *Pittsburgh* the next day. However, when the *Brooks* hoisted its international code flag signal and radioed a request for permission to enter Kiel, Ellyson was refused by uncooperative Germans, so he tied her up to a buoy. Eventually, a German sublieutenant came aboard and ordered the ship to leave. But Ellyson had his orders and refused. The language difficulties led Clark to summon a German-speaking sailor from the fire room, but the situation only worsened.

"Ve vill cannon you," declared the German sublieutenant.

"Cannon! Hell!" barked Ellyson, "I'll blow up your Kiel Canal if you try to cannon me." Then he added, "I'm going ashore."

He took with him two officers who understood some German and Clark's fireman, and he strapped on a pistol belt with two Colt automatic pistols. The exec Mullinix remained aboard as senior officer afloat, with Clark next in the chain of command. Ellyson's orders were "that if the Germans opened fire on us, we should return it and get out of there as fast as possible, leaving the skipper and his shore party behind. So we armed our torpedoes with warheads, loaded them into the tubes, and stood by the loaded guns."

Once ashore, the party was refused an audience with any senior authority until Spuds brandished his Colt revolvers. The ranking German officers still ordered him to leave, thereby ignoring the right of any Allied warship to stay under the terms of the 1918 armistice. Again Ellyson said no and returned to the *Brooks*, which he defiantly kept at its mooring buoy through the night. Jock was OOD about 0200 when the flagship *Pittsburgh* arrived, so he woke up Ellyson and got him ready to go see Admiral Huse.

Clark pleaded with Ellyson to report the incident, and the other officers agreed. But he did not, claiming that he and the admiral had too many other matters to discuss. Mullinix and Clark then begged him to write up a dispatch reporting the matter, but he avoided the issue. When the State Department learned of the affair from the German foreign office it questioned Admiral Huse, who, knowing nothing of it, recommended Ellyson's immediate detachment from the ship.

The Navy soon concurred, but Ellyson was allowed to call for a board of investigation, which eventually found him guilty only of failing to inform his superiors of the incident. The whole matter taught Clark an important lesson: "An officer should never keep his senior officer in the dark about any of his activities, no matter how adverse the action might appear."

Meanwhile, as these matters transpired, the *Brooks* assumed its Baltic patrol along with destroyers *Gilmer* and *Kane*, helping to strengthen the confidence of newly created Latvia, Estonia, and Lithuania against the expanding Russian Bolsheviks. During a three-week visit to Riga, Latvia, which had been holding off the Red Army, the *Brooks* was waiting to be relieved by the *Kane* when that vessel struck an unswept mine at the harbor entrance and called for help. Ellyson did not have time to round up anyone who was ashore, including Jock Clark, who was playing tennis with the skipper of the *Gilmer*, Lieutenant Commander Marion C. Robertson.

So Ellyson drafted the chief engineer of *Gilmer* to run *Brooks*'s engines and got under way in just 20 minutes to take *Kane* in tow to Copenhagen. And Robertson recruited Clark to direct *Gilmer*'s engine room for the overnight passage to Copenhagen, where Jock rejoined his own ship the next day.

The original orders for the *Brooks* were now instituted—proceed with *Gilmer* to Constantinople on the Black Sea to join the Allied fleet policing the politically turbulent waters around Turkey and the Balkans. After the two ships reached the Mediterranean, they refueled overnight at Brindisi, Italy, only to be struck afterward by a sirocco—a powerful, hot, dust-laden storm emanating from North Africa.

Clark was at the desk of his cabin when the ship began to pitch and pound heavily.

> All of a sudden a terrific wave hit us with a crash, and green water came down over everything—down the [smoke]stacks, down the companionway outside my room, and across the floor of my cabin. I ran up to the bridge and saw that a wave had crashed over it, buckling the chart house. I eventually went down to the wardroom, where I found Dr. [H. G.] Spiedel [ship's doctor] scared half to death.

The seawater foam went higher than the forward stacks. After the ship was rolled an extraordinary 53 degrees by winds that "must have reached 100 miles per hour, strong for the Mediterranean," Ellyson turned *Brooks* into the heavy seas to avoid her capsizing. Bulkheads buckled and the window of the chart house blew away. Ellyson conferred with Mullinix and Clark before deciding to head north for repairs. Detaching *Gilmer* to proceed on to Constantinople, Ellyson conned his battered ship up the Adriatic Sea to Pola (now Pula), an old Austrian naval base being turned over to Italy as spoils of war.

Such stress at sea likely heightened the skipper's undisguised passion for diversion at poker and other card games. In the wardroom one night he started losing at "red dog," in which each player holds three cards, with those with high cards betting against the pot. The betting started at 20 British pounds, and after Ellyson lost all his money he started tossing in IOUs matching the pot. He lost 17 straight times, including his last IOU for *60,000 pounds* sterling. His embarrassed officers bet no more than 20 pounds, which they left in the pot so Spuds could eventually win, which he finally did. Even so, Jock had to lend him $400 when he was detached from the ship to go home.

Ellyson's gambling taught Clark a lesson:

> Gambling on board is wrong. Officers have good pay but not enough to waste on gambling. 1) Gambling is against Navy Regulations. 2) Those officers who have families cannot afford to lose. And 3) officers aboard ship are among friends, whose friendship they should not jeopardize. I

decided right then that I would never again gamble on a ship, and I never did.

Ellyson's irresponsible behavior extended to the fitness reports he wrote about his officers—in which he said virtually nothing. In his second, and last, report regarding Clark he did manage a minimal yet accurate assessment: "even tempered, very forceful, very active."

When the *Brooks* reached Pola, Ellyson's relief was waiting for him, and he turned over command on 23 November 1920. The officers "felt very badly losing Ellyson, because we all loved him and thought he was a wonderful man." In the end, Ellyson's brash conduct with the Germans did not affect his career. He even returned to aviation, two months after leaving the *Brooks,* only to perish in a plane crash in 1928.

As his relief for command of the *Brooks,* the Bureau of Navigation selected an older, staid officer—Commander Victor Stuart Houston, 44 years old to Ellyson's 35, and class of 1897, eight years ahead of Spuds. Unlike the popular Ellyson, who had rarely interfered with any officer, Houston was meticulous about the minutest detail, seeming not to trust anybody. He likely had been briefed by his superiors about Ellyson's freewheeling style of command and advised to run a more taut ship.

Henry Mullinix simultaneously transferred stateside, and Jock Clark "fleeted up" to the job of acting executive officer. It was an unenviable role because the new captain kept everyone on edge. With tensions building, one day Clark went to Houston's cabin for a showdown. "Captain," he said, "I know you want an efficient ship, and I know you have excellent officers. We can give you what you want if you will only trust us." The captain immediately apologized, and thereafter the officers had no more difficulties with him.

Although some people, Clark surmised, "cannot be approached in such a manner, I had figured out this would persuade the new skipper that we were all on his side. Each senior officer has his personal characteristics or whims, and the junior has to find out what suits the 'old man' and act accordingly."

During Houston's year as skipper, Jock had to fill various "shoes," some simultaneously—exec, navigator, engineer, ordnance boss. Small wonder that Houston twice regarded him as "slightly irritable." But the captain also noted that Clark's five months as exec seemed to make him a more responsible officer. In the end he rated Jock as "an earnest, painstaking young officer with real promise." (1920–21 fitness reports)

Captain Houston received orders to delay again the *Brooks's* move to Constantinople by joining the Adriatic Patrol trying to stabilize postwar

As manager of the destroyer *Brooks* baseball team, Clark shares a postgame beer at an Adriatic seaport in early 1921 with two opponents from the *Reuben James:* Lieutenant O. O. Kessing and Ensign Eugene F. Burkett, who soon became navigator on the *Brooks* under Clark. *U.S. Navy photo*

tensions between Italy and the new country of Yugoslavia. The ship remained at Pola long enough for officers and crew—managed by Jock—to play baseball games with the team of the destroyer *Reuben James.* Then it moved to its new base, Yugoslavian Spalato (or Split), a former Austrian naval base from which *Brooks* towed the old Austrian battleships *Zyrini* and *Radetsky* to Italy as war reparations.

The region was quieting down, however, and the Adriatic Patrol began to break up in April 1921. Clark had accumulated two weeks' leave time, which he used "for a glorious vacation" in Vienna. On his return, the *Brooks* left the Adriatic to finally complete its odyssey to Constantinople. What lay ahead for Clark and his shipmates would not be more of the fairly passive observation chores of the preceding months. Instead, they faced a whirlwind of bloodshed, hatreds, and endless fighting: in the new Soviet Union, the Balkans, and the Middle East.

# FOUR

# Policing the World, Round One, 1921–1923

NAVAL HEADLINES OF 1921–22 FOCUSED ON THE TREATIES ENDING the U.S.–Japanese battleship-building race at the Washington Naval Conference, assuring peace in the Pacific for at least ten years. But dirty unsung small wars raged in the Balkans, the Middle East, and the Black Sea region, requiring small warships like the destroyer *Brooks* to try to restore some semblance of order. For the chief engineer of the *Brooks*, Lieutenant J. J. Clark, the ship's deployment in these troubled waters in the summer of 1921 turned out to be "the best duty I ever had in the Navy from the standpoint of seeing the world and of sheer enjoyment."

Happily for him, the United States high commissioner to Turkey and senior American naval officer present was none other than Rear Admiral Mark Bristol, Clark's old skipper on the *North Carolina* whom he sought to emulate. Headquartered ashore at Constantinople, Bristol enjoyed broad authority to attempt stabilization of the eastern Mediterranean and Black Sea areas. A related charge was to assist Herbert Hoover's American Relief Administration during the terrible Russian famine of 1921–22, even as the Bolsheviks achieved victory in the civil war there.

The *Brooks* made port calls at Middle Eastern cities liberated from Germany's wartime Ottoman Turkish ally and mandated by the newly created League of Nations to the care of victorious Britain and France. Clark carefully observed the occupation methods used by both these European countries, being "very impressed" with the British in Jerusalem, Palestine (now Israel). Their high commissioner over Palestine, Sir Samuel Hoare, kept a tight rein on the country but conserved his forces by employing military aircraft instead of large numbers of ground troops. This tactic apparently helped promote good relations between natives and administrators.

By contrast, the French forces in Beirut, Lebanon, suffered from the animosity of the native Syrians who pressed for independence. "In any case," remembered Clark, "Hoare's program was one of my first realizations of the great value of air power." Hoare returned home in 1922 to become the air secretary who enlarged the relatively new Royal Air Force (RAF), which absorbed the air arm of the Royal Navy as well as that of the British army.

British relations with Ottoman Turkey, unlike Palestine, were "openly hostile" in Clark's words, leading to the British occupation of Constantinople in 1920. When the *Brooks* arrived on the scene a year later Britain was supporting Greece in an effort to overthrow the traditional Ottoman Turkish authority in the Middle East. Britain especially wanted to keep the strategic Dardanelles strait open for international trade and also to control much of the raw oil in the region. Yet, that very summer of 1921, a new nationalist movement under Mustafa Kemal rejected Ottoman authority and successfully rallied the Turkish people to resist the invading Greek army.

Admiral Bristol, considering the Turks to be honest people who deserved the chance to reassert themselves as a new nation, maintained a strict policy of neutrality by the United States. This position so pleased Kemal and most Turks that it laid the foundation for future close Turkish-American relations. While the fighting raged, the *Brooks* passed through the Dardanelles and patrolled the Black Sea enforcing Bristol's policy.

The ship was anchored off Samsun on the Black Sea coast of Turkey in September 1921, when Jock Clark suddenly saw a familiar shape come over the horizon. It was his old 1914 midshipman cruise ship *Idaho,* the battleship he and his shipmates had turned over to the Greeks, who in turn renamed it *Kilkys.* Its captain threatened to bombard Samsun.

The Turkish authorities in Samsun informed the Greek admiral that if the city was shelled the Ottoman Armenians and Greeks who had lived in that coastal region for centuries would be relocated to the hinterlands. Such a deportation meant death in one form or another—by starvation or by liquidation at the hands of native Anatolian Turks. With these lives at stake, "our skipper, Commander Houston, talked to the Greek admiral and convinced him to give up his plans for bombarding Samsun."

When the *Brooks* returned to its new base of Constantinople, Houston reported his action to the Greek Orthodox patriarch of that city, who was very pleased. But Houston, sympathetic to the Greeks, who were Christians, also criticized Admiral Bristol's stand on neutrality, because most Turks were Muslim.

Word of Houston's criticism soon reached Bristol, who wrote Houston
a very curt letter pointing out that Houston had exceeded himself in
criticizing matters of policy, that the United States was a neutral in any
foreign war, and that Houston would be relieved of his command for
his indiscretion.

On its way home later, the *Brooks* stopped off at Gibraltar, and Houston was
replaced. Never again promoted, he was retired from the Navy in 1926.

The anchorage that *Brooks* used when at Constantinople was near the
Ottoman sultan's palace, located in a quarter of the city known as Dolma
Bagtche. Its pronunciation was settled one night when two sailors finishing
their liberty from the cruiser *Pittsburgh* hired a horse-drawn carriage, an
*arraba*, and told the driver, their *arrabaji*, to take them back "to the American ship."

The driver knew only of the American station ship docked at Topani
closer to the center of town, far from Dolma Bagtche. When the arrabaji
delivered the two sailors to Topani, one of them started cursing him as a
"dumb bastard!" "Ah!" responded the driver, "Dolma Bagtche!" and returned
them to their ship.

Clark and his peers enjoyed the many sights of the ancient city. They
relaxed in the evenings at Maxim's, a café run by a black American named
Thomas who had fled his Moscow restaurant with his White Russian wife
when the Bolsheviks took over. Dining there one night with Julian Gillespie, a commercial attaché to Admiral Bristol, Jock saw an Italian count
"start a fracas" with his friend and classmate Lieutenant "Bubbles" Fisher.
As the count started to break away, "Gillespie and I saw Bubbles go after
him. The count drew a pistol from under his coat, but Bubbles took it away
from him—a very brave act, I thought." Next day the count complained to
the Italian high commissioner, who told Admiral Bristol, who in turn found
out the truth from the two witnesses. "So nothing happened to Bubbles,"
Clark recalled.

At the end of September the *Brooks* left the Mediterranean, stopping at
Gibraltar to change skippers. Commander Charles S. Joyce had just completed a Near East tour of duty as captain of the destroyer *Fox* and would
bring back the *Brooks* before being reassigned. From the officers of the *Fox*,
Clark and his fellow *Brooks* officers learned that Joyce was "very particular,
meticulous, and a strict disciplinarian—in fact, a martinet."

As soon as Joyce came aboard Clark found him to be "very thorough"
and quite satisfactory. Because Jock was his executive officer Joyce took him
around the ship and told him what he wanted done before getting under
way next morning. Then that night his officers went ashore, drank too

much, and got into a fist fight, which Clark had to help break up. In the morning Joyce went ashore and apologized to the owners of the damaged nightclub. He then inspected his ship with his exec, noting that all preparations had been carried out as ordered: "I realized that although Joyce was a tight disciplinarian he was also a very efficient officer."

During the voyage home Clark spent many hours on the bridge talking with Captain Joyce. Having enlisted in the Navy during the war with Spain (1898), he rose to become an officer "because he had always done his work well and had known all he could about the ships on which he had served." Jock admired Joyce immensely and fully expected him to become an admiral someday. But Joyce said that as a mustang, an enlisted man who had come up through the ranks, he was something of an outsider and that his age was against him. "He was happy with his rank and did not expect to go much further." Joyce eventually made captain and retired as such.

Joyce particularly impressed Clark during one of their talks when he observed that Naval Academy graduates enjoyed "a spirit of camaraderie which is invaluable to you as you go up in rank"—always able to consult or just visit with a classmate on another ship for information on any subject including particular job assignments, all of which Jock knew very well. "Joyce did not resent being an outsider and was very philosophical about it. But what he had told me was something I thought valuable enough for every regular officer to know." As a consequence, "throughout my naval career I always judged a man on his merit" and never gave preference to any Academy graduate.

That Clark equally impressed Joyce was revealed in the fitness report the captain wrote on him after only one month together: "Lieutenant Clark is an excellent officer. His intelligent interest in his profession, devotion to duty and particularly, his loyalty make him a very desirable subordinate."

On arrival in New York the *Brooks* received word it would be visited by the Board of Inspection and Survey. The same mail brought orders detaching Commander Joyce. Having served on the board himself he knew exactly what its members were looking for and how to prepare for them. He briefed Clark in detail before he left the ship, and Clark carefully followed his advice.

Because the European deployment was over and no replacement orders for a new captain had been issued, Joyce recommended Clark for command of the *Brooks*. The Navy Department quickly agreed, and Jock now had the command he had so coveted ever since visiting the *Manley* after his graduation in June 1917. He took command on 3 November 1921.

The ship was in particularly "good shape" for the inspection board because, while overseas, it had hired many young Russian refugees to help the crew shine the brass and keep the ship looking trim. The president of the board that visited both *Brooks* and *Gilmer* was Rear Admiral C. P. "Cy" Plunkett. He commented very favorably on everything he saw on the *Brooks:* "To see ships in this condition restores my faith in the Navy!"

In the engine room Plunkett was amazed to find the usually rough-surfaced housing on the circulating pumps for the condensers ground down to a beautiful shine—the work, unknown to him, of the "Russian waifs." "Young man," he said to Clark, "you've done a wonderful job."

Replied Clark, "Sir, I had a skipper who taught me this. Captain Joyce is the one who did this."

"No, sir," said Plunkett, "you're the man. It all depends on the man on top. You're it!"

After the inspection, the board members and the officers of the *Brooks* assembled in the wardroom, where the inspectors complimented the officers on their fine job. In the midst of the meeting, who should walk in but Commander Joyce, who had friends on the board. As he sat down he remarked, "I just came back to see what was wrong."

"Wrong!" exclaimed one of the inspectors. "Everything is wonderful! We are going to give you an excellent report."

Whereupon Joyce turned to Clark and said, "There's the man who did it." Jock was amazed.

> Here was an exhibition of unselfishness I had never before witnessed; Joyce was big enough to pass on some of the credit to me when actually he was the one who directed the preparation of the ship for inspection. This quality was a mark of leadership I never forgot, and throughout my career whenever anyone merited praise I tried to give it unstintingly. One of the characteristics of a big man is to be able to pass down credit to his subordinates rather than arrogate everything for himself.

As skipper of the *Brooks,* Clark had nothing to do other than take the ship to Charleston, South Carolina, for the winter. Little happened there, except one night when he was awakened by a frantic young fireman who shook him, saying, "Sir, the ship is sinking!" Clad only in his pajamas, Clark rushed down to the engine room where he saw water over the floor plates. His experience as an engineering officer paid off, for he immediately realized that the fireman had opened the wrong valves: instead of pumping water *out* of the bilges he had hooked the overload discharge to the fire main, pumping water *in.* Clark promptly reversed the flow.

With only half a normal crew Clark kept the *Brooks* in such good condition over the winter and spring that he was rated "a very excellent first lieutenant" and "ship keeper" by the squadron commander, Captain Charles S. Freeman (1921–22 fitness reports).

Lacking sufficient seniority for a regular captaincy of a destroyer, Clark gladly accepted the invitation of a friend to become his exec. Commander Alfred W. Atkins—inevitably nicknamed "Tommy" because of Americans' admiration for this British soldier's sobriquet—had graduated from the Academy ten years earlier than Jock ('07) and now commanded the destroyer *Bulmer*. Because it was earmarked for a Mediterranean deployment, where Clark had had such a satisfactory though brief tour of duty, he gladly accepted. As soon as he transferred to the *Bulmer* in June 1922 it departed for "the Med" and Constantinople in the company of five other tin cans. His collateral duties included those of first lieutenant, navigator, and chief fire control officer.

Tommy Atkins did not turn out to be an expert ship handler, although he had many idiosyncrasies that made him a colorful skipper. When he gave orders for the helmsman or the engine room, he sometimes forgot them or got mixed up. A seaman at the annunciators (electrically controlled signal boards) relayed the order to the appropriate station. So Clark as exec positioned himself at the annunciators; whenever the captain gave the wrong intended destination, "I would hesitate and point to the correct signal without saying anything verbally to the seaman, who would ring the correct order."

> Once off Russian Odessa Atkins had the ship headed towards a minefield, and only after great effort was I able to convince him of his mistake. Occasionally, however, Atkins made a good landing, and I would usually say to him, "Captain, that's a mighty fine landing you made!" He would stick out his chest and puff up proud as a peacock. The officers all loved him, and we would have a big laugh after each such incident.

Atkins entertained several fetishes about the seagoing navy. Although the *Bulmer* had a perfectly good motorboat, whenever the ship put into some out-of-the-way port and had to call on the American consul Atkins would insist on going ashore in a four-oared dinghy. He would put on his full dress suit—railroad trousers, epaulettes, and the "fore and after" cocked hat that was still standard issue—climb into the back of the dinghy, and manipulate the rudder with two white lines attached to it. The officers had to laugh; they thought Atkins a little *too* ancient, going back beyond the sailing days to oars.

Another fetish was his refusal to paint the regulation black strip—"black watch cap"—around the tops of the smokestacks. He wanted *Bulmer* to be different from other destroyers, so he had each stack painted entirely battleship gray.

Soon after the *Bulmer* began operating in Near Eastern waters it had an occasion to hurry toward Constantinople at 18 knots, fast for *Bulmer*. It had to make a wide turn around a shoal in the Bosporus strait, which put it into a collision course with a two-masted sailing cutter from the Italian training ship, the ex-battleship *Vittorio Emanuele*. Not only was the cutter propelled by sail but it was also starboard of *Bulmer*, giving it the right-of-way on two counts.

Clark told the captain to give way to the cutter, but he said, "No, we're all right." When Clark insisted the *Bulmer* was in the wrong, Atkins replied, "Makes no difference," and the two vessels closed on each other. When Clark saw the collision was imminent he stopped *Bulmer*, but the sailing vessel crashed into the side. Its bow was pushed in by the blow, two Italian sailors were knocked overboard, and a young Italian lieutenant lost his "brand new beautiful, gold-striped hat in the water."

Trying to be equal to the situation, Tommy Atkins went to the side of the ship to assess the damage. Another idiosyncrasy of his was speaking French, which he did very poorly and which was a doubtful tool in this crisis with the Italians. Leaning over the side, Atkins yelled down to the furious Italian lieutenant, "Quel dommage?" which literally means "Which damage?"

But the Italian lieutenant apparently understood French, and "Quel dommage!" also is a French idiom meaning "What a pity!" Atkins repeated himself, "Quel dommage?" The Italian mistook the captain's meaning, shook his fist at Atkins, fished his cap and men out of the water, and sailed away in his damaged boat.

After Clark thought awhile about the mishap, he decided that the skipper might get into trouble and suggested that he, as exec, go over to *Vittorio Emanuele* and make amends or at least apologies. At first Atkins did not want to give his permission because he felt no harm had been done, but Jock finally convinced him. When he boarded the Italian ship he was met by the admiral's staff and escorted to the admiral's cabin.

The Italian admiral spoke perfect English and was most gracious, serving Clark a glass of his wine. Jock told him that the *Bulmer* would very much like to pay for the damage to his boat and that the crew was very sorry. "Young man," he said, "don't worry about that. That sort of thing just happens to people who go down to the sea in ships." Clark thought this approach to the problem was "very nice," while Tommy Atkins escaped any difficulty, which certainly would have followed had word of the incident reached Admiral Bristol.

The *Bulmer* assumed its patrol in Turkish waters and witnessed many Greek destroyers operating in the Aegean Sea and the Sea of Marmara, which connects the Aegean to the Black Sea. Little had happened in Turkey until the Greeks launched a summer offensive against Mustafa Kemal's provisional capital at Ankara. They were crushed in August and driven back toward the city of Smyrna (now Izmir) in southwestern Turkey. The Greeks tried to hold Smyrna, but the Turkish army reentered it in early September.

Several days later someone put the torch to the city, burning most of it. Each side blamed the other. About ten days after that tragedy the *Bulmer* put in there, and Clark saw what he termed "one of the saddest scenes in my life":

> Everything was reduced to ashes for a mile and a half along the shoreline and about two or three miles back. We were told some 500 bodies were found in the harbor after the fire. Some of us went ashore to look for souvenirs among the ashes, but we found nothing. I picked up a silver spoon that was oxidized to practically nothing by what must have been a terribly intense fire. We witnessed two Greek destroyers lob a few shots into Smyrna, but that was the end of the fighting.

The war was over, and negotiations began in earnest between Kemal and the Allies, leading to the creation of the Republic of Turkey in 1923.

The U.S. Navy continued its active role in the Greco-Turkish struggle by refereeing the exchange of refugees who wanted to be relocated—Macedonian and Thracian Turks to Turkey and Ottoman Greeks and Armenians to Greece—after hostilities ended. *Bulmer* and other destroyers rotated from port to port, acting as station ships and ensuring orderliness.

Often they spent six weeks at sea in the Mediterranean and perhaps three in the Black Sea and three at Constantinople. When the time came to shift destroyers, the *Bulmer* went into port to receive a portfolio of the latest information from the station destroyer, which then proceeded to the next port. Clark and several fellow officers, however, did manage some shore leave in Egypt to ride camels and see the Sphinx and the great Cheops pyramid.

The *Bulmer* assisted the American Relief Administration in Russia in many ways by acting as station ship at such key Black Sea Crimean ports as Odessa, Yalta, and Novorossisk. The sights the men saw dramatically illustrated the gruesome aftermath of war, the White Russian regime having collapsed late in 1920. Whenever the ship put in to a Russian port it established a food line for the endless numbers of hungry children, always giving them soup and sometimes even a full meal.

> One day in Odessa we had about twenty children in the soup line, and a little girl who could not have been more than three or four years old

Lieutenant Jock Clark (*left*), Ensign C. A. "Whitey" Whiteford (USNA '21), and two others visit the sphinx and pyramids of Egypt, ca. 1922–23. *U.S. Navy photo*

was being squeezed out of line by the older children. I stopped the proceedings and took her to the head of the line and saw that her cup was filled before the others. Another child was a walking scarecrow, and I made sure he had a square meal before he went on his way. We could not help but feel compassion for these innocent victims of the political upheavals.

American ships brought food to the Russian Black Sea ports and turned it over to the Russians for distribution. The communist Bolshevik government controlled the Crimea-Volga region now that the Russian civil war had ended, but it allowed the local magistrates to distribute the food. Many White Russians were fleeing the country, but most stayed, hoping that the new Soviet government would eventually become less communistic than the strict Bolshevik regime. Everyone around the Black Sea "was passively non-resistant to communism, but sometimes when people were alone with us they talked freely against it." Yet Russia's fate was already sealed as the Soviet dictatorship consolidated its rule.

Odessa was the largest port that the *Bulmer* visited and had by far the most intelligent people the Americans met, including many doctors and university professors who spoke very good English. The city also supported an opera that Clark and his mates attended several times. Everyone with whom he talked in Odessa complained about Russia under the czars. The old nobility had been very high-handed and tyrannical, so the intelligentsia of Odessa that Clark encountered explained their guarded hope "that any kind of government was better than the old czarist regime. And we don't have any place else to go."

On one occasion, the *Bulmer* transported Colonel William N. Haskell, the field head of the Allied and American relief programs, from Athens to Odessa. He expressed his hope to the officers that eventually the communist form of government in Russia would evolve into "a practical limited capitalistic system." Because Haskell was such an able administrator, the Bolsheviks around Odessa wanted to honor him with a party. They selected a local wine cellar in the city that had been in operation for over 400 years. Luckily, along with the American Relief officials, the officers of *Bulmer* were invited and "had a grand time" tasting wines.

Now and then while the ship was anchored at Odessa some sniper would fire at it. One morning during muster on the forecastle at about 0800 Clark heard a "zing." A bullet dropped at his feet, having hit the wooden beam of the overhead canvas awning. The crew found a few bullet holes in the smokestacks, but nobody got hurt. Clark figured the shooting was "the work of some crank" but realized that protesting to the Soviet authorities was useless, "since they had problems enough of their own."

One of Clark's several jobs aboard *Bulmer* was acting as intelligence officer. While the ship was operating off the Levant, Admiral Bristol learned the British were going to build a harbor at Haifa in Palestine. Two ports led to Jerusalem—Jaffa and Haifa—but only the latter offered some protection from the south winds. Captain Atkins ordered Jock to find out what the British intended to do at the harbor so that he could inform Bristol.

Clark went ashore at Haifa and finally got referred to a young British naval officer who was the equivalent of a U.S. Navy civil engineer. He was quite affable but regretted that the plans for the harbor were secret and could not be shown. Nevertheless, Clark invited him out to *Bulmer* for lunch and a tour of the ship, and he happily accepted. The *Bulmer*'s motor launch brought the British lieutenant to the ship:

> I noticed he had a roll of papers in his hand. I took him to my stateroom first, and while we were talking he laid the papers on my desk. Then we went to meet the captain. When I could gracefully break away

I hurried back to my stateroom, where I unrolled the papers to find the plan of the harbor. I realized that the Britisher did not want to be in the position of giving me something secret or confidential. But he did not want to deny the navy of the United States, so closely associated with Great Britain, the satisfaction of having the information.

Luckily I had on hand some tissue paper, and in the matter of a few minutes I traced the outline of the proposed harbor. Then I returned to my guest, entertained him at lunch, showed him the ship, and returned to my stateroom. Before leaving, he picked up his roll of paper, and neither of us mentioned it or the proposed harbor. Captain Atkins relayed the data to Admiral Bristol, and I had a feather in my cap. It was a neat job of intelligence but hardly of the cloak-and-dagger variety.

Clark's more routine duties in intelligence consisted of writing up an assessment or summary concerning each area the ship visited, and only one other time did he come into close contact with the Royal Navy. In Constantinople he met a British officer aboard His Majesty's destroyer *Wild Swan*, Lieutenant Neville Pisani, who was Italian only in name. They became good friends, dined aboard each other's ships on numerous occasions, and often spent shore liberties together.

"I say, it's high time that the United States and Great Britain get together and run the world the way it should be run," Pisani would remark. "I agreed with him," recalled Clark in retirement, "and still think the idea has some merit." They corresponded until Pisani died about ten years later.

Another good friend was *Bulmer* shipmate Lieutenant George "Egg" Mentz, the prematurely bald Academy classmate who had eventually graduated two classes behind Jock. One day Mentz informed Clark that he was going to marry a Russian girl he had met. Admiral Bristol's policy was to transfer home those officers who wanted to marry local girls, and Jock advised Egg against it. He seemed so resolved to marry that Clark informed Captain Atkins. Atkins called in Mentz and gave him an ultimatum: if he did not give up this Russian girl Atkins would send him home. Egg had to agree, but he was angry at Clark for interfering in his personal affairs. Jock told him, "What you want to do is wait till you get home, marry an American girl, raise a family, and settle down and have a normal life." But Egg would not listen.

The Russian girl tried to communicate with Mentz and sent him letters threatening to commit suicide. This news made him more miserable. Quite bitter about it all, he confronted Clark, saying, "You're just a murderer! You're going to be responsible for this poor girl's death." Jock replied, "I don't think that's fair. I don't think she loves you that much. You'd better wait a little while and see whether she goes ahead with it. If she does, you wouldn't want to marry her anyway, and if she doesn't then you ought to take your time and make sure." But Egg had let his emotions run away with him, and for some time he refused to speak to Clark or to anyone else on the ship.

Tommy Atkins solved the problem. He would always look up people's birthdays and do something for the occasion. The *Bulmer* left Constantinople on a cruise and had been at sea for a week—during which time Egg still refused to speak to anyone—when his 20 April birthday approached. The captain and the other officers decided to throw a party for him:

> We had a big dinner aboard ship, and everything was related in some way to eggs. The place cards were egg shells with little cartoons drawn by the captain, who was something of an artist. The first course was egg soup—soup with an egg dropped in it—and every other course had something to do with eggs. During the meal Egg began to realize that after all he had some real friends on the ship. He joined right in and became one of us again. We heard no more about the girl.

Clark found many of the Russian girls very nice, and some of "our people" had happily married lives with them, but one had to use discretion. Some of the girls were prostitutes, out of economic necessity. But in the case of his friend Egg Mentz, "I felt he had made a mistake that might have ruined his life." After he returned home he met and married a wonderful girl from Virginia. They raised a fine family, enjoyed a happy marriage, and Mentz had a successful career in the Navy, retiring with the rank of rear admiral.

In July 1923 the crisis in the Near East and Black Sea regions ended. The Treaty of Lausanne was signed, ending the Greco-Turkish war and proclaiming Turkish independence. That same month the American Relief Administration closed down its offices and returned to the United States. Clark had been at sea for over a year and realized he needed some shore duty. So he applied for a postgraduate course in ordnance.

Much depended on what Tommy Atkins had said in his fitness reports. The two men had gotten to know each other fairly well, going on "long hard walks" that helped strengthen Jock's slowly healing foot and ankle. Atkins took note of Clark's impatience with others and the less than perfect neatness of his uniforms. On the other hand, he commended him as an able, proud, and "exceptionally efficient officer."

In March 1923 Atkins rated Clark "one of the best officers of his years of experience I have encountered in the Navy." And in July:

> Lieutenant Clark . . . is able to observe and to apply the best ideas of
> officers with whom he serves. He is studiously inclined and has suffi-
> cient determination to make good on a project which he undertakes.
> He is loyal and efficient and I could not ask more than to have officers
> of his type serving under my command. (1922–23 fitness reports)

Instead of gunnery school, however, personnel officers at the Bureau of
Navigation assigned Jock as an instructor at the Naval Academy—choice
duty, in his opinion. He was to report in September.

Because the *Bulmer* was not leaving yet, he "hitched" a ride on the
*Gilmer,* heading Stateside. So on 12 July he bade farewell to his skipper,
Tommy Atkins, who remained in the Navy another ten years but was never
promoted; he retired at age 50 in 1933. To Atkins's lasting credit, however,
like many officers who had to retire while still relatively young, he returned
to active duty in 1939 as World War II was breaking out in Europe and
served throughout the war. He attained the rank of captain and retired for
good in 1945.

The captain of the *Gilmer* turned out to be Commander Martin K.
Metcalf, with whom Jock had been friends ever since Annapolis when Metcalf had been a lieutenant and duty officer. So "we enjoyed a pleasant voyage together. But little did I realize that my career in destroyers was over."

The tin cans or "small boys" had performed indispensable service in
handling the manifold chores of policing post–World War I hot spots. But
the American people and government rejected the role of world leadership
that entailed such unfamiliar and nebulous tasks, and the Navy soon
brought most of its warships home from the Black Sea and the eastern
Mediterranean.

Even many of the American admirals regarded such an unglamorous
and amorphous mission as uselessly diverting resources away from the
Navy's main business: operating the expensive Battle Fleet with its battleships, cruisers, and destroyers and the new technologies represented by submarines and aircraft carriers.

A few years later, when Jock Clark was serving on the staff of a battleship admiral, Montgomery Meigs Taylor, he related some of the highlights
of his postwar Mediterranean and Black Sea cruises. Taylor had been in the
office of the Chief of Naval Operations (CNO) about the time Clark came
home, and he had been instrumental in having the destroyers returned to
the United States. Said Taylor to Clark, "I thought it was time we got the
loafers back."

It was an innocent joking remark that Clark always remembered. In
fact, however, the United States rejected any postwar role of policing unset-

tled regions of the world; refused to join the League of Nations; reduced the size of the Navy and the Army; and laid up "in mothballs" the very destroyers that had done such yeoman service from 1919 to 1923.

In reality American talents and evenhandedness continued to pay handsome dividends, as in the case of Rear Admiral Mark Bristol, who was not sent home but retained in Turkey another four years. He performed the herculean task of cementing U.S.–Turkish diplomatic and trade relations so effectively that the Republic of Turkey remained staunchly pro-American for the rest of the century.

In 1927, with civil war raging in China, Bristol was promoted to full admiral (four stars) and appointed commander in chief of the small U.S. Asiatic Fleet. His task was to use his considerable diplomatic talents and experience to achieve a similar settlement between the warring factions. At this he was not successful, for the events in China closely involved imperial Japan, and the eventual outcome would be World War II in the Pacific.

Following that conflict, Jocko Clark would find himself back in the Mediterranean in the same role of policing tense war-stricken countries and the adjacent waters, but this time with the rank of rear admiral. His experiences in that region after World War I would prove invaluable.

# FIVE

# Flying with the Battleships . . . and Moffett, 1923–1931

No SOONER HAD JOCK CLARK REPORTED TO THE NAVAL ACADEMY to teach navigation in late September 1923 than he began to flirt with naval aviation again. It had made tremendous strides since the "crates" assigned to the *North Carolina* six years before. Battleships now catapulted scout planes; patrol planes and rigid airships flew from naval air stations; and the 11,000-ton experimental aircraft carrier *Langley* joined the fleet in 1924 to help train pilots. The pilots flew fighting, bombing, scouting, and torpedo-carrying planes. The new Bureau of Aeronautics (BuAer) coordinated everything (except air operations in the fleet) and was headed by a dynamic chief, Rear Admiral William A. Moffett.

After some hard thought, Clark decided to resubmit his application for flight training, but not before visiting BuAer to weigh his chances of being accepted. Particularly concerned about the limp from his leg injury, he consulted a flight surgeon at the bureau about his chances. After examining him the doctor proclaimed, "You can fly better than you can stand watch!"

"That does it," said Clark, and he immediately applied. The fact that he was 30 years old—slightly older than most student pilots—did not seem to matter to the Navy.

Hastening back to Annapolis he submitted his request to the superintendent, Rear Admiral Henry B. Wilson. This "old sea dog," as Clark regarded him, had no use for "such new fangled ideas as aviation." He called Jock into his office and turned him down, earmarking him instead to make the midshipman summer cruise. At Clark's insistence, however, Wilson at least agreed to forward the request.

Jock was fully aware that all requests for flight training were being granted in order to meet BuAer's needs. He hastened to the bureau and explained the situation to Admiral Moffett's aide, Lieutenant B. R. "Benny"

Holcombe, who said simply that he would be accepted. It was done, and less than two years later Admiral Wilson retired just as the Academy initiated a course in the theory and science of aviation.

Clark had yet to even ride in an airplane (his balloon ascent in 1917 hardly counted), so he welcomed an invitation from a former classmate to go up. Marine Corps Captain Ford O. "Tex" Rogers, class of '17, had left the Academy in 1916 to join the Marines (rising to major general in World War II). He flew Jock from the naval air station at Anacostia, D.C., to the Marine base at Quantico in northern Virginia in a two-seat Vought VE-9, a spotting plane for battleships.

After lunch with other Marine Corps pilots, the two men took off on the return flight, only to have the 180-hp engine quit over Gunston Hall, a palatial country mansion and estate. Tex glided the plane down to a meadow, from which he and Jock walked to the great house to telephone Anacostia for help. Treated to refreshments by the owners, they signed the guest book beneath the names of President Calvin Coolidge and Earl Balfour, the British delegate to the recent Washington Naval Conference.

Presently, a Navy plane landed in the field with a mechanic to make repairs. It was flown by Lieutenant Alford J. "Al" Williams, Admiral Moffett's favorite pilot in the National Air Races, which were a highlight of the "Air Age" aspect of the Roaring Twenties. The mechanic fixed the engine, and Tex Rogers flew the plane back to Anacostia. The experience cemented Jock Clark's eagerness to become a flyer himself.

Meanwhile, he taught navigation during the 1923–24 academic year. He was rated only average by his department head until the spring when he was considered "a very thoughtful and conscientious officer," superior in cooperation and courtesy. (1923–24 fitness reports by Commander John Downes) He did even better in the summer session as a volunteer athletic coach, lauded for promoting "excellence and good sportsmanship" among the midshipmen. (Fitness report by Commander W. J. Giles)

Clark reported to Aviation Class 21 at the Navy's air training center at Pensacola, Florida, on 12 August 1924, one of some 60 entering senior and junior grade lieutenants. The most senior of them was Gerald F. Bogan, another escapee from Admiral Wilson's clutches at Annapolis. The instructors had the same ranks as the students, having won their own "golden wings" only since the war, among them Jock's 1918 classmates Forrest "Fuzz" Sherman, Tommy Sprague, and John D. Alvis, who was assigned as Jock's instructor.

Each instructor taught four students the rudiments of flight in classrooms made muggy by the Gulf Coast summer. Radio code equipment—in those days before voice transmissions—required a towel for wiping moisture off the sending key. Graduating to the open-air cockpit, each student took the front seat, connected to the instructor in the rear seat only by the "gosport"—a voice tube through which only the instructor could talk; no backtalk from the student!

"Don't try to be the best flyer, only the oldest," especially when landing, cautioned the safety-conscious Alvis: "Any landing you can walk away from is a good one." An initial "uneasiness" gave way to self-confidence for those who expected to complete the course, Clark among them. In fact, he learned so quickly that he had extra time to play bridge and poker in the BOQ (bachelor officers' quarters).

Clark figured that "once I won my wings I would be up with the angels, with no obligation to do any work. But this illusion was soon shattered; when I received my wings, I was put to work and never had a chance to relax until I retired from the Navy."

The students began their actual flying in old multiseat wartime aircraft. First was the 150-hp single-engine basic Curtiss biplane: the JN-4B Jenny landplane with wheels and the N-9 seaplane version with single float pontoon. Clark moved easily into the "H boat"—as the Curtiss HS-2L flying boat was known. It was powered by a single 360-hp Liberty engine located behind the wings, the only "pusher" biplane that Clark flew. He handled it so effortlessly that instructor Alvis moved him on quickly to the larger twin-Liberty-engine F5L Canadian flying boat.

On his initial hop in the latter Jock was horrified to see another F5L go into a spin from which it never recovered. It crashed into the sea, whereupon Alvis and Clark landed alongside the wreckage. But the two petty officer pilots and three passengers had been carried down with the fuselage into the deep water. After taking off, Clark found that the fatal crash left him with "an almost insurmountable mental block" against turning at the required steep angle with wings nearly vertical. He then failed his five-hour-long check.

That night he spoke to Lieutenant Commander D. C. "Duke" Ramsey about his problem. Ramsey, personal aide to the air station commander, listened to Jock's fear that "some mistake of mine might result in someone else's death." Ramsey, who had earned his wings back in 1917, assured him that although crashes occurred and people lost their lives, it was nobody's "fault." Aviation was still in its infancy, and fatalities were "incident to service." They had to be accepted if naval aviation was to make progress.

Ramsey's logic made sense, Clark's mental block disappeared, and he had gained a lifelong friend in one of the rising leaders of the Navy's air arm.

Clark mastered the training syllabus, ensuring that he did so by obeying the one inviolable rule imposed on all student flyers: no drinking except on

Friday and Saturday nights. Each trainee had to sign the "Bevo" list, "swearing that we had not had a drink in the 24 hours preceding each scheduled flight." The name came from Anheuser-Busch's nonalcoholic beer-like Bevo drink. (Otherwise, beer and spirits continued to flow freely in the Navy during national prohibition until it ended in 1933.)

Though Clark was "somewhat slow to learn" and never above average, school commandant Captain John Raby regarded him as an excellent officer and generally "good" student. The attrition rate was fairly high, and when Jock received his golden wings as naval aviator on 25 March 1925 he stood 28th in a class of 37. (1924–25 fitness reports)

He remained at Pensacola another five weeks for advanced training in patrol and fighter aircraft. In twin-engine flying boats he moved from the F5L to the Curtiss H-16, a bomber armed with five Lewis repeater guns. In both planes he concentrated on improving his aerial navigation skills. He practiced aerial gunnery in the single-engine 180-hp VE-7 and VE-9 Vought fighter-observation landplanes. Clark and his fellow graduates honed their tactical skills on long flights. Ever alert, Jock became proficient in air-to-air dogfighting and formulated a motto that he followed throughout his career: "Watch every angle and fight for every inch."

Transferred to the Navy's premier West Coast naval air station, North Island in San Diego, in July 1925, Clark honed his flying skills in the fleet aircraft there. Much of the fleet was absent on a cruise to Australia, leaving as senior aviator present Commander John Rodgers, Naval Aviator No. Two, who had, like Ellyson, recently returned to aviation after a long hiatus.

Clark, however, like other bachelors among the 21 graduates arriving from Pensacola, was most interested in the social scene at Coronado Island—the resort connected to the air station by the "Silver Strand" of sand. One of them, Lieutenant Gerry Bogan, accepted a bet that he could drink a dozen pisco punches in an hour. This concoction consisted of a strong Peruvian brandy mixed with pineapple and grapefruit juices. Jock agreed to act as referee. So they climbed into Bogan's Ford runabout and drove across the Mexican border to a saloon in Tijuana notorious for its pisco punches. "In less than 45 minutes," recalled Clark, "Gerry downed 14 pisco punches and then drove us back to Coronado none the worse for wear."

Jock attended one of the weekly Saturday night social bashes with Lieutenant (jg) A. I. "Al" Malstrom, who was not a flyer. After leaving the party about 4 AM, Malstrom indulged his passion for ocean swimming by taking a dip into the surf in his shorts. Clark went home, only to be awakened at dawn by the town marshal saying that Malstrom's clothes had been found on the beach. Fearing that the violent undertow had swept him out to sea, Clark searched all day for him in a plane, unsuccessfully.

Just before midnight the phone rang. It was Al. After his swim in his shorts he had returned to the wrong beach. In the broad daylight, minus his clothes, Al took refuge in a garage, periodically calling out for help. Late that night he was finally heard and was able to telephone the base. His only attire was a rubber raincoat and rubber boots he found in the garage.

The incident became the talk of North Island, and Jock was later best man at Malstrom's wedding.

The biggest news was John Rodgers's anticipated and unprecedented long-distance flight from San Francisco to Hawaii with three flying boats. Rodgers, as reckless as he was fearless, faced the considerable problem of navigating beyond the sight of land for 2,100 miles. One day he sent for Clark and said bluntly, "What do you know about navigation?"

"Sir," replied Jock, "I taught it at the Naval Academy, and before that I navigated destroyers in the Mediterranean."

"Fine," said Rodgers, "from now on [15 July 1925] you are my ground navigation assistant for my flight to Honolulu."

Clark could not make the 2,100-mile, 28-hour flight himself because Rodgers had already selected the five-man crews for the three planes. But he was able to assemble, test, and even develop navigational instruments, keeping in mind the 1919 transatlantic flight of the three NC Navy flying boats.

To Rodgers's sextants, which Clark tested and adjusted, he added a newly developed bubble sextant for celestial navigating without a horizon. He assembled and adjusted the standard Navy navigational watch to serve as a chronometer. He developed a drift indicator for sighting waves to tell the actual direction over the water. And, perhaps at Rodgers's instigation, he "manufactured a roll chart from San Francisco to Honolulu with the latitude and longitude lines set at correct angles along the course with about 300 miles leeway on each side so that Rodgers could navigate the entire flight on one continuous strip map." (Illustrated in Dwight Messimer, *No Margin for Error*, 57, which makes no mention of Clark.)

Clark worked out tables showing the exact altitudes of each prominent celestial object—sun, moon, bright planets, and stars—for each time and date during the flight. This would enable Rodgers to use sight lines of any two objects to establish a fix for his own altitude. The two men tested this system on day and night flights off San Diego in an old H-boat (HS-2L), trading off between piloting and "shooting" celestial bodies with their sextants. They landed on the water to discuss navigational problems:

Rodgers was a rugged individual, courageous, but not always alert. Once as he brought our H boat down for a landing in an ocean swell, he bounced it very heavily, knocking a small hole in the bottom of the hull. But he kept on flying. When we returned to North Island, someone asked him about the hole, "What happened?" "We hit a rock in a cloud," Rodgers answered. This amusing remark, however, did not excuse careless flying.

Completing their preparations on 21 August, they flew to San Francisco the next day. That morning, however, Clark discovered the telescope of their regular sextant missing. Both men frantically searched for it until Jock noticed a bulge in Rodgers's pants pocket. Sure enough, there it was. Rodgers apologized, and they took off.

The expedition trained a week in the Bay Area for the 31 August flight, and Admiral Moffett arrived from Washington to observe its departure. A Boeing flying boat proved too heavy, so all hopes were pinned on two Naval Aircraft Factory twin-engine PN-9 flying boats. These, however, could not lift off the water early on the 31st until some of the heavy navigating instruments were unloaded. Finally, at midday, the second boat took off. Rodgers followed two hours later in the flagship, racing its engines for five hours to take the lead.

The trailing PN-9 broke a fuel line and suffered hull damage in a hard landing at sea, forcing it to be towed home, out of the running. Rodgers pressed on, aided by radio transmissions from station ships every 200 miles, enabling him to plot his position on Clark's roll chart. Rodger's last acknowledged receipt of such a position report was from the aircraft tender *Aroostook* at 1607 on 1 September.

After that, silence. Rodgers and his PN-9 had disappeared—likely down at sea. Unknown to the outside world, Rodgers and his crew were indeed in the drink after having flown 1,840 statute miles from San Francisco. The primitive loop antenna of the *Aroostook* had given Rodgers a reciprocal bearing—180 degrees from his correct position. So he headed far northward, where the PN-9 encountered strong headwinds, then ran out of gas.

The mood of the Navy's flyers, beginning with their leader, Admiral Moffett, awaiting news in San Francisco, was glum. With Clark out of a job once the PN-9 had departed, Moffett assigned him as temporary aide— "the beginning of a long and treasured friendship."

The sadness increased two days later, 3 September 1925, when the *Shenandoah,* one of the Navy's rigid dirigible patrol airships, was sent crashing to earth by a thunderstorm over Ohio. Fourteen men died, while the other 29 "free-ballooned" safely to earth with part of the gasbag.

Next morning in San Francisco Clark brought Admiral Moffett his railroad ticket for the return trip to Washington. Jock had already read the newspapers. Brigadier General William "Billy" Mitchell, crusading head of the U.S. Army Air Service, had launched a new attack. He used the losses of Rodgers's PN-9 and the *Shenandoah* to condemn the leaders of both the Navy and the Army for "incompetency, criminal negligence, and almost treasonable administration of the national defense" by neglecting to build safe aircraft.

Clark found Moffett pacing the floor angrily. "Did you read the morning papers? Did you see what Billy Mitchell said?" Clark replied that he had, knowing also that Mitchell had accused Moffett of being "a swivel chair artist," meaning that he was not a real pilot like Mitchell. (He had, however, completed the first half of the pilot training course at Pensacola to qualify as "naval aviation observer"—a stopgap Navy measure for obtaining more senior officers to command aviation forces.)

"That son-of-a bitch," roared the normally tactful Moffett, "is riding over the Navy's dead to further his own interests! I'm going back to Washington and put a stop to this!"

And he did, with a withering denunciation of Mitchell in a press release one week later. This contributed to the fury aroused by Mitchell in the Army and Navy officials he had criticized. In subsequent hearings, Moffett used Commander John H. Towers (Naval Aviator No. Three) to successfully discredit Mitchell's claims. The Army summarily court-martialed their outspoken visionary, reduced him in rank to colonel, and suspended him from active duty for his blatant insubordination. His ideas for a separate "air force" centered on long-range strategic bombers years ahead of the available technology. His methods were downright disloyal—unlike those of Moffett, who wisely worked within the system to advance the Navy's air program.

Meanwhile, on 10 September, good news: a U.S. submarine operating off the Hawaiian Islands had sighted and rescued John Rodgers and his crew in their flying boat. Using its hull, the five men had cut and fashioned the PN-9 wing fabric into a sail and sailed 450 miles before the trade winds for six days. The sub towed them the last ten miles to Hawaii.

This success—repeating the feat of Jack Towers in the NC-3 six years earlier—proved not only the grit of naval aviators but also their skills at seamanship and navigation. Rodgers honored Jock with a letter of commendation for having been

> of great service to me in the preparations for the West Coast Hawaii
> flight, particularly in connection with navigation. He prepared all the

necessary tables, and otherwise assisted me greatly as to navigation equipment. I consider him a proficient navigator of aircraft. (Rodgers to Commander, Aircraft Squadrons, Battle Fleet, 2 December 1925)

Still, Clark largely blamed Rodgers for having gotten lost in the first place, and he was not entirely surprised when—a year later—Rodgers suffered a fatal plane crash into the Delaware River near Philadelphia. This tragedy could not be passed off as "hitting a rock in a cloud." (Seven civilian flyers perished in the 1928 Dole pineapple company "race" from California to Hawaii before Navy Lieutenant (jg) William V. Davis Jr. and a civilian copilot succeeded later without mishap.)

Soon after Jock returned to San Diego he found a new and tough commander of the fleet's Aircraft Squadrons, the bewhiskered Captain Joseph Mason "Billy Goat" or "Bull" Reeves. The sturdy reputation of Captain Reeves stemmed from his football days at the Academy in the early 1890s, during which time he invented the football helmet! Reeves had rushed through the naval observer course at Pensacola during the summer of 1925 in order to be eligible for his new command, hoisting his commodore's flag in the carrier *Langley*.

Billy Goat Reeves electrified the airmen with often long but unforgettable speeches at his headquarters. The major one that autumn resulted in his famous "1001 Questions" that needed to be resolved in order for Aircraft Squadrons to serve the fleet effectively. Clark was fascinated by Reeves's four-hour lecture on the 1916 Battle of Jutland. (Wildenberg, *All the Factors of Victory*, 23–24, 126–27; Reynolds, *Navies in History*, 162–63)

Reeves condemned British Admiral David Beatty for having failed to keep fleet commander Admiral Sir John Jellicoe adequately informed when Beatty charged forward against the German fleet. As a consequence, the British fleet defeated but did not destroy that of the Germans. Lieutenant Al Buehler, sitting next to Jock at this lecture, summarized it in three words: "Beatty bitches battle!"

Reeves created the Navy's first utility squadron, VJ-1B ("V" the symbol for aircraft, "J" for utility, "B" for Battle Fleet), and assigned Clark as its flight officer. Shore-based at San Diego, it performed general utility tasks not done by the front-line squadrons of fighters (VF), scouts (VS), bombers (VB), or torpedo (VT) planes, and patrol (VP) or observation (VO) planes. The pilots of "Utility One" towed practice targets for ships' antiaircraft guns, conducted long-range searches, tested equipment, hauled passengers, and did miscellaneous tasks.

For six months Clark's squadron supported the fighters operating off the *Langley* (CV-1), and the gunfire-spotting float planes catapulted from the battleships. He voluntarily took a course on the use of catapults and became squadron navigation officer, giving admirable lectures on navigation to his fellow pilots. He continued his testing of new navigational instruments, notably an improved bubble sextant. Lieutenant P. V. H. Weems, beginning a lifetime of major improvements in aerial (and eventually aerospace) navigation, obtained all of Clark's instruments and data from the Rodgers flight and those in use by VJ-1.

Clark's successive squadron skippers gave him superlative fitness reports, remarking on both his love of flying and his abilities as a pilot. Lieutenant Commander J. F. Moloney found him "conscientious, willing and a hard working officer." Commander W. G. "Gerry" Child admired Clark as faithful and loyal: "I am very sorry to lose him from the squadron." (1925–26 fitness reports)

The reason was a step up to battleship duty. In April 1926, Clark was transferred to the small observation unit—part of VO-2 (Observation Squadron Two)—on board the battleship *Mississippi* as junior aviator. His orders were to learn the functions of operating the unit's two small single-engine 200-hp UO-1 seaplanes. After three months he was supposed to relieve Lieutenant Charles L. Hayden, a former classmate of '17, as senior aviator.

The Friday morning that Clark reported aboard the 33,000-ton battlewagon he followed the custom of immediately presenting his orders directly to the captain. Thomas C. Hart was an acerbic old-school skipper so humorless that junior officers regarded him as having been "weaned on a pickle." Known as "Tommy" Hart throughout the fleet, he ran the proverbial taut ship. When Clark presented himself, Hart looked up from the paperwork at his desk and saw only Jock's aviator wings.

"We've got too goddammed many aviators on this ship already!" he barked. "I can take you up on my quarterdeck and show you oil marks where the aviators have spilled oil. I can also show you Irish pennants [loose lines] hanging from the planes. You aviators are just not seamen!"

"This reception," Clark recalled, "took me by surprise, especially since I was fresh out of Pensacola with a high opinion of myself."

Jock managed to reply, "I don't know about that, Captain, but I am reporting for duty, and here are my orders." He slammed his orders down on Hart's desk, did a sharp "about face," and marched out. He eventually learned Hart had once published an article on aviation that he believed Billy Mitchell had plagiarized. But some of his animus was due to his own naval aviators, as Clark learned immediately.

That very afternoon Jock was catapulted in one of the float planes just for practice, soon landed off the stern of the anchored ship, and was hoisted aboard by the after crane. Charlie Hayden was waiting with the news that Captain Hart had inspected the living spaces of the enlisted aviation personnel and found them below par.

Hart had consequently put the entire aviation unit—five officers and 22 men—"under hack": suspended from duty and restricted to the ship, thus nullifying weekend liberty ashore. Clark inspected the compartment himself and "found it in such a messy state that I had to agree with the captain."

While mulling over some way to turn things around quickly he sat down to his first dinner in the wardroom. His department head and ship's gunnery officer, Lieutenant Commander Daniel J. Callaghan (who in 1942 as rear admiral was killed in the Naval Battle of Guadalcanal), stood up and made "a very flowery speech of praise for the new member of the mess. Gradually, it dawned on me that I was the subject of his welcome."

When Callaghan finished, other officers at the table applauded, calling out "Speech! Speech!" Taken by surprise, Clark cautiously rose to reply, whereupon cheers broke out, "Yea! Yea! Yea!" He never got to say a word, soon realizing this welcome was standard for all new officers. At least the officers did not seem to share their captain's disdain for aviators.

After the meal Clark decided on direct action to get his men out of hack. He gathered all 25 aviation personnel—except Hayden, who had "disappeared, furious with the Old Man"—in the offending spaces and told them that "the thing to do is to clean up this compartment, even if we have to work until four in the morning."

They agreed, and Clark did not leave until 0400, when he was satisfied that everything was "in good shape." He had to wait to see Captain Hart, who was preparing for the general Saturday morning personnel inspection: "Sir, the aviation compartment is now ready for inspection."

Hart frowned. "I've got to go ashore after personnel inspection. I don't think I'll have time to inspect it." When I hesitated, he softened, willing to go halfway. "Well," he said, "I'll have the duty commander inspect the aviation quarters and see what he says." Luckily the duty commander was an old friend from Naval Academy days, Lieutenant Commander Joseph H. Chadwick. Joe inspected the compartment, but what he said to the Captain I never knew. The restriction was immediately removed, and the aviators were allowed to go ashore.

Early Monday morning Captain Hart sent for Clark and said to him the moment he appeared, "You are now senior aviator of this ship." Charlie Hayden, though a year senior to Jock, was happy just to fly and stay away from Hart unless forced to do so because of his seniority.

Clark's principal activity was piloting a UO-1 in the front seat while Hayden or another aviator in the rear seat spotted the accuracy of the fall of the 14-inch shells near the floating target. They did their job well enough to earn plaudits from the battleship division commander, Rear Admiral Louis R. DeSteiguer. One day, after spotting fire for DeSteiguer's flagship, the *New Mexico*, Clark and Hayden experienced engine trouble on the 70-mile return flight to the *Mississippi*, anchored at San Pedro near Los Angeles.

Clark passed a note to Hayden, suggesting they return to land near the flagship, but Hayden—whose flying skills Jock respected—convinced him to proceed. Once over the horizon, however, Clark heard a loud bang as the top cylinder of the engine sailed over his head, followed by another. The engine had run out of oil, freezing the bearings, stopping the propeller, and causing the plane to shake "so violently that I thought it would fall apart."

Jock glided her down in his first emergency water landing, while Hayden radioed the *New Mexico*, 20 miles away. It sent a boat, which towed the plane to the ship's crane for hoisting aboard. Luckily for Clark, Hayden as senior lieutenant had to explain why the displeased admiral was forced to interrupt his training schedule for this incident. Hayden was soon transferred to Pensacola, where he died in a plane crash several months later.

All eyes were on the carrier *Langley*, however, which was establishing procedures to be applied to two 33,000-ton carriers (actually, and illegally under treaty agreements, 36,000 tons) then nearing completion, the *Lexington* and *Saratoga*. This included qualifying most naval aviators in carrier takeoffs and landings by making ten of them in the primitive UO-1s while the *Langley* was under way. Jock's turn came in July 1926 under the watchful eye of its executive officer and acting captain, Commander Towers.

He had no trouble touching down on the "Covered Wagon" (which the lumbering flattop *Langley* resembled), his tail hook grabbing one of the arresting wires to stop the plane. Several other VO pilots who qualified with Clark that month later became major leaders in the war against Japan: Arthur W. Radford and Calvin T. Durgin (USNA '16), Donald B. Duncan ('17), and Jock's classmates ('18) Tommy Sprague and Miles R. Browning. Whenever they had the time and the opportunity, they all practiced their onboard landings and powered takeoffs.

The fleet's endless training culminated annually in war games. Clark's first was Fleet Problem VII in the Caribbean during the spring of 1927. The VO units did their customary spotting for the battlewagons, and Billy Goat Reeves—now a rear admiral—used the occasion to demonstrate that the *Langley* needed tactical freedom to avoid enemy air attacks.

During the return voyage to the West Coast the battleships dropped off their seaplane pilots at North Island for landplane training and continued on to Seattle for maneuvers. By now Clark had become flight and executive officer of VO-2, commanded by Lieutenant Commander W. Keene Harrill. One of his many duties was indoctrinating new pilots in squadron procedures and tactics. The squadron flight officer was Lieutenant Miles Browning, a chronic complainer and critic of Harrill. On his desk in the hangar he even displayed an oversized key-shaped piece of aluminum with an attached shipping label inscribed "Key to the SOB Locker."

When Jock saw this piece of "typical sailor grousing" he jotted a note to his classmate to remove it "in the interest of squadron morale." Shortly, the irascible Browning—whom a great many fellow officers regarded as an SOB—dashed into Clark's office and announced loudly, "I'll be goddammed if I will remove it!"

"Browning," Clark replied, "that is an order, and in the Navy we all carry out orders."

Keene Harrill overheard this exchange and called in Browning for a talk. What the skipper said, recalled Clark, "I never knew, but Browning came to my office and apologized to me. The key was removed, but Browning never got over it. The episode marked the beginning of our differences that extended into World War II."

Jock's performance with VO-2 "in all ways showed exceptional ability" (fitness report by Calvin Durgin) and led to his assignment to the VO unit on the battleship *Pennsylvania*. When the battleships returned to southern California in September, the *Pennsylvania* was flagship of Rear Admiral Montgomery Meigs Taylor, commanding Battleship Division Three. When Clark's plane was hoisted aboard, the admiral's flag lieutenant greeted him with the words, "You are on the admiral's staff"—as aviation technical adviser, in addition to being senior aviator on the flagship. He could only guess that Captain Hart had recommended him; both of Hart's fitness reports on Clark (1926–27) credited him with establishing "harmony" between the aviation unit and the rest of the ship.

The new job brought Clark into close contact with admirals who strongly supported aviation—Reeves, Taylor, and the commander of the battleship divisions, Vice Admiral William V. Pratt. In fact, the latter two men were bringing about "a marked change for the better in the attitudes of the old-line battleship admirals and captains toward naval aviators." This led Clark to remember this year of duty as "one of the most constructive periods in my entire career."

Often in the late evenings Admiral Taylor would send for him, Clark recalled.

We would discuss future applications of naval aviation in modern warfare, especially as it might relate to a war with Japan. Most of the forward-thinking admirals accepted the premise that we were destined sooner or later to fight against the Japanese in the Pacific. During our conversations Taylor, who had a very sharp, incisive mind, would devise intricate and complex war problems, then solve them logically and systematically.

And Taylor was impressed with Clark, who had "excellent ideas in the broad subject of aviation." (25 June 1928 fitness report)

The year of being based in the Long Beach–San Pedro area afforded Clark opportunities to visit with Will Rogers, now living on a "ranch" (really just a home and 300 acres) in the hills above coastal Santa Monica and starring in motion pictures. The two attended nearby Sunday polo matches, followed by dinner with movie stars at the Rogers ranch. Sometimes Jock "took along" Admiral Taylor, who thoroughly enjoyed talking aviation with the humorist, a flying enthusiast ever since he had gone aloft in a Curtiss flying boat in 1915.

On one such occasion during the autumn of 1927 Rogers said he would certainly like to be catapulted off the flagship. The admiral lost no time inviting the entire Rogers family to the *Pennsylvania* to witness such a flight. So on 29 December Rogers got the grand tour of the battleship, followed by lunch in the flag mess area. During the course of the meal Will remarked, "Who is going to fly me off the catapult?"

From the opposite end of the table Jock piped up modestly, "I am, sir."

"I don't know," the droll cowboy observed to the amusement of all, "whether Oklahoma can afford to lose two good men at one time or not!"

Jock and Will adjourned to the "cat," which shot them out to sea. They circled back, landed in the harbor, taxied to the *Pennsylvania,* and were lifted aboard by crane. Crewmen swarmed over turrets, mast, and all parts of the superstructure for a view of the gangway as the Rogers party said its farewells to the admiral and ship's officers.

Will sneaked away. He walked over to a turret where two strapping Marine guards—the admiral's and the captain's orderlies—stood stiffly at attention. Will said to them in a low but audible voice, "What's the matter with you fellows? Won't they have anything to do with you?" The crew let out a roar. Will Rogers always played up the underdog.

The new year, 1928, brought the mammoth carriers to the fleet, *Saratoga* in February and *Lexington* in April. Both were too new and untried

Humorist Will Rogers with Rear Admiral Montgomery Meigs Taylor on board the battleship *Pennsylvania* in 1927 for his catapult shot with pilot Clark. (Photo courtesy of Harvey M. Beigel) *U.S. Navy photo*

to participate in fleet exercises, notably Fleet Problem VIII—a mock attack on the Hawaiian Islands—but little *Langley* and the VO squadrons did. Admiral Taylor and his spotting unit transferred to the battleship *New York* while the *Pennsylvania* underwent overhaul in the navy yard. Jock's unit continued its superlative performance, receiving commendations on the new flagship.

The only difficulty lay in its versatile new amphibian floatplane, the Loening OL-6. The plane was known as "Aimee" because it could set down on land as well as on the water; this is exactly what southern California evangelist Aimee Semple McPherson had done when staging her water "kidnapping" from a boat at sea and five-week "disappearance" in the California desert in 1926. Unfortunately, the plane tended to lose power halfway along the catapult and would sometimes bounce off the water. In rough seas this was risky, as Clark discovered off Hawaii, when his Aimee hit a six-foot wave and nearly "spun in" (crashed).

As his tour of duty with the battleships drew toward a close in May 1928, Jock considered his options. He preferred to stay with the fleet, but because he was due to rotate ashore he put in for Naval Air Station Anacostia, near Washington, D.C. Either way, he had the blessing of Admiral Taylor, whose fitness reports on Clark (1927–28) lauded him:

> A fine type. Inculcates fine spirit in subordinates. Loyal and intelligent. Fine disposition and excellent cooperation. . . . A fine officer and excellent pilot. Of a pleasing personality and likeable. Has a thorough knowledge of his duties and an excellent leader. . . . A most loyal and fruitful officer.

Clark toyed with the possibility of naval attaché duty in Peru—and use of his broken Spanish—until a more senior lieutenant won this posh posting instead. This proved fortunate, inasmuch as BuAer Chief Moffett personally approved Clark's request to come to Anacostia—and as its executive officer at that. The admiral constantly utilized the air station for travel, meaning Jock would continue to fly—and he felt that "being a pick-and-shovel aviator was better than being a diplomat."

Such transfers of duty stations usually provided leave time for extended visits with his family in Oklahoma. The small farming town of Chelsea did not change much over these years, except perhaps for the arrival of a young telegraph operator at the railroad station who passed the time strumming a guitar as he sang and yodeled Western songs—not unlike those of Jock's father and late father-in-law. In 1927, while visiting, Will Rogers heard and so liked 19-year-old Gene Autry that he advised him to try to sing over the radio—a very recently mass-marketed technological marvel. Within a year Autry was billed as "the Oklahoma Yodeling Cowboy," and by 1931 he was a star, headed for the movies.

Clark's extended family was starting to add a new generation. During the decade, sisters Stella and Lucy married men in the region and began having children; brother Bill's wedding followed in 1929. Their oldest sibling, Joe, lived a world apart. Not only did he often shift duty stations between coasts—the East (New York, Charleston, Annapolis, now Washington), the Gulf (Pensacola), and the West (San Diego–Long Beach)—

but he partook of the Roaring Twenties in these seaport cities. There, Jazz Age "flappers" (newly liberated women), illegal booze, and very relaxed morals prevailed.

So when he visited his relatives in Chelsea during his leave periods their "Joe" was something of an outsider. Socially, he was by now accustomed to a good time, steady pay, being catered to, and even driven about in automobiles by enlisted sailors. But Mama Lillie Belle was a staunch hard-shell Methodist who ruled her home unequivocally: no alcohol, no card playing, no movies (silent, then "talkies" after 1927), no dancing, and no makeup or knee-length dresses of the day for her girls.

At family reunions Lillie allowed only coffee or punch, although the men always went behind the barn for their "little drink." As a niece (Betty Joe Clark) remembered, whenever the men were "caught" there by the "little ones" they explained that the liquor was for "medicinal purposes," which satisfied the kids. Still, at Jock's age—pushing 35 when he crossed the country from West to East in June 1928—he was starting to long for a wife, a lifelong companion and one preferably young and attractive for the lively Navy social scene.

Being stationed at the nation's capital might have satisfied Clark's search for a mate, but in the end it did not. Professionally, though, NAS Anacostia was the place to be: it was naval aviation's showcase during the Air Age of popular flying in the nation. It included a Marine Corps and a Navy aerobatic team of three pilots each. The latter was called "The Flying Fish" and was led by Lieutenant M. B. "Matt" Gardner.

Clark's role as executive officer made him active in such high-profile activities as air races, testing new airplanes, and courting congressional support. Also, the station's commanding officer, Lieutenant Commander DeWitt C. Watson, insisted on a heavy flying schedule for Clark and the staff, even on weekends, to maintain their flying proficiency. This included air races, which drew massive crowds from the Washington area. The annual Curtiss Marine Trophy race in May 1929 drew 20,000 people and an ensuing commendation by CNO Admiral C. F. Hughes to Watson and his officers "for the manner in which the event was held." Watson, however, was quick to pass the praise along to Clark, who had organized the entire event. (24 June 1929 fitness report)

Everything done at Anacostia was coordinated closely with BuAer, headquartered a few miles away in downtown Washington. Admiral Moffett's two main subordinates reported aboard the same time as Clark. Both men, with whom Clark would interact frequently from then on, were brilliant and effective in different ways. The assistant chief was the hardboiled Captain Ernest J. King, who had earned his wings only the year before as a latecomer to aviation—at age 48! Commander Jack Towers, after 22 months in command of the *Langley*, became head of the Plans Division and two years later was promoted to captain.

As part of Moffett's policies of courting and supporting all facets of the nation's aviation, Clark met, transported, advised, and worked with America's budding commercial airline executives, aircraft and engine manufacturers, congressmen, and military and civilian racers and stunt flyers. In their own category were the many aviatrixes who passed through Anacostia, well-mannered and "quite ladylike." But one who landed a small plane en route to air races in Florida shocked the officer of the day—"a religious, soft-spoken young man"—when he asked if she planned to fly all the way to Miami. "Not that goddammed crate!" she snorted, leaving him aghast.

The Army Air Corps (formerly Air Service) shared Anacostia with the Navy until it soon opened its own airfield nearby. When the Army flyers, exasperated over the Navy's larger congressional appropriations, complained, Clark and other Navy aviators explained, "We have Admiral Moffett. He knows how to use publicity." Before long such techniques became the model of accelerated Army Air Corps showmanship, using the Navy example. It "soon out-Moffetted Moffett," Clark reflected four decades later, "and to this day has never stopped using publicity to good advantage."

Part of Clark's interservice duties involved attending meetings of the National Advisory Committee for Aeronautics regarding progress in aviation. They were held at the Air Corps' Langley Field near Hampton Roads and Norfolk. Army and Navy officers usually got there together by riding the night steamer *District of Columbia,* enabling Jock to talk with the outspoken and retired General Billy Mitchell.

> I listened to Mitchell by the hour, getting to know him quite well. His visions of aviation in the future were impressive. I had to admire him for his foresight, yet I realized that he was years ahead of his time. And I appreciated how much more effective was Admiral Moffett's suave personality than Mitchell's outspokenness.
>
> Moffett had a motto that was in direct contrast to Mitchell's technique: "Never make an enemy when you don't have to." I tried to practice Moffett's version throughout my own career. His way was better.

The Air Corps' most famous representative was Charles Lindbergh, because he had flown the Atlantic alone in 1927 and had already been an Air Corps Reserve pilot. "Lindy" had accomplished his great feat using an air-cooled radial engine, although both services used it equally with the water-cooled variety. Soon after Clark reported, Admiral Moffett's "star" racing pilot, Lieutenant Al Williams, turned over to him the supervision of an experimental project: substitution of Prestone for water in the engine radiator of a Curtiss F6C-3 Hawk fighter plane. Prestone's boiling point of 367 degrees Fahrenheit would enable the engine to run at a higher temperature, increasing its power and presumably its speed. Because the project was experimental, no publicity was allowed, except that the plane would be entered in the National Air Races at Cleveland, Ohio. The press consequently and inappropriately labeled it a "mystery plane," which only resulted in public curiosity.

When the Hawk was ready for testing Clark flew it on the measured speed track along the Potomac River. The engine overheated—"ran hot"—in reaching an increased speed of 186 mph, leading Jock to recommend a larger radiator. That meant canceling the plane's participation in the Cleveland race, which BuAer would not allow. So Clark flew it "as is" to Cleveland for the 75-mile race, in which the engine's temperature rose quickly to 345 degrees. Rather than risk blowing up the engine—and himself—Jock held it steady at 345 degrees, finishing fourth.

This mediocre performance, he recalled, "sealed the fate of liquid-cooled engines in the Navy's planes." BuAer turned to perfecting the air-cooled engine, while commercial aircraft companies streamlined the cowl around the engine that had caused a drag on the plane. For the next 15 years the Navy used the air-cooled radial, while the Air Corps used the water-cooled engine. So, "in the final analysis, I rendered naval aviation a service by not winning that race."

As part of Admiral Moffett's policy of promoting the new commercial airlines, Clark welcomed and serviced their planes that flew in to Anacostia. World War I fighter ace Eddie Rickenbacker of General Motors's Fokker Company flew the first Curtiss Condor to the air station, where Jock shared the cockpit with him for a flight. It was the very first American transport plane equipped with sleeping accommodations. When Clark piloted it himself in 1934 he lauded the Condor as "a swell plane." Juan Trippe brought in a Sikorsky amphibian en route to South America, initiating Pan American Airways. Two of Jock's naval aviator friends piloted the first Consolidated commercial flying boat from Buffalo to Anacostia. American Airlines's first pilot, Warren Vine, escaped after crashing into the Potomac while testing a Lockheed monoplane, but the Navy mechanic riding with him drowned.

Clark mainly flew the station's Ford Trimotor to transport the admiral and others around the country. With an engine in the nose and one on each wing, it was "rather noisy." On one occasion he and Marine Corps Colonel T. C. "Tommy" Turner delivered several other Marine aviators to the West Coast. Coming back, the Trimotor kept them barely ahead of a violent snowstorm until they landed at the Air Corps' Love Field in Dallas, Texas, which Marine Turner had in fact commanded during the war. The plane froze to the ground, "connected by huge icicles," for five days—during which Jock and Tommy partied with the latter's friends.

Soon after their return to Anacostia, the Ford Motor Company delivered a new Trimotor with improved engines and speed. The Anacostia flyers soon dubbed it the "workhorse of the air," and the company that became TWA (Trans World Airlines) soon initiated passenger service with it. Tommy Turner, however, carelessly walked into the spinning propeller of a Sikorsky amphibian before 1929 ended—another tragic fatality.

Such multitudinous activities required a well-run air station, and its commander, DeWitt Watson, commended Clark for having achieved just that after only ten weeks on the job: all "excellent" ratings in 15 categories—at the very top tact, cooperation, loyalty, and attention to duty. "He commands the respect of both seniors and juniors" and is "especially well fitted for promotion." (30 September 1928 fitness report)

Watson's accolades continued over the following year. He praised Clark for having "instilled a splendid spirit in the crew to the betterment of the station" and "by reason of his pleasing personality is an exceptionally fine leader of men." He regarded Jock as "a natural leader, hard working, intelligent, forceful and at the same time sympathetic and kind; brings forth the best efforts of his subordinates." (1928–29 fitness reports)

Clark's performance remained consistently high, even when he was acting station commander for a week in late June and early July, 1929; Rear Admiral A. L. Willard, commandant of the Washington Navy Yard, was amazed to "have been very favorably impressed by the manner in which Lieut. Clark 'carried on'" in that role. Watson's permanent successor, Commander A. Hugh Douglas, a man of few words, admired Clark as "enthusiastic, zealous, tactful, trustworthy, forceful and has initiative."

Like other superior officers earlier and later, Douglas marked Clark down a bit only on "military bearing" and "neatness of person and dress"—he *could* have rumpled shirts, and not only because he was a bachelor. Most important, however, Douglas found Clark "an excellent pilot of all types of planes." (1929–31 fitness reports)

Clark and his Anacostia pilots always had to be versatile, rarely knowing what Admiral Moffett would have them do. Late in 1929, for example, Jock was called upon to give a short flying course to three Mexican army pilots involved in putting down the latest revolution in their country.

At a weekend cocktail party in October 1929 talk centered on Black Thursday the 24th when the stock market had crashed and some despondent and penniless business executives were jumping from skyscrapers to their deaths. One of several aviators clustered around Admiral Moffett joked that he and his fellow pilots could show the world just *how* to jump—by parachute. Jock even offered to fly the plane for a mass drop. In fact, they quipped that they could do it on Navy Day, Monday the 28th. The publicity-conscious admiral

> thought it was a fine idea. Next day everyone forgot about it or dismissed it as mere cocktail conversation, but not Moffett. In the afternoon he called us all into his office and said, "I think it is wonderful that you are all going to make a parachute jump on Navy Day." None of the officers had ever jumped before, but no one was given the opportunity to back down.

Moffett placed the project in the hands of Jock's fellow Oklahoman, Lieutenant Apollo Soucek (pronounced Soo-check), who with five other pilots would make the jump: the station's medical officer, Commander Frederick A. Ceres (pronounced Sears); two lieutenant commanders; one lieutenant; and Marine Corps Captain Arthur H. Page, a classmate of Jock's and Anacostia's premier test pilot. Six aviation enlisted men, all experienced parachutists, would also jump—"to push anyone hesitating at the door of the plane." The dozen jumpers plus pilot Clark totaled 13 men, and superstition over that number would also be thrown to the winds. (*New York Times*, 29 October 1929)

Some 10,000 spectators gathered at Anacostia on Navy Day. Formations of Navy and Marine Corps planes paraded overhead, and Al Williams provided thrilling acrobatics, flying his plane low and upside down. Then Jock took off with his human cargo in "a giant tri-motored Ford transport plane," as the press described the lumbering sturdy workhorse of the air station. Clark leveled off at only 1,000 feet above Anacostia, whereupon the nervy dozen parachutists tumbled out in ten seconds flat!

The first chutist jumped too soon and landed in a tree, but the others alighted safely on the airfield. Moffett's coup garnered the attention it deserved, setting two world records: the most exits—12—by parachute from a single plane, and the ten-second speed at which the men jumped together. At least for Dr. Freddy Ceres, who was becoming a close friend of Jock's, the jump was not only his first one but his last.

This stunt carried no more risk than many flying feats of these and other naval flyers. In the spring of 1929 Lieutenant Soucek had set world altitude records in a 425-hp Wright Apache as a landplane fitted with wheels (39,140 feet), then as a seaplane with pontoons (38,560 feet). Captain Page in May 1930 won the last Curtiss Marine Trophy Race at the 164 mph mark in a Curtiss seaplane fighter over the Potomac, and two months later he flew a Vought 02U on instruments alone ("blind" in a hooded cockpit) 1,000 miles from Omaha to Anacostia.

Then, in September 1931, Page raced in a similar fighter for the Thompson Trophy in Chicago, quickly taking the lead only to inhale poisonous carbon monoxide and suffer a fatal crash near the finish. That flying was dangerous work was brought home often to Clark, as when another classmate (who stood 13th in '18), one of Anacostia's finest test and racing pilots, Lieutenant George T. Cuddihy, dived the wings off (diving at too steep an angle until the wings snapped off) a British Bulldog fighter there in November 1929. And, in the first week of 1930, Jock's former navigator on the *Brooks*, Lieutenant Eugene F. Burkett, suffered a fatal crash at San Diego.

Because good pilots were especially important for ferrying government officials to and from Washington, early in 1929 Clark selected one of the Navy's top enlisted (noncommissioned) pilots, Paul I. Gunn. Known to all as "P.I.," he had "an uncanny ability and engaging personality." That spring both men were returning from Detroit only to be blinded by a thick fog over Pittsburgh. When Jock spotted a road, Gunn, "by sheer guts and superb flying skill," brought the plane down to treetop level over a mountain route to land at Uniontown. During the Pacific war, P.I. proved invaluable flying Army B-25 medium bombers.

Admiral Moffett used Al Williams as his own personal pilot, but early in 1929 the chief of the Bureau of Navigation (personnel), Rear Admiral R. H. "Reddy" Leigh, ordered Williams to the *Saratoga* for sea duty he had never had. Moffett was away at the time, but his own assistant chief, Ernie King, endorsed the orders. Williams protested, and when Moffett returned he delayed the orders. He later explained to Clark that King had exceeded his authority by challenging Moffett and that he would therefore be transferred out of BuAer to command of the naval air station at Hampton Roads.

Simultaneously, Moffett's second term as BuAer chief came up for renewal, a third four-year term being virtually unprecedented for any bureau chief. The opposition was led by the Chief of Naval Operations, Admiral C. F. "Handle Bars" Hughes—so nicknamed for his splendid mustache—and seconded by the miffed Reddy Leigh, "both fast friends of Ernie King." They especially preferred Admiral "Billy Goat" Reeves, commanding the fleet's carriers. The staff members under Reeves were so confident he would be appointed that one of them, who was planning to command Anacostia under him, wrote a letter to Jock instructing him to get ready for the transition.

Over the week following Herbert Hoover's 4 March 1929 inauguration as president of the United States he twice received lists of candidates for chief of BuAer from Admiral Leigh but without Moffett's name on either one of them. Both were returned for "a wider selection" of candidates. Then the Sunday papers carried endorsements of Moffett by the captains of the aviation industry, notably Donald Douglas, and proaviation journalists.

> On Monday morning the irate Admiral Hughes summoned his aviation aide, Lieutenant Commander Ralph E. Davison. "Davison, who wrote all this? Who is responsible?" Davison replied calmly, "Why, Admiral, we thought *you* wrote it." Finally Admiral Leigh made a list that included everyone who had any qualifications for Chief of the Bureau; at the very bottom was Moffett's name. Immediately President Hoover sent back the answer, "Approved for Admiral Moffett."

At this news, someone sent a one-word telegram to Reeves's staff in California: "Unpack."

Moffett was reappointed on 13 March, Ernie King was detached in April, and on 10 May Moffett managed to get Al Williams awarded a Distinguished Flying Cross for contributions to testing aircraft and improving flight safety.

The admiral also kept Al Williams at Anacostia for more speed tests, but when Moffett left the country to participate in the London naval disarmament conference early in 1930 Admiral Leigh again issued Williams orders for sea duty. Jack Towers, who had succeeded King as assistant chief but was still only a commander, would not question these orders. But the temperamental Al Williams did and in a fury threatened to resign his commission.

Jock Clark, by now a close friend of Williams, "advised him, even pleaded with him, to accept his orders. His experience, I told him, would be invaluable to the new carriers." He would not listen to reason, however, and left the Navy.

A "deeply distressed" Admiral Moffett had "loved Al like a son and had given him a privileged status in the Navy." When he returned to Washington he told Clark that Williams's brash act—set off by Ernie King—had cost naval aviation "its prime publicity drawing card."

At least Clark profited by it by succeeding Williams as the admiral's personal pilot. Because Moffett—a "naval aviation observer" rather than pilot—still required monthly flight time *in* an airplane aloft, Clark usually flew him on a clear day to the Navy's dirigible base at Lakehurst, New Jersey, in the admiral's personal open-seat Vought O2U Corsair.

There both men boarded the rigid airship *Los Angeles*. Away from the bureaucratic wrangling of the nation's capital, the admiral enjoyed cruising over New York City as well as eating the meals provided by "an excellent cook who invariably prepared a fine steak dinner."

Moffett confided his views to me on the subject of lighter-than-air craft. He fully realized that dirigibles were unsafe and had no real military value. But they had given the Navy much publicity, and he felt they probably could have a future in commercial aviation. I must say that in my opinion too many risks were involved. Dirigible disasters cost the Navy many lives. Little did I suspect that one day Moffett's would be one of them.

The South Carolinian's "truly magnetic personality, with all the charm of the Old South," amazed Clark.

His genial disposition and gentlemanly appearance, enhanced by snow-white hair and ruddy complexion, were coupled with a remarkable gift for making friends. His popularity extended high and low, to people of all ages and from all walks of life. Few men have ever enjoyed the loyalty of their own organization as completely as he did.

And in Clark's case, and probably other pilots' as well, part of the reason was Moffett's wife, Jeannette. In a 1933 letter Jock wrote that she "has been almost as a mother to me."

Clark discovered just how diverse a following Moffett enjoyed when he flew the admiral to the National Air Races in Chicago in September 1929. So popular had he been while commanding Chicago's Great Lakes Naval Training Station during World War I that for ten days he was telephoned or visited by innumerable people—notably, wartime naval pilot turned millionaire William Wrigley, but also former enlisted shipmates. "His friends never forgot him; he always had a kind word for every one of them."

Closer to home—New York City—Clark flew the admiral to Long Island in May 1930 to inspect the Curtiss factory at Garden City while a hundred Navy planes flew over as part of a weeklong commercial and military air show at Madison Square Garden.

Moffett exhibited his political skills when he testified for naval aviation in congressional hearings, accompanied by a team of experts that included Jack Towers, Freddy Ceres, and Jock Clark. Inasmuch as he usually spoke without notes, they counseled him on his effectiveness as seen in the reactions of the committeemen. "If he left something out or made an incorrect statement, Ceres or I either pulled on his coattail or nudged him," Clark recalled. Moffett followed up by contriving to meet a congressman in the corridor after the hearing to clear up any confusion.

Moffett's "remarkable sense of timing" was embodied in three tenets that enhanced Clark's professional education:

1. Life is timing. Everything you do must be timed.
2. Never leave a job when the going is tough; things will always get better.
3. The time to leave a job is when the flags are flying and the bands are playing.

The admiral confided to Clark one of the most timely decisions of his own career: entering naval aviation. Just after the end of the World War Moffett had achieved the pinnacle for any naval officer of that day—command of a first-line battleship—the *Mississippi*. But Captain Henry C. Mustin, one of the earliest naval aviators, had spent a long evening convincing Moffett of the bright future of Navy air. Moffett had forthwith applied for the post of chief of the new Bureau of Aeronautics and gotten it in 1921. Also, "he appreciated the possibility of a war in the Pacific, and he visualized that the aircraft carriers were the best way to carry the war across the Pacific to enemy shores, rather than fight in our own backyard."

Clark as exec of Anacostia was sometimes caught in the middle of Moffett's wrangles with the CNO. Handle Bars Hughes regarded Moffett's policy of transporting government officials as a misuse of Navy funds to promote publicity not only for naval aviation but personally for Moffett. One example was courting Secretary of Labor James J. "Puddler Jim" Davis. This worthy made so many trips that after one he gave the Navy pilot a munificent tip . . . of one quarter! The pilot properly declined it.

Indiana Congressman Ralph Updike needed to get to the Indianapolis hospital where his pregnant wife had suddenly been admitted for childbirth. Assistant Secretary of the Navy for Aeronautics David S. Ingalls gave permission to Anacostia to transport Updike there, but a phone call of unknown origin ordered the flight cancelled just as the plane was warming up. The pilot took off anyway, just in time for the congressman to be at the hospital when his wife gave birth to twins. Next day a furor followed when the origin of the cancellation order turned out to be CNO Hughes. In the ensuing brouhaha between Hughes and Assistant Navy Secretary T. Douglas Robinson, the latter protected Clark and his pilot and pigeonholed Hughes's requests for an investigation.

In the summer of 1930 Clark became eligible for promotion to lieutenant commander after 11 years as a senior grade lieutenant. He allocated himself three weeks to prepare for the promotion exam, only to be distracted for half that time by agreeing to defend a fellow lieutenant he hardly knew who had been arrested for nonpayment of debts. All the judges in the court-martial case agreed the man was guilty, but Jock managed to obtain clemency from the court.

"Thus I succeeded in my only law case," he remembered, and he passed the promotion exam with flying colors. Unfortunately, his reprieved and ungrateful client left town, "leaving me to pay his bills at the Racquet Club, where I had put him up during the trial." The lieutenant resumed his old habits, soon faced another court-martial, and was found guilty and kicked out of the Navy.

Clark acted as "aviation aide" to Assistant Secretary Robinson's successor Ernest Lee Jahncke on a junket to Houston, Texas, in 1930 to visit the new cruiser *Houston* there on Navy Day. The entourage included Jahncke's daughter and three of her debutante friends. They were greeted at the airport by the usual dignitaries, with the exception of the *Houston*'s captain, Jesse B. Gay, who was miffed at being upstaged by a civilian appointee. Gay did attend the mayor's reception that evening, only to treat the assistant secretary rudely. When Gay decided not to fire the customary salute—a decision conveyed to Clark via the ship's exec, Commander W. C. I. Stiles—during Jahncke's planned visit on the morrow, Jahncke canceled the visit.

That evening Gay encountered Clark, only to learn the situation. When Jock suggested that the captain call on the secretary at his hotel Gay flew into a rage. But he went to the hotel immediately to make an appointment to see Jahncke the next morning. Gay remarked to Jahncke's Marine Corps aide, "That lieutenant commander I saw, that fellow Clark, didn't he have too much tea?" ("Tea" was a Prohibition Era reference to illegal bathtub gin or other spirits.)

"Captain," replied the Marine major, "if you mean what I think you mean, the commander did not have too much tea. I've been with him all evening."

Clark was acting aide to Jahncke the next morning at the hotel when in marched Captain Gay, "in full regalia—fore-and-aft hat, sword, and epaulettes"—to call on the assistant secretary. He blurted out bombastically, "Is the situation still tense?"—completely unaware that Jahncke could hear him through the slightly opened door to his room.

Jock simply opened the door all the way and announced, "Mr. Secretary, the commanding officer of *Houston*!"

All Jahncke wanted was a simple invitation to go aboard, but Gay brusquely demanded, "Mr. Secretary, when will you call on *Houston*?!" At that, Jahncke simply made excuses that he would not have the time. And that was the end of the interview—and of Captain Gay's career.

Upon Jahncke's return to Washington he passed word of his mistreatment to the new CNO, Admiral Pratt, who immediately relieved Gay and Stiles of their posts. Within five years both men were retired, without having been promoted. The lesson for Clark from this sad affair was that "a little diplomacy in the right place at the right time can save all manner of grief." (Both officers, incidentally, were returned to active duty in World War II, and Stiles made captain.)

This experience was underscored by the "somewhat chronic problem" at Anacostia of Congressman Melvin J. Maas. A Marine Corps Reserve aviator, he was a terrible, nearly blind pilot who often ground-looped his plane when landing. Moffett needed his vote in Congress, however, so the Navy let him fly, with Jock always keeping a crash truck at the ready—which he often had to use. A later commanding officer at Anacostia tried to prevent Maas from flying, even going to the Secretary of the Navy—and thereby losing any chance of promotion.

In the spring of 1931, near the end of his tour of duty, Clark was saddled with piloting the Ford Trimotor for a "Virginia Air Tour" of Governor John G. Pollard and Senator Harry F. Byrd (senior). Admiral Moffett, "a good South Carolina Democrat," apparently allowed their political stumping via naval aircraft. Pollard's aide, an elderly retired Army colonel named W. D. Newbill, arranged the details.

One day, as Jock waited in Moffett's outer office to see him, "in marched Colonel Newbill, right past me into the admiral's office." Clark could see what transpired through the slats of the swinging doors. Newbill halted before the seated Moffett, "stiffened to attention, saluted, and pompously announced himself: 'This is Colonel Newbill from Virginia, suh!'"

Whereupon Moffett "ceremoniously backed away from his desk, rose, went behind his chair, and returned the salute with equal pomposity, declaring 'This is Admiral Moffett from South Carolina, suh!'"

The "tour" took place without incident across Virginia, West Virginia, and eastern Tennessee, ending in Norfolk where several passengers departed. It was a huge success for Governor Pollard, who praised Clark and his crew for being "most cordial and accommodating." (Pollard to Assistant Secretary David S. Ingalls, 9 May 1931) Taking off for Anacostia, Clark relaxed at the controls of the Ford Trimotor and lit a cigarette, content that everything had gone so well. Then he tossed out the cigarette butt, only to have it blow back into the cockpit. He called the mechanic to look for it, without success. Soon the plane began to smoke, and Jock yelled to the mech: "We're on fire! You've *got* to find that cigarette or we'll burn up!" Figuring the smoke came from their parachute flares, the mechanic jettisoned them, and the fire stopped—coincidentally, as it happened.

Clark landed at a small field on an island in Virginia's James River, inspected the plane "from top to bottom," found nothing, and flew on to Anacostia with the last passengers. There, a more thorough search found the answer. The butt had followed the "course" taken by many discarded cotton wads that pilots and crewmembers had stuffed in their ears to ease the loud engine noise and vibrations of the plane: through a tiny hole in each of two baffle plates to a two-inch space about a foot long between the imitation leather upholstery and the outer skin of the plane. Then the butt had lighted the cotton, which smoked until it burned itself out.

"Never again did I smoke in an airplane," recalled Clark.

Nothing had spoiled the excellent three-year tour of duty that Admiral Moffett had given Jock Clark at Anacostia, a tour that ended in June 1931. He had served well, learned much, made many new friends and professional contacts, and requested command of a fighter squadron in the fleet. He now received his reward from the admiral—command of the already famous Fighting Squadron Two aboard the aircraft carrier *Lexington*.

Despite the deepening national and global depression, and the resulting cutbacks in the Navy's strength, Clark happily faced "the prospect of a bright future in aviation."

# SIX

# "Attacking" Pearl Harbor with Ernie King, 1931–1933

JOCK CLARK REPORTED ABOARD THE *LEXINGTON* (CV-2, "AIRCRAFT Carrier No. Two") in June 1931. By that time advocates of carrier aviation had become fully aware of its vital importance in protecting American interests and bases in the Pacific and in any future war with Japan. Early in 1929 Admiral Pratt had used the *Saratoga* (CV-3) during Fleet Problem IX for a successful sneak attack on the Panama Canal, and he planned to use both carriers for a similar surprise attack against Pearl Harbor, Hawaii, early in 1932. In September 1931, Japanese ground and air forces attacked and overran Manchuria in mainland China, an ominous signal of Japan's intentions to dominate East Asia and the western Pacific. From that moment on, the U.S. Navy gave increasing attention to the defense of Pearl Harbor.

Clark took command of Fighting Squadron Two B (VF-2B); the "B" stood for the squadron's assignment to the Battle Force built around the 25-knot battleships. Exactly one year later the "*Lex*" was reassigned to the Scouting Force of cruisers. The two carriers' top speed of 33 knots enabled them to operate with the cruisers independently of the Battle Force. In that organization Clark's squadron became VF-2S. In reality, these administrative designations proved meaningless as the fleet increasingly operated in temporary "task" forces. Tactically, the primary mission of the fighter planes was to engage enemy fighters in aerial combat—dogfighting—to protect the fleet and its bombing planes and to command the air over the enemy fleet.

The 18-plane "Fighting Two" was an enlisted men's unit, a crack outfit of the 12 best APs—"aviation pilots"—in the whole Navy. They were divided into six three-plane sections, each section led by an officer. For his own section, Clark arranged the transfer of the superb Chief A. P. "Pappy" Gunn into the squadron to be his right wingman. Fighting Two's best dog-fighter was Chief Verne W. "Pappy" Harshman. (One of the section leaders a year later, Ensign Raymond N. "Red" Sharp, impressed Clark sufficiently to call upon him as a key adviser during World War II.)

The high morale of this select squadron inspired Clark to seek a motto for it. On the advice of a Catholic Navy chaplain, he adopted the famous ancient Latin battle cry of Julius Caesar: "Adprimini!" (First to Arrive!). That slogan could have served as Jock's World War II credo as well—he was always striving to get his ships into battle ahead of everyone else. Alas, an administrative misprint in 1931 substituted "Adorimini!" which was approved and very loosely translated as "Up and at 'em!" (Scarborough, "Fighting Two," 20)

VF-2 was the last squadron in the fleet to receive the 410-hp Boeing F3B-1 fighter, soon replaced by the follow-on F4B-1 with its greater 450-hp engine. The *Lexington* had another 18-plane fighter squadron on board, VF-5B, "the Red Rippers," commanded since mid-1932 by Clark's classmate Lieutenant Commander W. M. "Gotch" Dillon. One of Dillon's pilots, Ensign J. H. "Jimmy" Flatley Jr., especially impressed Jocko both as a pilot and a writer of squadron reports—assets that Clark would draw on in the coming conflict.

The *Lexington* and *Saratoga* usually operated offshore during weekdays, returning to San Diego for the weekends. In port, Jock shared an apartment in Coronado with Gotch Dillon and Gerry Bogan, skipper of VF-1B on the *Saratoga*. On occasion the planes operated out of North Island. The fighter pilots would rev up their Pratt & Whitney engines to a maximum speed of 176 mph for dogfights. The fixed landing carriages prevented the biplanes from achieving higher speeds, and the two fixed .30-cal. machine guns provided only modest firepower—all reasons for new designs by aircraft manufacturers. The Boeings also had bomb racks as well as air flotation bags under the lower wings, should the pilot have to ditch at sea.

On 30 July 1931, one month after Clark reported aboard, his classmate and friend Lieutenant Bubbles Fisher was dive-bombing a radio-controlled target destroyer off San Diego using water bombs. As he pulled out of his dive, the air flotation gear suddenly inflated, causing the plane to disintegrate in midair.

> All that was recovered was Fisher's helmet and part of his brain. Sitting as a member on the Court of Inquiry that investigated the accident, I considered the possibility that Fisher might have pulled up too quickly from his dive, but there was no evidence to substantiate it. I had been best man at Bubbles' wedding and had the sad task of telling his mother the circumstances of his death. We kept the remains aboard ship for some months, then dumped them overboard to let the sea he loved claim all of him.

Skipper of Fighting Two, Clark poses with dress sword next to the squadron's "Flying Chiefs" emblem, "Adorimini" ("Up and at 'em!"), on his F3B plane. *U.S. Navy photo*

Even the most routine carrier flight operations entailed risks. Every landing was a particular challenge. The cardinal rule was that the pilot obeys the signal flags waved by the landing signal officer (LSO) during the approach. On 5 November Jock's fellow Oklahoman Lieutenant Commander Oscar W. Erickson ignored the LSO's signals and spun in as the plane flipped off the starboard side. Erickson struggled free of the sinking plane, only to drown. An additional challenge was night landings on the lighted *Lexington;* but the entire squadron qualified the night of 15 December.

The following summer Gotch Dillon had a hair-raising experience flying over the coastal waters. The tail surfaces of his fighter simply collapsed, eliminating any means of control. But Dillon managed to bail out, landing safely in the water. Flight operations were constant, evidenced during carrier qualifications, during which on 18 July 1932 VF-2's Lieutenant E. C. "Eddie" Ewen made the 11,000th landing on the *Lex.*

Careful pilots like Jock Clark were not immune from hair-raising moments. In a tight dogfight in October 1932 with Pappy Harshman at 17,000 feet inland of San Diego—using a camera gun to record "hits"— Clark could not shake Pappy off his tail, which meant sudden death in actual combat. He put his brand-new F4B into a spin to escape, but he could not pull out of it. After 14 spins (Pappy counted them) he was down to 4,000 feet and decided to jump. Grabbing the upper wing's handgrip, Clark stood up to pull his parachute lanyard, only to have the plane level off abruptly. He sat down and returned to the airfield.

Apparently, Clark's motion had "changed the air flow and weight distribution" sufficiently for the plane to recover. He shared his experience with the other fighter pilots on both carriers, including Lieutenant Commander Matt Gardner, who had relieved Gerry Bogan in 1932 as skipper of *Saratoga's* VF-1. Gardner repeated Clark's actions exactly. But his F4B did not level off, and he had to bail out, losing the plane. At least Gardner was added to the rolls of the "Caterpillar Club" of plane jumpers, entitled to wear a golden silkworm badge—because he had "hit the silk" safely—"an honor I did not envy him," said Clark.

Later, in April 1933, while flying back to the air station at San Diego, Clark's engine quit just short of North Island. He coasted down to the water, coming to a stop 150 yards from the beach. The Boeing fighter just sat there, damaged from the saltwater yet keeping the pilot dry, until the station's crash boat arrived and towed him in. Clark gained "a lot more faith in having to land at sea as a result of this experience."

The fighter pilots, charged with protecting the squadrons of scout-bombing and torpedo-carrying planes, worked endlessly to improve their tactical skills; both carriers usually operated one squadron of each type. San Diego's North Island airfield allowed for longer takeoffs and landings. Once at sea, however, the pilots' very survival depended on a well-run carrier and their obedience to its operating requirements. These were established and enforced by the ship's captain. On the *Lex* it was Ernest J. King.

Ernie King stood virtually unique as a class of naval officer. His razor-sharp mind had stood him in good stead for 20 years, especially on admirals' staffs. He had served with equal distinction as a submarine leader in the early 1920s, then—seeing the future—earned his wings at Pensacola in 1927 at age 48. "He ran a 'can do' ship"—in Clark's words; the *Lexington* "was by far the cleanest ship on which I ever served, a taut ship ruled with an iron hand."

"A tall, thin, wiry man with a deceptive twinkle in his eyes—certainly not one of kindness," King already had the reputation "of being a tough disciplinarian."

> He was a perfectionist, aware of every detail of the ship's operation. If a man knew his business, it was easy enough to get along with Ernie King. But God help him if he were wrong; King would crucify him. On the other hand, King was fair-minded and unfailingly gave credit wherever it was due. Feared but respected, he had the requisite qualifications for a dynamic leader.

Not long after reporting aboard Clark had a close call with King. The *Lex,* operating off the southern California coast, was landing 16 new replacement aircraft, a fairly routine procedure, with so few planes that a full flight deck crew was not required. Lieutenant Commander William Masek, the air officer, had called for only half the usual 400 enlisted "airedales," as the plane handlers were called.

Clark was topside watching his four new planes come aboard when the captain's orderly approached him and said, "Sir, the captain wants to see you on the bridge." Jock climbed the ladders to the bridge, where King grabbed him by the arm, pulled him to the side railing, and exclaimed, "Just look at that flight deck. Just *look* at it! There are supposed to be 400 men on that flight deck! Now, where are they?"

Trusting that his chief petty officer, J. C. Mettee, had all of VF-2's airedales on deck in spite of Bill Masek's order, Clark replied, "Captain, I'll bet you my men are present. I'll bet you $50 *all* my men are present!"

Just then two other summoned squadron commanders—George Dorsey Price (Scouting or VS-3) and Hugh Sease (Torpedo or VT-1)—

arrived on the bridge, whereupon King tore into them. Clark slipped away and rushed down to the flight deck where Chief Mettee confirmed that all his men were at their usual stations.

Jock ran back up the ladder to the bridge and interrupted King, still lambasting the other two squadron commanders, "Captain, my men are present!"

"That's fine," said King, who continued to rail away at the other two.

When King learned of Masek's order for only half a deck force, he put the air officer under hack—confined to his quarters and suspended from duty for ten days. In later years, Clark mused that perhaps King had used this incident as an excuse to end Masek's career for other reasons. In any case, it *was* ruined; he retired three years later, as did Clark's two fellow squadron commanders soon after. At the time, Jock believed Masek had been unfairly punished, but the incident "taught me to steer clear of Ernie King unless I knew I was dead right."

King was an innovator in developing the carrier doctrine that would eventually be used in the war against Japan. His first aviation duty had been in 1926–27 as captain of the seaplane tender *Wright,* flagship of Commander Aircraft Squadrons, Captain Harry E. Yarnell, to whom he had simultaneously been senior aide. Now, in June 1931, Yarnell, as rear admiral, relieved Billy Goat Reeves in this enlarged command, his flag in the *Saratoga.* Yarnell's chief of staff was Captain Jack Towers, and the three other key staffers were all brilliant aviators and lieutenant commanders: Ralph Davison, operations; Forrest Sherman, navigator; and Arthur Radford, flag secretary.

All these future combat carrier captains and admirals, like Clark, served under the supreme wartime command of Ernie King. Now—a decade earlier—they devised carrier tactics that would be used to eventually fight and defeat Japan. To further demonstrate the offensive capabilities of carriers—initiated by the 1929 mock attack on the Panama Canal—Yarnell and his advisers planned to launch a sneak attack on the Navy's base and the Army's adjacent defenses at Pearl Harbor in the Hawaiian Islands.

The *Lexington* departed with the fleet from California on 31 January 1932 to undertake Grand Joint Exercise No. Four and the follow-on Fleet Problem XIII. The attack on Pearl Harbor was designed to surprise the defenders at dawn on Sunday morning the 7th of February, when most of them were still in bed. Admiral Yarnell turned over detailed planning to Towers, who decided to put all the fighter planes on the *Saratoga* and the scouting and bombing planes on the *Lexington.* As senior fighter squadron commander, Jock Clark would lead the attack and "eliminate" enemy fighters. The bombers under Gerry Bogan could next pound enemy installations, including fuel storage tanks, on Oahu and the adjacent islands, and then support an amphibious assault by the Marines.

On Friday, 5 February, "Lady Lex" and "Sister Sara" with their escorting destroyers broke away from the battleships to form a separate task force. Next day this force made a 25-knot high-speed run to a position 400 miles from Pearl Harbor. During the night the ships endured heavy rainsqualls and rough seas as they ran in to the launch point 100 miles north of Oahu before dawn on Sunday the 7th. Yarnell had to slow down his carriers to minimize their rolling, thereby doubling the time allowed for the takeoff into a pitch-dark sky.

Clark rolled down the deck first, followed by the entire initial wave of fighters. Young Jimmy Flatley wrote in his logbook: "Dawn attack on Pearl Harbor." (Ewing, *Reaper Leader*, 18) Next came the bombers behind Bogan, who happened to be Flatley's cousin. Force radio listeners picked up no radio traffic, indicating that the island's defenders were unaware of any danger. Using searchlights at Kahuku Point as a beacon, Clark initiated the simulated attack just as dawn broke.

The attack produced the same shock as the real one by Japanese carriers against Pearl Harbor on Sunday morning, the 7th of December, in 1941. Yarnell's planes "destroyed" the Army Air Corps fields, ammunition depots, hangars, and barracks. But the Navy umpires allowed the Army planes to take off anyway to see what they could do. By the time they got off the ground, however, their Navy antagonists had departed the area so cleanly that the Air Corps could not discover the direction the attackers were taking back to their carriers.

The Army planes landed at about 0700, only to be clobbered by Yarnell's incoming second strike of fighters and bombers. This time some Army planes and a defending submarine reached the two carriers to score some "hits." The Army's airmen claimed they had seriously damaged both *Lex* and *Sara* and cried "foul" for having been attacked on a Sunday. And both umpires and admirals minimized the damage inflicted at Pearl, leading to justifiably loud objections by the attackers.

Over the following days Clark's fighters and Bogan's bombers attacked the islands, laying down a smokescreen over the Marines assaulting the beaches (little could Jock and Gerry know that together as rear admirals commanding fast carrier task groups they would support a real assault on Guam in 1944). The dogfights between Clark's fighters and angry Army pilots on the 10th got so realistic that the umpires terminated that phase of the exercise early.

Word of the surprise carrier attack on Pearl Harbor may well have impressed certain naval officers in Japan inasmuch as one member of Japan's

Naval Staff in 1936 advocated just such an attack to initiate war. (Evans and Peattie, *Kaigun*, 474) It impressed certain U.S. naval aviators as well, among them Lieutenant Commander Logan C. Ramsey who the following year predicted the Japanese attack in the *U.S. Naval Institute Proceedings*, an essay that profoundly impressed Clark, especially when it proved correct.

The actual Japanese surprise carrier attack on 7 December 1941 only differed from that of Grand Exercise No. Four in that it was launched at slightly longer range and after sunup, enabling their strikes to be made in broad daylight. On that day Ramsey "had the dubious distinction"—as chief of staff to the patrol wing commander at Pearl Harbor—of witnessing his prediction come true, "and there was nothing he could do about it!"

Fleet Problem XIII, purely Navy war games, followed the Pearl Harbor attack. Clark's squadron flew back to the *Lex* in Hawaii, and in March 1932 the fleet was divided up into separate task forces. The Hawaii-based "Blue Fleet" of the battleships, *Saratoga*, and an invasion convoy attempted to capture imaginary atolls along the California coast defended by a "Black Fleet" of the cruisers, the *Lexington* and *Langley*, and patrol flying boats. Planes from the big carriers inflicted "damage" on each other: 38 percent to *Lex*, 25 percent to *Sara*.

Ernie King did not like that, as Clark observed: "He would always make sure to win. It was said that King would change the rules or do anything to achieve victory." To make certain that the umpires would not allow the damaged *Saratoga* to be "rebuilt" overnight, King got permission from the cruiser commander, Vice Admiral William H. Standley, to operate independently. Just as *Sara*'s planes were coming back aboard in late afternoon after pummeling "Black" cruisers, no fewer than 48 planes from the *Lex*, led by Clark's fighters, attacked.

The umpires could not equivocate this time: *Sara* suffered 49 percent damage, meaning it had been put out of action. Next day, Captain William F. Halsey's "Black" destroyers added to the damage with a torpedo attack, and *Lexington*'s planes crippled the battleship *Pennsylvania*, flagship of the U.S. Fleet. "King's bold use of his carrier," recalled Clark, "contributed to the development of fleet air doctrine and gave him practical knowledge of carrier operations that served him well in wartime." But the battleship-weaned umpires and senior tacticians refused to accept the fact that both exercises had demonstrated "the complete helplessness of battleships against well-executed air attacks. The days of the battleship were numbered."

Clark exchanged such views personally with Admiral Yarnell and his staff—Jack Towers, "Raddy" Radford, "Fuzz" Sherman, and Ralph Davison—after they transferred from the *Saratoga* to the *Lexington* following the exercises and returned to San Diego.

So closely were air operations conducted between squadron skippers, captains, and the commanding admiral that the latter two wrote fitness reports on the squadron commanders. Clark received high marks from Admiral Yarnell, Captain King, and Captain Frank R. McCrary of *Saratoga*, from which VF-2 had operated during the mock attacks on Pearl Harbor.

Ernie King had nothing but accolades for Clark, whom he regarded as "cool and daring, a good pilot, and a very good squadron commander. Quick to act on any orders or to carry out suggestions." McCrary echoed King: "cool, level headed and efficient." Yarnell agreed: "able and intelligent," with "exceptional interest and enthusiasm" in his work. (1932–33 fitness reports)

In June a major personnel change occurred when King was transferred ashore to the Naval War College and relieved by Captain Charles A. Blakely. Jock took an immediate liking to the new skipper, who compared with King in ability but not personality: "kind, gentlemanly, and very intelligent; I found I could work with him easily."

San Diego offered many year-round recreational pleasures for naval officers, notably golf, one of Clark's favorite pastimes. Early in the year Jock encountered baseball pitching great George Earnshaw wintering in the area. Jock had attended one of the two World Series games in 1930 in which the powerful 6 foot 4 right-hander of Connie Mack's Philadelphia Athletics had overpowered the St. Louis Cardinals in two games to help win the fall classic. The two men struck up an "instant friendship" during which "Moose" Earnshaw showed Jock—in one of the most memorable rounds of golf in Clark's entire life—that he was just as commanding on the links as on the mound. They would meet again during the war.

An even more important meeting occurred that June—with the squadrons shore-based for the summer—when Jock met, and was immediately smitten by, a striking and intelligent 18-year-old young woman from Savannah, Georgia—Mary Catherine Wilson. "M.C.," as her friends called her, had been traveling after attending (1928–31) the Academy of St. Genevieve-of-the-Pines finishing school for girls in Asheville, North Carolina. There she excelled in French conversation and drawing, in marked contrast to Jock's education and interests but therefore cultured and fascinating to him. (St. Genevieve's transcript) She had come to San Diego to visit a former St. Genevieve's schoolmate of similar age, Marie Ceres. Marie had married the much older flight surgeon Freddy Ceres, who—after giving Jock his flight physical—had transferred with him from Anacostia to San Diego.

M.C. came from a seafaring family. Father Harry MacKenzie Wilson, Canadian born and nearly 66, was chief engineer of the merchant steamship *City of Savannah*. Her brother was its third engineer. The brownish-blonde, blue eyed, and golden skinned M.C. was quickly taken by the attentions of the uniformed 38-year-old pilot from Oklahoma. The lively San Diego–Coronado summer Navy social scene included Sunday drives to Rosarita Beach below the Mexican border with Jack Towers, his top pilots, and their ladies for beer parties; alcohol was legal there.

In spite of their 20-year age difference, Jock moved quickly toward the fluid Navy marital environment, specifically that of the carrier staff. A divorced Jack Towers had—at age 45 in 1930—married his French bride "Pierre" (from Pierrette), 17 years younger, though after a long courtship. She immediately welcomed M.C. Fuzz Sherman was securely married and a father. Arthur Radford and wife Dorothy were "among my finest and most cherished friends," Jock informed M.C., although they would divorce within a few years. Ralph Ofstie, the flag secretary, was a bachelor.

The divorced wife of one pilot (Morton Seligman) quickly married another (Stanhope Ring), but the most scandalous event regarding the carriers' flyers occurred in August 1931. The wife of Jock's fellow squadron commander George Dorsey Price was the victim of an attempted rape. In the event, Daisy Price fell from a hotel room window and died from the injuries. The scandal racked the carrier staff.

Junior officers like Jimmy Flatley were especially vulnerable in the heavy party atmosphere of the weekends. In a drunken stupor from too much Prohibition booze early in 1932 he had impetuously married a party girl in a ceremony he could not even remember next morning. The long annulment litigation was followed, happily, at the start of 1933 by his wedding to the schoolteacher who became his lifelong mate.

And the unremarkable 1916–27 marriage and divorce of early naval aviator and now air officer on the *Saratoga* Earl Winfield Spencer Jr. and Wallis Warfield (later Simpson) became news in 1936. That year she toppled the king of England, Edward VIII, so that she, a foreigner and commoner, could marry him. (Jock had met this future king, Prince Edward, in Hawaii in 1920.) And three years after that Arthur Radford married another divorced wife of Win Spencer.

The Coronado summer social whirl fed the mutual attraction of Jock and M.C., an attractive couple—he always well dressed, with pressed uniforms and natty civilian attire, she downright elegant. They became engaged within a matter of weeks and set the date for 15 August 1932—one day before her 19th birthday, three months before his 39th. While Mary Catherine visited cousins in San Francisco, Jock rented a "little white house" and welcomed her back in time not only for the wedding but the Olympic Games in Los Angeles, part of which they apparently attended.

The wedding took place in a Beverly Hills Episcopal church. Freddy and Marie Ceres—he was now Admiral Yarnell's medical aide—served as

Jock Clark marries "M.C." (Mary Catherine) Wilson, 15 August 1932, in Beverly Hills, California. They are flanked by the best man, flight surgeon Freddy Ceres, and his wife, matron of honor Marie Ceres. *Clark family photo*

best man and matron of honor respectively. After a honeymoon at the Grand Canyon (over which Clark had flown with his entire squadron in June) the newlyweds settled into the active Navy social scene. Jock adored M.C. as if he were closer to her own age, nicknaming her "Squeatie," and she reciprocated to her "Jock." She was athletic, and they shared a love of playing golf. She was an accomplished pianist; he enjoyed Dick Powell–Ruby Keeler movie musicals.

But both had problems. Jock, generous to relatives and friends alike, had developed bachelor habits that included restaurant meals and drinking, which meant picking up the tab for his pals, and the Navy had taken care of most of his basic needs. "He didn't know how to live in the real world," his brother John said later. "He did not make good personal decisions when it came to women, marriage, and spending money." Now, in the very depths of the Great Depression, he was forced to budget to meet basic household expenses, especially after the Navy cut pay 15 percent as an economy measure.

Though M.C. wanted amenities like new clothes and traveling, she instead had to endure Jock's entreaties to economize. Both of them, he implored her in a letter, must "squeeze the nickels until the buffalo [image on them] squawks." But she had deeper psychological problems, most likely due to a bipolar, manic-depressive personality—on the one hand spirited and vivacious, on the other antisocial. Countering this trait in the Navy officer social whirl may have been a major factor in her turning increasingly to alcohol, which flowed aplenty during happy hours and parties in spite of Prohibition.

The courtship and wedding coincided with the carriers being transferred from the Battle Force to the Scouting Force and a new flag officer, Rear Admiral John Halligan. Jock pleased Halligan and Captain Blakely over the autumn by honing his pilots' shooting skills with their machine guns.

On 11 November 1932, Fighting Two, using fixed camera guns, earned such high scores in gunnery practice that Admiral Halligan reported them to the CNO's office in Washington as unprecedented. Such scores reflected "intelligent and effective training" behind the firing, for which Halligan congratulated Jock and his men. (Halligan to CNO, 5, 27 December 1932; Halligan to Clark, 12 December 1932)

In addition, Clark began to refresh himself on the duties of the OOD and with "general ship work" in order to qualify as such on a carrier. (1932–33 fitness reports)

As the fleet prepared for winter maneuvers, which would keep the newlywed pilot at sea for long periods, he decided to save money by sending his young bride back to Savannah at the start of 1933. She could stay with her mother until the spring and then return to her husband in Coronado. He soon regretted the decision because he missed her terribly, and he could neither control her spending nor care for her. Also, he wanted "a little Jock." He wrote this on 26 February 1933, followed on 25 March by his expressed desire for "a sweet little baby." These remarks were from two of many letters Clark wrote during M.C.'s absences in early 1933 and again two years later—virtually the only surviving major correspondence from the letters he wrote throughout his life.

Until her anticipated return in the spring, Jock moved into the BOQ at Coronado with two friends and similarly temporary bachelors—Freddy Ceres, flat broke with a baby on the way, and Gotch Dillon, who had left his wife and newborn baby boy in Washington, D.C. All three men quickly grew to hate the boredom of the BOQ, which was no substitute for being at home with their wives.

M.C. took a coastal passenger liner up to San Francisco in January 1933, dined at the captain's table next to a pleasant Army pilot, then boarded the Army transport *Republic* for a trans-Canal passage to Washington, D.C. There she stayed with a girlfriend until Franklin D. Roosevelt's inauguration, which she attended with Gotch Dillon's wife Mary on 4 March. Until then, she spent some of her time socializing with Navy couples, including the Radfords. At one such soiree an obnoxious Army colonel pestered the Navy wives until M.C. "put him in his place."

Jock responded to her account on 26 February, threatening to "fix him good" but not surprised inasmuch as he regarded the army as "morally . . . pretty thoroughly rotten." The Navy had its problems too, he admitted, especially submariners, "but the gang that we know play a straight game." He was not equivocating. Naval aviators could be as wild as any off-duty officers, but Clark's "gang" had reached middle age along promising career tracks.

His 1933 letters recounted social activities only with fellow lieutenant commanders (and their wives) who would achieve flag rank and important wartime and postwar commands and who were familiar to one another by their nicknames from Academy days: Fuzz (and Dolores) Sherman, Gerry (and Katy) Bogan, bachelor Ralph Ofstie, Matt (and Helen) Gardner, Eddie (and Betty) Ewen, the Radfords, the nonaviator Mick (and Grace) Carney, and R. W. "Dick" (and Dee) Whitehead—the only non-Academy man but "a regular member of our gang" who gave "swanky" cocktail parties. (Letters, 26 February 1933, 17 April 1933, 1 April 1935)

Clark's career was developing well, so it was with some amusement when he read in the 4 March 1933 *Army and Navy Register* that Lieutenant Commander Clark had been assigned to "command of the *Lexington*." He immediately wrote a letter to the editors who printed it forthwith: "I appreciate the compliment, of course, but it seems only fair to state that the *Lexington* is commanded by a very able and efficient officer in the person of Capt. C. A. Blakely."

Sending a clipping of the correction to M.C. (25 March 1933), he observed wryly, "This should make Mrs. Blakely feel better." (Incidentally, Blakely got his command of the carrier in peacetime at age 50, 27 years after graduating from Annapolis in '03; by comparison, Clark got his first carrier command in wartime 1942 at age 48, 24 years after his '18 graduation.)

Early in the year Admiral Moffett arrived with Radford at San Diego for an inspection visit. They relaxed one evening over the border in Mexico with Jack Towers, Jock, and others discussing the future. Satisfied with the current state of the carriers, and their assumed primary role in any war with

Japan, the admiral expected to stay on as chief of BuAer until retiring at the end of the year. He hoped to be succeeded by Towers as head of the team Moffett had shaped, in spite of Ernie King's ambition to become chief of BuAer.

During this visit Moffett informed Jock of his next duty—as the aeronautical member of the Board of Inspection and Survey. This choice assignment, for which he had lobbied for a year, meant testing all the aircraft being designed and built for purchase by the Navy. For the third time—after Anacostia and VF-2—the admiral had given Clark "a choice billet," not least because it meant three years ashore during which Jock could start a family. Moffett's "confidence gave me the satisfaction of knowing that I was doing the kind of work expected of me."

On 24 January 1933 the *Lexington* headed for Hawaii for more fleet exercises to further demonstrate the offensive power of carriers. When heavy seas prevented air operations en route, Clark stood the watch as OOD and attended classes learning about the "internal workings of the ship," between which he read or played bridge. He had "a couple of run ins" with the ship's executive officer, Commander Victor D. Herbster, one of the earliest naval aviators, who was described by another aviator as "a small fussy officer with no visible talent."

Clark wrote to M.C. that "nothing short of murder would be his just desserts." In both clashes Jock "came out the winner." Herbster, "the rotten bounder [ill-mannered]," especially did not like a proposal of Clark's for a ship's "air commodore" to coordinate all four squadrons aloft (VF-2, VF-5, VS-3, VT-1, and a small Marine Corps scouting unit, VS-15M). The exec was now known as "Little Caesar"—after the gangster portrayed by Edward G. Robinson in the 1931 motion picture of that title. (Letters, 23, 24 January 1933) Soon transferred, Herbster retired in 1936.

Fleet Problem XIV was about to unfold. Building on the previous year's mock attack on Pearl Harbor, *Lexington* and *Saratoga* were to focus on the virtual destruction of the Navy's facilities there. Indeed, the planners assumed Japan would begin a war with just such a surprise attack (as it had done against Russia in 1904). Again, Jock Clark would lead the initial fighter sweep.

En route the carriers kept operating aircraft until the predawn and precarious recovery of George Price's squadron in mountainous seas on Thursday the 26th of January. All flying was cancelled "until we make the big raid on Honolulu," Jock wrote M.C. that day. On Sunday the 29th he told her, "We make the big attack [on Pearl Harbor] Tuesday morning," followed by strikes on Lahaina Roads and then the city of Honolulu over the ensuing two days.

It didn't happen. Suddenly, the government ordered cancellation of the mock attack in order to save money as the Depression worsened during the final days of the inert Herbert Hoover administration. Instead, the fleet was ordered to return to California and carry out Fleet Problem XIV against West Coast targets.

In the meantime, the fleet anchored at Pearl Harbor, and on 2 February Jock played golf, followed by a cocktail party and "tea dance" (that is, a late afternoon dance) at the Elks Club hosted by the Hawaii-based naval officers. Rubbing elbows with officers of every rank from admiral to ensign—and Gotch Dillon bedecked in numerous leis—Clark described the affair as nothing less than "a riot."

He then joined a large group of his peers for dinner, followed by dancing at the Royal Hawaiian Hotel, where he discovered that the Hawaii-based officers took their drinking "seriously": "The universal drink is the famous Okooleheon—a very poor approach to green rye or corn. It's beastly stuff. . . . I left at one o'clock in self defense." He missed his wife, finishing his 6 February 1933 letter with a pun-inflected plea: "You have to come back [to San Diego] in May if not before or I'll pine away to a nut."

Departing Hawaii to undertake Fleet Problem XIV, the fleet headed for the California coast, substituting San Francisco and San Pedro for Pearl Harbor as targets. *Lexington* participated in intense tactical exercises to further demonstrate the offensive power of the carriers. She and "Sister Sara" formed the nucleus of the attacking "Black Fleet," covered by the cruisers and commanded by another Clark—Vice Admiral Frank H. Clark. Inexperienced in carrier operations, this "black shoe" (nonaviator) planned to launch surprise attacks on San Pedro's docks and naval facilities by the *Saratoga* and on those of San Francisco by the *Lexington* on 16 February before the defending "Blue Fleet" of battleships appeared.

But on the 15th a *Lex* plane spotted smoke from a Blue submarine, leading the admiral to form his cruisers into a battle line before the enemy battleships could arrive. This unfortunately stripped the *Lexington* of her defensive screen (its destroyers were too undergunned to handle a battleship attack).

Just before dawn the following day, as Jock Clark was preparing to take off and lead the attack on San Pedro, two Blue battleships suddenly appeared some 4,500 yards off each side of the *Lex*. In their imagined broadside salvos the battlewagons put her out of action, according to the umpire, Admiral Billy Goat Reeves. Jock never took off. *Saratoga* managed to launch planes, only to be temporarily disabled by shore-based enemy bombers. Next day the *Sara* got off strikes against the San Francisco Bay area, only to be disabled by defending planes from the *Langley*.

Unlike the 1932 mock attack on Pearl Harbor, no surprise had been achieved against San Pedro or San Francisco. In the 3 March critique blame for the failure of the excellent plan was assigned to Vice Admiral Clark's mishandling of the carriers; as punishment, he was transferred to the General Board of the Navy in preparation for a premature retirement. He had failed to neutralize the enemy fleet before attacking shore bases, the very problem that would face naval commanders, including Jock Clark as an admiral, during World War II.

What the Navy needed before any such war broke out were more carriers. The small 13,800-ton *Ranger* (CV-4) was under construction, due out one year hence, while the new Franklin D. Roosevelt administration prevailed upon Congress to authorize construction of two 19,800-ton carriers—*Yorktown* (CV-5) and *Enterprise* (CV-6). In the meantime, Jock and the squadrons flew off the *Lex* and *Sara* each weekday, improving their gunnery and dive-bombing skills. He continued to stand OOD watch at sea and when the ship was in port, thereby qualifying for OOD on carriers.

The weekends offered respite in the usual parties, and when the ship laid over at San Pedro, Jock was able to enjoy the hospitality of Will Rogers at his Santa Monica ranch. On Friday evening, 3 March, he took with him Commander Ernest D. McWhorter, chief of the Scouting Force Aircraft staff, so both could invite Will to make a cruise on the *Lexington*. But the very busy movie star could not work it into his hectic schedule. (Letter of 4 March 1933)

One week later, late in the afternoon on Friday, 10 March, an unexpected enemy struck southern California—a severe earthquake. Clark immediately mustered his squadron's enlisted men as the fleet's first rescue party ashore. (Scarborough, "Fighting Two," 30) Navy families in the Long Beach area were evacuated from their damaged homes to the *Lexington* and other warships until the aftershocks subsided several days later. After two weeks' interruption, the carriers resumed rigorous weekday flight operations as their squadrons competed for the aerial gunnery and dive-bombing awards. And on 1 April the squadron returned to the Battle Force as VF-2B.

Then another blow hit the carriers and the Navy in general. On 4 April Admiral Moffett perished aboard the new airship *Akron* when an electrical storm brought it down off the New Jersey coast. As soon as Jock heard the news he penned a sorrowful letter to M.C.

> Just a note as I feel too sad to write because of the loss of Admiral Moffett. He was the greatest of the great, darling, and to me a true friend. He was the kind of leader that comes once in a century, and we are all going to feel his loss. (Letter, 4 April 1933)

Years later Clark reflected on Moffett's credo that "life is timing" and that consequently one should depart "when the flags are flying and the bands playing." Because the admiral had done just that, said Clark, "I believe he could not have wanted a better time to go."

Moffett's sudden death set off a brief power struggle within the naval air community over a successor. Most of the aviators favored Jack Towers, still only a junior captain. More senior men preferred Ernie King, already selected for rear admiral based on his broader experience—his abrasive personality notwithstanding. Two weeks later King won out, leading pro-Towers Clark to admit that King as skipper of the *Lexington* was "pretty tough but I got on with him very well and I think that altogether he is a very good selection." (Letter, 21 April 1933)

Jock had some competition of his own—his squadron was pitted against Forrest Sherman's crack Fighting One (VF-1) on the *Saratoga*. Clark's VF-2 proved superior in its machine gun scores, but in mid-April "Fuzz's outfit hung up a world's record" in bombing scores. "We'll have to do phenomenally good from now on as Fuzz has already made a marvelous score" toward winning the trophy. (Letter, 12 April 1933) And win it Sherman's squadron did.

Jock need not have worried. If fitness reports meant anything, he—like Sherman—had ample credentials for advancement. Admiral Yarnell added to them in his final fitness report on the VF-2B skipper:

> Lieutenant Commander Clark is a loyal and efficient officer, and a capable squadron commander. He is conscientious and industrious, and possesses to a marked degree that phase of loyalty which prompts him to exert himself to the utmost in the interest of his subordinates. His squadron is efficient and well led. Qualified for promotion.

Treating his own junior officers and enlisted men with the same loyalty he gave his superiors became a Clark trademark. He had learned it from many fine officers like Yarnell—and would learn it again from others.

Jock finally received his orders to Washington, looked forward to M.C.'s arrival by train in May, and planned for a few weeks of relative relaxation in Coronado to enjoy their reunion. He plotted their two-week return cross-country trip by auto to Washington via Chelsea. His mother Lillie, 61, had been ill for months and was reported to be near death. (Her son's visit may have provided the curative, inasmuch as she still had 25 years of life left in her!)

Thus he did not relish another "tough week at sea" when he went aboard the *Lexington* on Saturday, 29 April, then waiting another day for

decent weather to "let us have the field." Jock, perhaps the "most flamboyant" skipper the famous interwar Fighting Two ever had, eagerly awaited
his relief by Lieutenant Commander Thomas P. Jeter. (Scarborough,
"Fighting Two," 35) On 1 May he reflected in his final letter to M.C. before
their reunion, "This will be my last carrier duty for a long time and the way
I feel now I hope for keeps."

Little did he know! Clark faced future duty aboard nine carriers, from
the *Lexington* again to the rest yet to be built: the first *Yorktown*, the *Suwannee*, the second *Yorktown*, the second *Hornet*, the *Philippine Sea*, the *Midway*, the *Kearsarge*, and the *Bon Homme Richard*. His life was becoming
aircraft carriers.

# SEVEN

# Warplanes, Carriers, and Hawaiian Defenses, 1933–1939

L IEUTENANT COMMANDER J. J. CLARK REPORTED TO THE NAVY Department in Washington in late June 1933 for a normal peacetime three-year assignment. By the end of it, impending war would require accelerated and shorter tours of duty. Adolf Hitler had just come to power in Germany, which by 1936 would be transformed into a militarist Nazi state. Imperial Japan, party to naval arms agreements with the United States and Britain, abandoned them over 1934–36 and invaded China in 1937. Depression America would not and could not respond adequately to these threats of ultimate war. Its armed forces therefore had to make certain that what weapons they did develop within their restricted budgets were as qualitatively superior as technology allowed for fighting the next war.

Such was Jock Clark's new task for the Navy. Bypassing BuAer, he joined the Board of Inspection and Survey, an agency independent of the bureaus. Its members tested and judged all new warships and warplanes being built for the Navy and made recommendations for acceptance or rejection directly to the Secretary of the Navy. The board president was Rear Admiral George C. Day. Clark, the only aviator on the board, had specialist peers in ordnance (gunnery), engineering, naval construction, and submarines. On at least two occasions, however, he filled in for absent colleagues by inspecting a heavy cruiser and a sub.

Admiral Day had so much faith in these specialists that he gave them a free hand and accepted their recommendations so uncritically that Clark occasionally "had to insist he read my documents before endorsing them, as I thought he needed to know what he was signing." Day, however, quickly sized up Clark and in the first abbreviated fitness report even remarked on his "good appearance." In the subsequent four reports (1933–35), each covering six months, Day recommended that he be promoted "when due."

Clark himself had a staff of experts and a half-dozen of the Navy's best pilots at Anacostia and Norfolk to test the new planes submitted by the major aircraft manufacturers and by BuAer. This required travel throughout the country to visit the companies and naval air stations inasmuch as Clark insisted that he personally fly each plane being tested for possible purchase by the Navy. One of BuAer's expert airplane design engineers was Lieutenant John B. Pearson Jr., fifth man in the class of '23, formerly of the Construction Corps, and wings 1931. He was transferred from the Aircraft Scouting Force staff to Washington at the same time as Jock. "Jack" Pearson and his wife Doris became good friends of Jock and M.C.

Like the Pearsons, who were starting a family of two children, Clark was determined to enlarge his own as well and therefore rented a comfortable apartment on Connecticut Avenue in northwest Washington. By the following spring M.C. had become pregnant, and on 14 November 1934—two days after Jock's 41st birthday—she gave birth to a girl. They named her Mary Louise after Jock's second sister.

The 21-year-old mother was unprepared for her new responsibilities, although apparently Jock hired a maid or perhaps a black wet nurse like M.C. herself had had as an infant. And Jack and Doris Pearson generously lent helping hands when needed. Jock had to return to the West Coast for five weeks the following spring, at which time M.C. took four-month-old Mary Lou on a visit to her family in Savannah. It was Jock's turn during his summer leave in 1935 to show off mother and daughter at the annual Clark family reunion in Chelsea.

By then M.C. was pregnant for the second time, and when Jock had to return to San Diego for more aircraft tests in October, she and Mary Lou spent the month in Savannah. Jock wrote to her whenever they were apart, and she did not respond often enough to suit him. She doubtless did not appreciate his gentle reminders that she, like he, must "stretch" each check he sent her "as far as you can." Strains on the family budget forced him to borrow small amounts of money from fellow officers. At Jack Pearson's request he rented most of the apartment to the family of aviator Lieutenant Commander Lucien Grant, including four daughters, for a week during M.C.'s absence. (Letters, 3, 10 October 1935)

Still in all, while he "bached" it, fellow officers and their wives entertained him for dinner, bridge, and golf, or he had drinks while listening to football games on the radio at Eddie Ewen's house.

Jock decided that Navy doctors, who were considerably less expensive than the civilian doctors who attended Mary Lou's birth, should deliver the new addition to the family. Unfortunately, when M.C. went into labor on 17 February 1936 the medicos used the "twilight sleep" technique of the day—

injections of morphine and scopolamine to eliminate the pain and/or any memory of the birth and its pains. Catherine Carol Clark entered the world successfully. But M.C.'s encounter with morphine apparently added to her physical and emotional difficulties, and she turned increasingly both to alcohol and morphine for relief. Drug addiction eventually developed.

Both daughters, 15 months apart, turned out attractive and intelligent. Mary Lou proved to be the robust and independent firstborn. Cathy was afflicted with asthma and other ailments that led to dependency on others, including her father. He liked to protect and even dote on her as he did with anyone in need. But mother M.C., now 22, only worsened under these increased familial responsibilities and pressures.

In addition, only six weeks after Cathy's birth, M.C.'s father Harry Wilson died on board his coastal steamer, only four months shy of his planned retirement at age 70. M.C. flew to New York to meet the ship and, with her brother, still an officer on the same vessel, accompanied the body by rail to Savannah.

In spite of these mounting family tensions, Clark immersed himself in his demanding and critically important work of examining and testing all new aircraft under consideration for purchase by the Navy. The main categories were carrier-based fighters, scout-bombers, and torpedo-bombers; catapulted battleship and cruiser observation float planes; multiengine flying boats; patrol planes; and the naval airships.

Despite the fatal crash of the dirigible *Akron*, Clark and the board completed and approved the acceptance trials of her sister airship *Macon*. Fully loaded, this rigid had a maximum speed of 70 knots and a maximum altitude of 5,000 feet. Jock believed that no airship could survive an electrical storm, and after *Macon* crashed in such a blow off northern California early in 1935 he and the board rejected recommissioning the mothballed *Los Angeles*.

The Lakehurst pro-airship lobby, recalled Clark, "accused the Navy's gray-bearded admirals of interference, which faintly amused me because the decision was largely mine, and I was far from being gray-bearded." The Navy thereby killed its dirigible program but continued to use the smaller and safer nonrigid "blimps" for low-speed over-water reconnaissance chores.

Each new airplane of the competing manufacturers was considered experimental and initially designated with the letter "X." After the Navy received a new plane, Clark and his test pilots flew it and recommended modifications. They also traveled to the aircraft factories to observe company test flights and to fly the planes again. In Clark's three years on the board, from 1933 through 1936, the most impressive record proved to be that of the Grumman Company. It evolved a progression of ever sturdier carrier fighters, from the biplanes F2F and F3F to the monoplane F4F

Wildcat. Among the several test pilots he got to know was Lieutenant (jg) George W. Anderson Jr. (whose talents he later tapped). (Anderson transcript #3, 112)

The advent of steep-angle divebombing, a U.S. Navy invention, required a streamlined monoplane with dive flaps, doubling the plane's mission between scouting and bombing. The major result was the Douglas SBD Dauntless, accepted over six competitors. Douglas also produced the first carrier torpedo and bomb-dropping monoplane, the TBD Devastator. American carriers would enter World War II with a mix of these very same single-engine monoplanes: F4F, SBD, TBD.

No less important were training planes, notably the XN3N Yellow Peril biplane built by the Naval Aircraft Factory to be the primary trainer for pilot candidates. Clark flew it in air races against several Army Air Corps trainers at New Castle, Delaware. He beat them all, for which he received a silver cocktail shaker.

Two companies competed over the contract for a long-distance multi-engine patrol-bomber flying boat, adapted in a later version to be an amphibian that could make water-based takeoffs and landings, but fitted with wheels for shore basing. The board tested the Consolidated XP3Y at Anacostia early in 1935. Because the competing Douglas plant with its larger XP3D required ten days of testing, Clark obtained permission to have it done at the Douglas plant in southern California by three highly regarded naval pilots already based at nearby San Diego.

He had Admiral Day request the men from Admiral Billy Goat Reeves, now Commander in Chief U.S. Fleet, who approved. But instead of the three individuals requested by Clark, he was assigned three inexperienced pilots. So he tried another avenue; he went straight to Admiral King, chief of BuAer. "Who do you want?" Ernie asked in his usual terse way with icy glare.

"I want the flyers I asked for in the first place, but—"

"All right," King cut in, "let me handle it. I'll have the Bureau of Navigation order them to you."

Sidestepping the gruff Reeves, whose other nicknames were "Bull" and "Whiskers," worried Jock. "They're not going to like this on the West Coast," he told King. "These people will be furious with me."

"To hell with what they think," retorted King, his sharp eyes twinkling. "You get what you want!"

Jock got more manpower than that: the three men he wanted, the three already assigned by Reeves, and his civilian test expert, E. W. "Eddie" Rounds: seven in all, plus Clark, who took a commercial Douglas "sleeper plane" version of the DC-3 cross-country to Los Angeles via Dallas at the beginning of March 1935. Eight flyers to test one plane! After laying over at the aptly named Hotel Clark in L.A., he joined the plane at Santa Monica and with the company pilot flew it to San Diego on the 6th.

Upon reporting in to the office of the fleet's Commander Aircraft Squadrons, Vice Admiral Henry V. Butler Jr., Clark was directly ushered into the inner office by the dour chief of staff, Commander Richmond Kelly Turner. "Benjie" Butler stood behind his chair. He pointed to another chair and shouted to Jock, "Sit down!"

> Quite naturally, I hesitated, since the Admiral was still standing. Sharply, he repeated, "I said, *sit down!*" In short order I learned that being in the presence of an angry vice admiral is not healthy for a young officer.
>
> He blasted me because he could not spare the three requested officers. He was still the more indignant because now he had lost six pilots for ten days. I kept still while he spent the worst of his ire, until he had to pause for a break.
>
> Then quietly I told him that I needed only the advice of his men, that I could do all the flying myself. And to top it off I ventured to offer him a ride in the new plane. This seemed to pacify him. . . . Next day I took Butler up in the XP3D, and that did the trick. He was delighted.

The Douglas crew flew demonstration flights on 7 March and then spent several days modifying control surfaces to improve the plane. Jock socialized with the Bogans, Whiteheads, and others, notably Jack Towers, now commanding the naval air station. Jock wrote that the visit to date "has been a grand whirl." (Letter, 10 March 1935)

Testing of the big flying boat was extended three weeks, and more radio equipment had to be ordered. The additional time enabled Douglas representative Eddie Rounds to take a suite at the Coronado, which he generously shared with Jock and Jock's top test pilot, Lieutenant Ernie Litch—all three "living like kings." (Letter, 17 March 1935) Lieutenant Commander Wu Duncan—Jock's former classmate of '17—flew out from BuAer to join them. Clark's classmates of '18 in the San Diego area had a class dinner on the 16th. Arthur "Raddy" Radford was also flying a plane westward from the bureau, but when it failed him over Louisiana he was forced to bail out (safely).

Both competing flying boats required extensive modifications, and Clark was not fooling when he reported that his experts had "to practically redesign the hull of the Douglas boat." (Letter, 1 April 1935) But tests on this XP3D, as well as Consolidated's XP3Y, now proceeded to a rapid conclusion. Jock took the opportunity to telephone Will Rogers to come see the big Douglas boat.

The outcome of Rogers's visit was Clark spending eight nights at Will's Santa Monica ranch. Rogers was wrapping up a movie, *Steamboat 'Round the Bend,* and during long conversations with Jock exuded a great desire to take a long trip to see out-of-the-way places and to do it in a civilian amphibian.

Will's unbridled enthusiasm led Jock to remind the humorist, who was not a pilot, that airplanes required periodic checkups not readily available in the wilderness. Rogers just smiled and laughed it off: "Will's confidence in an airplane made him dangerously disregard caution." This fear of Clark's was realized in August when Rogers died in a crash with Wiley Post, pilot of the amphibian they were using to explore the wilds of Alaska. It was a tremendous loss to Clark personally and to a Depression-ravaged nation in need of Will's great and good humor.

Meanwhile, the tests of the XP3D by Clark and his fellow pilots revealed that the plane was slightly inferior to Consolidated's rival XP3Y, which won out. Clark then suggested to Ernie King that the winner be sent on a long-distance flight to demonstrate its capabilities. They believed that the plane could fly the 3,900 miles from Panama to Seattle, Washington. (Conversation with Paul E. Pihl) King wholeheartedly agreed and assigned Jock to arrange everything and to fly the plane himself in the fall.

Because Lieutenant Commander Paul Pihl, BuAer flight desk officer, had helped design the XP3Y, Clark selected him to be copilot. They modified the plane at Norfolk for a mid-October flight and were almost ready one week ahead of schedule. Unknown to Clark, on the 12th, the Saturday before the flight, King got in his required monthly four hours of flight time (to receive flight pay) by flying to Norfolk where he could check the progress on the plane.

There King found Clark absent instead of working around the clock. Worse, two days earlier Jock had flown to Annapolis to attend the Saturday Navy football game. When he returned to Washington an enraged King ordered Pihl taken off the flight, "knowing that would rile me." Clark confronted King in his office: "Sir, I think Pihl has earned the right to be on this flight."

That "merciless twinkle" came into King's eye as he responded, "Is that your recommendation?"

"Yes, sir."

Just 15 minutes later the head of BuAer, Commander Marc A. "Pete" Mitscher, informed Clark that the flight had been taken away from him and given to Lieutenant Knefler "Soc" McGinnis, who had already set long-distance records in the earlier P2Y. This was Jock's punishment, Ernie King style, and he felt "grossly mistreated. As a rule, I was not in the habit of wanting to shoot people. But on this occasion if I could have shot King without getting into trouble myself, it would have been a pleasure."

Clark's grudge only deepened when McGinnis set a world's record for distance. After flying the XP3Y to Panama, Soc and his five-man crew flew a record 3,443 miles for a seaplane from Panama to Alameda near San Francisco in October. It was "a very nice performance," Jock admitted to his wife, then in Savannah with the children, "but I think the plane could have made Seattle." (Letter, 16 October 1935) That was the additional 450 miles Clark and Pihl had originally planned to go.

Clark and Wu Duncan then recommended that the flying boat contract be split between Consolidated's XP3Y and the Douglas XP3D, the performance characteristics of both being virtually identical. Then Consolidated lowered its bid, and King awarded it the contract. The plane became operational the next year as the PBY Catalina, a future workhorse in the Pacific war.

The lone XP3D remained active as a transport for BuAer, but it crashed during a takeoff from Acapulco, Mexico, in 1937, with none other than Ernie King on board. King, by then commanding the fleet's patrol planes in the Pacific and the Caribbean, managed to scramble into a life raft. Meanwhile, the Douglas company sold the blueprints of the big-hulled flying boat to Japan. The Imperial Japanese Navy gave it two more engines in 1940 to become the Kawanishi Type 2 (or "Emily" to the Americans); throughout the Pacific war it was again a rival to the PBY, as Japan's best patrol bomber.

> I protested against this sale. But the Bureau answered that it was selling this design to a potential enemy 1) because the plane was outdated, 2) because the money received could be used to design new planes, and 3) because it would be an advantage for us to know one airplane of our potential enemy. The reasoning sounded dubious to me, but it was the policy at the time.

The need for long-range patrol planes to span the vast Pacific also led to consideration of a radical candidate built by the Hall Aluminum Aircraft Company—the four-engine XP2H. Its huge hull led aviators to nickname it the BMB, for "Big Mammoth Bastard." Very light weight from its aluminum parts, it was a biplane with two engines in tandem on each side. Clark flew it with Lieutenant John S. "Jimmy" Thach at Norfolk, and Thach alone was pilot on a nonstop 1935 flight from there to Panama. Despite this successful flight, pilots' fears over the BMB's light weight and apparent lack of strength led to its rejection.

Clark's resentment of BuAer chief Ernie King was shared by a great many of his peers. On the eve of the XP3Y flight, Jock received a revealing letter (dated 13 September) regarding King from Lieutenant Commander John Dale Price, operations officer to Base Force air commander Admiral F. J. Horne on the flagship seaplane tender *Wright*. (At the time the tactical officer on this staff was Radford, another great friend and now a full commander.)

> One of my operatives [i.e., informants] recently from Washington reports that the Chief is completely out of hand nowadays. I've used every known means trying to insult him into coming out here or writing but I think he mortally dreads and fears me. My agent also reported that he is still afflicted with insomnia, especially after the evening meal. Tell him Radford and I double dog dare him to come out here [before] Oct. 1 [when] the *Wright* shoves off [on a long cruise].

Perhaps Clark did try to broach this subject—obviously a sensitive one to the unpopular bureau chief—on his return to Washington in mid-April. If so, King may well have added fuel to a suspicion that some of his talented mid-rank officers—Radford, Price, and Clark—were conspiring against him. In some ways they were, but for positive reasons: more efficiency and higher performance. The "spy," who no doubt worked closely with King, might even have been the brightest of all the airmen, Fuzz Sherman (second in Jock's Academy class of '18). He had become director of aviation ordnance in the Bureau of Ordnance in Washington after transferring from VF-1 two years before. And King, whatever his quirks, certainly respected all of them.

A related officer on King's mind was Jack Towers, the flyers' acknowledged pioneer aviation leader, who was physically present with the fleet as the commander of NAS San Diego. But King groomed his own successor in mid-1936, a nonthreatening Arthur B. Cook. Jock, in his anger at King, wisely kept his distance, as did Sherman and Radford. But Johnny Price could not. King hardly feared him (or anyone else for that matter), for when King relieved Admiral Horne as Base Force air commander in 1936 he retained Price as staff operations officer. And when King ran the whole Navy during World War II he allowed Price to advance up the admiral ranks but never to hold a major combat command.

Clark did his job ably, and testing all the new planes whetted his appetite to return to sea—and the new carriers. In early 1934 he ran the acceptance trials of the *Ranger* (CV-4), commissioned that June. By 1936 tiny *Langley* was earmarked for conversion into a seaplane tender, making way for the two large flattops *Yorktown* (CV-5) and *Enterprise* (CV-6), which were commissioned in late 1937 and mid-1938 respectively.

Late in 1935 Admiral Day retired and was succeeded as president of the Board of Inspection and Survey by Rear Admiral John D. Wainwright. Like Day, Wainwright found Clark "an outstanding officer in whom one can place absolute dependence"—which Wainwright, like Day a nonaviator, indeed did. Clark then requested—and got—carrier duty and Wainwright's generous farewell: "I have the highest opinion of him personally and professionally. . . . He is well qualified for promotion and I most heartily recommend him for it." (1935–36 fitness reports)

Ordered to his old ship *Lexington* as assistant air officer, Clark drove cross-country to San Diego. Waiting for him on his arrival in early July was a copy of a letter of appreciation (dated 26 June 1936) from the new chief of BuAer, Rear Admiral A. B. Cook, to Wainwright. Cook specifically lauded Clark—"by his energy and splendid spirit of cooperation" between the board and the bureau—for enabling the 1935 aircraft trials at San Diego as well as at Anacostia and Pensacola to "have been accomplished with a high order of expedition and thoroughness. . . . I consider that his tour of duty, just ending, has contributed measurably to the improvement of Naval aircraft."

M.C. and the two girls moved with Jock to Coronado, but M.C.'s heavy drinking, frequent illnesses, and erratic behavior (possibly associated with morphine) led her to neglect the children. Worse, while Jock was at sea—usually during the weekdays conducting flight operations as part of fleet exercises—his wife began "running around" with other men. She occasionally left her young daughters home with baby sitters, sometimes without even that. As word of these difficulties reached Clark he understandably began to worry. And being at sea aboard the *Lexington* most weekdays or even longer over the next two years, he could not control his wife. His worries seem not to have affected his performance, except that an ulcer began to develop.

In July 1936 Clark reported aboard the *Lexington* to Captain Aubrey Wray "Jake" Fitch, "an outstanding officer," as was the popular exec, Commander M. S. "Chubb" Brown. Jock's '17 classmate Lieutenant Commander Felix B. Stump was navigator, replaced a year later by friend Buddy Wieber, class of '18. Fitch explained to Jock that his assignment as assistant air boss had been enlarged to "carrier representative." This was a newly created post for the senior pilot on board, the very same post ("air commodore") that Jock had proposed during his first tour on the *Lex*. Matt Gardner got the same job on the *Saratoga*.

Both men were charged with coordinating training of their ships' four squadrons, especially when shore based. Clark believed the squadrons needed to be coordinated by one person in battle as well. This became increasingly obvious, and by mid-1937 the term "air group commander" was being adopted over "carrier representative" (formally in July 1938).

Four squadrons comprised the "air group," as it came to be known: Clark's former squadron, Fighting Two (now led by an old friend, Lieutenant Commander Andrew J. Crinkley, who had just relieved Tom Jeter); Bombing Three; Scouting Three; and Bombing Five. For a short time VF-1 also operated from the *Lex*, having transferred from the *Langley* when it became a seaplane tender. One of the pilots of VF-2 briefly was Lieutenant (jg) George Anderson, another in VF-1 was Lieutenant (jg) Thomas H. Moorer. Both men were later key advisers to Clark, and each eventually held the post of Chief of Naval Operations.

The squadrons still retained the "B" suffix (e.g., VF-2B), but only for another year, inasmuch as tactical distinctions between "battle" and "scouting" were becoming blurred in carrier missions. In fact, Clark's task was to develop a new carrier air group attack doctrine, which embraced interplane voice radio communications and new rendezvous techniques after launchings and following attacks.

Naval warfare was customarily fought in daylight, but modern fleets were experimenting with nighttime air operations beyond simple takeoffs and landings. Clark led the *Lexington's* planes in the first coordinated night bombing attack against the old battleship *Utah*, converted into a radio-controlled target ship. It was carried out well beyond any light glow from California coastal towns, thereby creating the worst possible conditions for a pilot: no visible horizon. The planes had lights for following one another, but without the horizon the pilots "flew by the seat of their pants."

Clark's squadrons succeeded, however, proving night attacks "very feasible," although the pilots preferred moonlight in order to see the horizon for orienting themselves. Recommendations went forward for improving night navigating instruments, but in the meantime pilots were guided to the ship by its searchlight pointed straight up or toward the horizon. All carrier night flying would be discontinued at the outbreak of World War II— regrettably, because the Japanese became very adept at it.

Clark faced several personnel problems in the senior ranks on the *Lex*. In November 1936 a plane flown by exec Chubb Brown was reported down in the hills somewhere east of San Diego. Clark formed part of the aerial search and was the one who found Brown's plane and its dead pilot. He was replaced by early naval aviator Commander Wadleigh Capehart.

A growing headache turned out to be VF-2 skipper Andy Crinkley, a chronic writer of complaint letters. One touched a nerve on the staff of the new fleet air commander, Vice Admiral Horne. Crinkley wanted to change the flying rules at North Island. But Horne's chief of staff, Captain Jack

Towers, had just left after two years of commanding that air station very successfully. He stymied Crinkley by insisting on positive recommendations and detailed drawings beyond Crinkley's ability to make. This silenced the pilot until other grievances surfaced, thoroughly compromising him. Jock never liked "letter writers."

A steadily worsening problem was VS-3 skipper Lieutenant Commander A. S. "Ooks" Marley Jr., a classmate of Jock's who Jock had originally succeeded as skipper of Fighting Two in 1931 but who was "a troublemaker by nature." Ooks Marley chronically lied to Clark and to the normally congenial Captain Fitch, who became particularly enraged by it. Clark mentioned it to Raddy, Horne's tactical officer, who suggested that Marley might be "off the beam." When two of Marley's planes collided and crashed, Jock presided over the court of inquiry and witnessed Marley rambling on with hearsay evidence, all of which had to be expunged from the record. That very night on the *Lex* the ship's doctor found Marley on the floor of his stateroom raving madly and surrounded by hundreds of cigarette butts. He was taken ashore in a straitjacket, soon medically retired, and committed to a mental hospital at Anacostia from which he escaped. When caught, he declared that he wanted to kill "that fellow Clark for expunging my testimony."

A more positive experience was filming action scenes on board ship and in the air for the Hollywood motion picture *Wings over Honolulu*. Jock, assigned as liaison officer, was so impressed by the filmmakers' speed and efficiency that "I felt the Navy could profit by copying some Hollywood procedures"—a harbinger of his future wartime contacts with filmdom. What he did not like was having to round up 60 Navy wives to be extras for a large scene on the *Ranger*. But he was rescued when Jack Towers's wife Pierre took over the task. Then word leaked out that each woman would receive $20, whereupon over 100 of them showed up.

The fleet's exercises in early 1937 involved Admiral King. When the *Lexington*'s squadrons remained ashore during the ship's navy yard overhaul, they were assigned to King's shore-based Aircraft Base Force command. Clark as carrier representative was temporarily assigned to King's staff to help coordinate *Lex*'s planes with the patrol planes in the defense of San Diego against Admiral Horne's *Saratoga* and *Ranger* planes. The day before the exercise Clark reported to King aboard the seaplane tender flagship *Wright* anchored in the bay.

He first encountered Johnny Price, King's operations officer. He sat down, but as they chatted King stormed in and swore at his ops officer, "Goddam you, Price, I told you not to do that!" As King railed on, Jock just jumped up and exited down the adjacent stairway, "just to get away from him." King was "the only naval officer I ever knew who would curse his subordinates." Jock went straight to his stateroom and never did officially report in person to King. Price and Clark spent most of the night planning the air defense at San Diego. Clark simply avoided King.

King's night-flying Consolidated P2Y flying boats located Horne's carriers, which could not launch planes in the morning because of a heavy offshore fog. San Diego, however, had clear skies, enabling King's patrol-bombers and Clark's scout-bombers to hammer the *Sara* and *Ranger* from dawn until mid-morning when the umpires ruled both ships sunk.

Although the exercise officially ended at 10 AM,

> King, characteristically bent on making sure, kept the attacks going strong until noon. As usual, he covered himself with glory as the winner of this tactical exercise. He was always outsmarting the other guy. No messages passed between him and me until the exercise was over. He then called me in to say, "You did a fine job. Just magnificent." That was all that passed between us.

In fact, "everybody in the Navy lived in fear of Ernie King. They all felt he was a rough customer." The mild Duke Ramsey, for one, confided to Clark that he did not like King's style; things should be "done with a smile." On the other hand, whenever King went anywhere like Pensacola or San Diego, the parties lasted all night, and everyone, except King, needed two or three days to recover from his visit. The conclusion of fleet exercises led to the customary Saturday night celebration at the Hotel del Coronado. Sure enough, on this occasion, King was there with a big party, as was Clark but at another table.

During the course of the evening King sent over Lieutenant Bob (Robert W.) Bockius of his staff to invite Clark to come have a drink with the admiral. "You tell Ernie King," replied a still chagrined Jock, "that if he stays on his side of the fence I'll stay on mine, and everything will be alright." Bockius's eyes got "as big as saucers" at hearing a lieutenant commander deny an admiral's request.

But King got the message and either respected Clark for his forthright response or laughed it off, or both, because nothing came of the incident. In Jock's view, King was the one who built the "fence," and Clark made sure he avoided King in the future. Even no less a figure than Jack Towers believed that, as a result of his calling King a "penny whistle" (noisemaker) at one of these Coronado affairs, King forever after thwarted Towers's career. (Reynolds, *Admiral John H. Towers*, 263)

The fleet now planned for Hawaiian maneuvers, meaning a long absence from Coronado. Clark, hoping to curb his wife's nocturnal forays and to give her time to recuperate from her "illness," sent her and their daughters to M.C.'s mother in Savannah for an extended visit. Jock concentrated so heavily on his duties and with such success that Captain Fitch at the end of March 1937 rated him as "fitted for independent command ashore and afloat commensurate with his rank."

The *Lexington*, planes back aboard, sailed to Hawaii in mid-April 1937 for "the big war," Fleet Problem XVIII, another carrier attack on Pearl Harbor. On the eve of her departure from Hawaii's Lahaina Roads Jock wrote to M.C. extolling the virtues of his admirable seaborne "family":

> So far we have done very well in every thing we have undertaken and I am glad because it has been quite a feather in Captain Fitch's hat. He is very much a prince and the *Lexington* is all in all an unusually fine ship. . . . Tell Mary Lou to "be a good girl" [implying the same for her mother]. (Letter, 28 April 1937)

The Black Fleet of *Lex* and *Saratoga* reached the 180th meridian (International Date Line) west of Midway Island on 4 May. Their planes covered an amphibious assault on Midway, followed by the attack on Pearl Harbor, defended by the White Fleet of *Ranger* and Ernie King's flying boats. Results were unsatisfactory, due partly to the battleship mentality that had restricted the carriers' mobility. All three carriers were "damaged" by enemy surface fire. And Jock's divebombers did not perform well.

Worse, Clark became a real casualty. His ulcer suddenly began to bleed severely, and he landed in sick bay during the fleet's return voyage to California at the end of May. Because he needed immediate medical treatment, the *Lexington* had him flown to the naval hospital in San Diego. Jock spent a month there, during which time the ulcer was surgically closed, and he received medicines and was placed on a restricted diet of milk, cream, and eggs. Freddy Ceres, again flight surgeon on the carrier staff, looked in on him. The doctors advised Clark to remain on this diet—and to discontinue the use of alcohol and tobacco—for two or three years! And he obeyed. But his worries continued, including M.C.'s spending, exacerbated by his loss of flight pay while in the hospital. (Report of Medical Survey, 18 November 1939)

Jock wrote to her on 1 July that the *Lexington* would have a tight schedule over the coming year, mostly at sea, and that she should get well before returning to San Diego with "the babies." This may have been a thinly veiled attempt to give his daughters the protection of their Georgia grandmother.

On Clark's return to the ship he found that a new skipper, Leigh Noyes, had relieved the much-admired Captain Jake Fitch. Furthermore, Noyes elevated Clark from assistant air officer and air group commander to ship's air officer. He now headed the Air Department, which included aircraft maintenance as well as seniority over the air group commander.

This was a major career step up, a billet that required Clark's promotion to the full rank of commander as soon as practicable. And at age 43 he would do much less flying, for the job made him part of a ship's company and was a prerequisite to eventually becoming captain of an aircraft carrier. He was right in line with his most outstanding classmates of '18, especially those who had also survived the high risks involved with flying.

As Clark began to settle in to his new job, the *Lexington* made a leisurely run up the coast to Santa Barbara "to show the flag" on the Fourth of July weekend. It arrived on the 3rd, whereupon liberty parties rushed ashore. Suddenly, the ship received orders to return immediately to San Diego and then head to the South Pacific.

The famous aviatrix Amelia Earhart and her navigator Fred Noonan, near the end of a round-the-world flight in a twin-engine Lockheed Electra, had failed to land at Howland Island near the Gilbert Islands chain for a scheduled refueling. They had obviously gone down at sea, and the "Lady Lex" was among several warships being dispatched to find them.

First, sailors on liberty in Santa Barbara had to be rounded up by search parties and all pilots on leave in southern California recalled immediately to North Island. The *Ranger's* VS-41 lent 14 SBUs, among the other carriers that provided two-seater planes. (Foley, "Searching for Amelia," 210) The *Lexington* hastily reprovisioned at Long Beach on Independence Day, then rushed to San Diego. En route, Jock penned a letter to M.C., which he airmailed to Savannah:

> It may take a month, but my guess is that she [Earhart] will be found before we get there. In any case she should be able to float in their rubber raft a couple of weeks at least and perhaps longer. It will take almost a week for us to get there as it is 3800 miles via Honolulu. . . .
>
> We are going to have quite a naval force . . . about 70 planes, four destroyers, one battleship the *Colorado,* plus patrol planes from Honolulu. All in all Amelia will be the subject of the Greatest Woman Hunt in history. Probably [she will] have more men after her than Cleopatra.

Clark revealed his historical sense of this unprecedented naval event by jokingly comparing it to the pursuit and destruction of Antony and Cleopatra's Egyptian fleet by the Roman navy in 31 BC.

On 5 July the *Lexington* stood out of San Diego, landed aboard the entire air group, and picked up its destroyer escort. Captain Noyes rang up

30 knots to make Hawaii in just four days. Refueling quickly at Pearl Harbor, the *Lexington* continued on toward Howland but at a reduced speed to conserve fuel. The ship needed its oil for the broad search over a 150,000-square-mile area, as it turned out, and the return trip to Hawaii.

Lacking bases in that region of the Pacific, the Navy added this experience to its general need for underway fuel replenishment in order to give the fleet mobility. The first successful attempts from tankers were made a year later.

By the time the carrier reached the vicinity of Howland Island on 12 July, Earhart and Noonan had been missing for 11 days. It relieved the *Colorado*, which had used its three O2U spotting planes to search since the 7th. The Hawaii-based flying boats had been unable to reach the area.

> [Earhart and Noonan] should be afloat, and it is a question of how long they can survive in the broiling equatorial sun. Our plan is to search 90 miles on either side, with two miles interval between planes on the scouting line. In a day we could search an area 160 miles by 180 miles and we could keep that up indefinitely. . . . I think if we can get anywhere near the location where they landed we ought to find them. (Undated letter to M. C.)

*Lexington's* planes operated for six days in ideal weather. Between four and six aircraft, each with two pairs of eyes, flew in a group at about 500 feet altitude, sometimes up to 48 planes daily. (Foley, "Searching for Amelia," 211–12) But they finally gave up on 28 July, "after searching almost the entire Pacific Ocean," a disappointed Jock wrote in another letter. "It was a most irksome task. The heat was terrific, particularly at night, and day after day the same answer, 'no trace of the missing pilots.' Our aviators did a very commendable job though, and I don't believe that they missed any area." The ocean had apparently swallowed up Earhart and Noonan, and "Lady Lex" plodded homeward at ten knots to conserve fuel.

Captain Noyes gave special credit to Clark for having conducted the air search so admirably and extolled him in his fitness reports (1937–38), also recognizing his key role in developing the new air group command system.

> A superior officer of the highest personal and military character. Keen, able, cool, forceful and of sound judgment. Devoted and efficient in performance of duty. As a leader elicits admiration and confidence. Broad aviation experience and judgment, but also always has the best interests of the whole ship and service in mind. Well fitted for command. Highly recommended for promotion.

Finally, the promotion papers went forward, and as soon as Clark passed his medical exam in December he was promoted to the full rank of commander. He also became ship's athletic officer, one of his steady passions.

Even bigger news that July and in the ensuing months of 1937 was the Japanese invasion of China proper. After having absorbed Manchuria in the north six years earlier, Japanese militarists took on the herculean task of trying to conquer the rest of the world's most populous country. The U.S. Navy therefore welcomed the simultaneous arrival of its new carriers *Yorktown* and *Enterprise* and the new fighting planes in anticipation of the mounting probability of fighting Japan's equally growing fleet. The last carrier biplanes now entered service—the Grumman F3F fighter and Curtiss SBC scout-bomber—along with the first monoplanes: the Douglas TBD torpedo-bomber and Vought SB2U scout-dive-bomber.

No changes occurred in Clark's personal life, except that M.C. returned to Coronado with Mary Lou and Cathy. There he could exercise some control over her activities on weekends, when the ship was in port.

As 1938 began, Ernie King succeeded to the fleet carrier command in the rank of vice admiral, Jack Towers became skipper of flagship *Saratoga*, and Jock Clark kept the *Lexington*'s Air Department so efficient that its planes executed 4,000 consecutive landings aboard "without so much as blowing a tire—an enviable record!" boasted Clark. In fact, between November 1937 and May 1938 no aircraft accident of any kind occurred that required a major overhaul, and no personnel were injured. Said Captain Noyes of Jock, "I consider him one of our leading naval aviators, as well as an excellent all-around naval officer." (6 June 1938 fitness report)

Fleet exercises that March involved King's Black Fleet of the two big carriers attacking the southern California coast and the White Fleet of Captain John S. McCain's *Ranger* and two patrol-bombing squadrons of the new PBY flying boats under Jock's former *Lexington* skipper, Rear Admiral Charles Blakely. The senior "Gun Club" battleship admirals forced King to split his carriers between two battleship forces, which he rightly protested: late on the 17th—600 miles from the coast—in two separate bombing attacks, the *Ranger*'s aircraft and 36 PBYs put the *Lexington* out of action—dramatic proof of what the former XP3Y could do.

King's objections to his carriers' lack of independence from the battle line led his superiors to give him freedom of action in Fleet Problem XIX two weeks later—another surprise attack on Pearl Harbor with all three carriers. As the *Lexington* approached Hawaii, however, the crew was suddenly stricken by a virus. The apparent cause was a faulty dishwasher in which the water was not hot enough to kill the germs. Jock had 450 cots set up on the hangar deck, "but the ship was put out of action without having fired a shot." King excused the *Lex*, but even without her the *Saratoga* launched predawn strikes on 29 March that caught Pearl Harbor by surprise—again.

By the final phase of Fleet Problem XIX the crew's rest in the Hawaiian sunshine had restored the *Lexington* to fighting trim. The ship joined King's Purple Fleet and the *Saratoga* for successful attacks on the Green naval forces at San Francisco and off San Pedro on 24–26 April. These war games capped Clark's very successful two years on the Lady Lex, during which time he had honed his knowledge of fast, 30-plus knot, aircraft carriers.

That knowledge included the obvious vulnerability of the nation's major Pacific base, Pearl Harbor, to the mobility and striking power of carriers at the hands of potential enemy Japan. With the Navy building up its facilities there, Clark was pleased to receive orders in June 1938 to become executive officer of Naval Air Station Pearl Harbor, Honolulu, Territory of Hawaii.

He had five weeks' leave to relocate from Coronado to Honolulu, during which he brought M.C., now 25; her mother Laura Wilson; and daughters Mary Lou, almost 4, and Cathy, 2, on a summer voyage to Hawaii on board the luxury liner *Lurline*. Mary Lou was seasick for the entire voyage. M.C.'s mother returned home, leaving M.C., whose problems had only worsened, to tend to the children. Her erratic and out-of-control behavior weighed heavily on Jock. He enrolled his daughters in "the little red schoolhouse" at the Ford Island base in the middle of Pearl Harbor. They hated it.

M.C.'s nocturnal excursions and behavior eventually led to a blowup, and Jock decided to file for divorce. He banished her from their quarters, refused to allow her to visit with the girls, and depended on friends to pick them up from school and do other essential tasks.

Jack and Doris Pearson, already in Hawaii for a year, became substitute parents, treating Mary Lou and Cathy as virtual siblings of their own young daughter and son. A nurturing Doris firmly adhered to Jock's insistence that the girls not be allowed to see their mother. When four-year-old Mary Lou once asked why not, another officer's wife said simply, "You can't because your mother is a prostitute." The unfathomable word remained buried in Mary Lou's memory, especially after she later discerned what it meant.

M.C. soon left Hawaii for the mainland, leaving the girls with Jock; and the Pearsons remained at Pearl Harbor until July 1940 when they returned to BuAer in Washington. Jack Pearson headed its Fighter Design Branch where he played a key role in developing the Navy's two premier wartime carrier fighter planes, the F4U Corsair and F6F Hellcat.

Clark's Pearl Harbor office was located on Ford Island, alongside which carriers and battleships docked when in port. The island's major function was serving as headquarters of Patrol Wing Two, the PBY Catalinas commanded

Jock entertains his children and those of good friends and helpers Jack and Doris Pearson at a Pearl Harbor swimming pool in 1939. *From left*: Johnnie Pearson, Bev Pearson (behind Clark), daughters Mary Lou and Catherine Carol Clark. *Clark family photo*

by pioneer naval aviator Captain Kenneth Whiting. Commander J. W. Reeves Jr. was Fleet Air Base commander. He was nicknamed "Black Jack" (and no relation to the now-retired Admiral Billy Goat Reeves). Clark was his second in command as well as athletic officer to Patwing Two.

The wing's PBYs, in response to Japan's increasing truculence, regularly patrolled the waters around Hawaii. Ford Island held weekly antiaircraft drills, in which "all personnel would turn out en masse to man machine guns and every conceivable type of antiaircraft equipment." To prepare for a possible Japanese invasion fleet, the Navy mounted its longest-range guns—16-inch—"in hidden places" to help repel any enemy landing force.

And periodically, planes from Carrier Divisions One (Rear Admiral Bill Halsey)—*Saratoga* and *Lexington*—and Two (Vice Admiral Blakely)—newly arrived *Yorktown* and *Enterprise*—made more simulated attacks on Ford Island and the Air Corps' Hickam Field—always successfully.

> Thinking we were alerted to every possibility, I was shocked to learn, when Japan finally did attack Pearl Harbor [on 7 December 1941] how ineffective our defenses were. Of course, the element of surprise accounted for much of the Japanese success. But, in my opinion, we should have been able to offer better resistance.

For any war in the Pacific, the fleet needed a system of interlocking air defenses between Pearl Harbor and outlying islands, reaching as far westward as Howland (location of the Earhart search); to Johnston, Palmyra, and Canton to the southwest; and to Midway and Wake to the northwest. Clark met often and for long hours with Commander Henry F. Bruns, chief civil engineer of the 14th Naval District, planning airstrips and seaplane anchorages for these tiny islands—with the tacit agreement of the British government, which owned several of them. Often when Whiting's PBYs took training flights to these islands, Jock hopped rides to inspect the progress of the construction.

The newly created Civil Aeronautics Authority (changed to Board in 1940) participated in setting up these island airfield and seaplane bases because Pan American World Airways asked to use them for its mammoth new transoceanic passenger flying boats. William T. Miller of the CAA—a friend of Clark's since his Washington days—flew to Honolulu in Pan Am's first four-engine flying boat, the Boeing-built B-314 Clipper. There he and Jock discussed at length the commercial aspects of the new island air facilities.

Black Jack Reeves found Clark especially industrious and cooperative in carrying out "my policies and desires . . . in every possible respect." As a result, the annual inspectors of the fleet air base in April 1939 gave Reeves accolades for high standards in maintaining equipment, uniforms, and the messes with their excellent food.

Reeves generously passed along chief credit to Clark for "his personal attention to duties and . . . his leadership resulting in a loyal following by the other officers attached to the Base." What was more, his additional duty as Patwing athletic officer "has taken a large amount of time, has been done well, and has had a definite morale value." (1938–39 fitness reports)

No doubt his commitment to both the baseball and football teams offered a diversion from his domestic difficulties. As always, baseball was his passion and led to a championship team. He turned to the air station's personnel officer, Lieutenant Hubert S. Strange, for two things: Strange's wife to help run the team, and Strange himself to "recruit players from all over the Navy." Recalled Hubie Strange, "I could give the edge to a good pitcher." And it worked! (Strange, *A Full Life*, 48) For the football team Jock recruited recent *Lexington* shipmate and now PBY pilot Tom Moorer to be coach. (Moorer transcript #30, 1585)

Patwing Two commander Whiting had Clark make a survey of the large islands within the Hawaiian group for possible airfields. Jock and Whiting's flag lieutenant, Lieutenant Commander George L. Richard, accordingly flew low over these islands and landed where possible to examine the suitability of the terrain for landing fields. Then Clark and civil engineer Bruns drew up detailed plans for any location that had even a modicum of airstrip suitability.

Admiral Blakely, who relieved Ernie King as Commander Aircraft Battle Force in 1939, visited his former *Lexington* shipmate at Ford Island to discuss the airfield expansion program. Clark flew Blakely to the construction site at Kaneohe on the other side of Oahu to inspect what was becoming a major air station.

Incidentally, Clark learned that Ernie King had gone to the General Board. "Everybody was waiting and hoping to see the time when he would pass off the picture," Clark among them, still smarting over the XP3Y incident a few years before. The General Board was the traditional "kiss of death" for a flag officer's career. King reverted to his permanent rank of rear admiral. He and the other members of the General Board advised the Secretary of the Navy on general matters until each—according to custom—would be retired.

Jock's workload increased. Not only was he executive officer of the Ford Island air base, but in April 1939 Commander Reeves departed to take command of the new carrier *Wasp* (CV-7), leaving Clark as acting base commander *and* exec for one month. His immediate superior, Ken Whiting, was gratified that Jock proved "especially cool headed, energetic, industrious" and with "the ability to think, to plan and to do things without being told." (2 June 1939 fitness report)

Then, to add to Clark's already immense workload, Whiting was also transferred, forcing Jock to wear yet a *third* "hat" as acting CO of Patwing Two. As all three, Clark reported to the officer in charge of defending the Hawaiian Islands, Rear Admiral Orin G. Murfin, commandant of the 14th

Naval District. But he was evaluated by Admiral Blakely's relief, Rear Admiral Cook, who immediately took note of Clark's ability "to exercise independent command with firmness and decision." (27 July 1939 fitness report) Virtually every one of his immediate superior officers had for years recommended him for promotion and his own command.

The makeshift and divided responsibilities for defending "the Islands" against Japan reflected a peacetime mentality. In reality, for example, recalled Clark,

> we found many signs of Japanese espionage. For instance, on a flight to Midway, as my plane passed over Pearl and Hermes Reef, I sighted a small 100-ton Japanese fishing ship hard and fast aground. When our people went aboard, they discovered it was equipped with an ultramodern radio installation that confirmed our suspicions. We came to regard every Japanese vessel, large or small, as capable of rendering intelligence to Japan.

Testimony of inevitable war in the Pacific came from several visitors passing through Hawaii. Admiral Harry Yarnell turned over command of the Asiatic Fleet to Admiral Tommy Hart in July 1939, after having had the U.S. gunboat *Panay* sunk by Japanese bombers the previous December during the war in China. Yarnell and Jock "agreed that war with Japan was only a matter of time." Millionaire industrialist Sir Victor Sassoon passed through with a "plane full of gold" from his holdings in China, as did Egmont P. Walker from Australia. Walker's two nieces "expressed fear that if they remained in Australia they could expect to become Japanese concubines"—a remark that startled Jock.

Clark's workload decreased somewhat in August when Rear Admiral Arthur L. Bristol Jr., a man Jock greatly admired, assumed command of Patwing Two, and Captain Elliott Buckmaster took over the Ford Island air station. This easygoing officer quickly became very popular with the men and admired Clark's excellence for being "loyal, courteous, painstaking and efficient." (September 1939 fitness report) Early in September Nazi Germany invaded Poland to begin World War II in Europe. Within days Vice Admiral Adolphus Andrews arrived at Pearl Harbor with a large force of cruisers and destroyers to form the Hawaiian Detachment as an additional deterrent to Japan.

The mounting international tension, Clark's heavy workload, and his concerns about his wife and daughters led to occasional overeating and a queasy digestive tract. X-rays at the naval hospital on 14 September disclosed the return of his ulcer (under control since May 1937). The condition worsened, and on the 29th he was transferred to the hospital for treatment and rest. Clark gradually started to improve but not rapidly enough to return to duty.

Unable to care for his daughters and already indebted to the Pearsons and others, he resigned himself to sending the girls to M.C. at her mother's home in Savannah until his health could be restored. They boarded the *Lurline* for California on 14 November 1939, the day before Mary Lou's fifth birthday. Over 60 years later she reflected that the true cause of her dad's illness was likely "a broken heart when his dream of the beautiful family began to disintegrate."

On 24 November Jock wrote to his sister Mary that he was being transferred to the naval hospital at San Diego again for further treatment: "Can only hope for the best and it will take a long time." He was flown to San Diego in mid-December for a month of treatment, followed by three months' sick leave. (Report of Medical Survey, 12 January 1940) In addition to medicines received there to control the bleeding, he was counseled that the best possible deacidifying agent was a mixture of three-fourths milk and one-fourth cream. It worked, but he had to use it for many years to come. Eventually, canned Avocet goat's milk enabled him to control his ulcers. But it meant that he had to keep a large supply of it with him on whatever ship he served if he expected to continue his career.

The Navy assuredly wanted him to do this, as war clouds in the Atlantic and Pacific threatened the country, making talented and experienced officers like J. J. Clark valuable assets in the expanding conflict.

# EIGHT

## Into the Two-Ocean War, 1940–1942

THE NAVY GAVE JOCK CLARK A CLEAN BILL OF HEALTH IN MAY 1940—as Hitler's armies were overrunning western Europe and German warships assailed British merchant shipping in the Atlantic. Japan's war machine continued to ravage China, arousing American sympathy and aid for the Chinese, thereby adding to Japan's growing animosity toward the United States. America was frantically mobilizing, and Clark, anxious to be part of it, reported to Rear Admiral Jack Towers, Chief of BuAer, in Washington.

During June and July Congress authorized construction of a two-ocean navy to protect the country from the Axis aggressors. It included several new air training centers, the first 11 of many 27,000-ton fast 33-knot aircraft carriers of the new *Essex* (CV-9) class, nine 11,000-ton light carriers of the *Independence* (CVL-22) class built on cruiser hulls, and a bevy of Navy aircraft superior to anything belonging to the Japanese.

Clark would soon be part of it, but before he could return to the rigors of sea duty Admiral Towers decided he needed a shore billet to help him recuperate fully from his bout with ulcers. Towers therefore sent him to Buffalo, New York, to inspect Navy planes being built by the Curtiss-Wright and Bell Aircraft companies.

Jock's one great frustration, however, remained his children. The divorce settlement—generally agreed upon—had not been finalized and in fact dragged on until M.C. was eventually awarded custody and $100 a month alimony from Jock. In the meantime he hired a woman caretaker to be present whenever M.C. and the girls were together. Eventually, he engaged a portly part-time German-born governess, Frieda Heinan, to help look after his daughters. He later wrote to his sister Mary, "I am very much distressed about their surroundings. M.C. goes off periodically and if it were not for Frieda I should be much alarmed about them."

Proceeding to Buffalo in early June, Clark arrived at the Curtiss plant just as it was about to send 30 SBC-3 biplane scout-bombers to the French carrier *Béarn* anchored off Nova Scotia in Canada. No sooner had the planes been hoisted aboard France's only flattop than France surrendered to Germany, whereupon the *Béarn* was interned in the French West Indies for the duration. The fall of France galvanized American rearmament. Clark, conscious that the war threatened to drag in the United States, inspected the newest planes with even more rigor than he had when he was with the Board of Inspection and Survey four years earlier.

One new Curtiss plane that Clark inspected closely was the XSB2C Helldiver, the Navy's best hope for a powerful and rugged carrier-based scout-divebomber. However, the contract had been awarded as "a sop to Curtiss"—a longtime customer—and in the opinion of many naval aviators it "should never have been built." (Conversation with Paul Pihl) Clark soon discovered it to be "structurally weak," which was confirmed when the main wing beam collapsed during static tests. He wrote a list of defects seven pages long and recommended that Curtiss strengthen the plane accordingly. The first production model flew at the end of the year, after Clark had left Buffalo, and he had no way of knowing—yet—that his suggestions were not followed.

Bell Aircraft was building a fighter plane for both the Army Air Corps, the XP-39 Airacobra, and the Navy, the XFL-1 Airabonita. The only difference between the two was the stronger undercarriage and arresting hook for the latter to land on board carriers. Tests over the summer proved the undercarriage inadequate, and Clark and the Navy—unlike the Army—rejected its version, preferring instead Grumman and Chance-Vought fighters (F4F Wildcat and F4U Corsair respectively).

At least Clark was able to renew acquaintances with pioneer airplane manufacturer Lawrence P. Bell, who had been with the Consolidated Company during development of the XP3Y/PBY Catalina. At a gathering of Q. B. (Quiet Birdman) aviation developers in Buffalo, Larry Bell introduced Clark by chiding him about his recent illness:

> I want you to meet my friend Jock Clark, an old-time aviator and a great fellow. He has a stomach ulcer and something else—severe headaches. The other day he went to see a doctor, but a most thorough examination disclosed nothing wrong.
>
> The doctor asked, "Maybe you drink too much?"
>
> "Oh, I don't drink at all," said Jock.

> "Well, maybe you smoke too much."
>
> "No, I don't smoke."
>
> "Well, maybe you stay out late at night with the ladies."
>
> "Oh, no, I don't go round with the ladies."
>
> Still worried about the headaches, the doctor said, "Let me feel your head." After he felt Jock's head on all sides, he said, "I've got it! Your halo is too tight!"

Clark always appreciated such levity, which the country badly needed as it faced an unfriendly world and internal political repercussions. The Depression was ending, helped in no small part by the growth of new defense industries. But over the summer and fall of 1940 the question of America's participation in World War II found voice in the presidential election rivalry between Democratic incumbent Franklin Roosevelt—running for an unprecedented third term—and the Republican challenger, utility executive Wendell Willkie.

Many vocal isolationists opposed FDR because of his rearmament program and undisguised pro-British, pro-Chinese stance that threatened to lead the United States into the fight.

Clark had admired pro-Navy Roosevelt throughout the president's first two terms and strongly supported him again. Shortly after FDR's reelection in November Jock forcefully revealed his views in a (undated) letter to his sister Mary. They reflected his experiences abroad during and after World War I—fighting the Germans for the first time, then policing the Middle East—and revealed Clark's keen sense of America's next postwar future in world affairs.

> Am not sure . . . whether you were for Roosevelt or not[,] but I have a firm conviction that we ought to thank God for the fact that we have him at the head of the government rather than Mr. Willkie, who was a "phoney"—and fortunately the people were able to see through him.
>
> Unfortunately there are some who are still trying to cast aspersions on Mr. Roosevelt[,] and the only thing I can offer is that the election is over, and whether we prefer someone else or not the die is cast. All who have the best interests of their Constitution at heart should render the present Government their full support.
>
> For there are many hurdles ahead before we can *reach the position in world affairs that should rightfully be ours,* and the only safe way to cross over them lies in loyal unified cooperation, and not loyal opposition as Mr. Willkie would have.

Forgive this blast, but I have seen all sides of the picture, and I can speak with much feeling. (Emphasis added)

Clark's position on the election aside, the future admiral saw America's "rightful" position in the world as that of a global leader to protect democracy, eliminate the dictators, and maintain the postwar peace. This emerging internationalist viewpoint among Americans would culminate in the "Four Freedoms" proclaimed in August 1941 by Roosevelt and British prime minister Winston Churchill. They jointly declared that the ultimate Anglo-American goal was to bring four basic freedoms to the entire postwar world: freedom of speech, freedom of religion, freedom from want (poverty), freedom from fear (of dictators). But first the war had to be won and the German, Japanese, and fascist Italian dictatorships destroyed.

By late November 1940 Clark's health was "much improved" (letter to Mary) and he had laudatory fitness reports from the general inspector of naval aircraft, Ken Whiting. He visited the Bureau of Aeronautics in Washington to ask for sea duty, convinced that the United States would soon be in the fight. The assistant chief of BuAer, Captain Marc Mitscher, informed him that his orders had already been cut for duty as a student at the Naval War College, normally a prerequisite for promotion (but which Mitscher himself had managed to avoid). "I told Mitscher that if war came I wanted to be at sea where I could fight the war," whereupon Mitscher cancelled Jock's war college orders and promised him "the next available billet at sea."

Meanwhile, Clark returned to Buffalo, where his friends needled him about "the red woolen underwear" required for the frigid winter ahead. On 30 November, however, he received a long distance phone call from Mitscher saying that the new naval air training station at Jacksonville, Florida—opened only days earlier—suddenly needed a replacement for the executive officer, the station's second in command. Mitscher wanted Clark to be that person until a seagoing billet opened up for him.

Jock agreed, and next morning he drove through Buffalo's first three inches of snow to his office at the Curtiss plant. "Gentlemen," he announced to his friends, "I want to bid you all good-bye. I hope you all have a very heavy winter. I will be down in Florida. If it gets too cold for you, come visit me."

He left by noon and reported to "Jax" on 4 December 1940. The day after that Lieutenant Jimmy Flatley, his shipmate from his first *Lexington* tour of duty, arrived as one of the first pilot instructors. The air station was still being rushed to completion before the first trainees arrived at the end of the month—not only pilot candidates but also enlisted aviation mechanics, ordnancemen, and radiomen. On his very first day Clark met the man he was replacing, who "was in a great hurry to leave." This worthy simply handed Jock the newly completed station regulations, ready to be printed in time for the formal beginning of instruction on the first day of 1941.

When Jock looked over the regulation book he discovered it to be a virtual carbon copy of the "regs" for NAS San Diego—a fleet operating center, not a training station. He reported this to the station commander, Captain Charles P. Mason, who had no choice but to inform his officers in a special meeting that a completely new set of regs would not be ready by January 1st.

As the meeting broke up, Jimmy Flatley approached Jock, "Commander, can I help?"

Clark answered with a loaded question, "Jimmy, can we do it?"

"You're damned right we can!" came the reply Jock wanted—and likely expected.

Together, the two men got to work, but only at night; Clark's days were filled with getting the construction completed and the air station fully activated. Flatley "did most of the work," remembered Clark, "performing a colossal job in record time"—a book of regulations 160 pages long and carefully proofread. On the afternoon of New Year's Eve Clark presented Captain Mason with his personal copy. Training commenced the next day—on schedule.

By then, Jock, who had known Charlie Mason casually for years, now discovered him to be a "brilliant officer" who quickly "taught me a great deal about leadership."

> He had a quick, incisive mind that grasped all details and immediately transformed them into the right course of action. Mason knew what he wanted. No matter how intricate a problem was, he quickly assimilated it and gave a rapid answer, thus freeing me with time to work on other projects. He told me the "what," leaving me to figure out the "why" or "how" to do things. The expeditious clarity of his orders made my duties comparatively easy.

Talented senior enlisted men were as important as experienced officers in preparing the Navy's air arm for war. Clark struck up a friendship with Warrant Boatswain John E. Montgomery, a former FBI agent who immediately admired Jock's style of leadership. Clark "was a sweetheart who had two speeds—Stop and Go! He never got excited or yelled at a man." In fact, by the time Montgomery was serving under Clark's command in battle he consciously tried to pattern himself after Clark as a leader. (Conversation with Montgomery)

Additional talent at Jacksonville existed in the form of Naval Reserve officers called up for active duty, civilians from the business sector, and even some Academy graduates who for various reasons had left the service but were now readmitted. Few of them were more talented than Ensign Owen E. Sowerwine. He had graduated near the top of 432 graduates of '33 only to be forced to resign a year later due to his susceptibility to seasickness, of all things. Sowerwine impressed Clark sufficiently to utilize his talents throughout most of the war.

Jock moved his daughters into his quarters on the base. M.C., beset with her emotional and social problems, lived off the base and retaliated once by "kidnapping" the girls. Jock had the base police swiftly track them down and lock up M.C. in the brig overnight. The divorce had turned ugly, yet Clark adhered rigidly to his sparse diet and kept his ulcers under control.

Through it all he managed to fulfill social obligations to new neighbors in northern Florida. "He wears his uniforms smartly and his normal limp does not show when he dances," according to a *Life* magazine reporter. At an informal dinner at the sumptuous Epping Forest manor of philanthropist Jesse Ball DuPont (widow of Alfred I. Dupont), he arrived "in a sack suit" (jacket with an unfitted back). "Informal" to the upper set turned out to mean black tie and dinner jacket.

Instead of uncharacteristically taking the defensive amid the rarified atmosphere of these hard-core Republicans, this lifelong Democrat "started talking politics and soon was warmly praising his Commander in Chief and the New Deal. The emotions engendered among the other guests wilted many stiff collars that evening." (Gray, "'Jocko' Clark," 48)

A key political figure flew into Jax in December 1940—Secretary of the Navy Frank Knox. Jock was among those who met the plane and was surprised to see that the last person to exit it was none other that Rear Admiral Ernie King. Clark had not seen King since the Fleet Problem XVIII attack on Pearl Harbor four years before. Though King had ended up on the General Board, the traditional "kiss of death" for an admiral's career, seeing him with Secretary Knox made Clark realize that King "wasn't dead by a long shot!"

This was confirmed a few days later when King assumed command of the Patrol Force in the Atlantic and was elevated again to the rank of vice admiral. His job was to protect the eastern seaboard from German naval activity. Two months later, in February 1941, the Navy divided the U.S. Fleet between the Pacific Fleet and the Atlantic Fleet, the latter, an upgrade of the Patrol Force. King then became Commander in Chief, Atlantic Fleet, in the rank of four-star admiral.

As the third-term president prepared the nation for war, he himself visited Jax on 20 March. FDR was driven around the base in a convertible to inspect the flying activity and to be seen. Proud dad Jock had little Mary Lou and Cathy dressed in red, white, and blue, and they waved to FDR as he passed. Charlie Mason officially commended Jock for the success of the president's visit. (31 March 1940 fitness report)

The so-called Battle of the Atlantic of German U-boats attacking thinly escorted British merchant ship convoys was gradually drawing the U.S. Navy into the fight. The Navy used British Bermuda and West Indies island possessions to track and report U-boats and surface warships to the Royal Navy and even to escort U.S. convoys of Lend Lease military supplies partway to England. An undeclared naval war between the United States and Nazi Germany had begun.

Jock Clark therefore welcomed a phone call in May 1941 from Pete Mitscher. True to his word, Mitscher had a choice seagoing job for Clark: executive officer of the carrier *Yorktown* in the Atlantic. He would relieve his old friend Radford, about to develop naval bases in the Caribbean.

Excited at the prospect, Clark did not wait for his relief to arrive. As for his children, he had to leave them in Jax, only to have M.C. soon "kidnap" them again—this time successfully—to Orlando, where she enrolled Mary Lou in the first grade. Jock, after a short stop at BuAer in Washington, boarded a British flying boat at Baltimore that flew him to Bermuda, which had been established only the month before as forward operating base of the U.S. Neutrality Patrol. Jock relieved Radford in mid-May. The *Yorktown*'s captain was Elliott Buckmaster, with whom Clark had recently served in Hawaii.

The carrier had just arrived in Bermuda after a long voyage from Pearl Harbor via the Panama Canal. Its mission was to conduct "neutrality" patrols—five as it turned out—each about two weeks' duration, searching for and reporting to the British navy movements of German submarines and surface raiders. The *"Yorky"* became flagship of a task force under Rear Admiral Cook that also included the *Ranger*, a light cruiser or two, and three or four destroyers.

Late in May, the German battleship *Bismarck* sortied into the North Atlantic, sinking British merchantmen and warships for a week before Royal Navy forces were able to sink it. By the time the *Yorktown* cleared Bermuda on its first patrol 31 May the United States was unofficially at war with Nazi Germany. The ship's activities consisted primarily of search patrols by various combinations of fighters (F4F), scout-bombers (SBC, SB2U, BT, SBD), and torpedo planes (TBD). Neither their pilots nor the ships spotted any U-boats, let alone a surface raider. But the patrols provided excellent training, especially for the shipboard operators of the new CXAM radar learning how to use it to track aircraft.

The first two cruises proved uneventful, both culminating at Norfolk. Passing through Bermuda's harbor, however, led to one of the very few instances in which Rear Admiral Cook—an impulsive, showy individual—ever spoke to Clark, the ship's exec. This occurred when the ship bent its pitot log sword strip—the device that measured ship's speed and the water pressure beneath the hull—on a reef in the harbor. The instrument extended about three feet below the hull. The admiral's navigational notice had stated the harbor's depth to be 30 feet, whereas the instrument had bent at 28-and-a-half feet. When Clark questioned the accuracy of the depth in Cook's notice, Cook shot back, "Where did you go to sea? Where did you get your sea experience?"

"USS *Lexington,* sir," Jock replied, the very same ship Cook had commanded five years before. All the admiral could do was shake his head.

Early in July, the United States occupied Iceland as an interim stop for convoys, so the *Yorktown*'s next three patrols helped cover the sealanes between Bermuda and Iceland. The fifth patrol took the ship back to Norfolk in early September, another empty cruise except for the usual false alarms—"U-boats" that were schools of fish.

On 4 September, however, a German sub attacked the destroyer *Greer* in another patrol force, leading President Roosevelt to issue a "shoot on sight" order to all American warships that encountered submarines. This came as alarming news to Jock Clark, not because he feared the unseen enemy—which he did not—but because during his three months as exec he had found leadership on the *Yorktown* to be ominously deficient.

Clark considered the skipper, Elliott Buckmaster, to be "very much a gentleman and an excellent ship handler." However, he lacked "the brilliant but chilly presence" of Radford, the exec Jock had relieved and under whom morale had dropped due to Raddy's running the ship strictly "by the book." Nor did Buckmaster have the "flamboyant but opposite 'character' traits" of Clark—in the later words of one of the ship's bright recent ('40) Academy graduates, Lieutenant (jg) John E. Greenbacker. (Letter to author, 19 December 1967)

Worse, "I discovered soon enough," Clark recalled, that Buckmaster "placed too much faith in his heads of departments, failing to crack the whip when some of these officers made serious mistakes." What quickly became obvious to him was that several of them were simply "substandard." In fact, most had been passed over for promotion to commander. But, in the rush toward war, serious shortages in qualified personnel in all ranks meant the Navy had to rely on what was available.

Whenever mishaps occurred, Clark informed the captain that these officers were not doing their jobs.

"Well," Buckmaster would reply, "I have to trust my officers."

"They'll sell you down the river," Jock insisted. "They don't understand what they're doing!" But as the exec "I could only go so far" in pushing the skipper, he later reminisced.

Clark knew he was being considered for promotion to captain; his fitness report for 18 May–31 July 1941 was entitled, "Special Fitness Report for Selection Board." In it, Buckmaster strongly supported his candidacy: "An excellent officer. Loyal, efficient and a hard worker. Well liked by both officers and men. His personal and military character are of the highest order."

Most of this was true, with the exception of the officers' attitudes. In the checklist of 13 personal "qualities" on the fitness report form, the captain gave Clark the academic equivalent of straight As, except for a slightly lower mark on "judgment" and "neatness of dress" and a borderline A-minus on "intelligence." On the Navy's 4.0 numerical scale of general performance Jock received a 3.8.

Even after months of a rocky relationship, when Buckmaster received word of Clark's promotion, his final assessment was virtually identical. The only change was an overall 3.9 and an A+ for "loyalty"—a remarkable gift that likely reflected Buckmaster's honest realization that Clark would be a tough fighting skipper whose expected loyalty to superiors ought to be beyond doubt. And it certainly was in his treatment of enlisted men.

The *Yorktown*'s officers' loyalty to Clark, however, was not high. Twice the Air Department, headed by a lackluster commander, H. F. MacComsey, spilled large amounts of aviation gas on the deck while fueling planes; "with sheer luck it did not catch fire." During one call to General Quarters an enlisted man abandoned a fan supplying air to a shipmate below who then suffocated to death. When, on another occasion, fire from the incinerator spread to inflammable materials in the adjacent space, the ship's first lieutenant and damage control officer, Lieutenant Commander Clarence E. Aldrich, responsible for firefighting, did not respond to the call. Jock had no choice but to open the door himself and lead in the firefighters to extinguish the flames.

With defense against air attack prominent in his thinking, on one of the ship's layovers in Norfolk Clark paid a visit to the British carrier *Illustrious* at a nearby dock. It had been undergoing repairs for damage caused by six direct bomb hits inflicted by German divebombers near Malta in the Mediterranean early in the year. Captain Lord Louis Mountbatten of the royal family had been its skipper until relieved at Norfolk by the exec, Captain G. R.

Tuck, who gave Jock a personal tour of the *Illustrious*. It lasted four hours, during which Clark learned valuable lessons about firefighting and damage control.

> I shuddered to think what would happen to our ship. I even took some of our people over there and showed them what [the British crew] had done and how they had done it. But even so, they didn't seem to get it. They just didn't have the right attitude, I thought. It kind of scared me.
>
> Now, this is a very strange thing. I just had a premonition, a feeling that the ship was going to be sunk.

All but one of the department heads had stood in the middle or lower part of their graduating classes—in addition to Buckmaster himself (class of 1912), they were MacComsey ('22), Aldrich ('21), the navigator Commander Irving D. Wiltsie ('21), air group skipper Commander Curtis S. Smiley ('23), chief engineer Lieutenant Commander John F. "Jack" Delaney ('25), and gunnery officer Lieutenant Commander E. J. Davis ('25). Only the communications officer, Lieutenant Commander Clarence C. "Jug" Ray, had stood high in his class ('25); both he and Aldrich had even tried their hands in submarines. The cream of the officer corps had obviously been sent to battleships or other gun ships.

The ship's aerologist was Lieutenant Commander Hubie Strange (lower half of '26). He had had mixed feelings about Clark at Pearl Harbor and claimed in his memoirs that the department heads were "extremely capable" and that Clark's treatment of them irritated "everyone aboard." (Strange, *A Full Life*, 58) Yet doing other men's work, officer or enlisted, was something Clark had learned never to do back on the old *North Carolina*. If post hoc evidence is acceptable, none of these department heads, including aerology, ever made rear admiral, except as postwar honorary ("tombstone") promotions.

> I learned more about leadership by being executive officer of that *Yorktown* that I ever learned in my whole life before or since. I learned that—in order to get an honest day's work out of these fellows—I had to beg them and wheedle them and praise them and kick them in the rear or whatever you do to get a fair amount of work out of people. And Buckmaster, as the skipper, would not do anything about it.

So Clark turned to the backbone of any ship for getting things done—the senior enlisted men. Working through the chief master-at-arms, Boatswain Leonard C. "Pop" Austin, and his own yeoman Clark soon accomplished needed tasks. Another long-time acquaintance over the preceding decade, Aviation Chief Joseph L. Tucker, also proved useful. In truth, Jock got along best with the sailors, with whom he identified. They tended to respect both his brand of leadership and his humanity—like stepping right over an illegal crap game without saying a word (a page in fact out of Ernie King's book).

Not surprisingly, according to Strange, "this caused the officers to despise Clark, but Captain Buckmaster kept the peace and avoided confrontations." (Strange, *A Full Life*, 58–59) In fact, Jock's entreaties to Buckmaster to "lean on" department heads led to bitter exchanges between the two men, recalled one of the fighter pilots, Lieutenant Bill Leonard of VF-42, which augmented VF-5 on the ship. (1996 and 1997 interviews of W. N. Leonard by historian John B. Lundstrom)

According to Leonard, Clark was "a hard man," acerbic and a know-it-all, whose rough domestic life was known to some. Nor did he talk to the pilots—not that, technically, as ship's exec, he was necessarily supposed to. Neither did the air officer, MacComsey, for that matter, who, like Clark, did not fly much. The airmen respected Clark well enough professionally, but they saw him always scowling, his lower lip permanently curled in apparent disdain. Leonard said Clark easily got his nose out of joint—"a congenital nose out of joint guy!" (Lundstrom interviews)

One of the few times the exec actually intruded in air operations was in criticizing the bomber pilots' landing technique. The SBD pilots came in too high, shut off their engine, and glided down to the flight deck instead of using the standard "power-on" landing—shutting off the engine as the wheels touched the deck. The extra load of bombs now caused the SBDs to "squash down" heavily on the flight deck, breaking the fuselages of 17 of the squadron's 36 planes.

Both the admiral and the captain rejected Clark's recommendation for power-on landings—revealing their lack of practical experience in the cockpit as "JCLs," or Johnny-come-latelies, to flying, against Clark's unimpeachable qualifications. Buckmaster's and air officer MacComsey's solution for stopping the damage to the SBDs was to remove the depth charges rather than to train the pilots to make power-on landings. Jock was incredulous: "Without depth charges our bombers were impotent against the submarine menace, and here we were practically in a war!"

Clark and all the pilots knew that Buckmaster was a JCL to aviation. Indeed, he was one of the very last of the "black-shoe" attired nonflyers to shift to the brown shoes of the aviators—as a commander at age 46 in 1936. Such shortcuts had been necessary for the Navy to fill the senior ranks until the young career aviators gained sufficient experience and seniority to progress through the normal promotion cycles. Jack Towers had become the first full-fledged early airman to become an admiral, in 1939.

Bill Leonard may have inferred that Clark viewed Buckmaster as unqualified for a carrier command because he was a JCL. Indeed, so was Admiral Cook. In fact, Clark had admired and/or respected many excellent JCLs under whom he had sailed, notably Charles Blakely, Jake Fitch, even Ernie King. And William F. Halsey Jr. had joined their ranks in 1935 at 52.

"Some of the latecomers learned enough about the carriers to operate them," Clark recalled, "and some didn't." Among the latter Clark included Buckmaster, although he "admired him as a man and consider him a friend to this day [mid-1960s]." Such a remark was hardly gratuitous, a trait simply out of Clark's call-'em-as-I-see-'em character.

Clark's reputation among the officers of the *Yorktown* was not all that different from his own judgment and that of most others of Ernie King. King, however, did not have Jock's familial or medical problems as at least partial rationales for his gruff behavior. Regarding King, in fact, Clark was starting to develop a different perspective on the man. Although he disdained King's hot temper, especially when King swore at subordinates, even stomping on his hat in the process, Jock could "not help admiring King's stamina, driving power, and unflinching efficiency. In my opinion, some of *Yorktown*'s hapless department heads needed a lot of King's brand of discipline."

Suddenly they got it one day when, as Atlantic Fleet commander in chief King ordered all ships to hold 15 minutes of physical exercises at the conclusion of each morning's muster on the flight deck and before beginning the day's work. The department heads "grumbled and griped" to Clark when he briefed them, arguing that the calisthenics would interfere with their work. One of them even figured that because war with Japan was fast approaching "we'll be in the Pacific pretty soon, and we'll be out from under Ernie King. We won't have to put up with this foolishness!"

"I don't know about that," mused Clark in reply. "Unless I miss my guess, you'll be under Ernie King for a long time."

No doubt, as Clark approached his own advancement to senior rank, he realized why the Navy and the nation needed tough leaders of the King ilk to survive in a hostile world. Ernie King was "smarter than hell, even though nobody liked him." So with King as a veritable role model, Jock Clark as exec labored to whip the ship into fighting shape.

> With consistent effort I eventually managed to achieve a fair amount of success aboard *Yorktown*. But I resolved, right then and there, that

although I never subscribed to anyone's being a martinet, I would endeavor to command firmly, if ever I had a ship of my own.

That would surely happen, given the need for savvy captains as the conflicts in both oceans widened. In June, Hitler invaded the Soviet Union, leading the United States to extend its Lend Lease aid. The next month Argentia, Newfoundland, became a new operating base, to which the *Yorktown* headed in mid-September for another patrol. The overall commander of Argentia was Vice Admiral Arthur Bristol, another JCL and "an excellent leader with high administrative abilities." His superb operations officer was Jock's old friend Commander Mick Carney.

The ship first approached Argentia in a heavy fog the night of 21/22 September. Clark hit the sack about midnight. But the irascible Admiral Cook kept Captain Buckmaster and navigator Wiltsie up all night as he drew circles (arcs) of visibility on his chart, constantly rechecking the navigation—"a useless procedure, because the fog was too dense to see any light."

Clark returned to the bridge at 0500, the same moment that Cook picked up his chart and repeatedly exclaimed in a frenzy, "Who drew these circles on my charts?" Just then his flag lieutenant, Lieutenant Commander Hugh H. Goodwin, arrived and said calmly, "Why, Admiral, I saw you draw those marks on that chart yourself." "Cook," recalled Jock, "went straight to his cabin without a word." Clark regarded Cook's obvious attempt to emulate Ernie King as a flop because Cook "lacked King's dynamic qualities and sense of perfection." And Cook constantly criticized the ship's captain, Buckmaster, which an admiral should only do privately. But perhaps Cook was aping King subconsciously.

Happily, Admiral Cook shifted his flag to the *Ranger* during the Argentia-based patrol, at the end of which in mid-October the *Yorktown* headed for Casco Bay near Portland, Maine, to conduct flight training. Plans to overhaul the ship at Norfolk were cancelled due to new escort demands on it, and Clark enjoyed renewing acquaintances with the prominent Payson family of Portland whom he had befriended during a 1919 visit while aboard the *Aaron Ward*.

On 25 October the carrier sortied from Casco Bay as part of a powerful task force that included the battleship *New Mexico*, two light cruisers, and nine destroyers. They escorted six American merchant ships bound for British merchant service under the Lend Lease program. The heavy escort had become necessary because of increased truculence by German subs; one had torpedoed the U.S. destroyer *Kearny* a week earlier, killing 11 sailors.

On the 30th a U-boat attacked and sank the American destroyer *Reuben James* escorting a convoy outbound from Halifax, Nova Scotia.

The pilots and aircrewmen in *Yorktown's* unarmed patrol flights of SBDs and TBDs increased their vigilance. Sure enough, one TBD patrol saw something. When the flight leader, Lieutenant Harlan T. "Dub" Johnson, landed back aboard he raced up to the bridge to report. They had sighted a sub stalking a convoy out of Halifax.

"What are we waiting for?" said Clark to Buckmaster. "Let's load up and go get her." The skipper only shook his head, "That's not for us. It's out of our area. That's a job for Mullinix's patrol planes." Commander Henry Mullinix commanded the patrol wings of PBY Catalinas at Argentia, from which it would be a four-hour flight for the PBYs to the U-boat contact, plenty of time for the U-boat to escape.

Buckmaster did transmit a radio contact report to Admiral Bristol, who later criticized the *Yorktown* skipper for his inaction. "We had missed a golden opportunity to score the first American kill of the war," recalled a disgusted Clark. Buckmaster did not seem to grasp the wartime conditions. He now armed his SBDs and TBDs with antisub depth charges, yet he "shied away from abandon ship drills for fear of their effect on [the crew's] morale." (J. E. Greenbacker letter)

On the morning of 2 November the convoy and its escort reached the mid-ocean meeting point (MOMP), where it swapped convoys with a British escort force to take the merchantmen on to England. In return, the *Yorktown* force picked up eight British transports carrying 20,000 troops to escort back to Halifax, from whence they would travel around Africa to Egypt in order to help defend the Suez Canal. Later in the day one of the destroyers sighted what appeared to be torpedo tracks in the water and commenced dropping depth charges, with unknown effect.

On the return trip the force was buffeted by a ferocious gale and the highest waves Clark had ever seen. A force of six other destroyers arrived on 6 November to take the transports in to Halifax, while the *Yorktown* and her consorts returned to the Maine coast for more flying and gunnery exercises.

At month's end the ship and one escorting tin can departed Casco Bay for Norfolk, arriving on 2 December for boiler repairs and the postponed three-month refit. Jock Clark began his planned two-week leave by flying a Navy plane down to Jacksonville the following Sunday morning, 7 December, to visit his daughters in Orlando.

When he landed, the man who had relieved him as exec of the air station, former '17 classmate Commander George R. Fairlamb Jr., met him "with astounding news."

Pearl Harbor was under air attack by Japanese carrier aircraft. He took me directly to his quarters to listen to the radio. It was a calamity of the first magnitude. The news was all bad, except that none of our aircraft carriers were in port. This was the one ray of sunshine that lent hope to the otherwise dark picture in the Pacific.

Unable to see his daughters, 100 miles away in Orlando, Clark took off for Norfolk that night, expecting the *Yorktown* to be sent to the Pacific without delay. Fog forced him to land at Charleston, South Carolina, for a four-hour sleep until the fog lifted. He took off and reached his ship by 0800 that morning, the 8th.

Within hours the *Yorktown* received orders to return to the Pacific as soon as practicable. On 12 December it moved from Pier Seven of the navy base to the Navy Yard to receive additional antiaircraft guns, then back to Pier Seven on the 16th. All that day planes were hoisted aboard—those of the air group (VF-42, VB-5, VS-5, VT-5) and 29 other carrier planes (F4F, SBD) to bolster Hawaii's defenses. Several young sailors from Norfolk's boot camp came over to observe. Whenever Clark, roaming the pier, saw an idle swab, including several of these men, he barked, "Don't just stand there! Get aboard and lend 'em a hand!" They jumped to it.

The *Yorktown* cast off after dark, escorted by four destroyers, bound for San Diego via the Panama Canal. During crew's muster far out to sea next morning the master-at-arms informed Clark of an anomaly: "We got 30 more men aboard than we oughta. They're wandering around the hangar deck like a bunch of orphans."

"Get them up here" to the flight deck, Clark demanded. Upon arrival they were lined up, and Jock went down the line, asking the same question and getting the same answer: "Who told you to come aboard this ship?"

"You did, sir."

They were all curious "boots" that Jock had assumed belonged to the crew during the previous night's airplane loading; afterward, they were too scared to ask about returning ashore. They had no choice but to remain aboard until the ship reached Panama on the 20th. (Frank and Harrington, *Rendezvous at Midway*, 42–43)

Japanese forces were overrunning southeastern Asia and the western Pacific islands, while Germany and Italy declared war on the United States. The two-ocean conflict required a delicate balancing act by the Navy to hold back America's enemies in both the Atlantic and the Pacific until the newly authorized fleet—and army and air forces—could be built, manned, and trained to mount counterattacks in both oceans. That could not be realized before mid-1943, meaning that the prewar ships, planes, and personnel had to hold the line until that time.

It also required that the ablest leaders be advanced to high command, starting with the man at the top. On 20 December 1941 the Navy announced the appointment of Admiral Ernest J. King to be Commander in Chief U.S. Fleet. This came as no surprise to Jock Clark. "Nobody else," he said many years later, "had the intestinal fortitude to run the Navy as King did." At the time, to anyone who sought Clark's views on King's appointment, Jock recalled the many war games that King had won by hook or by crook: "We're sure to win the war now, because if we don't win it any other way, Ernie King will *steal* it!!"

In order to direct the Navy in both oceans, King elected to maintain his headquarters in Washington as "CominCh," while Admiral Chester W. Nimitz—with no experience in aviation, incidentally—carried out King's policies as Commander in Chief, Pacific Fleet, "CinCPac," from Pearl Harbor. In March 1942 King took over the additional top post of Chief of Naval Operations, making him "CominCh-CNO" for absolute unity of command.

Given the critical importance of the aircraft carrier—conclusively proved by the Japanese at Pearl Harbor—so too were the men who led the few of them into battle. The Navy kept only the smaller *Ranger* in the Atlantic, where the United States relied mainly on Britain's fleet. The older *Lexington* and *Saratoga* remained in the Pacific, except that a Japanese submarine torpedoed the *Sara* early in January 1942, forcing her to withdraw to the West Coast for repairs. *Yorktown* and sister ship *Enterprise* were soon joined in the Pacific by the newest flattops, *Wasp* (CV-7) and *Hornet* (CV-8).

The *Yorktown* passed through the Panama Canal on 22 December 1941—the Wildcats of VF-42 flying protective cover—and zigzagged northward to avoid Japanese subs known to be operating off the West Coast. (Reynolds, "Submarine Attacks on the Pacific Coast, 1942") Jock wasted no time inspiring the crew for the fighting that lay ahead.

> To the men of *Yorktown*, the ship was personified by Commander Clark. He was everywhere in those first days at sea, passing wrenches to mechanics, pushing planes across the deck. His gimpy leg was testament to his long service as a carrier pilot [unknown to the crew, caused by his anchor chain mishap on a destroyer in his pre-flying days]. Junior officers often feared Clark, but the white-hatted enlisted men loved him. "Let's go to Tokyo!" he roared. His enthusiasm was infectious. (Frank and Harrington, *Rendezvous at Midway*, 45)

One thing he did not like to hear was talk among the white hats who, in their ignorance, denigrated the defenders at Pearl Harbor as somehow responsible for having dropped the ball. Clark therefore issued a long memo to all hands on 29 December urging generosity, blamelessness, and comfort toward those "on the spot" in Hawaii during the sneak attack. The efforts and actions of the crew should be concentrated on winning "the righteous victory that will ultimately be ours." (Reproduced in ibid., 47–48)

The *Yorktown* reached San Diego the next day, and three days after that, 2 January 1942, Jock Clark received orders promoting him to captain. As a formality, it was a temporary rank, to become permanent after about a year if he measured up. Admiral King had taken absolute control of promotions to admiral and captain and the assignments of these men to the major combat commands, especially carriers. King wanted Jock to skipper a carrier. Conversely, a great many officers were surprised at Clark's promotion, including Admiral Halsey on the *Enterprise,* who expressed his amazement to that ship's exec, Commander Tom Jeter. (Conversation with Jeter)

Because no ship can have two captains, Jock made the formal offer to Buckmaster—which the latter accepted—not to add his captain's fourth stripe and eagle insignia to his uniforms until transferred off the *Yorktown.* No relief for him as exec was yet available, so Clark went into his first battle in the rank of commander.

Rear Admiral Frank Jack Fletcher, a cruiser division commander with no aviation experience, hoisted his flag aboard the *Yorktown* on New Year's Day 1942. His Task Force 17, including two cruisers and four destroyers, departed San Diego on 6 January 1942. It escorted four transports embarking 4,800 men of the First Marine Brigade, plus an oiler and an ammunition ship, all bound for American Samoa to prevent Japanese forces at Rabaul from moving into the eastern Pacific. Fighting 42 flew daily CAP (combat air patrol) and inner anti-torpedo patrols over the expedition.

The 5,000-mile voyage lasted two weeks, during which time the Japanese consolidated their control over the western Pacific as far east as the Gilbert Islands. They threatened to invade Samoa and cut the vital sealanes between America and Australia. Admiral Nimitz, at Admiral King's urging, decided to use his available carriers aggressively to divert Japanese attention away from Samoa with carrier raids on Japanese airfields and anchorages in the Gilbert and Marshall island groups of the Central Pacific.

Unloading of the Marines at Samoa commenced on 19 January with the *Yorktown* and Task Force 17 on station 30 miles to the south. Simultaneously, Vice Admiral Halsey arrived from Hawaii with Task Force 8, the *Enterprise* plus escorts, to cover the northern approaches to the island. Once all the Marines and their gear were ashore by the 25th, both task forces headed northwest—the *Enterprise* to strike the northern Marshalls, the *Yorktown's* planes the southern Marshalls and northern Gilberts. Each force included an oil tanker to refuel ships and planes.

Jock Clark thought that the targets in this first American offensive raid of the war were "insignificant compared to Rabaul." This superb anchorage on New Britain Island in the Bismarck Archipelago lies almost due west of Samoa. Occupied earlier in the month, Rabaul—according to intelligence— was teeming with hundreds of Japanese troop transports and other shipping. Clark reasoned that instead of hitting the Gilberts and Marshalls both task forces ought to run westward for two days, refuel, and then strike the Japanese at Rabaul. Their 150 planes could launch a surprise air attack there before Japan's navy had any task forces in the area. The carriers could then withdraw with impunity. He even suspected that no Japanese opposition would be encountered: "The United States would have a signal victory, the Japanese offensive would be slowed down, and Samoa would remain safe from Japanese designs. In my judgment, those transports had to be knocked out!"

When Clark recommended this plan to Buckmaster he said "No!" Then Jock asked Admiral Fletcher to break radio silence to request permission from Nimitz to strike Rabaul. Fletcher, who had impressed *Yorktown* officers as aloof ("eminence on high" as Bill Leonard put it in 1997), said the Marshalls-Gilberts plans could not be changed. Fletcher did not even have an aviator on his staff and was clearly reluctant to show his ignorance of carrier operations.

"No plan should be absolutely inflexible," reasoned Clark. Ernie King's flexibility in the prewar fleet problems was ingrained in his thinking, not to mention his own instincts. But Fletcher would not break radio silence, and any proposed change of plan would have had to be routed through Halsey on the *Enterprise*, then Nimitz in Hawaii, and finally to King in Washington for approval. Clark gave up.

The two carriers consumed an entire week running northwest and parted company on 31 January to proceed their separate ways. Clark did not like that either. Intelligence had revealed that the targets assigned the *Yorktown* in the southern Marshalls were poor, and Jock believed Halsey should have taken the *Yorktown* with the *Enterprise* to strike the more plentiful pickings at Kwajalein and other northern Marshalls targets. But the plan was set in veritable concrete as the admirals from Nimitz on down were feeling their way into this new war.

On 1 February the *Enterprise's* planes had clear weather for the many targets they hit at Kwajalein. Not so the *Yorktown's*, led by air group commander Curt Smiley, whose planes burned two flying boats at Makin in the Gilberts but suffered from lack of targets and rain squalls at Jaluit and Mili in the southern Marshalls. The *Yorktown* lost two torpedo-bombers, which collided after takeoff, plus two divebombers to antiaircraft fire. Two other TBDs, one flown by Dub Johnson, made a navigational error and ran out of gas. Both pilots and the four aircrewmen crash-landed on the reef at Jaluit and were imprisoned for the rest of the war.

*Yorktown's* CXAM air search radar—only now being introduced into the fleet—picked up a large image 32 miles out that had to be an enemy plane. Fighter director personnel vectored two F4F Wildcat fighters on combat air patrol to intercept it—the U.S. Navy's first radar intercept in wartime. Clark went to the fighter director control room to listen in on his pilots' transmissions. Then the plane came into view of the ship about seven miles out. Jock recognized it immediately as the four-engine version of the old Douglas XP3D flying boat, the blueprints of which the Navy had sold to Japan.

The Navy gave men's and women's names to Japanese warplanes; this was a Kawanishi Type 97 "Emily." After it crossed the *Yorktown's* bow, Ensigns E. Scott McCuskey and John P. Adams of Fighting 42 made three passes at it before it burst into "a spectacular mass of flames." Jock shouted out, "Burn, you son of a bitch, burn!" And the crew cheered as it plunged into the sea. A jubilant McCuskey informed the ship, his transmission piped throughout the ship, "We shot his ass off!" The radar had proved its worth and became a potent tool on all U.S. carrier operations. (Frank and Harrington, *Rendezvous at Midway*, 61; Lundstrom, *First Team*, 96–99)

Jubilation turned to chagrin and anger on the bridge, however, when, as the last planes were coming back aboard during the morning, word was received that one of the missing TBD Devastators had been sighted by returning squadron mates 20 miles astern of the ship—virtually on the horizon. Clark suggested that the force turn around and pick them up.

Buckmaster "would not listen." He said, "Oh no, we can't do that. This is war, the risk is too great!"

Jock went to Fletcher on the flag bridge and got the same response. In Clark's view, Fletcher "lacked confidence in our air protection," the flaming of the Emily notwithstanding.

> Utterly depressed to see three good Americans abandoned, I solemnly resolved that whenever I reached a position of higher authority I would never leave anyone adrift if there was even the least vestige of possibility for rescue. . . . The three men were never heard from again.

Apparently unknown to Clark, Fletcher *did* take his advice—and/or perhaps that of others—and dispatched three of the four screening destroyers to conduct a search in the stormy seas of late morning. They found an oil slick, suggesting a plane might have crashed and sunk, leaving no survivors. But neither Fletcher nor anyone else informed Clark of this search. (Lundstrom, *First Team*, 98, 634)

Clark would encounter the same lack of confidence by individuals throughout the war—excellent peacetime officers who were not up to the psychological demands of wartime. Indeed, he learned some two months later that a cruiser division commander, Rear Admiral John W. Wilcox Jr., had suffered a nervous breakdown and jumped overboard and was lost at sea. "Supposedly a crack officer," whom Clark had met, Wilcox seemed to be a worrier, like Fletcher, concerned "about what Japan would do." Aggressive, self-confident leaders flourished best in the very wartime conditions for which they had been preparing.

At least the distant Admiral Fletcher, to his credit, now began to warm up to the pilots, at first the air group and squadron commanders, later junior pilots too, to help him make decisions. (Leonard interview 1997) Though helpful, this provided no substitute, of course, for genuine expertise in carrier operations.

The pinpoint attacks by *Enterprise* and *Yorktown* planes on the Marshalls and Gilberts did alert the Japanese high command to the need to seek out and destroy America's carriers—a strategy that would culminate in the Battle of Midway in June. For the Americans, Admiral King had to keep pressing Nimitz to use his carriers actively and thereby keep the Japanese off balance and guessing. (Reynolds, "U.S. Fleet-in-Being Strategy of 1942")

To achieve this end, Pearl Harbor remained the forward U.S. base, to which Halsey's *Enterprise* force returned on 5 February. Fletcher's *Yorktown* force entered the next day. Jock Clark was standing on the bridge as the ship steamed into the harbor an hour before noon, the crew mustered in white uniforms on the flight deck. Like all his shipmates he was stunned by the wreckage of sunken, crippled, or simply damaged battleships, cruisers, and destroyers and the scars to the air station buildings at Ford Island. "It broke my heart," he recalled, but the sight proved to him that the battleship and battle line were no longer the heart of naval warfare. Japan's carrier planes had seen to that.

What really amazed him, however, were the cheers for the *Yorktown* from sailors working on the wreckage and rebuilding the shoreside facilities. "Hip, hip," one would shout to a chorus of "hoorays." "These men," Clark reflected, now "knew our carriers were there to continue the war." The most moving incident occurred that evening on the hangar deck of the *Enterprise* where Jock attended a movie. When Admiral Halsey arrived the sailors cheered him wildly, demanding a speech, which Clark had never seen swabbies demand of any officer.

Halsey finally obliged. He said simply, "I'm so proud of you I could cry." (These were his exact words, the careful Clark noted, disagreeing with the version given in Halsey's autobiography.) "The terrific roar of approval they gave Halsey," recalled Jock, "was the most moving demonstration I ever witnessed."

Once ashore, Clark encountered Rear Admiral Raymond A. Spruance, the skipper he had admired on the *Aaron Ward* over 20 years before and now commander of the cruiser screen in Halsey's task force. The two men had a long conversation about the war, during which Clark remarked that in his opinion the war would have to be won with carriers. Spruance—as inexperienced in carrier operations as Fletcher—"agreed with me." Both of these admirals had a great deal yet to learn from the aviators about carrier operations.

For the moment the most important individual Clark encountered at Pearl was a friend and contemporary, Commander Dixie Kiefer, carrying orders to relieve Jock as exec of the *Yorktown*—and very anxious to go aboard. This placed Jock in a quandary. He had no specific orders, other than to assume his new rank of captain. After briefly visiting Admiral Nimitz, he consulted friends on the CinCPac staff. They gave him a choice: stay aboard the *Yorktown* as exec in the rank of commander, with Kiefer riding aboard in "make-you-learn" status; or assume the rank of captain, in which case the staff would cut orders sending him to BuAer in Washington to be reassigned.

Jock lay awake an entire night weighing the alternatives. If he remained on board he was certain to see more action (as it happened, more carrier raids and the battles of the Coral Sea and Midway). If he went ashore he figured he would eventually get his own ship.

The decision really hinged on his superiors on the *Yorktown*. Finally, Clark reasoned, "I didn't think that Fletcher knew what he was doing, and I *knew* that Buckmaster didn't know what *he* was doing." (After the war, in 1949, Admiral King said of Fletcher to historian Walter Muir Whitehill, "Not much on brains. He had ideas but did not know how to work them out.")

Clark continued to harbor "great misgivings about the *Yorktown*," especially its department heads, who "were not on their toes." And he still had his "odd" feeling that, as a result, the ship was going to be sunk.

So, he figured he would get his own ship "and win the war the way I think it ought to be won than to waste my time here." He so informed the

CinCPac staff, which cut his orders to BuAer. On 14 February 1942 he turned over his exec's job to Kiefer and spent two days breaking him in. Kiefer (who had graduated near the bottom of the class of 1919) proved to be an easier-going exec whose demeanor would soon help improve shipboard morale.

But, alas, the *Yorktown* would indeed be sunk.

# NINE

# Carriers and Men and Battle, 1942–1943

A s Captain Clark headed home in February 1942 for reassignment, he left behind *Yorktown* and the other six U.S. carriers, which would continue to raid Japanese island bases and fight Japan's fleet in pitched naval battles for the rest of the year and well into the next. In the process, carriers of both navies were sunk or heavily damaged. In a broader and concurrent struggle, American and Japanese industry raced to turn out more and improved carriers and aircraft for them. Old or new, the flattops of both navies required the skills of superior admirals, captains, pilots, and crews.

The cost of unpreparedness for the war, sadly, fell on the tightly knit prewar generation of experienced officers, senior noncoms, and enlisted men who had grown up as shipmates and squadron mates in early naval aviation. They fought and often died in the fierce battles of 1942–43 in order to hold the line until the new machines were ready for the counterattack—manned by a new generation trained by the survivors of these early campaigns.

The U.S. Navy already had no doubt whatsoever that Jock Clark would become one of its foremost carrier leaders. In late February CominCh Ernie King, looking ahead, solicited BuAer chief Jack Towers (via Admiral Harry Yarnell) for a list of the current admirals and captains best suited for eventual wartime seagoing high command. Towers devised four criteria: their established professional ability, aggressiveness, physical stamina, and modernized conceptions—that is, the use of aviation in naval operations.

For expert counsel, Towers called in four of his brightest aviator captains then in Washington to collaborate with him in drawing up the list—Duke Ramsey, Raddy Radford, Fuzz Sherman, and Ralph Davison. All four were part of the "crowd" of skilled aviation leaders—and Academy graduates between 1912 and 1918—to which Jock had belonged since the late 1920s.

Out of the 77 names that Towers and his four advisers came up with were 26 aviators. Among these—including themselves, of course—were Bill Halsey, Pete Mitscher, Charlie Mason, Arthur Bristol, Jake Fitch, Henry Mullinix, Gerry Bogan, Johnny Price, Wu Duncan, and Jock Clark. All of these men had already proved or would prove their worth as effective leaders. (Reynolds, *Admiral John H. Towers*, 384–85)

Clark had known and admired at close hand the above named individuals, whether they had been senior to him or contemporaries. Charles Blakely was not on the list, having become ill and earmarked for retirement. Bristol, sadly, died while still on his North Atlantic duty in April. Mason made flag and served well until illness and grief over his son's death in battle removed him from combat. Nonaviators Fletcher and Spruance were on the list, but aviator Buckmaster was not.

Three other names omitted were Ernie King favorites Arthur Cook, who had revealed some of his shortcomings on the flag bridge of the *Yorktown;* Ernest McWhorter, whom Jock had known from his early *Lexington* days; and Leigh Noyes, Jock's last *Lex* skipper about whom he seems to have been indifferent and who as rear admiral later in the year lost the *Wasp* in the South Pacific.

Whether Clark was told of this list when he reported to Jack Towers at the bureau in early March is unknown. But if Towers did not inform him of it, Raddy, Duke, Fuzz, and/or Ralph likely did. As proof positive of their, and Ernie King's, confidence in him, they informed Jock that his new orders were to be prospective commanding officer of "a new converted aircraft carrier early in June. This is a grand task for me as I will be able to get in another poke at the Jap before long. It is exactly what I had hoped for and am very much pleased to get such a good assignment." (Letter to sister Mary, brother-in-law Ira, and nephew I. G. Jr., 6 March 1942)

Until the new *Essex*- and *Independence*-class fast carriers began to enter the fleet in 1943 several commercial vessels were being converted into small "auxiliary" or "escort" carriers for both the U.S. and British navies (they were designated AVG, aircraft escort vessel, until August 1942; then ACV, auxiliary aircraft carrier, until July 1943, when CVE, escort carrier, was finally adopted). Given a choice from the first ones under conversion, Clark selected command of the *Suwannee* (AVG-27), expecting its metamorphosis from an oil tanker to be completed in June.

This delivery date by the Newport News Shipbuilding and Dry Dock Company near Norfolk proved totally unrealistic and was soon revised to October 1942. Clark used the interim to serve the Navy—and his children—in other ways.

He purchased the small house of Owen Sowerwine in Jacksonville for M.C. and their daughters and engaged Frieda Heinan full-time as live-in housekeeper for the duration. Also, he endeavored, unsuccessfully, to "buy off" M.C. for full legal custody of the children. With the girls' very social mother often partying late or sleeping it off, Mary Lou and Cathy relied on Heinan, who proved to be an exceptionally skilled caregiver, despite quirks from her German past such as reciting their nightly prayers with her in German.

And now war was taking their "Daddy" from them—for almost the entire ensuing three years, as it turned out.

Clark's first interim task for the Navy over the spring of 1942 came as a result of musings about the Marshalls-Gilberts raids during his return trip home. The United States, he decided, needed a great many aircraft carriers to win the war in the Pacific. "Out of the air" he arbitrarily but realistically decided on a figure of no fewer than 150 carriers required for victory over the fanatical Japanese. Clark expected victory to occur no earlier than 1947—a view shared by most strategic planners until the end of 1944.

In spite of the Pearl Harbor attack, he knew that the conservative battleship-weaned admirals—the so-called Gun Club—would resist sacrificing battleships for carrier construction. So he was completely unprepared for an encounter with Admiral Tommy Hart in the corridors of the Navy Department soon after his arrival in Washington. Jock had not seen Hart, his former skipper on the battleship *Mississippi,* for many years, and they reminisced about "our old ship." To Clark's surprise and amazement, Hart suddenly remarked, "Battleships are no good. You fellows are going to win this war. It's all in the air now!" Hart had just lost virtually his entire command, the Asiatic Fleet, mostly to Japanese air attacks. "He had learned the hard way," mused Jock to himself.

Reporting in to Admiral Jack Towers at BuAer, Clark shared his idea for 150 aircraft carriers.

"You're absolutely right!" exclaimed Towers. "That is *exactly* what we need!" He sent Clark over to Admiral King's office to repeat the figure to him. King agreed with it, suggesting in turn that Jock try out the figure of 150 carriers on the director of war plans, Rear Admiral Richmond Kelly Turner.

The explosive Turner, on hearing Clark's idea, started to blurt out "That's sil—" but stopped before completing "silly," thought a moment, then remarked, "You can't get that many."

(As it turned out, Clark's almost arbitrary figure of 150 carriers was right on the mark. In addition to the seven prewar carriers, by 1947 American industry would have completed at least 40 fast carriers and 102 of the smaller and slower escort carriers—in addition to another 30 of the latter for the British navy. The figure was not achieved because the war ended in 1945. [Grossnick, *United States Naval Aviation 1910–1995*, 421–32])

Kelly Turner gave Clark a discourse on his own plan for victory. He would build up massive amphibious forces to retake Japanese island bastions in the Pacific. Jock responded, "You can't get there until aircraft carriers gain control of the air."

Turner conceded the point, to Clark's satisfaction. Yet Turner, who was King's top planner, had left aviation only four years earlier, believing it as less career enhancing than gun ships, which would eventually support his future island assaults. And when the first major amphibious attack did take place—at the Gilbert Islands in late 1943—Turner's role in restricting the carriers' mobility seriously jeopardized their safety and brought on the wrath of the air commanders, Clark among them.

In fact, Clark raised the very issue of tactical mobility and initiative by tactical commanders when he visited Ernie King on this occasion. He recounted his rejected proposal to Buckmaster and Fletcher during the Marshalls-Gilberts raid to go instead directly to Rabaul to knock out the Japanese troopships unloading there. King "gave me a long appraising look" before remarking, "Do you know, we almost ordered you to do that very thing from Washington?"

Jock seized the moment to elaborate his views about command to King, something he had never dared to do before King had become CominCh-CNO: "Here's a case where a commander on the spot should have had the freedom of action to change the battle plan and go down [to Rabaul] and hit the enemy in a vital spot without getting hurt."

"You're absolutely right," declared King. "That *must* be done."

Clark had in mind the basically conservative tactical philosophy expounded at the Naval War College, that all commanders had to "stay in line"—the battle line—and thereby contribute to the prescribed overall plan of battle. Clark never saw anything that King wrote down advocating tactical initiative but later summarized what King said during their conversation: "You tell the commander the *what*, not the *how* or the *why*. If the commander is not able to figure out how to accomplish his mission without being given the details of *how* or *why* then he shouldn't *be* the commander."

Of course, Clark had seen King do this very thing with his carriers during the fleet problems of the 1930s, although he first usually obtained permission from his superiors, virtually all of whom admired his pluck and customary successes. In Clark's words,

It's a high-level trust of the man on the spot, and when the enemy leaves himself open or offers a juicy target, then the high level commander should leave the [local commander] the latitude to take advantage of any new situation. And it might happen in the course of a battle. I was pleased to have Ernie King agree with me. I got to know him well enough that when I said anything he listened. Apparently, I had risen in his estimation by turning in a good score.

That "score" would add up as the war progressed. But first, carriers had to be built, and Admirals King and Towers decided to send Clark on a speaking tour around the country expounding his proposal for 150 of them. The first occasion was at a luncheon of the Overseas Press Club in New York. The master of ceremonies forewarned him, "We've got a man on the program you probably won't like."

"Who?" asked Jock.

"De Seversky"—Alexander P., a naturalized Russian aircraft designer, builder, and prophet whose new book, *Victory through Air Power*, was published that very day.

"Why, he's an old friend," said Jock. "He's for aviation, isn't he?"

"Yes," came the reply, "but he's pretty radical in his views. He's against aircraft carriers."

"If he's strong for aviation, we should get along all right," Jock insisted.

Clark spoke first, laying out his call for 150 carriers. De Seversky then propounded the view that land-based aircraft would win the war, notably the strategic bombers of the AAF, or U.S. Army Air Forces (upgraded from Army Air Corps in 1941). He criticized the carrier as vulnerable, but Jock was "certain he toned down his presentation because of our friendship."

In the question-and-answer period Clark said that enough carriers "could take the war right into the enemy's backyard, gain control of the air and maintain it in any area accessible by sea," unlike the strategic bombers, which lacked the round-trip range and staying power to maintain command of the skies over the western Pacific. To Jock, de Seversky seemed to echo Billy Mitchell's similarly extravagant claims. Clark argued that only a carrier-centered fleet could conquer and hold Japan's Pacific islands. He left the luncheon "with the definite impression that my arguments had scored heavily with the audience."

Similar presentations by Clark as far west as Indianapolis alerted audiences to the effectiveness of carriers, underscored by the sometimes exaggerated news reports of their success in battles in the Pacific.

The Navy also sent Clark to Canada over the spring as head of the Navy section of the Canadian American Selection Board. Its mission was to bring back American men who had been allowed to join Canada's air forces before Pearl Harbor in order to fight Germany. Traveling across Canada in a 17-car Pullman train, the board returned over 2,700 pilots to the AAF, some 300 to naval aviation—an excellent boon for the Navy. For his "tact and independent judgment" in achieving success Admiral Towers congratulated Clark—"an outstanding officer of great force and initiative." (23 June 1942 Fitness Report)

Wherever Clark went he closely followed events in the Pacific. Japan seemed unstoppable. Its forces overran the Philippines, destroyed the remnant of the U.S. Asiatic Fleet, and threatened Hawaii and even Australia. Nothing, therefore, prepared Clark for news of the thrilling Halsey-Doolittle bombing raid on Tokyo in mid-April 1942. Neither the Japanese nor the American people knew—although Clark soon learned—that Colonel Jimmy Doolittle's 16 B-25 Army medium bombers had been launched from Pete Mitscher's *Hornet,* escorted by Halsey's flagship *Enterprise.*

The psychological rewards were immense, lifting American spirits and shocking the Japanese. Then, three weeks later, in early May, Admirals Fletcher and Fitch fought a Japanese carrier force in the Battle of the Coral Sea, the first carrier battle in history. Planes from the *Lexington* and *Yorktown* inflicted heavy damage on the two large Japanese flattops and their planes, even sinking the small third one, to turn back a Japanese landing force bound for southern New Guinea.

Sadly, however, Jock's old ship "Lady Lex" suffered such severe damage that she had to be scuttled. Months later, he was able to discuss the battle with several of his former *Yorktown* shipmates. Neither he nor they could understand why the "Yorky" had not launched the planes on her deck when the *Lexington* was attacked. He surmised that Fletcher had displayed a poor understanding of carrier aviation during the battle.

No sooner had this action ended, arresting Japan's southern thrust toward American-Australian sealanes, than Japan hurled the bulk of its battle fleet toward Midway Island in June in an attempt to neutralize Pearl Harbor as the major U.S. base in the Pacific. Clark happened to be in Jack Towers's office at BuAer on 4 June, the day of the epic Battle of Midway. Towers personally informed him that the planes from the *Enterprise, Yorktown,* and *Hornet* had sunk all four large Japanese carriers in the battle.

Towers and Clark agreed "on the spot" that Midway was the turning point in the Pacific war. Japan's offensive had been blunted, Pearl Harbor spared, and credit for the victory given to Admirals Spruance and Fletcher. Jock learned that before the battle, Spruance, having replaced a physically ailing Halsey, had inherited Halsey's carrier staff, notably Captain Miles Browning as its chief. The petulant Browning, who had had a rocky relationship with Academy classmate Clark over the years, had provided crucial counsel to Spruance that helped him to win the battle.

Unfortunately, the *Yorktown* had been so badly damaged that Captain Buckmaster had decided to abandon ship. But he then returned aboard with a skeleton crew to get it moving again. Several days later a Japanese submarine fired torpedoes into the gallant ship, which was quickly abandoned. It then rolled over and sank. Clark later interviewed some of his former *Yorktown* shipmates and heard criticisms of the way the ship had been handled. He concluded that it had been abandoned too early. Clark always admitted, however, that because he had not been on the scene he was in no position to criticize Buckmaster and the officers—although he had his suspicions. His earlier hunch that the *Yorktown* would be sunk had been realized, and he was not surprised.

> It goes back to that winning spirit. If you don't have it in an organization, you'd better turn in your suit. War is something you can't play with. You've got to be out there to win, or you shouldn't be there. Playing marbles for keeps—that's exactly what it is.

For pilots on the scene at Midway, none was more critical of the loss of the *Yorktown* than the skipper of that ship's VF-3, Lieutenant Commander John H. "Jimmy" Thach, inventor or the "Thach weave" in winning dogfights; he shot down six Zero fighters in the battle. To his dying day (as a vice admiral) Thach laid the blame for the loss of the *Yorktown* squarely on Admirals Fletcher, Spruance, and Nimitz and Captain Buckmaster. (Thach, "A Beautiful Silver Waterfall," 62–64)

Clark had no intention of letting that happen to his first command, the *Suwannee*. "At long last," he recalled, "I could put into practice some of my ideas of how to fight the war with a ship of my own." To get some pointers on handling an escort carrier, he visited Captain Wu Duncan, then on Ernie King's staff. Duncan had brought the very first escort carrier, *Long Island*, into service one year before, in June 1941. Since then only two others had been commissioned, but three more were due out in August 1942, another three in September, and the *Suwannee* in early October.

The 18,000-ton *Suwannee* was one of four converted carriers of the *Sangamon* class, converted oil tankers. Jock's was formerly the Standard Oil Company's *Markay*. The oil tanks were left intact, providing each of the Sangamons with 7.5 million gallons of fuel. This not only gave them greater range but the capability to refuel other ships. Though they were sturdy vessels, their great bulk restricted their top speed to 19 knots, a far cry from the 30-plus knots of the large fast carriers.

Among other peculiarities of these escort carriers, Duncan counseled Clark, was that they would always have to catapult the first planes of any deckload launch. This would clear enough of the flight deck to enable the rest of the air group to make powered takeoffs using only their engines.

During the course of their discussion Duncan casually remarked, "There's going to be a party. But you can't get in on it"—because *Suwannee* would not be commissioned in time to participate.

The "party" meant a major military operation, but it was a top secret. *Suwannee's* sister ships *Sangamon, Chenango,* and *Santee* were scheduled to be commissioned between late August and mid-September. But *Suwannee's* early October commissioning date would prevent it from participating.

Jock knew something big was up—as he later learned, the Allied liberation of North Africa from Nazi control. So he asked Duncan why his ship would miss "the party."

"Your ship won't be ready."

"When do I have to be ready?" inquired Jock.

When Duncan told him, Jock quickly calculated that he could just make the "party" if the commissioning date of his ship could be moved up from early October to 24 September 1942.

As he bade Duncan farewell, he remarked, "Maybe I *will* be there!"

Formally appointed the *Suwannee's* prospective captain on 8 July 1942, Clark hastened to Newport News, the premier warship construction firm, especially of aircraft carriers, and well known for its overall excellence. It had built the *Yorktown* and was now constructing the *Essex* (CV-9), first in its class. Six days before the Pearl Harbor attack the shipyard had laid the keel of the second *Essex*-class carrier, *Bon Homme Richard* (CV-10). To preserve the memory of the sunken *Yorktown,* in a time-honored tradition of all navies, the Navy in September 1942 renamed the uncompleted *Bon Homme Richard* for the sunken carrier. Soon Jock Clark would become intimately linked to the "new" *Yorktown* (CV-10).

When Clark first met the superintendents of yard outfitting, A. S. Butterworth and Douglas Petty, he repeated what Wu Duncan had told him, and said, "I cannot give away any military secrets, but if you give me my ship two weeks early, I will put her where she will do some good!"

"Brother," one of them replied, "that's the kind of talk we like to hear. We, too, want to win the war." Then he reported in to the Navy's supervisor of shipbuilding there, Rear Admiral O. L. Cox.

Clark's no-nonsense zeal was immediately infectious. No doubt his frustrations over the mishandling of the old *Yorktown* helped account for his impatience and drive. But it was much more than that. He was a fighter.

He had been trained and honed to lead naval forces into battle. And he knew his trade intimately from the engine room to the cockpit.

In a word, Clark was a leader determined to win the war as directly and expeditiously as possible. He informed everyone who mattered of his motto for racing the *Suwannee* to completion: "Get things done yesterday; tomorrow may be too late!"

The Newport News people immediately found his forthright approach refreshing and worked closely with him to cut red tape—by careful planning, working long hours, and making instantaneous changes to the vessel. A typical example involved aluminum, preferred for several parts of the ship because of its light weight. But when it was not available, or would take precious time to procure, the yard substituted steel. This added perhaps 75 additional tons to the weight of the ship, but it worked.

Company and captain coordinated the shipyard workers with the officers and crew of the ship as they reported in. For his 120 officers Clark had little opportunity to request individuals; the lone exception was Lieutenant Owen Sowerwine from Jacksonville. The complement of sailors was 960, most of them quite raw recruits with no more naval experience than boot camp. Jock Clark was their first skipper, who they as novices accepted at face value.

The naval hierarchy quickly learned about him too. If a part was needed, Clark would have one of his officers flown to an East Coast facility to get it and fly it back the same day. The most sensitive equipment, radar, required Clark's personal attention. A closely guarded military secret, it was always installed at the Norfolk Navy Yard, across Hampton Roads from Newport News, after a ship was completed. Clark wanted it installed earlier, at Newport News, to save precious time.

So he personally flew up to Washington where he spent four hours going up the line to the chief of the Bureau of Ships to obtain permission to have the radar installed at Newport News. And he did!

> Following this experience, I established what I called my "sit 'em out" policy, which meant that if at first I was refused what I wanted, I would just sit there and talk—about everything, the weather or what not. Finally, to get rid of me, more than for any other reason they would give me something very close to what I had asked for.

More problematic was the policy of loading ammunition, absolutely forbidden in the builder's yard, lest a miscue lead to a conflagration. But waiting until commissioning to do it would consume precious time and force the *Suwannee* to miss "the party." So Clark simply went to aviators on the Atlantic Fleet staff and arranged to have two boxcar loads of ammunition rolled down to the dock, where the ship's crew feverishly unloaded it under the firm direction of Gunner's Mate H. T. "Tiny" Pickett.

Before long two shipyard managers appeared and announced to Clark, "You can't load ammunition in this yard!"

"Well, we're doing it!" said Jock. Period. End of discussion. They only blinked and walked away, obviously to consult Doug Petty. He had no objection but informed Clark the ammo's weight might make the ship so heavy it would rest on the sand, preventing it from moving away from the dock. But it did not. The loading took all night to complete—safely. An explosion could have conceivably caused sufficient damage to the shipyard to adversely affect the war effort, given the crucial role of Newport News ships in it.

By September Clark decided that the *Suwannee* would be ready in time to make the North African operation. He flew back up to Washington and informed Wu Duncan, "I'll be there." Duncan replied, "We are all pulling for you!" That included Admiral King. Soon the Board of Inspection and Survey—of which Jock was an alumnus—visited Newport News and pronounced the ship ready for service.

The date of commissioning was set for 24 September 1942. Still, the two weeks leading up to it would be critical, including the required ten-day shakedown cruise in the confines of the Chesapeake Bay (utilized instead of the U-boat–infested open sea).

After that, *Suwannee* had to join the other carriers at Bermuda in time to sortie with them into battle. The planners of the invasion wanted the ship to replace the smaller escort carrier *Charger* (ACV-30), which carried only 21 aircraft (all F4F Wildcat fighters) and did not handle groundswells in even moderate seas. The sturdy *Suwannee* had 38 planes—F4Fs and the new and more bulky Grumman TBF Avenger torpedo-bombers. Skipper of *Charger* was Jock's classmate Captain Tommy Sprague, resulting in a good-natured rivalry, with *Charger* in the lead by arriving at Bermuda first.

Clark arranged to move the entire ship's crew aboard the day before commissioning in order that they "turn to" as soon as the ceremonies ended. He got on the "bullhorn"—the ship's main microphone—and told the officers and enlisted men that they were going to war "to win. The way for us to get home is to fight—if necessary, fight our way back home." He was determined to prevent the lackadaisical attitude that had plagued the now-lost *Yorktown*. What was more, he informed the crew that no "abandon ship" drills would be conducted: "You boys are going to bring her home!" (Of course, he *did* have the drills, but with little fanfare.)

The vast majority of his listeners were "fresh out of the cornfields," meaning the land-lubbing civilian life. New to the Navy, they had no basis for comparison of their captain, figuring only that he was a typical rough-tough skipper. So the new "swabs" responded in kind. After a hearty breakfast the morning of commissioning day, each man received his assigned battle station. Then Clark held a fire drill so all hands knew what to do in such an emergency. Only then did the ceremonies proceed.

An amazed Admiral Cox, the supervisor, gave Jock all 4.0 scores on his fitness report (even for neatness!), an extraordinary accolade:

> He is enthusiastic about his work, instills the highest loyalty in his subordinates and was untiring in his efforts to aid the Contractor and the Supervisor's office to expedite the satisfactory conversion of his ship. Sound judgment and his vast experience was of great value to me. An outstanding officer.

Immediately after commissioning the *Suwannee* got under way on its shakedown cruise in the upper reaches of the Chesapeake. "Nobody knew their jobs," remembered Owen Sowerwine, "except the regular Navy men." If even one of the ten days of shakedown were lost, the ship would miss the North African operation. The crew had many scares. The main throttle of the big engines stuck, forcing the ship to drop anchor in Hampton Roads and make repairs. Already on a tight schedule, with many ships awaiting degaussing at the designated range, *Suwannee* just barely made its appointment for demagnetizing the hull against possible underwater mines.

The incredibly crowded roadstead resulted in the ship's navigator once running *Suwannee* aground. According to the story that spread throughout the Navy, after the ship was refloated Jock took over the conn himself and said to the navigator, "Goddam you, now it's my turn to run it aground." And he succeeded in doing just that! (Thomas H. Moorer transcript #30, 1586)

The ship's antiaircraft guns, 40 mm and 20 mm, had to be tested, but the gunnery officer, Lieutenant Commander B. W. "Skag" Arnold III, had forgotten to obtain the required sand-filled test projectiles. Arnold, an Annapolis grad ('23) who had early shifted to the Naval Reserve, exuded the kind of energy that Clark liked. But now Jock had to race the ship back to Norfolk overnight to get the test rounds and return to the operating area. Happily, the guns all functioned perfectly; any misfire of real shells could have threatened lives.

Very quickly, the captain's no-nonsense zeal began to take effect. Fairly typical among the personnel was a bright-looking lieutenant who came up to the ship's tiny bridge one morning and addressed Clark, "Sir, can I be of any help to you?"

"Yes," Clark answered quickly, "you can take the watch." Lieutenant Eric Lambart was thus handed the duty, fully competent to take it; he had earned a glowing reputation at Columbia University as stroke oar of its championship rowing crew. For the rest of Jock's life, whenever he encountered Lambart he laughed, "You took the watch that day on *Suwannee*, and as far as I am concerned you still have it."

Clark's demeanor became an object of curiosity among the green sailors. His gruffness, energy, sense of fair play, and alleged American Indian roots were enough to spark curiosity. He also walked with a pronounced limp, the cause of which (his old anchor chain injury) he surely never revealed. The skipper also had a slight paunch, though not from overeating. Indeed, the word got out from the cooks and supply clerks that the captain's cuisine consisted mostly of Avocet goat's milk to prevent a recurrence of his ulcers. His diet was

> more befitting a Park Avenue physician's lady patients . . . , with or without Cherokee blood to nourish. He eats no meat and finds all the energy he needs, apparently, in tenderized breast of chicken, which he consumes in careful small quantities along with a few other bland foods, the harshest of which are creamed vegetables. Considering the nature of [his] war against Japan [and Germany], which he pursues with the relentless hell-roaring energy of a Sitting Bull supercharged with firewater [i.e., alcohol], this is remarkable. (Gray, "'Jocko' Clark," 44, 46)

Finally, there was his nickname, "Jock." Surely, no *Suwannee* crewman knew the true origin of it (the Naval Academy). Nor did Americans think of the word as the Scots and Irish had since the sixteenth century—a nickname for John and from that a penis, as in jockstrap (indeed, Clark's sexual prowess was indisputable, known only to his close friends and certain ladies).

One may surmise, rather, that as his shipmates began to admire and talk about him among themselves, they soon added an "o"—as "old Jock-o is at it again."

Hence his new, enlarged nickname, which he made no effort to downplay. He remained "Jock" to his friends and peers, "Joe" to the family, but when the press discovered him he became "Jocko" Clark.

Nothing was more newsworthy than combat operations, and Clark's first as carrier captain was the assault on North Africa—"Operation Torch."

With shakedown completed, the two squadrons—fighting and "escort and scouting"—of F4Fs and TBFs were hoisted aboard, and the crew prepared for the voyage to Bermuda through a dangerous U-boat–infested sea. Everyone donned rubber life belts and life jackets, which they *never* took off, even when given the opportunity. Each person on the bridge, officers included, was issued a .45-caliber pistol to use as a makeshift antiaircraft weapon. They were *that* scared.

By the end of the operation all the rubber life belts were completely worn out from the constant friction caused by overuse, remembered Sowerwine, "and no one ever wore them again the entire war!"

*Suwannee* arrived at Bermuda unscathed and just in time to be included in the operation. Clark was greeted by congratulations from a disappointed Tommy Sprague, whose smaller *Charger* relinquished its position in Task Group 34.2 to *Suwannee*. Sprague even sent over some of the *Charger*'s antiaircraft ammunition to Clark for the battle and transferred a few experienced personnel as well. Among them, Chief P. P. Day helped remove two of the six .50-caliber machine guns from each of the F4F Wildcat fighters in favor of two additional bombs, balancing the planes' weight inasmuch as not much dogfighting was anticipated. Before long, Day could see that the *Suwannee* was a good ship—"no bubbleheads, no lazy people." (Conversation with Day)

Too little time remained for exercising flight deck gangs and pilots at Bermuda, and Clark had great difficulty even getting sufficient wind down the deck for powered takeoffs, so he had to depend on the catapult. On one of *Suwannee*'s few training sorties into the open sea "the eagerness of my crew to be ready ahead of time produced grievous results." Plane handlers prematurely hooked a plane onto the catapult, making it ready for being "shot" off the deck. This was not known to the "cat" operator, an experienced career sailor, who decided to test the firing mechanism.

The cat snapped forward, slamming into a dozen men lounging at the forward end of the flight deck awaiting the call for flight quarters. It knocked four of them overboard. Only two were recovered by a plane guard destroyer. A court of inquiry absolved Clark, blaming the accident on "a simple personal error which was not supposed to happen but did."

The liberation of Axis-held North Africa was the first Allied objective in the march to destroy Nazi Germany. American troops were to land from the Western Naval Task Force at Casablanca, French Morocco, on the Atlantic coast, simultaneously with two landings by Anglo-American forces in French Algeria inside the Mediterranean. The major defenders were the army, warships, and aircraft of Vichy France, the collaborationist regime allied to Hitler.

It was not the first amphibious operation to be supported by carriers. In the South Pacific in August the *Saratoga, Enterprise,* and *Wasp* had covered the successful Marine Corps landing at Guadalcanal, initiating a long and bitter campaign, but little was learned there to apply at Casablanca.

Rear Admiral Ernest McWhorter commanded the carrier task force and had direct charge of the flagship *Ranger,* the *Santee,* and the *Sangamon.* Buddy Wieber, Jocko's classmate, whose father had saved Jock's leg in 1918, skippered the latter ship. Clark had administrative control of a carrier division—his own ship and the *Chenango,* the latter acting only as a ferry for 78 AAF Curtiss P-40 fighters to be catapulted ashore as soon as the army had secured Casablanca's airfield.

Unlike the *Ranger,* the four escort carriers were all ex–oil tanker sister ships. Total carrier air strength (minus *Chenango's*): 108 F4F fighters, 36 SBD divebombers, and 28 TBF "torpeckers."

The five carriers sortied from Bermuda on 25 October, escorted by a light cruiser and nine destroyers. They rendezvoused in mid-ocean with the rest of the 150-ship Task Force 34. All maneuvered to avoid possible U-boats, unaware that German subs had been distracted away from the course of the invasion armada by a large Allied convoy. On 7 November task force ships separated to their assigned sectors for the next day's landings. *Suwannee* stayed with the *Ranger* to cover the main landings at Fedala and to attack Vichy French warships there.

Operation Torch was unique in several respects. Politically, the Allies had struck a secret deal with the Vichy defenders that after three days of token resistance against the invasion force—to assuage French national honor—they would cease fighting and switch over to the Allies. Yet, several French naval units defied the deal. In addition, the invasion fleet of unbloodied ships and crews endured much chaos. "Nobody knew nuthin'" on the *Suwannee,* for example, in the words of Owen Sowerwine, such as how to get the radios working even to report an enemy submarine sighting to the flagship.

Cherokee Jocko put his knowledge and experience to the test by fighting the battle in spite of everything. He launched the first strike of *Suwannee's* bomb- and torpedo-laden SBDs and TBFs of Escort and Scouting 30—under Commander M. A. "Lefty" Nation—before dawn on D-day, 8 November. With antisubmarine combat air patrols covering the landing ships, the Wildcat fighters shot up several parked French planes at Port Lyautey. The *Suwannee's* bombing planes and those from the *Ranger* combined to sink three French submarines in the harbor and damage the anchored battleship *Jean Bart.*

Next day the carrier planes attacked French reinforcements rushing to Casablanca in trucks and tanks and finished off the last French aircraft. On the 10th, however, the Vichy navy tried again. The *Jean Bart* fired its main batteries at the invasion fleet until silenced by task force aircraft. Several French subs escaped the harbor and missed hitting the *Ranger* but sank several small landing craft.

At one point a neutral Spanish fishing boat appeared near the *Suwannee*'s formation. Clark dispatched a boarding officer in a gig who ordered it to clear out, inasmuch as it might disclose the carrier's position to German subs. The Spanish skipper refused, until Jocko threatened to sink him.

The carrier planes had standing orders to sink all unidentified submarines, orders that were still in effect as the French defenders announced that the armistice would begin at midday on the 11th (the 24th anniversary of the armistice of 1918 ending World War I). Lefty Nation, however, was returning from an antisub patrol of four TBF Avengers—each loaded with depth charges—when he "sighted a submarine under the edge of a fogbank," Clark recalled. "He succeeded in getting right over the submarine by approaching from above the fogbank before it could dive. Nine depth charges ripped the submarine apart, and it was seen to sink." Although the sub was believed to be German, postwar records revealed it had been one of the Casablanca-based French subs.

The carriers, having completed their tasks, departed North African waters, recrossing the U-boat–infested Atlantic. *Suwannee* launched antisub patrols daily. Roaming the flight deck one day Clark noticed that one of the planes had an inscription in chalk near the nose—an unusual practice for carrier aircraft: "Rosenblatt's Reply." He was told that the plane had been damaged but fixed up to fly again, whereupon the fighter pilots had named it for their air combat intelligence officer (ACIO), Lieutenant Herman S. Rosenblatt. Jewish, he also conducted religious services on board.

A strapping 6 foot 2, the handsome, brilliant, and somewhat aloof Rosenblatt had Ivy League credentials. He had only two close shipmate friends. The one in ship's company was Owen Sowerwine, whom he nicknamed "Sowerwine-Zero" for unknown reasons (perhaps because that was how the name appeared on ship's muster: "Sowerwine, O.") In any case it was an appellation that remained with Sowerwine as long as he served under Clark.

The other friend was diminutive, droll Wildcat pilot Lieutenant Harry W. Harrison, a Yale man whom Rosenblatt encountered in Fighting 30. "A dignified fella" (according to P. P. Day), Harrison was nicknamed "Stinky." He put the "Reply" sign on his plane as an answer to Hitler's anti-Semitism and war machine.

Jocko sent for Rosenblatt, "who instantly impressed me. Indeed, he proved to be highly intelligent, energetic, and a tireless worker." He was so good, in fact, that as soon as the ship reached the States Rosenblatt was transferred to the office of assistant chief of BuAer, Rear Admiral Ralph Davison. In addition, Clark learned that Herman was the brother of Sol Rosenblatt, and that both of them were New York lawyers for President Roosevelt's family. Their uncle, Samuel I. Rosenman, had been Roosevelt's principal speechwriter, having coined the phrase "New Deal" in FDR's momentous first inaugural address in 1933. Now in 1943 he became special counsel to the President. Herman himself was close to Eleanor's entourage at the White House, including the Roosevelts' sons Frank and John—who had both become naval officers.

Although Sol Rosenblatt, an Army reservist, was now on active duty as a colonel in the AAF, Clark decided to engage his legal services to handle the divorce settlement with M.C. This cemented Jocko's connection to Herman and opened possibilities for Jocko to exploit the brothers' political connections if ever necessary. Clark always watched "for every angle."

After a brief layover at Bermuda the ship returned to Norfolk, where Clark, "to my great surprise," found orders awaiting him to report personally to Admiral King in Washington. There he gave King a full account of the operation. "You did a good job," King said warmly, a "totally unexpected" accolade to Jocko, whose "scores" continued to mount in the eyes of the top man.

While readying the *Suwannee* for transfer to the Pacific at Norfolk, Clark visited Newport News to share his North African success with supervisors Petty and Butterworth, who were overjoyed. At the end of November, Admiral McWhorter gave Jocko a letter of commendation for his zeal and ability in preparing and leading his ship in battle and his swift preparation of it "for distant service." Furthermore, he recommended Clark "for command of a new large carrier" and "strongly recommended" his promotion to rear admiral! (25 November 1942 fitness report) And he had received his permanent promotion to captain only in mid-December. The following April, Clark received a letter of commendation from the Atlantic Fleet commander, Admiral Royal E. Ingersoll, for his "high efficiency, outstanding performance and skillful handling" of the *Suwannee* during Operation Torch.

Meanwhile in the Pacific, furious land, sea, and air battles raged over the U.S. foothold on Guadalcanal. In August 1942 Duke Ramsey's *Saratoga* was disabled by its second Japanese submarine torpedo hit, though Ramsey's promotion to rear admiral was assured. In September another sub sank Fuzz Sherman's *Wasp*, but Admiral Leigh Noyes got the blame. In October enemy carrier planes sank Charlie Mason's *Hornet*. Admiral Halsey, now theater commander in the South Pacific, used the *Enterprise*, his last surviving carrier, to help repulse the last major Japanese naval thrust against the island in November.

With Halsey desperate for carrier decks, Admiral King dispatched *Suwannee* and *Sangamon* to the South Pacific as part of a carrier division under Clark. Early in December, escorting cruisers and destroyers joined up to create a task force that departed Norfolk for the Panama Canal. The force was commanded from a cruiser by a nonaviator, Rear Admiral Robert C. "Ike" Giffen, who was handicapped by total ignorance of the necessity for his carriers to turn into the wind in order to launch planes, then out of it again to resume the ships' normal course.

The former oil tankers squeezed through the locks of the canal with such hair-raising moments on the *Suwannee* that they became scuttlebutt throughout the fleet. For example, welders had to climb high aloft the island superstructure to cut off a protruding yardarm. Once into the Pacific the force headed straight for Nouméa, New Caledonia, operating its planes en route. When a Wildcat fighter suffered damage in a rough landing, Clark had his mechanics practically rebuild it to save time instead of sending it ashore.

The *Suwannee* pulled in to Nouméa on the fourth day of 1943, "ready in all respects for battle," as Clark announced in a message to Admiral Halsey. Given the ship's immense oil capacity, it did not even need to be refueled. Halsey was impressed and let Jock know it via Miles Browning, Jock's cantankerous classmate and still Halsey's chief of staff.

Also on hand to greet him was Vice Admiral Jack Towers, who only three months before had been promoted and transferred from BuAer to command the Pacific Fleet's air forces directly under Nimitz at Pearl Harbor. He had come to Nouméa to discuss aviation logistics with Halsey.

*Suwannee* quickly moved northward to Havana Harbor in the New Hebrides to join in the defense of Guadalcanal. En route, operations were hampered by Admiral Giffen's inexperience operating with carriers. Nevertheless, he generously rated Clark "an outstanding naval officer. Handled the Carrier Division in excellent and seamanlike manner. An excellent Shipmate. Well worthy of promotion." (21 January 1943 fitness report)

New orders dated 8 January awaited Clark at the New Hebrides. He was to return home as quickly as possible to become prospective captain of the new *Yorktown* (CV-10), still under construction at Newport News. The first carrier of its class, the *Essex* (CV-9), had only just been commissioned on the last day of 1942, Wu Duncan commanding.

Clark's assignment, like that of all captains of new carriers, was made personally by Ernie King, a fact Clark learned only later. The two men had obviously discussed a new and bigger ship for Clark during his brief visit to the department after his return from North Africa. Told to select an executive officer, Jocko had visited BuPers (Bureau of Naval Personnel) and been given a choice of available officers. At the mention of Commander Raymond R. "Raöul" Waller the search ended. Clark knew Waller, a former VF-2 pilot, only by his reputation "for getting a job done."

"Do you know he stammers?" remarked the detail officer.

"I don't give a damn about that," replied Jocko. "It's not how he talks that counts. It's what he *does!*"

At the moment Waller was handling all armaments for Navy aircraft at BuAer, but just before Christmas he received his orders to become exec of the *Yorktown*. Waller knew Clark's renown as a taskmaster but laughed off friends who pitied him. He regarded the assignment as an honor, as only the second member of his class ('24) to become exec of a large carrier.

In the New Hebrides Clark encountered Lieutenant Commander Jimmy Flatley, his former helper at Jacksonville and now veteran skipper of the celebrated "Grim Reapers" (VF-10) both on the *Enterprise* and shore-based during many furious air actions over the preceding months. Clark asked Jimmy to become commander of the *Yorktown's* prospective air group. He accepted without hesitation.

Similarly, Clark ran into former *Lexington* shipmate Lieutenant Commander George Anderson who flew in to Nouméa at midmonth as part of an inspection party headed by Admiral Nimitz and Navy Secretary Frank Knox. Anderson's brilliant mind had kept him at BuAer as a top planner for Admiral Towers since 1940. He and the new chief of the bureau, Rear Admiral John S. McCain, were accompanying Nimitz to examine aviation needs in the hard-pressed South Pacific.

Learning on their return flight to Hawaii that Anderson was due for sea duty, Clark wondered if he would like to become his exec on the new *Yorktown*, even though Waller had already been assigned. "Andy" replied simply that he was too junior, whereupon Jock said, "Well, how about coming as my navigator then?" Andy jumped at the opportunity, having been a "plank owner"—original crewmember—of the old *Yorktown* too. Clark had already been assigned a navigator, but he changed that when he reached Washington. (Anderson transcript #3, 112) Soon Anderson received his orders to the *Yorktown* and promotion to commander.

Jocko regretted leaving the *Suwannee,* but the new and much larger *Yorktown* promised to have a prominent role in the counterattack against Japan. And he was turning over the converted escort carrier to the very able Captain F. W. "Freddie" McMahon, the very same officer who had relieved him in 1928 as aviation adviser to battleship admiral Meigs Taylor. "I knew she was in good hands."

Obviously, Ernie King had great confidence in Jocko Clark, who spent the next eight months forging his new ship and its crew into an effective weapon and moving it to the Pacific. Everything he did over those months only confirmed the faith that Admirals King and Towers had in him. In late July 1943—before Clark had even taken his ship into battle—the high command selected him for eventual promotion to rear admiral, along with Duncan, Sherman, and Sprague, among others. (Reynolds, *Admiral John H. Towers*, 399, 429)

The Cherokee-weaned leader had finally come to the fast carriers, the revolutionary weapon system that would spearhead the Pacific offensive to destroy the Japanese empire.

# TEN

# A Civilian Navy Run by a Sea Dog, 1943

JOCKO CLARK WAS "ALWAYS FIERCELY LOYAL TO HIS FRIENDS AND their strongest boosters," George Anderson told me in 1965, shortly after retiring as Chief of Naval Operations. Anderson had been privileged to be one of those friends.

Friendship and loyalty meant everything to Clark—up and down. That is, throughout his life he reciprocated such personal relationships with subordinates—officers and enlisted men alike—and with civilians in sundry walks of life. Similarly, he remained faithful and close to peers and superiors he respected and who regarded him in kind.

Now, at the start of 1943, he was able to handpick several officers and senior noncoms for the new *Yorktown* to form the nucleus of its total complement of 360 officers, 3,088 enlisted crewmen, and 466 air group personnel. A few were former shipmates—like Jimmy Flatley for skipper of Air Group Five (so numbered in honor of the first *Yorktown*'s hull number). Some he knew only by reputation, notably Raöul Waller for exec. Others he requested from BuAer or the Bureau of Naval Personnel, selecting certain men who simply impressed him along the way. He eventually obtained about 35 of the individuals he specifically requested.

On the whole, remembered Anderson, "Jocko really assembled a marvelous group of officers and men for the *Yorktown*." (Anderson transcript #3, 113) The ship was destined to develop a unique personality. Like the entire wartime Navy, only the small nucleus of officers and crewmen was made up of career regulars. The vast majority joined up only for the duration—graduates and students from Ivy League universities and state colleges, businessmen, doctors, lawyers, shopkeepers, athletes, workers skilled and unskilled—a cross-section of America.

What made them unique was Jocko—the *Yorktown* story was his story, recalled Waller, and his style of leadership was unprecedented and pace setting.

By Clark's reckoning, time was of the essence. As with the *Suwannee*, the new *Yorktown* had to be completed as soon as possible in order to take the war to Japan expeditiously. Unlike the *Suwannee*, however, he did not want to cut corners—a policy endorsed by Admiral King. Still, Clark fully intended to waste no time in getting the ship ready for battle (which entailed *some* compromises) and to use his typical drive as before.

Furthermore, Jocko had a personal-professional stake in being expeditious. He wanted his ship to get into battle first, ahead of the three other new heavy fast carriers simultaneously under construction in order to show that *his* flattop was first and foremost in the new post–Pearl Harbor fleet. Their captains were classmates from both his Academy classes. Wu Duncan '17 had the *Essex* (CV-9), commissioned 31 December 1942 and still working up. Felix B. Stump '17 got the new *Lexington* (CV-16) into commission in mid-February 1943. And John J. Ballentine '18 had the *Bunker Hill* (CV-17), which was being built at the Bethlehem Steel shipyard at Quincy, Massachusetts; its projected commissioning date was still problematic.

But because *Essex* was the first of the new class and first to get into the water, Clark set his competitive sights on that ship. "Beat the *Essex!*" became his clarion call, inspiring his own men and provoking a response in kind. "Jocko Clark was a great driver," recalled Fitzhugh Lee, first air officer of the *Essex:*

> The contest was on. The rivalry was great. We thought that a lot of dishonest things were done to get things provided for the *Yorktown* which should have come to the *Essex* just so we wouldn't get finished in time, but we were never able to prove anything. (Lee, "First Cruise of the *Essex,*" 107)

In later years, when someone asked Clark the source of all this competition, he smiled, "I generated it!" Nevertheless, Duncan and his officers gave invaluable advice to help Clark learn from mistakes made building the *Essex*.

Unfortunately, none of Clark's frenzy would be felt until he arrived at the shipyard. And he was still in the Pacific on the launching day of 21 January 1943. Waller, the exec—who had reported only two days earlier—officiated at the ceremony.

The bitterly raw morning was deceptively sunny as the guest of honor arrived at Shipway No. Nine: Eleanor Roosevelt, the president's wife, who had christened the first *Yorktown* in 1937. Rear Admiral Buckmaster, last skipper of that ship and now chief of the Navy's primary flight training, gave the major address. The First Lady's breaking of the ceremonial bottle of champagne against the bow would complete the ceremonies. Then shipyard workers were to knock aside the "triggers" that held the ship in place, enabling it to slide down the ways into the waters of Hampton Roads.

Buckmaster compared the two *Yorktowns*, named for the nearby battleground on which General George Washington's army, supported by the French fleet, had defeated the British in 1781 to secure American independence. Then he addressed the shipyard workers: "Your efforts to weld together the natural resources of America that go into the construction of such magnificent fighting craft is beyond praise. . . ."

Suddenly, the great mass of steel before him quivered. The time was 1237, seven minutes ahead of the appointed moment, and the ship was starting to slip off its stocks. The triggers had failed to hold it in place. An alert Eleanor Roosevelt jumped from her seat and swung out the bottle, tethered to a line. It hit the receding hull with a thud and bounced back, unbroken.

She caught it over her head, gave it a Joe DiMaggio–style baseball grip, and smashed it against the receding ship, spraying her and Buckmaster with bubbly. The *Yorktown* gained momentum amid the resounding cheers of shipyard workers and sailors who took the event as the portent of a ship eager for battle. Jocko himself could not have planned it better.

The workers then began clearing away the debris on the empty shipway to start all over again—laying the keel of another *Essex*-class carrier, the *Ticonderoga* (CV-14). Arriving as its prospective commanding officer was Captain Dixie Kiefer, who had relieved Clark on the old *Yorky*.

The unfinished new *Yorktown* was tied up alongside a pier, where it entered into the "overboard" stage of outfitting. Until Captain Clark arrived, Raöul Waller (USNA '24) had charge, along with Commander James A. McNally ('25)—nicknamed "Blackie" as chief engineer of the "black gang" that operated the ship's four Westinghouse turbine engines and eight Babcock & Wilcox boilers. Among McNally's officers were two mustangs—given commissions after serving as machinists on the first *Yorktown*. They were part of a draft of veterans from the old ship that were supposed to cement the traditional link between the two vessels.

Meanwhile, a Navy flying boat transported Clark from the South Pacific to Pearl Harbor, where he had a brief conversation with Admiral Nimitz over the envisioned role of the new carriers in the coming Pacific offensive. He then flew on to California, and then to Oklahoma to visit his parents and siblings.

Clark used the time en route to consider the men he wanted for his ship, keeping in mind the poor example of Spuds Ellyson, his skipper on the *Brooks*. Ellyson "had brought too many of his friends on board and treated them as pets, with the result that the rest of the crew held resentment." Clark's understanding of "friend" in the Navy did not extend to pampering. Nor did it involve preferential treatment, unless rooted in superior performance.

He landed at Norman in central Oklahoma, home of the Navy's air technical training center, to visit his brother Bill, newly commissioned as a photo interpreter. He also planned to obtain use of a Navy car, a driver, and free gas for a few days to take him to hometown Chelsea, 150 miles away. Base regulations, however, prevented the duty officer at the motor pool, Ensign F. Robert Reynolds, from releasing any cars after 1700 (5 PM). Clark would have to wait until morning. Jocko insisted, but the new 26-year-old "90-day-wonder" (wartime ensign) could not and would not violate regulations for anybody.

Bob Reynolds did, however, offer to let the captain borrow his own spiffy white 1942 Buick Roadmaster, which he had obtained while operating his own trucking company in southern California. A graduate of Santa Barbara State Teachers College (now the University of California at Santa Barbara), Reynolds had also taught high school engineering drawing, talents he put to use at the Norman base.

Gregarious by nature, Reynolds tried to calm down the irate Clark with chatter, "Where do you go from here, Captain?"

"I'm going to Newport News to take command of a big new carrier, take her out to the Pacific, and kick the hell out of the Japs!"

"Gee, I sure wish I could go with you," said Reynolds.

"You really mean that?" replied Jocko.

"You *know* I do!"

Clark wrote down Reynolds's full name and serial number. The ensign still would not give him a car, but he had a Navy driver take Clark to plead his case with the base commander. This was one of the very early naval aviators, Captain V. C. Griffin Jr., who all hands referred to (behind his back) as "You-all" for his thick Alabama drawl.

Reynolds simultaneously knocked off work and returned to the BOQ. There he took off his tie and relaxed over drinks with other junior officers in the room of Lieutenant George Halas, the 48-year-old "father" of professional football. Halas had left his championship 1942 Chicago Bears for his second wartime service (he had also been in World War I). This time he was a "tunafish"—or "Tunney-face"—as part of ex-boxer Lieutenant Commander Gene Tunney's Navy athletic program to whip new recruits into shape.

Presently the phone rang. It was Captain Griffin calling Reynolds. "You-all" chewed him out for "talking back" to this captain. "Come over and apologize to him."

So Reynolds put his tie back on and hastened to Griffin's office, where he found Clark sitting on a lounge, laughing and having a good time. Griffin let Reynolds sweat a bit, while Clark said nothing, feigning anger. Finally, Griffin remarked that he hated to "give in" to Clark, "but he's asked to take you aboard the *Yorktown* with him. He wants you." Then the two captains had their laugh.

"Well, I sure do appreciate that opportunity," said Reynolds. "That would be fine, getting out there and doing a little fighting instead of standing here fighting people over cars!"

Clark had been immediately impressed by Reynolds's "clear eye and quick mind. He was smart, and I instantly liked the guy. It was instant mutual admiration, as sometimes happens." That Jocko reckoned he could somehow put Reynolds to work on the ship was a telling example of Clark's shrewd judge of character. He was also delighted by the fact that Reynolds had been born in San Diego, Clark's virtual second home.

Clark could not know, in fact, that Reynolds had already, and recently, smelled death. The previous November he and several other new ensigns had taken dates to Boston's Coconut Grove nightclub, only to have it erupt in flames that snuffed out nearly 500 lives, including his fellow officers and their dates. Reynolds had survived only by quickly locking himself in the basement meat freezer.

Another officer at Norman was Lieutenant (jg) Joe Tucker, commissioned an officer from having been aviation chief metalsmith on the old *Yorktown*, where he had served with Clark. At the Battle of Midway he had wrapped an American flag around his waist and jumped overboard when the ship was mortally torpedoed. Now Tucker was exec of the metalsmith school. When Bob Reynolds told Tucker of his encounter with Clark, Joe pleaded with him to ask the captain if he too could join the new ship. Jocko agreed immediately.

Bob Reynolds learned from Bill Clark that brother Jocko had already been told that he would be promoted to rear admiral. But first he had to take out the *Yorktown* for its initial combat operations. (One other brother, George Clark, saw military service. Drafted into the Army, he served with General George S. Patton's army in the push across Europe until the final victory, never receiving so much as a scratch.)

"You-all" Griffin provided the future admiral a car and driver to take him to Chelsea, where he was "Joe" again for a two-day visit with his Mama and Papa, both thriving in spite of health problems. He then visited his sister Mary in Tulsa, where local reporters regarded him as "looking surprisingly young" at 49.

"I certainly didn't protest the assignment" to command the new *Yorktown*, Jocko laughed when reporters asked about it, but he "brushed off" questions about his combat experiences to date. "After we get this war won," he grinned, "I'll come back and bore everyone to death with my stories." (Undated *Tulsa World* article)

Clark flew to Jacksonville to see his daughters. At the naval air station the officer of the day turned out to be none other than Lieutenant George Earnshaw. When Clark had been exec there in 1941 he had written a letter at the request of the former pitcher (who had retired from baseball after the 1936 season), recommending him for a commission. He had gotten it—like George Halas, a "tunafish/Tunney-face." However, at Jax he had become virtually permanent OOD—a "greeter" of visitors. Now Earnshaw asked Jocko to take him on board the *Yorktown*. Clark said yes.

He also wanted an associate from his Jacksonville duty, John Montgomery, the enlisted intelligence specialist who however had since been transferred. Clark learned that Montgomery had moved into foreign intelligence work and had been sent to Nassau in the Bahamas as liaison to the Duke of Windsor—the abdicated King Edward VIII, who was there with his wife the duchess, formerly Wallis Warfield Spencer Simpson. So Jocko wrote a letter to Montgomery, now a chief warrant officer, inviting him to join the *Yorktown* crew. Montgomery jumped at the opportunity.

Clark arranged to have Lieutenant Rick Lambart transferred from the *Suwannee* to the *Yorktown*. The new ship's assistant surgeon described the 6 foot 2 Lambart, English-born but now a naturalized American, with his crew cut and "continental manner" eating habit (pushing with knife; fork inverted) as "a fine and most interesting gentleman who has traveled over most of the world—all of Europe, Russia and Turkey." (diary of Dr. Raymond F. Gard) Lambart welcomed the chance to serve again with Clark.

Flying on to Washington, Jocko headed to BuAer, where the first person he encountered was Herman Rosenblatt. This individual's immense talents had led to his transfer from the *Suwannee* to the bureau as an aide to the assistant chief, Rear Admiral Ralph Davison. Rosenblatt now implored Clark to take him on the *Yorktown*, again as an ACIO. Jocko approached his friend Davison: "If you can spare that young aide in your outer office, I can put him to work on my ship."

Davison acquiesced, but Jocko advised Rosenblatt first to enroll in the new ACIO school at Quonset Point, Rhode Island, to learn the latest techniques for disseminating air combat intelligence. Herman left by train for Quonset that afternoon and soon proved extraordinarily talented in many ways: a lawyer, he was multilingual, athletic, musical, and a bon vivant and connoisseur of fine food, liquor, and cigars. This was in direct contrast to Clark, who otherwise lacked the social graces and contacts enjoyed by many of his peers.

"Herm" Rosenblatt deftly exploited this situation, so much so that other *Yorktown* officers viewed and caricatured him as a rank sycophant ("ass-kisser"). Many therefore feared him because he could go straight to Jocko; or they simply hated his guts. Undeniably brilliant, he quickly won Jocko's confidence and soon "acted as sort of an aide and political adviser to him." (Anderson transcript #3, 114)

That Clark fashioned his inner circle of advisers with individuals totally unlike himself or each other, except for their particular talents—as Waller, Anderson, Rosenblatt, and Reynolds showed—is proof positive of his exceptional abilities as a leader.

After securing Rosenblatt's transfer from Davison's staff, Jocko visited BuPers to get similar orders cut for Reynolds, Joe Tucker, George Earnshaw, and others. The detailing officer balked at "Big George," about to be promoted to lieutenant commander in the Tunney athletic program. Only seven billets existed for that rank on the *Yorktown,* and if Earnshaw occupied one of them, observed the detailer, the 6 foot 4, 210-pound athlete, then 43, would likely turn out to be "a white elephant."

"You give me George Earnshaw," roared Jocko, "and *I'll* worry about what to do with him!"

Further protests by the detailer proved futile, for Clark simply sat down and instituted the same "wait-'em-out policy" that had worked miracles for the *Suwannee.* BuPers gave in, and Earnshaw soon had his orders to the *Yorktown.* That settled, Jocko forgot all about Earnshaw or about alerting the exec Waller about him.

Waller was sitting at his desk at the Newport News shipyard one Monday morning when "a giant of a man" (his words) walked in, held out his hand—"which appeared about the size of a ten-pound ham"—and announced, "I'm Earnshaw!"

"I'm Waller. Welcome aboard," and they shook hands. The exec, no follower of baseball, had no idea what to do with this very senior lieutenant. So he began the conversation by simply asking Earnshaw what department he would like to be in.

"Sir," replied Earnshaw simply, "I'll do my best in any department you assign me to." Taken aback by this unorthodox yet sincere answer, which revealed an alarming ignorance of warships, Waller nevertheless took such wartime surprises in stride. After studying the ship's officer roster he figured that Earnshaw might fit in the Gunnery Department. So he ordered him to the antiaircraft gunnery school at nearby Dam Neck for instruction.

When Earnshaw later reported to the *Yorktown* he was assigned as assistant "gun boss" to the department head, who would teach him the ropes. This was Commander Cecil L. "Stroke" Blackwell, who had been an athlete at the Naval Academy ('25). In battle, Blackwell directed the anti-aircraft (AA) fire of one dozen 5-inch/.38-caliber batteries from within the ship, while Earnshaw ranged along the edges of the flight deck superintending the crews of shorter-range AA guns. These were eight quadruple 40 mms and 46 single 20 mms (to which 13 were added at Clark's insistence).

Whenever a gunner paused to look around instead of ahead for targets, big right-hander Earnshaw used his pitching arm to swat the man's helmet with a stick. That he learned to do once in battle.

During Clark's brief stopover in Washington he also paid a visit to BuAer and his old friend Radford, also a captain and director of aviation training, which included motion picture instruction films. Raddy introduced him to Edward Steichen, arguably America's premier living photographer, now a commander orchestrating the Navy's combat photography program. Steichen assigned a superb still photographer to the *Yorktown*, Lieutenant Charles W. Kerlee, whose black and white shots soon began to reach the public.

At the bureau Jocko also dropped in on early pilot Commander Frank W. "Spig" Wead (USNA '16). He had been retired since 1927, after a fall paralyzed him from the waist down, but had become a successful screenwriter of Hollywood movies portraying naval aviation. He told Clark he wanted to make a color motion picture of the new fast carriers in action, and Jock immediately volunteered the *Yorktown* for the task.

Wead concurred and soon convinced Clark to take on board a particular photographer to do the filming. This was Lieutenant (jg) Dwight Long, who had circled the world before the war in a 32-foot ketch, shooting color movies throughout and writing a book about it, both of which Wead showed Clark. Suitably impressed, Clark gave Long the run of the ship to take candid color shots of life on board.

Wead also had no trouble convincing Clark to utilize the *Yorktown* during its shakedown cruise as the setting for a commercial black-and-white Twentieth Century Fox motion picture, *Wing and a Prayer*. Based on the events leading up to and including the Battle of Midway, it was directed by Henry Hathaway (*The Lives of a Bengal Lancer*, 1935; and later, *True Grit*, 1969). The stars were veteran actors Charles Bickford (as the taciturn captain), Don Ameche (the no-nonsense air officer), and Dana Andrews (the savvy torpedo squadron skipper).

Although the script was already written and the scenes were filmed in Hollywood, the personality of Ameche's character bore an uncanny resemblance to that of the ship's real air officer, Lieutenant Commander Henry L. Dozier. On camera, one of the movie's aircrewmen expressed the ultimate enlisted man's disdain for the fictional "Commander Harper" (substitute Dozier) as "the only officer I ever knew whose men wouldn't give him a nickname."

The title of the movie was taken from the popular new war song "Comin' in on a Wing and a Prayer"—an odd selection, inasmuch as the lyric (written by Harold Adamson) celebrates a damaged multiengine AAF bomber: "Oh, with one motor gone, we will still carry on." Carrier planes had only one engine; when it quit, the plane went down! (That's Hollywood.) Obviously, the song itself could not be used in the film.

Remarkably, the ship received another excellent still photographer in an enlisted sailor, Jeff Corey, who had appeared in several movies as a supporting actor (*Syncopation*, 1942; *My Friend Flicka*, 1943). His job was to help provide entertainment in shows staged by the crew when the ship was in port or at anchor.

All such publicity was, however, almost incidental to Captain Clark's real task of forging his officers and crew into an efficient, hard-hitting combat team. From the bridge, navigator George Anderson and the officer of the deck (OOD)—always under Jocko's steady eye—maneuvered the ship in battle and throughout every day and night at sea.

Assigned to the ship were only seven very recent Academy grads, classes of '39 to '43 (the last three classes graduated early, just as Jocko's had during World War I). The most senior among them, from '39, was Lieutenant George J. Largess. All the other "deck" officers below the rank of lieutenant commander—more than 100—were 90-day-wonders with less sea time than he had, many with none at all.

Among the few who had previously "stood the deck" were six battle-seasoned veterans transferred from the *Enterprise*. These included Lieutenant Marshall Field IV of the prominent department store/newspaper family, who as a gunnery officer had been wounded in action.

"Jiggs" Largess was senior watch officer, charged with training virtually all the junior line officers as OODs to conn the ship. When he himself had the conn under the watchful eye of the skipper, Clark criticized his every move, ending with "What in hell *did* you learn at the Academy about responsibility?" And Clark harangued the 90-day-wonders equally, with the concluding statement, "You Reserves ain't got no sense of responsibility!" The bridge earned the reputation as the "can't win room."

Largess's regular assignment in the Hull Department included policing the ship—the people as well as the equipment. Commander Daniel J. Sweeney ('26), a lovable New Englander of Irish descent, was department head. His part in outfitting the *Wasp* three years before had prepared him for this task. Its captain, "Black Jack" Reeves, had been mean and disliked, creating an unhappy ship.

Some people regarded Jocko Clark similarly, including a former shipmate of Sweeney's who had suffered under Clark. Because Sweeney had recently received a knee wound aboard his gunboat fighting a U-boat, his friend advised him to get off the *Yorktown:* "Jocko will drive you crazy!" The amiable Sweeney laughed that off and quickly found Clark's style of leadership invigorating. When Jocko discovered Sweeney to be a good manager he left him alone.

The Hull Department was also known as C & R for its two parts (Construction and Repair), making Sweeney both first lieutenant and damage control officer, roles Clark regarded as critically important. Separate assistant heads divided these responsibilities. Jocko assigned Rick Lambart as assistant first lieutenant. Serving under him were the ship's fire marshal, Lieutenant (jg) Bernard J. "Barney" Lally, straight from the New York City Fire Department, and ship's sheriff—chief master-at-arms—Chief Bos'n Pop Austin, one of Clark's confederates on the old *Yorktown*.

Raöul Waller discovered the perfect choice for assistant damage control officer during a "sit-'em-out" pilgrimage to BuPers at Clark's behest. There behind a desk was an Academy classmate ('24) who had left the Navy until war came, Lieutenant John W. "Diamond Jim" Brady, a colorful fellow with a loud voice. "Raöul," he blurted out, "how in *hell* can I get on a big ship?"

"Well, Jim, if you're going to get on a big ship, why don't you get on the best ship, the *Yorktown?*"

"Gee, do you think I can?" Waller not only thought so but with Clark's help arranged it, and Brady plunged into his work with great zeal and humor. He maintained the stability of the ship, directed all repair parties, and quickly earned affectionate nicknames like "Socket-wrench" from equally fun-loving fellow officers.

Jocko Clark descended on Newport News on 15 February, inspected his ship, and got into a huddle with Doug Petty, the supervisor with whom he had rushed the *Suwannee* to early completion. The original pre–Pearl Harbor projected completion date for the *Yorktown* of September 1944 was now 21 June 1943. He learned that sister ship *Bunker Hill* was 85.2 percent completed against 73.8 percent for the *Yorktown.* He told Petty, "That ship is gonna go out first. I'd like to go with *it* instead of the *Yorktown.*"

"Captain," said Petty, "if you stick with us you'll go out first." He wanted to work with Clark again and to beat the Quincy-built *Bunker Hill* into the war, even though he knew that its captain, Clark's classmate John Ballentine, wanted to switch ships. "Bally's" wife had grown up in nearby Yorktown, where Petty had known her, and its namesake ship would have cemented her tie to the town. Jocko took Petty at his word.

The Navy moved up the *Yorktown*'s commissioning date to 15 April 1943, knowing that such deadlines for large carriers were never met. So Clark went straight to the company president, Homer L. Ferguson, for guarantees that this date *would* be met. Ferguson, an Academy man (1892) who had been building warships since leaving the Navy in 1915, was impressed with the *Suwannee* precedent and believed that the dynamic part–Cherokee Indian would make it happen for the *Yorktown.*

So Ferguson repeated his customary speech to Petty and E. F. Herd, general yard manager, "There's three ways to do a job: the right way, the wrong way, and *my* way." And he told Clark, "You can have anything you want!" (Conversation with Petty) The senior Navy supervisor at the yard, Admiral Cox, shared their faith in the man who had delivered the goods with the *Suwannee.*

Ferguson prevailed upon the Bureau of Ships not to divert any materials from the *Yorktown* to the *Bunker Hill* and gave Jocko carte blanche. The combined team of Ferguson, Eddie Herd, Petty, and Clark got to work to set a record—11 weeks "overboard" time from launching to commissioning, nearly four weeks of which had already gone by. Clark also intended to beat not only the *Essex* into battle but also the new *Lexington,* which was commissioned at Quincy virtually that day, 17 February.

Clark demanded, and got, radical departures from accepted construction practices. Cut corners, he said. Again, substitute steel if aluminum was unavailable. If hatches would not close to keep out leaking fuel, put coamings around them instead of rebuilding them. Enemy bomb shrapnel had punctured gas lines of other carriers in the hangar bay leading to the flight deck; instead of relocating them, install casings around them. Jocko seemed to break every rule of peacetime shipbuilding in the book.

The shipyard managers obliged him and found that most of his expedient changes could be adopted as standard solutions for all other new carriers. They did not even object when Clark told them to divert needed materials to the *Yorktown* from the other carriers being built in the yard— *Intrepid* (CV-11), the new *Hornet* (CV-12), and *Franklin* (CV-13).

Not only management but the Newport News workers—more than 4,000 of whom (out of 31,000 at the shipyard) eventually worked on Jocko's ship—understood that all his requests were essential, unlike those of most new skippers who simply asked for everything, including frills. Workers who had been indifferent to a speedy completion of the *Essex,* and Fitzhugh Lee's admonitions regarding their slow work, marveled at Clark's energy. They admired his determination and thus came to share his compulsion to make the *Yorktown* number one.

His officers and crewmen got the same Jocko treatment from both barrels as they reported in during and after the overboard period. Everywhere at once, so it seemed, he drove all the officers relentlessly until they—at best—dreaded his coming or—at worst—hated his guts. "Goddammit," he roared at them, "if you can't run, walk. If you can't walk, crawl. But get the job done. And if you can't get the job done, get off my ship!"

Some officers did, on his order or on their own initiative, but most— this being their first ship—did not know any better. The 90-day-wonders and sailors fresh from boot camp had no basis for comparison, figuring he must be a typical captain. He taught and commanded by example. He followed through on everything, and so must they. Submitting to his apparent tyranny, they worked to near or real exhaustion. He earned their respect and eventually much more. If nothing else, Jocko Clark was a true leader.

When Navy bureaus or civilian manufacturers proved slow or uncooperative, Clark or Waller would fly to the factories or to Washington. They usually went in a three-seat TBF piloted by Lieutenant Joseph R. Kristufek of Torpedo Five, soon to join the ship. He was selected because Clark insisted that the pilot must already have 1,000 hours flying experience and an instrument rating to fly in foul weather. Also, he had to be single, because Jocko did not want to take married men away from their families on overnight hops. On one trip he had Lieutenant (jg) James W. Campbell of VF-5 fly him in an SNJ trainer to New York, even sharing his hotel suite with Campbell.

In one regard, spare parts for the Engineering Department, the *Yorktown* was oversupplied. BuShips supplier personnel did not seem to realize that CV-10 had been renamed from *Bon Homme Richard.* They therefore sent two of everything to the ship, each item labeled separately for both ship names. The *Yorktown* became a virtual supply center and would never be put out of action for want of parts. This mistake was not corrected until another new carrier was named *Bon Homme Richard* (CV-31).

Clark lost one of his "sit-'em-out" efforts, though he succeeded in the long run. Though not a prewar churchgoer, he identified himself as an

Episcopalian. He often remarked, "You can't fight a war without religion!" He always carried a military service Bible containing words of faith written in it by his mother. (niece B. J. Clark Mayer to author, 26 June 2001) Even at the end of a visit with anyone, instead of saying "good-bye" Jocko said simply, "God bless."

In his customary way of requesting former associates whom he admired, he invited his chaplain from Jacksonville, Father Maurice S. Sheehy, to assume the same post on the *Yorktown*. Sheehy agreed, only to be transferred instead to a battleship. When Jocko protested to the chief of chaplains, Rear Admiral R. D. Workman, the latter agreed to move Sheehy to the *Yorktown* but only when the two ships were operating close together. Then Workman surprised Jocko by offering him two chaplains—unprecedented for any one ship—a Catholic and a Protestant. "Of course," Jocko replied. "I want the Lord on my side!"

So the *Yorktown* became the first ship to have more than one chaplain, both of them 40 years old. The Catholic was an eminent Dominican theologian and author, Walter A. Farrell, the Protestant a lanky Presbyterian, Robert L. Alexander. Both did well from the outset, so Jocko kept Farrell and allowed Sheehy to go to the *Saratoga* instead.

When Admiral Nimitz later marveled about his having two chaplains, the proud skipper responded, "By my orders, they pray full speed all the time. We have the Lord on our side, and we will not miss!"

Old-timers and newcomers alike appreciated the exec, Commander Waller, in a different way. Waller had a personality completely unlike Clark's, which is why Jocko had selected him. A soft-spoken Tennessean with a slight stammer, Waller was well ordered, efficient, reserved, with a penchant for keeping the ship clean. Raöul always seemed to be on the move to answer Jocko's every call. A man of slight build, he scurried briskly about, tending to walk so lightly on his toes that amused sailors referred to him as "Mr. Eggshells."

The skipper, preoccupied with finishing the ship, relied completely on Waller to organize the departments and assign officers to them as they reported in. The departments were Engineering, Navigation, Hull, Gunnery, Air, Communications, Supply, and Medical.

From the outset the bombastic Clark and the reserved Waller got along famously, inasmuch as the latter quickly learned how to deal with him.

> I never disagreed with Jock [except twice, though Clark recalled only once]. But he would listen very carefully to everything I had to say. When I got through he would say, "Well, Raöul, we'll do it this way."

Every time he listened me out I'd better do it because I'd end up doing
it that way anyway!

Waller was really a foil whose own expertise and style complemented
that of Clark. In his memoirs Clark called him a "trusted aide." He wrote,
"No money could buy the kind of loyalty he gave me. Not only did he
learn to anticipate my wishes, but he often gave me what was needed even
without my asking. He was the kind of executive officer I wished I might
have been."

The OOD was surprised one day when an ensign reported for duty carrying unusual orders to report directly to the captain. It was Bob Reynolds
from Norman, Oklahoma. Clark was out with visiting "brass" from Washington, so Reynolds sat down to wait. Presently, in walked Jocko with Assistant Navy Secretary Artemus Gates. Noticing Reynolds, Clark said, "Hey,
California, you made it!"

They shook hands and Clark introduced him to Gates, with the OOD
and other personnel looking on agape at such treatment for a lowly ensign.
"I don't want you to log in yet," Clark said to Reynolds, "we'll discuss it at
dinner tonight." That evening the captain informed him, "Just keep your
eyes open and help me. You're working for *me;* you don't have any other
boss." Jocko would teach him as much as he could about the carrier then tap
him for ideas and suggestions.

It was an unorthodox assignment, with duties much like those of an
admiral's aide. In fact, Jocko showed Bob Reynolds the two-star rear admiral's collar insignia he would put on as soon as the *Yorktown* was battle
weaned and the Navy needed him as flag officer. "If you do a good job with
me," he told Reynolds, "I'm going to take you with me"—on his staff.

On the last Friday in March, when the *Yorktown* looked like it just
might meet its 15 April commissioning date, Clark discovered the ship
lacked sufficient ready rooms to accommodate the three squadrons totaling
90 pilots and 72 enlisted aircrewmen of the bombers. He told Doug Petty
he needed a third ready room on the gallery deck, just below the flight deck.
Petty obliged but could not get it insulated for the air conditioning that kept
flyers fresh for battle. "Don't worry about that," Jocko replied. "Just put up a
light and some blackboards." The insulation could wait. The job was done
over the weekend.

To save several days from the time normally required to familiarize the
2,400 men of the crew now training at Norfolk, Clark took the unprecedented step of bringing them over daily in bunches of 200 men each to tour
the ship's spaces. They learned the basic layout of the 27,100-ton carrier,

heard the proper nomenclature, and witnessed workers testing shipboard equipment.

Clark's style of innovative thinking inspired several of his officers. One was the supply officer, Commander William L. Patten, a classmate ('24) of Waller's. Patten wanted to get some supplies brought aboard before the day of commissioning. Jocko approached Petty, whose bosses okayed it, and he worked out a schedule whereby boxcars full of provisions were brought alongside the ship and off-loaded at night, when there was less construction activity.

By the time the *Yorktown* was ready to be commissioned, it had 60 days of supplies on board. Clark was "tickled to death," in Petty's words. Furthermore, advice for feeding the crew was solicited from a top executive of the Pig n' Whistle restaurant chain, a boon for a healthy and happy crew.

April arrived and with it the shipyard's Trial Board to test everything on the ship, a process that usually took an entire week. Jocko told its members to do it in a day—and they did! Then, on the 9th, the Navy's Board of Inspection and Survey examined and approved the readiness of the *Yorktown* for duty. One of its members, Captain Ralph E. Jennings, who had relieved Clark on the board (1936–39) and returned to it, was incredulous.

"Of the many new ships I inspected while on the board," he said a year later, "she was in the best condition of them all as far as appearance and readiness for duty were concerned." Jennings was so impressed that he began to pull strings—successfully—to command her as Clark's relief when that time came.

Jocko had done it. His "indefatigable energy," in George Anderson's words, had resulted in a "monumental achievement."

The great ship was ready for commissioning on time, set for 15 April 1943—the first time that any heavy carrier had been completed on schedule. *Essex* and *Lexington* were already in commission but had had longer "overboard" periods. Clark had beaten the *Bunker Hill*, not commissioned until late May, and the *Intrepid*, commissioned in August. What was more, from this time forward Newport News and other shipbuilding companies adopted Clark's measures as precedent standards for constructing and outfitting all large warships.

And Doug Petty used him as a yardstick by which to measure subsequent prospective captains whose carriers Newport News was building. Happily, Dixie Kiefer of the *Ticonderoga* proved equal to Clark's example, and less bombastic. But Jocko's temperamental classmate Miles Browning was "very weak" with the new *Hornet* (CV-12). Admiral Cox, the yard's Navy supervisor, repeated the same fitness report assessment he had given Clark for his achievement with the *Suwannee*—straight 4.0s for "the satisfactory and expeditious completion of the *Yorktown* . . . in large measure" due to Clark's "assistance and cooperation. Recommended unqualifiedly for promotion." (15 April 1943)

Clark had the shipyard workers move the ship to the Norfolk Navy Yard one day early to take on the crew and assign them their battle stations. That evening he addressed his officers: "This ship will reach the combat zone in record time and in complete combat readiness. Therefore any officer who remains aboard will grade his own fitness report a perfect 4.0 since I will tolerate nothing less!"

Before dawn, at 0400 on the 15th, reveille sounded, and emergency drills were held. Despite bitter cold temperatures Jocko was confident. Waller was handling all the details of the commissioning ceremony, with Eleanor Roosevelt, whom Clark greatly admired, scheduled to be guest of honor just as she had been when she christened the ship so admirably in January.

Still, he was realistic about possible problems among his green crew. So he summoned Stroke Blackwell and Lieutenant Commander Raymond N. "Red" Sharp, assistant air officer—Waller's chief workhorses for the occasion—to his sea cabin on the bridge. "Now, boys, things are going to go wrong," he gently and uncharacteristically counseled them. "And a lot of these VIPs that you're going to be escorting are not going to like this or that. Just laugh it up!" (Conversation with Sharp)

Shipyard personnel moved the *Yorktown* to the commissioning pier, while designated officers went ashore to greet guests and admirals. Among them were Jocko's Oklahoma Congressman Wesley E. Disney and principal chief of the Cherokees J. Bartley Milam, a Chelsea banker with whom "Joe" had walked three miles to school 40 years before. Unfortunately, Mrs. Roosevelt failed to appear, sending a telegram with apologies that was received only five minutes before the noon ceremony.

The guest speaker, Assistant Navy Secretary for Air Artemus Gates, extolled the great new warship, proudly harkening back to the time when his Pilgrim forebears had landed on these shores. Then Cherokee Clark took the podium and responded with the old Will Rogers line that *his* ancestors had already been here to greet those of Gates. Several attentive crewmen chuckled as they witnessed Gates stiffen in his seat at the captain's jibe.

Then Jocko thundered to his men: "We're all going to do our job and do it well, and we can all come out with flying colors. A chain is only as strong as the weakest link. I'm not going to put up with any weak links! Anybody who is dissatisfied and doesn't want to go to the Pacific, step forward and we'll transfer you now!"

No one stepped forward; the crew was suitably dazzled.

Formalities completed, in late afternoon Captain Clark moved USS *Yorktown* to a dry dock for 12 days of finishing touches. He did not let up, except to relax ashore. In the evenings he enjoyed the local night life, having resumed dating.

Jocko depended on others for nonnaval chores like shopping in Norfolk. Requiring a driver, he was initially assigned Coxswain Henry E. Bolden. "Captain Clark has some peculiar habits," Commander Waller advised Bolden, handing him $200 in cash. "He tends to pick up things at a store and walk away without paying. Be there to pay for it! When you get below one hundred dollars see me—and try to keep a tab on what he buys." Jocko kept Hank Bolden jumping.

And he continued at flank speed (faster than "full speed") preparing the ship for combat. He had ammunition loaded from boxcars and flatcars. When challenged for the risk and illegality of having this done in dry dock, he retorted, "This is war, and we can't live by peacetime regulations." The additional antiaircraft guns were delivered, but the last "gun tubs" for them could not be installed on the starboard side until the ship had squeezed through the Panama Canal. All this and more increased the ship's displacement from 27,100 to 36,200 tons by the time it reached the Pacific.

Shopfitters installed pipes on the outside of the hull, but without the expansion joints necessary for riding out a typhoon. When chief engineer McNally noticed this, he alerted Clark, who demanded to know how long installing the joints would take. About a month, said McNally. "To *hell* with it," barked Jocko. "If we get into a typhoon we won't give a damn. Don't put 'em on."

The bare steel hull had to be painted, but when the shipyard could not do it in time to suit Jocko's timetable he ranted and then announced, "We'll do it ourselves!" Bright and early Sunday morning, 18 April, nearly all hands—junior officers included, an unheard-of indignity—were lowered over the sides on scaffolds to do the thankless work. Air-powered wire brushes in hand, serenaded by the ship's band, they scraped bare the hull, then painted it. Very few complaints were heard—it was simply part of the job: to win the war. But that did it for Lieutenant Marshall Field, who pulled some fast strings to wrangle a transfer to another ship.

At least the evenings were free for officers and men to have liberty ashore. But when sailors returned late, Clark held mast, chewed them out, and then gave light sentences. And he instructed their division officers "to break out the billy clubs" for the worst offenders (not literally, of course).

If Clark saw a man not doing his job, he said nothing to him except to note the sailor's name and division. Then he would chew out the fellow's division officer. When he walked by crewmen sitting during a break, they instantly jumped to attention—until, agitated, he barked, "Sit down! Sit down and rest! Never mind that!"

From his experience as a junior officer on the *Brooks* Jocko had resolved never to allow gambling on a ship of his own. He issued strict orders to that effect, threatening to demote anyone caught. Two ship's cooks were indeed caught, given a warning, then caught again and broken in rank to second-class petty officers. That solved the problem, at least among the crew. Gambling by officers, especially pilots needing diversion, was tolerated, however. A similar double standard existed regarding liquor on board.

Cigarette butts were especially abhorrent to Clark. Not two days had passed after commissioning before Raöul Waller—even more passionate than Jocko about a clean ship—walked through one space "ankle deep" in butts. He gathered all division officers and laid down the law: no butts! From that day forward the *Yorktown* gained a reputation as one of the cleanest ships in the fleet.

The effect of both men's treatment of the crew brought respect, even later affection in many cases. For example, they helped 18-year-old Private Robert W. Bender, one of their Marine Corps orderlies, "through the rest of my life."

> Both loved the enlisted men. They never once mistreated a man—never talked out of line to them. Usually when a man was on report and went before Clark or Waller—the bigger the lie they told and could make Captain Clark laugh, the easier he was on them.

Being captain's orderly, Bender was posted at the entrance to the bridge and the captain's sea cabin, always at Clark's beck and call and also available to receive unauthorized visitors. One morning, following reveille,

> a short young sailor came up to me on the bridge, had his breakfast tray with him, and asked to see the Captain. I figured that anyone with that much guts should see Captain Clark. The Captain had just got up, was in his shorts, and said he would see him. The young sailor stood in front of the Captain and said, "Sir, I cannot do a day's work on this kind of breakfast." (It *was* sorry.)
>
> Captain Clark looked at it, called his kitchen, and said, "Son, what would you like for breakfast?" The sailor ate breakfast with Captain

Clark—bacon, eggs, home fries, juice and coffee. Needless to say, Captain Clark had me bring the supply officer [Commander Patten] to him, and what he had to say would be unprintable!

Clark genuinely loved the enlisted men, empathized with them, and consciously promoted teamwork among all hands. "Many of the crew regarded me as slave driver at first," he conceded later, "and in a sense they were right." As for the feared and hated Japanese, who had sunk the battleships at Pearl Harbor and the prewar carriers (except *Saratoga* and *Enterprise*) in the battles of 1942, he regarded them as "a worthy and courageous foe." But he announced to his shipmates, the Japanese "could be beaten if we only used our American ingenuity. I told them I was confident that together we would find the way to victory."

One problem with feeding over 3,000 men was inefficient chow lines for distributing the cooked meals. So Clark put Bob Reynolds in charge of organizing them efficiently—which he did. This job, and Reynolds's own requests for a note (chit) to get himself a snack from the galley, led to his occasional nickname of "Chow-chit." Indeed, whenever the captain needed him for anything, the bullhorn boomed, "Ensign Reynolds, dial 2-2-2," summoning him to the bridge, usually a long hike up several gangways. (Conversation with Cooper Bright)

Jocko downplayed "abandon ship" drills, although he held "plenty of them," emphasizing instead alertness, damage control, and fire fighting. The first real fire—and alarm—occurred the night of 22 April when Navy Yard workmen using an acetylene torch on a 40-mm gun shield set fire to a life raft; the alert fire watch doused it in less than five minutes.

Known to very few on board, their captain received a physical setback the next day, the 23rd, when he was given a thorough medical examination at the naval hospital ashore. He had passed every test in his annual flight physical on board the *Suwannee* four months earlier. In that one he had been rated with perfect 20/20 vision. Alas, the rigorous Norfolk physicians discovered him to be far-sighted (20/100 right eye, 20/40 left), an inherited family trait, and prescribed reading glasses—not unusual for a 49 year old. He would use them sparingly in the privacy of his sea cabin.

The doctors also discovered that Clark had gained 26 pounds—up to 196—over those four months. This was surely inaccurate, but he obviously had gained weight and now had to adhere strictly to his lean diet lest he suffer a recurrence of his ulcers and thus lose his command. Still, the paunch would stay with him—as revealed by ship's cartoonists and, worse, by immediate superiors who in their fitness reports commented on his less than perfect neatness and physical bearing.

Still, Navy medical exams could be notoriously sloppy. Clark certainly did not shrink two inches in that four-month period—from 5 feet 11 to 5 feet 9 inches (the first figure was closest).

At 0400 on 27 April the dry dock was flooded; the ship became buoyant at 0505, and at 0600 it eased out into the Chesapeake Bay—still a refuge from German U-boats—for its sea trials. From the outset Jocko bellowed and cursed, especially at the OODs at the conn, as he put the ship through its paces. In fact, all officers quickly learned to avoid the bridge unless absolutely necessary, fearful they "were gonna be massacred by Jocko." (Conversation with Cooper Bright)

Officers and sailors alike discovered that the skipper, unlike the ship with its varying speeds of up to 33 knots, knew only two speeds: Stop and Go. And that it was usually GO! Adjusting to this pace was especially difficult for the landlubbers of all ranks—most of ship's company—who reeled from seasickness on these daily runs up and down the Chesapeake until they got their "sea legs."

Clark's greatest fetish was gunnery—shooting at target sleeves towed by planes from the air station. On the morning of the 30th the eager 5-inch gun crews opened fire prematurely and got off five rounds before Jocko stopped them. The guns soon passed their tests, as did the entire ship. On 1 May Clark reported to the Atlantic Fleet that the *Yorktown* was ready for duty and then congratulated "all hands on a job 'Well Done.' KEEP UP THE GOOD WORK."

The afternoon of 5 May, however, brought only frustration. The key to the long-distance reach of the fast carriers was the relatively new technique of underway replenishment, and Clark now tried to maneuver his ship alongside the equally new fleet oiler *Schuylkill* to simulate refueling at sea. But in vain. For two hours he failed to get abreast of it, because their similar deep draughts—27 feet for the *Yorktown,* 30 for the oiler—churned up the shallow bottom, keeping them apart.

Finally, the *Schuylkill*'s stern twice slammed into the *Yorktown*'s starboard side aft, ripping off the gangway and a radio antenna and scraping paint off the hull. All the while Clark—who believed himself a better seaman than that—screamed over the bullhorn, shaking a fist at the hapless tanker and telling its skipper where to go. Its captain obliged and left. Refueling drills would have to wait for open sea.

Next morning, at 0738, brought a happier event. With Newport News executives aboard, and a frosted cake from the galley to mark the occasion, Jimmy Flatley made the first landing aboard in a brand new Grumman F6F Hellcat—the fighter designed to defeat the Japanese Zero. This was followed by the other planes of Air Group Five—36 Hellcats, 36 Curtiss

SB2C Helldivers, and 18 Grumman TBF Avenger torpedo-bombers. The air operations continued for two more weeks—landing, then taking off to shore bases—while the *Yorktown* cruised up and down the Chesapeake.

Then, on 18 May, after the divebombers and "torpeckers" landed on the ship, they remained on board. The *Yorktown* tied up to the Norfolk dock that night, and next day the fighters taxied to the dock and were hoisted aboard by crane. That night final supplies were loaded on board for the ship's shakedown cruise, interrupted for an hour by an air raid alert. (Eastern seaboard sky watchers were still jittery about possible German attacks.)

Among the items taken aboard were two jeeps and two small tractors that had been spotted by Lieutenant Joe Tucker and his aircraft maintenance gang for possible flight deck uses. He bribed the Marine guards on the pier with several bottles of booze. The Marines told Joe, "If you need 'em, take 'em. There's plenty more where these came from!"

Clark welcomed aboard the movie crew of Henry Hathaway along with several engineers and mechanics from the Curtiss factory to work on the brand-new Helldivers. The plan was for the ship to proceed to Trinidad in the British West Indies, there to "shake down" into a fighting machine by conducting intensive flight operations and antiaircraft gunnery. After a month there, the *Yorktown* was scheduled to pass through the Panama Canal to San Francisco, and thence to Hawaii—*if* all went well on shakedown.

On the morning of 21 May 1943 the crew mustered on the flight deck as Navy Yard tugs eased the ship out into the channel. On the bridge Captain Clark instructed the bugler to blow the proper calls to salute the senior officer present afloat (a rear admiral) on one of the brand-new battleships docked nearby, the *Iowa*, first of its class. He obeyed, but blew too early.

Jocko pushed the bugler away from the loudspeaker and yelled at him, "You dopey no good sonofabitch! What the hell did you do that for?" He railed on in a tirade, oblivious to the mike still being "open"; his words went out over 3,000 watts to the *Iowa*. Its swabbies—like those of the *Yorktown*—doubled over with laughter. It sounded like Clark was calling their admiral a no-good SOB!

Passing out into the open Atlantic, the ship picked up three equally new destroyers as antisubmarine escorts—two in front, one astern. In addition, the Air Department prepared to launch Jimmy Flatley and a deckload of planes for a training flight. The air officer, "Hank" Dozier, orchestrated the launch and recovery from the island structure aft of the bridge. A classmate of navigator George Anderson ('27), Dozier not only was a loner with an utterly humorless disposition but he was handicapped by inexperience in

Jocko and senior ship's officers and guests are all smiles on 6 May 1943 following the first landing on his ship, the new *Yorktown*. The pilot, Air Group Five skipper Jimmy Flatley (holding gloves), landed in the F6F Hellcat behind them. *Left to right:* Herman Rosenblatt, Charlie Crommelin, Clark, AAF pilot C. B. Gaty, George Anderson (face hidden by mess steward holding ceremonial frosted cake), a Newport News executive, Hank Dozier, Flatley, AAF Colonel Sol Rosenblatt, Raöul Waller, and Red Sharp. *Bureau of Aeronautics*

such intricate operations. This soon became obvious, to the dismay of the captain, an expert from his days in the same post on the old *Lexington*.

By contrast, the flight deck officers had long experience as former enlisted mustangs—Lieutenant Pappy Harshman of old VF-2 and his assistant, Lieutenant Henry O. Warren, who waved each pilot down and off the deck. Hank Warren had launched Jimmy Doolittle's B-25 bombers off the old *Hornet* to bomb Tokyo the year before. "Crash One," landing signal officer Lieutenant (jg) Edward "Red" Volz, expertly waved each pilot back aboard with his colored paddles.

On their first flight off the ship in the open sea, the planes circled and landed uneventfully until Volz gave a TBF a "wave-off"—meaning, the pilot must circle around the ship and try again. The pilot, however, did not pull up fast enough. His tail hook caught one of the flight deck arresting cables, causing the plane to slew to the left and over the port side into the drink. The pilot and two crewmen were rescued by the plane guard destroyer, which took them back to Norfolk—where the tin can required repairs anyway.

Jocko was furious. Losing a $56,000 airplane was bad enough, but the departure of the destroyer reduced his antisubmarine escort to two cans. He paced the bridge, angry also that flight operations took so long that a lurking U-boat might line up a shot at the *Yorktown*.

Aside from exec Waller, only three career officers seem to have initially enjoyed Clark's confidence—George Anderson, Dan Sweeney, and Red Sharp. All the rest, along with the Reserves, he tested; if and when they satisfied him he tended to leave them alone. His very physical appearance was menacing: leaning over the wing of the bridge, often without a hat or cap, his thin hair blowing in the wind, his hump nose and protruding lower lip coated with zinc ointment or the lip swathed with a piece of cloth against the sun.

Jocko's bark was worse, felt most keenly by those nearest him—the OOD, assistant OOD, and junior OOD, each standing the usual four-hour watch. Gruffly and abruptly, he fired questions at each one of them, demanding immediate, confident, and *correct* answers. If—typically—they hesitated, or seemed intimidated, he let fly with a broadside: "Get off my bridge!" The victim simply returned to his quarters, under hack (or "in hack"). If all three duty officers got the axe, a call went out over the bullhorn for the senior watch officer: "Lieutenant Largess, report to the bridge."

When one brand-new ensign took the conn for the first time, the skipper suddenly asked him, "Is the ZB workin'?"—referring to the radio signal that gave the ship's heading.

"ZB, sir?"

"Don't you know what the ZB is?"

"No, sir."

"Get off my bridge, you knucklehead!"

When Clark's ulcers acted up, preventing him from sleeping, he would stagger out of his sea cabin, bedecked in "loud" pajamas, and pose a hypothetical problem. "We've been hit aft of Frame 105, and the rudder's jammed at 30 degrees right. What are you gonna do about it?" he once asked intelligence officer Robert W. Eaton.

"I'd just stop this sonofabitch and fix it?" replied the puzzled man.

"You're relieved of your post. Send up your relief."

The captain's challenges to his officers continued unabated, even in combat. Some would appeal to Raöul Waller to get him off their backs, and Waller would try to drop a careful hint to the skipper.

The head of the Communications Department, Lieutenant Commander James A. Morrison ('26)—a quiet, efficient individual—told the exec that the irascible captain was questioning his professional integrity. Waller smoothed that over. But he had difficulty writing a fitness report on a recent Naval Academy graduate ('42), Lieutenant (jg) Richard S. Bond, who never seemed to last a complete watch on Jocko's bridge. "Sweeten it up, Raöul," Jocko conceded. "It's just a conflict of personalities." He was thinking of Bond's career (although Bond died in a plane crash two years later).

But a few junior officers had enough sea knowledge and just plain guts to bluff the skipper, like Lieutenant (jg) James L. Lawrence. One day as the ship changed course Jocko shot out at Lawrence: "How'd you get that course?"

"Seaman's eye, Captain, seaman's eye," said Lawrence coolly. That satisfied Jocko. One good bluff deserved another. Lawrence's "reward," however, was a mixed blessing—always taking the conn at 0400 on combat days.

One day during flight quarters Clark observed the OOD, Lieutenant (jg) Ernest B. Kelly Jr. (an insurance executive in peacetime), chew out the Junior OOD for ordering a course change without informing him. Right then Jocko decided that Kelly, a combat veteran of the *Enterprise*, knew his stuff and made him OOD during all routine flight operations, a responsibility normally handled by the navigator.

Then there was Ensign Bob Reynolds, who roamed the ship to alert the captain to potential problems. A perennially happy guy, he soon took it upon himself to run interference not so much for Clark as for the officers summoned by him—either warning them or smoothing things over with the skipper on their behalf.

The one individual Clark never let up on was the air officer, Hank Dozier. Academy classmate George Anderson described him as "a serene, efficient, quiet type of naval officer who neither shouted nor became excited." Although a hard worker, he was the antithesis of Clark, who was "inclined to measure action by noise and activity. Thus Jocko boomed away at Hank, who took it all." Clark simply believed that the Air Department required aggressive leadership.

One of the department's officers, Lieutenant Cooper "Coop" Bright (also nicknamed "Buck" by some), believed Dozier displayed the peacetime naval officer's mind-set of always trying "to look good in order to be promoted" and blaming others for his mistakes. No one could get close to him. Indeed, his 1927 *Lucky Bag* observed, "A touch of Satan often causes him to get in trouble, but being a politician, he manages to smooth things over and come out on top." This simply did not work with Jocko.

One day Dozier complained to Anderson, "Andy, can't you possibly get the skipper off my back?" Anderson in turn alerted Waller, who got Jock to try to be patient with Dozier, but the stakes were too high—without efficient flight operations the carrier was dead meat to enemy planes. Even Bob Reynolds tried to befriend him, but he flatly rejected any help, much less admit to any problems, believing that he "had all the answers." He was genuinely disliked. Worse, Dozier seethed, occasionally taking out his frustrations on his own officers, which made Clark lean on him even harder.

Suddenly, on 23 May, Clark erupted. He was convinced the flight deck crews were not respotting the deck correctly—pushing the planes into their tight parking spaces for the night, only six to eight inches apart. Grabbing the handheld bullhorn from Dozier, he barked "Come on!" at Marine orderly Bender, and they clambered down the ladders onto the flight deck. To Dozier, right behind him, he yelled, "I'm gonna lock you up!"

Witnessed by over 1,000 men topside, Clark commanded, "Get out of my way," pushed Dozier aside and walked right past the flight deck officers. "Get them planes moving!" he bellowed at the plane-handling airedales and with his usual limp directed traffic, showing them how to spot the planes properly. They obeyed, with no little amusement, and were then treated to a lecture by the captain—standing on a *tree stump*—on the art of spotting the deck. And, of all things, cameraman Dwight Long caught the whole episode on color movie film.

The humiliated Dozier (who was *not* locked up, despite Clark's threat) returned to Air Plot near the bridge, seething. He blurted out, "I'm just on the verge of beating *the shit* out of that captain!" (Conversation with Cooper Bright) Instead, assistants Sharp, Harshman, and Warren pored over their "weegie [Ouija] board"—a six-foot model of the flight deck and tiny model planes—to test Clark's spotting schemes. Next day Sharp used the ship's two new tractors to simulate respotting schemes. It was going to be a long war.

Reaching the Caribbean, the *Yorktown* launched the fighters after sunup on 26 May to land ashore at Trinidad, and the ship passed through the antisubmarine nets into the island's enclosed Gulf of Paria. It briefly dropped anchor near the new *Lexington,* also on shakedown, enabling Jocko to check in ashore, then move the ship into the 80-mile-long lagoon for an afternoon of air operations.

One SB2C Helldiver lost power taking off and landed in the water, another broke its tail wheel on landing, and a third blew a tire. An F6F Hellcat fighter blew both tires in a hard landing, another ignored a wave-off then nearly hit the island structure, and a third snapped an arresting cable, which seriously injured one observer. Joe Tucker assigned some of his airplane mechanics to help Commander Dozier, who would not listen to them. One mechanic, a mustang, got so fed up with the air officer that he managed to wrangle a transfer off the ship within a month.

Clark had an officer note the time it took for the airedales to respot the planes: pushing all of them aft after landing and repositioned for launch. One day in the gulf after the respot Jocko leaned down from the wing of the bridge and yelled, "Mr. Warren, that took too long, and it's taken up too much space." As Hank Warren looked away in disgust, Clark continued, "I'll come down and show you how to do it."

Before Clark reached the 872-foot-long flight deck, Warren had Joe Tucker mark the spot where Hank had parked the forward-most plane, so they could compare Jocko's respot with Warren's. And he asked Tucker to time Clark's effort.

Shuffling about, Jocko again directed the plane pushers in respotting the planes aft. When they finished, he announced proudly, "Mr. Warren, *that's* the way to spot a flight deck!"

Warren turned to Tucker, "Joe, how much time did that take?"

"Almost two minutes longer than you took, Hank," replied Tucker, the customary and mischievous twinkle in his eye.

"How much space did we save?"

"He's eight feet further toward the bow than you were."

Warren turned to Clark and without blinking an eye said, "Captain, I promise never to come up there and try to run that bridge if you'll leave me alone and let me spot the flight deck."

Jocko stared at him as if to blow his stack, then a sly grin broke across his face, and he said, "I promise."

Both Hank and Joe wanted to explode with laughter but did not dare even to smile. Warren knew his stuff and had stood up to Jocko, who many times thereafter boasted, "Hank Warren is the best deck-spotter in the whole damned fleet!" Never again did Clark try to run the flight deck.

Joe Tucker now found a use for the two small tractors or "mules" he had purloined from the dock at Norfolk. He and his officers—11 of 13 of whom were mustangs like himself—had them rigged with tow bars to pull the planes and respot the deck. This not only greatly speeded up the process but conserved the energy of the airedales. But they needed more of them.

Another frustration was the slow rearming of planes with bombs and torpedoes brought up by elevators from magazines deep within the ship. Jimmy Flatley solved that problem by having the energetic Lieutenant (jg) James T. Bryan, a Yale man with the air ordnance gang, replace the incumbent arming boss by having the latter transferred to the new *Intrepid.*

And the speed and efficient recovery of returning planes was enhanced by "Crash Two," Red Volz's assistant landing signal officer Lieutenant (jg) Richard W. "Dog" Tripp. The latter won bets with the movie cameramen by accurately calling out which of the 12 arresting wires—six to nine—each plane hook would grab when he gave it "the cut" to cut off the engine and drop to the deck. (Grabbing #1 to #5 required too much time to taxi forward, #10 to #12 meant piling up in the wire crash barrier and valuable time lost being removed from it.)

A droll fellow, Dick Tripp did not always look around to watch the plane touch down. Instead, he would just look between his legs at it. Amid the general laughter, Jocko Clark would mutter, "Goddamm, that's not a good attitude." But he never interfered.

The many headaches of air operations fell directly on Commander Dozier, who never sought help, rejected any proffered him, never stood up to the skipper, and remained morose. Fellow officers called him "Hilarious Henry" behind his back. Late in 1944, while serving on staff duty aboard the *Ticonderoga*, Dozier would be lost overboard one night. Some *Yorktown*ers surmised that he had been pushed. Shipmates guessed he had lost his footing climbing an exposed ladder on the darkened carrier. (Vice Admiral Hugh H. Goodwin to author, 21 November 1965) Or could it have been a suicide? In any case, it was a sad fate.

All ship and air operations on the *Yorktown* were contingent on accurate weather forecasting—the responsibility of the aerologist or "weatherguesser," Lieutenant James J. Vonk. A ruddy Dutchman in ancestry, appearance, and uncanny skill, he held a master's degree in meteorology from Columbia. Clark, who remembered Vonk as "a very positive guy," appreciated his professional skill in judging Trinidad's tropical weather. Whenever a day dawned overcast he would bellow, "Get Vonk up here!"

One such morning in the Gulf of Paria a dark cloud led the worried skipper to summon Vonk to the bridge. "It'll clear up," announced Vonk, who then added, "Goddammit, it's *got* to clear up!" And it did, as usual.

A reporter once described Clark as "a fighting, shouting extrovert who yells at his officers in a rasping voice and expects them to yell back at him." (Alexander, "Carrier Revolution," 48) Vonk, however, was one of the very few who dared do so. After many a heated discussion with Jocko, Vonk decided to beat him to the punch. He climbed the ladders from his office to the bridge, where he saw Clark standing out on its wing. He burst into the enclosed bridge area and blurted loud enough for Clark to hear, "Where the hell is the Captain?!" That calmed down Clark, who appreciated and respected Vonk's forcefulness and expertise. (Conversations with Clark and Vonk)

At reveille one day, 0400, a particularly menacing sky greeted Clark, Vonk, George Earnshaw, and others on the bridge. Jocko remarked, "What's your prognostication, Mr. Aerologist?"

"Captain," intoned the deep-voiced weatherguesser, "anybody who would send a plane off the ship today is just fucking fate!"

*"What?"*

"Fucking fate!"

Jocko and the others roared with laughter. In fact, the skipper rarely knew when Vonk was putting him on. Often when the two were looking out to sea, Jocko would ask for an instant forecast. Vonk would lick his index finger, hold it up as a simulated weather vane, and with a perfectly straight face predict the weather. (Conversation with Bob Reynolds) Jocko innocently bought it—and many years later declared, "He *never* missed!"

Indeed, Red Sharp (eventually an admiral) remarked that Vonk "had the best nose for weather than anyone I have *ever* seen! He was even better than [the fleet's] Weather Central in the Pacific." These skills led to Vonk's eventually becoming aerologist for the entire Fast Carrier Task Force.

Every twilight, morning and evening, Vonk's men launched weather balloons to obtain data. These gave off good reflections of sunlight, so navigator Anderson occasionally tested his skills by trying to navigate the ship under them. And occasionally Stroke Blackwell's gunners fired at the balloons; if they could pop such a tiny, jerking target they would certainly be able to knock a plane out of the sky.

Most of the shooting off Trinidad, however, was aimed at target sleeves (the sock) towed by Air Group Five planes. The gunners had trouble hitting them, much less the tiny weather balloons. Clark was in a hurry, but he did not expect perfection (he often remarked to intimates, "There was only one man throughout history who was perfect, and they crucified Him"). Jocko's solution was to shoot down not just the towed target but the tow wire as well. The new antiaircraft proximity shell detonated close enough to an enemy plane to destroy it.

Stroke Blackwell countered that his gunners should only shoot holes in the sock so that he could count them. "Shoot *down* the goddammed sock!" snapped Jocko, and when they did everyone cheered as the whole apparatus plummeted into the sea.

But when they missed or took too long, Clark summoned Blackwell to the bridge and took him into his sea cabin—where no one could hear him. Then Jocko chewed him out so loudly that everyone nearby heard it anyway. A tall gentlemanly Virginian, Blackwell simply took it. But when the gunners began to improve, he cut off one of Clark's tirades: "I don't have to take this, and I'm not *going* to!" And Jocko stopped, for he actually did respect his gun boss.

The senior medical and dental officers were old Navy men who preferred battleship to carrier duty. Both proved so mediocre that their well-skilled assistants—directly commissioned from civilian life—soon took charge. Surgeon Raymond F. Gard was a 1927 product of the University of Kansas

Medical School. Frank J. Losey, a 1942 graduate of the University of Southern California School of Dentistry, had worked his way through school by leading a dance band and playing trombone. Waller assigned him collateral duty as ship's entertainment officer.

Jocko Clark, apart from his light diet and goat's milk, generally left the Medical Department alone—except for a standing order that all hands must brush their teeth twice a day. The dental office was open daily for checkups. If any sailor had cavities due to neglect, he was put on report and made to appear before captain's mast with resulting loss of liberty or pay. Jocko wanted no time or efficiency wasted on dental problems.

On 27 May, with his ship clean from seamen's teeth to main engines, Clark showed it off to Felix Stump, skipper of the new *Lexington* anchored nearby. Next day, noted Dr. Gard, "Shortwave radio from Germany says the *Yorktown* was sunk. That has been the topic of amusement today, with a few Bronx cheers for Hitler." Jocko began to invite several officers to join him for dinner, including Gard on the 30th: "A good dinner and splendid conversation."

> Busy, busy, busy. . . . The captain of this ship certainly doesn't belong to the union and he never heard of an eight-hour day. You should hear some of the men gripe, but you know I never had an eight-hour day either—so pour it on, Cap'n. (Gard letter to wife, 2 June 1943)

Air Group Five operated out of two Trinidad airfields, where pilots and aircrews were billeted when they were not practicing group tactics. The F6F fighters escorted the SB2C bombers dropping live 500-pound and 1,000-pound bombs at a target sled towed astern the *Yorktown*, and the TBF torpeckers dropped practice "fish" at the destroyers. The planes landed aboard the ship on only three of the 19 days spent in the Gulf of Paria. In addition, the ship's catapults were tested—to be used only when the flight deck had insufficient wind for powered takeoffs. Several fighters and one TBF were "shot" off two flight deck "cats," including one of both type planes from the athwartship cat in the hangar—the only time it was ever used.

Jocko arranged shore parties so that all hands could swim, have beach parties, and watch the *Yorktown* softball team win two out of three games against a destroyer team. George Earnshaw was the manager and the pitcher was TBF pilot Joe Kristufek (a prewar tennis star at Pitt, '40). These were pleasant diversions over two weeks, with yet a third week anticipated there before the ship headed for Panama and the Pacific war.

It was not to be, due to the malfunctioning divebombers. The powerful Curtiss SB2C Helldiver still suffered from many of the weaknesses Clark

The new *Yorktown* backs down—stern first (backwards)—in order to land planes over the bow during the shakedown cruise in Trinidad's Gulf of Paria, May–June 1943. A TBF Avenger torpecker touches down. *U.S. Navy photo*

had reported while an inspector at the Curtiss factory in 1940. Crackups ashore and afloat led to pilot nicknames for it—"ensign exterminator" and "the Beast." "Hydraulic nightmares," they had engines that stalled, faulty wing-locking mechanisms, landing gear that collapsed on touchdown, and tail hooks that, instead of retracting into the wheel well after takeoff, ripped through the fuselage and fell out—so often that the destroyers below them claimed the bombers were shooting tail hooks at them!

The onboard Curtiss engineers and Joe Tucker's mechs worked feverishly using the spare parts sent by the company. But 17 of the 36 bombers could not be repaired, and Tucker grounded them. They would have to be rebuilt, which the *Yorktown* was not equipped to do.

On 12 June six congressmen came aboard to witness flight operations. Air officer Dozier called Tucker on one of the ship's 1,100 telephones: "I want a maximum launch."

"We can't do it," replied Tucker, incredulous at Dozier's naïveté. "We can only launch about half of our SB2Cs."

"Why?" asked Dozier.

"I've got the others grounded."

"Will they fly?"

"Yes, they'll fly, but they're just as likely to crash on landing and end up in the barrier."

"I *order* you to fly them."

"Fine," replied Joe, "but I'd like to have an AVO [avoid verbal orders]. I'd like to have that in writing."

Dozier was furious but agreed, "I'll send it down."

The 32 Beasts were launched in the morning and, sure enough, when they landed the tail hooks pulled out of 17 planes, which piled into the wire crash barrier. The recovery seemed to take forever as the airedales labored to disengage the planes, strike them below on the elevators, and degas them.

Tucker said his officers "were ready to kill me" because their crews would have to stay up all that night repairing the planes—work aggravated by the usual turning off of the hangar bay lights as an antisub precaution.

By the time Tucker got down to the wardroom for a late lunch it was 1500, and he was boiling mad. Just then, ever-smiling Bob Reynolds appeared for a snack and asked what was wrong.

"I don't know why that goddammed fool ordered those planes flown over my order to ground 'em. As far as I'm concerned they can take this job and stick it! It's stupid, and I don't wanna be on this ship!"

"Joe," said the captain's troubleshooter, "how long have you known Jocko?"

"Well, since about 1930."

"Jocko handpicked you for this job," Reynolds pointed out. "He's got a lot of confidence in you. I've heard him say so. I've also heard him tell you that if you ever ran into a situation that he should know about, you ought to come out and tell him, regardless of who is between you."

"Bob," career man Tucker explained, "it's just that having grown up in military schools and then in the service, it's absolutely against my grain to bypass the right channels."

"This is one of those times when it's important enough," Reynolds countered. "These aircraft are not going to fly. They're going to keep us from going to the Pacific on schedule. If, in your analysis of the situation, you believe something ought to be done with these planes, then do it."

Tucker thought a few minutes and then made a beeline for the bridge. When he got there, he could hear Clark in his sea cabin roaring—livid at something. But so was Joe Tucker. "I'm Lieutenant Tucker," he told the orderly, "I'd like to see the captain."

"Joe!" exclaimed Jocko, "what in *the hell* is wrong? Come on in. Sit down."

He did and let it out straight: "I don't know what damned fool ordered those planes flown over my 'ground.' It's the most stupid thing I ever had. And, really, if that's all the ship thinks of me, maybe you'd better get rid of me and get another officer."

"Simmer down, Joe, simmer down. Tell me all about it." So he did. But Jocko shrugged his shoulders, "Well, Joe, the SB2C is the divebomber built for the new carrier program. If it doesn't work, we're in a helluva mess."

"We're in a helluva mess then," said Tucker, "because it's not gonna work until there are 200 or so modifications made that are all essential. It is not ready to go out there on carriers. The best thing in the world that could be done would be to return it to Curtiss-Wright and make them prove it before we put it on the new carriers."

Jocko eyed him, "If you were me, what would you do?"

Tucker thought a moment and figured he'd crossed all his bridges; he was doomed. "Well, if I was you, captain, I would sit right down and write a letter to BuAer and tell them—I wouldn't ask them; I'd *tell* them—to tell Curtiss-Wright to come and get their damned airplanes. And, I'd turn this ship right around and head back to Trinidad, and I'd put those SB2Cs ashore and *leave* 'em there!"

"What would you use in their place?"

"We're a lot better off with SBDs that'll fly than we are with SB2Cs that won't!"

Clark sat there, thought a few minutes, and said firmly, "You know, I agree with you." Then he yelled out the door, "Tell Commander Dozier to come up here! Andy, come in here!"

George Anderson stuck his head in first, and Jocko told him, "Set a course for Trinidad."

"What?!"

"Set a course for Trinidad. Cease operations!"

"Yes, sir!"

Then Dozier came in. He was staggered at the sight of Tucker sitting there. "Sit down here with Lieutenant Tucker," Clark ordered, "and compose a message to BuAer telling them to tell the Curtiss-Wright people to come get their SB2Cs. We're puttin' them ashore at Trinidad. They're not ready for carrier operations."

When both men went into the adjacent chart room to compose the message, Dozier muttered angrily, "How dare you go to the captain!"

"It's a long story," said Joe. "I'd be delighted to tell you about it. But let's get this done." Dozier could see that Tucker was visibly miffed, and he agreed. So while Tucker dictated the message, Dozier feebly wrote it down.

By the end of the day, the ship had anchored off Trinidad, and all night long the flight deck crews wore themselves ragged hoisting the derelict Beasts off onto barges, trying not to damage them further in the rolling waters. The undamaged ones stayed on the ship. While the crew worked, Dozier came back at Tucker, "What in hell did you mean by going to the captain over my head?"

> Commander, I didn't mean no disrespect for you, but I tried to tell you these aircraft don't work. You would not listen. The captain says the carrier depends on these aircraft, and they're just not worth it. Somebody had to take the chance. I've taken it. If you want to give me a black mark on my fitness report or put me ashore you can. I want to win the war. And I don't want to be killed!

Dozier backed off completely and never bothered Tucker again. Come dawn, four-engine flying boats landed nearby carrying personnel from the Curtiss-Wright factory. When they came on board, they told Captain Clark they'd repair their planes and put them back on the ship. "Absolutely not!" Jocko responded, and by mid-afternoon he had weighed anchor for Norfolk.

As for Hank Dozier—already selected for promotion to the full rank of commander—he continued his own peculiar modus operandi. He made out the Air Department's Plan of the Day (each department had its own) but would not show it to anyone. He kept it and all pertinent dispatches under the engineer's cap he wore so that no one else knew in advance what was to be done, much less why.

So when Jocko bellowed, "Where's the Plan of the Day?" Dozier would pull it out of his hat and read it aloud, detailing launch sequences and numbers of each plane type, their armament, and so forth. Then Jocko would take a look at it and toss it aside with a blast: "To hell with it! Launch the Fighters! Launch the Bombers!"

He just wanted a quick launch, which left others confused, even any admiral who might be on board. On an actual combat strike day the latter sometimes sent a messenger up to the ship's bridge from the flag bridge (one level below) to inquire exactly what was going on. Jocko would bellow, "I'm fightin' the Japs! And we're the first to launch!" (Conversation with Cooper Bright)

Three destroyers joined the *Yorktown* as it departed Trinidad on 13 June, heading north for Norfolk. Teams of fighters and torpeckers conducted the antisub patrols in place of the SB2Cs, though a few still on board did fly. When the ship turned into a southerly wind to recover them, one Helldiver pilot took two wave-offs before landing. An irate Clark called the pilot to the bridge: "Here I am trying to go to Norfolk, and you're taking me further south!" (Conversation with the pilot, Les Rector)

The morning of the 15th chief engineer McNally put the new carrier through a six-hour test run. From the cruising speed of 21 knots at 0630 Clark revved the ship up to the maximum designed speed of 33 knots by 0734. When he commenced a full-power run at 0800, the ship shuddered as it reached 34.9 knots—a record for any carrier. And he held this "flank speed" for four hours, leaving far behind his escorting tin cans—and any possible lurking U-boat. Resuming normal speed, the *Yorktown* registered its 1,000th landing—a Hellcat.

After refueling one of its escorting cans next day, the ship launched its F6Fs and TBFs to land ashore at Norfolk just as it ran smack into a thick fog while approaching the Chesapeake Bay. Navigator Anderson sweated over his charts, unable even to find the entrance buoy, and had to turn the ship around. Clark, who never yelled at Anderson, because of his prominence in the aviation community, did this time. "Where in hell is the ship?" he demanded of Andy in the chart room. Andy wasn't sure—maybe somewhere south of Norfolk.

The ship cruised around in the soup for three hours and finally sent off a plane to assist. When it landed ashore, the pilot radioed the *Yorktown* that it was parallel with Baltimore—far to the north! The radio screamed commands from the beach to head in. Anderson—his skills now in question—turned the ship south. All hands topside strained to spot Buoy No. One marking the outer channel.

Suddenly, from the bridge, a sailor named Moody hollered out, "There she is!" Jocko, greatly relieved, turned to Moody, "What's your rate, son?"

"Quartermaster First, sir."

"Now you're a chief!"

Clark had made the first of many spot promotions for excellence. Six VT-5 torpeckers took off from NAS Norfolk to fly antisub patrol for their carrier, relieved in the afternoon by a Navy nonrigid blimp that covered its entrance into Hampton Roads.

As soon as the ship docked at the Norfolk Navy Yard, Henry Hathaway and his *Wing and a Prayer* cameramen left to return to Hollywood. He showed his gratitude to his hosts by donating radios to the three wardrooms (officers, warrant officers, and chief petty officers) and $2,500 to Jimmy

Flatley to buy liquor for the air group. "Godammit!" roared Jocko. "The *ship* provided the services." So he confiscated the money and had the Medical Department purchase 2,000 cases of beer and 200 of whiskey in Norfolk. The stuff was loaded into the ship's double bottom, earmarked for a future beer bust on a Pacific island.

Hathaway thereupon gave another $2,500 to the flyboys without Clark's knowledge. Before departing for a few days of their unplanned leaves, the pilots entrusted the money to Herman Rosenblatt, the ACIO heading for leave in New York. There he purchased 300 bottles of Four Roses. Each pilot filled his metal cruise box with them for consumption on board, on the sly. These World War II pilots had no use for the old edict banning shipboard booze that Jocko as a midshipman had lamented back in 1914.

Also, several ingenious swabs—notably in the galley—eventually set up well-hidden stills to make their own stuff. Worst of all, the aerial torpedoes could be tapped for raw alcohol—potentially lethal though it was. The U.S. Navy may have been officially "dry," but the new *Yorktown* was going to sea "loaded." Sadly for Jocko, his ulcer diet kept him a teetotaler.

The major changes during this unplanned return to Norfolk were to the air group. The Navy (likely with Admiral King's tacit approval) had so immediately accepted Clark's initiative to unload his SB2Cs and return to Norfolk that 36 brand-new Douglas SBD-5 Dauntless divebombers were waiting for him there. Though slightly slower than the 2Cs, and lacking folding wings, the SBDs had proved their worth sinking the four Japanese carriers at Midway and more ships in other actions. Also, all the *Yorktown's* F6F fighters had their inferior self-sealing gas tanks replaced.

As for the ship, Clark had learned of a new plastic coating for the bottom of the hull. Sprayed on hot, it extended from one year to two the need for the hull to be scraped of marine organisms in dry dock. Jocko *had* to have it for the *Yorktown*, even though not scheduled for it, nor for navy yard workers to scrape off the paint so laboriously applied earlier by the crew. *And*, the ship had to depart for the war zone within two weeks. BuShips rejected his request for the spray. So Jim Campbell flew the skipper to Washington in an SNJ on 19 June where BuShips told him that the navy yard could not spare the manpower to scrape down the hull. And it would take too many days, further delaying the ship's deployment. Jocko: "Don't worry about that. My crew will do it—and in three days." BuShips officers knew that to resist him any further was futile. They agreed—as usual.

Waiting at Anacostia on the 21st to return to Norfolk, Jocko and pilot Campbell discovered over coffee a mutual love of quail hunting. Campbell sat in awe as the captain spun quail yarns, like the time Clark had a quail dog so good that it had once pointed to a covey of quail in an old stump hole, then covered it with his front paws and let the birds out one at a time! (The Japanese were in for trouble with *this* hunter!)

Back at Norfolk, Clark told George Anderson (acting exec while Waller was on leave) his plans for the plastic spray, and Andy appointed Red Sharp to oversee the job. On 23 June the *Yorktown* went into dry dock as Jocko announced, "Clear the bottom, 'cause in two weeks I'm gonna leave to hit the Japs!" They did it in the three days he promised BuShips. But then the rains came, soaking the hull, which required another full week for drying before the coating could be sprayed on.

"To hell with the rain!" roared Jocko. "Put on the stuff!" The shipyard performed the task, only to watch the coating peel off. Clark's gamble had failed, and the dry dock had to be reflooded, leaving the ship without coating *or* paint. Barnacles and algae began to adhere to the hull, slowing down the ship over the ensuing year. The lower hull looked like a forest of marine growth when dry-docked again 14 months later.

Some officers and crewmen were granted leaves of absence during the scraping episode. A divorced Joe Tucker was reluctant to propose to a Navy nurse named Dawson he had fallen for at Norman, Oklahoma, and who had just arrived at Norfolk. When the ship was being moved into dry dock Joe beat Bob Reynolds (as usual) in several games of acey-deucy (a form of backgammon) in the wardroom. Suddenly Reynolds challenged Tucker to three out of five games to propose to the lady on Joe's behalf. Bob beat him in three straight, telephoned Dawson, who accepted, and she and Tucker were married in a brief ceremony, with Reynolds as best man. A nurse who married was immediately discharged, and Dawson was put in hack by the hospital commander, a captain.

A desperate Tucker appealed to Jocko, who telephoned the naval district commander, a rear admiral—Clark "did this kind of thing for everybody." Upon Dawson's immediate release, Jocko granted four-day passes for the wedding party: Joe, Bob, Diamond Jim Brady, and mess officer Lee Foster. They and departing *Yorktown*er Marshall Field and his wife all spent the honeymoon together at Virginia Beach!

Most officers and sailors got only two days leave, except that Marine orderly Bob Bender "heard Captain Clark tell Commander Waller that anyone calling or telegraphing for an extra day—even if they said their grandmother broke a toe—give it to them." So he too managed to get an extra day.

Sailor Tony Yankovich was granted three days as well, except that he decided to visit his wife and young son in Kansas—some 3,000 miles round-trip by rail! Incredibly, he made it there and was delayed from returning only a day by floodwaters and so informed the ship by telegram. So

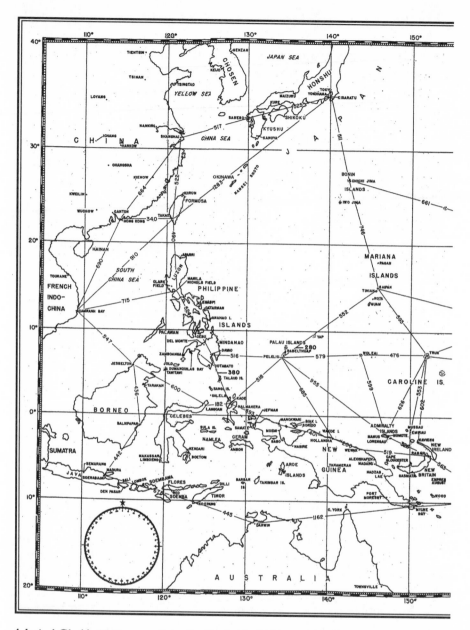

Admiral Clark's 1944 map of the Pacific (with Okinawa added). *J. J. Clark*

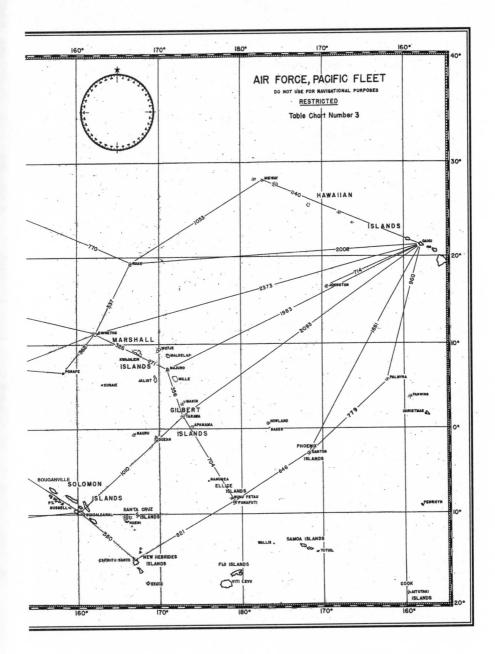

when Yankovich—a thin individual without any fat—arrived back on board he had to go to captain's mast:

> We were lined up on the hangar deck, and Jock and the executive officer was [sic] standing there, and Jock said he would make it easy on us because we did a wonderful job. The fire bell rang, and everybody ran for his G.Q. [General Quarters] Station, and it was a false alarm.
>
> When we lined up again, why, Jocko was mad, and he asked me where I'd been, and I told him, and he said why didn't I send a telegram, and I said I did, sir. And he asked the exec, where is the telegram, and he said he didn't receive one, and Jocko said, "three days bread and water." So there I was in the brig. When I got out I pushed on my stomach and could feel my backbone. I always was a heavy eater, and three days, that was rough.

Over the first three days of July Clark put the ship through its paces up and down the Chesapeake Bay. The bomber pilots qualified in carrier landings in their new SBDs, and Stroke Blackwell's best three 5-inch gun turrets repeated their earlier performance of shooting up target sleeves to earn a second battle efficiency award. Each of these gun crews now painted a hash mark over the "E" on the turret—denoting prizes for two gunnery years, the new year having begun on 1 July. This was a remarkable feat for a ship in commission less than three months.

Jocko Clark could hardly wait to get to the Pacific; he had lost valuable time. Air Group Five's planes were hoisted aboard the next two days, and the *Yorktown* pulled away from the dock at noon on 6 July 1943. Then— boom!—all engines stopped, the anchors ran out. A malfunction in one of the ship's four propeller shafts necessitated minor repair. Poor Jocko's ulcers. At 1430 anchors were hoisted, and the ship headed for the war—finally.

With Cherokee tenacity, an unorthodox naval leader had begun to mold a crew of neophytes and a handful of regulars into a team ready and able to "fight the Japs" as he so often put it. Indeed, the new *Yorktown*, as Coop Bright recalled, was manned by "a civilian navy run by a sea dog." Joe Tucker, long after completing his military career as a colonel in the U.S. Air Force, had a loftier appraisal: "I've had three heroes in my life—Christ, Buddha, and Jocko!"

# ELEVEN

# The Pacesetting New *Yorktown*, 1943

### "J. J. C. Takes the *Y* to Sea"

There were cynics who said he'd regret it,
They pulled out their dough and they bet it,
    He'd bit off, they knew
    Much more than he'd chew,
But he not only chewed it, he et it.

Don't none of you sailors forget it,
His vessel was not a corvette; it
    Was a flat-top enormous,
    And he'd often inform us,
'Twas our duty to aid and abet it.

He'd worry and sweat and coquette it,
At times he would coax it and pet it,
    When progress was slow,
    He'd scream and he'd blow,
He'd curse it and damn near upset it.

To all of the wise guys who said it,
Who said he would live to regret it,
    He paid them no heed,
    Just told them that he'd
A schedule to meet—AND HE MET IT!

—Anonymous *Yorktown* sailor

Jocko Clark sped the *Yorktown* and three escorting destroyers south from the Chesapeake Bay on 6 July 1943 for a three-day run to the Caribbean. They zigzagged to frustrate the aim of any of Hitler's ubiquitous submarines. Toward nightfall next day antisub patrols of *Yorktown*'s dive- and torpedo-bombers spotted a U-boat but did not attack it. On the 8th the ship launched five patrols while hurrying through the Windward Passage between Cuba and Hispaniola at 30 knots, even as a Navy patrol boat attacked but missed a U-boat in the area.

At twilight the ship prepared to recover its last patrol—12 TBFs—when escorting destroyer *Terry* signaled, "Torpedo on port side!" Jocko grabbed the wheel from the helmsman and gave it a hard right rudder (to starboard) in a 100-degree pivot to "comb" the reported "fish." The ship listed sharply, with dinner dishes sliding off tables where the crew was eating. No one actually saw a torpedo, and in any case none hit.

The three tin cans began dropping depth charges, and an excited Jocko dispatched his orderly with instructions for Chaplain Alexander. The Marine found the "padre" leaving the wardroom, snapped to attention, and reported, "Sir, the captain respectfully requests the chaplain to engage in prayer for the safety of his men and ship."

As darkness fell, tiny subchasers converged on the *Yorktown*, one nearly colliding with the bow, another impudently blinking out, "What is your course?" The bridge ignored it, unaware that these little guys had been pursuing one particular sub, the *U-579*, for seven long hours. The U-boat survived another two weeks before a Navy seaplane sank it in almost the same area.

The ship arrived at Colón the morning of the 10th. While preparing to enter the Panama Canal, Clark gave half the crew—including himself and Waller—a seven-hour liberty in town. He also issued special instructions to two officers from the Air Department—Lieutenant Commander E. E. Stebbins and Lieutenant Cooper Bright. Jocko was fed up with the feedback and breakdowns of the portable microphone system into which he had to scream while addressing the crew on the flight deck. He told the two men to go to a nightclub: "Buy the equipment that they use for comedians on the dance floor. It *has* to work; it's their bread and butter." Coop and Steb bought it right off the floor, and sure enough it worked every time Jocko bellowed into it.

By midnight all hands were back on board. Many, hopelessly drunk and battered, preferred sleeping it off on the flight deck on this hot moonlit night. Suddenly, one very inebriated airedale let out a whoop, dashed across the deck, and went over the side! Dick Tripp, standing his first Junior OOD watch at the after gangway, sounded the General Quarters alarm—sending all hands to their battle stations.

In the pandemonium, Jocko—"looking wild-eyed" to Tripp—staggered down to the hangar in his one-piece knee-length nightshirt and bare feet. "What the hell's going on?! Who's the stupid sonofabitch who pushed the button?" Tripp turned it off, and the drunken kid, planepusher Don Aitkenhead—one of a gang of roughnecks—swam to the dock unhurt, singing away until he was retrieved and brought to the captain.

Seeing Aitkenhead's drunken state, Clark gave him coffee and told him to hit the sack and sleep it off. This kind of humanity was what led John Montgomery to regard Jocko as "a sweetheart" and one of Aitkenhead's pugilistic pals, Charlie White, to revere him as "a wonderful man. No bullshit!"

Next morning Clark was in "great humor, very excited to be entering the Pacific," recalled George Anderson, who was apprehensive, however, because of tales of the *Suwannee*'s anxious transit. Jocko cleared the bridge of all unnecessary personnel, with Andy as OOD and the best quartermaster at the helm for the transit. The ship entered Gatun Locks, and Dwight Long's cameramen began to film the tight squeeze, only to be challenged by an Army sentry who "put a slug" into his rifle and ordered them to stop.

Waller and Jimmy Flatley rushed down to explain, but the soldier had orders that no one was to photograph the locks. Finally, the man's colonel was summoned, as was Jocko—and the cameras finally rolled.

During the tight transit, Clark—"a very different type of captain"—shouted and screamed at the crew. (Anderson transcript #3, 115) With only one foot leeway between the hull and the sides of the lock, the men utilized ropes and lines instead of bumpers to minimize the scraping. This also concerned Raöul Waller, who ran from one side of the flight deck to the other "like a fussy old maid about her cat." The Assistant First Lieutenant Rick Lambart did the same in the open hangar, except that he pushed against the wall of one side of the locks and then the other, calling for help: "Come here! Sonofabitch. Everybody push her off!" No one obeyed; they just stood there laughing.

At noon the *Yorktown* dropped anchor in Gatun Lake, waiting for the battleship *Nevada* to come through Culebra Cut from the other direction. Clark "dressed ship"—all hands in white uniforms to honor the *Nevada*, just back from the recapture of Attu in the Aleutian Islands. Each crew cheered the other, including naked swabbies bathing under the spray of fire hoses on the battlewagon's fantail and afterdeck. These Pearl Harbor veterans deserved it, in the opinion of the green *Yorktown*ers.

The *Yorktown* passed through Culebra Cut, then after dark through the Mira Flores Locks, anchoring at Panama City too late for liberty ashore—just as well, given the wild night at Colón. In all this, Jocko caught sight of something jumping around on the flight deck and yelled down, "Whoever's got that goddammed monkey, bring him up here!" The two culprits then confessed they had swiped it from the commodore commanding at Colón. The monkey was promptly put ashore.

So was Joe Tucker, in the jeep "liberated" at Norfolk. Clark ordered him to locate expected spare parts for the F6F fighters—but he found none. The ship radioed BuAer, which replied that the parts had been sent on to San Francisco, *Yorktown's* next port of call. Refueling at Balboa on the 12th, the ship stood out to sea only to receive orders to head directly to Hawaii—with assurances the spare parts would be sent there. The change suited Jocko, still in a hurry to beat the *Essex*—already at Pearl—into battle.

Jocko's departure from the Atlantic led to a final fitness report covering the shakedown cruise "and getting the ship ready for war" (16 April to 10 July 1943) by Rear Admiral P. L. N. Bellinger, the Navy's air force commander in the Atlantic.

> Largely due to his outstanding qualities of perseverance, initiative and industry, the ship completed *on schedule* a very strenuous training program and fitting-out period. Captain Clark is a forceful and aggressive commanding officer and it is expected that the ship he commands will distinguish herself in battle. Captain Clark is considered qualified for flag rank. (Emphasis in original)

No higher vote of confidence could be given any warship captain.

For 13 days and 5,000 nautical miles Clark concentrated on honing the skills of the 91-plane Air Group Five (37 F6F, 36 SBD, 18 TBF). Its popular skipper, Commander Jimmy Flatley, who flew an F6, inspired his flyers as a father figure, devout Catholic, and peerless aerial tactician. He sometimes clashed with Jocko over air operations, though such differences never threatened their deep mutual respect and friendship.

Fighting Five (VF-5), about to introduce the Hellcat into combat, was led by dynamic Lieutenant Commander Charles L. Crommelin, one of five brothers, all Academy grads, four of them flyers. Bombing Five (VB-5), led by Lieutenant Commander Robert M. Milner, suffered serious clashes of personalities after it was created by the merger of two squadrons. The smaller Torpedo Five (VT-5) was led by taciturn Lieutenant Commander Richard Upson, a fearless pilot and man of few words.

Key to the success of the flyers was their effective working relationship with ship's Air Department, headed by Hank Dozier and his assistant Red Sharp. The principal divisions were Operations (V-1), especially the flight deck; Aircraft Maintenance (V-2); and Air Operations (V-3), including

Radar Plot and Air Combat Intelligence (ACI). Strengths and weaknesses, already evident in each, became pronounced as battle neared, stretching whatever patience Clark had with those who failed to meet his exacting standards.

Wizened mustang Lieutenant Pappy Harshman ran V-1. At 41 but looking twice that, he had an efficient flight deck thanks largely to Hank Warren. Clark kept Pappy running up and down the flight deck, in spite of his age, wearing him out. Thankfully, Jocko would soon be able to move him up to a less physically demanding job and let another, but younger, seasoned mustang take it over—Lieutenant Virgil Irwin.

The head maintenance (V-2) officer, Lieutenant Commander Curtiss C. Watts, gained his Navy position based on his executive experience with the Black and Decker machine tool company. Though an amicable fellow, he had infuriated his boss Dozier by obtaining needed airplane parts on weekend visits directly from industry instead of going through channels. When the parts would arrive within two or three days, Dozier refused to sign for them. "You don't have to," explained Watts, "it's a gift to the United States Navy from [X company]." (Conversation with Cooper Bright)

But Jimmy Flatley also had some misgivings about Watts. He did not seem to be efficiently organizing spare airplane parts so that damaged planes could be expeditiously repaired. So during the transit of the Canal Flatley began sounding out Jocko's "man" Bob Reynolds about his prewar experiences running a trucking firm. Reynolds had no idea that Flatley was mulling over the very unorthodox prospect that he, a mere ensign, might replace Lieutenant Commander Watts.

Air Operations (V-3)—located at Air Plot in the island structure—kept the pilots informed in their ready rooms via ticker tape enlarged on a screen. It was run by Lieutenant Commander Stebbins, a non-Academy SBD pilot who had scored a direct hit on a Japanese cruiser and shot down two planes near the Santa Cruz Islands the previous October. Unable to land on his own carrier, the sunken *Hornet*, he landed on another one.

Lieutenant Cooper Bright assisted Stebbins. A Rutgers man ('31), this former business, newspaper, and real estate executive had a great flair for management—and an unmatched sense of humor. He was nicknamed "Skinhead" for his baldpate. Bright and Stebbins set up such superior ready-room data-display boards that these were adopted for all carriers.

Bright also supervised the ACI unit, officially run by smart, gentlemanly Lieutenant James A. Sutton, a Philadelphia lawyer and combat veteran. Sutton endured—being unable to counter—the brash arrogance of his brilliant assistant, Lieutenant Herman Rosenblatt, one of Jocko's pet officers, who had graduated second in his class at ACIO school. "Jim, you're my senior ACI officer," Coop counseled. "You stand Rosenblatt down! Close that big mouth of his. You're the boss. Stop him from wandering all over the ship and taking command!"

But the mild Quaker just "let Herman do more work than he wants," Coop recalled, while Sutton performed the few tasks Rosenblatt would not. Coop did not fault Sutton, because nobody but the captain seemed to get along with the man. Indeed, Jocko offered to make Rosenblatt senior ACIO, but the latter demurred—to his credit. Either way, Bright was still Rosenblatt's boss and regarded him as an SOB who tried to run everything by devious methods. So Coop stayed on the offensive with Rosenblatt, becoming a "constant irritant" to him, Stebbins remembered. Loyal only to Jocko, Rosenblatt "was never well liked by anyone," in the words of Waller, who did not trust him and—in deference to Clark—had to tolerate his outspokenness and insistence on perfection.

Clark kept a constant watch on Air Operations by bursting into Air Plot, talking to people, and chewing them out. One time when he appeared, Bright grabbed the nearest telephone and pretended to be talking to someone, whereupon the captain left him alone. When the other officers there caught on, they vied for the other two phones, leaving Stebbins to catch all of Jocko's wrath. After a half-dozen times Steb finally caught on and ordered Coop to let him pick up their receiver. Grabasser Bright just laughed and kept doing it.

Jocko—and therefore Stebbins and Bright—had a major problem with Radar Plot. Its major function was "fighter direction." Two air-search radars detected enemy planes out to 80 miles; IFF (identification, friend or foe) indicators determined which planes were foes ("bogeys," "bandits"); and fighter director officers (FDOs) "vectored" the ship's Hellcats by radio to intercept and destroy them. Radar Plot also housed homing beacons for returning planes as well as two surface-search radars to detect enemy ships out to the 20-mile horizon.

As in so many other components of the *Yorktown*'s operation, new Radar Plot doctrine had to be developed by the ship and its sister carriers. And Jocko Clark—as in everything—wanted to excel in this critical activity, thereby setting the pace. Unfortunately, BuPers assigned two Reserve lieutenants—Henry F. Billingsley and Edward V. Milholland Jr.—who had proved so utterly inept at it during shakedown that Clark had stormed into Radar Plot demanding better data. When they had the temerity to make excuses, he flew into a rage.

A new Navy policy required that a qualified aviator be assigned to Radar Plot to provide flying expertise. This was veteran combat fighter pilot Lieutenant E. T. Stover (North Texas State '39)—nicknamed "Smokey" for

"Coop" and "Steb" in *Yorktown*'s Radar Plot, 1943. Lieutenant Commander Edgar E. Stebbins (right), air operations officer, plots the location of the ship's aircraft, while his assistant, Lieutenant Cooper B. Bright (his "skinhead" covered), communicates with the pilots. Under their innovative leadership, Radar Plot quickly evolved into the CIC (combat information center) on all the carriers. (Photo courtesy of the Bright family) *U.S. Navy photo*

comic strip character Smokey Stover. The real Smokey had flown Wildcats from Guadalcanal where he had been wingman of Joe Tucker's brother Charlie when the latter was shot down and killed. Stover had won a game of "chicken" against a Japanese seaplane-fighter over Guadalcanal when he destroyed it by slicing off one of its wings in a dogfight. A fragment of the wing with the painted Japanese "red meatball" had embedded in the wing of Smokey's F4F. He kept it in his stateroom on the *Yorktown* for roommate

Jim Vonk and others to admire. But Stover regarded himself as "merely excess impedimenta" in Radar Plot.

With little to do, Smokey occasionally assisted the air officer at Pri Fly (primary flying control) outside Radar Plot near the bridge. On one such day during shakedown, Stover wrote in his diary,

> [I] happened to be in the way when our dear Captain got mad over something. Told Mr. Dozier, "What's this fellow doing out here? Get him out of here! I don't like him!!" One of the greatest shocks I ever had to hear—the captain of the ship come out with a statement like that. At any rate I got out and haven't been back. (Diary entries of 4, 10 June 1943, in Stover with Reynolds, *Saga of Smokey Stover,* 90–91)

Clark demanded that BuPers send more expertise to improve Radar Plot. And two days after the ship's return to Norfolk from shakedown two lieutenants (jg) had reported aboard to assist the incumbents. Both had top credentials: Charles D. Ridgway III, one of the Navy's first FDOs, had served over a year on the *Saratoga;* Alexander Wilding Jr. had graduated as top man in the newest class of Norfolk's FDO school.

Ridgway, a Princeton-weaned scholar, and Wilding, a USC grad and minor league baseball player, decided to room together. Their first visit to Radar Plot so appalled them that they agreed to "shake it up" if necessary, working round the clock "to make the *Yorktown* the best Fighter Director ship in the fleet." (Wilding to author, early 1970s)

Equally worrisome was radar maintenance. Radar Plot's officers and enlisted men could do nothing if the radar equipment did not function properly. One day one of the sets malfunctioned, leading "Bill" Billingsley, unable to solve such problems, to seek the advice of the radar maintenance officer of the air group, Lieutenant George H. Klaus. The latter's task was to service the airborne radars on selected TBFs and F6Fs.

Soft-spoken and mechanically adept in nearly everything, Klaus was "such a fine person" in the words of Dr. Gard (in a letter home) that he had "taken care of his mother and a younger brother since he was 12, worked his way through school, college and finally M.I.T. in radio."

Before Klaus and his technicians could repair the faulty equipment, Clark discovered the radar unit had failed, thereby compromising air operations. Angry, he summoned George Klaus to the bridge. But Jimmy Flatley, Klaus's superior officer, was right behind Klaus as Jocko chewed him out.

"Captain," Flatley interrupted, "what are you bawling out my radar officer for?"

"He didn't report the radar was on the bum."

Klaus started to explain, but Jocko tore into him until Jimmy cut in again, "Captain, George is trying to tell you something, but you won't let him talk. Let's hear what he has to say."

"O.K."

Klaus: "Captain, I helped your radar officer write the letter to you that the radar was out of order and that it couldn't possibly work in the position it's in, and it would have to be relocated. That was written last week."

Clark: "Well, what did you do with the letter?"

"Sir, I forwarded the letter through the chain of command. We gave it to the Radar Plot officer, Lieutenant Billingsley."

So Jocko summoned Billingsley to the bridge and "tore into him," then turned to Klaus, "I want that goddammed radar fixed. I know you know how to do it. You're gonna do it!"

Klaus protested that he didn't want his men to do the work, since it meant taking the motor out of the radar unit, which was situated near the top of the smokestack on the island structure. The fumes would make them sick.

"I don't give a damn," roared Clark. "I want that radar fixed!"

"Aye, aye, sir."

And Klaus did the work of removing the unit himself. But his exposure to the stack gases landed him in sick bay for three days. During that time his technicians repaired the radar unit, which indeed had been damaged by those very fumes. Then Klaus put it back himself. But he told the captain, "The radar unit is working. It's in very fine shape, but it won't last long because the stack gases are going to burn it up again. It'll have to be relocated."

Jocko was impressed. "Well, lieutenant, you did a fine job. I'm real proud of you. I can't offer you much. Would you like a cigar or a cup of coffee?"

"No, thank you."

"I'll write the letter" to BuShips, said Clark, "and you check the technical language, and we'll get it relocated. Thank you very much." So impressed was the skipper in fact that he made Klaus senior officer in charge of all radar on the ship as well as on the planes.

Maintaining this sophisticated equipment that connected ship to planes was so continuous and demanding that one of Klaus's officers, Lieutenant (jg) Joseph O. Hachet, wrote to his family that he "should have drawn a battleship or cruiser instead of a carrier because this maintenance work keeps you hopping all the time."

The Klaus incident was another example of a man earning Jocko's respect—and his unfailing loyalty. But the reverse was also true: those who did not measure up had to go. That meant Billingsley and Milholland if Radar Plot was ever to become effective. Cooper Bright resolved that as soon as the ship reached Hawaii he would pay a visit to Captain Ralph Ofstie, Admiral Nimitz's staff air officer. This friend of Jocko's also happened to be the beau of Coop's widowed sister and cofounder of the WAVES (the wartime Navy Women's Reserve), Lieutenant Joy Bright Hancock. Coop would arrange to have Ofstie transfer the incumbent senior lieutenants of Radar Plot.

Among Clark's favorite officers was photographer Dwight Long because of the fabulous color movies he was making on board. In Jocko's eyes Long could do no wrong and thus deserved to be elevated to the position of ship's senior photographer. This required transferring the incumbent. Lieutenant Les Johnson, a kindly soul and excellent photographer in his own right, was shattered at the news, as Coop Bright could plainly see.

Eventually, while the *Yorktown* was in port, Bright went to the bridge to confront the captain, knowing that "Jocko had a big heart, if you could get to him." Explaining Johnson's despondency over his relief, Coop asked Clark to give him a glowing fitness report. "Get him up here!" demanded Clark. "When's he leaving?" "He's all packed now, ready to shove off." Jocko summoned Johnson to the bridge, extolled him for his fine performance and for helping out Long, and handed him an excellent fitness report. Johnson departed with tears in his eyes.

Discerning junior officers, especially at the conn, began to appreciate the fine difference between Jocko's "Goddamm *it!*" and "Goddamm *you!*" If it was the latter, as was often the case, the addressee was in trouble.

The tip-off of when Clark was in his worst mood was the few times he put Herm Rosenblatt in hack. It meant simply that Jocko's divorce—being handled by Herm's brother Sol—was going badly. On one occasion when the ship was well out at sea a $3,000 paycheck arrived, but his "ex" M.C. had claimed $2,200 of it—no doubt for child support—on the accompanying garner sheet. The dispersing officer, rather than face Clark's wrath, sent a second class petty officer to deliver it. Furious, Jocko yelled and screamed.

For the two weeks' voyage between Panama and Pearl, the *Yorktown* relentlessly operated its planes—never launching or recovering them fast enough to suit the skipper. The divebombers pulled target sleeves for the fighters, and both dropped bombs (1,000-pounders by the SBDs) around the sled towed astern, while the torpeckers flew antisub patrols. The antiaircraft gun crews also fired daily at the sleeves, and Radar Plot tracked not only the planes but also the escorting destroyers. One day the ship refueled the three tin cans.

General air group performance did not please Clark. One day a young ensign fighter pilot (J. K. Pellow) panicked when approaching to land and took no fewer than six wave-offs. Jocko finally roared to Hank Dozier that if the man did not get aboard on his next pass he would have him *shot* down. He then landed and was immediately summoned to the bridge and Clark's wrath: "This ship is headed for Pearl Harbor, but we'll never get there by sailing east [to land planes] unless we go completely around the world!" Clark ordered him transferred.

On 17 July a rainsquall covered the ship before most of the air group could land. Using the homing beacon, all but one division of four SBDs found the ship. In Radar Plot new FDOs Ridgway and Wilding kept track of their location. Still they groped, burning up their gas, leading a furious Clark to pace the bridge, with Flatley and Charlie Crommelin trying to calm him down. Finally, at 1730, Jocko—acting in his temporary capacity as Commander Task Group 52.4—ordered his three destroyers to belch smoke to attract the wayward bombers. The scheme worked, and all four finally came in.

Clark thought that the badly divided Bombing Five was the worst squadron in speed of launch and recovery. So he got its skipper Bob Milner up on the bridge one day to observe the impressive performance of the fighters and torpeckers. "See, Milner," he said with obvious pride, "that's what I want—something like that!"

"Well," Milner replied sarcastically, "why don't you fire off your 5-inch guns at the same time?"

"Get off my bridge!" thundered Clark, enraged. Milner's days on the *Yorktown* were numbered. (Conversation with Cooper Bright)

As skipper, Jocko responded to the crew's obvious frustration with constant training, zigzagging, and air patrols instead of fighting. He issued a statement in the mimeographed Plan of the Day for 20 July taking note of the fleet's "resolute and splendid will . . . to attack the enemy" in the early battles of the war. Obviously remembering the first *Yorktown*, he remarked, "However, in few cases has our skill been equal to our will." Though eager to destroy Japan's ships and planes, "we must remember that contacts" with them "are rare. . . . Not only must we seek them out but we must be ready to make the most of [contacts] when they do come and to hit, both day and night, on those occasions when suitable targets are found."

Till then, training. As several TBFs began taking off at 0930 to patrol that day, the one piloted by Lieutenant James W. Condit Jr.—nicknamed variously "Pop" or "Junior"—started trailing white smoke from an oil leak. He circled for an emergency landing, but his engine froze as he came "up the groove" astern. The plane dove into the drink just behind the ship and stayed afloat long enough for Condit and his two crewmen to climb into their raft and be picked up by the plane guard destroyer. It later returned them by bosun's chair to the *Yorktown*, which sent back the traditional reward of 50 gallons of "gedunk" (ice cream), a delicacy not manufactured on destroyers.

Daily gunnery drills even had their moments of anxiety. One 5-inch shell proved to be a dud when it fell in the water close aboard. Jocko went into a tantrum and yelled to gun boss Stroke Blackwell, "What the hell are we shooting—*fish?!*"

When time permitted, Clark held mast on sailors guilty of earlier serious breaches of regulations—like Seaman Second Class W. R. Schaffer, AWOL from Norfolk for nine days and 20 hours. On 21 July he socked Schaffer with a huge $162 fine and recommended a bad conduct discharge, which he would remit only if the man performed well for the next six months. Bill Schaffer not only did so but he became a tireless, loyal worker.

Next day, Jim Campbell's F6F Hellcat lost power on takeoff and then splashed down near the port side destroyer. The plane sank in 20 seconds, leaving a smooth slick for another 60. Then, abruptly, Campbell's head popped up. He had been trapped in the cockpit by his parachute harness but managed to pull the toggles on the $CO_2$ bottles of his Mae West life preserver and shoot to the surface. The destroyer's whaleboat picked him up. Such mishaps became part of the carrier's routine.

A subtle and not-forgotten separate war festered on the *Yorktown* thanks to New Jersey native Coop Bright's "attacks" on Southern shipmates; he did this to inject levity into the constant and dangerous work. One of his "targets" was launching officer Hank Warren, who spoke with a drawl. Alabamian Joe Tucker had a small Confederate flag fashioned by the signal flag shop to replace Warren's regulation checkered launching flag. The first time Hank held it up to launch a Yankee pilot he got a shake of the fist in return!

When Jocko (forgetting his own ancestral Indian Territory rebel roots?) gave Tucker hell for it, Joe drawled with his puckish smile, "Why, Captain, it's only the state flag of Alabama!" Which it was. The flag stayed and helped in a small way to ease the anxieties of pilots heading off for battle.

The older pilots with a sense of humor knew how far they could push the Old Man, among them diminutive Harry Harrison, who had come to VF-5 from the *Suwannee*. A Yale ('33) man, he rolled down the deck wearing a blond woman's wig. A roar of cheers went up from those who saw it, all except Jocko: "Goddamm, that ain't funny!" (George Anderson had seen Harrison do the same thing with a Father Time mask when Andy was launching officer on the old *Yorktown*.)

As the ship and her escorts neared Hawaii Clark received a message from Pacific Fleet headquarters ordering him to launch an air "attack" on the battleship *Washington* on the morning of 23 July, then accompany her back in to Pearl. The *Yorktown* launched a predawn search of eight TBFs, one of which made contact at about 0700 and remained overhead for 45 minutes. Jocko sent out a deckload strike of 45 planes that went out 200 miles, only to find nothing. To Clark's dismay, the Avenger pilot had made a potentially fatal navigational error of 8 degrees. More work was needed.

Between radar and voice radio the *Yorktown* pinpointed the "target" at 160 miles. Jocko waited till afternoon to launch a second "strike," by which time the *Washington* and two destroyers were only 25 miles away—just over the horizon. Following the mock attack, she came into view at 1430 wearing the flag of Rear Admiral Willis A. "Ching" Lee, commander of the Pacific Fleet's battleships, as the ships and their destroyer escort joined up.

Jocko sent a message by blinker light to Lee pronouncing that the USS *Yorktown* was "reporting to duty" to the Pacific Fleet. He also went down to the flight deck to meet torpecker pilot Lieutenant Douglas A. "Tex" McCrary and present him with the traditional frosted cake after making the 2,000th landing on the ship. In Radar Plot Charlie Ridgway wrote in his diary, "One year and almost two months after the sinking of the *Yorktown* at Midway [on 7 June 1942] the *Yorktown* returns to avenge itself. High words, those, but perhaps prophetic."

The *Yorktown* presented its real credentials to Pearl Harbor with a predawn strike next morning, the 24th. At first light, however, Air Group Five was intercepted en route by patrolling Navy PBY Catalinas and Army P-40 fighters that thoroughly outmaneuvered Flatley's Hellcats. The air group then encountered a bombing strike against the *Yorktown* from the *Independence*, first of the 11,000-ton light carriers to arrive in the Pacific. The skies over the *Yorktown* were soon filled with so many Hawaii-based attacking planes that two midair collisions (nonfatal) occurred, causing the mock attack to be called off.

Most of Air Group Five landed at NAS Barbers Point, while Jocko eased the ship into the harbor. A blinker light signaled a message from Admiral Nimitz: "The *Yorktown* carries a name already famous in the Pacific, and in welcoming you we anticipate that you will maintain the high reputation of your predecessor." To which Clark replied, "Many thanks for your message. That's what we came here to do."

All hands mustered at quarters topside as the site of the former "Battleship Row" came into view. They were dumbstruck—the *Arizona* in her shallow grave, the newly righted but stripped-down *Oklahoma*, the overturned hulk of target ship *Utah*, along with bullet holes in the Ford Island hangars and outside office walls of Vice Admiral Towers, commanding the Pacific Fleet's air forces. Sight of the wreckage and damage had the cumulative effect of pulling everyone closer together.

But the future beckoned too. The crew of the *Independence* gave the *Yorktown* three hearty "hip-hip-hoorays." Sister ship *Essex* was there too. It had arrived at the end of May, well before the *Yorktown*, but Clark still had every intention of beating her into battle. Felix Stump's *Lexington* and John Ballentine's *Bunker Hill*, commissioned in February and May respectively, had yet to arrive.

Clark brought the *Yorktown* alongside Pier Fox-9 near the *Utah* in midafternoon. Two days later, the new light carrier *Belleau Wood* pulled in—yet another addition to the massive buildup for the coming offensive.

Jocko kept all hands busy preparing the ship for the coming inspections by Admirals Nimitz and Towers and gave one-third of the crew liberty ashore each day (until sundown). Liquor and women were both plentiful, especially for the pilots. Each flyboy was issued a "booze card" for one fifth at any of Hawaii's six officers clubs. While Clark looked the other way, most of the whiskey and beer was loaded into the bulky TBFs to be flown aboard. If one had ever crashed on landing, the pilots worried that the resulting alcohol fire would burn a hole through the flight deck!

The most convenient bistro for ship's officers was the Ford Island O-Club, scene of a big afternoon party. As it was ending, a particularly "smashed" Jim Vonk, the weatherguesser, played soccer with George Anderson's white dress hat. Once outside, Vonk spotted the captain heading for his Navy car and driver with "that gimpy walk" from his old ankle injury. Without thinking (or unable to!), Vonk fell in behind Jocko, imitating his limp.

Jocko, sensing something amiss, suddenly stopped and turned around. Vonk was so drunk that "I walked right into him!" he recalled.

"What the hell you doin'? Mocking me?"

All Vonk could manage was "that silly shitty grin that a drunk guy gives"—and Vonk, as serious as he was on the job, often had a big smile.

But Jocko understood at once. "That's some kind of party there," he remarked to his highly respected aerologist, "and you were getting too much party. Come on, I'll drive you back to the ship. You probably need the rest."

Once there, Vonk and his pals headed to the wardroom mess for chow. The main course was a whole turkey—as was appropriate for their holiday mood. They celebrated like it was a Roman carnival. "The only thing missing here," Vonk announced, "are the Vestal Virgins"—priestesses of ancient Rome. "That's not easy to remedy, but we can do the rest of it." So Vonk and his pals ripped away at the cooked turkey, each throwing the bones over his shoulder like a Roman aristocrat. When informed next day what he had done, all Vonk could do "was feel like a horse's ass." But such revelry provided relief from the pressure of satisfying the skipper's endless demands on the weatherguesser for accurate forecasts.

If the ship's cleanliness did not pass Clark's daily inspection, the guiltiest third of the crew remained on board and kept working—which happened more than once. Still, the men were beginning to appreciate their skipper, and, as in the Vonk incident, they lampooned him with backhanded admiration. One example was graffiti in one of the heads: "How does Jocko keep us on our toes? He raises our urinals three inches!"

Similarly, cartoon sketches of the skipper, most of them the work of sailor John Furlow, were passed around. He exaggerated Jocko's foibles in funny but pointed ways: his Indian heritage, as in scalping Japanese premier General Tojo; his goat's milk regimen; and even one depicting Rosenblatt with padlocks on his pockets so no one could reach in them to steal the Spearmint chewing gum Herman was saving for Jocko as an offering. (Alexander, "Carrier Revolution," 48)

According to an unconfirmed story, about this time Rosenblatt left the ship temporarily to undertake a secret and hazardous mission into the Soviet Union to obtain information about its progress in aeronautics, accompanied by a young aeronautical engineer from Lockheed Aircraft. The account has a ring of authenticity to it but cannot be confirmed. (Numerous conversations in the early 1980s with Bernard Rosson, né Rosen, who had accompanied Rosenblatt; Rosson's reminiscences of the mission dictated to his wife on his deathbed in October 1986, courtesy of Irene Rosson)

Clark and Waller kept the crew working furiously in anticipation of Admiral Nimitz's initial inspection. Admiral Towers's office was situated near the pier, and as Jocko entered it one day on a visit the noise from his crew's air hammers chipping paint was deafening.

"How do you get your men to work like that?" asked Towers.

"Raöul Waller, my exec, knows how to keep men busy. We will gladly stop if you like."

"Oh, no," replied Jack, "I never interfere with anyone working!"—a policy of Jocko's as well.

Nimitz brought his inspection party on board the morning of 27 July. Clark was ready for him, attired in a freshly pressed khaki uniform with tie and overseas cap. (Reynolds, *Fighting Lady*, 25) One thing Jocko did not bring to the Pacific was the gray uniform designed and ordered for all officers by Admiral King himself, Clark having heard that Nimitz had not bought one (neither had most others in the Pacific theater).

Nimitz immediately noticed the three gun turrets emblazoned with gunnery awards. "Jocko," he marveled, "is it legal for a ship in commission so short a time to have three Es with a hash mark?" Clark proudly assured him it was. After a thorough inspection, Nimitz remarked to Jocko and Raöul, "This is the cleanest carrier I have ever inspected!"

Old friend Arthur Radford, newly promoted to rear admiral without ever having commanded a ship, came aboard for a three-day training cruise. And Admiral Towers, responding to Cooper Bright's initiative, sent three officers to observe the troubled Radar Plot at work. The *Yorktown* put to sea on the 29th, the air group flew aboard, and the cruiser *Mobile* and three cans constituted the screen.

Jocko returned to form. When one particular foul-up occurred in the engine room regarding the speed of the ship, he became so furious that everyone on the bridge retreated when he summoned the assistant engineer, Lieutenant Commander Walter T. Hart Jr. "Bill" Hart was a short, soft-spoken native of Charleston, South Carolina, who had left the Navy four years after graduating from the Naval Academy in 1920, only to age prematurely under the weight of the Depression. His drawl irritated Clark, who would often impatiently cut him off and turn away. When Hart arrived on the bridge, Jocko began a tirade, "I asked for that [certain] speed, and you *lied* to me!"

But Hart had begun to understand Clark, and he came away chuckling, "The Old Man's a little disturbed this morning. We've got to get the cook to make those eggs over easy. It gets the man upset every time. It gets his ulcers going." (Conversation with Cooper Bright)

The next day each SBD dropped a 1,000-pound bomb near the target sled until one bomber went into a flat spin and crashed 300 yards astern. It disintegrated on impact, leaving no traces of the pilot or radioman (Elmer Parkes, Cameron Edgar). Squadron morale worsened. But combat training could not be interrupted: the AA guns blazed away at aerial sleeves all afternoon and at a "radar target" 90 degrees to starboard at night (1900 to 2230).

Sleep was short, with a predawn launch at 0400 on the 31st. The tiny task formation squeezed together in a tight disposition—the *Mobile* 1,000 yards astern, the lead destroyer 2,500 yards ahead. Radar Plot guided the defensive CAP fighters to intercept the air group's attack, and Jocko used the close formation to sharpen his skills as a ship handler.

He sped the ship out of the screen for launching planes into the wind and thereafter back into the formation using an unorthodox but effective sharp "fishtail" or "flipper" turn. He left the details to the OOD. On one occasion this was Lieutenant (jg) William Griffin, who had to decide whether to turn 180 degrees right or left to reenter. Figuring it was a toss-up, he had given the order, "*Left* full rudder, all engines ahead flank [speed]."

Jocko, giving no reason, loudly condemned him for turning left. However, next morning, "Griff" found himself in exactly the same situation, with the same trade winds and base course. So he ordered, "*Right* full rudder, all engines ahead flank."

Again the captain cursed him out. "Why in hell did you turn right?"

"To be honest, Captain, because I turned left in exactly the same situation yesterday and you gave me hell."

Jocko: "Christ, you young sonofabitch, ain't you got the courage of your convictions?!" No wonder the bridge was regarded as the "can't win room."

The *Yorktown* returned to Pearl late that afternoon to Radford's congratulations for the ship's performance but only lukewarm remarks about the air group. The ComAirPac observers, unimpressed with Radar Plot, recommended that Billingsley, Milholland, and a third officer be detached. Raöul Waller recommended that Clark make the change, allowing Stover, Ridgway, and Wilding to take over the critically important role of fighter direction.

Jocko demurred, telling Waller of his loyalty to Billingsley, a personable, hard-working individual who was still learning the ropes. Waller replied that loyalty was not as important as competence in the war zone. Clark would not budge, so Waller let the matter drop and was not surprised when Jocko renewed their discussion next day. But Waller, untypically, held his ground.

In the midst of these deliberations, on the first day of August "we had communion for the first time aboard ship," Dr. Gard wrote to his wife. Clark attended every religious service that he could, including this one, which was Protestant. Chaplain Bob Alexander's sermons invariably impressed the surgeon.

> Everyone attending, from the Captain and executive officer down to the lowest ranking Negro mess boy, kneeling together on an armored [hangar] deck, receiving into his mouth a wafer dipped in wine—"This do in remembrance of Me."
>
> A communion service never meant so much to me. When all show and all veneer of convention is gone and men on a mission such as this one kneel in prayer and communion, it is to me an evidence of the value and power of our faith.

Similar evidence of this faith appeared on the bridge one day in the person of a black mess attendant, William E. Davenport, who asked to see the captain. Clark obliged, asking Davenport what he wanted. He replied that he "had the call" and wanted to do some preaching. Jocko thought the idea a good one: "No ship could do well in war unless it had religion," even beyond the Protestant and Catholic chaplains preaching "fore and aft." Any man who had the call should "carry out the Lord's work." Jocko had the exec give the sailor some Bibles and "preaching books" and asked him to report on his progress.

Davenport's services turned out to be Southern Baptist revival meetings, highly popular and well attended for their lively Negro spirituals. Weeks later, when the ship was far out at sea, Davenport returned to the bridge. Jocko asked him how he was getting along.

"I'm just gettin' along fine, Captain," he reported. "I've got 'em givin' up the gamblin',' givin' up the drinkin.' I've almost got 'em giving up hankerin' after the flesh."

"Well, that's fine. You just keep on, and maybe they will start giving up hankering after the flesh!" (Conversation with George Anderson)

This example of Clark's treatment of minorities was a cut above the Navy's traditional exploitation of them—which, however, wartime manpower requirements were subtly undermining. In his earliest youth his black "Mammy" had saved him from rattlesnakes, and his 1914 encounter with the black machinist Johnson on the *Maine* had taught him that color was not the measure of a man.

When "Brother Davenport" and his mates were not serving up chow in the galley, they manned the 20-mm antiaircraft guns along the flight deck aft and became crack shots. Each had come to the *Yorktown* rated second class seaman—and would finish the war in the same rate. Such callous indifference by the Navy toward racial minorities led Cooper Bright to observe contemptuously years later, "Domestic help doesn't get promoted."

Clark's two personal "mess boys" were not African American but Filipino, the other large minority in the fleet. Jews had never been prominent in the prewar navy, and Jocko's absolute admiration of Herman Rosenblatt—who flaunted his "Jewishness"—curbed any biases on that score. As for homosexual personnel, as on all warships, when discovered they were quietly transferred and discharged.

Such social concerns aside, the skipper remained focused on the demands of streamlining ship's operations. The most pressing challenge as August began was Radar Plot. Clark wrestled with the problem of its officers and finally sent for Waller again. He announced to his trusted exec,

> I'm going to follow your recommendation, even though I don't necessarily agree with you wholeheartedly. What you have said is sound. I have a great deal of loyalty to our present Radar Plot officer, and I feel I am doing him an injustice of having another officer ordered in to replace him. But I'm going to follow your advice.

On the afternoon of 3 August air officer Dozier passed the word to Radar Plot, where Ridgway and Wilding rejoiced at the news. And Smokey Stover informed both of them that they—junior in rank to him—would run it. He preferred to act only as a figurehead and would follow them as an excellent fighter director until he could be returned to flying status with VF-5 (which Dozier and Flatley had promised him). Furthermore, Radar Plot was now divorced from Air Plot as a separate division of the Air Department, much to the relief of Stebbins and Bright, whose Air Plot responsibilities were growing to embrace all air operations. (Wilding diary, 1, 3, 5, 6 August 1943)

Admiral Towers's ComAirPac officers, no doubt strongly influenced by the *Yorktown* experience, simultaneously ruled that Radar Plot on all carriers be renamed Combat Information Center (CIC). With Ridgway in charge, Wilding as intercept officer, and six other officers, CIC sent air combat information to Air Plot, the pilothouse (the captain and OOD), the flag bridge (the admiral), and to Gunnery and its lookouts.

Jocko's *Yorktown* was setting the pace.

The ship, with Admiral Radford still on board, sortied again the morning of 9 August to test the new CIC arrangement. Its FDOs successfully tracked a mock attack by planes of the new *Lexington,* now reporting to Hawaii for duty. Then the battleship *Indiana* and British carrier *Victorious* came over the horizon. Clark asked his signal officer Lieutenant Ernie Kelly, "What do the flags say, Kelly?" *Indiana*'s signal flags were hanging so limp and soggy in the humid heat, however, as to be unreadable. So Kelly hastened to the signal bridge where he had a signalman read the flags on the leading destroyer, enabling him to fake it and avoid Jocko's wrath.

The ship then launched its combat air patrol (CAP) of F6Fs, successfully directed by CIC to intercept the rest of Air Group Five, which then landed aboard. "For the first time," Alex Wilding applauded in his diary, "the Radar Plot of the *Yorktown* was functioning smoothly and competently." Intercepts of large numbers of incoming planes based at Maui followed over succeeding days.

On the 11th the *Independence* joined up, and Rear Admiral Charles A. Pownall was flown aboard in a TBF to observe operations. Red Sharp particularly welcomed him, having admired "Baldy" Pownall as captain of the *Enterprise* when Sharp had run its flight deck.

Another TBF was readied to fly ashore and return the next day with Admiral Jack Towers. Jocko told the pilot, "Now, you'll have a damned valuable cargo. You gotta be particularly careful."

"Captain," the pilot retorted, "when I'm in that airplane there's damned sure nothing more valuable than *I* am!"

Nighttime cruising with two carriers and five cans in close formation was tricky at best. Clark retired to his sea cabin one night, leaving Ensign H. Shackleford Moore ('43) at the conn. Ship's surface "bug" radar scopes—PPI (plan position indicator) and DRT (dead reckoning tracer)—enabled him to ensure the safe intervals between ships. At one point, however, they indicated the *Independence* was starting to close on the *Yorktown* at 20,000 yards.

Moore rang up the captain on the phone to inform him, receiving only Jocko's customary "umgrumph" when disturbed from his slumber. When the interval continued to narrow he repeated the warning and got the same "reply." At 15,000 yards Moore telephoned him again, and Clark said, "I'll be right out."

But when he did not show, Moore made his fourth call. With *Independence* now at 10,000 yards he requested permission to maneuver away from the base course. Within seconds Jocko came out, tying his bathrobe and angrier than usual at the disturbance. After making the necessary course change he chased Moore off the bridge for not having told him when the *Independence* was crossing ahead at 12,000 yards.

The "can't win room," day *and* night.

But Shack Moore learned from Jocko Clark how to handle a big ship—notably the "fishtail" turns when running the carrier in and out of the formation to operate aircraft. This future admiral recalled that all ship handling compared to Jocko's was "minor league," and the next 29 years for Moore were all "downhill!"

One day Clark was surprised to see a little gray dog barking down on the flight deck. "There's a goddamm dog barking on the deck," barked Jocko in his own way. "What the hell's going on here?"

"Captain," a sailor responded, "we call him 'Jocko.'"

"Well, that's all right. He can stay."

The pooch had been "liberated" at Pearl, preferred for his small size because he could walk under the spinning propellers. Most swabs called him "Scrapper Shrapnel"—"Scrappy" for short, or just "Bozo." Of course, he crapped all over the place, to Raöul Waller's dismay.

(After the war, pilot Harry Harrison bought a pup he let sleep with him until it bit him in the fanny one night. So he named it "Jocko" because, as he explained to his wife, "Jocko was always chewing everybody's asses!")

Scrappy figured in more than one tall tale, including the time he was supposed to have ambled up behind two "boot-assed" ensigns chatting on the flight deck and used one's leg as a fire hydrant. The victim looked down in disgust, then amazement, and remarked, "How in the world did that dog know we were ensigns?"

Early on 13 August a Hellcat made a poor landing on the *Independence*, fouling its flight deck and forcing the remaining planes to land on the *Yorktown*. Among them was the fighter skipper, the celebrated "ace" (five kills or more in dogfights) Lieutenant Commander E. H. "Butch" O'Hare. While the *Yorktown* refueled the wayward fighters, O'Hare visited with Jimmy Flatley, his former flying instructor. Both had worked with Jimmy Thach in developing the famous "Thach Weave" fighter tactic that helped defeat the Zero. (Ewing, *Reaper Leader*, 119–20, 183, 185, 256)

Most of the planes from both carriers flew ashore later in the day, and their ships returned to Pearl. Admirals Towers and Radford went ashore, but Admiral Pownall remained on board to prepare for a combat operation—a carrier raid against insignificant Marcus Island in the north-central Pacific. It was to be in effect a realistic training mission, not to be announced to the crews and pilots until the ship and its consorts were en route to the target.

Meanwhile, the ship's baseball team went ashore on the weekend to defeat the *Belleau Wood*'s nine, and the ship stood out to sea for more gunnery and air exercises. One of Nimitz's training specialists in antiaircraft gunnery, Commander Ernest M. Eller, rode aboard each of the new carriers at Pearl and was "quite impressed with Jocko Clark's handling of the *Yorktown*. Jocko was a hard master and a tough Indian. But he ran the ship well. He had a good ship." (Eller transcript #11, 618–19) Its performance was so successful in fact that Admiral Radford now instructed the other carrier captains to emulate the *Yorktown* in both gunnery and air operations.

Joe Tucker's maintenance crews managed to obtain five more tractor "mules" from a warehouse by bribing the sailors there with whiskey. Fitted with tow bars, each of the ship's seven mules did the work of some 25 men in moving one plane. This so speeded up respotting the deck that the *Lexington* asked Towers's office to move half of them over from the *Yorktown*.

This order was written up but not sent before it was pigeonholed by Clark's friend Captain F. W. "Horse" Pennoyer Jr., ComAirPac matériel officer, who told Jocko about it. Suitably alarmed, Jocko had a sign posted— "Off Limits to *Lexington* Personnel Without Seeing Captain Clark First." When Felix Stump of the *Lex* assured Jocko that his men would not "steal" any of the mules, Jocko took down the sign. Other carriers wanted them as well, so Admiral Towers arranged to have "mules" become standard issue for all carriers.

The story spread, and months later, when Clark hoisted his rear admiral's flag in the new *Hornet*, his new boss, Admiral Pete Mitscher, sent him a message: "Do you recommend that the *Yorktown* give the *Hornet* its tractors?"

Jocko replied, "If the *Yorktown* wants to give them, the *Hornet* will be happy to receive them." Mitscher laughed over Clark's careful sidestepping of his question.

Regarding the still missing spare parts for the F6F Hellcats, however, the *Yorktown* had not received them from San Francisco, as BuAer had promised, and Fighting Five simply could not go into battle without them. Joe Tucker had alerted Clark, who simply figured Tucker would find a solution.

But when the day of departure for battle was set for 22 August, Tucker convened his officers and chiefs for ideas. One of them knew of more than 100 new unassigned Hellcats parked ashore at Ford Island. The idea of more "midnight requisitions"—as in obtaining the "mules"—immediately came to mind: sneak ashore, convince the guards, and fieldstrip the planes of all easily removable parts; these could be replaced by *Yorktown*'s spare parts when they arrived.

Tucker agreed to let leading Aviation Chief Machinist Mate Louis T. Pisarski (which Joe pronounced "Pizecky") and his fellow chiefs handle it. All they needed was use of the ship's after crane.

Tucker went to Clark for approval to use the noisy crane in the middle of the night. When Jocko asked why, Tucker replied, "Captain, if you want spares for the fighters, just give us the crane and don't ask any questions."

Jocko eyed his old friend carefully, then said, "O.K."

At sunset on the 20th the chiefs went ashore. Half an hour before midnight the crane started working, hoisting aboard great quantities of gear. The noise continued for three hours. Then silence. Pisarski reported to Tucker, "Tell the captain to get the ship under way."

Tucker understood, aware that the ship was ready to move after sunup to 1010 Dock to take on fuel. But the Marine orderly would not let Tucker awaken Jocko until he ordered him to. Jocko looked awful.

"Captain, we have *got* to get the ship under way." Clark said that *nothing* was allowed to move in the harbor at night but accepted Tucker's suggestion to cast off at very first light.

Clark called up George Anderson, "Andy, prepare to get the ship under way."

The sleepy-eyed navigator protested, "What's the hurry?"

"No questions! Just do it. We move at daylight."

"Aye, aye, sir."

All the needed crewmen were aroused and carried out the move, while Tucker and his crew sorted out the haul: spare tires, engine harnesses, tail hooks, hydraulic gear, carburetors, fuel lines—clearly enough for the squadron of 36 Hellcats. In fact, Pisarski's guys had purloined enough equipment for *three* squadrons; it would last a year and a half!

No sooner was the *Yorktown* out in the harbor than the Ford Island signal tower lit up "like a Christmas tree." Clark had his signalmen ignore it. Furthermore, he had "Off Limits" signs posted to deter non-*Yorktown*ers while the ship refueled at the oil depot.

Admiral Pownall came aboard with a completely makeshift staff, having arrived in Hawaii on short notice. He temporarily drew upon the staff officers of Admiral Towers, who, under Captain Forrest Sherman's direction, had been hastily hammering out operating procedures (PAC 10) for the new multicarrier task formations. Notable among them was Commander Wallace M. Beakley, Towers's carrier specialist, to handle air operations for the force. Pownall swiped signal officer Ernie Kelly from Jocko's bridge to be his flag lieutenant. (Reynolds, *Fast Carriers,* 72–73; conversations with Beakley and Kelly)

Later in the day, ominously for the crew, several war correspondents reported on board for an extended stay. It looked like the real thing was about to happen.

Significantly, Clark's *Yorktown* became flagship of the new fast carriers in their first offensive operation. Task Force 15 included Wu Duncan's *Essex* and George Fairlamb's *Independence*—the prototypes of their classes. But Jocko's ship got the honor of carrying Pownall's flag, surely because of Clark's aggressive leadership. The "wild Indian" thereby ensured that his *Yorktown* would indeed beat the *Essex* and all the other new carriers into battle.

At 0831 the morning of 22 August 1943 four yard tugboats eased the *Yorktown* away from the dock and into the harbor. As usual, the crew was mustered on the flight deck to the strains of "Aloha 'Oe" from a Navy band on the dock. The ship's band responded with "Anchors Aweigh" and other marches. All hands returned to their morning chores as the ship backed around into the channel. It fell in behind three destroyers and was followed by the *Independence* and another can.

As the ship moved into the open ocean, the Ford Island signal tower blinked out a message of farewell: "You look good out there, hunting." This was a faint allusion to the fact that enemy waters and islands were being increasingly referred to as "Indian Country"—an Old West allusion not particularly associated with Cherokee Jocko. Then the tower changed the last recorded word in the message to "honey," giving all hands a laugh. Unknowingly, the revised message accented the femininity of the ship that would become Hollywood's "Fighting Lady." (Oliver Jensen's handwritten notes; Jensen, *Carrier War,* 47)

Once beyond Hawaii's horizon, the ship's crack 5-inch gun crews shot down three target sleeves being towed at 12,000 feet altitude. Air Group

Five flew out from Barbers Point in the afternoon for a mock attack, the SBDs bombing the sled. Clark adroitly maneuvered the ship at varying speeds to "avoid" the planes. But the fighter attack was completely "botched up" (wrote Harry Harrison in his diary) due to the slow recovery of the bombers on board, for which Jocko raged at air officer Dozier.

With actual combat fast approaching, the stakes rose. Even rehearsals could be deadly. Two patrolling antisub SBDs had engine trouble as they entered the landing circle. One simply coasted into the drink astern of the ship for the occupants' rescue. The second turned too sharply "into the groove" for landing, spun in 200 yards short of the ship, whereupon its depth charge exploded, blowing to bits plane, pilot, and gunner (Arthur Johnson and Freeman Conner, respectively). The spectacle unnerved onlookers and increased Clark's low opinion of Dozier and VB-5 skipper Milner.

By dawn of the 23rd the *Yorktown* was surrounded by a sea of warships, mostly new: carriers *Essex* and *Independence* (total planes of all three flattops: 96 VF, 72 VB, 45 VT), battleship *Indiana,* two cruisers, ten destroyers, and one fleet oiler. In addition to Admiral "Baldy" Pownall on the flagship, Rear Admiral Alfred E. Montgomery rode the *Essex* in "make-you-learn" status (before commanding a task force or group).

All off-duty officers gathered in the wardroom where Commander Waller informed them of the target—the Japanese naval weather station at remote Marcus Island, 2,700 miles west of Hawaii and less than 1,000 miles from Tokyo. Raided by Admiral Halsey and the *Enterprise* in March 1942, it still had several defending aircraft. Because the Japanese were known to be fairly set in their ways, Commander Beakley used their 1942 patrol plane search patterns to time the task force's approach behind these planes on the return leg of their patrols. Except for Admiral Montgomery on the *Essex,* others questioned this hunch, but it proved correct.

Late on the 24th Clark took the *Yorktown* out of the task formation to recover the four TBFs on antisub patrol—the "Baker" maneuver. Then he called for 25 knots, turned the ship "right full rudder" straight back into the formation, through the destroyer screen and past the *Essex,* executing a sharp "left full rudder" to slow the ship—his "fishtail" maneuver. It worked handsomely, as usual, to the admiration of his officers and cheers from flight deck personnel.

But not his boss. Admiral Pownall dashed up from the flag bridge. "He was just shaking," remembered Anderson, and scolded, "Clark! Clark! Don't *ever* do that again! It's too dangerous!" And he moaned, "Why did I ever come to the carriers?" Jocko, flabbergasted and dejected by this rebuke, was left speechless—a rare event for him. But after Pownall left, Clark said, under his breath, "The yellow son of a bitch"—a phrase he would utter

The "Baker" maneuver consisted of a carrier like this one charging out of the task formation of escorting gun ships and other carriers in order to turn into the wind to launch or recover its aircraft. Clark was so expert at it that he unnerved Admiral Charles Pownall by executing it with an abrupt "flipper" or "fishtail" turn to race out and again back in, invariably avoiding any collision. As an admiral, Jocko instituted the "modified Baker" method in which all ships turned together with the carriers into the wind for air operations. *U.S. Navy photo*

whenever Pownall faltered. Yet he felt better when Wu Duncan signaled congratulations from the *Essex*.

But this was the occasion when Clark "made up his mind he was going to get rid of Pownall," somehow. (Anderson transcript #3, 120)

As the day of battle neared, minor irritations were magnified. On the 24th Alex Wilding, at his battle station in CIC for the 0530 G.Q. (General Quarters), had breakfast, showered, and hit the sack, only to be aroused to muster with the crew on the flight deck for Jocko's calisthenics. "Exercises," he bitched in his diary, "—what asinine things they can think of. The only ship in the [task force] that was called to muster and exercises." 'Twas another mark of its uniqueness, thanks to the skipper.

On the day of battle, one week later, with the first planes being readied for the predawn launch, Raöul Waller went up to a loud and frenzied Air Plot and ordered Ed Stebbins to clean the head. Steb, unnerved by this untimely order, passed it on to Coop Bright, who only looked at the exec in disbelief. "*Now! Now!!*" repeated Waller. Incredulous, Skinhead broke out the buckets, took some of his talkers off the phones, and cleaned the head.

After Air Plot got the planes off, Waller returned there, took one look, and said, "Mr. Bright, clean the head again. You didn't do a good job." "This guy must be a complete ass," Coop thought to himself, "here we are trying to fight a war!" And Stebbins was beside himself. Before long, however, both men learned an important lesson from this incident: cleanliness brings order to a ship, and the *Yorktown* was always clean, one of its distinguishing characteristics.

On the 25th 2,000-pound bombs were loaded into the torpeckers and belly tanks of extra aviation gas placed on the fighters to extend their time aloft. "You can feel the tension growing a little tighter every day," recorded Wilding as the ship passed 80 miles north of Midway. It went right over the spot where the old *Yorktown* lay far below, in which Clark showed absolutely no interest.

The weather began to worsen as the force moved into ever more northern latitudes, often preventing flight operations. On one such dense foggy day Vonk the weatherguesser came up to the bridge about midmorning and said, "Captain, you'd better get your fighters ready. It's going to clear up any minute now." Jocko disagreed, and the two got into a shouting match.

Cooper Bright happened to be climbing the ladder to the bridge, which he always tried to avoid. Much as he grew to love the skipper, he never got used to Clark's shouting. Whenever Coop was the brunt of Jocko's wrath it took him a full day to recover. On this occasion he heard the usual screaming going on and thought, "Somebody's gettin' it."

The loudest voice was Vonk's. And *he* wasn't getting it—Jocko was! Clark yelled, "Goddammit, I know the weather. It's gonna be clear over here," and he pointed to a different area on the chart. The Dutchman thundered back, "You're crazy as hell!! It's over *here!*" Both were pointing with wild gestures. A few minutes later the sky began to clear near the task force, as predicted by Vonk.

So he exclaimed to Jocko, "Didn't I tell you so?!"

"Yeah, you did," Clark thundered, whereupon the weatherguesser walked away, visibly shaking from each such traumatic exchange. He was the only man Bright ever saw "who could stand up there and give the Old Man hell."

Vonk's reward for his talents and his integrity was Clark's undying trust and respect. And small favors, to the resentment of Vonk's roommate Smokey Stover: "I doubt if there are a half-dozen officers in the Navy, even regulars, who have had as much liberty as he." (Stover diary, 19 October 1943)

The *Yorktown* refueled from the tanker *Guadalupe* on the 27th, and next morning Clark mustered the crew topside to witness a demonstration of the largest bomb in the *Yorktown*'s arsenal. Ship's company could thereby share the air group's punch—a sound idea to cement teamwork. Wilding noted it in his diary that a TBF "cut loose a 2,000 lb. daisy cutter astern so that all hands would have an idea of what one looked and acted like. Shrapnel flew 1,000 yards in every direction. Hope we don't receive one of those amidships on the 31st," the day of battle.

Throughout 28 August, Flatley led the air group's first tactical exercise of the cruise; the force passed 800 miles north of Japanese-held Wake Island; and ship's radio direction finders picked up a wireless station in the Kurile Islands north of Japan and another from Tokyo itself. The submarine *Harder* passed just south of the force, en route to prey on Japanese coastal shipping. Another sub reported tracking an enemy convoy and escorts, including a carrier, south of Wake, heading west. (Wilding diary, 28 August 1943)

"My heart," Jimmy Flatley addressed a letter to his wife Dottie the same day, "We're getting further and further away from anywhere. . . . Can't be long now. . . . Every day I go up and see Jocko and each day he becomes more lovable and obstreperous. One thing is certain. We will never disappoint him." And Clark welcomed a torpecker making the 3,000th landing on the ship.

By dawn, Sunday the 29th, the *Yorktown* was 800 miles from Marcus, 860 from Wake, and 1,360 from Tokyo. By circling around to the north of the target island the force avoided Japanese patrol "snoopers" out of Wake. It aimed for a launch point only 800 miles from Japan—closer than the Halsey-Doolittle raiders of 1942.

Worsening seas and temperatures were augmented by a radio message from Pearl reporting a weather front heading south from Alaska. Vonk and Flatley calculated that the task force could conceal its run-in to the target by maneuvering into that storm and using it for cover. Admiral Pownall's staff agreed and adjusted the line of approach.

Church services were heavily attended—led by Father Farrell for the Catholics, Bob Alexander for all Protestant denominations, and layman Herm Rosenblatt for Jewish crewmen and airmen. Baldy Pownall and Jocko Clark debated attacking not only Marcus but the Japanese convoy to the south inasmuch as it seemed to be on a collision course with the force near

Marcus. Then, as final refueling of the escorts took place, the enemy convoy moved away and out of the picture altogether. (Wilding diary, 29 August 1943)

By the dull wet dawn of 30 August, Marcus Island lay 550 miles southwest of the *Yorktown*, which launched four fighters into the murk on CAP and two F6Fs and two TBFs on intermediate patrols. All hands did their daily half-hour exercises, after which (recorded Wilding)

> Captain Clark came on the loud speaker and said we were 850 miles from Tokyo. That this was the opening of the central Pacific battle and we would clean up the central Pacific (which means Wake, Marshalls, and Gilberts) before moving south. Everyone was to wear shirts with long sleeves, flash clothing [all against bomb hit flashes], helmets, life belts, gas masks and the officers' side arms. Good luck and good hunting.

Nearly everyone was scared before his first battle, but, as on the *Suwannee* off North Africa, such extraneous accouterments as gas mask, .45 automatic pistol, and hunting knife were soon to be discarded as utterly superfluous on a carrier.

Ensign C. A. "Sandy" Sims, who had spent his youth in Japan with his businessman-missionary father, had been temporarily assigned to the ship as Japanese language radio intercept officer. He reported Radio Marcus oblivious to the approaching danger and that a dozen Jap patrol planes had just landed there. This was "just 12 less for them when we get thru" veteran Harry Harrison sneered in his diary.

The heavy weather caused a last-minute change in the attack plan for the morrow. *Yorktown*'s planes would make the first attack—"thus beating our rivals, the *Essex*, to a draw," noted pilot Harrison. "We've accomplished as much in six months as they have in a year and a half." He meant Air Group Five, commissioned in mid-February, against *Essex*'s Air Group Nine. As for the two ships, the only "draw" was their going into the new fast carriers' first battle together. *Yorktown*'s planes were scheduled to make the first strike against the target, however. Jocko had seen to that.

The pilots did not like the prospect of the predawn launch: takeoff, rendezvous, and navigating in the dark. Their leader, Jimmy Flatley, gathered his young charges in the wardroom in early evening for a final briefing, ending with words of reassurance:

> Say your prayers tonight. We're out here fighting for Christian ideals established by our God. Ask Him for strength and courage to do your job well. . . . You have the best equipment in the world. Use it effec-

tively. Make the Jap pay through the nose with every bomb and every
bullet where it will do the most good. We are the best Air Group on the
best ship in the Navy. Let's prove it tomorrow. (Mimeographed copy of
his attack memorandum)

Each squadron commander said a few words, followed by Admiral
Pownall, who expressed his confidence in them to do their job. Then they
adjourned to a fitful sleep.

Their captain was arguably the best carrier skipper in the fleet, surveying his domain from the bridge. Their admiral, however, was an unknown
quantity. In complete contrast to the boisterous, profane Clark, Pownall was
a short, pleasant man, easy to work for and with. A prewar skipper of the
*Enterprise,* he was very professional. But he was also clearly nervous—a
chain smoker who paced the flag bridge as Dog Day—attack day for Marcus—drew near.

Pownall's new flag lieutenant, Ernie Kelly, had seen combat on the signal bridge of the "Big E" working with three superb admirals—Halsey,
Spruance, and Frederick C. "Ted" Sherman. Unlike these battle-hardened
leaders, Pownall asked advice of everyone around him—and got it and
many unsolicited opinions as well. Inasmuch as some of his staff had not
seen action either, much of the advice turned out to be less than helpful.

Of the men on the *Yorktown,* however, only Jocko Clark needed to be
concerned with Pownall. Officers and crew, most of them "kids," whatever
their fears this night, already had faith in the skipper's ability to fight and
protect them in battle. He had—virtually overnight—forged them into a
team. "Let's go get 'em!" was his attitude, remembered Coop Bright. Those
who did not play on the team "just disappeared"—transferred—as "there
was no place for them." Also, unlike other carriers, no friction or fights
occurred between ship's company and the air group.

Jocko's charisma had already forged the men of the new *Yorktown* into
a close team, almost a family, even before their first action. As the sun set on
30 August, Jimmy Flatley joined Clark on the bridge. Jocko reflected,
"Jimmy, we've waited a long time for this. We've worked and slaved. I *know*
we won't fail." (Ewing, *Reaper Leader,* 192)

Marcus was just the beginning, and Jocko Clark would set the pace.

Jock Clark in his Boeing F3B fighter flying over the *Lexington* (CV-2) off Southern California, ca. 1932. *U.S. Navy photo*

Admiral Marc Mitscher (*left*) and Jocko Clark, his most trusted task group commander, at a meeting of carrier admirals—probably on board the new *Lexington* (CV-16) sometime during the summer of 1944. *From the motion picture* The Fighting Lady

Admiral Ernest J. King—"Ernie"—in 1944. *U.S. Navy photo*

Rear Admiral J. J. Clark—"Jocko"—seen in 1952. *U.S. Navy photo*

# TWELVE

# Pacific Offensive, 1943

MOST OF THE CREWS AND PILOTS OF TASK FORCE 15 REGARDED the 31 August raid on tiny, insignificant Marcus Island as a fairly bold operation. It marked the beginning of the Central Pacific offensive and the first combat for most of them.

The target lay some 130 miles southwest of the *Yorktown* when Air Group Five's pilots arose at 0200 for the customary battle day steak-and-eggs breakfast. On the bridge, Captain Clark received word from Air Plot of two "bogeys" 50 miles out—obviously patrol planes from Marcus. Because the fighter pilots had not been trained for night combat—unlike the Japanese—no interceptors could be launched.

Then the "snoopers" turned away, on the return leg of their patrol, confirming Captain Beakley's prediction that Marcus had not changed its search patterns in a year and a half. At 0300 "Flight Quarters" called the pilots to their ready rooms for a final briefing, followed by reveille for all hands at 0330, then at 0400 loud gongs and the call to "General Quarters! All hands, man your battle stations!"

Weatherguesser Vonk's cooperative storm front had cleared away, leaving such a glassy, calm sea that Clark had to ring up 28 knots to create a 35-knot wind across the deck for lifting the lumbering TBFs into the sky. The flight deck was dark "like a ghost spectacle," noted Alex Wilding, while scattered clouds so thoroughly obscured the horizon that the pilots would not be able to judge their proximity to the water when they cleared the deck.

Clark had a solution to this unforeseen development: create an artificial horizon. He recommended to Admiral Pownall that some of the destroyers be swung into a semicircle ahead of the formation, each to display its screened truck lights at the masthead—not only "creating" a horizon but also enabling each plane to avoid the ships themselves. Pownall refused, citing the possibility of a lurking Japanese submarine. But Jock insisted; no slow sub could keep up with ships speeding along at nearly 30 knots. The pilots *had* to have a horizon.

Baldy Pownall talked it over with his makeshift staff, which convinced him to accept Clark's recommendation. But the admiral began to pace the flag bridge nervously, going through one cigarette after another, as the tin cans maneuvered ahead. Jock even had his tractor "mules" parked at the forward end of the deck with headlights ablaze to enhance the false horizon. Neither worked very well for all pilots; some of them would simply guide on the plane in front as they cleared the deck.

The flight deck was so dark that airedales had to help the pilots and air crews feel their way to each plane at 0415, just as Clark began to turn the ship into the wind. Forty-eight airplane engines roared to deafening life, and VF-5 skipper Charlie Crommelin eased his Hellcat into the lead position for takeoff. At 0423—seven minutes ahead of schedule—Crommelin roared down the deck and into the black sky.

Jocko and the *Yorktown* had won their race—launching a full hour ahead of the initial *Essex* strike. Light carrier *Independence*'s planes helped provide combat air patrol and antisub vigilance for the task force.

Seven more *Yorktown* Hellcats joined up on Crommelin, followed by all 18 torpeckers—most armed with 2,000-pound blockbusters—under VT-5 skipper Dick Upson. Bombing Five's commander Bob Milner taxied his SBD into the launch spot in order to lead 11 others aloft, only to have his engine suddenly quit. Rather than let someone else lead the squadron into its first action, he preempted another pilot while his own plane was pushed aside. All this resulted in a 15-minute delay, sending Jocko into an almost apoplectic rage on the bridge. Milner finally led his division of six Dauntlesses into the night, each carrying a 1,000-pound bomb.

When the second division, five bombers, took off it failed to rendezvous in the correct sector. The sky being so black, the division leader informed Ed Stebbins in Air Plot that he refused to head for the target until first light. Charlie Crommelin even flew alongside and gestured for them to follow him, only to give up when he got no response.

A dozen more F6Fs began to taxi forward, when one rammed into another, disabling both planes and causing the loss of more precious minutes. The rest then took off, the last being air group commander Jimmy Flatley. These planes continued to circle, however, because of the wayward division of five SBDs. At 0504 flight leader Dick Upson—his TBF equipped with an airborne radar to guide "Run One" to Marcus—took the initiative and headed off for the target. The rest began to follow him, strung out in some confusion.

Back on the bridge, a furious Jocko Clark stalked into Air Plot, grabbed the primary strike frequency mike from Stebbins and bellowed into it for the five orbiting bombers to get the hell going to the target. "Steb," a decorated SBD pilot much admired by Clark, convinced the skipper to speed things up by delaying the second SBD division's departure until "Run Two," now being prepared for launch.

The effective initial strike group of 18 VT, 12 VB, and 14 VF was thereby reduced to 18, 6, and 13 plus three fighters on CAP over the task force: 37 planes instead of 44. Jocko had "had it" with Milner, whom he blamed—somewhat unfairly—for the botched rendezvous and weakened Run One. The captain decided to replace Milner as soon as possible.

The *Yorktown* as flagship was positioned at the center of the formidable task force, surrounded by an inner circle of the carriers *Essex* (90 planes) and *Independence* (33 planes), battleship *Indiana,* and light cruisers *Mobile* and *Nashville*—beyond that by an outer screen of ten destroyers. Unseen was submarine *Snook,* submerged 20 miles north of Marcus on lifeguard duty to rescue downed flyers—an innovation initiated by Admiral Pownall and perpetuated for the rest of the war.

Pownall continued to pace nervously throughout the day, constantly asking questions of his makeshift staff, from Captains Beakley and H. S. Duckworth to flag lieutenant Ernie Kelly. He had not liked launching planes in the dark, despite Clark's insistence that it would guarantee surprise for the attackers. The admiral and his advisers were concerned about possible counterattacks by Japanese planes based at Chichi and Iwo Jima—four hours flying time from the force, meaning possibly any time after midnight.

The admiral occasionally discussed the situation over the TBS (talk-between-ships radio) with Rear Admiral Alfred E. Montgomery, riding in makee-learn status on the *Essex.* This carrier launched a four-plane CAP at 0531—taking an inordinately long time, thought observers viewing it from the *Yorktown,* a contrast very pleasing to them.

In the *Yorktown's* Air Plot Stebbins and his radio listeners heard only occasional pilot chatter until 0605—about first light—when Upson announced to his pilots, "There it is, boys, over on the left!" The flyers could just make out lights on the triangle-shaped island through thin clouds, just seven miles away. The lights and lack of AA fire indicated surprise had been achieved. Then Jimmy Flatley's order was overheard: "Carry out run!"

Suddenly, the Japanese "woke up," and flak began to burst in the skies around *Yorktown's* planes as they bombed and strafed—flaming seven long-range Mitsubishi "Betty" patrol torpedo-bombers. Back on the ship, Run Two—12 VF and 12 VB led by Harry Harrison—commenced its launch at 0628, joined by the still orbiting five bombers and two fighters.

Simultaneously, radio listener Sandy Sims picked up and translated a plain-language transmission from Marcus radio to Tokyo, which he broadcast over the ship's public address system: "Being attacked by four American planes!"—and the reply: "You are crazy. Get off the air until weather is forecast!" It got even funnier when the Marcus radioman yelled ridiculous orders in broken English to *Yorktown* pilots to return to base.

After the last plane of Run Two cleared the deck at 0640 the entire task force began to turn around. It lay 117 miles from Marcus, the closest it would get. The plan called for opening the distance to prevent possible enemy counterattacks—planes from Wake or the Jimas, submarines, even the Japanese fleet, about which little was known.

Indeed, exactly at sunrise, 0652, radar operators reported a bogey 54 miles out. Nine minutes after that Air Plot heard a report that a Hellcat had shot down a Betty. And successive runs throughout the day imagined Zero fighters over the target.

Not one of the reports proved real, but all had to be checked out. The reported bogey made Admiral Pownall visibly nervous, and he turned to an equally apprehensive Captain Duckworth for advice. The response—to send a whole group of fighters—did not satisfy the admiral, who then turned to Ernie Kelly, his young flag lieutenant.

What did Kelly think that his former admirals on the *Enterprise*—Spruance or Halsey—would do in a similar situation? Kelly calmly suggested that he send out two or three fighters to investigate the contact. Pownall did just that, and they reported the "bogey" to be TBFs with their IFF signals turned off.

Meanwhile, Jimmy Flatley coordinated the attacks over the target most of the day, his Hellcat kept aloft by auxiliary gas drop tanks. He reported how each run spread destruction to the island's installations, confirmed by pilot's reports to the ACIOs after returning aboard. Two fighters and Junior Condit's torpecker were shot down by flak during the morning, but returning pilots spotted two life rafts, toward which the lifeguard sub *Snook* headed.

Pownall's fears only worsened, and at 0711 he had the *Independence* launch all nine of its TBFs to search 200 miles to the west for possible Japanese fleet units. This was followed an hour later by a *Yorktown* SBD antisub patrol—catapulted off the deck because returning planes were about to be recovered.

Jocko Clark and most other ship captains did not share their admiral's anxiety—quite the opposite. The skipper called Flatley and several pilots to the bridge as soon as they landed for personal reports. Encouraged by what he heard, he recommended the force stay another day and get in closer in order to launch more strikes. Captain William M. Fechteler of the battleship *Indiana* agreed. In a message to Pownall, he suggested going in much closer—to less than 20 miles offshore—so that his 16-inch guns could be used to bombard the island. Barring that, Clark and others suggested attacking Wake Island on the way back to Hawaii. (Conversations with Beakley and Bright)

Clark went down to the flag bridge and presented his recommendations to Pownall. At that, a distraught admiral blurted out, "The ruination of the Navy will be these damned carriers!" Shocked, Jocko returned to his bridge where he repeated Pownall's words to George Anderson, exclaiming, "We don't need an admiral with *that* kind of attitude! We're here to *fight!*" (Overheard by Bright)

As the carrier planes pummeled Marcus and a hapless Japanese cargo ship north of it, Sandy Sims heard the long-silent island radio return to the air at 1120 announcing the exact position of the task force (located by radio direction finding). Nervous staff officers advised CIC intercept officer Alex Wilding that "we should be under attack from Yokosuka in three hours." That was in Japan itself but over 800 miles away. (Wilding diary)

All the while, the search for Pop Condit and his two crewmen continued—by surfaced sub *Snook*, two catapulted floatplanes from cruiser *Nashville*, and each run of *Yorktown* planes. In midmorning Lieutenant (jg) Louis Richard of Bombing Five found and buzzed the three men, who frantically waved back. Returning to the ship, he rushed the location report by having his rear-seat gunner write it on paper, place it in a weighted oilskin drop bag with a red cloth streamer, and drop it onto the flight deck as Richard flew low. It was rushed to Pownall in Flag Plot.

Sadly, neither Condit's raft nor the one sighted earlier belonging to one of the two downed fighter pilots (Clem Morgan, Lonnie Towns) were ever located by sub, floatplanes, or carrier planes. And by early afternoon the nervous admiral was ready to head for home, especially after receiving a message from submarine *Whale* reporting a four-engine Japanese "Mavis" patrol plane 660 miles to the west. Then a returning plane jumped the arresting cables and ended up in the crash barrier—a possible indication of pilots tiring. And, over Marcus, Flatley reported its installations 80 percent destroyed.

Time to leave, decided Pownall, as soon as Run Six was recovered. Jocko Clark was incredulous; no downed pilots should be abandoned. Just then Ed Stebbins and Coop Bright approached him: "We think if we send out one more search [in a certain direction] we'll pick up Junior Condit," even if it meant turning around the entire task force. They recommended using TBFs.

"We'll launch it!" proclaimed Clark—either immediately or by remaining another day. He descended again to the flag bridge to get the admiral's approval. Pownall said, "No!" In his view it would be too hazardous.

Jocko, livid, came back and reported to Steb and Coop, "By God, they can take this command of this ship away from me when we get back to Pearl Harbor, but goddammit I'm gonna get my pilot and launch that damned search!"

He then sent a dispatch to Pownall—a distance of about eight feet between the captain's bridge and the flag bridge—followed by a series of messages between them.

Finally, Pownall climbed the ladder to discuss the proposed search. Except for George Anderson, the lookouts on the bridge, and the captain's talker on the phones, Charles Coburn, they were alone. The exchange was seared in the latter's memory (and differed only slightly from Bright's recollection of it).

"We'll go back and get them in the morning," said Clark.

"No," Pownall countered, "I'm afraid they are expendable."

Jocko, sticking out his jaw, exploded right in Pownall's face:

> You got the widest yellow streak up your back of any admiral I've ever seen in my life! Goddammit, I don't care if when I get back to Pearl Harbor I don't have a ship and I don't have any command. You can make me a Seaman Second tomorrow. But this is my ship, and these are my boys out there, and *I'm going* to send out a search for them! Do I have your permission?

Pownall backed down, "All right. Send them out now, 75 miles."

"They're going out 125 miles!" Clark shot back. But before he calmed down he raised it to 200—all the way back to Marcus, although the actual distance was 160.

After Run Seven—a four-Hellcat CAP—was launched at 1345, eight of Condit's squadron mates took off and formed a search line five miles apart on a true bearing of 245 degrees from the ship. En route, Joe Kristufek unloaded his four leftover 500-pound bombs at low level on top of the burning Japanese cargo ship, blowing it sky-high.

But the popular Condit was never spotted, to the chagrin of the pilots and especially Clark, who made no attempt to hide his tears from Anderson and others on the bridge. Equally sad were the deaths of the two downed Hellcat pilots. No one on the ship could know that from their raft Pop and his crew (Ken Kalberg, Gordy Marshall) had seen their squadron mates off in the distance nor that they were picked up by a Japanese trawler, beaten, and sent to a brutal prison camp near Tokyo for the duration.

They were not only the first *Yorktown* flyers captured but the only captured *Yorktown* flyers to survive the war. And, they would be present at the Japanese surrender in Tokyo Bay! (Reynolds, *Fighting Lady,* 43–45, 205–6, 322–29; Gamble, "First Mission Blues")

Jimmy Flatley brought Run Five back aboard at 1441, radioing ahead permission to lead one more strike to finish off Marcus. Pownall turned him down, and, as the planes were landing, a destroyer reported an enemy sub 20 miles to the west of the screen. False alarm, reported the CAP that investigated. The admiral nevertheless ordered more Hellcats aloft until sundown, 1900. Seventy-five minutes later another tin can reported a definite surfaced sub contact, but it soon submerged and evaded the force. It was eventually diagnosed as a probable whale.

Clark and his officers now learned, but found difficult to accept—in the words of Anderson—"that Pownall wanted to terminate any operation just as fast as he could." (transcript #3, 121)

The *Yorktown* remained at G. Q. all night, while Jocko ordered gedunk for all hands, and the ACIOs compiled probable damage inflicted on Marcus based on interviews with the pilots and gun camera photos. Certainly Air Group Five, having been the first to hit the island, exceeded the amount of damage inflicted by *Essex*'s Air Group Nine.

Yet, typical of damage assessment based on pilot reports, it was unintentionally exaggerated. According to Japanese records, the 1,400-man garrison of their island called Minami Tori-shima suffered only 37 casualties, with seven parked planes of the Yokosuka Naval Air Detachment destroyed. Men and planes were easily replaced and damaged facilities repaired.

As *Yorktown*'s assistant engineer, Lieutenant Raleigh A. "Country" Lancaster, observed, "Attacking Marcus was like knocking a grain of sand off a mountain. We'll *never* get home!"

The task force withdrew at high-speed—30 knots—under strict radio silence and in an arc northward to avoid possible enemy air searches from Wake Island. Just before midnight a U.S. submarine patrolling off Tokyo radioed that "a large Japanese task force left Tokyo at noon heading in our direction." (Wilding diary) Admiral Pownall, who, like others, was rattled by this news, changed course straight for Hawaii and maintained strict radio silence all the way.

The Marcus strike, however, had achieved its larger purpose. The new carriers, planes, and tactics had proved successful and given confidence to pilots and crews. Not all personnel, however, had performed well. Jocko Clark came away with flying colors; Admiral Pownall never registered a formal complaint against Clark's tongue-lashing of him. And perhaps now that Pownall had been through his first action, he would develop more self-confidence.

Such was not the case on the light carrier *Independence*. During the attacks against Marcus the ship's captain, George Fairlamb, had lost his head—and lunch, too, vomited all over the bridge. He had succumbed to the stress of combat command and was soon quietly replaced.

Especially gratifying for Clark's command was the realization, however mutually grudging, that regulars and wartime-only personnel—officers and enlisted alike—could work together effectively. This was due in no small part to the leadership genius of their skipper. But the griping, of course, never ceased; it never does among military people.

After Alex Wilding had "caught hell" from Captain Duckworth of the staff for failing to inform him of a minor bit of information en route to Marcus, the skilled assistant fighter director had shrugged to himself that "such is life in the Navy."

> The indoctrination schools say officers should not only be officers, but also gentlemen. I know some Academy officers that need to have that impressed upon them. The Navy is the greatest caste system in the world. Not based on brains or ability but solely on rank, years in the Navy. I could write a dissertation on that. (Diary, 26 August 1943)

Neither Jocko Clark nor Jimmy Flatley was of that sort, however; both judged their subordinates on performance only.

Flatley, returning over the ship from Marcus in midafternoon, was alarmed at seeing sunlight brightly reflected off the Plexiglas canopies of the planes parked on deck. These reflected rays made the *Yorktown* an easy mark for enemy planes. On landing, he informed Jocko, who in turn alerted the exec. Waller knew that the heavy oilcloth covers had been removed because they caused moisture on the Plexiglas, delaying launching by several minutes.

Waller handed the problem to Parachute Rigger Second Class Jesse Rodriguez, who in a matter of hours fashioned canopy covers out of bunting that was lightweight enough for the enlisted "plane captains" to easily remove and carry them rolled up in their belts. "Rod" had them cut, sewn, and dyed, then installed on the parked planes.

Next day, prior to a CAP launch, from the bridge Jocko noticed the new covers being removed and rolled up by the plane captains. He yelled over to Hank Dozier at Pri Fly, "Where the hell did you get those?"

"The rigger made 'em."

"He did? That's exactly what we want! Advance that man a rate!"

When the order was passed to Rod's division officer, the latter protested to Clark, "He just made second class a few months ago."

"Well," came the reply, "he's a first class now." Such spot promotions endeared the skipper to the crew.

Nor did Clark give preferred treatment to Academy-trained pilots over those who had come into the Navy via the Aviation Cadet (Avcad) program created by Congress in 1935. In this program, college graduates or near-graduates took one year of flight training and served three on active duty before receiving commissions in the Naval Reserve. Commissioning was speeded up in 1939, enabling the Navy to integrate more pilots as war approached. And the next year Congress extended to these flyers eligibility for careers in the postwar Navy.

Ed Stebbins was one of them (Pop Condit too), having been a commercial airline pilot who enrolled in the program. He had been a superb SBD pilot in the battles of 1942, and Captain Clark admired his work as air ops officer. Jocko wanted Steb to be the VB-5 skipper as much as he wanted to get rid of Bob Milner—Annapolis '35—over that squadron's fumbling during Run One to Marcus. Also, Milner had failed to eliminate the bitter factionalism among his pilots.

On the return voyage to Pearl Jimmy Flatley sounded out Steb about whether he wanted to take over VB-5. "Hell, yes!" Steb replied. The change was soon made, to the mutual embarrassment of old friends Stebbins and Milner, the latter returning stateside to be a test pilot. When Steb first assembled his pilots he asserted firm leadership, expecting their loyalty "to one commanding officer—me—to *Yorktown*, and to Captain Clark!" Then he introduced new bombing tactics that soon won their respect.

By the time BuPers got the word that Clark on his own authority had fleeted up "one of his own" from ship's company to lead one of the squadrons it could only admonish him. Equally unorthodox, the sudden change meant that Cooper Bright—a nonflyer—moved up to replace Stebbins as air operations officer. Jock admired Bright as well and refused to let BuPers replace him.

The bureau simultaneously made its own changes as the *Yorktown* headed back: Jimmy Flatley, long overdue for a shoreside training assignment, was ordered to relinquish command of Air Group Five to Charlie Crommelin, who was promoted to commander en route to Pearl. One of his division leaders, Lieutenant Commander Ed Owen, another Avcad product, took over Fighting Five. And Avcad graduate Harry Harrison got transfer orders to bring out a new F6F squadron.

Torpedo Five did not change. The overbearing skipper, Avcad alumnus Dick Upson, had been resisted by Junior Condit, now gone. And Upson turned on the other division leader (after himself), Joe Kristufek. Jealous of the handsome and athletic Joe's successes with a Navy nurse or two, Upson (his face partially scarred from a crash) blamed Kristufek for the failure to spot Condit's raft.

Stunned by his accusation, Kristufek said, "I felt like shooting myself." When Clark got wind of this altercation he called both men to the bridge, told Kristufek he was "the hero of the battle" for sinking the Japanese cargo ship, and ordered Upson to apologize. By way of revenge Upson restricted Kristufek to the ship during its stay in Pearl and tried, unsuccessfully, to force him to transfer out.

Another personnel problem in the Air Department had developed during the battle. Matériel officer Curtiss Watts had stayed in his bunk for four days, terrified. Jocko put him in hack and ordered him transferred. Worse, Watts had completely failed to organize the airplane gear and spare parts. No one knew where anything was—"he didn't know shit from Shinola!" observed one wag. Eleven F6Fs and ten TBFs were "down"—unable to fly, some in need of replacement electrical engine harnesses that could not be found anywhere on the ship.

Jimmy Flatley asked Bob Reynolds what was the difference between airplane and automobile engines. "None," said the former trucking company operator. Next day Flatley recommended that Reynolds relieve Watts as acting matériel officer, and Jocko concurred. This change was extraordinary in the extreme: the position called for a lieutenant commander, and Reynolds was still a lowly ensign, though Jocko soon nominated him for "jg."

Recalling from his youth a card file system of auto parts used by a Ford garage in his hometown, Chino, California, Reynolds set up a three-part index card system, one for each plane type: F6F, SBD, TBF. On the ship's return to Pearl he got a plan of the ship showing the location of the holds from Dan Sweeney, the first lieutenant. All airplane parts had simply been randomly dumped into the holds.

The two men worked closely, Sweeney providing 35 sailors to work an entire night opening up the holds. Later, avoiding the main structural beams, Reynolds utilized acetylene torches to have holes cut in bulkheads in the after hangar bay. Then he had the spare parts hung in and around them. No one interfered or questioned him, and gradually the system began to work. And that was all that mattered to J. J. Clark.

As Task Force 15 pressed homeward, the ship received a message early on 3 September from a submarine stalking a Japanese seaplane tender and two destroyers 500 miles to the south. "Did we want to change course and attack?" (Wilding diary) Admiral Pownall said no, so the sub tried to attack the ships but without success.

Two days after that the *Yorktown*'s and *Essex*'s entire air groups—160 still operable planes—went out 130 miles then roared back in a simulated attack on the force from all directions. Charlie Ridgway's fighter directors vectored the *Independence*'s two dozen Hellcats to intercept them. "We topped the *Essex* in both take offs and landings," exulted Wilding in his diary. Jocko never missed.

Plans called for the pilots to carry out much-needed night qualifications south of Oahu on the 7th, then return to Pearl Harbor the next day. But at 1530 on the 6th the force detected a Japanese sub. The destroyers tracked it for an hour, dropping depth charges before losing contact. Also, Hawaii reported that three Army tugboats had been sunk during the day by a sub off Pearl. So the force cancelled the night "quals" and took a shortcut to arrive on the 7th.

An excited Alex Wilding recorded all this and nearly everything else in detail, including his severe case of jock itch in the tropical heat and humidity. Keeping diaries was forbidden, but he had obtained special permission in order to have a detailed record of evolving fighter direction techniques.

On the evening of the 6th the officers gathered in the wardroom for a final assessment of the attack on Marcus. They congratulated themselves, noted Alex, for being a part of "the first of the new carriers to see action."

> Old Navy men say the *Yorktown* is destined to be the hottest ship in the fleet.... Her Captain wants to fight.... [All hands] have shaken down so that it doesn't resemble the ship that put into Pearl two months ago. Everyone ashore looks at her and speaks of her as the leader of all the carriers. It's true she's a taut ship now—but she was a heller three months ago.

Just after sunup next day Flatley led Air Group Five off the ship for the last time, heading for NAS Barbers Point. No sooner had the planes disappeared over the horizon than Jocko was surprised to see them return. Jimmy had arranged them into a formation that spelled "J. J. C." The tribute was shared by most of the crew. And tears filled the eyes of their emotional and immensely proud skipper. The *Yorktown* then led the task force into Pearl.

The high brass showed their satisfaction over the Marcus raid by giving out medals. *Yorktown* and *Essex* skippers Clark and Duncan and their air group commanders received theirs in Admiral Towers's office, after which they threw them away—"they didn't amount to a hill of beans" for such a minor operation. (Conversation with John Raby, *Essex*'s Air Group Nine commander)

Admiral Pownall did not receive an award. Instead, he transferred his flag to the *Lexington,* from which he led two light carriers and escorts in a similar raid against Tarawa atoll in the Gilbert Islands two weeks later. There, again, he behaved erratically, but not enough to alarm his superiors. (Reynolds, *Fast Carriers,* 84–85)

The best news for all hands on *Yorktown* and *Essex* was orders for an immediate high-speed 84-hour transportation run with Army Air Forces and Marine Corps veterans to San Francisco and a return with fresh Marines and supplies. Cots were set up on the hangar deck for them. One passenger was Harry Harrison, headed for his own Hellcat squadron, who recorded the overall confusion and the behavior of Jocko's favorite ACIO: "'Horrible Herman' wanders around looking important as hell but not saying anything. Probably doesn't know anything anyway." (Diary, 7 September 1943)

*Yorktown* cleared Pearl Harbor on the afternoon of the 9th, followed by the other ships, all ringing up 25 knots for the entire voyage. Most personnel relaxed, but not the Old Man. On one occasion he got so angry at OOD Lieutenant (jg) John C. Lovci that he chased him off the bridge and down the ladder, shouting, "Goddammit, you're *never* coming back up here. You're finished!" Lovci told his friends, "I'm not going up there if *God* commands me!" But of course he did.

Clark simply never let up in running a taut—and the best—ship, always "lividly angry when things did not go as he wanted them to go." (Alexander, "Carrier Revolution," 48) As often as not he cursed individuals and in quite the same manner as ferocious Ernie King had. Though in postwar years Clark criticized King for having cursed people ("damn *you*" instead of "damn *it*"), he himself did it and often.

Indeed, tension on the *Yorktown* was constant as long as Jocko Clark commanded. He insisted the ship be the first to launch *and* with the most planes, the first to strike the target and to achieve the highest scores. He invariably volunteered the *Yorktown* for all manner of tasks. He did these things because "he was a *soldier,*" as Cooper Bright put it: "By God, he was a *combat man.* I loved him, just the way he'd operate. I didn't give a damn about his screaming. I didn't like it. I never got used to it. I just took it in my stride; I'd come back laughing."

Clark admired any man who stood up to him with a different point of view. But if Jocko clearly got under someone's skin to intimidate the man, he would rub it in. And from his post on the bridge, he seemed all-seeing, all-knowing about matters large and small.

He thought the one-minute bosun's whistle calls that preceded announcements, especially "chow call," over the PA system were too long— "they upset the whole ship." So he had them abbreviated to about four seconds. He had all hands assemble each morning on the flight deck not only for exercises but also for a muster to ensure that no one had fallen overboard or was otherwise unaccounted for.

The unpopular calisthenics especially irritated Vonk, who did not want to work up a sweat after his morning shower. Feeling quite "smart," he would find an inconspicuous spot where the skipper could not see him and then fake it. Then one morning after his alleged workout when Vonk appeared on the bridge with the weather report Clark remarked, "Just what the hell kind of goddammed exercises were *you* doing?" He never missed a trick.

Ever conscious of cleanliness, Clark one day declared, "We've got to air the bedding on this ship!" So he had lines rigged up over the deck, onto which everyone's blankets were then draped, creating "an awful sight." When the men started to beat them a big cloud of dust arose "to the heavens" obscuring ship and sea—a veritable smokescreen! "Jeez-sus Kee-rist!" Vonk exclaimed on the bridge. "How can you get that much dirt aboard the ship??"

With nearly everyone choking and laughing so hard, Jocko finally declared, "Knock that off!"

He constantly bellowed at everyone, with the notable exception of navigator George Anderson, part of Admiral Towers's "in" crowd.

Because the navigator had the collateral duty of maintaining the ship's library, one day he perused a newly received book—*The New York Yankees* by Frank Graham. Because Clark was always talking about baseball, and the Yankees were his favorite team, Anderson read through the book and had an idea. He casually approached Clark, who was intensely watching everything on the flight deck, and remarked, "Jock, here's a very interesting book. You ought to read it."

"I have no time to read books," he replied. "I've got to get this ship ready to fight a war."

But later Clark went into his sea cabin and skimmed though it. Soon he emerged and remarked, "Andy, I've got some work to do." And he went back inside and closed the door. He spent much of the day reading it, emerging in midafternoon with book in hand and announced, "That's the way to do it! The way the New York Yankees do it: teamwork! They watch for every angle and fight for every inch. This is the way we'll run this ship! This is the way we'll run the war!"

He required *all* hands, especially the pilots, to read the book. Even Raöul Waller, who had always ignored baseball, soon learned much from the assignment.

But Clark returned Anderson's "favor" by assigning him the unusual task of tutoring Herman Rosenblatt—"an exceptionally able young man" in

Jocko's "weatherguesser" Jim Vonk advises a crewman regarding aerological matters on board the newly arrived escort carrier *Liscome Bay* during the fall of 1943. The winsome Varga pinup calendar girl from the January 1943 issue of *Esquire* magazine "peers" over his shoulder. (Photo courtesy of the Vonk family) *Bureau of Aeronautics*

Andy's view—in the duties of a flag secretary, which Herman was to become when Clark put on his admiral's stars. This was "a little bit different" from the usual way naval officers learned, in Anderson's understated recollection.

Rosenblatt moved all his gear, including (to Anderson's amazement) cigars and special gourmet foods he had brought aboard, to the charthouse. There Andy taught him to navigate and stand flag staff watches. An "apt pupil," Rosenblatt learned quickly and well—and remained on the bridge.

By contrast, Anderson never even spoke to Jocko's other "pet" on the bridge, Bob Reynolds, or to most other junior officers. Yet en route to San Francisco Alex Wilding—happily anticipating a short reunion with his wife there—marveled that the aloof navigator "and I had a 15 minute talk—kidded around a bit." (Diary, 10 September 1943)

In fact, Anderson was not an outstanding navigator, nor was Clark the perfect ship handler for that matter. But their spirits soared as the *Yorktown* followed the *Essex* under the fog-topped Golden Gate Bridge the morning of 13 September. They dropped their anchors at 1100 just short of the Oakland Bay Bridge to await a favorable 1430 tide to take them in to NAS Alameda. Andy took note of the current running port to starboard and advised Clark to move to port as the ship was drifting sideways, but Jocko insisted on simply following the *Essex* in.

When the *Yorktown* raised the hook to start in, an alert Raöul Waller noted that the current had caused the ship to drift sideways, then pick up speed, toward the concrete-steel bridge piling off Yerba Buena Island. But three long starboard outrigger radio antennas were positioned horizontally, flush with the forward flight deck. At the very least, they would be snapped off. At worst, the *Yorktown* might crash into the piling, seriously damaging the bridge and the ship.

While Jocko and Andy argued over whether to turn to port, the observant Waller rushed over and tried to break in. Clark took one look and screamed, "Left full rudder! Raise starboard antennas!" Some unknown hero had already pushed the button to start their slow rise toward the vertical position. Breaths were collectively held as the ship passed close by the piling, whereupon Clark barked to the helmsman, "Right full rudder!"

The stern swung the other direction, clearing the piling by 15 feet—except for two of the rising antennas, which snapped off their three-foot-long tips. Junior OOD Bill Bowie, a peacetime lawyer headed for a postwar career as a Maryland judge, described the two antenna ends as "hanging there like two limp pricks." Jim Vonk congratulated Clark on his smart maneuvering, adding, "You just avoided becoming Seaman First." (Anderson transcript #3, 116; conversations with Clark, Waller, Bowie, Vonk, and several former crewmen)

And Jocko immediately ordered Bowie not to note the incident in ship's log—illegal as hell but protecting not only Clark's career but navigator Anderson's as well. In fact, the scare was the only time Bob Reynolds ever saw George Anderson excited. Too much was at stake, making the lie justifiable. The near collision, admitted Clark, "was the nearest I ever came to a court-martial."

For two days officers and crewmen rotated between loading new cargo and spending a few hours ashore living it up and making phone calls. Anderson and other aviators paid a visit to the legendary Mom Chung, the hospitable first American-born woman of Chinese descent to become a physician, who over drinks bestowed on them her special designation as her "fair-haired bastards." (Anderson transcript #3, 117)

Audacious Herm Rosenblatt used Anderson's name to get lodgings at a major hotel for his mother and two sisters in from New York. Bob Reynolds tried telephoning his oldest brother—a Los Angeles shipyard worker—and family five times before he got through. He later apologized in a letter for keeping "that little devil" three-year-old nephew up too late: "Tell him I couldn't shake those Frisco babes off to get back to the phone." But at least he had heard me crying! (Letter to Bill, Alma, and Clarkie Reynolds, 25 September 1943).

While half the crew relaxed ashore, the other half—including the captain—began loading 256 trucks and jeeps, several AAF planes, and 2,000 Marines and soldiers. Next morning, Clark and the other half waited anxiously for the ferryboat to take them into town. When it did not arrive on schedule "Captain Clark blew his top," recalled orderly Bender:

> He personally got on the radio, said half his men were waiting for their liberty, and if he did not see a ferry coming out to the ship in ten minutes he would run the G. D. ship right up on the beach! They evidently knew him or believed him, because in less than ten minutes you could see the ferry moving.

Come dawn the 15th, the ferry had all hands back on board for the 25-knot run back to Pearl. Jocko chafed at his own ship playing ferryboat and was particularly galled when an audacious AAF "second looey" pilot remarked to him en route, "This is a fine fast transport."

"Young man," replied Clark coolly, his lower lip stuck out more than usual, "this is a fighting attack carrier and *not* a goddammed transport!" To demonstrate, he carried out gunnery drills for all to witness. An impressed Army pilot remarked to Alex Wilding that "they never realized a ship could throw up so much lead" and hoped they would never have to attack one. (Diary, 18 September 1943)

The second morning out, Joe Tucker's cumshaw artist (purloiner of "gifts") Chief Pisarski successfully rigged a tow bar to one of the Marine Corps jeeps and discovered it could pull a plane faster than the mule/tractors could, 20 miles per hour instead of five. He convinced Joe to sequester four of them below for the use of the ship. When the ship reached Pearl a Marine colonel checking off his equipment came up four jeeps short.

When Tucker made excuses, the colonel remarked, "Son, don't worry about it. We can get along without four jeeps. It's not going to stop the war. So what?" To which Joe responded, "Colonel, you're a nice, understanding gentleman" who he then invited to his room for a drink. Tucker did not tell Jocko about the jeeps and had them painted Navy gray and given phony stenciled serial numbers.

During the Frisco-to-Pearl run, the *Yorktown*'s bridge—or "can't-win-room"—was untypically quiet when Bill Griffin assumed the conn as OOD from Shack Moore, who repaired to an anteroom to write up the log of his watch. Soon both heard Clark boom out from his sea cabin, "Osser de deck!" Griff jumped to the captain's summons, but Jocko said, "Naw, not you. The other guy." "Oh, no," thought Shack, "where did I blow it?" Trembling, he presented himself to the skipper, who looked up and said calmly, "Have a piece of choklit candy?"

So rarely could the CO allow himself to relax that he used such occasions to converse with crewmen. He asked one swabbie what he ate when the ship was buttoned up during G. Q. "Horse cock sandwich," came the reply (actually spam or baloney). "What do you mean?" Sailor: "Horse cock in the middle and horse cock on both sides." At that, Jocko chewed him out, went back to his room, and laughed uproariously.

He remained intolerant of gambling and put enlisted offenders in the brig "to give them time to think." But a story circulated that on the *Suwannee* a professional gambler (in civilian life) had cleaned out the entire crew until one night he had disappeared while sleeping on the flight deck.

The closer the *Yorktown* got to the tropics the more the rising temperatures and humidity increased the number of seasick troops. Also, the hangar deck, buttoned up tight, "is filled with the odor of gastric content," noted Dr. Gard, who also had to isolate six cases of mumps and two of scarlet fever lest an epidemic break out. At least morale was lifted by a "happy hour" jazz concert by Frank Losey's 13-piece big band and singing by mess stewards in the style of the popular Ink Spots.

The ship entered Pearl Harbor at midday, 20 September, disgorged its cargo, and prepared for the next operation, this time against Wake Island.

Two mornings later, Clark suddenly learned that Eleanor Roosevelt, the ship's sponsor, would come aboard that very afternoon for a visit. Clark admired her immensely and kept a framed and autographed photograph of the president in his office. He immediately sent most of the crew over the starboard side—next to the pier—with paintbrushes. The men labored four hours, only to have the First Lady arrive with Admiral Towers in his gig on the port—unpainted—side!

At 1630 Raöul Waller, according to regulations, passed the word, "Man the rails!" But when Jocko saw the entire crew, in dress whites, running to the deck edge as ordered, he yelled, "What the hell's goin' on? To hell with that goddammed stuff. Put 'em on the flight deck!" So the crew formed up there, with Roosevelt family intimate Herman Rosenblatt showing off as her escort. She then gave a sensible and impressive five-minute talk.

Bob Reynolds missed seeing her in order to enjoy a 24-hour leave playing golf with George Earnshaw at a lush course overlooking Waikiki Beach, as he informed his future golf pro brother. He then spent a fun evening at the Moana Hotel but "damn near broke my back the next morning trying to ride those darn surfboards." Without revealing the presence of four battleships—the most in Hawaii since that fateful December 7th—he wrote, "P. H. has more fighting power now than anyone can imagine, so don't be surprised if something big happens before long." (Letter to Bill, Alma, and Clarkie, 25 September 1943)

To prepare for that the *Yorktown* stood out to sea on the 24th in company with the *Essex* and the new light carrier *Cowpens*. As the ship prepared to conduct carrier qualifications for the pilots of shore-based Air Group One, Joe Tucker had the four ex-Marine Corps jeeps brought up from the hangar. As the airedales quickly respotted the newly landed planes aft for launch, Clark called down to Tucker, "Where the hell did you get these?"

"Captain," the grinning Tucker yelled back, "they just fell from heaven!"

Jocko had the speed of launch and respotting timed and compared with that of the nearby *Essex*. He found that the *Yorktown* could launch 30 percent faster. Soon the other carriers ordered jeeps. But the pilots did not like them; they made the launches *too* fast. So the *Yorktown* soon abandoned them in favor of the slower mules.

During a lull, a call came to Pappy Harshman at Pri Fly, "Request permission to launch one putt-putt." Figuring it was a plane, he said "O.K." The after elevator rose, only to reveal a squat little scooter—"a cushion on two wheels" (swiped during the August raid for F6F spare parts). It had a little propeller that turned and two small wings. Bos'n Dick "Junior" Meyer gunned the motor to go "roaring" down the deck and was "waved" to take off by Hank Warren. Then Meyer reached the forward elevator and was promptly lowered out of sight.

By now, Jocko was wondering "What the hell!?" Tucker figured as much and started for the bridge. When he was halfway up the ladder the PA sounded, "Lieutenant Tucker, report to the bridge!" Meanwhile, all hands topside were laughing at the whole spectacle. The *Yorktown* was a happy ship.

Cooper Bright was one reason for this, but now that he was acting air ops officer—though not a pilot—he knew he had to prove himself. He was all business when he arose before G. Q. next day. He particularly wanted to be certain about the ship's position for the pilots of the predawn launch. So he walked into the charthouse to get it from the navigator, Anderson, still sound asleep.

Coop woke him up—one hour early—and made his request. "God-damm you!" Anderson thundered. "Getting me the hell out of the sack at this hour of the night! Get out of here!"

Bright beat a hasty retreat to Air Plot and just stood there in the dark-ened room wondering what to do. Soon Anderson walked in, still in his pajamas, and said finally, "Bright, I want to talk to you."

"Yes, sir!"

"I shouldn't have talked that way to you."

"Well, commander—"

"No, I shouldn't. Because you're trying to do a job, and you're up here only because you're new. I feel like hell having done that to you. By God, you can get me out of the sack any time you want from now on!"

Coop admired Anderson for that but realized he had to plot the navi-gational data himself—and several times, because some errors were inevitable. If he gave the pilots the wrong data they might get lost and not make it back to the ship. He also realized that Andy made errors, once even admitting to Coop that he took a star sighting only to discover it was a light from a cruiser on the horizon.

Another time Bright made an apparent navigational error himself, which led Hank Dozier to jump on him: "You sonofabitch, we've gotta get an aviator in this job! We're gonna put you ashore!" Dozier was going to take Bright to see the captain personally about his mistake, until Coop discov-ered and revealed that Anderson had made the error in the ship's log. Then Dozier and Anderson covered it up, after which the latter became quite friendly with Bright. (Dozier was friendly with no one.)

During the launch of a TBF armed with antisub depth charges, the plane's engine failed. It "spun in" and immediately sank. The crew escaped, but the depth charges detonated close aboard amidships. Worrying about possible damage to the hull, Clark had underwater divers inspect it upon the return to Pearl. They found nothing wrong—yet.

Air Group One flew ashore early on the 26th, whereupon Air Group Five landed on the ship, was respotted, and took off again. It flew out 100 miles, then attacked the force and returned aboard—but mortifyingly slower than *Essex*'s planes. The ships then reentered Pearl Harbor.

A new operation was in the making—a two-day raid on isolated Wake Island. Preparations now went into high gear for this final live "training" operation by an unprecedented *six* fast carriers. To further speed flight oper-ations, Clark heralded an innovation of arming boss Lieutenant Jim Bryan: instead of loading bombs and torpedoes onto their "skids" (wheeled mount-ing racks) on the flight deck—a 20-minute process—it was done in the hangar in a record three or four minutes. Then the ordnance was hoisted by bomb elevator to the flight deck where the fuses were installed and the projectiles mounted on the planes. Bryan and his crews thereby gave the *Yorktown* 30 percent faster respots and launches.

Coop Bright also saved more time by moving chief fighter director Charlie Ridgway from Air Plot outside to the bridge with his earphones so he could talk directly to the captain instead of the two men shouting through the door to one another. Charlie, businesslike and methodical, got along well with Jocko.

Air Group Five was raring to go, not least the bombers, who were inspired by Ed Stebbins. The new VB-5 skipper and Torpedo Five's Dick Upson had worked out coordinated attacks—with the fighters strafing ahead of them. The pilots liked these tactics and used them to startle new ships arriving at Pearl. Steb also had his rear-seat gunners use tracers with all their .30-caliber machine gun rounds to form a "cone of fire" from 18 planes (thus 36 barrels) astern against Japanese Zero interceptors as the SBDs made their dives. In the predawn darkness this tactic was "an awesome sight."

Steb also speeded safer predawn takeoffs by having the gunner in the lead SBD of each division carry an Aldis lamp for the others to follow off the deck to the rendezvous. Their subsequent quick departure for the target thereby "got them the hell away from the carrier and watchful eyes of Cooper Bright and Captain Clark." The pilots were now eager to show Jocko just how good they were.

On the afternoon of 29 September the *Yorktown* pushed away from Pier Nine toward the harbor entrance, bound for Wake Island. As it moved along at six knots, and was just short of the main exit, the rudder suddenly jammed 20 degrees right. Clark screamed into the loudspeaker, "Back it down! Full speed astern!" as the ship headed toward the beach. Had it run aground, the *Yorktown* might have blocked the harbor entrance for a week.

Fortunately, Blackie McNally's engine crew reacted swiftly enough to stop the ship's progress 60 feet short of a mud bank. Then they shifted to emergency rudder control, enabling the ship to clear the harbor without further ado. The depth charges from the sinking TBF days before had damaged the steering engine circuit breaker, which suddenly tripped. But this was simply the kind of unpreventable surprise that "accounts for some naval officers' hair growing gray at an early age," recalled Clark, who concluded that "I was born lucky; the Good Lord was on my side." (A contradiction actually; typically, he was covering both fronts—sheer chance *and* divine intervention!)

Next day Task Force 14 came together south of Oahu. It was commanded by Rear Admiral Montgomery in the *Essex*. Its sister ships *Yorktown* and *Lexington* were the other heavies, and the light carriers were *Independence, Cow-*

*pens,* and *Belleau Wood.* Three heavy and four light cruisers and 24 destroyers provided antiaircraft and antisub protection. Two fleet oilers would replenish the latter, and submarine *Skate* provided lifeguard services.

Just before evening chow Clark informed all hands of their destination—a two-day attack on 5–6 October that would probably *not* be a surprise to the enemy. "No one is excited," reflected Alex Wilding as one of many new veterans. As for Wake, "We should blow it out of the water."

Japanese broadcast propagandist Tokyo Rose reached the ship's radio receivers. She urged the Americans to give up the fight, which resulted only in smiles from captain and crew. But when she announced that a Japanese sub had just sunk the *Yorktown* Jocko stomped his feet in fury and used every foul word he knew to curse her. Chaplain Alexander quietly gave the skipper "my own special brand of Presbyterian absolution."

Clark ran his ship taut as ever, day and night. Sleeping in pajamas in his emergency sea cabin, he occasionally wandered out onto the dark bridge and started feeling heads. When he found the round dome he thought to be the navigator's, he said, "Andy? Andy?" Often as not, however, it was that of Shack Moore with a cranium shaped much like Anderson's.

On Sunday, the 3rd, during Protestant services in the hangar and just as the worshippers lowered their heads in prayer, the tail gunner of a TBF cleaning his .50-caliber machine gun accidentally triggered it ("I didn't know it was loaded"). Captain Freddy Pennoyer, on board observing as Admiral Towers's matériel officer, ran down from the bridge to investigate.

The accident had wounded three men and damaged a plane. A furious Jocko dressed down the guilty sailor on the bridge, broke him in rank to seaman second class, and said, "You won't be able to fly anymore!"

This last punishment shattered the man, and tears welled up in his eyes. News of this type of punishment soon got around the ship: Do your job, or you don't fight! Proving oneself in battle to the Old Man and to one's peers was the ultimate test and success. (Conversation with Anderson)

During the attack on Wake Captain Pennoyer was watching the planes take off when he spotted the offending TBF roll down the deck. He remarked to Jocko, "I'll bet the tail gunner for that airplane feels like hell."

"Don't you worry," Clark said wryly. "He is in there alright." Jocko had lifted the ban—quiet evidence of his sense of fair play and shrewd leadership.

At least humor resulted from the faux pas of a sailor testing a fire hose on the island structure just as two officers walked below him on the flight deck—unseen. It was Jocko himself with Pennoyer. In a word, both officers were soaked before frantic witnesses on the bridge were able to get the hose shut off. To say the least, the culprit was soon "in the doghouse." (Anderson conversation)

Otherwise, the task force spent the 3rd refueling the escort ships. With the *Yorktown* positioned alongside one tanker, the cruisers refueled one by one on the other side of the oiler, while one destroyer "topped off" on the far side of the *York:* four vessels steaming in line abreast, connected by hoses. Underway replenishment had come to stay, giving the fast carriers true mobility. In fact, in order to refuel safely, the entire force steamed eastward—away from the target—all day the 3rd in order to remain beyond the range of enemy air searches from Wake 420 miles away and Maloelap in the Marshall Islands 600 miles distant.

During the night the force turned west again in a high-speed 25-knot run-in toward Wake, launching TBFs on antisub patrols, F6Fs on CAP after sunup. Two bogeys were tracked on radar over the course of the day, and Clark kept crew and pilots well informed, thereby improving morale. "When these announcements came over the loudspeakers," observed Lieutenant (jg) C. Roger Van Buren (Pop Condit's replacement in VT-5), "you could see everyone begin to get interested . . . to smile and laugh, making all sorts of remarks and speculations." (Diary, 4 October 1943)

The initial launches before daylight on 5 October occurred 90 miles from Wake and were plagued by intermittent rain. One torpecker bumped into a 5-inch gun turret and plunged overboard, with the three men retrieved by a tin can. Engine failure sent an SBD into the sea 30 miles out, killing the pilot (Joel Eshoo), but his gunner survived. Stebbins's Aldis lamps failed to act as beacons because of the dense rain, which also messed up his new bombing tactics. The bombers nevertheless pounded Wake.

As sunlight filled Wake's skies, so did Japanese fighter planes and AA fire. VF-5 Hellcats tore into the Zekes (Zeros) in wild but one-sided dogfights. Ed Owen's pilots sent eight Zekes down in flames, then—with the other air groups—strafed parked Betty bombers. On the return to base, five *Yorktown* fighters that were low on fuel landed on four other carriers. (Reynolds, *Fighting Lady*, 50–52)

Fighting Five's Lieutenant (jg) Jim "Izzy" Pickard took a burst of flak that blew off both wing flaps (airelons) and part of the rear tail assembly (horizontal stabilizer). He was given the option of ditching in the water or coming aboard. He elected the latter and surprised everyone by catching the number two wire in a perfect landing. Clark called him to the bridge for a "well done."

In fact, Jocko often played landing signal officer by screaming over the bullhorn "Too high!" or "Wave him off!" as a plane came up the groove before the pilot cut his engine to land. He called returned pilots to the bridge to question them on what they had seen, chew them out, and/or congratulate them. And before engine warm-ups in the predawn, he bellowed his own war cry over the horn: "Get out there and strike a blow for liberty!" (Gray, "'Jocko' Clark," 46)

Every day of flight operations provided unique incidents. Torpecker jockey Van Buren was coming up the groove to land after bombing Wake when the safety on his machine gun in the bubble turret broke loose, and the gun fired straight aft, cutting off the tail (vertical stabilizer). Van Buren managed to land anyway, with Jocko barking, "Tell that pilot to report to the bridge!" Van was so excited from his flight that he forgot to take off his parachute and other gear and was exhausted by the time he reached the bridge. Jocko roundly criticized him, then said, "Good job!" But neither Van nor his gunner could explain how the safety had failed.

Admiral Montgomery, unlike Pownall at Marcus, fully utilized the power of his task force. The cruisers moved in close to Wake and shelled it. Weatherguesser Vonk predicted—and got—heavy storms for the morrow. But TF 14 remained in the area overnight and clobbered Wake again next day. Unfortunately, the predawn launch in the murk led to five deaths: a Hellcat pilot (Thomas D. Crow) suffered vertigo, causing him to plunge into the sea, and two Dauntlesses collided in midair, killing the pilots (Robert Byron, Robert M. Gregg) and aircrewmen (Anthony P. Zanotti Jr., Fred L. Marty).

Everyone wanted to eliminate the hazardous predawn launches, but all the air admirals for the rest of the war insisted they were essential to ensure the element of surprise. And the complaints continued in kind.

The *Yorktown* was not scheduled to launch another strike, only to provide CAP. But returning air group leader Charlie Crommelin informed the ship that some of Wake's installations still remained unscathed, and he recommended another strike. Clark agreed, as did the admiral. Crommelin led it off at 1140, and an hour later it commenced its attack. Sadly, a burst of flak knocked off the wing of one strafing fighter, sending down the pilot (Cotton Boies) to his death. A second stricken F6F made a water landing next to submarine *Skate*, which took the pilot aboard. The later afternoon CAP, vectored by Charlie Ridgway in CIC, splashed a Japanese Nell medium bomber 30 miles from the force.

But the mood had changed from jubilation to disgust. Several downed pilots from other carriers had been spotted in life rafts, but Admiral Montgomery rejected several requests to have destroyers dispatched to rescue them. Jocko Clark took his ship—now fully bloodied in battle—back to Pearl, confident that it was ready for the first amphibious operation of the Central Pacific offensive.

En route, he finally agreed to qualify his pilots in nighttime takeoffs and landings. Clark had consistently opposed night air operations as unnecessary, but the hazards of predawn launches, rendezvous, and squadron cohesion en route to the target had changed his mind. In fact, Clark had Air Group Five practice after sundown on the way back to Pearl, where they would continue nighttime training.

The other innovation affirmed at Wake was the use of color motion picture film in the gun cameras of the fighter planes. Dwight Long was flown ahead to Pearl Harbor to develop the spectacular footage taken during the battle—added to that from the Marcus and Tarawa raids. This done, he spliced together an eight-minute montage for Clark to show to Admiral Nimitz.

In later years Clark insisted that he had had the film shown to Nimitz and his top advisers and commanders on 9 October 1943. Or perhaps this occurred the next day. For either date, Clark would have to have been flown to Hawaii ahead of the ship. The afternoon of the 11th seems more likely for the showing of the film, after the *Yorktown* tied up alongside Ford Island's pier Fox Two.

The showing was dramatic. In endless meetings ComAirPac Admiral Towers and his key senior airmen had been arguing with the "battleship boys" (or "Gun Club") for the primacy of carriers over battleships in the Central Pacific offensive that was about to shift into high gear. These "black shoes" insisted that their 16-inch guns or "long rifles"—"peashooters" to their opponents—should spearhead the attack.

Towers himself had to leave for a logistics conference in California but left his chief of staff, Captain Forrest "Fuzz" Sherman, to represent him at these discussions in his absence. As Nimitz listened, Sherman with "brown-shoe" air admirals Halsey, Jake Fitch, Ted Sherman, and nonaviator Mick Carney argued for the carriers against the black-shoe admirals Spruance and Kelly Turner. (Reynolds, *Fast Carriers*, 88–90; Reynolds, *Admiral John H. Towers*, 436–41)

Clark and Dwight Long first showed their movie footage privately to Jocko's old friend and classmate Fuzz Sherman. Then Sherman reconvened the strategy meeting by preempting the ongoing discussion: "I'm sorry. We haven't time for this. I have a film here that Captain Clark has brought in. I want you to see it."

As far as Jocko was concerned, the aerial views of fires burning on Marcus, Tarawa, and Wake and gun camera shots of the Nell bomber being ignited by *Yorktown* Hellcats near Wake "settled all arguments." No one had anything to say after that, thereby ending the discussion. The evidence was irrefutable: "You couldn't go anywhere [in the Pacific] till you went in with the aircraft carrier and you took command of the air and destroyed the enemy air." That still had to be proved in an amphibious operation, which would be the case—painfully—during the invasion of the Gilbert Islands in November.

As far as the high command was concerned Jocko Clark was performing up to expectations. Admiral Jack Towers now articulated the Pacific Fleet's satisfaction in his fitness report on Jocko (23 November 1943):

> Captain Clark is an outstanding naval aviator of long experience. He runs a smart ship and is a bold and fearless leader. His ship and air group have been brought to a high state of combat efficiency as demonstrated in the attacks on Wake and Marcus. He is well qualified for a flag command afloat.

# THIRTEEN

## Admirals Must Fight! 1943

O N 12 OCTOBER 1943 REAR ADMIRAL BALDY POWNALL REESTABLISHED
his flag on Jocko Clark's *Yorktown* as Commander Fast Carrier Forces,
Pacific Fleet. Despite doubts in many officers' minds—Clark's foremost—
about Pownall's abilities as a combat leader, he had three excellent "fighting"
admirals to lead his task groups—Montgomery, Radford, and Ted Sherman.
Clark, already earmarked for promotion, now received a letter of commendation from Admiral Jack Towers for his role in the Marcus and Wake raids.

In addition to the flagship *Yorktown*, the five other heavy carriers were
skippered by confident leaders like Clark (though none of them nearly as
bombastic), all of them friends of his: Felix Stump in *Lexington,* Matt
Gardner in *Enterprise,* Ralph Ofstie in *Essex* (succeeding Duncan), John
Ballentine in *Bunker Hill,* and John H. Cassady in *Saratoga.* Five light carriers gave Pownall 11 flattops in all, plus eight escort carriers assigned to the
amphibious forces.

Similarly talented aviation leaders were also needed to orchestrate the
complex and sprawling administration and logistics of ComAirPac. Admiral Towers obviously entertained no thoughts of wasting Clark's fighting
talents behind a desk at Pearl Harbor. But he had no hesitation about tap-
ping some of Jocko's best men for critical posts in orchestrating the air war
in the Pacific.

The task of assigning the thousands of aviation personnel throughout
the expanding Pacific Fleet required a person of meticulous administrative
skills. Towers asked Jocko to give up Raöul Waller to assume this critically
important job. Clark had no choice, but Raöul had told Jocko that he would
very much like to continue their close association—if possible as Clark's
chief of staff when Jocko was promoted. So Clark elicited from Towers (or

*thought* he did) a promise to that effect. Waller was transferred ashore and promoted to captain.

Desperate for a new exec, Jocko thought the best and simplest solution was to move George Anderson into the post. Andy was amenable, especially because the *Yorktown* was just getting started in the fighting. Admiral Towers, however, needed Anderson to be his plans officer (he had allocated all Navy aircraft for Towers at BuAer in 1940–42). Both he and Clark protested his transfer, but in vain. Anderson "hated to leave" the *Yorktown*, but as Bill Bowie remarked to him as he was leaving the ship, "Commander, you and I have had our run-ins, but you're going to go to the top!" And he would—to CNO.

With no remaining ship's officer senior enough to "fleet up" to be executive officer, Clark had to accept someone assigned by BuAer. It was Commander Cameron Briggs, Annapolis '25 and a crack prewar pilot. Loud and gruff, he was the complete opposite of the soft-spoken Waller. In fact, his personality resembled that of Jocko—a fighter. They would soon get into shouting matches, but in port they would go ashore and have a beer together.

A combined farewell-and-welcoming cocktail party was held at an O-club (officers' club), followed by a steak dinner aboard ship. Dr. Gard in a letter described mustachioed Cam Briggs as having "close cropped hair, two big fists and is plenty tough. Everybody likes him very much and so do I." But "Jocko's speech was an embarrassed effort. He can fight better than he can speak."

The fleet was growing so rapidly that many transfers were occurring in order to spread experience among the new carriers. To replace departing officers, Clark usually succeeded in moving up his own people. He shifted assistant air officer Red Sharp, now a commander, to navigator and brought Pappy Harshman up from the flight deck to the bridge to succeed Red.

Cooper Bright as Stebbins's successor measured up to Jocko's standards as air ops officer, in spite of the fact he was not an aviator. But dour air officer Hank Dozier did not like Coop, so Clark assigned a veteran VB-5 pilot, Lieutenant Alfred Wright Jr., to be Bright's assistant. Coop found Wright, a prewar writer for *Time* magazine, very congenial as they played word games during idle moments. But Wright had one problem—he had grown a goatee. And Jocko *hated* beards.

When Clark wandered into Air Plot he immediately encountered bewhiskered Al Wright, who loved to stroke his new goatee. "Stand up!" Jocko shouted. "That damned beard! You're ugly enough!" One day Clark actually put Wright in hack just for having it. Still, Al refused to shave it off and wrote to Henry Luce, his old boss at *Time,* to pull strings to get him transferred.

The first major task facing the *Yorktown* before the invasion of the Gilbert Islands was qualifying Air Group Five's pilots, temporarily based at NAS Puunene on Maui, in night carrier operations. The *Yorktown* and *Lexington,* escorted by four tin cans, left Pearl on 15 October and landed the planes in daylight. After sunset they took off, their visibility aided only by a partial moon, and came in for landings guided by lighted wands waived by LSO Dick Tripp. Each pilot made two landings to qualify and all succeeded, although three fighters and a torpecker ended up in the wire barrier.

Next day the *Independence* joined the formation for gunnery and air operations, and again the *Yorktown* beat both carriers in speed of launch and recovery. During the booming of the 5-inch, 40-mm, and 20-mm guns, Clark stuffed cotton in his ears. This made quite a sight, added to the customary white salve applied to his protruding lower lip and white cloth cover over his hump nose to prevent sunburn. On one occasion the cotton was hanging out of his ears when he ambled through Air Plot. When he was gone, Coop Bright blurted out, "Who the hell was that who just walked through here—Santa Claus?" (Conversation with Walter J. Spiess)

During flight operations Clark made sojourns back to Pri Fly where he yanked the megaphone from Pappy Harshman with both hands. He blew into it first, making a sound "like a damned hurricane." Then he would yell through it at the airedales on deck. Once when Jocko grabbed it, Pappy's thumb stayed in the megaphone, hurting him. "Goddammit," thought Pappy, "next time I'll be ready for him!"

So when Harshman next spotted Jocko coming from the bridge, he carefully turned the speaker part of the megaphone around. Clark grabbed it and blew into it. No sound. No "hurricane." He blew and blew "till his ears turned pink," recalled Pappy. Still no sound. Finally, he looked at it with an odd expression until it dawned on him what had happened.

Then he looked at Pappy, never said a word, and handed him the megaphone—and never came back to Pri Fly to do it again. He had gotten the message from one of his most trusted lieutenants, and the matter was settled, Jocko style.

On 17 October Jesse Rodriguez and his fellow parachute riggers broke out their thousandth-landing cloth banner, amended to show 4,000. When a Hellcat flown by Lieutenant Harry E. Hill grabbed the wire for number 4,000, Jocko greeted him on deck with the customary frosted cake. The air group then flew ashore, and the *Yorktown* headed in.

As Clark conned the ship toward pier Fox Nine, starboard side to, he welcomed the harbor tugboats to assist, inasmuch as a steady breeze across the starboard bow was pushing the bow to the port side and the stern toward shoal water. The tug *Mamo* moved in under the flight deck overhang and the flare of the bow to push. Unfortunately, the tug bent its smokestack against the hull, a not uncommon problem that the older tall-stack tugs had with the new carriers.

*Mamo*'s skipper backed off to avoid further damage. Jocko had his radio talker send a message, "Tug *Mamo*, come alongside and push." The tug answered with its whistle but did not close in to push. At that, Clark had the bos'n bark the order over the bullhorn—only to receive the same response. The shoals were getting ominously closer. "I'm gonna blow these Canucks out of the water," he growled, "if they don't pull me in far enough." (It's not known where he learned the pejorative French Canadian nickname, Canuck.)

The Junior OOD, Shack Moore, handed a megaphone to Clark. He looked at it but could not decide whether his lips went inside or outside of the mouthpiece. Finally, afraid that his ship would drift into the shoals, he mounted his little round stool on the side of the bridge, service collar open, cap 30 degrees off center, waving the megaphone, and screamed out with his powerful voice: "Goddamm you, *Mahoi*, come alongside and push!"

He had even forgotten the name of the little boat, and the expletives rolled out across the water. "*Mikki, Mikki*, move that tug! If you Canucks can't do it, *I'll* get down there and pull it in myself. You sons of bitches!"

The crew of the *Yorktown* exploded with laughter during Jocko's "little talk with one of the tug captains," as Dr. Gard put it. "Some fun. A lesson in seamanship cursing that I have never heard even remotely approached. It was a masterpiece of naval eloquence." Although *Mamo* never did push, other tugs did, and the *Yorktown* was finally eased into Fox Nine.

Ten days of alterations to the ship at the Navy yard were followed by three weeks taking on supplies for the invasion of the Gilbert Islands. This allowed some leisure time. No letters Clark wrote to his family survive, but Chaplain Bob Alexander once caught him writing a letter on pink stationery to "his fiancée" (name and circumstances unknown). Jocko also sat for an excellent portrait by combat artist Seymour Thompson, although when he presented it to Clark he got the response, "Since when are my eyes blue?" An overnight touch-up turned them brown. (Conversations with Alexander and J. J. Vonk)

Still an avid and excellent golfer, fiercely competitive, Clark managed to squeeze in a few rounds in Hawaii, sometimes with Earnshaw and/or Reynolds. In a foursome with Admiral Towers's medical officer, Captain George D. Thompson, Jocko guffawed when Thompson—flailing away at a ball buried in hilly rough—fell down a small ravine. Later Clark had his metalsmiths fashion an oversized replica of a Purple Heart medal, denoting a battle wound. He then presented it to Thompson with great fanfare.

The ship's preparations for major combat were scheduled to be judged during a major inspection by the top brass. To prepare for it, Hank Dozier ordered Cooper Bright to arrange haircuts for all Air Department personnel. Coop had to improvise for its hundreds of men: he convinced Jim Vonk to let him set up a temporary barbershop in the weather balloon room in the island, and he recruited ordinary sailors to serve as emergency barbers. They butchered the men's heads ("Got a haircut to end all haircuts," wrote diarist Wilding). And then the medicos ordered the balloon room evacuated as unsanitary for the sailors who bunked there. When the cut hair was swept out, it blew all over the flight deck.

A laugh a minute, it seemed, but *Yorktown*'s cleanliness became obvious to men who visited other ships. "I'm glad I'm on this one," Dr. Gard wrote to his family. "It seems from all I can hear that I picked the aristocratic sea duty. Everyone I meet wants to go on this ship or tells me how lucky I am."

Bob Reynolds certainly shared that view. As acting matériel officer he had helped clean up the *Yorktown* by his most unorthodox alterations to the aircraft maintenance spaces—the holes cut in bulkheads, aircraft parts hung in and around them, a storeroom of several well-arranged holds, the meticulously ordered file card inventory of parts, and working spaces with counters for each plane type.

He had the system working smoothly by the time of the prebattle inspection by several admirals and captains, some from BuAer in Washington. They included Captain Jack Pearson, the former caretaker of Jocko's young daughters.

All hands mustered for the inspection, decked out in dress whites. During the ceremony Reynolds, still only an ensign, stood with the other department heads—all commanders. Afterward, each one reported to his working area for the brass to inspect it. For Reynolds, this was the after end of the hangar, near the fantail. And he had ensured that everything there was spick-and-span.

Ere long, he saw Jocko approaching with three admirals and Captain Freddie Pennoyer, ComAirPac matériel chief, and other brass. "Uh-oh," thought Reynolds, "it will hit the fan now."

After the officers had looked over his work spaces, Pennoyer remarked to Reynolds, "This is pretty good looking. I don't know where you got the right to cut the bulkheads. But it looks like it really functions. Who's your boss?"

"I don't have a boss. I'm it!"

"Ah, come on, this ship doesn't run by ensigns!"

After Reynolds explained the fate of Lieutenant Commander Watts, he had to review his background as an engineering drafting teacher and trucking company operator and to explain that *nothing* in the air matériel department had been functioning when Clark had given him carte blanche.

Pennoyer then walked over to Clark and said, "Jock, what's all this matériel hanging from the bulkheads? What would happen to them in a storm?" and other implied criticisms.

Jocko said he had wondered too but managed to successfully defend Reynolds's performance.

Presently, Pennoyer returned to Bob, "I had to put up a front because you skirted the regulations by doing this yourself. But I admire you. By God, we've got some good civilian ideas in this navy. Now," he warned, "a Captain Pearson is going to come to you."

Pearson soon walked up and remarked to Reynolds, "Hey, I want to see the wonder boy!"

"I don't know what you're talking about," replied Reynolds.

"The guy who's Jocko's matériel officer on the *Yorktown*."

"That's me."

"By God," said Pearson, "you got Pennoyer's attention, and from now on the plans of these ships are going to follow *this* one!" He went on questioning the "wonder boy"—one of several on this remarkable ship. A few days later Reynolds's promotion to lieutenant (jg) came through, making him a little less junior to his fellow department heads.

As supplies were brought aboard, some of the edibles—including Admiral Pownall's fruit cocktail—were pilfered by crewmen for their own enjoyment. But Clark had to draw the line at his Avocet goat's milk. "One time he lined up his Marines," orderly Bob Bender recalled, "and let us know we were stealing him blind in his kitchen, but would we stay away from his fresh milk. He needed that for his ulcers and stomach. We did."

After the planes of Air Group Five flew over from Maui to Ford Island, they were hoisted on board by crane on 9 November. The pilots walked aboard. "There isn't any power that can withstand the force that is gathering in this broad Pacific," Ray Gard wrote to his family that night. "The end is a question of time and space. It is as inevitable as the setting of the sun. Tojo did the wrong thing when he slapped our face."

With the crew mustered on the flight deck the *Yorktown* cast off its mooring lines at 1530 next day, 10 November, and headed out. As it cleared the harbor entrance the band played "Farewell to Thee" ("Aloha 'Oe"), making Alex Wilding wonder "if it had any special significance." Dr. Gard had no such doubts as the ship rendezvoused with other vessels of Task Force 50.

Rendezvous!!—and how! Never will I forget that marvelous sight. Are there any other ships anywhere? There is more of everything here than I've ever seen before and I have not the slightest fear or doubt about its successful ending. A splendid Captain, a good ship and the finest planes that have ever gone into the air.

Actually, the rendezvous comprised only two of the four task groups: 50.1, personally headed by TF 50 commander Pownall—*Yorktown, Lexington,* and *Cowpens;* and 50.2 under Radford—*Enterprise, Belleau Wood,* and *Monterey;* plus a plentitude of accompanying battleships, cruisers, and tin cans. As they formed up, the ships learned that the two other groups were with Halsey attacking the big Japanese base at Rabaul in the South Pacific: Montgomery's 50.3—*Essex, Bunker Hill,* and *Independence;* and Ted Sherman's 50.4—*Saratoga* and *Princeton.*

Days later, the latter groups were to proceed northeast, rendezvous with the other two, and begin pounding enemy airfields in the Gilberts and Marshalls. Then all would join the eight escort carriers softening up the landing beaches at Tarawa and Makin and be prepared to engage the Japanese battle fleet should it sortie from Truk in the Carolines.

In *Yorktown's* CIC Alex Wilding did not share Dr. Gard's optimism. He worried about enemy airdromes to the north as well as submarine bases in the Marshalls.

I really believe we will be torpedoed or bombed this time. I don't see how we can miss. For three weeks we will stand in range of 5 Jap air bases [Kwajalein, Wotje, Maloelap in the northern Marshalls, Mili and Jaluit in the southern] and take everything they can throw at us—they say the Japs have about 250 planes on these islands [plus possibly several hundred carrier planes with the enemy fleet at Truk].

In spite of the 660 planes at Task Force 50's disposal, "Somehow I'm worried about this trip and don't feel the security I usually feel on these missions"—actually, he had only two under his belt, Marcus and Wake, and they were minuscule by comparison. "I'm making all preparations to abandon ship at any time."

Many in the high command shared Wilding's concerns, and they acted accordingly. Admiral Nimitz had appointed Vice Admiral Spruance—the victor at Midway—to command this Central Pacific Force. Under him were Pownall of the carriers and Rear Admiral Kelly Turner leading the amphibious forces. These included the eight escort carriers to provide close air support for the Marines and Army troops assaulting Tarawa and Makin in the Gilbert Islands.

Against the arguments of all aviation admirals, including Towers, who insisted that the fast carriers should exploit their offensive mobility to destroy enemy air and sub bases in the Marshalls, Spruance and Turner tied them down in confined defensive sectors off the two Gilbert islands during and after the assaults on them.

This was anathema to Jocko Clark as well, and the problems that he had had with Pownall during the Marcus raid began to resurface. Tensions mounted during the week before the final run-in to the targets. At least Pownall had a superb chief of staff in Captain Truman J. Hedding—a tall, cool, confident, neatly attired officer who smoked with a cigarette holder. He was a marked contrast to the short, nervous, chain-smoking admiral.

One logistical problem the *Yorktown* faced was having sufficient fresh water. Because the crew and pilots, perennially soaked in sweat from the tropical heat, kept taking showers, supplies always ran low. Raöul Waller had therefore instituted designated "water hours" morning and night for showering; otherwise, no water.

Now his successor, Cam Briggs, declared, "To hell with water hours!" At that, the crew rushed to the showers, creating such a shortage that the exec simply had to shut off the water from nonessential uses. Some confined compartments, especially during G.Q., now stunk so badly as to be unbearable. "You gotta get these guys to bathe!" the medicos told Briggs. So back the ship went to water hours. (Conversation with Jesse Rodriguez)

On 13 November good news: Captain Hedding announced that Montgomery's planes had shot down 88 Japanese planes over Rabaul in the south. "This proves what *those* ships can do. Let's see what *these* ships can do!"

Four days later a sad event occurred. A young medical corpsman, Ken Rayford, died from apparent asphyxiation by fumes and was buried at sea with appropriate funeral services—the crew's first, and therefore sobering. (Reynolds, *Fighting Lady*, 60–61, 110; letter from Dr. Charles A. Turner, former ship's corpsman, 22 August 1987)

The *Yorktown* launched its first CAP the third day out, 12 November, and next day a reported Japanese submarine contact did not materialize. On the 15th a TBF returning from an antisub hop had engine failure coming up the groove and ditched close aboard; pilot and crew were rescued by a tin can. Rough seas that day and next made topping off destroyers hairier than usual. The final run-in on the 17th and 18th produced no bogeys—incredibly.

With the landings at Tarawa and Makin set for 20 November, Admiral Pownall placed his task group between the Gilberts and Marshalls for predawn strikes on the 19th. Bucking foul weather, *Yorktown's* Hellcats braved the flak to shoot up parked and taxiing planes at Jaluit and Mili in the Marshalls—180 miles northwest and 80 miles north respectively. But they lost the excellent pilot who had splashed the Nell at Wake, John F. Furstenberg. Glide-bombing torpeckers flattened buildings and blew up an ammo dump at Mili. Later, Ed Stebbins and his SBDs "visited" the island with 2,000-pound blockbusters and 500-pound Torpex depth bombs.

No enemy planes approached the task group, leading everyone to expect night air attacks at which the Japanese had become adept in the South Pacific. Yet none came as the *Yorktown* and TG 50.1 moved overnight to a point some 70 miles due west of Makin by dawn of D-day, the 20th. There they and Radford's *Enterprise* group supported the Army's landings.

Charlie Crommelin led the first mission to strafe and bomb in front of the landing barges as the troops hit the beach at Makin. Unfortunately, Jocko Clark's penchant for fast launches put the 19 VF, 19 VB, and 8 VT over the target at 0720, an hour earlier than scheduled and into the teeth of a heavy rain squall. So FDO Charlie Ridgway ordered Crommelin to orbit nearby until the assault began at 0815. The landing went fairly well, in contrast to the one at Tarawa, where the Marines battled an exceptionally low tide and fanatical resistance to suffer heavy losses. Then Crommelin led another strike to Jaluit to pound enemy merchant ships and seaplanes.

During the course of the day *Yorktown* radio listeners picked up a Japanese order for its carrier force to depart its anchorage at Truk in the Caroline Islands "to intercept us, also for every submarine to hurry to this area and for land-based bombers on Kwajalein to find us and attack as soon as possible." (Wilding diary) Afternoon air searches from *Yorktown* out to 150 miles found nothing, while one from *Lexington* shot down a lone snooper.

Part of the Japanese message proved all too accurate. At dark, Montgomery's group splashed six torpedo-laden Bettys, but another one got through to score a hit on the *Independence*. It limped away to a South Pacific base for repairs. This left the rest of the fast carriers—now deprived of their mobility by Spruance's defensive cruising sectors—to gird themselves for more expected torpedo attacks, by air and by submarine.

Jocko Clark darkened ship at sunset this 20th day of November and turned the *Yorktown* into the wind to receive its last four-plane CAP. Suddenly, *Lexington's* CIC vectored these Hellcats to intercept a bogey 50 miles out. They complied, only to discover it to be a single AAF B-24 bomber, its guns all trained on the CAP leader when he flew alongside to copy its serial number.

Then the leader took his division back through a rainsquall, only to land in the dark mistakenly on the *Lexington*. Its CIC soon received word from the AAF that this particular B-24 had recently been shot down over Bougainville in the Solomons—and had obviously been refurbished and flown by the enemy to "snoop" the American fleet.

At 0245 on the 21st *Yorktown*'s CIC radars registered two separate flights of six to eight bogeys 20 and 34 miles due north of the ship, heading south, obviously from the northern Marshalls. Clark sounded G.Q. as Ridgway tracked both flights to nine and 24 miles until they headed off to the east, having missed seeing the task group. A third contact of four to six planes closed in, and Admiral Pownall slowed ships' speeds to eight knots to reduce the visibility of the ships' wakes.

It seemed to work, inasmuch as these bogeys finally faded from the radarscopes at 0348. But Pownall kept his ships buttoned up on the assumption—correctly—that daylight would bring back the snoopers. At 0540 *Yorktown* and *Cowpens* each launched a division of fighters, vectored to the intercept by Smokey Stover. A *Cowpens* fighter beat VF-5 to the kill of one Betty 46 miles to the southeast. The raid did not close.

All three *Yorktown* squadrons took off at dawn to bomb runways and AA positions on Mili, but the damage they inflicted did not prevent the enemy from staging in more planes by afternoon. Chief of staff Captain Hedding called up the VF-5 ready room for eight fighters to reconnoiter the island for any bombers there. If so, another full strike could be sent to Mili.

Charlie Crommelin, though group commander, hustled up to the flag bridge and asked to lead this recon. "Certainly," replied Hedding, "but just fly over and take a look and tell us what you see. Do not try to attack."

After a 120-mile flight to Mili Crommelin ordered the other six Hellcats to orbit while he and his wingman flew down for a closer look. He soon sighted several twin-engine bombers taxiing into position for takeoff. The temptation was too much for Charlie. Ignoring Hedding's order, he bored in and set a Nell bomber afire. Without even calling in his squadron mates, he came around for a run at 1,000 feet on a Betty.

Suddenly, a medium-caliber AA shell hit his plane and exploded in the cockpit. Shrapnel peppered Crommelin's body, inflicting over 200 separate wounds, and damaged the plane. In spite of searing pain, he managed to level off at three hundred feet and fly all the way back to the ship—guided by a fellow pilot flying wing.

"Clear the deck!" Jocko Clark yelled over the bullhorn. "Charlie's comin' aboard!" Freshly landed planes had already been spotted forward, but a thoroughly upset Pappy Harshman at Pri Fly implored through his megaphone: "Get those planes spotted forward closer! The air group commander's wounded! Get 'em up there!" His exhortations continued until Hank Dozier cut him off, "That's enough."

Crommelin, looking at his wingman, obeyed LSO Tripp's signal to "cut" his engine, and the plane hit the deck and caught a wire. He even taxied it forward to park but collapsed trying to climb out of the cockpit. Dwight Long caught the whole drama on film. In sick bay Dr. Gard managed to save a badly injured eye. When Charlie regained consciousness he instructed one of his pilots, "Tell Captain Hedding that I'm sorry I did not do what he told me to do"—only reconnoiter, not attack. Hedding was damned sorry too.

Jocko, already thinking ahead, passed the word over the loudspeaker, "Lieutenant Commander Stebbins, report to the bridge."

When he arrived Clark said to him, "Stebbins, can you fly a Hellcat?"

"Negative."

"O.K.," said Jocko, knowing better, "you go up in one this afternoon."

VF-5 skipper Ed Owen checked him out in an F6, and Steb took off and flew around the ship so all could see and trust him in a fighter. He made a perfect landing, whereupon Clark named him to replace Crommelin as air group commander. (Jensen, *Carrier War*, 7) The cocky exec of VB-5, Lieutenant Daniel J. Harrington III, moved up to squadron command.

Again, Clark had selected a "chosen son" from his own ship—and a bomber instead of the usual fighter pilot at that—rather than waiting for ComAirPac to assign a new group commander. In the middle of an operation it was understandable. Besides, Stebbins recalled, by Clark appointing one of his own, he preserved the distinction of having "the Number One air group on the Number One ship under the Number One skipper!" And, most unusual, the carrier's air group commander and two of the three squadron commanders (Owen and Upson) were Avcad instead of Naval Academy graduates (Harrington '38)—but that was typically pragmatic for the unorthodox skipper Jocko Clark.

Stebbins immediately briefed the three squadrons on his expectations for teamwork and assured them he would never commit Crommelin's mistake of attacking enemy planes instead of coordinating the air group.

Finally, Steb could work easily with his lively bald roommate and former Air Plot colleague Cooper Bright. With six carriers here, rather than the three used in the Wake operation, Coop suggested that the airborne Steb broadcast "blind" on high frequency during each attack. Bright could switch over from VHF to HF on a simple Hallicrafters radio receiver that the two men had bought on the advice of an old warrant officer at Norfolk. This would enable them to provide a play-by-play account of the battle for Jocko and the admiral—and make the *Yorktown* the first carrier to get news of the battle.

Stebbins agreed, enabling Coop to "take possession" of 728 megacycles as his own personal radio frequency. Beginning with Steb's first sortie as group leader, Bright heard Steb's transmission: "Skinhead, this is 99 Cairo. First report follows." Stebbins also learned to use the K-28 automatic camera to go in low over the target (as Crommelin had) for good, rapid pictures. These were developed quickly in the ship's photo lab, with the wet prints flown immediately to the amphibious commander—another *Yorktown* first.

All this was possible because of Jocko Clark's faith in the expertise of his best officers. He was clearly exasperated, however, by the defensive tactics that kept his ship vulnerable to both enemy planes and submarines. On the 22nd, after the *Yorktown* launched more strikes against Mili, a sub was sighted at periscope depth, but it went deeper.

Admiral Pownall ordered additional antisub patrols, meaning TBF torpeckers—18 in a squadron—most of them now armed with bombs to drop on Mili. Bright had no choice but to inform Clark out on the bridge, "We can't cover the antisubmarine patrol *and* get the bombs over the target the way they've made out this operation plan. The staff has made a bust!"

Clark turned to Bright and in his customary way screamed, "Goddamm you! I've got a job to do up here. *You've got a job to do.* The only thing I do is fight the Japs! To hell with the submarines! Fight the Japs! Get the hell off of here!" Bright retreated to Air Plot and "put damned near everything that had a bomb on it and sent it to the target. To hell with the antisubmarine patrol." The admiral later summoned Clark down to the flag bridge and asked him "what the hell I was doing." He replied, "Fightin' the Japs!" Later on, when Coop returned to the captain's bridge, Jocko said to him, "By God, you did a great thing today. You cut out that goddammed antisub patrol!"

It *was* a bold move, inasmuch as none of the subs already detected were American. That same day frustrated torpecker pilot Van Buren told his diary, "We know damn well that there are Jap subs out there, but we can't seem to find them. Or maybe they can't find us." (22 November 1943)

The regular antisub flights and the sonar gear of the destroyers on the screen continued the vigil, of course. But Clark simply refused to commit more of his few TBFs to the task—a hard choice, a calculated risk. His intuition (based on expertise and experience) told him that the many enemy torpedo-bombers staging through Kwajalein to Mili and Jaluit likely posed the greater threat than a sub or two.

Returning from a strike against Mili that day, Ed Stebbins went out of his way for three hours to direct the lifeguard sub *Plunger* to the successful rescue of a downed pilot in a raft—no more lost Pop Condits. During early evening, the *Yorktown* learned that a destroyer had forced a Japanese sub to the surface, rammed and sunk her, capturing survivors. So Clark's orders for the morrow were purely defensive, with two CAPs and two antisub patrols, *and* to provide protection for the island of Makin, where the last enemy troops had perished and the damaged airfield was being made serviceable.

A large midmorning raid of Zero fighters from the Marshalls on the 23rd led Smokey Stover in CIC to vector *Lexington's* CAP to intercept them, while *Yorktown* scrambled 22 Hellcats. *Lex's* pilots splashed them—at least 16 bandits—before VF-5 even arrived on the scene. Continuous air operations by the fast and escort carriers led to several wayward pilots needing refuge on any flattop, even after the sun set.

Clark agreed to take aboard five FM Wildcat fighters from the escort carrier *Liscome Bay,* who were being led by a VB-5 SBD to the darkened *Yorktown.* Dick Tripp waved the first one aboard at 1834, then two more. But he gave the fourth one a wave-off. The panicky pilot ignored it but came in too high to land, dipped, then tried to regain altitude, only to have his tail hook grab an arresting wire. This stopped the Wildcat's momentum, but it jumped the barrier and slammed into the parked planes.

In seconds, four airedales were crushed to death, fire engulfed the forward flight deck, and Jocko sounded G.Q. and bellowed over the horn, "Fire marshal and fire brigade, lay up to the flight deck on the double!"

John Montgomery grabbed a hose and led his terrified youngsters into the blaze, then used a mule to tow out burning planes (two Hellcats, two Wildcats) to be jettisoned overboard. Joe Tucker started generating fire-retardant foam to pour over exposed bombs and planes, then hurried down gangways to the hangar, which he saved by turning on the overhead sprinklers. Exec Cam Briggs rushed down to the flight deck to direct the firefighters forward, as fire marshal Barney Lally reached the flight deck and maneuvered more fire hoses into the conflagration. (Jensen, *Carrier War,* 76–77)

Jocko kept the helm into the wind to blow the flames away from still-unscathed planes, slowed speed from 20 to 18 knots, and thundered at his shipmates, especially one in an asbestos suit with a hose near the island, spurring them on: "Get that fire out! We can do it! We've done it before! We're not gonna lose another ship! You're not gonna let me lose *this* ship! It's all we've got!"

He turned to go into Air Plot to check on any enemy planes, but the door was locked shut under G.Q. "Open the goddammed door!" he roared, and once inside he learned a Japanese torpecker was approaching. "Stand by to repel enemy attack off the port bow!" the loudspeaker roared. Clark yelled to the helm, "Hard right!" The ship turned sharply to evade it. But the plane was probably the last *Liscome Bay* fighter, now diverted to the *Lexington.*

Alex Wilding, asleep in his room after a hot, grueling day in CIC, bolted upright at hearing G.Q. He struggled against "a solid mass of humanity" jammed into darkened passageways and fought the fresh water from the hoses in hatchways and hangar. Finally reaching the flag bridge, he had to duck as bullets from belts of aircraft machine guns exposed to the fire "splattered the bulkhead. But what I saw left me breathless. The whole ship was afire amidships on the flight deck. Flames were shooting a hundred feet in the air—five planes were in flames with their gasoline tanks exploding."

Other ships in the task group figured the *Yorktown*—all aglow—was finished. Then a nearby submarine contact was reported—false alarm, thank God. But Clark kept his ship twisting and turning as long as its fires made it a sitting duck. Suddenly, at 1905, they ended, only 16 terrifying minutes after the crash.

Clark immediately descended to the flag bridge and asked, "Admiral, may I go below and work on that flight deck?" Pownall believed a skipper's place to be the bridge, but Clark "was so energetic . . . I let him go." (Pownall transcript #2, 139) Following cleanup, only two small scorch marks on deck marked the maelstrom. And Clark obtained the Navy and Marine Corps Medal for Tucker, Montgomery, Lally, and other deserving firefighters.

Among the men left walking around in a daze was the pilot of the crashed Wildcat, Lieutenant Foster J. Blair. As a squadron mate of Smokey Stover at Guadalcanal he had shot down enemy bombers, and Charlie Ridgway had been a shipmate on the *Saratoga*. A skin rash had given Blair his nickname of "Crud"—which led Ridgway to reflect: "some suspicion that his nickname is appropriate." Assigned to Harry Harrison's squadron in Hawaii, he had been transferred to the *Liscome Bay* for failing to appear for his night carrier landing quals. Blair's fear of them had finally caught up with him.

At least by crashing onto the *Yorktown,* Crud Blair had coincidentally saved his own life. A few hours later, at 0513 on 24 November, the lookouts were startled as the inky predawn horizon lit up from an explosion. A Japanese sub had finally found a carrier—the *Liscome Bay.* The glow brightened as the "baby flattop" exploded, burned, and sank. Out of its crew of 916 men, 644 perished, including two of Clark's former shipmates—Rear Admiral Henry Mullinix, his exec on the destroyer *Brooks,* and the carrier's captain, Irving Wiltsie, the former navigator on the old *Yorktown.*

The new *Yorktown* immediately launched its fighter CAP and an anti-sub patrol of six dive-bombers, one of which sighted a submarine periscope only 20 miles out and made a bombing run, forcing it to dive deeper. This was at 0935, just as the ship was holding its second burial at sea—for five shipmates, William J. Cody, Joseph Coppi, Gilbert R. Howk, David S. Kasakow, and John J. Martin.

Jocko, moved by the tragedy that had befallen the *Liscome Bay*, decided not to reprimand Crud Blair. When the man apologized to Clark for his crash landing, Jocko simply replied that his mishap was "incident to service" and that at least he had not gone down with his ship. Blair and his two squadron mates were later transferred to the *Saratoga* for passage to Hawaii.

At midday, after a strike on Mili, fighters from the *Lexington* intercepted perhaps 20 Zeros and some Bettys near the island, 102 miles north of the *Yorktown*. Admiral Pownall, expecting an attack, had Clark launch all the planes on deck and have those in the hangar manned. But the fight was near Mili, where more Zekes jumped the *Lex* Hellcats. *Yorktown* dispatched 20 fighters hence, only to discover that *Lexington*'s VF-16 had repulsed the bandits, shooting down at least ten and chasing the rest back to Kwajalein at a cost of one *Lex* pilot.

Captain Felix Stump of the *Lexington* was pleased to have his guys finally succeed on both days before those of his old friend Jocko could even reach the battle. Stump "never heard Clark say anything unfavorable" about his ship "or that any ship was luckier than" Jocko's. But Clark did send a nice signal to Stump: "Well, you've beat us out so far. I hope we have better luck next time." (Conversation with Stump)

He never stopped competing and even had his two telephone "talkers" on the bridge watch different carriers to let him know exactly when they launched and recovered planes so he could compare their times with *Yorktown*'s. (Conversation with Richard E. Drover)

No planes attacked the task group, but the admiral received a message from Pearl Harbor saying Japanese naval forces were moving into the Marshalls, leading to speculation over a possible surface engagement. But it never matured, and the task group withdrew to the south to refuel, replaced by Radford's *Enterprise* group.

The increasing nighttime combat activity led Clark to rely on his very best OODs, among them Lieutenants (jg) Julian D. Porter and Dick Drover, to conn the ship. Porter was one of the few OODs who could coolly and deftly take the ship through the screen, then back in, during air operations. Clark called upon Drover, an architect by profession, so often that he became "duty happy," yet all in a day's work.

When bogeys were reported during the night, Clark required that the OOD knock on the door of his sea cabin and tell him exactly what had been seen on the radar, notably the course and speed of the bogey. When it seemed to be threatening, he would get up and take over. (Conversation with Drover)

The next day was 25 November 1943, and the Plan of the Day announced: "TODAY IS THANKSGIVING DAY—WE HAVE PLENTY TO BE THANKFUL FOR!" The Plan of the Day was written by Cam Briggs, the new exec who favorably impressed all hands. Alex Wilding compared him to gruff movie actor Wallace Beery—"very human and a good Joe." (Diary, 24 November 1943) Dr. Gard regarded Briggs as "splendid . . . , smokes (and chews) a dozen cigars a day and is a real guy. Everyone likes him very well." (Letter to family, ca. 28 November 1943) Although the usual feedback from officers was criticism, and Briggs even resembled a "Russian bear," he would always say "thank you" at least once to any hard worker. As was the case with Jocko, Briggs "had a lot of kindness in him." (Conversation with Cooper Bright)

As author of the Plan of the Day, Briggs inserted a holiday battle cry:

## LOCAL - - - FLASH

THE ADMIRAL AND THE COMMANDING OFFICER WISH ALL HANDS A VERY HAPPY THANKSGIVING. WE ALL HOPE TO HAVE WITH OUR ROAST TURKEY, A DESSERT OF "COOKED JAP GOOSE"!!

The meal that was served to the officers that morning was exquisite holiday fare, centered on roast young tom turkey with giblet gravy. For the 3,200 men of the crew and air group, however, the day was devoted to gunnery practice. All that long day the cooks held off serving the dinners until the guns stopped.

Whenever a lull occurred, Clark, oblivious to the prepared birds, yelled, "Get to firing the guns." Finally, Bob Reynolds, in charge of the chow lines and knowing that the cooked turkey meat was starting to dry up, told him, "Captain, we've *got* to serve those dinners. We'd better stop shooting." Jocko failed to understand: "To hell with that! Take another run!"

The cooks had no choice. During another lull, Clark asked Reynolds what he had done with the meal. Completely frustrated, Bob replied, "I just threw three thousand two hundred turkey dinners over the side!" Clark: "Well, there's nothing we can do about it now. Shoot off some more guns!" (Conversation with Cooper Bright)

At 1905—shortly after refueling was completed—came word that Radford's entire task group was under heavy night air attack—in the very location where it had replaced Pownall's. Twenty-five minutes later the *Yorktown* went to G.Q. and at 0200 headed back into the fray. The ship was located exactly on the Equator.

Night air attacks were something the high command had not anticipated. Task Force 50 had to improvise a defense. Night carrier landings and
takeoffs were not the same as dogfighting in the dark—fraught with danger
of mistakes and collisions. Radford had formed a makeshift night or "bat"
team on the *Enterprise* consisting of two fighters and a radar-equipped torpecker under the celebrated Butch O'Hare.

The high command at Pearl—Nimitz and advisers Towers and Forrest
Sherman—five days earlier had ordered Spruance to send the fast carriers
north to knock out Japanese air strength at Kwajalein and other Marshall
Island fields. This became a reality at sunup on the 26th when four heavy
cruisers and more tin cans joined Pownall's task formation, and brand-new
planes—ferried in on escort carriers—landed aboard to replace those lost
or with old engines. (Reynolds, *Fast Carriers*, 103–5; Wilding diary, 26
November 1943)

An insecure Admiral Pownall questioned the wisdom of these new
orders. Over the hectic preceding days he had resumed asking advice from
so many people around him that Captain Hedding informed everyone in
the flag bridge area to refrain from giving Pownall advice without clearing it
first with him. This, and word of the admiral's erratic behavior during the
Marcus and Tarawa raids, led Nimitz to order Rear Admiral J. L. "Reggie"
Kauffman, Pacific Fleet cruiser/destroyer type commander, to the *Yorktown*
to observe Pownall.

That afternoon Japanese-language staff radio listener Ensign Sandy
Sims intercepted an enemy pilot reporting a task force 20 miles from
*Yorktown*, namely the *Saratoga's*. One hour later he learned that 15 Bettys
had taken off from Mili. In the fading dusk two of these snoopers circled
the *Yorktown* and dropped flares—spotted from the ship—but without
sighting anything. Jocko held his fire from the AA guns, lest they reveal the
*Yorktown's* position, and he slowed down in order to leave no visible wake.

Soon the lookouts saw flashes over the horizon—Radford's *Enterprise*
group under air attack. "The Big E" launched Butch O'Hare's night team,
which proceeded to shoot down three Bettys and drive off the rest. Sadly,
however, the TBF crew mistook Butch's Hellcat for a Betty and shot *him*
down—fatally. This tragedy prompted Clark to address the new menace
immediately.

No more attacks occurred during the night, and next morning the heavy
cruiser *Baltimore* and the new antiaircraft light cruiser *Oakland* joined the
task group. The latter was commanded by Jocko's classmate "Sol" Phillips
(who had become a dirigible pilot in 1932, only to return to surface ships
two years later, after the crash of the *Akron*). These reinforcements were part

of a reshuffling of task groups. The fighting on Tarawa finally ended. But its development, and Makin's, as bases would be subject to continuous air strikes from Kwajalein, where no fewer than 60 torpedo planes had been detected, waiting to strike U.S. shipping.

Admiral Towers insisted, and Nimitz ordered it, that the fast carriers immediately knock out these deadly nighttime torpeckers. Over the protests of Admiral Pownall—who preferred to return to Hawaii as planned—he was directed to lead two task groups in the attack on Kwajalein, set for 4 December. Pownall remained in direct charge of TG 50.1—*Yorktown, Lexington, Cowpens;* Montgomery took over 50.2—*Essex, Enterprise,* and *Belleau Wood.* Ted Sherman would be stationed near the Gilberts with *Bunker Hill* and *Monterey* as backup.

Jocko Clark, however, called a meeting that very day, 27 November, to devise makeshift tactics against the night-flying Bettys, expecting an attack that night. And he wanted to avoid a repeat of the O'Hare tragedy. Captain Hedding attended on behalf of Admiral Pownall, with air group skipper Stebbins, squadron leaders Owen of VF-5 and Upson of VT-5, and four other pilots.

Clark began by saying that he himself would like to fly this dangerous night, but obviously his place was with the ship. Clearly the best pilot at the meeting was Lieutenant Melvin C. "Boogie" Hoffman, prewar VF-2 enlisted AP, who had flown a captured Zero and knew how to beat it. But Boogie told Clark that his Hellcat was just not equipped for night fighting. Jocko countered that simply Hoffman's presence "up there" would intimidate the Jap pilots. No, replied Boogie; so many airborne Japs would not care about just one plane.

Jocko then asked—not ordered—the other three pilots, all of them experienced, if they would go up at night, knowing the extreme danger. As they talked it over, F6 pilot Jim Campbell observed that if the ship was under attack, or if Japanese snoopers were in the area, the ship would not be able to recover the planes without being endangered.

Jocko, without hesitating, looked Campbell straight in the eye and said, "You fly about 100 miles ahead of the ship and land in the water. I'll pick you up in the morning."

The men believed him, based on his reputation for going after downed aviators, and replied that they would do their best. Clark thanked them and turned to the question of a more permanent night-fighting organization. All agreed to work up a doctrine based on O'Hare's techniques.

Two teams of two VF and one radar-equipped VT were designated—Scarlet Bat Team One led by Lieutenant John Gray and including

Campbell and Team Two under Boogie Hoffman. That very night snoopers dropped flares, and Gray's team climbed into their cockpits, but the bogeys never found the ships.

Throughout late afternoon and dusk hours for several days the two Bat teams drilled, vectored by CIC to within four miles of a makeshift bogey, at which distance it appeared on the TBF's scope. At 600 to 400 yards away, the lead fighter saw the bogey's blue exhaust flames and closed in for a stern shot with all six machine guns, while the other two planes broke away. Though a kill was preferred, merely breaking up the enemy formation would protect the task force.

Clark put three of his best OODs, Julian Porter and Lieutenants (jg) Joseph S. Hurley and William W. Ray, to work maneuvering the *Yorktown* out of formation then back into it after dark. The reality was dawning that naval warfare was no longer a strictly daylight affair but was round-the-clock and all-weather in nature.

Such virtually continuous air ops taxed everyone's patience and nerves—ship's company as well as air crews. Clark's ulcers acted up. Little irritations were magnified, like the time his toilet flusher failed to close, and the air blew up into the bowl. He called the shipfitters' shop and told the man who answered (Thomas Whitney), "Get somebody up here! The wind's blowing on my ass!"

Clark fully appreciated that the long hours, often at G.Q., exhausted all hands. After several arduous days, recalled Marine orderly Bender,

> he was going to his in-port cabin for some rest. We would not go the regular way unless we made the airedales who were all sleeping in the passageways get up. He said let them sleep, they need it. We walked the flight deck to the bow, down a ladder to the hangar deck, and back up to his in-port cabin.

Task Force 50 was reshuffled. Pownall's TG 50.1 screen now included four heavy cruisers, Sol Phillips's AA light cruiser *Oakland*, and six destroyers. Admiral Reggie Kauffman boarded the *Yorktown* to "spy" on Pownall. And Admiral Radford, now appointed chief of staff to Admiral Towers, in which capacity he would help resolve the night-fighting dilemma, departed for Pearl Harbor with the *Saratoga* and *Princeton*. These ships sent over several Hellcats to the Kwajalein-bound flattops in exchange for less-necessary SBDs, in order to bolster the new night-fighting defenses. *Yorktown* thus changed from 36 to 39 F6F, 36 to 28 SBD, retaining 18 TBF.

A destroyer rammed and sank a Japanese submarine on the 27th, picking up three survivors who were then transferred to the brig on the *York-*

*town.* Next day the force plowed through a heavy sea that quieted down as the force approached the Marshall Islands. Final refueling took place on 30 November and 1 December at a point 1,000 miles northeast of the target island.

On the latter date Admiral Montgomery was flown from the *Essex* to the *Yorktown* to discuss the attack plan with Pownall and the six air group commanders of Task Force 50. The schedule called for an attack on Kwajalein on 4 December, but details now had to be worked out. Captain Stump of the *Lexington* did not like the idea of only one strike if it did not eliminate all Japanese air at Kwajalein. So he told his air group commander, Lieutenant Commander Ernest M. Snowden, to argue for a fighter sweep the afternoon of the 3rd, followed by full deckload strikes next day. Captain Hedding agreed with him.

This would neutralize whatever Japanese planes were there on the first day, enabling the six air groups to work over airfield installations and shipping next day. But it also meant exposure to enemy night air attacks from several Marshall bases on the first or on both nights—aided by a gibbous moon (between the full and third quarter phases), setting after midnight. And it would be the first action for the makeshift Bat teams.

Montgomery argued forcefully against the proposal, calling it too risky, backed up by Admiral Pownall. That settled it. The force would hit Kwajalein all morning of the 4th, then hightail it out of there in the afternoon, possibly hitting Wotje and Maloelap on the way. Jocko Clark did not like it, but he had not been invited to the meeting. (Truman Hedding transcript, 45–50) "Pownall was scared of his own shadow," remembered Bob Reynolds, who felt sorry for him—"a gutless wonder."

To save time, evening night fighter drill was cancelled, and the two task groups turned northwest at 1630 on the 1st. Both operated in visual contact, making 17 knots, and maintained strict radio silence. All detailed messages between admirals were dropped in pouches by planes flying between the *Yorktown* and *Essex.*

The task force swung into an arc north of the Marshalls and commenced its final run-in at 0800 on the 3rd. Two hours later Ensign Sims translated a Japanese radio message that a flight of their planes was moving from Wake to Maloelap. And warships and cargo vessels (*maru*) were expected to be at anchor at Kwajalein.

Miraculously, no snoopers detected the force before it reached its launching point on 4 December. G.Q. sounded at 0550. The sky was clear, the moon aglow in the twilight. Jocko Clark entrusted the conn to his best OOD, Joe Hurley. The first plane of the deckload strike—22 Hellcats, 24 Dauntlesses, all 18 Avengers—took off one minute ahead of schedule, at

0629. Air Group Five broke its own record by clearing the deck in 31 minutes—with less than 30-second intervals between planes.

At 0706 strike leader Ed Stebbins informed Coop Bright the rendezvous had been completed, and Skinhead released them to the target eight minutes later—in company with the other air groups. At 0756 Bright heard Steb announce his arrival over Roi Island of the sprawling Kwajalein Atoll. A few airborne Japanese Zeros and heavy antiaircraft fire immediately greeted the carrier planes. Hellcats waded into the Zekes, while the bombing planes attacked the Japanese cargo ships and the few warships at anchor.

Fighting Five's pilots easily bested the Zeros in brief dogfights, but the flak was so heavy that several planes were hit. During the fighters' devastating strafing attack on seaplanes in the lagoon, Lieutenant Herb T. Gill took a hit and had to parachute. Boogie Hoffman and others tried to strafe the Japanese soldiers running toward Gill when he landed in the lagoon. There were too many, however, and they gunned him down instead of taking him prisoner.

Two enraged squadron mates smoked another bandit. When its pilot bailed out they machine-gunned him—fair retribution for Herb Gill's killing, they reasoned, in spite of the Geneva Convention outlawing it. (Conversation with Melvin C. Hoffman)

Then, after the rendezvous for the return flight, Hoffman's four Hellcats were jumped by some 20 well-piloted Zekes. VF-5's defensive "Thach weave" failed to protect them completely, and one F6F was shot down in flames, killing pilot Karl B. "Si" Satterfield.

Ten Zeros pounced on squadron skipper Ed Owen after he flamed one himself. They thoroughly shot up his plane before being driven away by his division mates. He radioed the ship that most of his instruments had been shot out.

"We'll turn into the wind for you" to land, he was told. "Where *are* you?"

"I'm about five miles at 1,000 feet. I got nuthin'!"

Then some cheerful guy flew alongside and radioed over, "Hey, you don't expect to land that crate, do you?"

Just then, Owen's engine quit. And one look at the 30-foot waves convinced him that his "crate" would disintegrate if he ditched at sea. So he bailed out, hit the water, inflated his Mae West, and waited forlornly. Suddenly, a destroyer appeared, threw him a line, hoisted him aboard, and delivered him by high-line to the *Yorktown* three hours later.

Surprised though the Japanese were (as Sims's radio intercepts revealed), their tenacious resistance convinced Admiral Pownall that counterattacks would come soon. *Yorktown*'s planes straggled back aboard for over a full hour, while the ship put up a 16-fighter CAP and four-SBD antisub patrol out to 40 miles.

Meanwhile, while leaving Kwajalein, Stebbins spotted and photographed an entire airfield full of up to 60 Bettys—totally unscathed.
*Essex*'s Air Group Nine had been assigned to destroy them but had failed to
do so. An inexperienced Ernie Snowden of the *Lex* had not coordinated the
attack very efficiently.

Those untouched Bettys would obviously be used for a counterattack
against the task force, probably at night. When Steb was 50 miles from the
ship he radioed CIC. Alex Wilding took the call: Steb "recommended that
another strike group be launched immediately. I advised Admiral Pownall,
and he said negative."

Pownall and Admiral Kauffman discussed the alternatives. Except for a
planned strike against Wotje, no more missions had been scheduled.
Another strike would keep the force within enemy bomber range at least
another day and two nights. So the admiral decided to turn the task force
around and run for Pearl Harbor.

He ordered Clark and the other carrier captains to cancel further air
strikes. A "dumbfounded" Clark pleaded with the admiral: "You'd better get
back there and knock out those Bettys, or they'll come and get you!"

When Stebbins and squadron skippers Dick Upson and Dan Harrington landed they all ran up to the bridge and urged Clark to let them lead
another attack on Kwajalein. Clark agreed with their point of view, but
Pownall would not listen, except to go ahead with the planned strike against
Wotje.

At noon the *Yorktown* began launching the latter, keeping other planes
and their pilots on standby. Suddenly, "a lot of black puffs" were seen "on the
other side of the *Lex*," which was about 300 yards to starboard of the *York*.
(Van Buren diary) The targeted bogey blew up from AA fire, then another
did as well, while an aerial torpedo passed astern of the *Lexington*.

"Scramble all planes!" yelled Hank Dozier as Stroke Blackwell's gunners
and every other ship in the formation opened fire. When the first planes
roared off the deck, Alex Wilding looked out from CIC and took in this
attack by single-engine "Kate" torpeckers:

> They had sneaked in undetected, coming in just skimming the water.
> Another one burst into flames and went down off our starboard quar-
> ter. Our CAP came screaming down from their high altitude. Torpe-
> does rushed by ahead of us and astern—all missed. . . . How could they
> have gotten in undetected?

This was a fair question from one of the men responsible for directing
the fighters to intercept and destroy them. The answer was: by flying below

the radar beams the Kates skillfully hugged the water, where the high-flying CAP pilots were not looking.

The firing stopped after ten wild minutes, and the CAP Hellcats began to land aboard. Suddenly the bullhorn blared, "Torpedo planes off the port beam!" Still-airborne fighters splashed all but four of these attacking Kates. Flak brought down the first survivor, its "fish" passing harmlessly by the *Lexington.* The other three climbed over the cruiser *San Francisco* and made runs on the *Yorktown.* George Earnshaw's shorter-range 40-mm and 20-mm guns opened fire, while Stroke Blackwell held back his 5-inchers lest they hit the cruiser. The second Kate burst into flames from the concentrated ack-ack and crashed astern the *San Francisco,* its torpedo missing.

The third Kate took flak from all three gun calibers, the 5-inchers set to local range. Kate's rear-seat gunner sprayed the *San Francisco* as it crossed its bow, while the pilot fired his fixed wing guns at the *Yorktown.*

Jocko Clark stood foursquare on the bridge, shaking his fist at the Japanese planes. At one point he noticed his nervous "radar talker," Bill Small, nearby, and handed him a stick of chewing gum. "Don't worry, son, we're going to get out of this O.K." (Small, *The Johnnys, Jocko, Tiger and Me,* 116–18) The visible tracers—every third bullet of the AA guns—laced the skies to port, engulfing the plane, highlighted by its yellow propeller hub. The closer it got, almost level with the ship, the flatter was the trajectory of the shells. Bullets from the *Yorktown's* port-side gun galleries began crashing all around the *San Francisco* beyond—and then into her.

"Cease fire! Cease fire!" Admiral Pownall yelled up from the flag bridge to an incredulous Clark. "You are firing on that cruiser!"

Jocko ignored him, determined to save the *Yorktown.* Flight deck personnel dived for cover as the Kate bored in. In addition to ship's gunners, two men with cameras held firm—Dwight Long with his movies and Photographer's Mate Al Cooperman rapidly clicking off stills.

At 300 yards the Kate took a shell in its left wing root, and flames erupted. With smoke trailing out, the torpecker veered from the port to the starboard quarter and skimmed by the flight deck at less than 100 yards. It seemed headed for the deck edge elevator; a torpedo hit there (Clark reckoned later) could have taken the ship out of the war for months, if not sunk it outright.

But the Kate's left wing broke off, and the burning plane plunged into the sea close aboard and exploded in a ball of smoke, flames, and airplane fragments.

The fourth torpecker turned out to be a Betty and tried to escape, but a Hellcat brought it down.

Blackwell's gunners had lived up to the efficiency "E"s on their turrets, but the surprise appearance of these "wily Jap" planes had stunned all hands. Pownall signaled the *San Francisco* for a casualty report from the effect of the *Yorktown*'s guns firing into her. One man killed, 22 wounded came the reply. But Pownall never mentioned to Clark his order to cease firing.

Neither did the captain of the *San Francisco,* A. Finley France Jr., a classmate of Clark's who realized Jocko had no choice if he was to save the *Yorktown.* Clark in fact believed that Pownall himself had come to that conclusion.

Clark was so impressed by Cooperman's photos of the kill that he titled the one showing the Kate's wing breaking off "Flaming Kate" and had over 3,000 copies made as Christmas presents for every member of the crew and air group. He autographed many of them to the man by name but always with the inscription: "This is how we did it [sometimes adding "on the USS *Yorktown*"] J. J. Clark Captain [Comdg]." *Life* magazine eventually recognized the photo as its "Picture of the Week."

And Dwight Long's footage of the shoot-down became a classic sequence that would find its way into innumerable Hollywood productions about World War II in the Pacific for the rest of the century (beginning in 1952 with the twelfth program in the *Victory at Sea* series, *The Conquest of Micronesia: Carrier Warfare in the Gilberts and Marshalls*).

Meanwhile, the ship launched a large CAP and antisub patrol while Admiral Pownall discussed his plans with Reggie Kauffman and signaled Rear Admiral Ike Giffen in the *Oakland* for another opinion. The immediate reply came by blinker light: "We better get out of here before we get our tail full of arrows."

This unintended simile better befitted the task force's own "Indian"— the Cherokee-weaned warrior with his own brand of "arrows." Throughout the afternoon this flabbergasted skipper—whom many of his friends now addressed as "chief"—repeatedly pounded navigator Red Sharp's chart table, exclaiming, "Goddammit, you can't run away from airplanes with ships!" (Honolulu *Star-Bulletin,* 27 January 1944; conversation with Sharp)

The Wotje strike returned in midafternoon, having destroyed the paltry five enemy planes found there—while 60 remained unscathed at Kwajalein. One landing Hellcat pilot accidentally triggered his guns when he grabbed the wire, hitting no one. But Jocko summoned him to the bridge for an admonition, adding, "We've had enough excitement here today without all these pyrotechnics."

As the last plane came aboard at 1506, Clark and the task force rang up 25 knots for full speed to escape Kwajalein's waters. But high winds increased the height of the ocean swells up to the hangar deck level and over the bows of the destroyers, slowing the tin cans' forward progress to 18

Japanese torpedo-bomber with a yellow propeller hub is hit by *Yorktown* AA gunners and photographed by crewman Al Cooperman from the flight deck edge on 4 December 1943 during the Kwajalein raid. The photograph appeared as *Life* magazine's "Picture of the Week." *U.S. Navy photo*

knots. Pownall had no choice but to slow down the carriers and big-gun ships to that speed—executed at 1617.

Suddenly, two minutes later, the loudspeaker blared, "Man overboard!" An airedale, Seaman Second Jim Blazejczak, had slipped on the flight deck, broken his arm, fallen into a catwalk, and been swept away by a high roller. Miraculously, the can *Nicholas* scooped him out of the water eight minutes later and eventually returned him to the carrier. Clark summoned him to the bridge to learn the particulars of his ordeal, then scolded him, "You picked a helluva time to go swimming. Now go below before you get court-martialed!"

By the time the sun set at 1809, the radars were tracking blips of Kwajalein-based snoopers flying expanding squares in search of the task force. Captain Hedding took over as force OOD, and Clark kept a tired Joe Hurley as "battle OOD"—"my best ship handler whom I had specially trained for the job." Given the bright moonlight, Hurley would exploit the few clouds to keep maneuvering the ship—and thus the task group—under them.

In the final sequence of four photos the remains of the Kate burn after hitting the water and exploding on the starboard quarter (right side, aft) of the *Yorktown*. Note the radio antennas in the "down" position. The island superstructure is flanked fore and aft by twin 5-inch, .38-caliber antiaircraft gun turrets, while above them are quadruple 40-mm guns. Outboard of the island structure single 20-mm barrels are seen against the sky. No enemy bomb, torpedo, or suicide plane ever hit the *Yorktown*, "the Fighting Lady." *Bureau of Aeronautics*

An equally cool Charlie Ridgway became task group CIC director—not for the planes, which never took off, but for the gunners. Pownall had no intention of using his untried Bat teams, lest the Butch O'Hare tragedy be repeated—or worse. The night was to be a long one, in which Ridgway "never hesitated, never repeated himself," remembered Clark. "His voice to the ships was clear as a bell, his diction perfect."

Cruiser *New Orleans* steamed directly ahead of the *Yorktown* as the guide, while Sol Phillips's *Oakland* took station astern. "You stay between these cruisers," Clark ordered Hurley. "They're our best protection." This was a challenge, inasmuch as the carrier in its turns tended to fall back from the sleeker cruisers. With formation speed 25 knots, Hurley had to keep the *York* at 27 or 28 to stay between the cruisers.

About 30 Bettys in small groups began an hour of attacks on Montgomery's *Essex* task group seven and a half miles west of Pownall's group. To augment the moonlight, the enemy torpeckers flew in teams of two—the first plane to drop parachute flares to illuminate the ships, the second one to attack.

Soon Sandy Sims translated a snooper's radio message from 18 miles out pinpointing the *Yorktown's* position. At 2057 Ridgway detected two groups closing in astern, and soon the *Oakland* opened fire on them. That seemed to convince the Bettys to withdraw, and a tense two-hour respite followed.

When innumerable bogeys (eventually perhaps between 30 and 50) began to register on radar scopes, Captain Sol Phillips of the *Oakland,* just astern of the *Yorktown,* personally got on the TBS radio and in plain language (ignoring call signs and other coded lingo) called Pownall: "Request permission to drop back ten miles astern of the formation, light ship, and shoot the bastards down as they come in."

This "electrified things for a while" as Pownall and Hedding granted the request, and *Oakland*—especially designed and equipped as an AA cruiser—began to draw them in "like flies" and shoot them down. (Conversation with Felix Stump)

Shortly after 2300 Yorktowners topside saw Montgomery's guns bring down an enemy plane, then another—closer. Suddenly, at 2323, the sky lit up from a string of four parachute flares two miles off the port bow, then three more on the port quarter, probably from the same plane.

Simultaneously, the Betty's teammate penetrated the destroyer screen at 6,800 yards off the starboard bow. Wilding plotted its run for Stroke Blackwell's gunners, but too many ships in the line of fire kept the 5-inchers from shooting. The 40 mms opened up at 4,000 yards, but the Betty pressed on. At 3,000 yards Clark yelled, "Hard right!" to turn the ship into the attack, "combing" any torpedo at the bow. At 2,000 yards the 20s opened up.

At 1,000 yards, a lookout yelled, "Torpedo splash starboard bow!" Alex Wilding counted off the 20 seconds for the 40-mph "fish" to reach the ship.

The Betty completed its two-minute run by passing some 50 feet over the deck—illuminated by the flares and tracers—while its torpedo passed harmlessly by the bow. Earnshaw's port side 40s and 20s took her under fire, and she plunged into the sea burning, 1,500 yards on the port quarter.

Bogeys continued to swarm, the moon to shine, and Jocko to curse. "Hard right rudder!" he roared as another torpecker made a run, and the ship combed the fish as it crossed the stern. The Betty escaped, and Clark made four course changes in as many minutes to confuse his attackers, which were everywhere.

Sol Phillips's *Oakland* fired almost continuously, then *Essex* and *Enterprise,* which at 2330 shot down a plane that crashed onto its deck. Onlookers saw it from the *Yorktown* and also saw that the fire was quickly extinguished.

Then another bogey closed on the formation, which Wilding recorded for future reference:

> . . . 5400 yards, 5000 yards, etc., then the plane shot over our deck, wing
> guns blazing, and disappeared into the night. Now the seconds, 1, 2, 3,
> 4 . . . 18, 19, 20, and the deep breath—when suddenly a terrific roar and
> flames leaped 200 feet in the air just 600 yards off our port quarter—
> the *Lexington.*

Hit in the rudder, *Lexington* lost steering control, its speed cut from 28 to 18 knots. Pownall ordered Clark to reduce *Yorktown*'s speed from 27 to 20 knots, turn left, and protect the stricken carrier. Using his call sign, Jocko assured Felix Stump, "This is Stork. We will watch you and stay with you." So did cruisers *Oakland* and *New Orleans* and one tin can, all throwing up a terrific fire at the relentless enemy torpedo planes.

At 2347 Jocko swung the *Yorktown* hard left to comb a Betty at 7,000 yards to starboard, and it quickly turned away in the face of heavy AA fire. The *Oakland*'s shooting was continuous, and its Captain Phillips avoided sundry attacks as well.

Just past midnight, 5 December, *Lexington*'s crew regained steerage, having rigged emergency gear, and it moved to the rear of the formation to zigzag against possible aerial torpedoes.

Sandy Sims listened in on a Japanese transmission calling for simultaneous attacks from both sides, but the pilots all lost heart and turned away in the face of withering flak from all ships. They dropped their fish but too far out to find a mark.

All hands anxiously watched the neutral moon sinking in the western sky and breathed easier at 0127, as noted in the quartermaster's log: "The moon has set—Thank God!" A few torpeckers made torpedo runs in the dark but missed, all heading for home by 0200. The seven-hour battle was over.

At 0215 Jocko gave the order over the horn: "Secure from General Quarters. All gunners sleep at their guns." The force had splashed or repulsed between 40 and 60 Bettys and Kates.

Less than two hours later, 0400, G.Q. sounded again; the ship was expecting a dawn torpedo plane attack to finish off the crippled *Lexington*. Steering by its engine, it was unable to reverse course into the wind to operate aircraft, so *Yorktown* had to do all the flying.

At 0555 Fighting Five's CAP began taking off, followed by eight Torpedo Five Avengers for antisub patrol. During the launch the ship suddenly rolled, causing the left wing of Jake Kilrain's TBF to strike the deck and send the plane plummeting over the side. He and his crewmen (Don Wellman, Herb Smith) climbed out and inflated their life raft. But the sinking plane's two 500-pound depth charges went off, exploding the 400 gallons of aviation gas, which killed all three men instantly.

When no bogeys appeared by the 0644 sunrise, the *Yorktown* secured from G.Q. and raced for Hawaii—leaving all hands and their captain exhausted, thankful, proud, and very disappointed at having had to endure such a sustained enemy attack. Not one ship had been sunk, but neither had the enemy's air strength in the Marshalls been eliminated.

On the return voyage Clark had an inkling that his promotion to rear admiral was about to come through. So he decided that, in addition to autographing the "Flaming Kate" photo for his shipmates, he would give each man an additional keepsake—an autographed and dated photo of himself. He had excellent penmanship, and these mementos would be prized by most of the recipients for the rest of their lives (not by all, however, for some of them simply hated him for his coarse treatment of them).

His most important piece of business was the problem of Admiral Baldy Pownall. In the eyes of Jocko Clark and a great many others, Pownall lacked the requisite aggressiveness to lead in battle. His performance at Marcus had been questionable, as it had during the Tarawa raid and Gilberts landings. But his endangering of the entire task force in the Kwajalein raid was intolerable.

So committed was Clark to removing Pownall from combat that he did three extraordinary and risky things, all involving Herman Rosenblatt. First, both men, with input from other selected officers, composed an unsigned white paper setting forth the evidence of Pownall's lack of aggressive leadership. It would be circulated among the key admirals and captains at Pearl Harbor.

Second, when the ship docked, Rosenblatt—accompanied by Bob Reynolds—made a long distance telephone call to the White House. Exploiting his contacts as a personal lawyer for the president and Eleanor Roosevelt, Herman briefly set forth the reasons why Pownall should be relieved of command.

Third, after the call, Rosenblatt was sent back—George Anderson remembered—"on a quick trip to Washington to get the word to the President to have Admiral Pownall removed and get another admiral in there who had greater fortitude in fighting the Japs."

These three measures were done at considerable risk to Clark's career, let alone his impending promotion to flag rank. "Well, it was going to help win the war," he said in justifying his action. "Everything he did," recalled Anderson, "was with the idea of winning the war and, of course, enhancing the position of Jocko Clark as the premier fighter." Success depended on how much confidence his superiors had in him and his own judgment as a combat leader. (Conversations with Clark, F. R. Reynolds, and Raöul Waller; Anderson interview #3, 119–20)

He need not have worried about that, inasmuch as he would soon receive the Silver Star medal—

> For conspicuous gallantry and intrepidity as commanding officer of the USS *Yorktown*, during operations against enemy-held islands in the Central Pacific Area, from August 31 to December 5, 1943. . . .
>
> During the day and night of December 4, when the *Yorktown* was under severe enemy attack, almost continuously for one five-hour period at night, he maneuvered his vessel so expertly that all attacks were repelled without damage. . . .

Jack Towers utilized his October-to-December fitness report of Clark to cite the praise of other authorities:

> Task Group Commanders under whom he has served in these operations [actually, only Pownall] have unanimously reported him outstanding in the performance of his duties. He has the complete confidence of officers and men in his ship. He is the aggressive-confident type of naval officer who can and will carry through on any assignment.

Neither did Jocko's flyers have any doubt about their skipper, who, they had heard rumors, was about to be detached. When the *Yorktown* neared Hawaii on 9 December, Air Group Five took off—85 planes in all—to return to shore bases. Once over the horizon, however, the pilots repeated their surprise to him following the Marcus raid. They flew back over the ship in parade formation, spelling out the letters "Y—JJC" for *Yorktown* and Joseph James Clark.

Officers and men on the bridge said nothing as an emotional Jocko Clark again fought back tears.

# A Jocko Clark Cartoon Gallery

Yorktown *Radarman John A. Furlow, 1943–44*

Cherokee Jocko scalping Emperor Hirohito of Japan. The artist originally drew a slightly different version of this cartoon entitled "Marcus" for the 31 August raid. The scalp was labeled "Tojo" for the Japanese general and prime minister who fell from power after the loss of the Mariana Islands in July 1944. (For the original cartoon, see Reynolds, *Fighting Lady*, 46.)

A nighttime ulcer attack requires Avocet goat's milk.

This parody of Admiral David G. Farragut's Civil War battle cry at the Battle of Mobile Bay in 1864 captures Clark's style of command. Contrary to several wartime and postwar newspaper articles, though, Jocko did not utter the phrase when he ordered the lights of his task group turned on the night of 20 June 1944 following the Battle of the Philippine Sea. Similarly incorrect, of course, are the spellings of "damn" and "torpedoes."

# FOURTEEN

# Mitscher and Task Force 58, 1943–1944

A S SOON AS THE *YORKTOWN* DOCKED AT PEARL HARBOR ON 9 December 1943, Captain Clark reported directly to Pacific Fleet headquarters. He went straight to old friend Fuzz Sherman, now Admiral Nimitz's assistant chief of staff for planning and a rear admiral. Jocko showed him Stebbins's aerial photos of the Bettys left unscathed at Kwajalein on the 4th that had counterattacked that night.

Sherman, astounded by this evidence, opened the door to the next room and called to Rear Admiral C. H. "Soc" McMorris, Nimitz's chief of staff, "You want to see the fish that got away?" Both men immediately agreed that a blunder had occurred when Admiral Pownall failed to eliminate the "fish"-dropping planes there. The entire operation also confirmed that Kwajalein would have to be captured.

Pownall transferred his flag ashore on the 14th, never to return to active combat command. Criticisms of him by Admirals Towers, Kauffman, and other officers and the damning Clark white paper—all of which generated a stout defense of Pownall by Admiral Spruance—consumed several weeks. Pownall feebly justified his failure to launch a second strike on Kwajalein because of "tired pilots, tired airplanes." (Pownall transcript, 129)

Whether the Clark paper and Rosenblatt's telephone call and visit to the White House played a role is not known, but they would not have been necessary. Admirals King and Nimitz were not happy with Clark's political tactic but let it go. (Anderson transcript #3, 119–20) And Admiral Nimitz was wise enough to trust his advisers, notably the aviation leaders, which had not always been the case. What was more, Nimitz decided to make Towers his deputy Pacific Fleet commander.

Aggressive leadership was essential for the continuous carrier and amphibious operations of the next several months. They would entail the capture or neutralization of Japanese island bastions at Rabaul and Truk, coastal defenses in New Guinea, and within the Marshall and Marianas island groups. Beyond these lay the Philippines and the coast of China—all held by Japan.

Pownall was relieved as carrier commander on 3 January 1944 and replaced three days later by Rear Admiral Marc Mitscher. The fast carrier force—growing in strength daily—was designated Task Force 58 as part of Spruance's Fifth Fleet. TF 58 flagship remained the *Yorktown*. (Reynolds, *Admiral John H. Towers*, 446, 449–52)

Jocko Clark could think of no finer person to be carrier leader than "Pete" Mitscher, whom he welcomed aboard on the 13th. Captain Truman Hedding stayed on as chief of staff, thereby ensuring continuity by breaking in Mitscher to the job. Clark had unbounded admiration for Mitscher,

> a truly great fighter. A thin, wiry little man, completely bald, with sharp blue eyes, he would scarcely talk above a whisper. I had to learn to read his lips to understand him. But I welcomed the opportunity to serve under him in the forthcoming invasion of the Marshall Islands.

Meanwhile, the process of endowing Jocko Clark with his own set of rear admiral's stars proceeded apace. The Pownall case likely delayed Admiral Ernie King's formal approval of Clark's promotion until the start of the new year. Orders were then cut for Jocko to hand over command of the *Yorktown* to his designated successor, Captain Ralph E. Jennings, as soon as Jennings could catch up with TF 58 at the successful completion of the Marshall Islands invasion—in early February.

Inasmuch as the customary initial assignment for breaking in a new admiral meant shore duty, Clark had orders to become commander of the Atlantic Fleet's patrol planes headquartered at Quonset Point, Rhode Island. He could also use that opportunity to assemble the staff that would accompany him back to sea. But Admiral King received a strong word from Admirals Towers and Sherman that they needed Clark as admiral to remain in the Pacific and immediately be given command of a carrier division. So when his orders reached Ernie King's desk, King drew a line through "Quonset Point" and wrote in a carrier division command, initialed with his customary "K."

Clark had already earmarked several officers for his staff: Lieutenant Herman Rosenblatt for flag secretary and Lieutenant (jg) Bob Reynolds as flag lieutenant. He approached ComAirPac Towers to make good on the promise to return him Captain Raöul Waller to be chief of staff, but Towers refused. In just two months on the job Waller had already become indispensable in assigning aviation personnel throughout the Pacific Fleet. During 1944 the numbers would jump from 8,000 officers and 80,000 enlisted men to 25,000 and 240,000 respectively. Towers could simply not spare Waller, although Clark would keep asking for him.

Chagrined at this broken promise, Jocko looked for someone else. George Anderson visited him immediately after the *Yorktown's* return to Pearl Harbor to "milk him for his keen observations" on the Gilberts and Kwajalein operations. Andy regarded the benefits of his former skipper's "unconventional competence" as invaluable to the ComAirPac staff.

Clark used this occasion to invite Anderson to be his chief of staff. Andy accepted eagerly. But Admiral Towers again flatly refused. Anderson was so indispensable to strategic planning that Towers kept Andy as his assistant when he became Deputy CinCPac. This rejection was one of the "greatest disappointments" of Anderson's career—not to go to sea as Clark's chief of staff. But Anderson would visit Jocko whenever the carriers returned to Pearl Harbor after the completion of subsequent operations in order to tap his mind.

Clark resigned himself to accepting whomever BuPers and BuAer gave him. It was Commander John O. Lambrecht, class of '25. No sooner had "Johnny" joined the staff, however, than Jocko encountered him at a party—drunk. Clark told Radford, still ComAirPac chief of staff, "I can't use a guy that gets drunk." So Raddy moved Lambrecht to Montgomery's staff and had BuPers assign Captain W. V. R. Vieweg. Raöul remembered that "Bowser" Vieweg, an Academy '24 classmate and physically large man, was "as intelligent and stubborn as Jocko." Clark found Vieweg too slow a thinker for the younger officers of his staff. Events soon proved Jocko and Bowser as simply incompatible. (Strange, *A Full Life*, 79; Hedding transcript)

The staff required an overall operations officer. BuPers assigned Commander M. T. Evans, a '27 classmate of Anderson and Dozier. Though competent, "Empty" Evans did not satisfy Jocko, who would gradually cast his eyes back to the *Yorktown* to find a replacement for him.

Although no billet existed for a staff *air* operations officer, first Stebbins and then Bright had so ably performed in this capacity on the *Yorktown* that Clark simply created the position—the only one in the carrier forces—and asked Bright to transfer to his staff in the same capacity. Having a nonaviator directing air operations for an entire task group was unorthodox in the extreme. Bright realized that it would be "a big job," but he declined the offer for two reasons. First, he assumed that Clark would go ashore first like any new admiral, and he wanted to stay at sea, especially on the *Yorktown*.

More than that, however, was something Bright would not tell Clark: he had no intention of being undermined by the devious Herman Rosenblatt. On the ship Herm was under Coop's control, but as Jocko's right-hand man on the staff he would be free of Bright's seniority. So Skinhead begged off. (By contrast, Bob Reynolds joined the staff in spite of the fact that he "hated Herman's guts.") Bright, however, recommended torpecker pilot Lieutenant Joe Kristufek for staff air ops officer, whereupon Rosenblatt countered by recommending one of Kristufek's squadron mates, Lieutenant Douglas A. McCrary. As usual, Jocko accepted Rosenblatt's counsel.

McCrary, like Herm an Ivy Leaguer (Yale '37), hailed from the Lone Star State and had the nickname "Tex." McCrary's brother John, who carried the same moniker, was well known as chief editorial writer of the New York *Daily Mirror* before joining the wartime AAF. This older Tex McCrary would soon marry beauty queen–starlet–champion swimmer Jinx Falkenburg. After the war they would create and host the first radio talk show, among other achievements. (*New York Times* obituary, 30 July 2003) Such hobnobbing motivated Rosenblatt—and Jocko vicariously.

A billet did exist for a gunnery officer to handle task group antiaircraft defenses. Jocko convinced *Yorktown's* gun boss, Stroke Blackwell, to take the job. It did not work out, however, and Clark turned to BuPers, which assigned him Lieutenant Commander David Suggett Brown, '36, an experienced destroyerman. Nicknamed "Sugar" from his middle name and his pleasant Mississippi accent, he proved absolutely expert at this job and Jocko happily kept him. Furthermore, Clark upgraded the title to "ships operations officer," coequal to McCrary in air ops and both subordinated to the overall operations officer.

Clark invited *Yorktown's* communications officer Jim Morrison to take the same job on the staff. Though grateful, Morrison had to decline, having received orders to Admiral Harold R. Stark's staff for the upcoming Normandy invasion in Europe. Then Owen Sowerwine, still communicator on the *Suwannee*, accepted.

Lieutenant Commander L. Thorne reported, but Clark had been spoiled by the outstanding work of Charlie Ridgway on the *Yorktown* and lobbied over the spring to get him.

Finally, Jocko arranged the transfer from the *Yorktown* to his staff of his two Filipino chief stewards for his mess as well as his four Marine Corps orderlies for their sundry tasks as his messengers, escorts, and guards.

Meanwhile, personnel changes occurred on the *Yorktown*, which Clark still had to take into the invasion of the Marshall Islands. He gave up his ace ship handler, Joe Hurley, by granting his request to enter flight training as a reward for his brilliant performance off Kwajalein. By contrast, in January Jocko was glad to be rid of bearded Al Wright, who transferred from Air Plot to the same job on the *Enterprise*. (Married in '43 to a gorgeous model,

Jocko and several staff officers pose on the new *Hornet* in 1944. Herman Rosenblatt (flag secretary) hams it up beside a smiling, bespectacled Owen Sowerwine— "Zero" (communications). The admiral and David "Sugar" Brown (ships operations) ignore him, while a disapproving Bob Reynolds (flag lieutenant) gives archenemy "Herm" a furtive glance. *U.S. Navy photo*

Wright would leave her after the war in order to marry actress Joan Fontaine, one of whose later husbands, ironically, turned out to be Hank Dozier's brother.)

Clark had to deal harshly with many disciplinary cases among crewmen unwinding during their shore leave in Hawaii. Several of the officers, on the other hand, took advantage of Rick Lambart's friendship with the prominent local Waterhouse family to attend a sumptuous luau with charcoaled steak at their mountainside home. Jocko played golf with Earnshaw and Reynolds, and Smokey Stover cracked up a car driving on the Pali mountain road. And a tipsy diminutive LSO Dick Tripp belted a rowdy commander from another ship for calling the *Yorktown* a "rusty, dirty old boat."

Coop Bright, no drinker himself, bumped into a snockered lieutenant (jg) from Texas staggering out of the Ford Island O-club. Robert W. Eaton had gone ashore with the Marines at bloody Tarawa as a photo interpreter and had just drowned his sorrows upon learning he would be doing the same at Kwajalein. In no condition to get to his beach house at Waikiki, Eaton welcomed Bright's invitation to spend the night at his place.

"Where's that?"

"The *Yorktown*, parked right here by the O-club."

So Skinhead took him aboard, where he slept off his liquor while Coop and ACIO Jim Sutton decided the ship needed just such a specialist to interpret aerial photos taken of enemy island defenses—especially to deter-mine gun calibers. Eaton was very receptive to the idea, so Bright took him to see the captain. As they talked, Clark learned that Eaton had known his brother Bill in Texas where, ironically, both had been petroleum geologists and were now military photo interpreters.

Finally, Clark said, "Can you be back aboard in an hour?" The answer was an exuberant "yes" (though it took him 90 minutes!). Clark had Bob Eaton's orders changed. He had found an invaluable photo interpreter, the first to be assigned to any carrier.

Another personnel change involved the air group and Air Plot. Crack fighter pilot Boogie Hoffman left to command his own squadron and was replaced by Smokey Stover, who had been badgering Clark and Stebbins for weeks to get out of Air Plot and back into the cockpit.

The major change in the air group was the development of Bat teams at the instigation of Admiral Radford. He immediately established a Bat training school at Puunene on Maui, staffed initially by only marginally experienced night pilots—from the *Enterprise* and *Yorktown*. Clark sent over Alex Wilding (now a senior grade lieutenant) to be air controller along with three F6 and two torpecker pilots. Their first practice intercepts of a bogey were "like shooting fish in a barrel," but only because Wilding controlled the altitudes of both target and Bat team. "The Japs will not be so cooperative." (Diary, 22 December 1943)

As a result, ComAirPac decided to drop the TBFs and establish night fighter Bat teams of four planes and five pilots for each large carrier. Some teams flew the F4U Corsair, those on the *Yorktown* and other flattops the Hellcat. In mid-January 1944 Detachment B of VF (N)-76 was assigned to the ship. Its skipper, Lieutenant Russell L. Reiserer, reported directly to Captain Clark through torpecker pilot Tex McCrary as liaison simply because they made their home in the VT-5 ready room. Also, Wilding visited the *Enterprise* to instruct its CIC in the art of night fighter direction. (Reynolds, *Fast Carriers*, 130–31)

In recent operations the flight deck airedales on "the Big E," skippered by Matt Gardner, had challenged the *Yorktown*'s record-setting speed for reloading, refueling, and respotting planes, only to be beaten by 41 minutes. Such performances led the *York*'s crew to begin referring proudly to their ship as "the Lucky Y." Captain John Ballentine, on arriving with the *Bunker Hill* off the Gilberts, had signaled a friendly challenge to Jocko that his ship would outclass the *Yorktown*. Tommy Sprague finally brought out the *Intrepid*, already "the Unlucky I" for having been damaged going through the Panama Canal—no challenge there.

Clark took on all comers and in so doing stimulated other carriers of the growing fleet to excel. Even the light carriers had to keep up, and Jocko welcomed to Hawaii his old pal Gotch Dillon, captain of the new *Langley.* He even decided that the new *Yorktown* might well beat the old *Yorktown's* record of 104 continuous days without returning to port. It would indeed, although not while Clark was on board. (After departing Pearl Harbor on 16 January 1944, the ship's 105th day out occurred on 2 May. The ship did not return to Hawaii until 11 June—114 days out, but by then such long deployments had become commonplace.) (Jesse Bradley diary, 9, 27 April 1944)

The invasion of the Marshall Islands was set for late January 1944, and thanks to Admiral Mitscher working directly with assault commander Kelly Turner, the fast carriers would not be too tied down to the invasion beaches as in the Gilberts but allowed to operate freely to destroy Japanese air power in the Central Pacific.

To prepare for this offensive posture Clark exercised the ship out of Pearl Harbor. A new carrier admiral, "Black Jack" Reeves, hoisted his flag on the *Yorktown* in mid-December to observe four days of gunnery exercises, carrier quals for several squadrons, and Bat team drills. It got quite real for the crew when a Hellcat simulating an attack on the *Yorktown* accidentally strafed the port side, wounding four men.

Newly arrived light carrier *Cabot* was initiated into fast carrier maneuvers on this occasion. Its captain, erudite Malcolm F. Schoeffel (top man at Annapolis in 1919) could not understand why "Jocko yapped at the half dozen destroyers [of the screen] all the time" over the TBS intership radio. Unhappy with the tin cans' failure to keep pace with the carriers' movements, Clark kept shouting at them, "Small boys, get going!" and stronger epithets. (Schoeffel transcript #5, 214–15)

No sooner had one morning CAP been launched than Fighting Five pilot Ensign Richard L. Newhafer radioed the ship, "Stork Base, this is Stork 42, I've got to come aboard. This is an emergency!"

"Wait," Air Plot responded, inasmuch as planes parked aft had to be respotted forward. Newhafer grew impatient and repeated his call with greater urgency. Finally, a response: "Stork 42, do you read?"

"Stork Base, this is Stork 42. It's too late. I've already shit in my pants!"

After a pause, during which Air Plot personnel erupted in sidesplitting laughter, Skinhead Bright radioed back, "Don't get any shit on the deck!"

Newhafer caught the wire and taxied forward, all the while shaking his first at Captain Clark up on the bridge. Jocko was laughing so hard that tears poured out of his eyes. It continued as the pilot parked and climbed down from his plane, pant cuffs tucked into his boots, and waddled to the showers. (Conversations with several VF-5 veterans)

All hands fought holiday homesickness, but dentist-musician Frank Losey staged a magnificent Christmas Eve program and service in the hangar that impressed the attendees, not least visitor George Anderson, a devout Catholic. The senior officers of the ship went ashore for a Christmas night cocktail party at which they toasted their captain, expected to be detached while at sea.

Next morning the ship pushed away from the dock for another four-day practice cruise, only to suffer loss of steering control and run aground in the soft mud at the edge of the channel. Newly reported signal officer Ensign George A. Wille marveled at his new skipper: "Jocko didn't know whether to jump through the bull horn, or wrap his mouth around it" as he bellowed to the tugboats: "Back it down! Back it down!" By smart seamanship Clark restored the steering, though not before his ulcers erupted after "too much Christmas." Between 0800 and noon he chased *every* OOD off the bridge, then started over at the top of the list. (Wille diary, 26 December 1943)

The new year brought the first draftees to the *Yorktown*, precipitating fears by Chief Master-at-Arms Pop Austin and other chiefs that someone might be killed by the plank owners, who had enlisted on their own. Rather than bother the skipper they met with Joe Tucker to work out a solution. They agreed to let the crew, under close supervision, settle it among themselves. After a few fistfights—unknown to Jocko or exec Briggs—the draftees were accepted and soon became proud shipmates on what they soon discovered to be "the best ship in the fleet." (Conversation with Tucker)

On 10 January 1944, at the conclusion of another four-day training foray, Jocko put on his tie to greet and be photographed with the pilot making the 7,000th landing on the ship—Smokey Stover. Three days later Admiral Mitscher hoisted his flag above the *Yorktown*.

Jocko also welcomed aboard another old friend, Commander Spig Wead, recently appointed by Admiral Towers to head the ComAirPac planning division. He would witness the Marshalls operation but also advise Dwight Long about the motion picture they were making that was focused on the *Yorktown*. The only problem was getting Wead—a paraplegic with heavy leg crutches from his early injury—all the way up to the bridge. Clark had a special lift rigged on the outside of the island structure for hoisting him. Spig swallowed his pride and tried it once—and rejected it. Instead, he used his powerful arms to muscle his way up the seven gangways to the bridge every day.

"What happens," Admiral Mitscher asked Jocko, "if he has to abandon ship?"

Replied Clark, "I don't expect to abandon ship. Neither does he!"

Wead normally worked and slept in Jocko's regular in-port quarters beneath the flight deck—hence the long climbs—where he could work with Long's combat films while they were still wet. Jocko slept in his own sea cabin anyway. Inasmuch as Wead was writing a script for the eventual movie, Clark showed him an old book written by a chief petty officer about the Spanish-American War era battleship *Texas*. Focused on the lives of the crew, it was entitled *Come On, Texas!* Wead liked it so well that he took the same approach for the screenplay of what would become *The Fighting Lady* movie.

On the morning of 15 January the crew mustered in whites, officers in formal uniforms with choker collars, for an awards ceremony honoring some 300 officers and men of the fleet for outstanding performance during the battles of recent months. Admirals Towers and Radford presented them, with Clark's Silver Star medal at the top.

During the afternoon, these two admirals, Mitscher, and three task group commanders convened for a final discussion of the coming operation: Reeves (TG 58.1), Montgomery (58.2), and S. P. Ginder (58.4). Ted Sherman (58.3) would later rendezvous at sea with them. Baldy Pownall was also present as an unofficial "adviser" to Spruance—a sop to the latter for having failed to prevent Pownall's relief as carrier leader. Indeed, when Spig Wead encountered Pownall, the pilot-turned-screenwriter loudly damned him for having run from the enemy on 4 December. (Overheard by Dwight Long)

An "audacious fighting spirit" had permeated Jocko Clark's crew and air group, reported an (unnamed) official observer to the admirals in Washington. Unlike on most carriers, Air Group Five's flyers and ship's company did not grumble at each other: "Mutual admiration societies as enthusiastic as this one are not easy to find." As examples, the sailors had begun to cheer announcements of the aviators' achievements over the loudspeaker, while the pilots had lined the island to yell encouragement to the gunners that wild night off Kwajalein.

The *Yorktown*, marveled this observer, "is an exuberant ship, proud of all the records" thus far set, "proud to be the cleanest of all the carriers, proud that in every action she launched the fastest, flew the most, dropped the most bombs on the enemy."

It was by no means a perfect ship, but several crewmen were disturbed by an editorial in *Our Navy*—the magazine of enlisted men—saying that the Navy had a serious morale problem. The essay indicted many sailors for fostering divisiveness—between regulars and Reservists, Navy and Marines, "shore feather merchants vs. salty guys," black-shoe nonaviators and brown-shoe airmen, even ship against ship.

Jocko Clark's competitiveness was never mean-spirited; it aimed at setting the highest possible standards of performance and teamwork in order to "beat the Japs!" Friendly rivalries could only help the common goal. His men appreciated him for that, and some now discussed the idea of putting together a ship's newspaper to express their concerns. They started gathering items for the first issue of SEA-V-TEN.

One was an essay that took exception to the *Our Navy* piece. Impressed "with the overwhelming evidence that our ship's personnel are not hopelessly damned with bigotry, narrow-mindedness, class, racial and religious distinctions," these Yorktowners implored their own shipmates who were the exceptions to this profile to fall into line. "We are not out here to beat each other. We are all on the same ball club. We have only two guys to lick— Tojo and Adolph—and all that they stand for. Let's lay off each other." (SEA-V-TEN, vol. 1, no. 1, March 15, 1944)

No greater testimony bespoke Jocko Clark's leadership as he took his beloved *Yorktown* into battle for the last time. The ship pushed away from the dock at 1307 on 16 January, passed out to sea, and conducted gunnery practice as it joined up on its escorts.

Mighty Task Force 58 headed for Kwajalein waters with twice the strength of the force on the 4 December raid—no fewer that *twelve* fast carriers (six heavy, six light), the largest carrier battle fleet in history by the time all its units joined up over ensuing days. With Pete Mitscher's flag in *Yorktown*, Black Jack Reeves commanded TG 58.1 from Matt Gardner's *Enterprise*. The center of this task disposition was rounded out by light carrier *Belleau Wood*, Captain A. M. Pride.

"Mel" Pride, like Clark, had an unorthodox but brilliant career of unique achievements that helped transform the character and style of the Navy. Unlike Jocko, however, he had a keen scientific mind. Pride had been a mustang before earning his wings and commission during World War I. He had then designed the arresting gear for the first carrier, *Langley* (CV-1); done postgraduate work in aeronautics at MIT; and become a major test pilot and aircraft designer in the Navy. Four years younger than Clark, and much more the thinker than the fighter, Pride too had just been selected for rear admiral, additional evidence of a navy in transition.

The inner circle of heavy gun ships of TG 58.1 was comprised of three fast battleships (*Massachusetts, Washington, Indiana*) and Sol Phillips's trusty cruiser *Oakland*. The battlewagons could be drawn out of the formation to join others in a battle line for a surface engagement with the Japanese fleet, should it appear.

Most of their gunnery, however, would be antiaircraft, augmented by the outer screen of nine destroyers. A new innovation was the posting of a radar-equipped picket destroyer, covered by CAP fighters, well ahead of the task group formation to help flagship *Yorktown*'s CIC provide better fighter direction.

*Yorktown*'s mission was to attack the Japanese airfield at Maloelap the first day, then spend the next six days operating between Maloelap, Wotje, and Kwajalein in support of the assault troops. Twenty enemy submarines were reported to be operating in Marshall Islands waters. En route, Air Group Five "attacked" the *Yorktown* en masse, the bombers making runs on sleds towed behind it and the Big E. Predawn launches and night fighter quals underscored the new reality of round-the-clock naval warfare.

Little irritations returned as battle day neared. Cooper Bright always signed air ops orders with his initials, C. B., until exec Cam Briggs came to him: "Don't use that! The captain just ate *my* ass out!" Crash One Red Volz got so disgusted with one pilot's poor approaches and wave-offs that he finally threw his paddles in the air and stuck his fingers in his ears. But before the operation was over, Tokyo Rose would be referring to the *Yorktown* as "Mitscher's Gray Ghost."

A more immediate dread than the hated "Jap" was the prospect of the task force crossing the International Date Line and the Equator at the same time. This unusual but convenient ploy by the planners enabled the ships to "delay" the war with the time-honored and rowdy initiation ceremonies for the latest violators of King Neptune's realm. For two days, some 35 "shell-backs" and "dragonbacks" who had already made the crossings "punished" the 3,000 or so "pollywogs" who had not.

On the afternoon of 21 January a burly Davy Jones (Chief Bosun W. J. "Frenchy" Beaudette) took charge of the proceedings. Captain Clark came down to the flight deck to greet him formally next morning. The butt-swatting revelry and other indignities left many initiates unable to sit down for days. And so many heads were shorn so outlandishly that Jocko had to order haircuts for many victims. But tradition had been served. (For details and pictures, see Reynolds, *Fighting Lady*, 85–87.)

In the midst of the second day of festivities Clark received the official word that President Roosevelt had approved his promotion to rear admiral. Furthermore, for purposes of seniority and pay, it was backdated to 23 April 1943. (Secretary of the Navy Frank Knox to Clark, 31 January 1944) The promotion made the national news on the 24th, followed two days later by a statement of high praise from Admiral Nimitz.

Clark also received orders to relinquish command on the 31st. But he could not replace his captain's insignia until his replacement, Ralph Jennings, arrived and relieved him. That could be weeks, inasmuch as Jennings was in New York and the ship was in battle. Another message revealed that the ship would not return to Pearl Harbor after the Marshalls operation but would remain anchored near one of the captured islands, probably further delaying Jennings's arrival.

The *Yorktown* dodged two submarine contacts, as tin cans dropped depth charges on 24 January, and next day oiler *Cimarron* topped off its oil and aviation gas tanks. Air and gunnery exercises resumed until the 28th when the force began its high-speed run into Marshall Islands waters. Added firepower included the fighter planes carrying racks of 100-pound bombs and the return of the big SB2C Helldiver—an allegedly improved version—to other carriers. Also, during the "battle," an F4U Corsair night fighter from another carrier accidentally landed on the *Yorktown*—a first for the ship, as the plane was now being phased in to carriers to complement the Hellcat.

By 0330 predawn of 29 January Jim Vonk was "guessing" the weather from the flag bridge when Admiral Mitscher quietly ambled up and asked him what the weather would be like.

"Shitty, Admiral, perfectly shitty!" said the Dutchman. Mitscher immediately liked this frankness and several months later would make Vonk his own aerologist for the entire task force.

But the dismal black rainy night—ceiling 700 feet—meant danger for the initial predawn launches. Admiral Reeves had given his flagship *Enterprise*'s fighters and bombers, instead of *Yorktown*'s, the honor of leading the first strike on Taroa Island of the Maloelap Atoll, accompanied by several *Yorktown* torpeckers.

Neither Clark nor VT-5 boss Dick Upson liked the ominous weather, and they recommended delaying the launch until first light (sunrise being 0711). Reeves turned them down, arguing that 45 to 60 enemy fighters had been reported at the target in spite of weeks of pounding by AAF bombers.

Jocko, furious, shouted curses into the night, with no recourse but to obey. At 0520 Upson took off first into the murk, completely unable to see the truck lights on the destroyers ahead. Then four more TBFs followed, equally blind. Suddenly, a brilliant flash was seen ahead of the ship: two planes had collided, all hands lost (William Meehan, aircrewmen Robert Olds, George Haigh; Donald R. Simenson with Robert L. Parks, Philip W. Atwater).

Clark delayed further launchings, hoping the weather would improve, but when it did not he sent off the rest per Reeves's orders. The seven TBFs circled aimlessly for 45 minutes until a lightening sky enabled them to join up with other planes and proceed to Taroa. There they bombed parked Bettys, with mixed results. Three more *Yorktown* attack groups braved the weather and AA fire throughout the morning to pound the Maloelap area, while several CAPs extended their coverage to cruisers shelling Taroa and Wotje.

Flak scored a direct hit on Ensign Thomas E. McGrath's TBF, which crashed in flames in the lagoon, killing pilot and crew (Richard C. Robinson,

Edwin A. Haselgard). Those who made it back to the ship cursed the weather and Admiral Reeves; "I hope the bastard is satisfied," grumbled fighter pilot John Gray. (Diary, 29 January 1944)

When Joe Kristufek returned from the predawn mission, the electrical system of his TBF failed. He used a hand crank to lower his wheels and tail hook—except that the latter did not respond. Planes were parked forward, but Joe radioed for permission to land anyway, hoping to be stopped by the wire barrier. Clark, knowing him to be a good pilot, granted it.

Just as Kristufek's front wheels crossed an arresting wire, an alert barrier operator, "with split-second timing, flipped his cable up and caught it in the tail wheel," slamming the plane to a halt.

"What is the name and rate of that barrier man?" shouted Jocko from the bridge.

"Casey, Aviation Machinist's Mate, Second Class," came the reply.

"Tell Casey that he is now an Aviation Machinist's Mate, *First* Class!" (Alexander, "Carrier Revolution," 48)

This was Clark's third spot promotion on the ship, again a richly deserved one. Gerald F. Casey's action had likely saved lives, planes, and serious damage to the ship.

TF 58's planes had a field day destroying parked Bettys without interference from any enemy aircraft—until late in the day. At 1753 a flight of ten bogeys was seen approaching low in a classic torpedo run out of the setting sun. Battleships and destroyers opened fire. *Yorktown* Hellcats closed in but broke away upon noticing their white star insignia—AAF B-25 medium bombers! *Enterprise*'s CAP did not see it and shot down two. All but one of the 12 flyers were rescued from the water—a tragic mistake all around. Clark was angry at Reeves and *Enterprise* skipper Gardner for having let it happen.

Dick Upson wrote an action report damning the predawn launches, which infuriated Admiral Reeves, who, however, admitted his error. He ordered the destroyers to display brighter truck lights for a visible horizon next day. Admiral Mitscher on the *Yorktown* did better by ordering the first launches delayed until after sunrise.

On the 30th, one day before the amphibious assault, the *Yorktown* moved to within 34 miles of Kwajalein itself to launch its strikes. Air Group Five spent the day vying with the battleships and destroyers in blasting gun emplacements, pillboxes, and troop-filled transports and barges. "The Japs are getting the living Hell kicked out of them," noted Alex Wilding.

But air ops were always dangerous, as when one fighter was approaching to land with a 100-pound bomb "hang-fire"—dangling from the bomb rack. Jocko agonized over whether to let it land. He considered having the pilot parachute, then pick him up, but he hated to lose a perfectly good airplane to the sea. He decided to take a chance.

Air ordnance boss Jim Bryan, at his station on the flight deck, watched the plane hit the deck and bounce three times. On the third bounce the bomb fell free to the deck, popping up the arming wire in the fuse. The vane on the fuse then apparently turned in the wind, arming it. If anybody touched one of the fins the bomb would probably explode.

As the bomb rolled around at mid-deck, Bryan walked over to it, stopped it with his foot, and calmly picked it up, avoiding touching a fin. He walked over to the deck edge and threw it into the sea. It did not go off, indicating that it had not armed itself. Jocko decorated Bryan on the spot. (Conversations with Bryan and F. R. Reynolds)

Task Force 58 completely controlled the air and sea in the Marshalls. Instead of running away from Kwajalein during the night (as on 4 December), the *Yorktown* moved to within sight of the island, only ten miles away.

Come dawn, the carriers were prepared to do expertly what they had not done at Tarawa in the Gilberts—provide effective close air support of the assault troops and thereby minimize casualties. In spite of continuing rain, Ed Stebbins as senior air group commander led the first strike of TG 58.1 planes. Once over the target, the airborne ACIO in a Torpedo Five Avenger assigned targets that were identified by radio from the amphibious command ship.

At 0910, as the first assault craft appeared 2,000 yards off Kwajalein's beach, Steb sent in the bombing planes ahead of himself and the strafing Hellcats. The soldiers hit the beach and pushed the Japanese back so quickly that Mitscher cancelled further air strikes at noon. But Reeves launched more anyway and kept CAP fighters aloft for two grueling hops totaling eight to nine hours—"anus patrols" for the seat-numbed pilots.

Next day, 1 February, Air Group Five resumed its close air support of the infantry, and Stebbins dodged bullets down to 400 feet photographing targets. On landing back aboard, however, he discovered that Dwight Long had forgotten to load his camera with film. "Jocko nearly had apoplexy," noted John Gray, as Clark chewed out Coop Bright when Long could not be found (he had hopped aboard a departing bomber with his camera to escape the skipper's wrath).

In late afternoon, pilot Smokey Stover investigated a two-masted sailing vessel with cargo on deck and received permission to attack it. Eventually, eight fighters, five torpeckers, and one SBD "threw some lead at it," more than it was worth. But Air Plot broadcast all the planes' transmissions throughout the ship. When they landed, Jocko called the pilots up to the bridge to congratulate them. "Some feat, sinking a Japanese man-o'-war like that!" mused Stover. (Diary, 1 February 1944)

Only mopping up continued ashore, so Clark took his ship close to the island next day for all hands topside to witness the gun flashes, smoke, and carnage as final resistance ended—a sweeping victory.

Also, four VT-5 planes prepared to strafe a small motor sailboat until its four crewmen waved their hands in surrender. A tin can picked them up and delivered them to the *Yorktown*, where Jocko had them locked in the brig. Sandy Sims interrogated two of them there, first in English—no response—then in Japanese, at which they opened up like magpies, in perfect English.

The *Yorktown* headed for Majuro Atoll, two hundred miles east of Kwajalein. It had been seized without opposition for its sprawling lagoon to act as a forward anchorage. Only one other Marshall island was assaulted and captured for the same purpose, Eniwetok. The rest—once-dreaded Maloelap, Mili, Jaluit, and Wotje—were bypassed. Their garrisons were being left to wither away as live practice targets for U.S. planes based on Kwajalein.

Majuro Atoll had only one big gap in it—at the north end—through which ships could pass. A survey ship had already taken soundings and made new charts of the anchorage, but the *Yorktown* had not yet received its copy. As force flagship it would lead the rest of the fleet in, but a promised harbor pilot did not come out to assist, causing navigator Red Sharp to advise Clark against trying to take the ship in unassisted.

Jocko thought it over then sighed, "Oh, goddammit, we can go in anyhow!"

He ordered the ship deballasted to lessen the draft, reduced the speed to a crawl, and leaned over one wing of the bridge to gauge the ship's maneuvering room. A reluctant Sharp leaned over the opposite wing to gauge the channel's depth. At 1405 the *Yorktown* began creeping into the passage.

Suddenly Red yelled to Jocko, "We're getting too close over here. Recommend we come to the right a little bit!"

Clark ordered the helmsman to do it, then countermanded himself: "Hell, we're on the beach over here!" Many jagged coral heads reached up and would have to be blasted out later.

The *Yorktown* squeaked through and took two hours to reach its assigned anchorage 500 yards off Majuro Island on the south side of the atoll. By day's end it had been joined by eight other fast carriers, four escort carriers (two bringing replacement aircraft), 11 battlewagons, eight cruisers, countless destroyers, and a dozen tankers, plus tugboats. (Ridgway diary)

Hellcat pilot John Gray surmised "one smashing raid soon" against Truk, the mighty forward—and feared—Japanese fleet base in the eastern Caroline Islands. (Diary, 4 February 1944) Captain Clark confirmed it next day to all hands over the bullhorn.

He gave the crew a rundown about Truk—its history, the Japanese fleet, and the many aircraft there, then finished with a battle cry: "We'll fight them yellow bastards if we have to fight them in a rowboat!" Seaman First Class Ed Spangler, a quad 40-mm gunner, thought, "This is the time to get *off* this thing! This is no place to be!" One of his shipmates remarked, "We're fightin' for a crazy guy!"

The Navy Department had finally issued a press release about the *Yorktown*, a copy of which now reached the ship at Majuro. It made a hero of Clark as "a turbine of driving energy." That he was, a war correspondent learned, but "inconsolable" and "harder to live with than ever" in his desire to take the ship into the Truk operation before his relief arrived. Indeed, when a tanker came alongside to refuel the carrier, it scraped against the hull, chipping away paint. "Get out of here, or I'll *sink* you!" roared Jocko, shaking his fist. The tanker obeyed, and stayed away. (Alexander, "Carrier Revolution," 48)

Admiral Mitscher told Clark he would need a full day to turn over command to Jennings. Until then, Clark would indeed remain in command for the Truk operation. Jocko dreaded Jennings's arrival.

Meanwhile, he broke out the beer donated by the movie company of *Wing and a Prayer* for riotous parties on the beach for three consecutive afternoons. The officers took their own whiskey ashore for similar relaxation. "The whole ship was drunk for three days," veterans recalled. Clark also permitted diving and swimming off both sides of the ship, but not off the stern after a few swabs almost got swept away by the lagoon's currents.

With 10 February set as date of departure for TF 58 to attack Truk, the deadline of having a full day—the 9th—to transfer command of the ship was fast approaching. So at 1700 on the 8th Jocko figured he would indeed go on the Truk operation.

Alas, 15 minutes later, he heard the unmistakable "ticking" of the four engines of a big PB2Y Coronado amphibian that had set down alongside the ship. He knew instinctively that it was Jennings.

Sure enough, the man he knew as "Al" quickly hopped out of the flying boat into the *Yorktown's* whaleboat, and the Coronado dramatically took off for Kwajalein. The Naval Air Transport Service had whisked Jennings all the way from New York in just three days. He climbed up the ship's gangway at 1732.

Clark greeted Jennings and lost no time in briefing him about the *Yorktown*. The two men spent all next day, the 9th, inspecting the ship, with Clark introducing Jennings to the department heads.

Generally speaking, ship's officers and crew, although prepared for Clark's leaving, were not happy about it now that his departure was at hand.

Charlie Ridgway shared the feeling of several diarists, "We feel unhappy about changing skippers at such an important moment." "Nobody," observed 40-mm gunner Coxswain Jesse Bradley, "wanted to see him leave because he sure was a good man." Jim Bryan remembered how the crew worried "about changing horses in midstream." VF-5 diarist John Gray believed "Captain Clark a rough, tough old S.O.B., but the pilots have a lot of confidence in him. . . . Old Jocko can lead me into a fight anytime."

Dwight Long, just before departing Majuro for the States with his latest film footage, had already given Clark his rear admiral's shoulder boards. Coop Bright's sister Joy Hancock of the WAVES had entrusted them to Long during his previous trip to Washington.

Next morning, 10 February, Clark packed his bag and invited all heads and assistant heads of departments to his stateroom to say farewell. "Tough old Jocco," wrote Dr. Ray Gard (who had obviously never seen the nickname written down), "almost broke down."

Mustered on the flight deck were officers and crew plus a visitor on hand for a squadron commanders' meeting—Harry Harrison, fighter skipper on the *Intrepid* after having flown for Clark on *Suwannee* and *Yorktown*. Jocko stood behind the mike on a small platform and tried to address his shipmates: "I know this is a right ship. She does everything right. She hasn't missed a schedule. She's met the enemy in combat, and she's turned in a good score."

His well-known "gale-force" voice cracked a couple of times. Then, for the first time anyone could remember, he choked—at a complete loss of words for the crew.

His puffed-up lower lip was visibly quivering as he finally, with a thick voice, blurted out, "This is the best group of fighting men in the Navy." At that, reported *Life* magazine, "He wept like a mother leaving her child." (Gray, "'Jocko' Clark," 46)

He then read his orders aloud, as did Jennings his. Turning finally to Clark, Jennings said, "Sir, I relieve you." "Aye, aye, sir," Jocko replied, according to decorum. They shook hands, appropriately beneath the gunnery efficiency "E" and hash mark of a 5-inch mount.

The band struck up "Aloha 'Oe" as Clark crossed the flight deck, picked up his belongings, and descended to the hangar. There he was startled to find about two-thirds of the crew (over 2,000 men) lined up as side boys, officers in front—a spontaneous final gesture of affection. Each officer shook hands with Clark as he made his way through the throng of shipmates, whose warm smiling faces bespoke their feelings.

Jocko, Chaplain Bob Alexander, and numerous crewmen could not hold back their tears. Many of them, recalled Machinist's Mate Ron Radke, also a *Ranger* (CV-4) veteran, had hoped he would never make admiral and stay with them "forever." Jocko may have chewed out a man, but he rarely "messed up" his service record.

Rear Admiral Clark saluted the ensign and was piped over the side, accompanied by his aides, Rosenblatt and Reynolds.

"He hated very much to leave the ship," observed Dr. Gard in a letter, "and many of us hate to see him go, although the new skipper looks to be very fine." Indeed he was. When Jocko was in command, remembered Cooper Bright, there was constant tension on the bridge. The minute Al Jennings—a basically calm individual—ascended to the bridge, "all the tension disappeared."

A case in point was the first time Jennings took the *Yorktown* outside the formation to operate aircraft. Coming back in, he simply let the OOD handle the maneuvering. The captain said nothing as the ship roared back in between ships. But as the OOD smartly executed the fishtail or flipper turn, Jennings held on tight to both arms of his chair in disbelief. That was the last fishtail maneuver the *Yorktown* executed as an individual ship.

In Clark's final fitness report as skipper (8 April 1944), Admiral Towers lauded him as "an able, aggressive carrier captain. The *Yorktown*, which he commissioned and brought up to a peak level of efficiency, is one of the best carriers in the Navy. His personal conduct during battle has been exemplary." Towers gave Jocko an overall 4.0 mark and the equivalent of straight A+ in ten categories of performance, with a slightly lower rating for "intelligence" and "judgment." Deserving only a "middle A" was Clark's "neatness of person and dress." Towers—himself a very smart dresser—personally initialed the latter mark, doubtless to let Clark and other readers know it was not a typographical error!

Such an obvious poke at Clark's rumpled shirts and fairly casual appearance likely mortified the new admiral enough to object, because just two weeks later Towers submitted another fitness report on Clark (backdated to 3 April). In it he changed the "neatness" mark to A+—but then, asserting his own pique, lowered his assessment of Clark's "judgment" one niche and of his "initiative" two niches, both to middle A, with "intelligence" dropped down two niches to a lower A. But then Towers wrote, "I consider him extremely well qualified for the duty he now has" as a carrier division commander.

Apparently, Clark did not forget what he seems to have regarded as a slur on his excellent war record because after the war, in early 1946, he likely asked that this February 1944 fitness report be replaced by a new one for that period. The peacetime form was different, and Baldy Pownall—of all people—filled it in. He kept the top mark for Clark's "bearing, dress, character, etc." but realistically, and only slightly, marked down Clark on a few other items.

Though his shirts were often freshly pressed, talkative Jocko (*left*) seemed chroni-cally unkempt—partly the fault of the tropical heat and humidity. His superiors usually criticized his appearance and bearing in their fitness reports. *U.S. Navy photo*

The measure of any captain's success in the minds of the crew was and is whether they could boast of having served on "a happy ship." That the new *Yorktown* assuredly was, most of the veterans who served under Jocko Clark agreed—and it would be under Jennings as well. *Suwannee* and *York-town* alumnus Chief Ordnanceman P. P. Day thought each ship had "a great personality" under Clark's excellent leadership. Neither crew had "bumble-heads" or lazy people. Day was later transferred to the *Franklin* (CV-13), "not even 30 percent" the quality of the *Yorktown,* and that was due to a ter-rible and pompous skipper (L. H. Gehres). Airedale Charlie Murray subsequently served in many carriers well into the postwar period, but none ever had an esprit de corps like this one under Clark's leadership.

The *Yorktown*—without Jocko—sortied from Majuro with the rest of TF 58, after a two-day delay, on 12 February to clobber Truk. Although the Japanese fleet had departed, the air battle was furious, and losses sustained, but the American victory was overpowering. With the Japanese so weak, TF 58 continued westward and ten days later successfully pounded airfields in the Marianas.

On the ship's return to Majuro late in the month, Captain Jennings gave his first formal address to the crew: "In Pearl, on the [West] coast and in Washington before reporting on board, I heard that the Lucky Y was the best, and what I have seen since taking over is proof enough that she is still out in front." He intended to keep her there, an obvious inference to the preeminent place Jocko Clark had put her. (Reynolds, *Fighting Lady*, 110)

Clark spent the night of his relief at Majuro on board the battleship *Washington*, damaged in a collision with another battlewagon, *Indiana*. While there he received a parting message from Admiral Mitscher on the *Yorktown*: "I want you back here in TF 58 soon." He certainly wanted to return but was flown back to Pearl Harbor still expecting to go ashore at Quonset Point, Rhode Island.

His old friend Radford pinned his two stars on the collar of his khaki shirt. Raddy then informed him that his orders had been changed to stay in the Pacific. Jack Towers's and Fuzz Sherman's recommendation had obviously paid off, although Clark did not learn for months that Ernie King had personally approved it.

Clark's promotion to captain exactly two years earlier had amazed most officers. Now, with his selection for flag, "*everybody* was pretty surprised," as Admiral Tom Jeter remarked in 1965.

> Old Jock, step by step, just moved along to one of the finest combat records of any officers in the war. And even to this day, when you run into people that knew him, it's the rule rather than the exception to have fellas shake their heads and say, "By damn, I don't see how he did it." They just never expected him of it. (Interview with the author)

Each seagoing carrier admiral held a carrier division command—only for administrative purposes (i.e., paperwork), given the fluid task group carrier organization. With Clark's appointment, the Fast Carrier Force (TF 58) had six "cardivs," each with two or three heavy or light carriers arbitrarily assigned to it. Mitscher was senior as ComCarDiv Three. Clark became

ComCarDiv 13, a new designation. The others were Ted Sherman, Reeves, Ginder, and Montgomery. In July 1944 CarDiv 13 would be abolished and Clark made ComCarDiv Five.

Clark gathered most of his staff at Pearl Harbor in late February and early March. Then Admiral Mitscher assigned him to the newly arrived *Hornet* (CV-12) for the customary makee-learn cruise before assuming a task group command. Clark hated this passive role and blamed Truman Hedding, Mitscher's chief of staff, for it. But Mitscher required it of all prospective carrier task group commanders.

Nor was Clark happy over the fact that the *Hornet's* captain was his old nemesis Miles Browning. Some three years younger than Jocko, he had graduated only six numbers behind him in the Class of '18. A smart air tactician, Browning had rendered invaluable service as chief of staff to both Spruance and Halsey, at Midway and Guadalcanal respectively. But his irascible personality had alienated not only Clark but virtually every peer officer with whom he had served.

Worse, after Midway, Browning had been caught in bed with the wife of a fellow officer—a skilled boxer who had unmercifully beaten him up. Clark and his "gang" had long abhorred such immoral behavior by officers, especially against one of their own. After the war, Ernie King concluded simply that Browning was "no damn good at all." (Reynolds, "The Truth about Miles Browning," 214–15; Clark to M.C., 26 February 1933; conversations with George Anderson and Herbert D. Riley about the boxing prowess of Commander F. Massey Hughes; King 1949 interview by Walter Muir Whitehill)

King and his admirals had lured Browning away from Halsey in July 1943 by offering him the new *Hornet;* his detractors, likely including Clark, suspected he would not measure up. Already complaining about his ship and an allegedly undertrained air group when both arrived in Hawaii the following March, Browning insisted—and got—its Air Group 15 switched for Air Group Two.

The enlisted men had little trouble with him, however. One of them, Chief Yeoman Cecil S. King, saw him simply as a perfectionist and "gung ho fanatic" who "acted as if he was going to win the war himself with one airplane." (Cecil King transcript, 219–20)

Ships' officers and pilots, however, caught his wrath. A bomber pilot remembered him as unable to delegate authority, "a chain-smoking martinet who prowled the bridge of the *Hornet* like a caged animal. Every order was a snarl, and his subordinates reacted to him with fear and hatred." (Buell, "Death of a Captain," 92–93)

Admiral Mitscher was sufficiently concerned about Browning—he later recalled to Admiral Nimitz—that he assigned Admiral Clark to the *Hornet.* Jocko had "specific instructions that I wanted him to advise [Browning] and assist in straightening matters out in so far as he could, as I consider Clark one of the best carrier captains that it has ever been my pleasure to serve with." (Mitscher to Nimitz, 24 May 1944) Of course, this meant that Clark was a virtual spy regarding Browning's conduct and general performance.

So the first time that Jocko was piped aboard the *Hornet* at Pearl Harbor, and Browning met him at the gangway, Clark noticed "a look of consternation cross his face" at having to welcome a long-time rival. Jock immediately assured him "that, regardless of our former differences, I would recommend him for promotion if he did a good job."

Clark and the staff were flown out to the *Hornet* in the rear seats of VB-2's SB2C Helldivers on 8 March. Passenger Herm Rosenblatt used the occasion to show off by detailing to his pilot (Hal Buell) the forthcoming mission: steam to Majuro, then join TF 58 for air strikes against Japanese airfields and possible warships in the Palau Islands group of the western Carolines, all in support of General Douglas MacArthur's drive along the coast of New Guinea—a clear violation of secrecy. (Buell, "Death of a Captain," 94)

As Clark and his staff settled in, crew and air group gradually became aware of them. The administrative officer of VF-2, Lieutenant Charles Farrell, a tall and handsome former silent film star, initially had great difficulty just finding his way around the ship. One day when Flight Quarters sounded he dashed off looking for the fighters' ready room, only to slam his head on a pipe suspended from the overhead and collapse.

Still groggy and utterly lost as he revived, Farrell headed up a ladder toward the flight deck but encountered "a weatherbeaten individual with an engineer type cap on coming down the ladder." Charlie said, "Say, Chief, can you tell me how to get to Ready Room One?"

"Take a good look at me," came the instant reply. "I am Admiral Clark, and don't call me Chief again!" (Roy Johnson letter, 6 April 1966)

En route to Majuro, as part of a convoy under Pownall, Clark instituted the practice of doing his own navigation without anyone's knowledge, lest an erratic skipper like Browning have a mishap that would reflect against Clark. He also forewarned Admiral Mitscher in Tom Jeter's *Bunker Hill* and all the other carrier skippers and admirals about the protruding coral head the *Yorktown* had dodged at Majuro Atoll the month before. Unknown to Jocko, however, ComAirPac had already informed them all, including Browning and his officers, that the hazard had been removed. So everyone ignored Clark's warning, which angered him.

Jocko's staff was like family, and he had Bob Reynolds autograph this March 1944 photo to his own parents in Oklahoma. Said Bob of their son, "He's a great naval officer and a grand person to serve under." *U.S. Navy photo*

When the *Hornet* started straight into the lagoon entrance, Clark ran up to the bridge yelling, "Captain, you are going aground!" Browning replied simply, "Oh, no, I'm all right," and continued on. Clark later recalled that a destroyer blew a warning whistle about the supposed obstruction and that Browning corrected his course. But *Hornet*'s popular exec, Commander C. H. "Dutch" Duerfeldt, remembered otherwise, that in fact Clark was embarrassed when Browning and Duerfeldt explained that the channel had been cleared. (Duerfeldt interview by John J. McClaire Jr.)

Such potential "dents in Clark's armor" may have alerted his aide Rosenblatt to start snooping around and report any potential problems on the *Hornet* to his boss.

At Majuro Browning created his own problem by disputing Admiral Montgomery over some operational matter, then having the temerity to write a message to Montgomery that Clark—after the mandatory look at it—regarded as "insubordinate in substance." He went immediately up to the bridge and urged Browning not to send it; Jocko believed that its transmittal would result in Montgomery demanding Browning's detachment. So Browning did not, and Clark figured he had saved Browning's career.

Jocko took more interest in the crew and the pilots, having just left his own beloved ship. In his first address to them after coming aboard he announced, "The *Yorktown* is the best ship in the Navy, but I expect you to beat her." The first time he revisited the *Yorktown* he informed his old shipmates that the *Hornet* was out to beat her—thereby instigating a healthy rivalry.

*Hornet's* crew admired both Clark and Browning as true fighters, but "Jocko Clark was as different from Browning as day is from night," according to Cecil King. "I think he got the same results but in a different way. He was just universally loved, respected, and admired on the *Hornet.*"

Clark was "such a colorful guy . . . totally oblivious to his appearance." He would come out on the flag bridge at night—including during G.Q.—wearing pajamas drawn from sick bay; "sometimes his hairy stomach would be sticking out." So would his lower lip, perpetually sunburned. As on the *Yorktown,* the *Hornet's* doctor insisted that in daytime Clark wear a four-by-four-inch gauze pad

> with a string over his ears so the 4 x 4 would hang down over his lip. Jocko did it, but it made him madder than hell. I've seen him snatch three or four of those things off in the course of a couple hours. "Goddammit!" He'd tear it off and throw it down. And here would come the doctor and make him a new one. (Cecil King transcript, 220–21; edited version in Wooldridge, *Carrier Warfare,* 278–79)

During March 1944 the Fifth Fleet and TF 58 were streamlined to facilitate the drive westward. Spruance became a full admiral and Mitscher a vice admiral. Mitscher transferred his flag from the *Yorktown* to the *Lexington,* just repaired from the hit it had taken the previous December 4th.

Furthermore, a new edict by Admiral King ordered the integration of black-shoe and brown-shoe officers on the respective staffs of their commands. Each senior air admiral (of a fleet or task force) must now have a nonaviator chief of staff and vice versa. So Captain Arleigh A. Burke, a celebrated destroyer leader in the Solomons, reported to the *Lex* virtually in makee-learn status to eventually replace Captain Hedding. Whatever Clark thought about the new policy at the time, after becoming a task group commander under the Mitscher-Burke regime he "considered Burke the best choice in the entire Navy" for the job. (Clark, "31-Knot Burke," 54)

As rear admiral, Clark posed for photographs on the flag bridge of the *Hornet* with his most trusted officers, who autographed copies of it for one another. Air operations officer Douglas "Tex" McCrary inscribed this one to Bob Reynolds in March 1944: "One helluva good shipmate on Jock's staff. If we can just kill the Japs the way you slay the gals it will be smooth sailing." *U.S. Navy photo*

The new Commander Task Group 58.3, "Cy" Ginder, hoisted his flag on the *Yorktown*, which moved southward with part of TF 58 to Espiritu Santo in the New Hebrides. From there and Majuro the entire task force would converge on Palau at the end of the month, protecting General Douglas MacArthur's northern flank in the New Guinea campaign.

TG 58.2 sortied from Majuro on 22 March under Montgomery in *Bunker Hill* and days later joined up with the other two task groups from the south—11 carriers total. Jocko and his staff had little to do as virtual bystanders on the *Hornet*. As such, Clark could only sympathize with Browning when several remodeled SB2C Helldivers of VB-2 were so handicapped by problems that Browning had some of them pushed overboard! (Conversation with Jeter)

Bob Reynolds and other staffers occupied the gunner's rear seat on several of the operable 2Cs as observers during bombing missions. When idle, Jocko and several of the staff engaged in word games in Flag Plot. Herm Rosenblatt had the temerity to make monetary bets with the admiral, who then had to pay up when the Ivy Leaguer won. (Conversation with Reynolds)

Japanese snoopers spotted the force on 25 March, enabling the enemy fleet to evacuate Palau for points west. Four nights later their customary torpeckers appeared, only to be clobbered by the heavy flak thrown up. Mitscher simply did not like using his Bat teams or engaging in any night flying. Too many risks were involved in night launches and especially in recoveries.

Next day, 30 March, TF 58 launched a fighter sweep that encountered and shot down some 30 airborne Zeros, then destroyed about the same number on the ground by strafing. Jocko was pleased to see his old squadron, VF-2, go into action. The 70 or so mostly small vessels in the harbor fell victim to low-level skip bombing (off the water), conventional dive and horizontal bombing, and aerial mining. Bob Reynolds took movies from a high-diving SB2C, seeing "lots of Japs . . . die with my own eyes." (Letter to Alma, Bill, and Clarkie Reynolds, 10 April 1944)

The enemy flew in about 40 more planes during the night. Flown by clearly inferior pilots, all were shot down by Hellcats at first light on the 31st. More bombing decimated Palau, and next day the carriers hit the island of Woleai. TF 58 lost about two dozen flyers over the three days, though most were picked up by lifeguard subs. By the time the delay-action mines finished the job, about 130,000 tons of Japanese shipping had succumbed to the Palau raiders. They had neutralized the island from being a threat to MacArthur's western advance across New Guinea.

In the midst of the operation, however, Admiral Ginder suffered a nervous collapse on the flag bridge of the *Yorktown*. His staff stretched him out on the deck, applying cold compresses to his head, as shipmates like Jim Vonk looked on uncomprehendingly at their leader. Ginder had simply broken under the emotional strain of combat command and would have to be replaced on the return to Majuro.

Admirals Nimitz and Forrest Sherman happened to be visiting Majuro when TF 58 returned on 6 April. Mitscher went directly to Nimitz, who immediately gave him permission to replace Ginder with another admiral. Mitscher had just the man, ready and eager. Before the day ended, Ginder was gone, and Jocko Clark was appointed as his relief. Clark kept his flag in the *Hornet.*

ComAirPac Admiral Baldy Pownall, similarly relieved earlier for his questionable leadership in the Gilberts campaign, was riding as an adviser to Spruance and opposed Ginder's summary relief. Spruance agreed with Pownall, who then tried to stall Ginder's replacement. The result was a confrontation at Pearl Harbor ten days later at which Nimitz sided with Jack Towers and Forrest Sherman to support Mitscher's decision and thus Clark's succession of Ginder. (Reynolds, *Fighting Lady,* 118–19; Reynolds, *Fast Carriers,* 149–51)

It was the first time that Mitscher appointed a task group commander, as well as firing another. And his judgment in subsequent replacements was never questioned again. Such changes would be directly influenced by the fact that Clark immediately lived up to Mitscher's confidence in him. Indeed, Jocko Clark quickly became Mitscher's most trusted task group commander for the rest of the war.

# FIFTEEN

# Carrier Admiral, 1944

WITH OVERPOWERING STRENGTH, THE U.S. PACIFIC FLEET WAS driving westward so fast that Japan would soon be forced to commit its battle fleet—bigger than ever but smaller than Nimitz's. And its pilots were grossly undertrained, their fighter planes inferior. Furthermore, the dual American advance confused Japanese leaders about where the next major landing might occur—in western New Guinea or the Mariana Islands of the Central Pacific. In whichever direction TF 58 went, Japan's carrier fleet would have to fight it.

The American strategy, largely the work of Admiral King, was two pronged: (1) an amphibious assault at Hollandia, New Guinea, in April 1944 as MacArthur leapfrogged westward, bypassing major Japanese ground forces; and (2) a similar operation to take Saipan in the Marianas in June, bypassing Rabaul and Truk. The Fast Carrier Task Force with its great mobility would support *both* landings and meet the Japanese fleet in battle whenever and wherever it appeared. That event turned out to be the Battle of the Philippine Sea—the largest carrier battle in history.

In King's view, the Marianas held the key to the offensive. By taking Saipan—followed by Tinian and Guam—the Pacific Fleet could drive thence straight to the coast of China, cutting off Japanese oil imports from Indonesia, and begin the blockade of Japan itself. Furthermore, the AAF's "very long range" B-29 strategic bombers could base in the Marianas and bomb Tokyo and other major Japanese industrial and population centers.

TF 58's timetable was first to support the Seventh Fleet's assault on Hollandia in April. Two months later it would attack the Marianas and neutralize Japanese airfields at Chichi and Iwo Jima to the north while supporting successive Fifth Fleet landings at Saipan, Tinian, and Guam. In addition, the fast carriers had to fight and destroy the Japanese Mobile Fleet during the course of these operations. Bypassed island strongholds would be kept inoperative by land-based planes from captured islands.

It was a tall order that required skilled leadership. Admiral Spruance commanded the overall Fifth Fleet, with Kelly Turner his amphibious commander and Pete Mitscher leading the fast carriers. The latter's task group commanders were Reeves ('11), Montgomery ('12), and Clark ('18). Because Jocko Clark was very junior to both of them, as he had been even to the ill-fated Ginder ('16), "I realized that only by turning in a top-notch performance could I hope to keep my job."

Mitscher, however, had such confidence in him from the outset that he gave Clark command of the first task group—58.1—during this and every subsequent operation. Inasmuch as he was the first in order, Jocko intended to perform equally as *the best*.

The key to his success he believed to be a superior staff. Clark insisted that he get the men best suited to work with him *and* his inner circle: Herm Rosenblatt (flag secretary), Sugar Brown (operations officer for ships), Bob Reynolds (flag lieutenant), and Tex McCrary (operations officer for air). Jocko was not pleased with his chief of staff, Captain Bowser Vieweg, simply because both were strong-willed (that is, stubborn) individuals, always competing with each other. Vieweg for his part went to Truman Hedding of Mitscher's staff and begged to be transferred. Clark desperately wanted Raöul Waller back for the job, and while at Majuro he visited ComAirPac Baldy Pownall to insist on it.

Pownall finally agreed but said Waller simply could not be spared until later in the year. Clark was willing to wait, but he did not want to keep Vieweg either. Admitting that their differences were due to a personality clash, Clark gave Vieweg a glowing fitness report, recommending that he be given his own ship. It meant that Bowser would be transferred soon, leaving Clark without a chief of staff for several months until Waller reported. Jocko assured Pownall that the staff would fill in for him until then. After the Hollandia operation Vieweg would be ordered to command of the escort carrier *Gambier Bay*, only to have it sunk later at the Battle of Leyte Gulf.

Clark also wanted three of his most-admired *Yorktown* officers transferred to his staff: navigator Red Sharp to be overall operations officer, replacing the one assigned to him, M. T. Evans; superlative fighter director Charlie Ridgway replacing Thorne for the same job on the task group staff; and Vonk the weatherguesser. To get them, however, he had to convince his successor on the *Yorktown*, Captain Al Jennings. So he paid a visit to his old ship at Majuro.

Jennings was not pleased by this raid on the ship's officer cadre. Vonk was not available; Admiral Mitscher had already claimed him. Jennings did not want to give up the superb Ridgway but agreed to do so, figuring rightly that Alex Wilding could easily fill his shoes. Losing his navigator was another matter, even when Jocko offered to "trade" Evans for Sharp. Jennings suggested that Sharp be given the choice, to which Jocko agreed.

Summoned to the bridge by the captain, Sharp was surprised to see Clark there and to hear Jennings's immediate question: "The Admiral wants you to come over to his staff. I've told him that I don't want to let you go. What do you want to do about it?"

Embarrassed, Red finally consented to go with Clark, but Jennings got Jocko to agree that Sharp would be the last officer he could have from the *Yorktown*. Meanwhile, Clark put Empty Evans ashore at Majuro to await his formal transfer to the *York*. Sharp and Ridgway would join Clark's staff after the Hollandia operation, and Sharp quickly became the fifth and final member of Clark's inner circle.

During Jocko's visit to the *Yorktown* he renewed acquaintances with Cooper Bright and George Earnshaw by inviting them to dinner at his mess on the *Hornet*. All they had to eat was Spam, the bland staple of every fighting front. Ere long, Clark asked them, "How's *the ship* getting along since I left?" "Not quite as sharp as you were, Admiral," they lied, inasmuch as Jennings kept it running smoothly—and "without all the bombast." (Conversation with Bright)

Another *Yorktown* guest was Dr. Ray Gard, who afterward wrote of Clark in a letter: "He is a most dramatic character. I was glad to see him, and he me. . . . But his heart is still here"—on the *Yorktown*, as was that of Gard, unhappy with transfer orders to the battleship *Pennsylvania*.

Jocko's sentimentality for his former ship showed whenever he saw her from the *Hornet*'s flag bridge. He would gaze at her nostalgically, saying quietly and repeatedly, "That's a wonderful ship." And when certain things went wrong on the *Hornet*, Clark would often assert, "We didn't do it that way on the *Yorktown!*" The flagship's officers put an end to that by never referring to the *Yorktown* by name, only as "the *Nameless*." (Alexander, "Carrier Revolution," 50)

One of Clark's first innovations as Commander Task Group 58.1 was to institutionalize his famous fishtail or flipper turn for all four carriers in the formation. The maneuver—a carrier hastening at 25 knots outside the 18-knot formation to operate aircraft, then returning—was dubbed the "B" or Baker method. It also saved fuel for the other ships, kept at the slower speed. Now, however, if aircraft operations were prolonged due to the constant demand for more planes in a battle, Jocko ruled that the entire formation should turn *with* the flattops—"Modified Baker"—until the battle was over.

When he held a meeting of all his ship captains to explain the new system, the cruiser skippers protested that it risked collisions, making the time-honored "rules of the road" difficult to obey. Clark countered, "Just forget about the right of way and all the other rules of the road and get out of the way" of the carriers if a collision seemed imminent. The carriers simply *had* to be properly positioned in order to operate their planes. Jocko called it "gentleman seamanship."

It worked, and Admiral Mitscher adopted it immediately for all the carrier task groups. Modified Baker was only one more example of the carrier task organization replacing the battle line; battleships and cruisers now had to give way to carriers on a daily basis.

One thing bothered Mitscher about TG 58.1, and that was the flagship. For the predawn launches, Miles Browning would ring up only 25 knots, not enough for all the planes to keep above the water after leaving the deck. The very first time two torpeckers were launched, they just plunged into the sea—all six men lost. Later a divebomber went in, and the pilot got into his raft but was never picked up. Air officer Roy Johnson advised Browning of the problem, but he refused to listen. (Johnson transcript #1, 89–90)

Although such "operational casualties were running quite high," Mitscher later told Nimitz (24 May 1944 letter), "I gave the *Hornet* the benefit of the doubt and sent her to the Hollandia operation." But he told Jocko, "I know what's wrong with the *Hornet*. It's the captain. He's wrong."

"Admiral," Clark reminded Mitscher, "the man is a classmate of mine. I can't make a recommendation against him unless he commits an overt act." So far, he had not. Part of Mitscher's animus toward Browning stemmed from the Solomon Islands campaign one year before. Browning, as chief of staff to theater commander Halsey, had been "pretty overpowering and ruthless" even with admirals like Mitscher. This behavior "started sort of a feud" between the two. (Johnson transcript #1, 84)

Browning's task as skipper was not made easier by the interference of the ubiquitous Herman Rosenblatt, prowling about the ship. The chief engineer, Commander Joseph T. Hazen, ran him out of the engine room for interfering with the work of the black gang. The air officer, Commander Leonard T. Morse, similarly stood up to Rosenblatt. Rosenblatt retaliated by turning Clark against both men and thus getting Browning to replace them. (Conversations of John J. McClaire Jr. with Hazen, Morse, and several other former *Hornet* department heads)

The Air Department did have many problems, which Browning blamed on air officer Morse. Its operations were understandably Clark's special concern. So at Majuro he sent several of its officers over to the *Yorktown* "to see how we operate." (Wilding diary, 7 April 1944) Such well-meant interference by Jocko in the *Hornet*'s operations did not make Browning's life any easier.

Air Group Two had wanted to keep its original—and more dependable—SBDs, much as Clark had done on the *Yorktown* by trading in VB-5's SB2Cs for SBDs. But the *Hornet* had received spare parts only for the Helldiver. And Browning did not want to go to the considerable effort of emptying his storerooms of "2C" parts for those of SBDs. As a result, VB-2 had had only a week in Hawaii to convert to the "2C." (Johnson transcript #1, 82–83)

Clark continued to hate the plane that pilots had nicknamed "the Beast." When several of Bombing Two's SB2Cs proved to be duds he recommended trading in several for more TBFs torpeckers, better at attacking land targets with bombs (ComCarDiv 13 Action Report, serial 0029, 10 May 1944). But it did not happen.

Something that Clark liked, though Mitscher did not, was the nightfighting Bat teams. He even had Lieutenant Russ Reiserer's four-night Hellcat detachment transferred from the *Yorktown* to the *Hornet* and his direct control. He never wanted to relive the nightmarish 4 December withdrawal from Kwajalein.

Admiral Herb Riley recalled:

> Clark never lost sight of the pilot's point of view. He was always very conscious of doing everything he could to make things as easy for the pilots as he could because he'd come up the hard way himself as a pilot. He knew it right from the cockpit. He never forgot this in his task group command. Mitscher was the same.

Admiral Ted Sherman, frequently compared with Jocko Clark, was just as aggressive but a latecomer to the cockpit. Older than Clark—in fact, a classmate of Mitscher ('10)—he had been "such a poor pilot" trainee that he had passed the course at Pensacola only on the orders of BuAer chief King in 1936. "He had unlimited personal courage," remembered Riley, "and would charge in, in the face of anything, and try anything. But as far as he was concerned, the pilots were expendable. . . . He didn't have any feeling whatever for the human side of things. He never saw the full picture." (Riley transcript #4, 277–78)

Because of this, some of Sherman's aviator staff officers disliked him intensely. A notable exception was Commander Roland H. Dale, air group commander on Sherman's flagship *Bunker Hill* in the battles of late '43 and early '44, then his staff operations officer. "Brute" Dale had just been loaned out to Rear Admiral Keene Harrill for the Marianas operation while Sherman returned stateside for a much-deserved breather.

"The pilots of the air groups liked to work under Sherman," recalled Dale, contradicting Riley, "because they knew he would take care of them," for example by holding up predawn launches in foul weather until first light. And, like Clark, "he had the courage of a lion and would go to great lengths to rescue downed pilots." (Dale to author, 14 April 1966)

Whether one liked or hated sluggers like Clark and Sherman depended very much on one's personality. For combat, after all, is not for the timid, indecisive, or sensitive—as Jocko had discovered of Pownall, and Brute Dale would of Harrill.

When Task Force 58 sortied from Majuro on 13 April, bound for the attack on Hollandia, Jocko Clark was in fine fettle. In addition to his flagship *Hornet*, TG 58.1 consisted of three light carriers (*Belleau Wood, Cowpens*, and *Bataan*), four light cruisers under Rear Admiral L. H. Dubose, and the customary destroyers. The two other task groups each had four carriers as well—an even dozen. All girded for the usual low-altitude torpecker attacks beneath the ships' radar beams. Clark, however, helped solve that problem by appointing several visual fighter directors on his carriers to spot them and vector CAP fighters to the intercept. (Reynolds, *Fast Carriers*, 153)

The force bucked heavy weather over much of the ensuing week, with several tankers joining up with 58.1 in the stormy predawn darkness of 19 April for a scheduled refueling. Clark put them astern of his carriers, which he ordered to make the Baker turn at 0515 in order to launch the morning CAP. The *Hornet* increased its speed to 25 knots and at the appointed moment turned right 20 degrees.

But the rest of the task group turned *left* 20 degrees! Clark saw the *Hornet* was cutting directly across the bow of the tanker *Platte*, whose captain, F. S. "Monty" Gibson, happened to be a classmate of Clark and Browning. It was headed for the starboard beam "on a direct collision course," recalled bomber pilot Hal Buell, sitting in his plane on deck for a dawn antisub search. The OOD triggered alarm whistles and horns, whereupon Buell cut his engine and leaped from his cockpit, expecting a collision: "The onrushing ship's bow appeared as tall as our flight deck."

Browning, initially ignoring warnings by junior officers, took the conn, ordered full speed ahead, and came full left to port as the *Platte* "went to full reverse." The oiler's bow just missed hitting the carrier's stern, with credit being given Monty Gibson rather than Browning. Some said the miss was between 20 and 60 feet, others "with only inches to spare" if indeed the ships did not actually touch.

"Captain, captain!" Clark shouted as he rushed up to the bridge in his bathrobe, "don't you *ever* do that again!" Whether Jocko "saved" Miles, as he later claimed, is problematic, but the two men "got into a heated exchange

. . . in front of several junior officers," after which Browning "just walked away shaking his head and went below to thank chief engineer Hazen for his quick response to the helm." (McClaire conversation with *Hornet*'s navigator, then Commander Evan E. Fickling; Buell, "Death of a Captain," 94; Mitscher to Nimitz, 24 May 1944; my conversations with Clark)

That afternoon, with Clark's TG 58.1 in the van, the carriers encountered a few Betty snoopers from Truk that the CAP easily splashed, one by a *Cowpens* fighter from Clark's group. But neither enemy planes nor major ground forces contested MacArthur's landings at Hollandia on 22 April. His AAF squadrons had already neutralized enemy air, with most Japanese troops having been evacuated.

Endless foul weather was the major foe while Clark's planes attacked installations at Sawar and Sarmi and an airfield on Wakde Island. At night, Clark sent in his cruisers and several destroyers to bombard coastal targets, and Mitscher finally exercised the Bat teams.

In full command instead of a mere observer, Clark was just as active as he had been on the *Yorktown*. Indeed, his former shipmates on that ship were amused to hear his verbal tirades over the TBS radio when he got excited. Especially attentive to *Hornet*'s flight operations, whenever he received a particularly good report during battle he often roared, "Put her there, pal," and shook hands with everyone in Flag Plot. (Conversation with Red Sharp; Gray, "'Jocko' Clark," 46)

Unlike the customary flag officer on his flag bridge, observed a war correspondent,

> Rear Admiral Clark, the Cherokee, is a fighting, shouting extrovert who yells at his officers in a rasping voice and expects them to yell back at him [but few did]. . . . The nickname [Jocko] is used affectionately and with admiration, for Clark is one of the most effective carrier fighters in the Navy and a born killer. . . .
>
> He is a mercurial, glandular man and has a long, floppy lower lip which protrudes far out when he is angry. He has a bulging unNavy-like abdomen and the ungainly kind of physique which makes it impossible for him to keep a shirttail tucked in. (Alexander, "Carrier Revolution," 48)

Before dawn on 23 April a *Hornet* night fighter shot down a lonely Betty. Destroyer *Cowell* reached the wreckage in time to pick up its pilot and his charts and instruction books. Staff Japanese language officer Ensign E. B. Beath added the material to information he had intercepted from radio messages. Next day another *Hornet* Hellcat on CAP splashed a second

Betty snooper, from the wreckage of which tin can *Burns* was able to recover an aircraft codebook. Beath copied it immediately, and Jocko sent it to Mitscher—"a veritable gold mine of information." Indeed, the Japanese continued to use this code for another four months, enabling TF 58 to track their airplane movements throughout the entire Marianas campaign.

That very evening of the 24th *Hornet*'s radar picked up three large groups of bogeys to the west. But Russ Reiserer's night fighters drove them off before they could sight the force. Next day Clark's task group covered the other two task groups as they refueled, and the CAP shot down a Betty 33 miles out. The can *Bedford* retrieved survivors, a boon to intelligence that Clark again utilized—another example of his ability to exploit opportunities.

Meanwhile, AAF bombers attacking Truk had encountered large numbers of enemy planes there, forcing Admiral Nimitz to order TF 58 to return to Truk and knock it out once and for all as an active airdrome. "Plaster Truk," Mitscher informed his carrier admirals, "with everything you have including empty beer bottles if you have any." Clark's group refueled on 27 April en route and battled the seemingly endless bad weather to reach the launch position 80 miles south of Truk at dawn of the 29th.

Just as the initial fighter sweep encountered perhaps 60 Zeros over the target, other Zekes escorted "Jill" torpedo-bombers in attacking the task force. All bandits were destroyed by the carrier planes and ships' fire, but Japanese AA claimed several Navy planes over Truk. With command of the air, TF 58's fighters and bombers strafed and pounded Truk's installations, parked planes, and a few minor ships. One of the destroyers in TG 58.1's screen detected and sank an enemy submarine south of the island bastion.

During the afternoon, reports of several downed airmen in Truk waters revealed that the lifeguard sub *Tang* could not find and rescue all of them (although it did pick up a phenomenal 22!). This realization motivated Herman Rosenblatt to recommend that the staff break radio silence and direct cruiser floatplanes to pick them up. Jocko enthusiastically forwarded the request to Mitscher. "When he said nothing in reply," recalled Jocko, "we knew he approved."

Clark put Herm in charge, and he carried out the task masterfully that day and the next, dispatching destroyers to retrieve pilots from the open sea and Vought OS2U Kingfisher floatplanes from the cruisers to land in Truk's lagoon for others. Admiral Mitscher thereafter appointed an overall task force pilot rescue coordinator.

The intense attacks resumed next day until heavy weather led Mitscher to cancel further strikes in midafternoon. Truk had been dealt a mortal blow as an airdrome and anchorage, to be kept neutralized by land-based bombers from southwestern Pacific air bases for the rest of the war. Clark's cruisers shelled nearby Satawan Island on the second day, and on 1 May his planes covered Admiral Ching Lee's seven fast battleships as they bombarded Ponape Island.

Pete Mitscher gave Clark a "well done" for his first performance as a combat admiral and sent his task group to Kwajalein and Eniwetok, while the others were sent to Majuro to prepare for the Marianas operation. But Jocko was determined to do something to improve air operations on his flagship. He admired the air group skipper, Commander Roy L. Johnson, but not the air officer, Commander Leonard Morse.

Likeable but unaggressive, Morse had, for example, been supplied with tow bars for the *Yorktown*-inspired mules that pulled planes forward on the flight deck. No tow bars yet existed, however, for respotting the planes aft. Morse knew that other carriers simply fashioned their own, but he would not do it for the *Hornet*. And Clark kept meddling until Morse asked Browning to replace him.

Before word of this reached Clark, Morse ran a snooping Herman Rosenblatt out of Air Department spaces. Herm headed straight to Jocko and threw a "temper tantrum," one device he used to get support from the Old Man. Clark immediately went to the captain's bridge, ordered Browning to fire Morse, and summoned Roy Johnson to the bridge.

When Johnson arrived, Jocko asked him his immediate plans.

"Well," he replied, "I'm still with the air group and, when we finish, go back, rehabilitate, and then come back and finish the war."

"No," countered the admiral. "Tomorrow, you're the air officer. I'm firing the guy we've got now because he can't do the job. And if you don't do the job I'll have to fire you, too." (Johnson transcript #1, 87–88)

Johnson turned to Browning, who, having been bypassed, said with disgust, "You're it!" and walked away. (McClaire interview of Morse) ComAirPac Pownall tried to stall the change so that Morse could defend himself formally, but Mitscher rejected Pownall out of hand. (Mitscher to Nimitz, 24 May 1944) VT-2 skipper Lieutenant Commander Jackson D. Arnold fleeted up to air group command; he would direct his pilots from a TBF instead of a fighter.

While each carrier prepared by day for the invasion of the Marianas, in the evenings a movie was shown forward of the parked planes in the hangar bay. Needless to say, the admiral and senior staff and ship's officers always sat in the front row on folding chairs. Because of the close proximity of highly flammable materials, smoking was absolutely forbidden there. Often, however, Jocko would put a cigarette in his mouth, strike a wooden kitchen match on the deck, light up, and smoke during the movie—"and not one person ever said anything about that." (Cecil King transcript #2, 234)

One evening during a film, with the *Hornet* anchored off Eniwetok, Clark and Browning were sitting in the front row as usual, with the staff, ship's officers, and air group pilots just behind them. Perhaps 2,000 men were on hand, some sitting on airplane wings, engine stands, and overhead catwalks.

Somebody in the back accidentally tripped a $CO_2$ fire extinguisher off the bulkhead. When it hit the deck, it let out a terrible screeching noise and took off "like a rocket" banging along on that steel deck. Some wag who saw it loudly remarked, "Look out, it's a plane loose, and here it comes!" (Johnson transcript #1, 85)

Whereupon another man, who had not seen it but only heard the racket, yelled, "It's a bomb!"

And another, "Fire!"

Other cries were accompanied by mass panic, "a human tidal wave action rolling from the rear toward the front," as bomber pilot Buell, sitting in the fourth row, put it. The hundred or so combat-weaned flyers instinctively kept their heads and did not panic but held their ground against the stampede. In so doing, they acted as a buffer for Clark and Browning. (Buell, "Death of a Captain," 95)

Clark thought that the panic-stricken sailors had seen his admiral's insignia and avoided him, but it was too dark for that. The rioters indiscriminately pressed others against bulkheads, or knocked them down, injuring 32 men who ended up in sick bay. Then, as lights came on and the panic subsided, somebody yelled, "Man overboard!" (Mitscher to Nimitz, 24 May 1944; Johnson transcript #1, 85)

Searchlights were turned on and swept the waters around the *Hornet*. Sure enough, a sailor was spotted and "fished out of the drink." He remarked that another man might also have been knocked into the water. So the duty department head, navigator Evan Fickling, kept the searchlights working and suggested a boat be lowered over the side. Clark ordered Browning to take a muster. But Fickling—who incidentally had helped Clark set up NAS Jax in 1941—assured the captain several times that all hands were accounted for. So no boat was lowered and no muster taken. (Buell, "Death of a Captain," 95; McClaire interviews of Fickling and other *Hornet* officers; Johnson transcript #1, 85)

Browning asked Clark if he could just forget the movie, but Jocko turned him down and told him to let everyone see the rest of it. First, however, with the moviegoers reassembled and the chairs set up again, Browning rightly scolded the crew for its shoddy behavior. Clark kept his own thoughts to himself, to wit: "If this is what they do at a peaceful movie in a secure harbor, what will they do in battle?"

Nothing else happened until the following midday, when a body floated to the surface near the gangway. There had been a second victim after all who, however, as Roy Johnson recalled, had "probably drowned right away." Still, a search should have been made and a muster taken, as Clark had ordered.

Browning convened a board of investigation headed by Captain Guy V. Clark, skipper of the antiaircraft cruiser *San Juan* (who had stood very low in Jocko's original '17 class). It criticized no one person and found only technical problems such as the lack of safety nets. The tragedy was simply something that could happen in wartime, it said, and that no individual was culpable. (Johnson transcript #1, 86)

Admirals Clark and Mitscher, however, regarded the incident as the "overt act" they needed to rid the *Hornet* of Browning. Clark ordered a second board with the same membership but instructed it to assign blame for the tragedy. This court called Clark and Browning as "interested parties" and quickly found Browning (and the exec Duerfeldt) guilty of negligence. Clark, in his endorsement of these findings, recommended that Browning be relieved of command.

The *Hornet*, Mitscher wrote to Nimitz (24 May 1944), "is a jittery ship" and Browning "a driver, but not a leader." The carrier was "not fully ready for war operations, in comparison with the other ships of the force." The first change needed was a new captain "who is calm, cool, and at the same time a man who can get results thru respect rather than by fear of the consequences." He recommended Captain William D. Sample, "an excellent man" who had commanded the escort carrier *Santee* in the North African landings when Clark had had *Suwannee*.

On 29 May Browning was relieved by Bill Sample and sent home to report directly to Ernie King, who made sure he would never return to sea.

Sample's arrival improved morale and efficiency immediately, especially among the officers. He was, in Jocko's opinion, "a forceful yet thoughtful and kindly leader who became an inspiration to his crew." Pilot Hal Buell saw him as "strong yet gentle . . . almost fatherly." (Buell, "Death of a Captain," 95; Cecil King transcript #2, 229–30)

Roy Johnson agreed, and the *Hornet* became "a different ship" under Sample, "even though you still had to contend with Jocko Clark. He was a fighter, I must say," but "you had to kind of walk a tight wire rope with that guy." (Johnson transcript #1, 86, 89)

Clark for his part saw in Johnson "a high type of leadership" exhibited as air group commander, air officer, and eventually exec of the *Hornet*. Such praise played no small part in helping Johnson advance eventually to four-star rank and command of the Pacific Fleet during the Vietnam War (1965–67).

Clark now welcomed the arrival of his last two staff officers from the *Yorktown*—fighter director Charlie Ridgway and Red Sharp as overall operations officer. Red looked forward to working with the chief of staff, Bowser Vieweg, whom he had known for years. But he was completely unaware that Clark had arranged for Vieweg's transfer and that Sharp would serve as acting chief of staff until Raöul Waller became available later.

Coming aboard the *Hornet* at Eniwetok, Sharp reported as was the custom to the chief of staff, who he knew as "Bows" (pronounced "Bouz"). As they were talking, Clark happened by and saw them together. The next thing Sharp knew, a Marine orderly was at the door: "The Admiral wants to see you right away!"

Excusing himself, Red reported to Jocko. "Now look, Sharp, goddammit," Clark scolded, "I want to know whose side you're on right now!" Sharp only then learned that Clark had not gotten along with Vieweg and had arranged his transfer. After assuring the admiral of his loyalty, Sharp learned he would temporarily fill in as head of the staff after Bowser left a few days later.

By the beginning of June 1944 and the Marianas operation, therefore, Clark had the key members of his team intact for the next six months:

Cdr. Raymond "Red" Sharp, air operations officer and acting chief of staff

Lt. Cdr. David "Sugar" Brown, ships operations officer

Lt. Cdr. Owen Sowerwine–"Zero," communications officer

Lt. Charles "Charlie" Ridgway, fighter director

Lt. Herman Rosenblatt, flag secretary

Lt. (jg) Frank Robert "Bob" Reynolds, flag lieutenant

In addition, Lieutenant (jg) Beath handled Japanese radio intelligence, while an ACIO and a senior watch officer rounded out the staff.

"Just like a family" recalled Sowerwine-Zero, these men discussed and brainstormed all matters involving task group operations. Jocko listened to each one for suggestions. And "he *listened!*"—carefully—before deciding on a course of action.

Rosenblatt was customarily aloof, but closest to Sowerwine, who acted as a buffer with the others because they generally disliked him. All, however, greatly admired Herman's incredible skills in smoothing out Clark's operations orders, then assembling and distributing them. Smart, fast, and witty, he knew how to get things done—literally, anything. In addition, his job required that he be Clark's "hatchet man." (Conversations with Sharp and Sowerwine)

Reynolds was gregarious, full of ideas, and the interference runner for others dealing with Jocko, as he had been on the *Yorktown*. Jocko "thought the world of Bob" except just once when Reynolds did something that so enraged the admiral that he bawled him out and even put him in hack overnight, then chewed him out again—the only time that Sharp ever saw Jocko treat a staff member so harshly. (Conversation with Red Sharp)

Admiral Mitscher rewarded Clark for his initial performance as admiral by assigning the *Yorktown* alongside the *Hornet* in Task Group 58.1 for the Marianas campaign. The two light carriers were *Belleau Wood* and *Bataan*. Replacing Mel Pride, now rear admiral, as skipper of the *Belleau Wood* was Captain John Perry, whom Mitscher regarded so highly as to have recommended him for the *Hornet* if Bill Sample had not been available. (Mitscher to Nimitz, 24 May 1944) The captain of *Bataan* was V. H. "Val" Schaeffer, 1919 classmate of Sample, Jennings, and Jeter.

An old friend of Clark's, Rear Admiral Ralph Davison, reported to the *Yorktown* in makee-learn status for an eventual fast carrier task group command. He was a bright, talented, and very intellectual officer (third in the class of '16), "an excellent leader" in Clark's opinion.

The carrier revolution over gun ships accelerated the arrival of many other of Jocko's contemporaries in the Pacific by mid-1944. Rear Admiral Gerry Bogan had survived a bad fall from the flight deck while skipper of the *Saratoga* and gotten Ernie King's blessing to command an escort carrier group in the Marianas operation. (Alexander, "Carrier Revolution," 46, 48) Commander of support aircraft was Captain Dick Whitehead, charged with coordinating the planes of all carriers bombing and strafing ahead of the assault troops at Saipan, Tinian, and Guam.

Mitscher assigned Clark and TG 58.1 to the van for these and all subsequent operations. It would always be closest to the enemy—when TF 58 attacked Japanese targets, and bringing up the rear when the force withdrew—always ready to engage the enemy. Mitscher trusted Jocko that much.

Warhorses Montgomery and Reeves remained in place, leading task groups 58.2 and 58.3 respectively. So many new fast carriers were arriving that each of these three task groups was now assigned two heavy and two light carriers. Montgomery rode in Tom Jeter's *Bunker Hill*, Reeves in Matt Gardner's *Enterprise*; Mitscher had his flag with the latter group in Ernie Litch's *Lexington*. Yet three more carriers enabled Mitscher to create a fourth group, 58.4, made up of Ralph Ofstie's *Essex* as flagship and two CVLs, one being Gotch Dillon's *Langley*.

The new task group was headed by Rear Admiral W. Keen Harrill, Jocko's old skipper in battleship spotting planes (when they had wrangled with the young hothead Browning). A 1914 Annapolis grad, Harrill joined "Monty" ('12) and "Black Jack" ('11) in following the very junior Jocko ('18) into and out of each battle.

Because Clark's group would always be the one nearest to Japanese air attacks, it was supplied with plenty of antiaircraft power by speedy, maneuverable cruisers: heavy cruisers *Boston, Baltimore,* and *Canberra* under Rear Admiral L. H. Thebaud and antiaircraft light cruisers *San Juan* and Sol Phillips's *Oakland.* Fourteen destroyers made up the outer screen, with Phillips the overall screen commander.

The rotation of fresh air groups accelerated due to the increased pace of the offensive, its casualties, and the battle fatigue of pilots and air crews. The *Yorktown*'s exhausted Air Group Five was finally rotated home after nine months aboard. Its replacement Air Group One would serve less than three months, so grueling would be the Marianas campaign.

Clark moved his task group from Eniwetok to Kwajalein, from which it headed out to sea on 6 June to rendezvous with the other three groups out of Majuro. As the *Hornet* weighed anchor, over on the *Yorktown* Radar Fire Controlman Joe Chambliss celebrated the occasion in his diary: "Our new air group aboard is rarin' to go and so is the ship after learning that 'Jocko' Clark is going to be the Task Group Commander."

# SIXTEEN

## The Great Carrier Battle, 1944

JOCKO CLARK'S TWO FAVORITE CARRIERS *YORKTOWN* AND *HORNET*, along with light carriers *Bataan* and *Belleau Wood*, formed the heart of TG 58.1 as it departed Majuro midday of 6 June 1944. The task group assumed the lead as the other three groups joined up later in the day. Scheduled for initial predawn strikes against Saipan, Guam, and Tinian on the 12th, ships and planes exercised and refueled en route.

On the 7th, however, fleet intelligence indicated "the Jap fleet was getting restless—starting to move around a bit" in the far distant South China Sea. So recorded fighter director Alex Wilding on the *Yorktown*, happy to be working again—by radio—with his former teammate Charlie Ridgway over on the flagship *Hornet*. This was the first hint that a major fleet engagement might be in the offing.

Good weather boded well for the operation, but by the same token the enemy enjoyed it too; force radars picked up snoopers the night of the 8th. They did not sight the carriers, nor did others two nights later when an Eniwetok-based B-24 attacked a not-too-distant Betty. Radio listeners heard the Betty pilot radio his position before being shot down. Clark then dispatched fighters that succeeded in splashing two more snoopers only 47 miles out.

To better protect his task group, Clark requested Mitscher to let him send two destroyers ahead of the formation with their own fighter directors and a special CAP overhead to intercept snoopers. Mitscher agreed, and early on the 11th Clark dispatched two tin cans 50 miles ahead and a third one to 25 miles on "picket" duty. This was soon followed by the approach of several long-range snoopers.

During a brief lull, *Hornet*'s Air Plot informed the ready rooms on ticker tape that Admiral Clark had arisen early to time the launching of the

*Hornet*'s CAP with that of the *Yorktown*'s: "THE YORKTOWN TOOK OVER 6 MINUTES LONGER, AND THE ADMIRAL, APPEAR-ING ON THE BRIDGE IN LOVELY GREEN PAJAMAS, WAS HEARD TO REMARK, 'I'LL BE DAMNED IF I KNOW WHAT SHIP THAT IS, SURE CAN'T BE THE YORKTOWN.'" (Reynolds, *Fighting Lady*, 140–41)

Alex Wilding on the *Yorktown* vectored the CAP to intercept the bogeys. A Hellcat of *Bataan*'s VF-50 promptly shot down a twin-engine Helen medium bomber 30 miles out, and Jocko gave Wilding a "well done" over the TBS. But another one got away. Wilding and the picket destroyers shared fighter direction chores, and minutes after the noon hour some 50 miles out VF-1 splashed two four-engine Emily flying boats and a twin-engine Irving; VF-2 got another Emily. From one of them picket destroyer *Burns* retrieved two aviators, many charts, three bags of official mail, and a large amount of "window"—strips of aluminum dropped to create false radar blips. All were delivered to the *Hornet*.

Clark sent another "well done" to Wilding and signaled his old ship, "Your CAP has turned in the usual and expected top-notch performance. Congratulations." Charlie Ridgway on the *Hornet* vectored *Yorktown* Hell-cats to destroy a Betty only 30 miles away and *Hornet* F6Fs to bag yet another Emily, the last interloper of the day.

Meanwhile during the course of the morning Admiral Mitscher and his staff decided to speed up the operational timetable to catch the enemy off guard. Instead of the customary predawn fighter sweep on the morrow, they decided (with Admiral Spruance's approval) to launch it that very afternoon.

At 1300—192 miles east of Guam—211 fighters began taking off, along with ten SB2C bombers that carried life rafts, instead of bombs, for any pilots shot down. All of TG 58.1's carriers launched Hellcats—16 each from *Hornet* and *Yorktown*, 12 each from *Belleau Wood* and *Bataan*.

The ruse worked. The afternoon fighter sweep caught the Japanese completely by surprise. Clark's squadrons, led by *Hornet*'s VF-2 skipper Lieutenant Commander William A. Dean, attacked Guam and small Rota while the other groups hit Saipan, Tinian, and little Pagan. They strafed and dropped 500-pound bombs onto the airfields, destroying buildings, guns, and parked planes. Some 30 Zeros rose to intercept them and were all shot down, and the AA fire was particularly heavy.

By the time TF 58's attackers departed they had destroyed some 150 enemy planes (most on the ground) at the cost of 11 Hellcats; three pilots were rescued. "Damn well done," Clark informed his task group. "Upwards of 30 [airborne] enemy aircraft destroyed against one of ours shot down," probably by flak.

Occasional snoopers visited the force during the day and were splashed, 58.1 ending up with 41 kills in the air on 11 June. At 1830 the force intercepted a Japanese radio message reporting the carriers' position to Tokyo, and after midnight three bogey contacts brought the ships to G.Q., but none closed. One of Russ Reiserer's *Hornet* night fighters failed to find any of them.

Admiral Mitscher, now more confident about the Bat teams, had both big carriers launch their four night fighters at 0230 on the 12th, two as CAP, the rest to "heckle" Guam's and Rota's airfields. These strafed sporadically for over two hours, keeping the Japanese awake and off balance for the first incoming strike. Defensively, Alex Wilding directed the *Bataan*'s CAP to destroy two Judy divebombers near the force at dawn.

At the same time, Clark sent off deckload strikes to Guam armed with the customary 100-, 250-, 500-, and 1,000-pound bombs and fragmentation clusters and incendiaries, as well as, for the first time, wing rockets for the torpeckers. Pounding Guam, they drew heavy flak that claimed several planes; the most remarkable was a VB-1 divebomber, whose pilot (Richard James) coasted into the water just beyond the reef. He and his gunner (David Smith) then sailed their life raft eight miles for five hours to the lifeguard sub *Stingray*.

Clark had also launched a long afternoon search-strike to the southwest to hit a reported enemy convoy. It returned without finding the convoy, but two night fighters succeeded the next morning, the 13th, in spotting a half-dozen transports and escorting destroyers 270 miles west of Guam. In the morning Clark dispatched a radar-guided search-strike of 21 bomb-laden *Yorktown* and *Hornet* Hellcats on a grueling five-hour, 350-mile round-trip that scored only one bomb hit on a vessel. The failure was laid to fighter-pilot inexperience in bombing. So they dropped their loads on Guam, while other *Hornet* planes scattered leaflets to the island's Chamorro natives, promising their pending liberation.

Amid all the activity Clark received a message from his old Annapolis pal Sol Phillips on the *Oakland:* "Tokyo Rose has announced on the radio that all our ships are sunk."

Replied Jocko, "Do not believe Tokyo Rose. When the rising sun goes down she will sing a different tune." This interchange initiated many to follow between the two friends—and riveted the attention of all hands, which was their real intent.

The morning of the 14th—D minus One Day for the Saipan landings—Clark's group and Harrill's TG 58.4 refueled and received replacement aircraft from escort carriers. At 0905 a *Bataan* "anti-snooper" F6 splashed a Betty 60 miles out. Lieutenant Beath and other Japanese language radio listeners had pieced together Japan's aircraft situation (thanks largely to the code book recovered off Hollandia). The Marianas were now stripped of planes, due not only to the carrier strikes but to MacArthur's push into western New Guinea. Many enemy planes had been diverted there only to be destroyed by the AAF.

More important, the next intelligence revealed large numbers of enemy planes being staged south from Japan to the Bonin and Volcano island groups, specifically Chichi Jima and Iwo Jima, collectively referred to as the "Jimas." There, enemy planes were refueled and rearmed to fly the 700 miles south and attack the Fifth Fleet off Saipan. Admiral Spruance therefore ordered Mitscher to detach half his force—two task groups—northward to destroy those planes on the 16th and 17th.

The Jimas were the closest islands to Japan—only 500 miles away— ever to be attacked by carrier aircraft. Afterward, the two task groups would rejoin the other two off Saipan before the Japanese fleet could sortie from its base at Tawi Tawi in the southern Philippines to defend the Marianas.

Mitscher decided to send the freshly replenished groups of Clark and Harrill. His choice of the aggressive Jocko was understandable, but Keen Harrill was still unproved. Oddly, however, Mitscher did not give overall command to the veteran Clark, or to Harrill, four years Clark's senior. Instead, the order was in the form of "a multiple-address dispatch" to both admirals as equals. In it he instructed them to remain "tactically concentrated." Jocko later learned that Mitscher did it "to give me freedom of action." Furthermore, Clark had four carriers, Harrill only three. One may surmise that Mitscher trusted his aggressive Indian to solve any command problem that might arise over carrying out his orders.

Clark, in any case, did not want to go north; he was afraid that while away he might miss the big battle with the Japanese fleet should it appear off Saipan. When both task groups rendezvoused north of the Marianas, Clark personally got on the task force TBS radio command circuit and argued his case to Mitscher's staff. Its chief, Captain Arleigh A. Burke, always did Mitscher's talking. Hoping to touch Jocko's vanity, he cleverly informed the flag radioman at the other end, "Would you please tell Admiral Clark that the staff over here thinks he is absolutely right, that it's a very dangerous and a difficult mission." That did it, and Jocko replied that indeed he was rarin' to go. (Conversation with Burke)

Then Harrill decided against making the long trip north. To his staff he "stated quite emphatically" that even though his ships had just taken on oil, they did not have adequate fuel for the long voyage. His ops officer, Brute Dale, checked with the staff logistics officer who replied that "we had ample fuel for the operation." Harrill insisted that as an "expert" he knew they were low and that he planned to so inform Admiral Mitscher. Chief of staff Captain H. E. "Blackie" Regan, Dale, and others tried to dissuade him. He nevertheless sent a message or two to Mitscher's staff and one to Clark. (Dale to author, 14 April 1966)

Jocko was stunned. Not believing that Harrill meant it, he got on the TBS and tried to convince him to change his mind. Remarkably, remembered Commander Lloyd M. Mustin (a nonaviator) on the cruiser *Miami* in Harrill's group, the entire discussion between the two admirals was "plainly audible to everybody in the two task groups." The weather made flying too risky, argued Harrill, to Clark's riposte that (as Mustin recalled it) "by God, they'd been sent up to strike this place . . . if it was feasible, and as far as he could tell it was."

> This was the beginning of an appreciation of Jocko Clark by me that . . . here was a great man. Somebody else invented dynamite, and somebody took a bundle of sticks of dynamite and tied them all up and put a blasting cap on the end and a fuze and lighted the fuze and handed it to Jocko and said, "Jocko, go throw this over here."
>
> Jocko didn't know and didn't care who invented the dynamite, or what made it go off, he was going to throw it! (Mustin transcript #20, 777–78)

But Harrill would not budge. So at 1240 Jocko had Tex McCrary of his staff fly him over to Harrill's flagship *Essex* in a torpecker. There he was surprised to hear more excuses from Harrill—bad weather was closing in on the Jimas, the Japanese fleet might come out to attack the invasion forces, and so on. Clark and Blackie Regan spent three hours trying to convince Harrill to change his mind; the Japanese air threat in the Jimas *had* to be stopped. (Conversation with Clark; Regan to author, 14 April 1966)

An astute war correspondent riding with Harrill, Morris Markey, could not mention him by name in relating the admiral's behavior, but his play on Harrill's name identified the admiral to anyone in the know: "He had an almost *harrowing* difficulty making that decision. It was plain to any eye that he had lived a life of conciliation, of reasoned compromise. He was almost incapable, temperamentally, of uttering a simple yes or no. In the end, other men really made the decision for him. . . . He did not belong at sea." (Markey, *Well Done*, 117–18)

Finally, an exasperated Clark said, "If you do not join me in this job I will do it all myself!" Only then did Harrill agree, without enthusiasm. "Formerly a top flight officer," recalled Clark, who flew back to the *Hornet* at 1600, "he now seemed to have lost his zip."

Indeed, several days later, while looking out on his task group, Harrill remarked pensively to ops officer Dale, "I must be getting old. I find I can't make decisions like I used to"—even small decisions, forcing Regan to prod him. But a mustang lieutenant of the staff, who as an enlisted man had served with Harrill, then an ensign, said that Harrill had *always* been indecisive. (Dale to author, 14 April 1966)

Harrill got worse. When Commander Dale worked out the schedule for strikes on the Jimas Harrill cut the number of planes in half, keeping the rest on CAP to defend the ships. Dale argued that the fighter sweep was the best defense, but it took him a long time to persuade his admiral.

After the carriers received replacement planes from the escort carrier *Copahee*, the two task groups continued northwest the night of 14–15 June for air strikes on the 15th and 16th. While en route, they received word from Mitscher that U.S. submarines had reported the Japanese fleet leaving its base at Tawi Tawi and heading for the Marianas to give battle. Spruance considered "canceling the Iwo strike when we knew the Japanese were coming out" because "it was a gamble whether the force involved would get back in time to take part in an action with the Japanese" fleet. (Spruance to author, 17 February, 3 December 1961) He therefore ordered Clark and Harrill to shorten their Jima strikes to one day, the 16th, and hasten back to rejoin Montgomery's and Reeves's groups by the 18th for the big battle.

Jocko was eager for that but believed the airdromes in the Jimas needed the original two days of strafing and bombing to eliminate the air threat there. So he rang up 25 knots and sped north to get in an afternoon strike on Iwo a day earlier—the 15th—and that in the face of stormy weather and high seas. Then he would have all day the 16th to finish the job. Harrill followed reluctantly and only managed to launch his CAP late on the 15th.

One hour before noon on the 15th antisub and "antisnoop" teams of F6Fs and torpeckers attacked and set fire to a 1,900-ton transport only 30 miles from the task formation—the *Tatsutakawa Maru*. Clark detached *Boyd* and *Charrette* from the screen to complete the sinking and pick up any of its 400 survivors who preferred survival to the "honorable" death espoused by Japanese tradition. Only 118 obliged, to which were added another 16 picked up later. They were delivered to the *Hornet*, where Marines guarded them and translator Beath quizzed them; he learned only that most of them were civilian laborers en route home from Truk.

They remained on board a couple of days, which "Jocko didn't like a damn bit because it interfered with the readiness of the ship," recalled Cecil King. After developing a fondness for American bread, they were transferred by high-line to the tanker that next refueled the *Hornet*. Two or three at a time were put in the transfer bag and sent over. Midway across during the third transfer one prisoner yelled "Banzai!" ("10,000 years!") and jumped into the water, where the four screws of the carrier or the two of the tanker acted as "meat grinders," leaving only pink foam in their wake.

Asked what to do, Clark said simply, "Let's keep them going. If they want to dive over, we got to get going." Only one more did, joining his ancestors according to the Shinto faith. (Cecil King transcript #2, 221–23, also in Wooldridge, *Carrier Warfare*, 279–80)

Clark thanked tin cans *Charrette* and *Boyd* for the rescue and transfer of these prisoners by sending the vessels the customary vanilla ice cream that a carrier gave to a tin can for returning a pilot. His accompanying message alluded to the coming encounter with the Japanese fleet: "For the destroyers it may be good training for taking care of some more [prisoners] that we expect to get from *Shokaku* [a Japanese carrier], *Fuso* [a battleship], et al. We promise they will not eat your ice cream."

Meanwhile, midafternoon of 15 June, Clark reached his point option (the launch position) 135 miles south of Iwo and sent off a 200-plane strike from all four of his carriers. Pilot visibility was restricted to 7 miles because of moderate to heavy seas with a 12- to 15-foot swell, an 18-knot surface wind, and a solid blanket of rainsqualls and heavy broken clouds between 2,000 and 30,000 feet. His planes split up to hit Iwo, Chichi, and tiny Haha Jima.

Wild dogfights over Iwo led to the overwhelming success of Hellcats against Zeros, but the fighter sweep took some losses against excellent pilots fresh from Japan. A composite strike of Hellcats, Helldivers, and Avengers to Chichi braved a small typhoon to pummel cargo shipping, troop barges, moored seaplanes, and airfields. Flak over both targets brought down several carrier planes, while at least two dozen Japanese planes were destroyed aloft and more on the ground.

The Chichi Jima typhoon spread southward as Clark's planes returned to base late on 15 June. Big carriers *Hornet* and *Yorktown* kept their flight decks steady for landing planes, but the fragile CVLs *Bataan* and *Belleau Wood* pitched badly. One plane jumped the barrier on the latter, causing a fire that spread to the hangar. Captain Jack Perry's crew put it out without any fatalities but lost several planes to the fire. Eight others that were still airborne had to land on the *Yorktown*.

Clark launched two night fighters to heckle Chichi Jima and frustrate any attempt by surviving planes to attack the task group. He need not have worried. But the typhoon led Admiral Harrill to renege on his promise to support Clark. He now informed Jocko that because of the stormy weather he was ending TG 58.4's part in the operation and heading south to rejoin Mitscher instead of attacking the Jimas next day.

Gun camera of a Fighting Squadron 50 Hellcat off the *Bataan* records the plane's strafing of a moored Japanese flying boat in the harbor at Chichi Jima, 15 June 1944. Over succeeding days the enemy mounted machine guns in caves on the adjacent mountainside; they proved deadly to Clark's flyers on the Fourth of July. *U.S. Navy photo*

Another heated exchange ensued, with Clark roaring that he was staying no matter what Harrill did. After a pause, Harrill let out a wail, hands to his temples, and bemoaned Clark's indictment. Again Clark tried to shame him into fulfilling his combat obligations, but Harrill refused to participate in the morrow's attacks.

Both groups moved southward for the night amid storms that never abated. Eight-foot swells brought green water over the pitching flight decks, making the next morning's planned launches impossible. Still determined, Clark had an idea. He spent all morning topping off the tin cans with fuel, which required masterful heavy-weather ship handling by all hands involved. Then as TG 58.1 ran north, at noon Jocko turned it eastward, out of the storm into the clear for a 1300 launch against Iwo Jima. Then the ships went back into the soup and out again twice more to operate planes. "This worked swell," recorded Joe Chambliss on the *Yorktown*, "for the Japs never expected an attack during such weather."

In a devastating fighter sweep and two deckload bombing strikes Clark's planes pounded the Jimas—Harrill did not participate—catching all the surviving Japanese planes grounded by the weather. They were demolished by strafing and bombing. Jocko's planes returned aboard by 1710; more refueling of destroyers began at 1720 on a westerly course, and 12 minutes after that Admiral Harrill suddenly turned southeastward with his task group, abandoning Clark altogether. (TG 58.1 Action Report)

Word had been received early in the morning that U.S. subs reported Japanese fleet units moving through San Bernardino Strait in the Philippines toward the Marianas to contest the invasion. That night, 16–17 June, Mitscher ordered the returning Clark and Harrill to search southwestward in hopes of sighting the enemy fleet, known to include at least three carriers. If they did not find them, their orders were to rejoin the rest of TF 58 by the 18th off Saipan for the expected naval battle.

While refueling destroyers at dawn of the 17th Clark launched a search-strike of ten VF and ten VB to 325 miles south, west, and northwest looking in vain for the Japanese fleet. At 1337 he sent a Hellcat search to that plane's extreme range of 350 miles, keeping them aloft a phenomenal seven and a half hours. During their absence Clark needed three and a half hours to top off the rest of his tin cans, which had to be fully "fed" in case the enemy fleet was sighted.

American submarine contacts revealed that the approaching Japanese fleet contained nine carriers plus supporting ships. As Clark steamed southward in its direction and to recover his search planes throughout the day, he remembered Admiral Billy Goat Reeves's lecture in 1925 about the 1916 Battle of Jutland. Britain's Admiral Beatty had charged forward with his

*Bataan's* planes, including the TBM torpedo-bomber at upper right, pummel parked enemy aircraft—fighters, bombers, transports—at Iwo Jima on 16 June 1944, as revealed by the K-20 gun camera. ("Conf" means the photo was "confidential.") *U.S. Navy photo*

swift battle cruisers trying (though unsuccessfully) to cut off the enemy fleet from its bases in Germany. Why couldn't, Jocko asked himself, he and Harrill—with a total of seven carriers—do the same thing to the approaching Japanese fleet?

By steaming southwest all night Clark figured that he and Harrill with their seven flattops would be west of—and behind—the Japanese fleet by dawn of 18 June, blocking any retreat to its bases. They could attack from the west. Mitscher with Montgomery's and Reeves's eight carriers could simultaneously attack the enemy fleet from the east. Jocko discussed it with his staff, and then got on the TBS with Admiral Ralph Davison, riding on the *Yorktown,* who liked the idea. Then he called Harrill, who not only rejected the scheme but was already steaming full bore to the southeast to rejoin Mitscher.

Clark could not break radio silence to discuss the idea with Mitscher lest Japanese radio direction finders use the transmission to pinpoint Clark's position. In that case all nine Japanese carriers might attack his four. He realized his own group might have been clobbered—"sunk myself"—if so exposed. But, "I would have had an attack group over them at dawn before they had gotten on me." (1964 conversation with Clark) His planes would at least have hurt the Japanese fleet. As one of his pilots observed on hearing of these deliberations, "What I want to know is, who's trapping whom?" (Jensen, *Carrier War*, 150)

Had Mitscher commanded the Fifth Fleet, Jocko might well have seized the opportunity, he admitted later, but in the circumstances Mitscher had to answer to Spruance. Indeed, Mitscher later told Clark he should have attacked from the west, and that Mitscher in fact had almost sent him such an order.

"Finally," Clark recalled, "I asked myself if I were not about to take the whole world on my shoulders." And he did not want to risk somehow "bitching the battle" as Beatty had done at Jutland. Clark's staff officers agreed with him. The inferior Japanese fleet—though 700 miles away—was still approaching the Marianas and would certainly be crushed in any case. So Clark sped south with TG 58.1 to rejoin Mitscher.

"*Speed, speed*—these ships were built for it and Jocco drives like Jehu," wrote Dr. Gard, still on the *Yorktown*, in his diary. "That is the reason the old––– made us fuel in a storm! On and on—rendezvous," as 58.1 rejoined the rest of TF 58 off Guam the morning of 18 June. "Lord, what a bunch of ships—where are the Nippos?" (from Nippon, meaning "Land of the Rising Sun," the Japanese name for Japan).

At 0532 on the 18th, still 60 miles from the rest of TF 58, Clark sent out yet another search-strike of ten VF and ten VB 350 miles to the west and southwest. Submarines were tracking the enemy fleet, and one even reported (correctly) that it had sunk a Japanese carrier. But the air search proved fruitless, as did a follow-up in the afternoon by Clark's and Montgomery's planes.

Mitscher prepared TF 58 to head west—with Admiral Ching Lee's fast battleships in front for a possible night engagement and follow-up daylight air strikes from all 15 fast carriers. Enemy snoopers, probably from the Jimas, kept making brief appearances on force radars, and one of Clark's CAP Hellcats splashed a Tony fighter 250 miles to the northwest. At midday Jocko ordered his pilots to prepare for a strike, only to rescind the order.

Admiral Spruance had changed his mind. Lee expressed no confidence in fighting a night action. Spruance had some evidence that the enemy fleet had split up to approach from two different directions, one for a possible

"end run" from the southwest. And he believed the carriers could best protect the landing forces—fighting ashore on Saipan since the 15th—by
remaining offshore on the defensive instead of heading west to sink the
Japanese battle fleet.

Mitscher, Clark, and most of the other carriermen were incredulous.
Spruance simply did not understand that no enemy force could run around
his carriers, whose aircraft had ranges out to 350 miles. (Reynolds, *Fast Carriers,* 180–90) What was more, Spruance formed a battle line from the bombardment ships just west of Guam made up of older battleships, escort
carriers, cruisers, and destroyers. Rear Admiral Gerry Bogan, commanding
a division of escort carriers, had no fears of any "end run" and kept his
planes flying ground support missions over Saipan without interruption.
(Conversation with Bogan in 1961)

The task force turned east after sundown, which it had to do anyway to
operate planes, because the wind was coming from that direction. "This was
definitely not closing the Japanese," recalled Clark, for radio direction
reports placed the enemy fleet 355 miles to westward. Half an hour before
midnight Admiral Mitscher made one final attempt to change Spruance's
mind and head west.

"To my great surprise," Clark recalled, Spruance replied in the negative
an hour later, just as a snooper circled Clark's task group, the tin cans firing
away at it. The *Yorktown* catapulted a night fighter, which could not catch
the interloper. In the *York*'s CIC diarist Alex Wilding's reaction to Spruance's decision was typical of others: "The Navy brass . . . turned yellow—
no fight—no guts. . . . Spruance branded every Navy man in TF 58 a
coward tonight. I hope historians fry him in oil." (Reynolds, *Fighting Lady,*
147–48)

Of course, Spruance had plenty of "guts"—demonstrated at Midway
and elsewhere. What he lacked was intimate knowledge of, and therefore
confidence in, the Fast Carrier Task Force, the expertise of its admirals, and
the overwhelming superiority in numbers and abilities of its 900 pilots and
their aircraft. His own weapon of choice ever since his Annapolis days (class
of '07) and three tours of duty at the Naval War College had been the battleship. (Reynolds, *Fast Carriers,* 165–69, 179–90; Buell, *Quiet Warrior*)

Admiral Clark was as stunned as Mitscher and the other aviators that
Spruance actually believed that by heading westward to engage the Japanese
fleet TF 58 would be leaving the landing forces at Saipan vulnerable to an
"end run" by part of the enemy force. (The troop transports were safe anyway, wisely withdrawn 200 miles to the east of Saipan out of harm's way.)

The troops fighting ashore, Jocko knew instinctively, "could have been
protected just as well from 250 miles further west"—the general fighting

range of TF 58's carrier planes—and "with our radar, our search planes, and our submarines keeping us informed of the movements of the enemy fleet. In my judgment we should have steamed west at every opportunity."

To make matters worse, the admirals were relatively certain—in fact, correct—that the Japanese carriers would launch their planes from 400 to 600 miles to the west of Saipan, well beyond the 350-mile radius of Mitscher's longest-legged planes (the Hellcats) as long as TF 58 remained near the islands. The enemy's planes would attack the fast carriers there, land on Guam, refuel, and take off to return to their own carriers—still beyond U.S. carrier plane round-trip range.

At first light on 19 June Clark stepped out on the flag bridge and was chagrined to see Guam on the horizon. Just as destroyers in the screen splashed a snooper from the south, Mitscher had Clark launch a 325-mile search to the southwest from the *Hornet*, but it found nothing. At 0528—as the sun rose—*Belleau Wood* launched a dozen Hellcats and TBFs as task group CAP and antisub patrol. The *Yorktown* sent four VF and four VB southeast toward Guam to intercept any bandits shuttling in from the enemy fleet far to the west.

At 0619 Spruance ordered TF 58 to head due west—except when the carriers had to steam eastward to operate aircraft. As it turned out, this would continue to take place virtually all day long.

Alex Wilding in *Yorktown*'s CIC at 0628 detected a bogey on his radar 100 miles due south and got a confirmation from Charlie Ridgway on *Hornet*. Charlie had Alex direct a division of four *Belleau Wood* CAP fighters to intercept it. Alex rechecked his instruments only to discover the bogey "was growing rapidly in size."

Pete Mitscher himself then called Wilding from the *Lexington*, "Send help to Guam!" Alex immediately vectored the other two *Belleau Wood* CAP divisions to the scene. The Japanese had sneaked in some two dozen Zeros, possibly from Truk to the southeast, during the night. Wilding recalled the outnumbered Hellcats, who nevertheless shot down ten Zekes on their way back.

The so-called Marianas Turkey Shoot had begun—the first phase of the epic Battle of the Philippine Sea.

Ridgway informed Clark, who concurred without question, that he was sending 24 more Hellcats to Guam—eight each from *Hornet*, *Yorktown*, and *Belleau Wood*. Clark was not able to tell Mitscher before Ridgway signaled the latter, "Many planes at Guam, require help."

Mitscher to all task groups: "Send fighter assistance to Guam immediately."

Clark to Mitscher: "Help is on the way."

Guam lay 94 miles southeast (138 degrees True) of TG 58.1. Mont-gomery's 58.2 and Reeves's 58.3 were south-southeast of Clark's group 22 miles (167 degrees) and 11 miles (160 degrees) respectively, with Harrill's 58.4 20 miles to the west (290 degrees) and Lee's battleships 25 miles to the southeast (244 degrees). The entire force tried to continue westward toward the Japanese fleet but had to keep steaming to the east to launch and recover aircraft. The fighting over Guam did not last long, as Hellcats overpowered the clearly outclassed Japanese pilots.

About 0900, staff communicator Sowerwine-Zero intercepted a cor-rected contact report of a PBM flying boat sighting of the enemy fleet. Its original transmission more than seven hours earlier had been delayed, plac-ing the Japanese carriers 360 miles to the west.

Minutes later, newly arrived *Bataan* fighters shot down a Rufe float-plane fighter, and the screen's guns splashed another bogey. Many radar blips alerted the task group to more bogeys to the north. *Yorktown* planes returning from Guam encountered them and got two more Jakes, a Kate torpecker, a Zeke, even a big Emily flying boat, all probably island-based.

Suddenly, at 0942, Ridgway and Wilding detected the first of many groups of enemy carrier planes approaching 130 miles from the west. At 1000 Clark ordered all available *Yorktown* fighters scrambled, amazing Ridgway that Jocko had not bothered first to consult Mitscher. But this revealed precisely how much Mitscher trusted Clark. He also shifted *York-town* planes from Guam and *Bataan*'s CAP to intercept this "Raid One."

Admiral Mitscher now ordered all divebombers and torpeckers armed with bombs and rockets to take off and crater the airfields at Guam and Tinian and thereby hinder the approaching enemy planes trying to land and refuel there. With the bombers away, the carriers could concentrate on oper-ating the fighters during the almost continuous dogfights to the west. Fly-ing at 25,000 feet the Hellcats easily spotted the bandits down at 18,000 due to the unprecedented contrails behind each one (contrails usually formed above 25,000 feet). Hellcats from all 15 fast carriers converged on the incoming bogeys. The few Japanese airplanes that did get through then had to endure a veritable wall of flak from the gun ships.

At 1100 VF-1's Lieutenant Commander B. M. "Smoke" Strean in-formed Wilding on *Yorktown* that the "first round" was over: no more enemy planes, and none had gotten closer than 55 miles to the force. Alex then directed the last 58.1 fighters aloft to fly CAP over the flagship. Ten minutes later, his radarscopes registered a fresh wave of bogeys—including Jill torpeckers—120 miles out. While Wilding handled fighter direction of *Yorktown* and *Bataan* Hellcats, Charlie Ridgway did so for *Hornet* and *Bel-leau Wood*.

Many bandits got as far in as Reeve's TG 58.3 just south of Clark's, while others chose to attack Lee's battleships—heavy AA destroyed them all. Clark's CAP remained a perfect "umbrella" for 58.1.

Whereupon Jocko—referring to an earlier Japanese radio announcement that the Marianas had suffered no damage—fired off another all-hands signal to Sol Phillips in *Oakland:* "What if Tokyo Rose could see us now?"

Phillips: "I believe you have made a liar out of Tokyo Rose."

Clark: "We haven't finished yet."

The slaughter of Japanese planes—with their clearly inferior pilots—continued into the afternoon. Ridgway and Wilding deftly traded off 58.1's fighter direction for *Hornet*'s Fighting Two and *Yorktown*'s Fighting One. The task group kept steaming eastward—100 degrees—all day, almost to Rota Island and away from the enemy fleet. Still, at 1330 Jocko sent nine *Yorktown* planes west-northwest out to 315 miles on a fruitless search.

Then another large raid tried to reach Guam, only to be annihilated by fighters from *Hornet* and Harrill's group. This included Russell Reiserer's night fighters. When they returned aboard, their leader modestly reported to Clark on the flag bridge that he had personally shot down five planes over Guam—making Reiserer an ace. Jocko made sure he eventually received the Navy Cross for this. But Clark ordered the Bat teams to stand down, lest they be needed for night chores.

By 1600 the skies and radars were clear of bogeys. Charlie Ridgway entered the "box score" for the day on his fighter director's chart: Clark's task group shot down 109 planes (29 of them over Guam, trying to land), plus 15 probables, out of 402 kills for the entire task force. The Ridgway-Wilding team had directed 80 shoot-downs. The eventual official count was virtually identical to these remarkable figures. Some 40 U.S. pilots had been shot down, but several were rescued.

Admiral Spruance finally realized that Japan's carrier planes had been virtually annihilated, that no "end run" would occur, and that TF 58 must now head west in search of the retiring enemy fleet. The carrier admirals had been anticipating this and preparing for it during the course of the day. All, that is, except Keen Harrill.

Clark had wisely topped off his destroyers with fuel at midday, but Harrill in 58.4 had not and asked Admiral Mitscher to leave his task group behind. Mitscher agreed, fed up with Harrill's lackluster performance.

When Jocko heard that, he signaled Mitscher, "Would greatly appreciate remaining with you. We have plenty of fuel."

"You will remain with us all right," came the immediate reply, "until the battle is over."

TG 58.4 with its three carriers broke away from the force at 1300 and continued to bomb Guam. Harrill suffered from an attack of appendicitis a week later, but that was not the reason Mitscher soon relieved him of command. He had simply failed as a combat leader.

At 2000 Clark's task group took its customary lead of the force at 23 knots—alongside Lee's battleships for a highly unlikely gunnery duel—as TF 58 turned west (260 degrees) in pursuit of the Japanese fleet. The lineup was 12 U.S. carriers with virtually full air groups versus seven Japanese with only a few planes after U.S. submarines had sunk two carriers during the day. Because of possible enemy subs, Mitscher's carriers sacrificed valuable time by zigzagging at 18 knots.

Jocko and his staff issued their attack plan: *Hornet's* air group would lead any strike on the Japanese fleet, fighter interceptors up front, followed by *Yorktown's*, with *Bataan* and *Belleau Wood* to provide CAP. During the night, as the ships passed over the waters of the "Turkey Shoot," one of Clark's destroyers sighted and rescued three aviators in a raft.

The two large carriers launched eight-fighter predawn 325-mile searches to the northwest at 0529 on 20 June. Both ships then respotted a composite deckload strike for launch as soon as the Japanese fleet was sighted and planned for a second one. About 0900 the searching VF-2 Hellcats shot down a Jake float plane and a Kate torpecker, obviously searching for evidence of TF 58's progress westward. Minutes before noon, Admiral Mitscher changed fleet course to the northwest (330 degrees), shrewdly reasoning that the enemy was heading for Japan. At 1325 he launched another 325-mile search.

Mitscher informed the task force at 1439 of ships being sighted, then at 1512: "Indications are that our birdmen sighted something big. Speed 23 knots."

Suddenly, at 1545, task force radios picked up a transmission from a searching *Enterprise* torpecker: Japanese fleet sighted 275 miles to the west-northwest. Mitscher confirmed it at 1551. Jocko Clark did not wait for orders; the next minute he selected the *Yorktown* deckload to participate in the first strike.

One minute after that Mitscher threw caution to the winds and ordered the launch—"a sample of Mitscher's indomitable leadership," in Clark's opinion. This was in spite of the fact that the strike would have only pre-sunset daylight to execute its attack, followed by a long trip back in the dark and a night landing, for which most pilots had had little practice, if any.

Likely as an expression of Old Pete's confidence in Jocko and the way he had molded the *Yorktown* into the premier carrier, Mitscher designated its VF-1 skipper Smoke Stream to lead the 216 planes from the three task groups. VF-2's leader Bill Dean told Clark it was late in the day and that his men were too tired to make such a long flight, much less land in the dark, to which his admiral replied, "We have to make the best of it. Carry out your orders!" (In the end, Fighting Two did not lose a single man.) Clark's two light carrier air groups also contributed to the strike along with most of the other carriers present.

But as the *Hornet* pilots started their engines at 1610 they were surprised to see an airedale holding up a chalkboard giving a corrected position report of the enemy fleet—one degree of longitude or 60 miles further west. Other air groups got the word over the radio once airborne. It meant that the sun would be near the horizon when the planes reached the target, requiring hasty uncoordinated attacks and much luck for the divebombers. And, their fuel capacity would be at its limit, meaning a possible water landing at night.

For those who made it back aboard, the total length of the flight would be some 700 miles. Mitscher cancelled the second strike and soon ordered all ships to test their searchlights and the cruisers to be ready to fire star shells to assist the returning pilots. (Conversation with Arleigh Burke in 1977)

As the planes began rolling down the decks, Jocko signaled Sol Phillips, whose code name in the cruiser *Oakland* was "Ramshackle": "Ramshackle, tell Tokyo Rose to stand by for a ram."

"Good luck," came the reply. "Ram where it will do the most good!" (obviously meaning up her "stern").

Suddenly, at 1647, task group radars detected a bogey only 30 miles due north and closing. Alex Wilding vectored the CAP to the intercept, and tin cans in the screen opened fire on the twin-engine Nell medium bomber, but it got away.

Except for four *Yorktown* planes that soon returned with engine trouble, the strike force of 212 planes pressed on for two hours. Finally, at 1840, with the sun touching the horizon, fighters from other squadrons took on the 75 or so Zeros that rose from the enemy carriers to meet them, shooting down most of them. Intense flak of all gun calibers licked up at the diving and glide-bombing SB2Cs, SBDs, and TBF/TBM Avengers. The F6Fs dropped light bombs, and only *Belleau Wood*'s VT-24 carried torpedoes (bombs having become generally preferred).

*Yorktown*'s Air Group One commander, James M. Peters, was unable to coordinate the attacks, as the planes raced the fast-fading tropical dusk to hit their violently maneuvering targets. Orbiting overhead, however, Peters was soon able, at 1850, to radio the *Hornet:* "Five or six carriers sighted— two on fire and smoking."

Japanese ships maneuver wildly to avoid the late afternoon strike by Task Force 58 planes in the Battle of the Philippine Sea, 20 June 1944. Only one of the seven carriers was sunk—by a torpedo from Warren Omark's TBM of the *Belleau Wood* in Clark's task group. *U.S. Navy photo*

The biggest carrier, *Zuikaku*, fell victim to direct hits from several of 13 SB2Cs of *Yorktown*'s VB-1, led by its skipper, Commander Joseph W. Runyon. Several *Hornet* VT-2 torpeckers added bombs to the same flattop, which the Japanese ordered abandoned. In fact, however, the flames burned themselves out, and this last surviving carrier of the Pearl Harbor attack limped back to Japan. Bombs from other squadrons scored hits and near misses on other carriers but not sufficiently to sink any of them.

The only "fish"-laden torpeckers in the flight, however, did sink a carrier. Four from *Belleau Wood*, which had flown antisub patrols in the morning, joined up for the flight with *Yorktown*'s planes. Over the target they made runs on the medium carrier *Hiyo*. Flight leader Lieutenant (jg) George P. "Brownie" Brown dropped his torpedo (which missed), took flak that forced his two crewmen to bail out, and then flew down the length of the enemy carrier.

While its AA gunners concentrated on Brown, Lieutenant (jg) Warren R. Omark planted his torpedo into the *Hiyo*, which exploded in flames. After his gunner managed to fend off two Zeros on their tail, Omark flew alongside the badly wounded "Brownie" (his arm visibly covered with blood) but lost sight of him in the fading light. Sadly, he disappeared into the dark sea on the return flight. Two hours later, his two crewmen in the water watched the *Hiyo* sink beneath the waves. (Reynolds, *Fighting Lady*, 158–62; Reynolds, *Fast Carriers*, 197–200; Omark remarks during a 1984 symposium at Pensacola)

Many other hits and sinkings were claimed in the failing light, but nothing could be certain until after the end of the war: only one carrier sunk, the *Hiyo*, and that by Jocko Clark's task group; two oilers scuttled; 65 enemy planes shot down.

*Hornet*'s air group commander, Jack Arnold, tried to get his own pilots together for the return flight in the darkness, contact the ship, then have all his planes land in the same vicinity, lash together their life rafts, and be picked up as a group. But this was impossible. As the planes started back, effecting such a rendezvous would waste time, energy, and fuel; navigating was difficult; plane damage and pilot fatigue took a toll; and distant heat lightning, which resembled ships' lights, drew some flyers off course.

At about 1900 Jocko Clark heard Commander Jim Peters report his attack was over and that two enemy carriers were burning. Mitscher's three carrier task groups were still separated by some 15 miles, heading northwest (315 degrees True) toward the returning planes.

Clark, planning ahead, at 1945 signaled Mitscher for permission to launch his eight night fighters at 0300 next morning, long after the attack force returned, in order "to heckle and turn" away any counterattacking enemy planes. Mitscher agreed after checking with Black Jack Reeves, whose group would then launch a night search and attack against the enemy fleet. (CTF 58 Message File, 20 June 1944) Such preparations proved premature and ultimately impossible, however.

With TG 58.1 guiding on flagship *Hornet*, Charlie Ridgway stayed glued to his radars when the first returning planes registered at 1957, heading in from 307 degrees. Clark immediately ordered the entire task group to turn east into the wind—from 300 to 100 degrees True. Flagship *Hornet*, light carriers *Bataan* and *Belleau Wood*, and several escort ships began the turn within the minute, with the rest taking longer. (Times are taken from their action reports and deck logs.)

During the afternoon, as soon as everyone had realized the planes would be returning late, Clark and the staff had begun discussing which lights would be turned on to aid the pilots in landing back aboard. It was never a question of *whether* to turn them on. Each ship was equipped with two dim truck lights at the masthead, and the carriers also had a dim glow light and tiny runway lights. These were only visible right on the horizon from just aft of the carrier and were utilized as part of night-landing procedures.

The discussion centered on what *other* lights should be employed. "You don't just say 'Turn on the lights' just like *that*," recalled Red Sharp, snapping his fingers. "That would have done more harm than good, because too many lights would create confusion," as had occurred when Clark was with the fleet in the early 1930s. What had worked best back then was when each carrier had beamed one searchlight straight up as a singular beacon. Jocko ended the discussion by making the decision to do just that.

At 2001 flight leader Smoke Strean reached the task force and called Wilding to say he had sufficient fuel (the fighters carried extra drop tanks) to orbit overhead. But, he added, "Expedite recovery, as many aircraft are very low on fuel. Some have landed in the water along the track from the target." (TG 58.1 Action Report; Wilding diary)

Jocko Clark was startled by this news, and one minute later, 2002, he ordered several destroyers to make smoke as signposts and at 0212 reversed course back to northwest to save the fuel-hungry bombers a few more miles. All hands topside now (2015) witnessed the returning planes racing in to land quickly. (TG 58.1 Action Report) Wilding told them, "Land on any base. All are recovering."

After Al Jennings turned the *Yorktown* back into the wind at 2020 to take aboard any comers, Clark ordered the entire task group to do the same thing at 2025. (*Yorktown, Belleau Wood, Oakland* deck logs) Three minutes later Admiral Montgomery turned TG 58.2 as well. A stampede ensued, with pilots ignoring wave-offs, crowding out rival planes, piling into barriers, and fouling most decks for many precious minutes.

On the *Yorktown* Pappy Harshman had started rigging cargo lights under Pri Fly to illuminate the flight deck. A desperate Captain Jennings came to him for ideas, whereupon Pappy explained his solution—the cargo lights. So Jennings immediately ordered these lights trained on the deck to assist the incoming pilots, and Cooper Bright broadcast, "*Yorktown* is lit up." Jennings had no choice, he later explained, because an "exchange of messages [with Clark and others] would have taken precious time."

Then, at 2030, Clark acted to aid the planes in their homing. He ordered the *Hornet* to turn on its 24-inch carbon arc searchlight and point it straight up into the sky as a beacon—and he immediately informed Mitscher. One minute later, he ordered heavy cruisers *Canberra* and *Boston* to fire star shells for additional help. They responded at 2035—followed by the *Oakland*—firing from their main batteries at a 65-degree angle. (TG 58.1 Action Report) This was a mixed blessing, as it turned out, because of the potential danger it posed to returning planes. (Rear Admiral J. D. Ramage, then commander of VB-10 on the *Enterprise,* to author, 20 November 1986)

A Hellcat touched down on the *Yorktown* at 2034 and helped convince Captain Jennings to take extra time to rig its second 24-inch searchlight, which lit up at 2048. The lights from both looked like "two great white pillars sticking into the night . . . quite spectacular." (*Yorktown* Action Report; George Wille diary)

At 2040 Jocko's light carriers *Bataan* and *Belleau Wood* lighted up, whereupon two *Yorktown* fighters touched down on the former, the *only* two planes to land on it the whole time. Also at 2040 Admiral Mitscher ordered each task group commander to have one destroyer in the van turn on a vertical searchlight—another dubious measure inasmuch as fatigued pilots mistakenly lined up to land on what turned out to be a tin can.

Planes were crash landing on carriers—most flattops were still showing only running lights—fouling their decks. So at 2044 Mitscher ordered the course changed to the east for all of TF 58—meaning Reeves's 58.3, the one in which Mitscher was riding on the *Lexington* and the only task group still needing to do so. (*Lexington* deck log)

One minute after that Mitscher instructed each task group to turn on one searchlight and for planes to land on any base, measures that Clark and Montgomery had already taken. (Mitscher TF 58 Action Report) And at 2046 Jocko had his screening destroyers display their lights. (TG 58.1 Action Report)

This detailed sequence of events reveals that between 2003 and 2044 Clark—and his individual ship captains, plus heavy cruiser leader Admiral Leo Thebaud—initiated the lighting up of Task Force 58. The fact that his task group was closest to the returning planes enabled him to do these things first. But the initiatives were largely his own—typical of his performance throughout the entire war. He informed Mitscher of most of them, many of which obviously influenced Mitscher to follow Clark's example.

The fact that one of Clark's task group torpecker pilots, Omark, sank the only carrier in the air attack on the enemy fleet was a bonus for his group's superb performance.

The wild night of 20 June entailed many deck crashes, sometimes followed by darkening the ship to clear the wreckage; ditched planes out of fuel, their pilots and aircrewmen in the water between ships displaying flashlights; and lost planes. The *Hornet* even dropped orange crates or anything else that would float for ditched flyers to cling to. (Cecil King in Wooldridge, *Carrier Warfare,* 284)

Captain Bill Sample, *Hornet*'s new skipper, had to maneuver the flagship away from destroyers—and an occasional cruiser—darting about to pick up flyers from the waters. This forced him to lose the wind for landing planes, and Clark shouted up to Sample from the flag bridge, "Can't you keep this ship heading into the wind?"

"No, Admiral, I can't." (Captain E. E. Fickling to author, 25 February 1977)

And that was that, as everyone tried to work miracles saving the flyers.

Even a lost Japanese plane was seen by several pilots and hundreds of topside hands and even tracked on radar by Alex Wilding on the *Yorktown*. Sol Phillips saw it from the *Oakland* and so informed Jocko.

"How do you know it's Japanese?" Clark responded.

"I can tell by the red balls on its wings!"

The last plane back to the flagship was the TBF of Air Group Two skipper Jack Arnold, who had circled overhead until all others had landed. But he came in too fast and went through the wire barrier, setting his plane on fire. He and his crew escaped, and the airedales routinely pushed the wreckage overboard—without knowing that invaluable combat photographs went with it. Because he "had been so unselfish and had been airborne so long," recalled Clark, "I could not find it in my heart to censure him."

Then there was 58.1's hero of the battle. During the return flight an utterly lost Warren Omark, who had sunk the *Hiyo*, called the *Belleau Wood*: "Just wanted to let you know, I'm back. I made it!" His VT-24 squadron commander happened to be in ship's Air Plot and used its radar to direct a night fighter from a big carrier to Omark's location and lead him in—to the *Lexington*, as it turned out.

At 2330, half an hour after the last plane landed, Admiral Mitscher turned the task force west again in pursuit of the fleeing Japanese fleet. He had each task group detach one destroyer to search the area for more airmen—which continued the following day as TF 58 passed over the track of the previous day's sunset attack. Many more flyers were retrieved, not only by the tin cans and cruiser floatplanes but also by Saipan-based seaplanes and four lifeguard submarines. Final total losses were 55 men and exactly 100 planes.

The carriers launched the postponed second deckload strike at dawn 21 June. And at 1050 Spruance sent Ching Lee's battle line in pursuit with the *Bunker Hill* and *Wasp* from TG 58.2, moving over its CVLs *Cabot* and *Monterey* to Clark's 58.1, giving him six carriers. But a long-legged search plane soon spotted the battered enemy fleet 360 miles to the northwest—too far away for another extraordinarily long strike given the ships' limited fuel supply, and too close to Japanese airfields in Formosa/Taiwan and the Philippines. Instead, wayward pilots flew back to their own carriers, and at-sea burials were conducted as TF 58 withdrew.

Jocko Clark's reflections on the battle never changed. Much as he admired Admiral Spruance, he put the blame squarely on the Fifth Fleet commander for the missed opportunity to sink all nine enemy carriers instead of one by his own task group and two by submarines. "Spruance had what I call an overcautious attitude, because I don't think he understood the technique of operating carrier aircraft," Clark said in later years. He agreed with analysts who said that Spruance's primary duty was to protect the landing force but added that "the best way to do that was to sink the Jap fleet." (Conversation with Clark in 1964)

During the operation, Jocko had written on his track charts, "Go west, young man, go west"—the famous words of Horace Greeley, nineteenth-century newspaperman and proponent of westward expansion, but Clark meant them for Spruance on 18–19 June 1944.

One thing that rankled Clark after the publication of his autobiography in 1967 was that

> some enterprising young naval air historians have tried to rule me out on "turn on the lights" at the Battle of the Philippine Sea.
>
> The facts are that I turned on the lights on my own initiative and told Mitscher, whereupon he signified his approval by turning on all the lights in Task Force 58.

Although Clark added that he didn't "want any undue credit," he asked Tex McCrary for assistance "in setting the record straight." (Letter, 30 March 1970) McCrary, then chairman of the board of a bank in Calvert, Texas, merely consulted the TG 58.1 Action Report to prove Clark's case. (McCrary to Clark, 13 April 1970)

Years later, after Jocko Clark was gone, Tex checked with his friend Joe Bryan, principal author of the 1945 book about the attack and recovery, *Mission Beyond Darkness*. Bryan replied that he had been in the *Lexington's* Flag Plot that night, where he saw

> Mitscher take off his cap and rub his forehead, and say in his almost inaudible voice, "Turn on the lights!" It never occurred to me that he was only following Jocko's lead. I assumed that . . . Mitscher gave the order, and others followed. I must have been wrong. (Letter to McCrary, 15 October 1981)

Joe Bryan told McCrary he had done his research in less than one week after that night and during his immediate return to the States on board the *Enterprise,* talking to its Air Group Ten flyers.

Jocko Clark was no braggart. He was simply satisfied that the documentary evidence "should establish for all time that I turned the lights on on my own initiative." (Letter to McCrary, 28 May 1970) He died a year later, having been equally pleased, I might add, with my account of his role on that long night. (*Fast Carriers,* 201–2)

Several days after the battle, eminent historian Samuel Eliot Morison, on Naval Reserve duty chronicling the naval war, came aboard *Hornet* for a visit. Clark told him, "A chance of a century was missed"—the twentieth century. Had TF 58 sunk the entire Japanese fleet, which it was overwhelmingly capable of doing, the Pacific war might have been considerably shortened, mused Clark. But neither good naval officers nor wise historians dwell on fruitless speculation. The war simply went on, relentlessly.

# SEVENTEEN

# Outstanding Fighter,
# Unexcelled Task Group, 1944–1945

Rear Admiral Clark has conducted the combat operations of the task group under his command with great distinction. His spirit is highly aggressive, and this combined with his ingenuity and alertness to seize upon and exploit every opportunity to damage the enemy, mark him as an outstanding officer. The record of his task group is unexcelled.

This high praise of Clark and Task Group 58.1 completed Jocko's next fitness report by Vice Admiral Mitscher. It also gave him straight 4.0 ratings and A+ marks in all categories of leadership. It was *not* written in late June 1944 or at the completion of a particular campaign or battle like the Philippine Sea. Mitscher wrote it covering almost an entire year: from 1 April 1944 (on the eve of the Hollandia operation) through 28 February 1945 (after the conquest of Iwo Jima and the first fast carrier attacks on Tokyo itself).

The appraisal demonstrates that the Marianas campaign and naval battle were but mere highlights of Jocko Clark's hard-hitting and superior leadership—so consistent and reliable that no need existed for periodic fitness reports. Such leaders within armies and navies are rare in history, and looking for historical comparisons is inexact and risky. Nevertheless, Douglas Southall Freeman's Civil War trilogy of the early 1940s, *Lee's Lieutenants*, is instructive. It revealed General "Stonewall" Jackson to have been Robert E. Lee's ablest "lieutenant," and for much the same reasons that Marc A. Mitscher had his own first lieutenant in Jocko Clark.

The feeling was mutual. To his dying day Clark regarded his association with Mitscher as symbiotic: "I consider myself Mitscher's Number One right-hand man. I never made a recommendation that Mitscher did not approve. Never did I make one that was not carefully thought through."

(Conversation with Clark in 1964) The two men thought alike and commanded alike, in spite of exactly opposite personalities—Mitscher the quiet one, Clark the tiger.

Let it be said also that good subtle humor passed between them on occasion—as when Mitscher allowed his staff to assign the new code name "Romeo" to Clark for the Marianas campaign—likely an allusion to Jocko's amorous ways as he hunted for a new mate when ashore. As Clark recalled:

> The senior-junior relationship that existed between us made it easy for me to succeed. In all our fighting [the enemy] together this mutual regard and respect prevailed. He continuously let me know that he held me in high esteem. This mutual confidence, I am glad to say, made for success in battle.

A typical example of their rapport occurred on 23 June 1944, the very morning of Task Force 58's refueling after the big battle just before returning to Eniwetok. Mitscher instructed Clark first to strike Pagan in the northern Marianas. Jocko was more concerned about the airdromes in the Jimas, which he now considered "my special property." Lieutenant Beath's intercepted enemy messages had revealed that more than 100 planes had been flown into Iwo and Chichi, with more waiting in Japan for the weather to improve. So at 1400, while heading north toward Pagan, Clark radioed Mitscher, "Unless otherwise directed I will strike Iwo Jima on the morning of 24 June while en route to Eniwetok."

Mitscher and his staff enjoyed this understated initiative while "en route" indeed! They replied briskly: "Plan Jocko approved." Clark's delight with this appellation was reciprocal.

Lack of sufficient aircraft due to the wild night recovery of 20 June plagued all four of his carriers. After the *Belleau Wood* launched its strike to Pagan, skipper Jack Perry signaled Jocko, "Launched nine fighters," leaving the ship only "one torpedo plane, four tractors, two jeeps."

An amused Jocko replied, "Keep tractors and jeeps in Condition 11 [ready for launch]. We may need them!"

Even funnier, a story was circulated regarding the fighting on Saipan: "A Japanese plane landed on the Saipan airfield recently and taxied up to the line for reservicing. The pilot was quite surprised and embarrassed to be taken prisoner!" (Printed in *Yorktown*'s Plan of the Day, 23 June 1944)

But tiny Pagan was no joke as heavy flak damaged or destroyed several attacking planes, killing pilots, while one Betty and five Zekes eluded *Bataan*'s CAP to approach the task group. Alex Wilding quickly took over fighter direction, enabling *Bataan*'s Hellcats to shoot down all six bandits.

During this busy day the task group passed through the very waters where on 12 June it had launched some of the initial strikes against the Marianas. On that day one of Tex McCrary's friends, Lieutenant Commander Robert H. Price, skipper of Air Group 25 on the *Cowpens*, had been shot down and lost. Now, this morning of the 23rd, after Tex woke up he told Bob Reynolds, "You'll think I'm nuts, but I had this dream."

"Tell me about it."

"I saw Bobby Price in this yellow raft, asking for somebody 'to come pick me up.'"

"You really had a premonition about it?"

"Yep. He's alright, in his rubber raft. Should I tell Jocko?" he asked, afraid Clark would think him nuts.

Reynolds, knowing how to handle the Old Man, said, "No, you told me. *I'll* tell Jocko."

So he went up to the flag bridge and explained the dream to the admiral, who responded, "Get that McCrary up here right now!"

When Tex appeared, Clark asked, "Can you find out what sector he was flying?"

Tex, Bob, Rosenblatt, and Sowerwine-Zero pored over the ship's charts and plotted his last known position 11 days before, figuring he would now be north to northwest of the force. With a slight course change, they figured the task group could pass the area en route to hit the Jimas.

McCrary then informed Jocko and insisted that a search for Price be launched. Clark, "following my rule to attempt the rescue of all downed flyers, regardless of how slim the chances," detoured the entire task group 100 miles off course and at noon launched four cruiser scout planes and four Hellcats to search in four sectors.

At 1350 destroyers in the screen sighted a life raft, only to find a dead Japanese pilot in it. Soon afterward the search planes returned, having seen nothing.

But just after 1600, the tin can *Boyd* spotted another raft and threw out a line. The emaciated occupant waved. It was Price! He had drifted for 11 days with only one pint of fresh water and trapped rainwater to drink. He rationed other emergency supplies and was blessed when two small fish jumped into his raft together. He ate them as well as birds that landed on his head "to shit on him!" Toward the end of his ordeal, however, he was too weak to eat a seagull that he had grabbed when it had come aboard. (Conversations with Reynolds, McCrary, and Clark)

Jocko greeted Price when he was transferred by breeches buoy from the *Boyd* to the *Hornet* and pinned a Purple Heart on him. (Photograph in

Jensen, *Carrier War,* 163) Reunited with McCrary, he was nursed back to health by the flagship's medicos, who discovered he had lost 28 pounds.

Eventually sent stateside for rest and recuperation, Price soon returned to the *Cowpens* as its acting air officer, out of harm's way as a pilot. Sadly, he would be washed overboard during a typhoon later and lost forever.

The very same day of Price's rescue the force retrieved a Japanese survivor from a cargo ship sunk by a U.S. sub on 6 June—17 days earlier. But he died of exhaustion within hours.

Plowing through heavy seas and rain squalls at 22 knots the task group was sighted before dawn of the 24th by an enemy snooper, which got away. "Operation Jocko" commenced at sunup 240 miles south of Iwo Jima. With *Belleau Wood* providing the CAP, *Hornet, Yorktown,* and *Bataan* sent 51 bomb-laden Hellcats on a 235-mile fighter sweep to Iwo and Chichi Jima. Rescue sub *Archerfish* reported some 50 torpeckers and as many Zeros at Iwo alone, of which at least 70 took off at 0700 to meet the Hellcats and to attack the task group.

Most of the F6s jettisoned their bombs as they came within sight of Iwo and waded into the swarm of very skillful enemy pilots. Clark's flyers splashed at least 24 Zekes and five Bettys in severe dogfights but at a cost of six of their own. The rest of the sweep returned aboard just before a 1004 enemy torpecker attack on the carriers. Alex Wilding vectored *Hornet's* and *Belleau Wood's* CAP to nail 15 Kates before they could execute their runs. (Reynolds, *Fighting Lady,* 169–70)

Jocko himself witnessed so daring a *Belleau Wood* fighter that he later signaled Captain Perry, "Believe it would be in order for you to recommend a Navy Cross for your fighter pilot who came through our AA fire to shoot down that Kate this morning. It was a magnificent piece of work."

"Concur and wilco," came the reply. "For your information he is a replacement pilot named Smith who crashed and had a fire on his second landing aboard. Has been doing a fine job since and we cannot keep him out of a plane."

Ridgway and Wilding directed their fighters in frustrating further attacks on the force as it retired eastward toward Eniwetok throughout the day. Jocko followed the action through Ridgway on the bridge. As one bogey bored in on the *Oakland,* Clark grabbed the TBS radiophone and called Sol Phillips, "Ramshackle, there's a plane coming at you. Have you got him?"

"I've got the son of a bitch," replied Phillips as his gunners brought it down.

Wilding tracked an illusive Jill torpecker for an hour and a half during the afternoon as it deftly evaded the *Hornet's* CAP. The pilot obviously knew how to elude radar by changing altitude and dancing among the clouds. But Alex discerned a pattern in his tactics, so when the VF-2 Hellcats needed to refuel he called Ridgway on the flagship for a fresh division of *Bataan* fighters to get the snooper.

"O.K.," replied Charlie, adding, "I'll give you a bottle of Scotch if you get him." It took only 21 minutes for Wilding to vector *Bataan*'s Hellcats to the kill. Lookouts saw the snooper plummet in flames 20 miles ahead. Admiral Davison personally congratulated Wilding, and Jocko sent him a "well done." But Wilding did not get his bottle of Scotch from Ridgway— until Christmastime in 1951, Chivas Regal at that! (Reynolds, *Fighting Lady*, 171)

Simultaneously, two large new radar blips meant fresh attacks from Jima-based bandits. Wilding sent two *Bataan* F6F divisions to make the intercept as *Yorktown* scrambled four from VF-1. Then *Hornet*'s CAP entered the fray some 80 miles out. The Kate and Judy torpeckers proved easy targets, but the Zekes put up an able defense. Clark's flyers shot down about 70 planes during the day—at a cost of several Hellcats, including the loss of *Bataan*'s fighter skipper, Lieutenant Commander R. S. Lemmon.

On the *Hornet*, Cecil King was impressed that sometimes when a wounded pilot landed back aboard,

> the doctor, the emergency crew, and Jocko would get to him all about the same time. Jocko would bend over the stokes litter [wire basket] and pin a medal on the guy right there on the stretcher. You know pilots appreciated that. He was really and truly a great man. (In Wooldridge, *Carrier Warfare*, 279)

Or, he would pin the medal on a man as he lay in the basket litter before being transferred to a hospital ship or ashore. (As seen in Jensen, *Carrier War*, 163)

Clark continued the task group's eastward course, frustrated that his planes had not been able to reach Iwo Jima's airfields. Low on replacement aircraft, fuel, and ammunition, he decided to continue on back to "the barn," Eniwetok, but determined to make a return visit to the Jimas.

On the 25th he passed command of the task group to Ralph Davison on the *Yorktown* for some final makee-learn experience before Davison got his own task group. Admiral Nimitz sent congratulations to Clark and 58.1, which Jocko shared with all hands. They had shot down 311 enemy planes and dropped 225 tons of bombs so far during the Marianas operation.

Admiral Thebaud of the heavy cruisers responded to Clark's statistics with amazement and congratulations, a Gun Club black shoe admitting only now how he fully appreciated the effectiveness of naval air power. But he showed his ignorance of it too by crediting the theories of Alexander de Seversky, advocate of land-based strategic bombing. "Your message very much appreciated," replied Jocko. "Believe that had Seversky been there he would have learned something about carriers that he needs to know."

Next day Thebaud's cruisers were detached from TG 58.1 to another task group. To Clark's parting message of thanks, Thebaud generously replied, "It has been a grand cruise, and you and your people have been an inspiration. May your star rise even higher."

Such cordiality pleased Jocko, especially because Thebaud ('13) was five years senior to him. So was Rear Admiral Larry DuBose, whose four light cruisers now returned to Clark's group. Out of tactical necessity, the carrier revolution was transforming the higher commands. Sol Phillips in the AA cruiser *Oakland* remained in charge of the screen with its 14 destroyers.

On 27 June TG 58.1 entered the Eniwetok roadstead, so crammed with warships and auxiliaries that Phillips signaled Clark, "This is more crowded than that jail in Boston," recalling one of their midshipman escapades. "Affirmative," responded Jocko, "much worse."

After anchoring, Clark made a beeline to the *Yorktown* in a motor launch to congratulate Alex Wilding for his fine performance as FDO. He also had an ulterior motive. Ralph Davison had tried to get Al Jennings to release Wilding to be his fighter director, but Jennings turned him down. Also, Jocko's staff had intercepted dispatches that Vice Admiral John S. McCain, earmarked to eventually relieve Mitscher, had requested Charlie Ridgway's transfer to his new staff. If Clark lost Ridgway, he wanted Wilding to replace him. But he could not tell Wilding these reasons.

Clark said nothing about it to Wilding until after a general task group meeting on the *Hornet* two days later. "I can't understand why Clark wants me on his staff," mused Alex in his diary, then turned him down, telling the admiral he "preferred to stay at home—the *Yorktown*." Jocko need not have worried, because the ComAirPac personnel officer who received McCain's request for Ridgway was none other than Captain Raöul Waller, who immediately pigeonholed it.

Clark had no trouble convincing Admiral Mitscher to let him have another whack at the Jimas, this time with more firepower—two task groups instead of one. Clark gave up the *Belleau Wood*—detached to Pearl Harbor for overhaul—and kept *Hornet*, *Yorktown*, and *Bataan*. Ralph Davison assumed command of TG 58.2—*Wasp*, *Franklin*, *Monterey*, and *Cabot*, as well as Thebaud's heavy cruisers. Davison, senior to Jocko by two years ('16), nevertheless asked him to plan the next operation, given his combat experience.

Clark's group sortied on 30 June and rendezvoused with Davison's next day, heading straight for the Jimas—Iwo, Chichi, Haha, Muko, and Ani. Because this was the admiral's third foray against these troublesome islands they were occasionally referred to in the task group as the "Jocko Jimas." All ships conducted intensive gunnery exercises en route in anticipation of an enemy aerial counterattack in response to the Fourth of July carrier raid.

During the final run-in after sunup on the 3rd, Davison's radars picked up an elusive snooper, which likely informed its base at Iwo of the carriers' presence. "1200—All plans changed," noted Alex Wilding. "Jocko has decided to kick off a fighter sweep this afternoon. 60 VF to hit Iwo." At 1252 Davison's CAP splashed an Emily, likely the same snooper that had been tracking the carriers. Armed with bombs, the fighters took off at 1400.

Alas for the Japanese, they had *not* spotted the carriers and were completely surprised when the sweep struck Iwo Jima. Their Zeros quickly scrambled aloft, only to have VF-1, VF-2, and *Bataan*'s VF-50 shoot them down close to the water and higher up—while dodging flak throughout. Clark's squadrons destroyed about 30 planes in the air and strafed and bombed others on the ground. The carriers lost one pilot.

Then, calamity! The Helldivers, after releasing their ordnance, recovered beneath the top of Chichi's high cliffs and flew into a deadly crossfire from AA batteries hidden in caves. Several planes were destroyed, although a few airmen managed to bail out, only to be captured and then eventually executed. Five more composite strikes by both task groups pummeled the Jimas throughout the day, shooting down 59 planes, burning several others on the airfields, and sinking or pounding at least two destroyers and 16 marus. (Reynolds, *Fighting Lady,* 174–76, 182)

Clark's air groups suffered unusually high losses—11 planes, with *Yorktown*'s Air Group One alone losing five pilots and three aircrewmen. Coastal targets could be more safely clobbered by naval guns, so Admirals Thebaud's and DuBose's seven cruisers went in close to shell Iwo Jima during the afternoon. Then the force withdrew without opposition.

Jocko was ecstatic. He knew that his third visit to the Bonin and Volcano island groups had been devastating, although he was unaware that the enemy now recalled its 54 surviving planes to Japan, only 500 miles distant. Such a clear-cut victory so close to the Japanese homeland made the excited Clark anxious to tell the whole world with a radioed report to Mitscher at Eniwetok. But staff communicator Owen Sowerwine stalled him. Radio silence was mandatory lest the enemy pinpoint the transmission and attack the force.

Jocko responded that "we ought to let the enemy know where we are, so we can have more of his planes to shoot down"—an idea he later proposed to Admiral Nimitz. He was inconsolable, but Sowerwine-Zero held his ground, until Clark turned in at midnight. Up again at 0400, he resumed his entreaties. Sowerwine doggedly held him off about four more hours, at the end of which time he said, "Admiral, my facilities are at your disposal. What do you want to say?" (Conversation with Red Sharp)

And so Clark radioed the results of the battle to Mitscher, who passed the word along to Spruance and Nimitz. Their congratulations to Clark and Davison were immediate, with Nimitz remarking on their holiday "fireworks close enough to Tokyo to burn the enemy up."

Jocko also heard from Davison, "Thanks for your help on the 3rd and for your heavy blows yesterday. I owe you a good night's sleep and will pay off at first opportunity." Clark had great respect for Davison and therefore appreciated his message. A superb task group commander, Davison stood in marked contrast to Keene Harrill on Jocko's first Jima strikes.

Indeed, Harrill's former task group, 58.4, still operating off Guam, received a new admiral in Jocko's old pal Gerry Bogan, who temporarily inherited part of Harrill's staff. Commander Brute Dale's month with Bogan became "the happiest I spent during the entire war." Bogan was "a cool fighter, aggressive but smart, the typical 'fighting cock' type of naval officer—distinct from the 'fighting bull' who has the courage but can hardly be considered to be smart." (Dale letter, 14 April 1966)

Pete Mitscher was finally honing a team of superb combat task group commanders—Clark, Montgomery, Davison, and Bogan—for the complete liberation of the Marianas and beyond.

As Clark and Davison headed for the Marianas on 5 July Jocko had *Bataan* launch a 24-plane search for its missing fighter skipper R. S. Lemmon, shot down in these waters on 24 June. But their good fortune in finding Bobby Price was not repeated. In the afternoon, *Bataan's* planes bombed Pagan in the northern Marianas.

Next day the two groups rejoined Mitscher, who sent a destroyer to fetch Clark and Davison to the *Lexington* to discuss preparations for the assaults on Guam and Tinian later in the month. Mitscher would take the other two task groups back to Eniwetok for a short breather, leaving Clark and Davison to alternate each day attacking Guam and Rota by air and destroyer bombardments.

That very afternoon Clark took station 75 miles southwest of Guam and launched 60 Hellcats on a sweep to Rota, only to suffer the first of many ensuing pilot losses to deadly flak from the two well-gunned islands. Escort carriers provided a steady flow of replacement pilots and planes, especially for the perpetually unreliable SB2C "Beasts," which continued to kill their own pilots and crews. Admiral Mitscher interviewed the last SBD pilots and realized this "Old Reliable" to be a much superior and safer bomber. But its production was just ending. (J. D. Ramage letter, 20 November 1986; Reynolds, *Fighting Lady*, 176, 178)

Clark in his next action report condemned the Helldiver and recommended that each heavy carrier turn in its 36 bombers in favor of 36 fighter-bombers, Hellcats carrying bombs and rockets. In addition, he recommended that each carrier keep the 36 regular day and 4 night fighters and increase the torpeckers from 18 to 20. These recommendations helped convince his superiors to change each group from 36 VF, 4 VF(N), 36 VB, and 18 VT to 36 VF, 36 VBF, 4 VF(N), 15 VB, and 15 VT by the new year. (ComCarDiv Five Action Report, 16 August 1944; Reynolds, *Fast Carriers*, 289–90)

Clark sent his planes against Guam's defenses on 7 July and in the evening admired the night-fighter direction of both Ridgway and Wilding. They brought down two Bettys (possibly Truk based)—which had dropped aluminum "window" to confuse radarmen—in full view of the ships. This led to wild cheers from those topside who witnessed it. The experience convinced Wilding that night-fighter direction had become so "perfected we can now feel a higher degree of security from night attacks." (Diary, 7 July 1944)

Shortly before dawn of the 8th the five survivors of the second Betty suddenly appeared in their life raft off the starboard bow of the *Yorktown*. Clark ordered the tin can *Helm* to pick them up, only to have them paddle away. At that Jocko lost his patience and bellowed over the TBS: "Hit them over the head with a shillelagh and drag them aboard!" The Irishman's club proved unnecessary as the prisoners were hauled aboard the *Helm*. Also, the can *Brown* recovered ten charts and data about several enemy island airfields. "Well done, destroyers," Jocko signaled. "You always deliver the goods."

Task group planes dropped incendiary bombs on Rota that afternoon, putting its airfield out of commission, then blasted Guam next morning—with enemy AA always taking a toll. Throughout all the air operations Al Jennings on Jocko's favorite ship, the *Yorktown*, never escaped his close eye (and ear, via the TBS radiophone).

The landing aboard of damaged planes especially concerned the admiral, who always preferred getting the plane aboard to ditching alongside, which risked drowning the pilot. Even if the plane was a wreck, at least its expensive clock and other gear might be salvaged before jettisoning. One day off Guam Clark overheard Jennings order a pilot approaching the *Yorktown* in a shot-up plane with a jammed tail hook to ditch. Jocko called Jennings and ordered the plane taken aboard. Just as it touched the deck, the tail hook dropped down and caught a wire. Jennings immediately transmitted what Clark regarded as a "generous" message: "Thanks, I stand corrected."

Captain Sample on the flagship *Hornet* had to endure even closer scrutiny, until he was relieved during the campaign by Captain Austin K. Doyle. Unlike the soft-spoken Sample, "Artie" Doyle could "handle" Jocko whenever he tried to interfere in respotting the deck, among other meddling. "What a great guy he was," remembered Roy Johnson of Doyle. (Johnson transcript #1, 88–89)

Even Johnson as flagship air officer could not escape Clark's vigilance. When a low weather ceiling over Guam obscured targets one day Johnson radioed the strike leader to shift over to less-cloudy Rota to "dump our bomb load there."

> Unfortunately, Jocko heard the transmission and "hit the overhead." We were told not to waste bombs, the country had paid a lot of good money for them and expected us to use them in the most effective way possible against the enemy.

While considering how to respond, Johnson was pleased to overhear one of his disgusted (and quite anonymous) pilots over Guam send a radio message to Clark, "Hello, Romeo [the call sign], how is the weather on the flag bridge?"

Johnson caught hell from the admiral, who demanded to know the identity of the smart-aleck pilot. Johnson never found out—if he even really tried. (Johnson letter, 6 April 1966)

On 10 July, while planes from *Hornet* and *Bataan* were working over Guam, the destroyer *McCall* on offshore air-rescue duty picked up a heliograph signal (hand mirror reflecting sunlight) from the island. Its captain, Lieutenant Commander John B. Carroll, dispatched a motor launch with armed sailors to investigate. They found a man standing in the surf who yelled to them that he was an American. They had him swim out and hoisted him into the launch.

He was Radioman First Class G. R. "Ray" Tweed. He had reported for duty on Guam in August 1939 and eluded the Japanese ever since their takeover in December 1941. Other such sailors had eventually been rounded up or killed, but Tweed had remained hidden by Chamorro natives and by his own cunning. He now pinpointed targets for the gunners on destroyers *McCall* and *Gridley*.

Next morning *McCall* transferred Tweed to *Hornet*, where he renewed prewar acquaintances with Chief Yeoman Cecil King. The crew treated him royally, starting with his first real haircut in 31 months, a dental checkup, and a fresh khaki uniform. "He was very edgy at first," recalled King. "You couldn't get behind him or anything, and he was spooky because he'd been by himself that long." Tweed recalled to King he had been selected for chief radioman just before Pearl Harbor but never received his rating. King immediately sent a dispatch to BuPers requesting it.

Soon Herman Rosenblatt summoned King and asked how come Tweed was not a chief yet, saying, "Admiral Clark wants him to be a chief." King replied that he had just sent such a dispatch to BuPers, expecting a reply on the morrow. But, "hell, I don't need a brick to fall on me," thought King, who returned to his office and typed out the promotion, which ended with "Authority verbal orders of CTG 58.1."

Then Jocko invited Tweed to his sea cabin, and upon stepping through the door the man announced, "Radioman First Class Tweed reporting, sir."

"You mean Chief Radioman Tweed," Jocko happily responded, to Tweed's immense satisfaction. Then he picked out more targets for Clark and flag lieutenant Reynolds. Meanwhile, Cecil King gave the promotion paperwork to the ship's paymaster, an ensign, with the authorization for Tweed's "three years' back pay coming, retroactive, as a chief."

"I ain't going to pay him," was the reply.

"You can have the same experience I did if you want," King responded, meaning the Rosenblatt treatment. The ensign grumbled and counted out several thousand dollars for the man everyone was starting to call "the Ghost of Guam." (King interview #2, 234–35) Then Clark sent Tweed to Admiral Kelly Turner, the assault commander for Guam, for a complete debriefing on details about the island's defenses.

Meanwhile, at 0330 on 11 July, a *Yorktown* night fighter splashed a Betty in full view of the force—another score for FDO Wilding. At dawn its planes pounded Guam. Next day Rota got it, while a tin can dropped depth charges on a submarine contact but without results. Simultaneously, the *Bataan* sent some of its best planes to the *Hornet* and *Yorktown* as it departed for Pearl Harbor and an overhaul. The *Cabot* took its place.

With the assault on Guam set for 21 July, the routine proceeded like clockwork—Guam struck on the 13th, Rota the 14th, then Guam, then Rota, then Guam, and on the 18th Captain Dick Whitehead commenced directing all close air support strikes against Guam's beaches in less than perfect weather. Cooper Bright announced to the pilots in *Yorktown*'s ready rooms, "It may be of interest to know that *Hornet* planes reported they were unable to get through to the target. Jocko's reply was that the *Yorktown*'s planes did—'you get in there.' After many attempts they did succeed." (Reynolds, *Fighting Lady*, 178)

Clark had anticipated that such endless operations would prevent the return of his ships and their crews to the fleet's Marshall Islands anchorages for a break ashore. So he had ordered beer for the *Hornet*, just as he had when he was skipper of the *Yorktown*. Two or three hundred cases of beer had been stowed in a storeroom up forward, and one division of ship's company at a time held a beer party, two or three cans per man, up on the forecastle. "That's the kind of thing," remembered Cecil King, "that made Jocko so beloved." (In Wooldridge, *Carrier Warfare*, 283)

TG 58.1's planes concentrated on Guam during the final three days of prelanding attacks. At one point Captain Sol Phillips remarked to Jocko about the almost routine war-making by the indomitable TF 58, "I note a partial eclipse of the Japanese sun."

"The rising sun of Japan is not all the way down yet," replied Jocko, "but, says the rabbi, it won't be long now."

At dawn on 21 July, assault day, Clark's fighters began strafing directly in front of the Marines and Army as they hit Guam's beaches and moved inland. By noon, 58.1's work was done. Escort carriers and land-based planes from the airfield at Saipan took over close air support. Admiral Mitscher then granted Jocko's request to anchor in Saipan's Tanapag Harbor next morning to take on more bombs.

During the lull, on 22 July, Jocko and Bob Reynolds donned their dress whites and went ashore in a landing barge. They presented medals to the wounded at Saipan's field hospital. In their absence, topside hands could see the gun ships pounding nearby Tinian, preparatory to the assault there two days hence. The stench and swarms of flies from enemy corpses being burned ashore at Saipan frustrated attempts at sunbathing.

Having successfully secured control of the skies and waters around the Marianas, TF 58 now turned westward to strike the Palau Islands and look for potential fleet anchorages ever closer to Asian and Japanese waters. The task groups of Clark, Montgomery, and Davison departed on 23 July, leaving Bogan's to support the troops on Guam and Tinian.

Foul weather slowed 58.1's progress until the afternoon of the 25th, when Clark readied his strikes against the Palaus. Just before noon, however, several radar blips had to be investigated. *Yorktown*'s CAP splashed a Kate within view of the force, but Charlie Ridgway had to let two others escape in order to vector Hellcats to a radar contact 85 miles out. They started to make a run when they saw plainly that the bogey was a four-engine land-based Navy PB4Y Liberator on patrol. The pilot had failed to turn on his IFF signal identifying him as a "friendly."

Clark radioed Mitscher, "The Liberator can be charged with allowing two Japanese Kates to escape by not turning on his proper identification."

Soon, Mitscher received a long complaint from the Liberator's wing commander, Rear Admiral Frank D. Wagner, protesting that Clark's fighters had dived on his plane. Mitscher replied by sending Wagner Jocko's

Jock and Bob Reynolds aboard a landing barge taking them from the anchored *Hornet* in Tanapag Harbor to the field hospital at Saipan, 22 July 1944. They presented medals to the wounded there. (Photo courtesy of Bob Reynolds) *U.S. Navy photo*

message to him. (One can speculate that Wagner had a certain pique toward Clark. After several months in makee-learn status for a task group command as ComCarDiv Five, Wagner had not measured up and had instead been given the patwing command. Then Clark became ComCarDiv Five on 1 July 1944.)

Clark's planes attacked and photographed Ulithi, Yap, Ngulu, Sorol, and Fais in the western Carolines, returning over the next three days to concentrate on Ulithi and Yap, destroying about a dozen parked planes at Yap. On the first day a *Cabot* torpecker was hit by flak, but the three men bailed out. Two VF-1 Hellcats circled them in their raft until a Kingfisher float-plane landed. A shore battery took the rescue under fire, only to be silenced by more Hellcats. Jocko sent the pilots a hearty "well done." A downed Helldiver pilot was similarly rescued the next day.

Nobody liked this foray of photo taking, notably the inactive cruisers. When Clark's classmate Captain Jerauld Wright of the *Santa Fe* pointedly asked him about the results of the air ops on 27 July, Jocko shared his frustration. The strikes "have been highly successful: no enemy targets, no air opposition, very little antiaircraft [fire], many photographs. In fact so many that if they are carefully studied there will be little time left to fight the war."

Sol Phillips was also tired of commanding the task group screen and asked Jocko to request that his ship *Oakland* be reassigned to a regular cruiser division. "Prefer that you retain command until arrival Eniwetok," Clark replied. "We ought to take one more swipe at Tokyo Rose."

He recommended that his task group be allowed to attack Woleai in the western Carolines, but Admiral Spruance turned him down. Woleai was situated within General Douglas MacArthur's Southwest Pacific theater, and Spruance's staff feared that MacArthur's bombers and Clark's planes might encounter each other over Woleai and exchange fire. (Buell, *Quiet Warrior,* 299–300)

The photographs taken by the carrier planes enabled Admiral Nimitz to select Ulithi Atoll, which was large enough to accommodate the entire Fifth Fleet, as the next major forward anchorage.

Heading back toward the Marianas on 29 July, Clark's and Davison's task groups swapped two carriers. Davison—en route to Eniwetok—sent over the *Franklin* in exchange for the *Yorktown,* which was earmarked for overhaul in the States. Clark declared a "draw" in the *York's* friendly competition with the flagship—*Yorktown* had sunk more ships, *Hornet* had shot down more planes. Jocko bade his beloved ship a fond farewell, "As always the *Yorktown* is a first-class fighting ship. Well done, good luck, and hurry back."

The next night brought Clark a touch of excitement when the destroyer *Boyd* on picket duty reported a "skunk"—unidentified ship—28 miles north of the *Hornet.* Alarmed, Clark replied, "*Boyd,* attempt to identify skunk," whereupon, much to his relief, Admiral Bogan broke in, "I believe I am your skunk." His TG 58.4 was still supporting the troops on Guam.

During refueling on the 31st Admiral Mitscher ordered Clark to search for a PBM Mariner flying boat reported down 200 miles northwest of Guam. Clark sent ahead two destroyers, but the rest of the task group bucked heavy seas during the night, unable to launch a search until dawn. Around 0700 on 1 August the leading tin can *Izard* made radio contact with the PBM, whereupon Clark sent ahead four more cans to act as radio relays.

*Izard* sighted the flying boat just as the planes arrived. It took off the 12-man crew and then sank the PBM—a shining example, recalled Clark, of "the pains we took to rescue our aviators."

Heavy seas frustrated attempts to take on more bombs, but TG 58.1 managed to refuel on the 2nd. This was just in time to respond to Mitscher's sudden orders for Clark's and Montgomery's groups to head north. Yet once more, the "Jocko Jimas" were being reinforced with at least 18 more planes and an approaching convoy. With Mitscher in overall command, both groups charged north throughout the 3rd to launch after daybreak on the 4th.

"The barn"—Eniwetok and its sandy beaches—Clark told his group, "ought to look good after cleaning out this place. The best of luck to all and give them hell!"

Learning that the assigned lifeguard submarine had spotted an 11-ship convoy—possibly including a light carrier—steaming north from Chichi Jima, Jocko increased speed from 18 to 25 knots to launch a fighter sweep and bombing strike at 0918 against Iwo and Haha Jima. "It looks like a fine day for scavengers," he remarked. (Gray, "'Jocko' Clark," 46) Lest the convoy escape, however, he obtained Mitscher's permission to proceed independently at high speed to catch it. *Hornet* and *Franklin* launched at 1017, their SB2Cs unloading their bombs an hour later—without scoring one hit!

Then at 1245 Clark learned that other enemy ships were fleeing Chichi, whereupon he detached Larry DuBose with all five cruisers and four cans to sink any enemy ships already crippled by bombs. Mitscher sent four of Montgomery's destroyers to assist. The hapless expenditure of his last bombs over Iwo concerned Jocko, who remarked to air ops officer Tex McCrary, "Are you going to let the cruisers do this job?"

"Don't worry, Admiral," replied the former torpecker pilot, "we loaded this last strike with torpedoes. They'll let in the water instead of the air."

That they did. The Avengers planted their "fish" into all 11 vessels, leaving only two freighters afloat. DuBose's cruisers reached the scene at sunset and finished off the two crippled marus. Total tonnage sunk—20,000.

By dawn of 5 August TG 58.1 lay but 421 miles from Honshu, the main home island of Japan, the closest any large naval force had gotten to Japan. In heavy seas, Clark launched a search-strike to the north, getting as close as 193 miles from Honshu, and shot down an Emily and a Betty likely from there.

When three enemy patrol boats suddenly appeared near the screen about 0800 Jocko let the 5-inch gunners on his big carriers shoot at them—a unique event for these AA crews, so untrained in shooting at surface targets that the CAP and destroyers had to complete the job. Hellcats also nailed a snooping Betty, while three strikes shot up targets on Chichi,

Muko, and Ani Jima. Next morning DuBose's four light cruisers plus *Oakland* moved in close to bombard Chichi's AA batteries and airfields.

And, in the afternoon, a nervy Emily from the homeland eluded the CAP and AA fire that was so thick that Clark ordered a cease-fire lest one of his ships be hit. It turned away, only to be splashed by returning planes from the *Bunker Hill* in TG 58.3.

"Tokyo Rose identified," signaled Sol Phillips for all the force to share, "from crow's nest at coordinates 82.5-48.2, Sasaki Airfield. Second salvo from *Oakland* blew her kimono wide open. Kingfisher pilot reported she was smoking and down by the stern."

"Congratulations and well done to *Oakland* for giving Tokyo Rose such an appropriate serenade," replied Jocko. "Would appreciate further details. Question: Is it true [that she is full of shit] and what was the color of kimono?"

"Admiral, it may be true, but visibility was indifferent and lookout excited. Kimono was stained brown. Signed, Phillips."

This contemptuous snort at the "Jap bitch" was the two men's final colorful exchange in their last battle together; Phillips was being transferred to staff duty. The two task groups retired, having neutralized the Jimas yet again, though at a cost of six planes and eight men to AA. The less-than-perfect shooting by 58.1's own AA batteries led Clark to conduct gunnery exercises during the retirement on 7–8 August. Nevertheless, congratulations came in not only from Nimitz but also from Ernie King in Washington.

After dropping the hook at Eniwetok on the 9th, the *Hornet* welcomed aboard Admiral Mitscher to present awards. The task force commander pinned a Navy Cross on Clark's uniform in recognition of "his professional skill, high personal courage, and superlative leadership" in seeking out and sinking the convoy and inflicting more damage to the Jimas over the two days.

Jocko's brother Lieutenant Commander Bill Clark came aboard for a visit. As a photo interpreter, he assured "Joe" that all those pictures his pilots had taken over the western Carolines were indeed important.

The pilots of Air Group Two decided to commemorate their four visits to the "Jocko Jimas" by issuing themselves mock shares in the "Jocko Jima Development Corporation." Jocko made certain that Mitscher received Stock No. One; the pilots issued Clark No. Two, a gesture that pleased him immensely.

Big changes reshaped the key fleet commands during the respite at Eniwetok. In order to keep constant pressure on Japan, Admirals Spruance and Halsey were now designated to command the fleet in a two-platoon system. While one of them led it in one campaign, the other would plan the succeeding operation. So Halsey now relieved Spruance for the liberation of

AIR GROUP TWO · · U.S.S. HORNET

*This is to certify that*

*is the holder of*

ONE SHARE

*in the*

JOCKO JIMA DEVELOPMENT CORP.

*EXCLUSIVE SITES IN THE BONIN ISLANDS*
*"JOCKO JIMA RETTO — CLARK ISLAND GROUP"*

*Choice Locations of All Types in Iwo, Chichi, Haha & Muko Jima*
*Only 500 Miles from Downtown Tokyo*

CERTIFICATE NO._____                          J J Clark _____ PRESIDENT

the Philippines. Fifth Fleet was retitled Third Fleet, Task Force 58 became TF 38, TG 58.1 changed to 38.1, and so forth. When that operation ended, Spruance would resume command under the Fifth Fleet rubric, with Halsey returning to Pearl Harbor to prepare for the next round.

Mitscher retained command of what now became TF 38 but only until his relief was ready to take the helm. This was Vice Admiral John McCain—another "Jock" but usually nicknamed "Slew" (for slue-foot). He and his air operations officer, Commander Jimmy Thach, had observed the Marianas fighting from Spruance's flagship, but they still lacked the experience of leading a large carrier force. Thus McCain relieved Clark in command of TG 38.1 on 18 August for makee-learn experience preparatory to the larger task force command. He would eventually move up to relieve Mitscher during the course of the Philippines campaign.

Clark had served a full year of combat command (since August 1943) and now deserved shoreside duty like most of his seagoing peers. But he also wanted to return to the fight (as Ted Sherman was doing) after a rest and told Mitscher so. When Pete informed Jocko that he too would likely go home about October, Jocko suggested that Mitscher give him a short leave simultaneously. Then both could return to the fleet and resume their partnership when Mitscher eventually rotated with McCain. Mitscher agreed immediately.

In the meantime, Clark stayed on board the *Hornet* to advise McCain whenever necessary. He was also to remain available to resume a task group command if necessary as the available reserve carrier admiral.

When McCain hoisted his flag in the *Wasp,* Jocko sent over his key staff officers to educate McCain's during the initial stage of the Philippines fighting. Red Sharp helped Jimmy Thach in overall operations, Tex McCrary assisted with aviation, and Sugar Brown took over ship operations for a time. Sowerwine-Zero advised the staff communicator, while Charlie Ridgway briefed McCain's FDO but remained on *Hornet.*

In order for McCain to gain maximum experience for task force command, his task group was assigned five carriers: *Wasp, Hornet,* and the CVLs *Belleau Wood, Cowpens,* and *Monterey.* Gerry Bogan's 38.2 and Ted Sherman's 38.3 each had the customary four flattops, and Ralph Davison's 38.4 had three.

The 16 fast carriers sortied from Eniwetok on 28 August to attack Japan's air forces defending the Philippine Islands. Mitscher at the helm was ably assisted by his new operations officer and Clark compatriot Commander Jimmy Flatley. The timetable called for supporting invasion forces in the Palau Islands on 15 September and at Mindanao, the main island of the southern Philippines, on 15 November 1944.

For the first two weeks at sea McCain and his staff relied heavily on Clark's team as TG 38.1 pounded Wake, the Palaus, and airfields on Mindanao. Japanese aerial resistance was so feeble that Admiral Halsey moved up his schedule, headed north, and sent his planes over Leyte and the central Philippines, which were not scheduled to be invaded until late December.

On 11 September one of VF-2's pilots, Ensign Thomas C. Tillar, was shot down over Leyte but rescued and hidden by native Filipinos who alerted the fleet. A PBY Catalina flew in near the beach, picked him up, and took him back to the *Hornet.* Interviewed by Clark, Tillar revealed that his rescuers insisted the Japanese had virtually no airplanes defending the Leyte area. Jocko immediately transmitted this revelation to Halsey.

Halsey realized at once that the projected invasion of Mindanao was no longer necessary, that Leyte could be assaulted instead—and well ahead of schedule. He boldly recommended the bypassing of Mindanao and an early major assault at Leyte instead. It was approved virtually instantaneously— 14 September—by the American and Allied high commands. The date for General MacArthur's landings on Leyte was advanced from Christmastime to 20 October 1944.

Throughout the rest of September the fast carriers supported landings at Peleliu in the Palaus and Morotai in the Molucca Islands, ranged the Philippine coast with impunity, and pummeled shipping and mostly parked aircraft as far north as Manila: nearly 900 planes and 67 ships destroyed.

Slew McCain was shocked, however, by Japanese planes getting through the CAP off Luzon late in the month to strafe both flagships *Wasp* and *Hornet*. He summoned Clark to the *Wasp* via destroyer high-line and said simply to him, "What can we do to stop this strafing?"

Jocko replied that all he needed was a good fighter director—like Charlie Ridgway, who had helped break in McCain's FDO. Little did Clark know that McCain—even before Jocko got back to the *Hornet*—sent a request to ComAirPac for Ridgway's transfer from Clark's staff to his own. When Jocko returned aboard the *Hornet* a copy of the request was waiting for him.

But McCain did not know that Clark had his own man at the other end of the pipeline—ComAirPac personnel boss Raöul Waller. "Smelling a rat," as Jocko put it, Raöul sidetracked McCain by asserting (quite falsely) that Ridgway required advanced instruction at the fighter director school in Georgia, to which Waller immediately sent him. It was a timely act in another way—Waller now had his own orders to report as chief of staff to Clark as soon as Jocko returned from leave.

As September drew to a close, and with the *Hornet* earmarked to replace its battle-weary Air Group Two with a fresh Air Group 11, Admiral Mitscher decided to detach Clark and his staff for their leave period. Admiral Jack Towers, as Nimitz's deputy, concurred. Both changes could occur after TG 38.1 retired to yet another new fleet anchorage—Seeadler Harbor at Manus in the Admiralty Islands near New Guinea.

En route, on the 27th, Clark and staff attended a farewell dinner given by the ship in honor of Air Group Two and the popular departing exec Dutch Duerfeldt. The printed menu included a musical program of bogus song titles dedicated to key individuals on the ship. A jazzy foxtrot number recognized their flamboyant admiral, "The Jocko Jima Jive."

As the task group entered Seeadler on 29 September Clark was dazzled at the sight of perhaps 500 transport and cargo ships gathered there for the upcoming liberation of the Philippines. Two days later he and his staff boarded a plane for Hawaii. On their arrival they discovered that while Jack Towers had wholeheartedly approved their leaves, Nimitz had deliberately not. Concurring with Forrest Sherman, now deputy chief of staff, Nimitz did not trust McCain to develop into a skillful carrier leader. Both men wanted Clark to remain on the scene should McCain fail to measure up. (Reynolds, *Admiral John H. Towers,* 489)

Of course, Nimitz had nothing against Clark—quite the opposite. The Pacific Fleet commander now personally pinned the Distinguished Service Medal on Clark "for exceptionally meritorious service" as task group commander between April and June 1944 at Hollandia, Truk, the Marianas, and the Jimas. The award specifically recognized his "keen foresight and resourcefulness, indomitable fighting spirit and heroic leadership."

Towers argued successfully for Nimitz to let Clark take his well-earned rest, explaining Mitscher's earnest desire to have Clark ready to resume his role as lead task group commander whenever Mitscher himself returned from leave. Nimitz, however, insisted that Clark be on call in the event he was suddenly needed in the Pacific. So Jocko and his staff departed by air for San Francisco on 5 October. Two days later Arthur Radford arrived in Hawaii, giving Nimitz at least one experienced task group commander on standby.

Clark was returning to the States as something of a celebrity. Oklahoma as well as Honolulu newspapers ran occasional stories that fed his Native American image, notably the "deep tan and high cheek bones of an Indian. He looks slight and . . . is full of nervous energy, walks with a quick, springy step and has the light of battle in his eyes." And he was very quotable:

> Let's tell the Japs when and where we'll strike—the exact hour—and invite them to come out. If they do, we'll wipe out their fleet. Then we can steam on into Tokyo Bay and knock out Japan. (*Honolulu Star-Bulletin*, 27 January 1944, article by Charles McMurtry)

The *Saturday Evening Post* provided national exposure (16 September 1944), featuring Clark along with Gerry Bogan, Arthur Radford, Forrest Sherman, John Ballentine, Mel Pride, and John Dale Price in "They Sparked the Carrier Revolution" (by Jack Alexander). Jocko was characterized as one of the "pure sluggers of the Halsey type, who would wither away and die if placed behind an administrative desk."

Clark's Cherokee roots allegedly made him what in future years would be regarded as a racial-ethnic slur: "a born killer . . . , a hell-roaring spectacular fighter whose current bludgeoning of the enemy must please his ancestors . . . , an inveterate bellower [who] can rarely be induced to speak in a conversational tone."

*Life* magazine (22 January 1945) gave him the ultimate coverage, a long biographical profile entitled simply "'Jocko' Clark." Author William P. Gray interviewed several unnamed officers, one of whom elaborated on Alexander's account of Jocko's appearance:

He looks like an unmade Navy bed. For comfort's sake aboard ship he invariably wears his khaki trousers with the belt just below his sizable paunch and leaves the top button unbuttoned. Enlisted men on his staff frequently make bets on how soon the Admiral's pants will fall off. The impression of sartorial disaster is heightened by his habit of chewing gum.

Only one of the three photographs accompanying the article hinted at this description, showing also his engineer's cap, while he is standing with several Air Group Two pilots. The other two photos are posed, with Clark immaculate in a freshly pressed khaki shirt. One of them has him smiling over a game of backgammon ("acey-deucy" in the Navy) with Bob Reynolds, whose sleeves are rolled all the way up, making Clark look better dressed in comparison. The other photo is captioned, "His men say their admiral does not have to look for Japs. His long nose smells them out."

Like the *Post* story, *Life* could not resist concluding with the trite notion that Clark's Red Indian forebears had somehow bequeathed him warlike proclivities:

With such lineage it seems entirely possible that, whatever his diet, Jocko Clark will increase in ferocity for some years yet. The Jap may not last long enough to know the Admiral's real possibilities.

Below that passage is *Yorktown* cartoonist John Furlow's sketch of him as tomahawk-wielding Indian chief scalping Emperor Hirohito.

Finally, a former *Life* staffer, Lieutenant Oliver Jensen, wrote the book *Carrier War* at the Navy's behest. Covering the fast carriers through the autumn of 1944, it appeared early in the new year. Jensen had spent the spring of '44 on board the *Yorktown*, after Clark had left it, but still gave him prominent notice in the book—"a prowling captain, as opposed to the sedentary order." (48)

Jocko's greatest wartime renown, however, was cinematic—in the movie about the *Yorktown* pieced together by Dwight Long. Long had shown the raw silent footage to ship's sponsor Eleanor Roosevelt (and even had her simulate the christening on film, something that was later cut from the movie). And with difficulty he had gotten Admiral King to lend his approval after viewing it with five other admirals while Long narrated.

Dwight was waiting for Jocko when he landed in San Francisco on 6 October. Of the original 60,000 feet of Kodachrome color film footage, Long had pared it down to 800—one hour's worth. To make a coherent story line, he had taken additional scenes on the *Ticonderoga*, showing its captain, Dixie Kiefer, and used footage from several other carriers and air groups. But if any one individual could be considered the star, it was Jocko, seen and heard more than any other individual in the film.

Long informed Clark that Twentieth Century Fox had agreed to release it, with all proceeds going to Navy Relief. He had entitled it *The Fighting Lady* as symbolic of all carriers, had gotten the studio's premier composer Alfred Newman to provide a musical score, and had obtained actor Robert Taylor (now a naval aviator himself) to do voiceovers. Two Fox screenwriters had redone Spig Wead's original script.

Clark did not like the title—until Long took him down to Hollywood to view the finished product. Only then did Jocko realize that nothing could be changed; as far as he was concerned it was perfect!

Problems still existed, however. Long told Clark that the Navy's film censor did not like the title. Furthermore, this worthy claimed the movie showed top secret radar on a battleship, meaning the whole picture would have to be redone. But producer Louis de Rochemont refused, and narrator Robert Taylor was no longer available.

Jocko disagreed with the censor, who turned out to be one of his Academy classmates and a black-shoe battleship man at that, Captain Jack Phillips. So Clark put in a long-distance phone call to Rear Admiral John Cassady at the Deputy CNO's office for Air. He instructed Cassady to show a copy of the film to Assistant Secretary (Air) Artemus Gates in order to get an approved release of the movie "as is."

The very next morning de Rochemont received a phone call from the Navy Department unconditionally approving the release of *The Fighting Lady* for public showing. Twentieth Century Fox timed its premiere for the last week of the year in order to make *The Fighting Lady* eligible for an Academy Award. In a word, the film received rave reviews by film critics and the Oscar as best documentary motion picture of 1944.

Clark flew east to spend a few days with his parents in Chelsea, Oklahoma, and with his daughters and estranged wife M.C. in Jacksonville, Florida. He proceeded next to the Navy Department in Washington to discuss specific operational matters like the terrible SB2C Helldivers and the need for fighter-bombers. Secretary of the Navy James V. Forrestal welcomed Clark and had him speak at a press conference, with a message—"we are winning the war because the fast carrier task force has the power to establish and maintain command of the air."

On the morning of 24 October (25th in the western Pacific) Jocko Clark paid his respects to Admiral Ernie King. As he entered the office, King was storming, pacing back and forth "like a tiger in a towering rage." King, seeing Clark, stopped, welcomed him, and in a few words praised his excellent performance in combat. Indeed, Clark found King so "nice" about it as to realize that finally "I was persona grata!"

Suddenly, King reverted to the unbridled anger that Clark had witnessed in him all too often in the past. But this time "Ernie King was madder than I've *ever* seen him!" The Navy's commander in chief was furious at Admiral Halsey and declared to Clark, "He has left the strait of San Bernardino open for the Japanese to strike the transports at Leyte!"

MacArthur's army had landed at Leyte on the 20th, supported by Vice Admiral Thomas C. Kinkaid's bombardment forces of prewar battleships and other gun ships and Rear Admiral Tommy Sprague's 18 escort carriers providing close air support for the troops. The Japanese navy had reacted with an ingenious plan aimed at capitalizing on Halsey's legendary bullheadedness.

During the night of 23–24 October (western Pacific date) two forces of enemy gun ships moved from the South China Sea eastward through the San Bernardino and Surigao straits of the Philippines to attack Kinkaid's amphibious shipping at Leyte Gulf. Simultaneously, another force built around four carriers ran south from Japan to a point northeast of the Philippines, announcing its presence by heavy radio traffic. This was done deliberately to lure Halsey with the fast carriers away from Leyte Gulf, leaving the shipping there at the mercy of the two gun forces by morning.

Mitscher's TF 38 carriers had driven back the "center force" from San Bernardino Strait the previous day. And around midnight Kinkaid's gun ships had destroyed the "southern force" in Surigao Strait. Yet Halsey had taken the bait and run north during the night in order to sink the decoy carriers of the "northern force" at dawn. And the "center force" had simultaneously reversed its course to the eastward through the San Bernardino Strait. Nonaviator Kinkaid in Leyte Gulf, however, had naively assumed that Halsey had detached Admiral Lee's TF 34 battle line (without air cover) from TF 38 to guard the strait. But Halsey had not done that, nor had he bothered to keep in touch with Kinkaid.

So the "center force," spearheaded by the superbattleship *Yamato*, had struck Kinkaid's transports, escort carriers, and tin cans at Leyte Gulf in the morning. The Japanese gun ships sank Bowser Vieweg's *Gambier Bay* and other vessels, just as Halsey and Mitscher were sinking Japan's four carriers (planeless, as it turned out) hundreds of miles to the north.

Nimitz at Pearl Harbor radioed Halsey, "Where is Task Force 34?"— adding "The world wonders" (from Tennyson's "Charge of the Light Brigade") as padding and/or an expression of his frustration. Either way, the message enraged "Bull" Halsey. For Lee's TF 34 battleships had remained with the TF 38 fast carriers, where they had always been throughout the

Pacific offensive. But neither King nor Nimitz—who relayed messages to King—knew that, due to Halsey's silence on the matter.

Ernie King immediately assigned primary blame to Halsey, as Jocko Clark witnessed first hand. In the event, even the Japanese "center force" commander figured Halsey *was* closing in behind him, so he suddenly fled Leyte Gulf with the *Yamato* and its entourage to escape back westward through San Bernardino Strait and toward Japan before Halsey could cut him off.

Clark, like King, realized Halsey did not need Lee's battleships to sink the Japanese carriers and that Halsey could conceivably have left Lee's battle line off the straits (presumably with some CAP as air cover against land-based bandits). (Reynolds, *Fast Carriers,* 255–78)

So Clark witnessed King's fury "at Halsey for taking those battleships north." From Nimitz's messages, King "knew what was going on too. . . . The one chance in all the history of the ages for a modern battleship engagement [off San Bernardino Strait] was lost because Halsey chased aircraft carriers with battleships."

When Clark passed through Pearl Harbor on his return to the fleet in November he reported first to Admiral Nimitz where he found Tommy Sprague already present. Jocko listened to his classmate spell out to Nimitz how Halsey had left Sprague's escort carriers at the mercy of the Japanese attack at Leyte Gulf.

Then when Clark rejoined the fleet he discussed the battle with Radford, who said that part of Halsey's problem was his chief of staff, Rear Admiral Mick Carney, a nonaviator. Raddy and Mick had been feuding for years, recalled Jocko, who "was on Radford's side. But I love Carney, a great friend" ever since Academy days. Clark concluded Halsey's decision to run north had been his own, not based on Carney's advice (and Carney never discussed the event for the rest of his 95-year life).

Clark's opinion of Halsey had been generally high up until the Battle of Leyte Gulf. But when Jocko returned to the fleet, he witnessed Halsey acting erratically in trying to juggle such multitudinous and often unforeseen challenges as Japanese suicide planes, typhoons, supporting more landings, and coordinating his ever-growing Third Fleet.

Clark began to realize that Halsey's faulty decision-making at Leyte had been the first evidence of his deteriorating leadership: "I claim that in the overall aspects that the war got too complicated for Halsey. There's no other answer!"

(During a conversation in 1964 I observed to Clark that Halsey as Third Fleet commander was in fact virtual fast carrier commander only, *never* having simultaneously commanded both the carrier and the amphibious forces as Spruance had while leading the Fifth Fleet. He reacted, "Leyte!" I replied no; that had been Kinkaid with MacArthur. Clark replied, "I never thought of that!")

At the end of October Mitscher turned over TF 38 to McCain and returned stateside for his leave period. Clark met him in San Diego early in November to discuss mutual concerns. (As the two admirals were standing together chatting at the naval air station, Bob Reynolds's older brother Joe—a wartime Navy dentist and boisterous prankster—sidled up to Bob to welcome him. Upon spotting the diminutive three-star admiral Mitscher conversing with Clark, however, Joe said out loud to Bob, "Who's this, Reynolds, *your aide?!*" Everyone but a mortified Bob had a great laugh.)

Mitscher and Clark agreed on the need both for more fighter-bombers on the fast carriers and for ways to counter the kamikaze suicide planes that had first appeared at the Battle of Leyte Gulf. Among the ships crashed by them, though not sunk, was Jocko's old command *Suwannee*. Having used Marine Corps pilots on the old *Lexington*, Clark recommended that they be assigned to the fast carriers, flying their F4U Corsair fighters. Mitscher convinced King, and the change received high priority. (Reynolds, *Fast Carriers*, 288–90)

The Battle of Leyte Gulf, including the advent of the kamikazes, convinced Clark, "not knowing what would happen next," to return to the war zone. "I thought my place was out there. So I foreshortened my leave, and I went back."

On 19 November Jocko and part of his staff flew from Alameda to Pearl Harbor. Reporting to Admiral Nimitz, Clark alluded to Leyte Gulf, "I guess I missed the best battle of the war." "Oh, no," Nimitz corrected him, "the best battle will be the *last* battle!"

Clark arranged for the staff and their baggage to be flown to the new forward anchorage at Ulithi in the western Carolines aboard five R4D long-distance rescue planes. He and Bob Reynolds flew out in one equipped with bunk beds, leaving the rest of the staff to follow with 40 cases of "the best bourbon money can buy" and other liquors purchased by Herm Rosenblatt. (Reynolds to Bill, Alma, and Clarkie, 24 December 1944)

Secretary of the Navy James Forrestal allowed ships to carry alcohol but only for consumption at shore parties. But Jocko had already "scotched" that! His ulcers prevented him from imbibing, but he set up a (strictly non-regulation) wine mess on the flagship for staff parties. The staff now had difficulty deciding whether to send the booze to Ulithi in one plane or among all four—just to be safe. They finally decided on one R4D and assigned an old chief bosun's mate to guard it. The entire cache arrived safely at Ulithi—minus one bottle of gin. The chief's gratuity, no doubt. (Conversation with Red Sharp)

During the summer Admiral Towers, with Nimitz's approval, had composed a list of the top men for fast carrier task group commands: Clark, Montgomery, Davison, Bogan, Gardner, and Ted Sherman. (Reynolds, *Admiral John H. Towers*, 480) Radford had been excluded, being "stuck" in Washington at the time. When Jocko reached Ulithi on 25 November no vacancy existed for him, especially because recent battle damage had eliminated the equivalent of one task group. He was happy to see that the *Yorktown* had returned from overhaul again as Montgomery's flagship in TG 38.1. But he preferred to await Mitscher's return to task force command anyway, so he simply restored his flag aboard the *Hornet*—on the same standby status as Radford.

Clark reported in to McCain, who bemoaned the fact that kamikazes had been following his strike planes back to their ships, then attacking. Clark described his picket destroyers with overhead CAP in front of his task group to weed out snoopers. McCain immediately adopted the scheme for TF 38, and he and his operations officer Jimmy Thach enlarged and improved it as the kamikaze menace increased. (Reynolds, *Fast Carriers*, 290–91)

On 1 December 1944 TF 38 sortied to support the Mindoro landings in the western Philippines. Clark and the *Hornet* were in Bogan's TG 38.2, but only until sunset when the operation was abruptly postponed due to continuing heavy kamikaze attacks at Leyte. The ships reanchored at Ulithi, where Raöul Waller reported aboard the *Hornet* next day—finally—as Clark's official chief of staff.

Jocko was overjoyed; as Red Sharp explained, to Clark "the sun rose and set on Raöul." As Jocko's former exec, he was glad to be back, and he asked Clark how he liked task group command.

"Raöul," Jocko eyed him, "just remember one thing. In your entire career you'll never have a larger command than your own ship!" Clark missed the *Yorktown*, which would never return to his task group, because it had been appropriated instead by Radford for flagship.

Because the staff had developed into a well-oiled team, Jocko cautioned Waller, "You're coming into a working organization. Don't start slinging the bull in all directions. Don't start giving orders. You'll just have to sit back and let the wheels turn. And you'll work into it over time." In short, Waller needed a makee-learn period. It wasn't easy, especially since he had been executive officer over half of the same officers on the *Yorktown*.

Clark now had his "perfect" staff—Waller as chief, Sharp for overall operations, Sugar Brown for ship ops, Tex McCrary for air ops, and Sowerwine as communicator (he screened all incoming messages for Clark's eyes only—the "Ultra" category—usually decoded Japanese messages). Sowerwine-Zero also continued to act as the "moderating influence" between flag secretary Rosen-

In "razzle-dazzle" camouflage paint designed to confuse attacking planes, five *Essex*-class carriers of TF 58/38 are moored in a row at Ulithi Atoll in the western Carolines in November 1944. *Front to back: Wasp, Yorktown, Hornet, Hancock,* and *Ticonderoga.* A lone battle-gray sister ship and two light carriers are seen to the left, among other vessels. *U.S. Navy photo*

blatt and the rest of the staff, including Waller. Charlie Ridgway remained fighter director, though loaned temporarily to McCain when the latter's FDO took ill. Reynolds continued as flag lieutenant, and Beath was still the Japanese radio listener.

Lieutenant Commander Charlie Kerlee, formerly of the *Yorktown*, returned to Clark as special photographer. And Rosenblatt, always milking his connection with the First Family, convinced Clark to request the president's youngest son, the quiet Lieutenant John A. Roosevelt, to be staff supply officer. He reported two months later. Jocko also settled in again with the flagship's excellent skipper Artie Doyle and became acquainted with the pilots of Air Group 11.

One day, the exec of VF-11, Lieutenant Robert E. Clements, peeked into Flag Plot just to "say hello." An idle Clark grabbed his arm and pushed him into a chair: "Why, hello, son. Sit down. Have a cigar. How're things going? Tell me *all* about it!" Jocko loved the pilots, and Bob Clements never had another case of jitters in flag country. (Courtesy of Barrett Tillman)

With the Mindoro landings rescheduled for 15 December, Gerry Bogan's TG 38.2 sortied from Ulithi on the 11th. Bogan had his flag in the *Lexington*, in company with McCain in the *Hancock*, Clark in the *Hornet*, plus light carriers *Cabot* and *Independence*. The latter ship had become the fleet's first "night" carrier, skippered by Jocko's old friend Eddie Ewen and expected to operate independently, engaging bandits only between dusk and dawn. Each heavy carrier, however, still retained its own four-plane Bat team.

Montgomery and Sherman each led four-carrier task groups as TF 38 neutralized enemy air forces on Luzon before, during, and after the assault on Mindoro. Heading north toward a fueling rendezvous on the 17th, Halsey minimized, and thus failed to avoid, an approaching typhoon. That night it struck the fleet, capsizing three tin cans, which, along with ten other ships, suffered heavy personnel losses.

Bogan's radars had seen the storm approaching, and he had recommended to McCain that the force turn south at ten knots to avoid it. McCain and Halsey ignored Bogan and entirely mishandled the force. Indeed, in contrast to Pete Mitscher's "professional" style of command, when McCain ran the task force "it was a goddam circus," according to Bogan. "He'd come up with one screwy idea after another." (Reynolds, *Fast Carriers*, 293–95; Bogan, "Kamikazes, Typhoons, and the China Sea," 241–42)

Clark worshipped Mitscher, had little to say about McCain, and was already questioning Halsey's command abilities. Aide Bob Reynolds likely reflected the boss's frustrations in a letter (to my parents and me) that Christmas Eve, as the *Hornet* again dropped the hook at Ulithi: "They have too many old men out here trying to run this show."

Actual age was hardly the problem—Halsey was 62, McCain 60; Spruance was 58 and Mitscher turned 58 a month later. (By contrast, Jocko was 51 and Bogan was 50.) Halsey and McCain simply *thought* and *acted* aged for reasons Reynolds hinted at in his letter:

> Lots has happened since we returned to the war zone. We were in the worst typhoon of the Pacific. Have been in two scrapes with the Japs. Losses very high on our side. These suicide planes of the Japs are really something. They very rarely miss their objective. And it seems that the objective is usually a carrier.

Admiral Nimitz (age 59) dropped in at Ulithi Christmas Day to check up on Halsey and to report his findings to a very displeased Ernie King (66).

The very next day TG 38.1 commander Alfred Montgomery (53) suffered a serious chest injury when he fell between his gig and the gangway of a carrier he was visiting at Ulithi, thereby depriving the fast carriers of his considerable abilities.

Partly because of Clark's former association with the *Yorktown*, Montgomery's flagship, Jocko was not allowed to replace him, so Radford (48) took over 38.1. (Reynolds, *Fast Carriers*, 295; Reynolds, *Fighting Lady*, 207)

Another "youthful"-thinking task group commander arrived at Christmastime, Rear Admiral Matt Gardner (47), aboard the *Enterprise*. The "Big E" had been converted into a night-operating carrier and now joined with the already night-equipped *Independence* to operate as TG 38.5 at night. During the day these two carriers cruised with Bogan's 38.2 of *Lexington*, *Hancock*, and *Hornet*, respective flagships of Bogan, McCain, and Clark. With Gardner, this meant four carrier admirals in one task group. Also, the first Marine Corps fighter squadrons reported aboard several day carriers.

On 30 December TF 38 sortied to cover MacArthur's landings at Lingayen Gulf on the west side of Luzon, scheduled for 9 January 1945. Because the fleet's "back" was to the South China Sea and adjacent landbased enemy air forces, the carriers ranged as far north as Formosa/Taiwan and Okinawa between the 3rd and 9th to neutralize them. Halsey then headed for French Indochina waters to sink two battleships fitted with short flight decks that had survived Halsey's attack on the "northern force" during the Leyte Gulf battle. He feared they might attack MacArthur's beachhead.

Jocko Clark shared the view of many officers that these two hybrid ships were already helpless and thus not worth attacking, especially when Japanese radio traffic revealed a large convoy east of the task force. Clark always thought—then and to the end of his life—it was comprised of 120 ships, but Alex Wilding on the *Yorktown* noted 20 marus and five escorts. (Diary, 10 January 1945) Either way, this was "a very juicy target," thought Clark, but Halsey did not want to betray his position so he let the convoy go—and never did find the hermaphrodite battleships! (Reynolds, *Fast Carriers*, 296–97)

Nevertheless, TF 38 planes decimated other enemy shipping and aircraft from Hong Kong to Saigon on the 12th and 13th until a monsoon forced Halsey further south. The strain of these demanding operations led Halsey to decide to avoid the storm-whipped waters north of Luzon by heading south then east through the confined Sibuyan Sea and Surigao Strait. Clark was completely baffled by this strange plan. Even Halsey's chief of staff, Jocko's old friend Rear Admiral Mick Carney, begged him not to do it—until Nimitz finally ordered Halsey to wait until the monsoon cleared, then head north of Luzon. (Taussig, *Warrior for Freedom*, 115)

The carriers then ranged between Formosa and Okinawa, pummeling Japanese airfields and shipping but against ferocious kamikaze counterattacks. On 21 January a suicider smacked into the *Ticonderoga*, killing 143 men and wounding Captain Dixie Kiefer and 201 others. Two more days of combat ended the carriers' and Halsey's role in the Philippine campaign, and TF 38 reentered Ulithi on the 25th—where all hands were sobered seeing the battered flight deck of the anchored *Ticonderoga*.

Pete Mitscher was there to greet Jocko as his premier task group commander for the final—and most deadly—push against Japan. Spruance relieved the exhausted Halsey in the two-platoon command shift. And Admiral Nimitz moved his headquarters forward from Pearl Harbor to Guam in order to better coordinate the campaigns against the "Jocko Jimas," Okinawa, and the Japanese homeland.

# EIGHTEEN

## On to Tokyo, 1945

ADMIRALS MITSCHER AND CLARK RESUMED COMMAND OF TASK Force 58 and Task Group 58.1 respectively at Ulithi on 27 January 1945. The campaign that lay before them was embodied in three names: Tokyo, Iwo Jima, Okinawa. Once the operation began, it would be incessant and brutal—the Japanese empire fighting for its very survival.

Clark's staff was the most experienced one among the fast carrier task groups. Those of Davison (58.2), Radford (58.4), and Gardner (58.5) all dated from after the Battle of the Philippine Sea, while Sherman's (58.3) had just reorganized after his extended leave stateside, giving Bogan a break. For this reason, as well as Mitscher's unbridled confidence in Clark as a leader, Jocko's group would always remain in the van—or bringing up the rear during the retirement—nearest the kamikaze and bomber bases.

And if any admirals and carrier captains at Ulithi doubted Clark's talents as a gruff leader they were shown a shining example of it the evening of 5 February on the *Yorktown*. The occasion was the fleet premiere of *The Fighting Lady*, introduced by Radford. The featured "star" was identified on film only as "Jocko," who now swelled with pride—as did several "costars" among the *Yorktown*'s crew. (Reynolds, *Fighting Lady*, 222–23) (This was about the same time that I—all of five years old—first viewed it, in southern California, according to a letter acknowledging the fact from my "Uncle Bob," 16 March 1945)

The timetable called for TF 58 to attack Tokyo and its environs for two days, 16–17 February, then join the escort carriers supporting the Marine Corps assault on Iwo Jima. Depending on the scale and effectiveness of Japanese resistance, and on damage to TF 58 ships and planes, the fast carriers would then range Asian coastal waters from Formosa to Tokyo before and during the Army's assault and conquest of Okinawa in April and May.

"JOCKO" ON THE WARPATH!
(DESTINATION: TOKYO)

P. D. Guttman

Mitscher replaced Jocko's detested "Romeo" radio call sign with the pleasing "Bull Durham"—for his preferred image of an embattled bull as well as the popular brand of tobacco that he used for his cigarettes.

Clark commanded four of Mitscher's 16 carriers—the three heavies *Hornet, Wasp,* and new *Bennington* (CV-20), and light carrier *Belleau Wood.* For the first time, he was assigned battleships—*Massachusetts* and *Indiana* under Rear Admiral J. F. "Fat Jack" Shafroth—for their much-needed anti-aircraft batteries. The cruiser division of Rear Admiral F. E. M. "Red" Whiting consisted of light cruisers *Vincennes* and *Miami* and antiaircraft cruiser *San Juan.* As usual, Clark was very junior to both black shoes Shafroth ('08) and Whiting ('12). Captain Jesse H. Carter ('21) commanded the 15-destroyer screen.

As the carriers prepared for battle, Clark had Tex McCrary fly him around Ulithi in a Kingfisher floatplane to get in his monthly flight time—and the extra pay that went with it. They would put down near each anchored ship of the task group and personally deliver operations orders. On one occasion, a whaleboat from tin can *DeHaven* maneuvered alongside the bobbing plane. Jocko climbed out on the wing to hand the bag of orders to an officer.

Suddenly, the admiral slipped and fell but grabbed the wing strut before he went over into the water. "Goddam you, Tex," he bellowed, "keep the goddammed plane steady!" The currents of the lagoon were not so obliging, and the destroyermen had to restrain their laughter as they muscled him back up onto the wing.

The new campaign brought a welcome guest to the *Hornet* on 6 February—Ernie Pyle, Jocko's old reporter friend. They had not seen each other since Clark's Anacostia days, and Ernie was now a famous war correspondent from the European theater. He refused Jocko's in-port stateroom and flag mess, preferring to live with his beloved enlisted men. Pyle brought Clark a copy of his best-selling book *Brave Men,* which he autographed, "Whoever would have thought that some day you would be an admiral and I would write a book."

But Ernie needed a quiet place in which to type his stories without any distractions. So Jocko gave him Bob Reynolds's stateroom while he wrote. Clark counseled his aide to give Pyle a bottle of good bourbon and let him write: "It's O.K. to lay on your bunk, but don't bother him; he hates officers!"

Reynolds took him down to the room and had him set his typewriter on the pullout drawer of the desk. Bob produced a full bottle of Early Times, broke open the lid of the cap, "and set the bottle on the desk. He'd take a sip out of it and set it on the floor."

Pyle: "You going to get some rest now?"

Reynolds: "Yeah, I'm gonna listen to that typewriter click away."

Bob fell asleep but awoke when the clicking stopped. He was amazed: "When the bottle was empty, the story was done!" And Ernie followed the same pattern the three days he was on board. After leaving the *Hornet* on 9 February, he made his way to the amphibious forces in order to join the troops bound for Okinawa.

TF 58 sortied from Ulithi next day and immediately commenced daily gunnery drills in anticipation of the kamikazes. Jocko had Red Sharp and Sugar Brown stand "watch on watch" at night because of their expert conning of the task group, alternating every four hours at the conn. Also, at 0400 every day he had Sharp check the secret Ultra message board to see what had come in during the night, withholding any "rough stuff" until he had had his breakfast.

The weather worsened each day, making flight operations increasingly difficult. On the 15th, as the distance to Tokyo shortened, Clark dispatched three destroyers ahead of the formation to reinforce the radar picket line for detecting bogeys. Late that afternoon the force increased speed to 20 knots for the final run-in toward Tokyo under cover of the overcast.

The first massive carrier attack on the Japanese capital was a complete surprise. Clark launched his fighter sweep into leaden skies at 0647 on 16 February, 136 miles from the Japanese capital. Half that distance was flown over airfields from which enemy fighters rose to meet the Navy's Hellcats and the Marine Corps' F4U Corsairs. Many zealous U.S. pilots forgot their teamwork discipline—the Thach weave—and instead, to their peril, attacked singly. Five veteran pilots from the *Wasp* alone were among 60 lost that day, some claimed by the heavy flak. By contrast, however, Japan lost 341 planes in aerial combat.

The low ceiling frustrated subsequent bombing strikes aimed at airplane factories, so these planes had to divert to secondary targets that pilots could see. One of Clark's strike leaders even resorted to dropping his bombs into the sea. When he landed, Jocko "took him to task."

> He said that he did not want to kill innocent civilians, an inhumanity which of course I did not want either. But any damage to the enemy in war contributed to destroying his will to fight. I told [him] he should have dropped his bombs on Mount Fuji [Japan's sacred extinct volcano], visible above the overcast, rather than waste them.

Very few snoopers or kamikazes even approached the task force, and the destroyer *Brush* shot down the only one that came near Clark's group. Gardner's two night carriers, the prewar *Saratoga* and *Enterprise,* launched strikes

Famous war correspondent Ernie Pyle, Clark's old friend, is escorted from the *Hornet* by Bob Reynolds after a three-day visit; Ulithi lagoon, 9 February 1945. *Bureau of Aeronautics*

at dusk, although they could not see anything even to aim at. Nevertheless, their presence overhead discouraged enemy interceptors from taking off. At last, the exclusive Japanese proclivity for night air operations had been stolen and turned against them.

In spite of the rain and overcast Mitscher ordered the next day's follow-up strikes on schedule. Red Sharp as TG 58.1 duty officer passed the order to Clark's four carriers. After about a fourth of the planes had taken off, Raöul Waller appeared on the flag bridge. Surveying the mediocre flying conditions, he ordered Sharp to stop the launching.

"The admiral's not going to like this," Red remarked to Waller, with whom he had always worked smoothly.

Waller replied simply that the weather was "terrible" for flying. Sharp, obviously accustomed to Clark's "nose" for weather conditions, agreed that they were "a little questionable" but not dangerous.

When Clark appeared, his trusted chief of staff informed him of the "stand down" order. Jocko simply said to Sharp, "Go ahead. Get the planes up."

Red resumed the launching as Clark and Waller went below. Presently, the admiral returned alone, having had a set-to with Waller, and said, "Now, look, Sharp,"—whom Clark never called "Red"—"I've had a little under-standing with the chief of staff. And as far as flight operations on the bridge are concerned, *you're* the boss. You and I have had an understanding on this since we've been working out here for months now. We know what we want to do. So I don't think we'll have any more trouble with the chief of staff."

Clark's absolute faith in Waller never wavered, no more than did his respect for Sharp. He simply knew how to balance their respective talents as he shaped the specific responsibilities of each member of the staff. Clark's final wartime staff was set, even though former *Yorktown* dynamo Lieu-tenant Commander Joe Tucker, "bored to death" at a desk in Washington, wrote to Bob Reynolds begging for a transfer: "I'd rather be with 'Jocko' than with anyone else in the world." But the admiral had been promised a stateside training command at the end of the campaign.

The 17 February morning attacks on Tokyo included dogfights above the cloud layer and inaccurate bombing of factories beneath it. At midday the weather closed in, leading Mitscher to cancel the afternoon strikes, and the task force turned south toward the Jimas. Clark and *Hornet* skipper Artie Doyle agreed that too many fighters on antikamikaze CAP had weak-ened the strike forces. For more fighter planes they joined Radford in rec-ommending that each light carrier trade in its nine TBMs in order to have all fighters, 36. It was not accepted. (Reynolds, *Fast Carriers,* 334)

Clark's return to the Jimas was devoted to supporting the Marines' 19 February assault on Iwo—fanatically resisted—and keeping Chichi and Haha neutralized against planes staging in from Japan. Fast carrier strikes began on the 18th and continued for five days. Enemy bombers and kamikazes attacked day and night, eluding defensive CAPs, to cripple night carrier *Saratoga* and sink one of the 11 escort carriers flying close air support missions.

The furious battle for Iwo—where the defenders in caves avoided the bombs—was won on the ground, and Admiral Mitscher soon shared with his task group commanders the stunning photograph of the Marines raising the flag atop Mt. Suribachi. Admiral Spruance released most of TF 58 the night of 22 February for more attacks on Tokyo two days later. But the foul weather obscured targets there on the 25th and at Nagoya the next day, leading Mitscher to cancel further efforts.

Fortunately, the weather did not affect the new B-29 Superfortress AAF bombers operating daily from airfields in the Marianas to fly above the clouds and hit Japanese cities and defenses. Their massive formations could be observed from the carriers, as during refueling after the 17 February strikes when "we got to see some 300 B29s pass overhead on their way to Tokyo. That was some sight to see." (Bob Reynolds to me, 16 March 1945) When enemy flak crippled a B-29 it could now make an emergency landing on Iwo Jima—the primary reason for the island's capture.

Mitscher swung TF 58 south to photograph the next target—Okinawa—before a breather at Ulithi. Clark began his 23-knot run to Okinawa on 28 February. Next day, 1 March, brought clear skies for the photos of Okinawa and strikes there and at other islands of the Ryukyu group. Mitscher had Clark detach Admiral Whiting with his cruisers and tin cans to bombard Okino Daito Shima during the night.

Task Force 58 then retired, reaching Ulithi on 4 March to prepare for the Okinawa operation. Because the landings and prolonged conquest of the island by the U.S. Army would occur within range of enemy planes based in Japan, the fleet could not return to Ulithi periodically to replenish. Instead, every three days a task group would withdraw just beyond enemy aircraft range to refuel and to carry out underway replenishment of all supplies and ammunition, including bombs. Lieutenant John Roosevelt, Clark's first and only staff supply officer, had his hands full.

Unlike this quiet Roosevelt, his brother Frank Jr., skipper of a destroyer escort, was "a wild-assed bastard." At Ulithi he would steam right up to the *Hornet* (ignoring speed limits within the lagoon), slow down, and yell over the bullhorn, "Hey, how about dinner tonight aboard the carrier?!" The OOD would convey the message to the staff, which invited him accordingly, and he "shot away" in his ship—returning later for chow. (Conversation with Bob Reynolds)

Jocko worked his gun crews relentlessly, anticipating the inevitable kamikaze onslaught off Okinawa. Waiting at Ulithi for target practice were gas-operated, radio-controlled, and highly maneuverable midget drones. In Clark's task group the battleship *Massachusetts* catapulted them over the other ships in simulated kamikaze maneuvers. Admiral Shafroth invited Clark aboard to witness the first use of these. Jocko was so impressed that he convinced Mitscher to require all ships to utilize them.

Red Whiting protested, and he got Mitscher to let his cruisers get machinery overhauls instead. All the other gun crews fired on the drones, although Clark had several of them placed on Whiting's flagship *Vincennes* for gunnery practice en route to Okinawa. During one of those days at sea a drone got out of control and crashed into the *Vincennes*. Jocko immediately signaled Mitscher, "Suicide drone crashed *Vincennes*." Mitscher knowingly replied, "Maybe *Vincennes* needs some gunnery practice." Whiting learned quickly, and his flagship gun crews would shoot down many bandits over the ensuing weeks.

The respite at Ulithi enabled Clark to consider his future. He was long overdue for shoreside duty, having been in and out of combat since August 1943. Mitscher wanted him to remain with TF 58 until the end of the Okinawa operation, and that depended on the anticipated fanatical resistance of the Japanese. During his recent leave Clark had been guaranteed a training command. He had lobbied for Jacksonville, in order to be reunited there with his daughters while keeping them in the local schools. But Andrew C. McFall was already entrenched there, and Jocko eventually got Corpus Christi, Texas. (Letter to M.C., 5 March 1945)

Clark also canvassed his staff, all of whom except for Waller were equally due for a change away from combat. He could only tell them that they would return to the States during the summer. But he elicited several promises that, no matter what, they would remain with him until July. (Bob Reynolds to me, 30 April 1945, and to his brother Bill, 19 May 1945)

Evidence of Clark's eventual relief arrived at Ulithi in the person of Rear Admiral Tommy Sprague. He was assigned to the *Wasp* in makee-learn status, expected to relieve Jocko as Commander Task Group 58.1 some time during the Okinawa campaign. Sprague would become the first fast carrier task group commander not to be senior to Clark; they had been classmates at Annapolis.

On 10 March Mitscher convened his task group admirals on board flagship *Bunker Hill*, including Sprague and Gerry Bogan, recalled prematurely from leave to be available. Mitscher confessed to them that he had no idea what the Japanese would do next. He did not have to wait long to find out. The very next evening Clark was roaming the forward end of *Hornet's* flight deck "when I heard an airplane passing directly over my head. Looking up, less than 20 feet away I saw the two red balls under the wings of a Japanese kamikaze."

It was heading straight for the carrier *Randolph* anchored in the berth next to *Hornet* and taking on ammunition starboard quarter aft under a cargo light. The suicider hit the mark, fires erupted, then explosions, causing many casualties. A second kamikaze crashed harmlessly into an islet, both having flown over 800 miles. The heavy damage put the *Randolph* out of action—but only for three weeks, thanks to herculean repair workers.

The calamity left idle the *Randolph's* Air Group 12, giving Jocko the opportunity to test a brainstorm. Because the task group always had so many planes over each target, he believed that one pilot should coordinate them in order to improve efficiency. Just the man was now available—Air Group 12's skipper Charlie Crommelin, who had so effectively coordinated Air Group Five's strikes from the *Yorktown* until wounded over Mili in the Gilberts 16 months earlier.

Clark requested Admiral Mitscher to assign Crommelin temporarily as TG 58.1 strike coordinator as an experiment. Mitscher agreed, and Charlie reported aboard the *Hornet* at the same time as its new Air Group 17. Crommelin had doggedly recovered from his wounds, although his injured eye was not perfect. Yet he had bagged a Zero over Japan one month before, and Clark "had great faith in him to do the job to perfection." (Bruce and Leonard, *Crommelin's Thunderbirds*, 192–93)

It would be a challenge indeed. With the invasion of Okinawa set for 1 April, TF 58 would range the waters north and south of the island. Planes and ships were to engage kamikazes and conventional aircraft primarily from Kyushu, southernmost of the home islands, as well as attack their airfields. Round-the-clock air operations were expected, meaning that each heavy carrier's Bat team would be kept busy. The *Enterprise,* the only remaining night carrier, was assigned to Radford's task group.

On 14 March Clark's TG 58.1 sortied from Ulithi in its customary position in the van. It was comprised of the same four carriers and two battleships as before, with the light cruiser *Vicksburg* in place of *San Juan,* which was still undergoing overhaul at Ulithi. One additional tin can increased the screen to 16 in all. Constant gunnery practice and reinforced CAPs kept all hands busy day and night.

Crommelin coordinated the task group's initial strikes against Kyushu on 18 March. Kamikazes and conventional bombers responded in kind, damaging three fast carriers (including the *Yorktown*) though none in

Clark's group. After midnight, bogeys began to register on task force radars. Suddenly, at 0450 on the 19th—with TG 58.1 only 38 miles off the coast of Japan—snoopers began dropping flares. The screen opened fire as Jocko rang up 22, then 25 knots and made 12 course changes in one half-hour period to dodge bombers and suiciders.

The CAP and initial strike planes were in the launch spot just as a kamikaze plunged into the sea a thousand yards astern of the *Hornet,* and *Bennington's* gunners brought down two more. Then the fighter sweep took off for Kyushu on a 134-mile flight. Over Japan they ran into a swarm of what turned out to be some of Japan's last surviving veteran fighter pilots— and suffered losses accordingly. But the hundreds of Hellcats and Corsairs otherwise prevailed. Jocko even dispatched an OS2U Kingfisher floatplane from the *Massachusetts* to pick up a downed flyer in Kagoshima Bay, "practically in the enemy's own back yard."

Meanwhile, the ceiling over the task group remained under 500 feet, making Clark's ships "sitting ducks" for their attackers. Suddenly, about 0700, Jocko noticed a patch of clear sky to the east and immediately turned the task group toward it. He simultaneously informed Mitscher, who ordered the other three groups to follow. Also, Mitscher informed Jocko that the *Franklin,* Ralph Davison's flagship in 58.2, had just taken two bomb hits and was burning furiously.

Just two minutes after that, when Clark's 58.1 was about ten miles short of the break in the clouds, an enemy bomber suddenly dived out of them. As Jocko watched helplessly, it dropped a bomb squarely on the *Wasp,* killing more than 200 men and wounding as many others. But *Wasp's* Captain Oscar Weller and his crew had their ship operating again within 15 minutes. This hit turned out to be the only one ever suffered by a ship under Clark's overall command.

Meanwhile, long-range searches had discovered Japanese carriers and other warships at Kure on the Inland Sea between the home islands of Shikoku and Honshu. Crommelin led the ensuing strike, whose bombers inflicted heavy damage to light carrier *Ryuho* and slightly damaged the battleship *Yamato* and heavy carrier *Amagi.* But flak and a bevy of Japan's last experienced fighter pilots brought down 13 of Clark's planes.

Further attack missions were cancelled so that the task force could concentrate on defending its own ships and covering those already stricken. The heavy cruiser *Pittsburgh* took the stricken *Franklin* in tow, and Mitscher assigned Clark and his task group to provide a defensive CAP over them. (Stephen Jurika interview #18, 643–44) As Jocko continuously maneuvered his vessels to avoid enemy planes his fighters shot down many of them in several separate raids. But during one the battleship *Massachu-*

Bombs from Task Group 58.1 planes coordinated by Charlie Crommelin score a near miss on the new Japanese carrier *Amagi* in the harbor of Kure on the Inland Sea, 19 March 1945. An SB2C can be seen (far right of *Amagi*) recovering after its bomb missed one of several anchored oil tankers. *U.S. Navy photo*

*setts* and cruiser *Vincennes* used their AA batteries almost simultaneously to splash three attackers each. And as the *Bennington* dodged another, that ship actually managed to land one of its own damaged planes downwind.

For the rest of the day enemy aircraft concentrated on trying to finish off the *Franklin* but failed to score another hit. The carrier's martinet of a captain, Leslie H. Gehres (a mustang and social friend of Jocko's a decade earlier), had failed to initiate precautionary damage-control measures early enough and then tried to put the blame on the crew, more than 700 of whom died in the conflagration. Nevertheless, heroic damage control saved the *Franklin*, a feat, recalled Clark, that "stands out as one of the great accomplishments of all time."

As Mitscher slowly withdrew his bloodied task force, Clark's group brought up the rear—remaining closest to the enemy as usual. Bogeys continued to pester the force all day 20 March, during which Jocko's planes searched for downed pilots. Just after midnight on the 21st the *Yorktown* in Radford's group launched two night fighters. Radford immediately passed fighter direction to Charlie Ridgway on the *Hornet*. At 0312 Charlie vectored one of the Hellcats to shoot down a Betty 35 miles to the north. (Reynolds, *Fighting Lady*, 258–62)

During midmorning Ridgway directed *Wasp*'s CAP to shoot down one bogey, while fighters from other task groups splashed two more near 58.1. Simultaneously, Ridgway was confused by a blip directly overhead—a Tinian-based AAF B-24 Liberator bomber, as it turned out. Fortunately, no guns fired at it.

Suddenly, in early afternoon, cruiser *Vincennes*'s radar picked up a large formation 90 miles out. Ridgway vectored the CAP, which Clark increased to 24 F6Fs, and Sherman added more from his 58.3. Fighting 30 of the *Belleau Wood* made the intercept at 60 miles—no fewer than 27 Bettys escorted by perhaps 17 Zeros. The latter tried to break away, but the Bettys were weighted down by what appeared to be "piloted bombs"—Clark's ships were the first to encounter them. (Clark interview, *Tulsa Daily World*, 1 July 1945) They were indeed manned suicide bombs—what the Americans soon labeled "baka," Japanese for fool.

All were defenseless against the Hellcat pilots, who handily destroyed all but one baka-laden Betty and most of the Zekes, which however shot down two F6Fs. This desperate suicide device had never gotten close enough to the carriers to be used and would in any case never be tried again in larger than three- or four-plane formations. Unlike the conventional kamikazes, they proved totally ineffective.

Task Force 58 withdrew overnight to refuel and reorganize for the Okinawa landings. Its planes had destroyed perhaps 500 Japanese aircraft on and over Kyushu and adjacent waters, but at a cost of some 100 of its own, due primarily to heavy flak. The enemy's air forces were sufficiently humbled at least temporarily, enabling the carriers to concentrate on supporting the assault forces. Mitscher reshuffled the task force on 22 March some 150 miles southeast of Okinawa.

Clark remained in *Hornet* but had to release the *Wasp* for repairs, forcing Tommy Sprague to shift his flag to the *Bennington*. Veteran light carrier

*San Jacinto* filled the gap, skippered by Captain M. H. "Ugly Mike" Kernodle. Light carrier *Belleau Wood,* Captain W. G. "Red" Tomlinson, remained, as did Jack Shafroth's two battleships. Rear Admiral L. J. "Jerry" Wiltsie reported with his heavy cruisers *Baltimore* and *Pittsburgh.* Captain Thomas H. Hederman took over the screen, its two light cruisers augmented by the *San Juan* and *St. Louis,* its destroyers increased by three to 19.

Sherman's TG 58.3 was enlarged to five carriers, while Radford's 58.1 kept its four. Ralph Davison took the damaged *Wasp* all the way back to Pearl Harbor, while the *Franklin* steamed to the States and out of the war. At the same time four British heavy carriers joined up as another task group. Such momentous changes in midocean demonstrated the incredible staying power of the fast carriers even in the midst of fanatical enemy retaliation.

The Japanese now broadly exploited an earlier discovery that U.S. radars could not detect planes flying just above the water. They approached from altitude and then came in low, forcing the ships to depend increasingly on visual spotters instead of radar. Nevertheless, on 23 March, when 58.1 commenced three days of Crommelin-led strikes against Okinawa, lesser islands, and shipping, the CAP and destroyer screen knocked down all attacking bombers and kamikazes.

The morning of the 24th Clark detached Shafroth's two battleships and six cans to participate in the first day's prelanding coastal bombardment of Okinawa. Then, an hour before noon, one of his search planes reported an enemy convoy northwest of Amami O Shima. Two hours later Jocko sent off 112 planes to attack it—two troop transports, an ammunition ship, and five escorts. With bombs and torpedoes, the planes blew up the ammo ship and handily sank the rest.

Admiral Mitscher later commended Clark for this achievement, "Well, you earned another Navy Cross," remembering his award for the convoy his planes had destroyed in the Jimas months before.

"I've never had a Legion of Merit," Jocko joked, "so just give me a Legion of Merit. It's a pretty medal."

Mitscher acceded to this off-hand request but waited until Clark's planes sank another two destroyers and splashed several bandits in the southern Ryukyus four days later. This added success strengthened the medal's special words lauding his "aggressive attacks, careful planning and indomitable fighting spirit."

That night of the 24th, Shafroth's battleships returned to the formation, followed by Rear Admiral Louis E. Denfeld's bombardment force of the Navy's three newest fast battleships—*Missouri, New Jersey,* and *Wisconsin*—as well as Admiral Spruance's flagship heavy cruiser *Indianapolis* and four cans. The swollen task formation of four carriers, five battleships, eight

Swinging side to side, to the amusement and wonderment of onlookers, Clark crosses between his flagship and a destroyer going the same speed in a high-line canvas basket for a meeting on another carrier (via another high-line). (Photo courtesy of Patriots Point Museum) *U.S. Navy photo*

cruisers, and 24 destroyers was the largest Clark ever commanded tactically, if only for one night. *Indianapolis* and *St. Louis* left next morning, Denfeld's force a day after that.

Everything was running well, although Jocko's staff worried that Charlie Crommelin was being overworked as the only strike coordinator. They discussed it with him the night of 27 March, suggesting that he rotate with other pilots to give them experience. He was scheduled to lead two strikes next day, so Tex McCrary offered to let someone else do it. Charlie replied, "Let me fly the one in the morning, and take me off the one in the afternoon."

While Crommelin was leading next morning's strike on Okinawa, Clark received a message from Admiral Spruance at 0933: Japanese fleet units were apparently heading southeast of Kyushu, presumably including superbattleship *Yamato*. They were reportedly moving down toward the west side of Okinawa. Jocko immediately turned his task group north at high speed, advising Spruance and Mitscher—as he had done before— "unless otherwise directed."

His two superiors did not question his initiative, but they did get into a heated argument over the TBS that was overheard by air ops officer McCrary and the staff. Spruance wanted a surface engagement and ordered preparations for his battleships to move from the east to intercept the enemy force on the west side of the island. Mitscher questioned such unnecessary risking of lives in a gunnery duel when airplanes could do the job better and more economically. Old Pete indicated that he would launch a bombing strike regardless of any order by Spruance to the contrary.

Clark said to McCrary, "Where's Crommelin? Tell him to get back here immediately." Jocko not only wanted Charlie to coordinate the attack on the *Yamato* but was recalling many of his planes from their Okinawa shore targets in order to rearm them against ships. Tex relayed the message via CAP fighters to Crommelin and got in reply a request from Charlie to make one more photo run over Okinawa. Clark consented, reluctantly.

In the event, Crommelin collided with another photo plane he had obviously not seen—due likely to his impaired eye. The news profoundly shocked Clark, who rated Crommelin as "the bravest man I encountered during the entire war." He showed his loyalty to Charlie by listing him as only "missing in action" so that his widow could receive benefits for a year. (Conversation with Raöul Waller)

As 58.1 headed north, Clark's planes found nothing. When they were 255 miles from the *Yamato*'s supposed position he launched a search-strike with orders to attack enemy airfields on Kyushu if the *Yamato* could not be found. He had Shafroth prepare his battleships for a surface battle if the bombers could at least cripple the enemy ships. The strike planes found nothing and went on to hit Kyushu.

Still hopeful, Clark launched a 146-fighter afternoon sweep-search after having the pilots briefed on night-landing procedures. They had already qualified after the 20 June 1944 recovery fiasco in the Philippine Sea, and the half of this flight that had to return aboard in the dark suffered no losses—immensely pleasing to all hands, especially their admiral.

This success only encouraged Jocko to launch yet another fighter search at midnight, which sighted the *Yamato* and other warships at dawn of the 29th—safely anchored at Kure naval base. An equally frustrated Mitscher signaled Clark, "How do you like going on a wild goose chase?"

Reply: "It was not a wild goose chase. I found the *Yamato*. She has not yet come out. Otherwise we would have done battle."

Then 58.1 resumed station at the north end of the task force—closest to enemy airfields on Kyushu—and bore the brunt of air attacks the next several days. The Army landed on Okinawa on 1 April and moved inland with relative ease under cover of planes from TF 58 and a dozen escort carriers. To give Clark's task group a breather, Mitscher shifted it to the south end on the 3rd, relieving the British carriers attacking the Sakishima Islands. Instead of a rest, however, 58.1 caught the brunt of Kyushu-based bombers that survived runs on the carriers to reach Formosa and then head back to Jocko's group.

The Japanese did not react in force to the Okinawa landings until 6 April. Just after sunup, large blips began to fill the radar screens of 58.1 and Sherman's 58.3 (58.4 was refueling to the east). Simultaneously, the *Yamato* was reportedly leading other gun ships south toward Okinawa. Admiral Mitscher chose to meet the kamikaze menace first by ordering all flight deck crews to strike below their bombers and torpeckers, enabling the fighters to have free rein all day long dealing with the suicide planes. He ordered the destroyer screens to prepare to use torpedoes against the enemy warships if and when they appeared.

At ten minutes before noon the reinforced CAP of Clark's and Sherman's task groups waded into the first of seven raids that day. All ships of 58.1 kept firing almost continuously as they twisted and turned. The *Bennington* suffered steerage malfunctions even as a kamikaze splashed nearby. What turned out to be a Hellcat trying to land drew heavy fire: shrapnel hit the *Hornet,* causing damage and injuries. Flak brought down a bandit just 50 yards in front of the *Belleau Wood.*

About 1315 the AA batteries almost simultaneously shot down three kamikazes inside the task formation, a fourth again just missing *Belleau Wood,* while yet a fifth crashed near the *San Jacinto*'s bow. The destroyer

*Taussig* in the screen received a near miss by a bomber set afire by a *Bennington* fighter. The Japanese pilot bailed out and was picked up by *Taussig*, which transferred him to the *Hornet*. There he boasted to Lieutenant Beath that another mass attack would occur on the 11th, information that Clark passed up the line.

The onslaught did not finally end until almost midnight. No ships had been sunk and none of 58.1's picket destroyers had been hit. Clark informed Mitscher that his pilots and gunners had shot down 154 enemy planes and three probables—Jocko's single highest day score during the war. What was more, top squadron honors went to a 24-plane light carrier squadron instead of one of the big carriers with 72 fighters. It was *Belleau Wood*'s VF-30 with 47 kills. Ship's captain Red Tomlinson radioed Jocko: "Does this exceed the bag limit?"

"Negative," replied Clark the lifelong crack rifleman. "This is open season. There is no limit. Well done."

During the night 58.4 rejoined. This gave Mitscher all three task groups from which he drew no fewer than 386 planes to deal with the *Yamato*, a light cruiser, and eight destroyers. Admiral Spruance prepared for a gunnery duel, but since TF 58 was closest to the enemy force Mitscher had Clark launch predawn searches to the north to make it a carrier battle. At 0823 Sherman's *Essex* planes sighted the *Yamato* force, whereupon Mitscher ordered the task force north at 25 knots.

Clark instructed Commander E. G. Konrad, skipper of the *Hornet* air group, to arm his TBMs with torpedoes rather than bombs "to let the water in." At 1018—238 miles from the target—58.1 began launching deckload strikes. Its planes were the first to reach the target an hour and a half later. They dived through the early afternoon overcast.

Jocko's torpeckers put at least one, maybe more, "fish" into the side of the *Yamato*, causing it to list. It increased with ensuing hits by other air groups. But the largest warship in the world did not roll over until 1423, after *Yorktown*'s VT-9 planted six torpedoes into its exposed underbelly. The cruiser and four tin cans were also sunk. (Reynolds, *Fighting Lady*, 272–83)

Over the next two months TF 58 continued to destroy hundreds of enemy planes and support the troops ashore, while kamikaze hits caused several more carriers to be withdrawn to Ulithi for repairs. Clark's ships were never among them, and much of the credit for their relative safety was due to FDO Ridgway, who occasionally also vectored fighters of other task groups.

Late on 7 April Gerry Bogan reported back to battery with three repaired carriers to re-form TG 58.2. Jocko gave him heavy cruisers *Baltimore* and *Pittsburgh* plus destroyers. But that task group survived as a unit only ten days,

Torpeckers from Clark's task group plant at least one, if not more, "fish" into the side of the 75,000-ton *Yamato*, the largest warship in the world, seen trying to evade its assailants early in the afternoon of 7 April 1945. These hits caused the superbattleship to develop a list, exposing her underbelly to fatal blows by six TBMs from Jocko's beloved "fighting lady" *Yorktown* about an hour later. *U.S. Navy photo*

being dissolved again due to more kamikaze hits. (ComCarDiv Two War Diary, correcting Reynolds, *Fast Carriers*, 341–42) At that time Clark got back his two heavy cruisers plus another one, the *Quincy*.

Bogan's availability was critical, inasmuch as the superb Ralph Davison had not returned to battery after delivering the *Wasp* to Pearl Harbor. A shy and quiet, though efficient, tactician and task group leader, Davison had been a lifetime bachelor, which was highly unusual for prominent naval officers of the era. Like Jocko, he enjoyed word challenge games with his staff during breaks—for example, defining "retromingent" and "meretricious." His only fault was relaxing ashore by getting drunk—"not nasty drunk but thoroughly, joyfully, playfully, even silly drunk." (According to his former chief of staff, then Captain James S. Russell, letter to author, April 1966) Such an incident, and perhaps a sexual misdeed, had cost him his combat command. Worse for Clark, Davison was transferred to the training command at Jacksonville that Jocko wanted.

Bogan remained on standby on the *Randolph*, while Rear Admiral C. A. F. "Ziggy" Sprague soon reported in makee-learn status on the *Ticonderoga*. He had been the most heroic of the escort carrier admirals at the Battle of Leyte Gulf. Tommy Sprague (no relation) continued as makee-learn in *Bennington*, with Jocko periodically passing him tactical command to gain practical experience. Clark and both Spragues were Academy classmates, Jocko and Tommy age 51, Ziggy 49. The younger men were taking over.

A different kind of blow than kamikazes struck the fleet before dawn on 14 April when it received word that President Roosevelt had died. Owen Sowerwine handed the message to Jocko, who immediately went to John Roosevelt's stateroom, woke him up, and handed him the dispatch. With the *Hornet* now taking on fuel from a Guam-based tanker, Clark offered to put John on it. From Guam he could grab a plane to Hawaii, thence home to be with the family.

"My place is here," the son of the late president replied simply, a devotion to duty that Jocko deeply admired. A dispatch soon arrived from mother Eleanor saying that John's father would have wanted him to "remain on station and do your duty." After the war Jocko had occasion to tell Mrs. Roosevelt—much to her satisfaction—that her son had made his decision before her message had been received.

On 15 April Mitscher sent many fighters on a sweep over Kyushu simply to draw more kamikazes to the task force and away from the amphibious shipping and the troops battling fanatical resistance ashore on Okinawa. Next day they came, focusing on the picket destroyers, and Jocko's group knocked 72 of them out of the sky.

At night a snooper eluded the heavy flak of the entire formation as it passed overhead, only to be brought down by the tin can *Taussig* on the picket line. Clark signaled *Taussig*, whose call sign was "Terrific": "Terrific, you are terrific!"

While Clark's planes struck targets on Okinawa on the 18th, Radford asked for assistance against a reported enemy submarine. Jocko sent destroyer *Collett* to help the *Mertz*. Together, they sank it. Otherwise, news from one of Okinawa's satellite islets, Ie Shima, was heartbreaking. Ernie Pyle had been killed by a Japanese machine gun; the enlisted men had lost a buddy. Three days later, en route to refuel, Jocko had cruiser *San Juan* bombard another smaller island, Minami Daito.

The Japanese army had dug in at Shuri Castle and adjacent points, and Marine Corps F4U Corsairs were landed at recently captured airstrips to help the escort and fast carriers. But they too were soon preoccupied battling kamikazes, so that Rear Admiral Mel Pride—who replaced Captain Dick Whitehead in the upgraded close air support command on 18 April—called in heavy carrier strikes on Shuri next day. Shuri and its cave network held on tenaciously and would have to be taken by ground forces at heavy cost. (Reynolds, *Fast Carriers*, 342–43)

The destroyers also took endless poundings supporting the big ships. Unusual by this point in the war, a single Japanese torpecker attacked Clark's picket line. It dropped its fish just before passing over destroyer *Brush*. The torpedo bounced off the water then went right through the ship and exploded harmlessly in the air after exiting. Not one man was killed, and the ship was left with a clean hole through it. Sadly, en route to Ulithi for repairs it broke apart in heavy seas and sank.

Another can (name unknown) on the picket line suffered such severe damage that it began to sink. When the *Hornet* received its call for help Jocko immediately told Red Sharp to ring up 28 knots for the entire task group to steam up there—perhaps 50 miles—to save the crew and the ship if possible. "Jocko would go to no end to rescue somebody." When the group arrived, the can was down by the stern, but Clark had a cruiser stand by, send over medical supplies, and take it in tow. Crew *and* ship were saved.

Foul weather curtailed air operations so dramatically that on 27 April Admiral Mitscher detached 58.1 to return to Ulithi for a ten-day period of rest, overhaul, and replenishment. Clark conducted gunnery exercises en route, an unpopular chore for the pilots who had to pull the target sleeves. The task group entered the lagoon on the afternoon of the 30th after 47 consecutive days at sea.

Jocko's orders were to become Chief of Naval Air Intermediate Training at Corpus Christi, Texas. But Mitscher insisted to Admiral Nimitz that

Clark remain as his ace task group leader until the Okinawa campaign ended. Clark stayed on.

Ulithi enabled him to throw a big party on the beach at Mog Mog for his "Bull Durham" admirals and ship captains. The admirals posed giddily wet from sweat, beer, and whiskey: Clark, Shafroth, Whiting, Wiltsie, and Sprague. When it ended Jocko, *Hornet*'s Artie Doyle, and *Belleau Wood*'s Red Tomlinson, an "old pal" from prewar days, lingered. Presently, a Filipino mess boy happened along who they promptly designated "Ambassador of the Philippines" and posed with him for photos. The mood was joyous.

Another party presently joined them. Its senior officer was Vice Admiral Jesse B. Oldendorf. As the hero for having destroyed the Japanese southern force at Leyte Gulf, he was revered by everyone, and he became the center of attention. A cruiser division commander was with him, Rear Admiral Charles Turner Joy (whom his peers addressed as "Charles"; later, during the Korean War, he preferred "Turner").

As everyone put away more drinks, Joy blurted out a common frustration of black-shoe nonaviators, "I think I ought to be able to command a carrier task force."

"Why yes, admiral," remarked Red Tomlinson, "you could command a task force if you can qualify. There are only ten reasons why you couldn't qualify: you have to make ten landings on a carrier and three of them at night."

That ended the conversation, leaving Joy very unhappy. But all naval aviators of the day believed strongly that one had to experience naval operations from the cockpit before one could lead carriers.

Jocko returned to the *Hornet*, but Oldendorf's barge hit a buoy and he broke his collarbone (not a serious injury, as he soon took command of a surface striking force). Next day Clark jokingly upbraided Tomlinson and Doyle for ruining the party by getting drunk, cavorting with the Philippine ambassador, angering Joy, and causing Oldendorf's injury!

On pulling the hook from Ulithi on 9 May, the *Hornet* shared good news with the entire fleet—Germany had surrendered! "But it doesn't make a damn bit of difference to us out here," Bob Reynolds wrote to his brother Bill (19 May 1945). He spoke for all hands, who believed that Japan's fanatical resistance would never end.

Admiral Mitscher experienced this dramatically on 11 May when a kamikaze slammed into his flagship *Bunker Hill*, killing more than 350 men, including 13 of his own staff. He shifted to the *Enterprise*, only to have a suicider smack into the ship three days later. The bald admiral remarked to ops officer Flatley, "Jimmy, tell my task group commanders that if the Japs keep this up they're going to grow hair on my head yet." They

# BULL DURHAM ADMIRALS

Party time on Ulithi Atoll in early May 1945 was a welcome break from the grueling Okinawa campaign for the admirals of Task Group 58.1, which was code-named "Bull Durham." Feeling no pain are, *left to right*, Red Whiting, Jocko, Fat Jack Shafroth, Jerry Wiltsie, and Tommy Sprague. *U.S. Navy photo* then moved to the *Randolph* where they joined Gerry Bogan. (Reynolds, *Fast Carriers*, 345)

Clark arrived on line with his task group on 12 May and next day resumed operations off Okinawa. He soon had to dispatch light cruisers *Vicksburg* and *Vincennes* to provide additional shore bombardment and eventually had them replaced by *Atlanta* and *Duluth*. The number of air attacks steadily declined, however, and the Army captured Shuri Castle ashore before month's end, heralding the end of the campaign.

The fighting abated so dramatically that on 26 May Clark received no requests for air support ashore, nor did kamikaze attacks occur. Jocko was so encouraged that he ordered the task group to assume "holiday routine except for refueling destroyers."

Captain Tom Hederman of the screen spoke for all exhausted hands in a signal to Clark, "See Hebrews 13, verse 8."

On checking the Holy Bible, Jocko read the passage: "Jesus Christ, the same yesterday, today, and forever."

Jocko passed it on to the entire task group, adding, "No irreverence intended."

Then he sent another message to Mitscher, misquoted as "What the hell are we doing out here anyway?" (But he wished he had said it that way.)

Mitscher replied in kind, "We are a high-speed stationary target for the Japanese air force."

By this time, Clark had learned the disturbing news that Admirals Spruance and Mitscher were suddenly about to relinquish command of the fleet and carriers to Halsey and McCain. Jocko regarded such a change in the midst of an operation most unusual. He figured Halsey simply wanted to get back in the war before it ended, and he discussed it over the TBS with Radford. Clark told him he "did not want to be party to that other team."

But he had no choice. The two-platoon shift occurred at sea on 27–28 May, a sudden change that left even Mitscher in the dark about whether he might even remain a while longer. Neither did he know which admirals would command the four carrier task groups at the start of the final campaign against Japan one month hence.

Sherman would be leaving after taking his task group back to Ulithi— after its record 87 days at sea. Clark would soon follow. Jimmy Flatley wrote a letter to Jocko on the 28th: "We are all so proud of you and your outfit that it hurts to leave you. . . . Can you use a junior Captain at Corpus Christi?" Flatley had this very day received word of his promotion to the rank.

Flatley simultaneously sent a separate and heartfelt letter "To All of Admiral Clark's Staff" expressing not only his views but those of Mitscher and chief of staff Commodore Arleigh Burke:

From where I sit, in a relatively easy job, your ability, planning, administration, and operations have been outstanding in Task Force Fifty-
Eight. I can tell you your just being around when the going was tough
has always been a source of comfort and confidence to all of us. I am
sorry I never had the honor to be one of you. . . .

I am sorry I didn't get to see more of you. Thanks again for doing a
top job in a fast league for the two top guys in the U.S. Navy, Rear
Admiral Clark and Vice Admiral Mitscher.

Clark hoped he could get transferred before the erratic behavior that
had characterized Halsey's previous period in command of the Third Fleet
resurfaced. But it was not to be.

As Ted Sherman departed, he transferred the battleship *Alabama* from
his TG 38.3 to Clark's 38.1, and Commodore Rodger W. Simpson took
command of Jocko's screen as Commander Task Flotilla Six. The weather
worsened immediately, forcing Halsey to cancel air support strikes to Okinawa on 30 May. Clark refueled his task group next day, but stormy seas and
skies prevented him from helping the troops ashore over the first three days
of June. So he remained with Rear Admiral Donald B. Beary's replenishment force. Admiral Ching Lee left with Spruance, making Jack Shafroth
in Clark's group the senior battleship admiral. Jocko turned over tactical
command to him just to give him experience in the (unlikely) event of a surface engagement.

Meanwhile, Halsey charged north with Radford's group for extraordinarily long-range air strikes against Kyushu's airdromes on 2–3 June. The
weather, however, steadily worsened as Clark began refueling on the morning of the 4th. His task group assumed an easterly course, hoping to find
clear weather in order to join the attacks on Kyushu.

But a tropical storm was developing to the south, forcing Clark to discontinue fueling before noon. He rang up 14 knots in order to draw away
from the storm. Halsey ordered him to continue eastward to avoid it, saying
that he, with Radford's group, would rejoin later. The weather eased sufficiently to enable Clark to complete replenishment between 1630 and 2000.

Resuming tactical command from Shafroth, Clark was joined by Radford's group, including Halsey in battleship *Missouri* and McCain in the
new carrier *Shangri-La* (CV-38). The latter assumed tactical command of
TF 38 as it continued eastward 110 degrees, well ahead of the storm to the
southwest as reported by Guam's weather central. About 2230 Halsey suggested McCain shift the course to 150 degrees, but he demurred, preferring
110 degrees. The eastward storm was soon reported to have grown into a
typhoon.

Shortly after midnight, 0050 on 5 June, Halsey radioed McCain that a course of 300 degrees—northwestward—was better, and he ordered it—to Clark's "great surprise and dismay."

> We were already well clear to eastward of the storm, and if we had continued to the east, the storm would have passed well astern, but now Halsey was taking us right back into the track of the storm. Because Halsey was quite as well aware of the situation as I, there was nothing for me to do but carry out orders.

Admiral Radford on the *Yorktown* reached the same conclusion and repeatedly recommended—in vain—to McCain that he change course away from the approaching storm. But McCain replied that the decision was Halsey's. (Conversation with Radford)

Clark's alarm stemmed from an experience Wu Duncan had shared with him in 1943 when Duncan was captain of the *Essex*. Concerned about the structural integrity of the steel I-beams that supported the forward overhang of the flight deck, Duncan had once personally and alone watched heavy wave action on them in high seas until he was almost washed overboard. Portions of the catwalk had been carried away by a big wave, revealing a structural weakness that might be inherent in the I-beams as well. Since then, Clark had tried to avoid heavy seas with carriers—not only of the *Essex* class but the light carriers and escort carriers too. Several of the latter type were in Beary's group carrying replacement aircraft.

Now, at about 0230, the blackened seas rose in violent winds amid an equally dark sky. On *Hornet*'s radar Clark and his staff could see the tight typhoon spreading westward between 233 and 259 degrees. It was about 60 miles distant, traveling generally northeast at some 25 knots. At 0246, Admiral Beary in the refueling group near 38.1 signaled McCain that the 300-degree course was running them back into the storm. McCain, in Radford's TG 38.4 some 16 miles north of Clark, then changed course to due north (000 degrees) at 16 knots.

That was alright for 38.4, but it pointed 38.1 and the tankers directly on to an intercepting course with the eye of the typhoon. Jocko was not surprised when Beary informed McCain that he intended going back to 290 degrees at ten knots—executed at 0353—thereby enabling his escort carriers to ride easier. Such was not the case, however, for his fat oilers and supply ships.

At 0400 Halsey and chief of staff Mick Carney discussed the situation and decided the storm "possibly was not a typhoon after all." (Court of Inquiry Proceedings, 48) Yet, one minute later Clark informed McCain that my radar clearly showed the eye of the typhoon bearing 245°, distance 30 miles, moving on course 030°—moving directly to intercept us. McCain did nothing. If he had promptly released me, I could at that time escaped the intense whorl at the center.

With the wind howling up to 120 knots, Clark and the staff knew they were within the edge of the typhoon. Red Tomlinson and Mike Kernodle, respective skippers of light carriers *Belleau Wood* and *San Jacinto*, reported their ships to be rolling dangerously. Destroyer *Maddox* rolled as much as 53 degrees but, incredibly, did not capsize as had three hapless tin cans during Halsey's first typhoon.

The tin can *John Rodgers* (named for Clark's 1925 long-distance flying boss) took on so much water that one of its engines quit, and it briefly lost steerage. Jocko slowed down the entire task group to 12 knots until the destroyer regained enough power to make 16 knots. At 0419 he set the entire group to conform to that speed.

Hoping to avoid the center of the maelstrom, Clark signaled McCain at 0420, "I can get clear of the center of the storm by heading 120°. Please advise."

McCain replied, "We have nothing in our scope to indicate storm center."

"We very definitely have," Jocko shot back. "We have had one for one and a half hours."

Clark intercepted a McCain message to Halsey asking for advice. Halsey replied "Posit"—meaning, keep your relative position with respect to the guide. This applied to Clark as well, whereupon Jocko ordered his photographer to take continuous pictures of the radar screen.

With TG 38.1 embroiled in the midst of the typhoon, Radford's 38.4—including McCain and Halsey—was 16 miles to the north, just far enough away to avoid the worst of it.

McCain's staff agonized over Clark's plight and his 0420 request to change course, and—at 0435—they asked him the exact position and bearing of the storm's eye.

Five minutes after that McCain signaled, "We intend holding present course [000 degrees]. Use your own judgment."

Later, at the court of inquiry, McCain weakly apologized, "If twenty minutes' delay made any difference, I'm sorry." (Court of Inquiry Proceedings, 55)

Too late. Clark had been sucked into the maelstrom. Searching for a suitable course to ease the rolling of his light carriers, he tried 330 degrees at 0507, just as daylight was starting to break. *Hornet's* air officer Roy Johnson had just come to the bridge when suddenly "we hit this mountain of water. Gad, it must have been ten times as high as a house." It crashed down on the flight deck and carried away everything. The forward edges of the deck were bent down, the radio antennas and catwalks swept away, while airplanes went over the side. "We were in bad shape." (Johnson in Wooldridge, *Carrier Warfare*, 244–46)

After changing course to 270 degrees at 0515, Clark informed McCain the winds were 80 knots and the waves up to 70 feet: "We are maneuvering to find best course, should be out soon."

As the *Hornet* neared the eye of the storm, the carrier kept swinging to the left, forcing Clark to transfer the role of task group guide to the heavier battleship *Massachusetts* at 0528. Jocko slowed task group speed to ten knots, but Captain James B. Sykes of the *Bennington* reported losing steerageway at that speed on a course of 270 degrees. But several course changes did not work either—200 degrees at 0535, with all ships to maneuver independently to avoid collisions—190 degrees at 0538, and 180 degrees at 0550.

Like the *Hornet*, the forward flight deck overhang of the *Bennington* collapsed, further confirmation of Wu Duncan's 1943 warning to Jocko about *Essex*-class carriers. At 0556 Clark changed course 160 degrees, which finally suited the two *Essexes*.

One half hour later, however, the entire bow of the heavy cruiser *Pittsburgh* ripped off in the churning seas. The ship did not sink due to excellent damage control and smart ship handling. Clark had the *Baltimore* stand by it, and that ship suffered damage too. The bow of the light cruiser *Duluth* buckled, causing minor flooding, and battleship *Indiana* lost rudder control for 17 minutes.

About 0700 on 5 June TG 38.1 entered the dead calm of the storm's eye, with a patch of blue dawn sky overhead. Minutes later, the typhoon closed in again, and the battered ships rode out another five grueling hours. Clark reported the *Belleau Wood* and several destroyers missing, but at 1052 the *Yorktown* in 38.4 catapulted several search planes that soon located them all. Before the storm ended, it had claimed only six men lost overboard and four seriously injured, but 76 airplanes were destroyed and 70 damaged by the battering.

Shortly after noon, Clark redesignated the *Hornet* as task group guide, course 200 degrees at six knots, then up to ten knots in midafternoon. As he reassembled his scattered vessels, he discovered that not only had he not lost a single ship, but he had *gained* one. It was the merchant ship *Luxembourg Victory* from Beary's group. Clark assigned it to the screen until nightfall, when two cans escorted the ship "home."

Mountainous waves break over a carrier's deck during one of Halsey's typhoons.
*U.S. Navy photo*

He immediately appointed Captain Donald R. Osborn Jr. of the *Duluth*
to head a task unit of his and other damaged ships to proceed to Guam. The
*Pittsburgh* went in two sections; two cans pulled its broken-off bow, dubbed
by one swab as "the suburbs of Pittsburgh." Three damaged destroyers and
two destroyer escorts from Beary's formation went back as well.

To replace Clark's departing cruisers, Rear Admiral C. F. Holden joined
the formation next day with light cruisers *Topeka* and *Oklahoma City.* So did
the brand-new night carrier *Bon Homme Richard* and another tin can. And
Jocko put Sugar Brown and Red Sharp to work gathering evidence and
Herm Rosenblatt to collating it for the expected court of inquiry over his
part in the typhoon.

Early on 6 June Clark transferred by breeches buoy to the destroyer
*McKee,* thence to TF 38 flagship *Shangri-La* to call on McCain. "Jock"
Clark pointed out to "Jock" McCain that he could have avoided the worst of
the storm had McCain allowed him to alter his course. McCain, out of loyalty to Halsey, remained vague about assigning responsibility but finally said

as Clark departed, "I am sorry you had to get *your* ships damaged." This rankled Clark, because when press releases announced the fast carriers attacking the enemy they were always *his* ships.

Clark then called on Halsey aboard the *Missouri,* but very little conversation passed between them. According to Jocko, "He knew and I knew who
was to blame for my ships turning back into the typhoon." Some time later,
Halsey's chief of staff and Jocko's old friend Mick Carney, well known for
his Irish wit, "started to rib me for getting into this typhoon. I properly
squelched him by saying, 'Now, Mick, you know who the typhoon king of
the world is!'" (Letter to Vice Admiral John T. Hayward, 6 May 1968)

Returning to the *Hornet* at midday, Clark was determined to join Radford for the planned strikes against Kyushu. But the pilots on the *Hornet*
and *Bennington* worried about disturbed air currents over the collapsed forward end of their flight decks. The first plane off the flagship, an F4U Corsair fighter, lifted off, but on reaching the bow suddenly flipped over and
spun into the sea. Luckily, the pilot scrambled out.

"We can't launch with this," remarked air officer Roy Johnson. "It's nonsense."

"O.K., I agree," said Jocko. "Now, what to do is to get those blow torches
out and cut those bent flight deck edges off." That meant cutting armored
steel, but Captain Artie Doyle agreed. It would take many hours at least. (In
fact, it was soon stopped as impossible for a ship's crew to undertake.) In addition, the crew ran inconclusive tests using smoke over the bow. Navy archi-
tects eventually showed that the damage had created a no-wind condition,
with a bubble of circling wind over the bow. (Conversation with Red Sharp)

"All right," said Clark to Johnson, "try to find us a way of launching airplanes." In meeting his attack schedule, "the guy never gave up," recalled
Johnson. They agreed to back down the *Hornet* at 18 knots and launch its
planes over the stern. The *Bennington* followed suit—an unprecedented
maneuver in wartime. The scheme worked, but it played havoc with the
ships' engines, adding to both carriers' need for an overhaul in the shipyards.
(Johnson in Wooldridge, *Carrier Warfare,* 246)

Clark put up a large CAP over Okinawa next day, 7 June, controlled by
FDOs in the picket destroyers. That night he organized a task unit under
Tommy Sprague to take the *Bennington* to the new advanced base at Leyte
Gulf, escorted by three cans. It would be repaired there. Next day, *Hornet,*
*Bon Homme Richard, Belleau Wood,* and *San Jacinto* sent 96 planes to strafe
and bomb Kanoya airfield on Kyushu.

McCain had Clark's bombers destroy shore defenses on Okino Daito
Island on the 9th using napalm bombs to demonstrate the effectiveness of
their jellied gasoline contents. On the 10th Halsey ordered Jack Shafroth

with his three battleships and five tin cans to shell Minami Daito Island. Clark's Hellcats and Corsairs spotted targets for the 16-inch guns.

Ironically, in Clark's final combat action leading carriers in World War II, he had employed them not to destroy ships or planes but in their original role of gunfire spotting that had inspired naval aviation way back in 1910–11. (Reynolds, *Admiral John H. Towers*, 29–32) The Okinawa campaign was over, and on the night of the 10th Jocko turned TG 38.1 south for Leyte. He was ready to go home, figuring that the war would end soon anyway, and he had no interest in remaining under the control of Halsey and McCain.

As far as many fighting men of his task group were concerned, Jocko Clark stood on a par with Halsey as a great leader and fighting man. "Patsy" McCoy, a swab on a tin can in 38.1, said so in a poem to his family about this time:

> . . . Me and Halsey and Clark
> Have sure got the Japs on the run,
> We're driving them wacky
> In old Nagasaki,
> We're setting the damned rising sun.
> Kyushu, Kobe and Kure
> Are wonderful ruins to see.
> We've got them like gophers a-seeking a hole.
> The way they burrow is good for the soul
> And everything out here is under control
> By Clark and Halsey and me. . . .

En route to Leyte, Clark and the staff prepared what amounted to their defense against the obvious implication that they—rather than Halsey and/or McCain—had been responsible for the fleet's having blundered into its second typhoon. They expressed their true feelings in a short screenplay parody entitled "WAS CHET CHECKMATED? or WHAT TYPHOON? A Halsey Productions Classic." Excerpt:

CHET [CHESTER NIMITZ]: Didn't I hear something about a storm?
BULL [HALSEY]: What storm?
CHET: Well! A typhoon.
BULL: Which typhoon you talking about?. . . . Recently. Oh, that bit of a blow. Nothing at all. . . . Goddam it, I know enough to keep out of typhoons.

CHET: Seems the others don't have that much sense. How'd they get into it?
BULL: They was joining up on me. I told 'em to. And when they goes and
gets into the center of the storm and I tells 'em to use their discretion
getting out, they foul up my orders. Goddam kids of two-stars and
captains. Bad as those yeller-bellied bast—. . . . (Full text in Reynolds,
*Fighting Lady*, along with "Ode to the BIG Wind [Halsey]," 299–303)

During the voyage to Leyte Clark and the staff packed their bags to
leave the *Hornet*, itself homeward-bound for repairs. On arrival, Jocko
finally relinquished his two commands—TG 38.1 to Tommy Sprague and
the administrative Carrier Division Five to Rear Admiral Arthur C. Davis,
Spruance's chief of staff. Davis inherited Captain Raöul Waller to be his
chief of staff but let Raöul "off the hook" when he was offered his own ship,
the escort carrier *Petrof Bay*. Of the staff, Jocko kept Sowerwine, McCrary,
Rosenblatt, and Reynolds for his move to Corpus Christi.

Within an hour after the *Hornet* dropped anchor in Leyte Gulf the
afternoon of 13 June Clark received orders to appear before the court of
inquiry on Guam two days hence. He flew there immediately with his aides.

The court consisted of three vice admirals—two aviators, John H.
Hoover and George D. Murray, and Pacific Fleet submarine commander
Charles A. Lockwood. For four days, 15–18 June, the court heard testimony.
Clark gave clear and uninterrupted testimony the first day, then became an
"interested party"—allowed to cross-examine others. He introduced Herman
Rosenblatt as his counsel. (Court of Inquiry Proceedings, 39–40, 52)

This shrewd peacetime lawyer tore into Halsey and his chief of staff
Mick Carney so viciously that Jocko took Rosenblatt aside at the break.
"Herman, you can't talk to a four-star admiral like that."

"Admiral," replied Herm, "that's the only way I know to prove your
innocence." He offered to "pull out" if Clark felt embarrassed by his treatment of the high brass, "but I can tell you that your throat is going to be cut
from ear to ear unless I can hang the blame on the one man who is responsible, and that is Admiral Halsey."

And he did, after getting Clark's permission to continue. When it was
all over the court recommended that Halsey and McCain both be relieved
of their commands and given other duties. Nimitz officially rejected this
finding because of their "outstanding service records." But in questioning
Clark at length about the storm after the hearings, Nimitz expressed "his
great displeasure with Halsey and to a lesser extent McCain. He minced no
words in charging Halsey with gross stupidity in both typhoons, especially

the latter, where Halsey had good weather information." (Conversation with Clark)

But Nimitz dared not touch the hero of Guadalcanal, nor did Ernie King, even though they both put the blame squarely on Halsey for blundering into both typhoons. Halsey's fame was simply too great; his picture even appeared on the cover of *Time* magazine in July. The court mildly assigned lesser "blame" to Clark and Beary "for operating against their better judgment." Nimitz did deal with McCain, however, ordering him to turn over command of TF 38 to Jack Towers in August.

As the Pacific war raced to its inevitable conclusion, fitness reports and accolades were hurried or forgotten or influenced by the euphoria of victory. Admiral Mitscher awarded Clark a Gold Star in lieu of a second Distinguished Service Medal for having directed operations "with brilliant and forceful leadership" against Iwo Jima, Tokyo, and Okinawa between February and May 1945.

Because of Mitscher's sudden transfer back to Washington he never filled out a fitness report as Clark's commanding officer for those months—until March 1946, when he wrote a letter expressing the same accolades as in previous evaluations. The letter was attached to a formal fitness report form submitted by Admiral George Murray recommending (successfully) Jocko's formal promotion to the permanent rank of rear admiral.

Although Clark was not present at the finish of the fighting, the major missions facing the fast carriers had already been accomplished. Halsey and McCain spent July and early August 1945 ranging the coast of Japan with the task groups of Sprague, Bogan, Radford, and the British, attacking airfields and defenses. The air-sea blockade of Japan was complete, while B-29s pounded the homeland. Then, between 6 and 15 August, B-29s dropped two atomic bombs on Japan, and the Soviet army crushed the main Japanese army in China. Only then did the Japanese agree to stop fighting.

Jocko Clark's final wartime fitness report was dated 2 September 1945 and written by McCain for the period of 28 May to 15 June when Clark had served under his direct command. McCain's generosity in it was likely a gesture to make up for his failure to rescue Clark's task group during the typhoon.

> Rear Admiral Clark has aggressive leadership of the highest sort. He has performed one of the outstanding jobs of the war. He is one of the best Naval officers in the Navy.

McCain likely signed this report on board Halsey's flagship *Missouri* in Tokyo Bay while attending the Japanese surrender ceremonies held on that ship that very day of 2 September. Exhausted, he died of a heart attack four days later in San Diego.

Many of Clark's superiors had inspired him long before and throughout the war, in spite of differences with some of them in certain cases. King was "unquestionably the best-fitted officer to lead our Navy in wartime." Nimitz was "the one great leader in the Pacific with an untarnished record all the way. He had no dent in his armor, and never did I hear a shred of criticism against him."

Spruance, admired since he had been Clark's first skipper in 1919, "blazed a trail across the Pacific from Tarawa to Saipan," making but one great mistake—failure to sink the Japanese fleet in the Philippine Sea. And the aggressive Halsey had saved Guadalcanal and the South Pacific theater but made "tragic mistakes" in the Central Pacific, the worst at Leyte Gulf and in the two typhoons.

Then there was Mitscher, in Clark's opinion a carrier combat commander "without a peer." Before Mitscher had taken command of the fast carriers they had not been employed very aggressively.

> It goes back to that winning spirit. If you don't have it in an organization, you'd better turn in your suit. Because war is something you can't play with. You've got to be out there to win, or you shouldn't be there. Playing marbles for keeps—that's exactly what it is.
>
> I think that we finally got a team in the Central Pacific that had that winning spirit. And we got it from Mitscher. We kept it, and it went right on through to the end of the war.

Jocko Clark had proved himself as Mitscher's foremost "player" on that team. Unfortunately, as he knew from his naval experiences after the end of World War I, victory alone did not solve the major problems of the world. In order to make the fruits of victory of World War II lasting, the world now had to be properly reconstructed—and policed.

# NINETEEN

## Policing the World, Round Two, 1945–1950

JOCKO CLARK AND HIS FOUR STAFF OFFICERS FLEW HOME FROM Pearl Harbor in high style—on a plush RY-1 transport plane (a modified AAF B-24 Liberator bomber) because it needed an overhaul at Corpus Christi. Better yet, Clark was allowed to keep it there for official travel. During the layover at San Diego he visited with Pete Mitscher, about to leave for Washington to assume the top aviation job in the Navy—Deputy Chief of Naval Operations (Air).

The big plane landed at Corpus Christi on 27 June 1945, a typically sweltering Texas day. As Clark exited the plane, he was greeted by the incumbent staff officers all wearing their prescribed uniform ties. Coming from an equally unpleasant tropical Pacific, Jocko barked his first order: "Take off those neckties!" The welcome response to this command made it "by far the most popular order I ever gave in the Navy."

As Chief of Naval Air Intermediate Training, Clark was part of the overall Naval Air Training Command. Its chief and his boss was—of all people—Rear Admiral Baldy Pownall, clearly better suited for this work than combat. Pownall's headquarters was at Pensacola, the other training station besides Corpus Christi, which was under Clark's authority for inter-mediate training (between primary and advanced). Together, the two air stations turned out some 12,000 pilots a year. Jocko also had responsibility for about 5,000 German prisoners of war awaiting repatriation and had to restrain their Marine Corps jailers from mistreating them.

Clark immediately undertook a flying tour of several satellite air sta-tions combined with a long-awaited family reunion. On 29 June he flew to Clinton in western Oklahoma to inspect the station there. Hours later he flew on to Tulsa where his sisters Lucy and Mary met him and drove him to the parental home in Chelsea, where his daughters had already arrived.

There, reported the *Tulsa Tribune* (30 June 1945), Clark "found eating watermelon and wandering among the hollyhocks with his daughters Mary Louise, 10, and [Cathy] Carol, 9, a far cry from life aboard a fighting ship."

All smiles, Joe Clark impressed one reporter as a "quiet spoken Navy commander and pilot, about whom more legend than fact has been printed" (wrong on both counts!). Photographing him with mother, daughters, sisters, and a niece (as well as his father), a newspaperwoman declared him "following the Navy tradition of being surrounded by girls when ashore." (Betty Baughman, "Sooner Admiral Says Nip War Woe Grows," *Tulsa Daily World,* 1 July 1945) Jocko certainly promoted that so-called tradition as he settled in.

He flew on to Washington for a quick visit to the Navy Department, thence to inspect NAS Atlanta on the Fourth of July. More inspection tours and family reunions would fill his days. During one of them, the town of Chelsea honored him with a special "Joe Clark Day." He moved his daughters from Jacksonville to Corpus Christi to be near him, also their mother M.C.; he set her up in a small house to continue raising the girls. Aside from a powerful hurricane that hit Corpus Christi, life there was not difficult.

Clark quickly gathered an official family like the one he had had in the Pacific. In addition to incumbents Sowerwine, McCrary, Rosenblatt, and Reynolds, he obtained his last exec on the *Yorktown,* Captain Cam Briggs, to be chief of staff. And he made good on Jimmy Flatley's request to join him—as director of training, in which capacity Jimmy deftly handled the administrative details just as he had for Jocko at Jax before the war. (Ewing, *Reaper Leader,* 270)

Although Clark kept up with the news of virtually unopposed carrier attacks on Japan, he was completely unprepared for the atom bomb dropped on Hiroshima on 6 August. Although he "had access to the highest secret information," like most high-ranking officers he had "no inkling that a fissionable bomb had been constructed."

"Instinctively," Clark perceived that the aircraft carrier could serve as "a good vehicle for carrying the atomic bomb overseas," and he immediately flew to Washington to sound out Mitscher. Old Pete agreed with him but revealed that the 45,000-ton *Midway,* first of its class of "battle" carriers (CVB-41) and due for commissioning in one month, was still too small to carry the 10,000-pound A-bomb, as were existing carrier planes. Mitscher only said that studies had begun for an even larger "supercarrier," eventually to be named *United States,* and a heavy bomber for it.

Jocko was not surprised when Japan soon called it quits, but he was unprepared for the frenzy of officers and sailors alike demanding to be returned at once to civilian life. Many enlisted men—"otherwise fine young citizens"—simply left for home. After ten days of being absent without leave (AWOL) they faced a mandatory court-martial, and Clark was soon reviewing up to five cases a day. He appealed to Navy Secretary Forrestal, who soon established separation centers to expedite discharges.

Contrariwise, terminated pilot training programs brought protests from trainees charging "violation of contract" and who insisted on continuing. Again, Forrestal bailed out Jocko by granting their requests—thereby making them available when the Navy soon needed pilots to help police the postwar world.

Clark used his own initiative locally by charging Sowerwine, McCrary, and Rosenblatt to set up a separation center at Corpus Christi. They did so with alacrity, separating themselves *first* from the Navy. Only Bob Reynolds of the original wartime staff remained, but for only a short while longer.

As the Navy rapidly downsized during the autumn, it amalgamated primary and intermediate flight training programs under Clark as the new Chief of Naval Basic Training, leaving advanced pilot training at Jacksonville. He and Flatley were constantly flying between bases, especially to Pensacola where Jocko personally pinned the golden wings on each graduating pilot. A major Flatley innovation was getting the SNJ monoplane to replace the N3N biplane as the primary training plane. (Ewing, *Reaper Leader,* 270–71)

Jocko's native Indian roots and his title as chief of basic aviation training led many personnel under his command to refer to him in both senses as "the Chief." He exploited it to the full. In September, Rear Admiral Min Miller, Chief of Information, flew him and Fleet Admiral William D. Leahy, chief of staff to President Harry Truman, to Yankton, South Dakota, in an old Beechcraft. There they helped local farmers and Indians celebrate Midwest Farmer Day on the 3rd.

Clark was already an honorary chief of the Cherokees and had to get permission from the real chief of the Cherokees to receive the same title from the Sioux as Chief Thunderbird ("Wakijan Zatha Pa"). Iowa-born Leahy received it also, Iowan Miller already had it, and in the morning, on the banks of the Missouri River, the three officers donned headdresses and did an Indian dance with their hosts. "It was fun," recalled Miller, "the most amazing thing [being] this old boy"—Admiral Leahy, age 70—"hopping up and down like an Indian." (Miller transcript #3, 164)

As featured speaker at the evening program in the local college football stadium, Jocko proclaimed to the 25,000 Midwesterners present his vision of the coming years: "If we are to enjoy the peace we have won, we must maintain a large navy as the best guarantee of that peace, and that navy should have a large number of aircraft carriers." (*Yankton Press and Dakotan,* 4 September 1945) Clark later posed, headdress-adorned, with comedian Bob Hope.

Comedian Bob Hope passes judgment on Jocko's borrowed Sioux headdress awarded him at Yankton, South Dakota, in September 1945. *U.S. Navy photo*

Fleet Admiral Nimitz, who replaced the retiring Ernie King as CNO at the end of the year, honored Clark by having Jocko ride with him in the victory parade during the American Legion convention in Chicago. Nimitz introduced Jocko as "the fightingest admiral in the fleet." Texan Nimitz also took Jocko with him to his homecomings at Fredericksburg as well as Dallas. Pete Mitscher inspected Corpus in December and used the opportunity to tell Jocko that he had been Mitscher's "best carrier admiral" in TF 58.

While Clark's war record held him in good stead throughout the rest of his career, by no means did it "carry him." His same leadership skills—minus the now unnecessary tirades—were needed in the postwar Navy. But known primarily as a fighter, he sometimes found himself serving under former peers or even more junior admirals who advanced more rapidly due to their diversified talents.

Yet, universally, *every one* of his immediate superiors between 1946 and 1953 wrote fitness reports giving him superior ratings and recommendations for promotion to vice admiral until he eventually got it. Their names, here listed chronologically per their fitness reports of him, reveal also the rapid takeover of the Navy's leadership by its aviation community: Pownall, Wagner, Radford, Ramsey, Duncan, Price, Bogan, Stump, Forrest Sherman, Ballentine, Murray, Wilder Baker (nonaviator but McCain's chief of staff in TF 38), Tommy Sprague, and Robert P. Briscoe (nonaviator).

Although Jocko returned to his hobbies of hunting and playing golf once he was in Texas, what he craved most was a wife. The busy south Texas social scene soon led him to Shannon Kelley Weiss Jensen, a 40-year-old thrice-married owner of a bank in Pharr, 100 miles south of Corpus Christi. She was active with the leadership of the state's Democratic Party. Admiral Nimitz introduced them at a Texas "brag" dinner (where rattlesnake was served!). Described in the new Atomic Age parlance as having "the energy of an unrestrained atom" (1945 *American Magazine* article), redhead Shannon was a brilliant if earthy businesswoman, wealthy but generous too. (Conversations with Mary Lou Clark; assorted articles)

Shannon was a social climber, no doubt dazzled by Jocko's uniform and renown—although at the time she met Clark she was dating Corregidor hero General Jonathan Wainwright, Fourth Army commander. Clark's high society contacts counted too, not least with the DuPonts of Jacksonville. Jocko and Shannon's whirlwind courtship resulted in their marriage on 12 May 1946 at "Epping Forrest," home of Clark's prewar acquaintance Jesse Ball DuPont. The announcement of the crossed-swords Navy ceremony even made the *New York Times*. (10 May 1946)

Jocko took Shannon to several family gatherings at Chelsea. At their first one after the wedding, they used a bedroom in which Clark's five mis-

A proud "Daddy" shows off his girls at Corpus Christi in early 1946, Cathy, nine (*left*), and Mary Lou, 11, behind whom stands chief of staff Cameron Briggs; at right is flag lieutenant Bob Reynolds. *U.S. Navy photo.*

chievous teenage nieces had rigged several alarm clocks to go off simultaneously in the middle of the night! "We heard them go off, and we had some giggles about it," recalled culprit Betty Joe (Clark) Mayer, "but Uncle Joe never said a word next day." On another visit, his having started to imbibe again, he gave "B.J." and his own daughter Cathy a quarter to spike the punch. When his brother John found out, they "had words outside behind the barn." Nothing more was said, but Uncle Joe "winked at us and said we did good." (Mayer letter, 3 November 2001)

Neither Clark's relatively easy workload nor his connubial bliss could hide the fact that the euphoria of global peace was steadily evaporating. By the time CNO Nimitz inspected Corpus Christi in mid-June, a truculent Soviet Russia threatened to engulf southeastern and even Western Europe. The Chinese civil war resumed, with the Communists starting to drive the pro-American Nationalists off the Asian mainland. Admiral Jack Towers reluctantly transferred ships and planes from his Pacific Fleet to Admiral Pete Mitscher's Atlantic Fleet in the face of rampant American demobilization.

Compounding this start of the "Cold War" was the renewed crusade by the AAF's strategic bombing leaders for their own armed service—the "Air Force." What was more, they intended that such a U.S. Air Force should monopolize atomic weapons. The air generals called for the unification of the Army, Navy, and this new Air Force, by inference all dominated by the latter service. Because these crusaders regarded the aircraft carrier as vulnerable to nuclear weapons and therefore obsolete, Admiral Nimitz assigned two of his top CNO deputies, Vice Admirals Radford and Forrest Sherman, to orchestrate the opposition.

Navy public relations director Min Miller and later Rear Admiral Eddie Ewen often called on Clark among other available flag officers to outline the Navy's arguments at public meetings. Jocko's light workload freed him to do it often and with great force. Sherman joined him speaking before the Conference of Southern Governors meeting in New Orleans. The intellectual Sherman, who was more measured in his arguments than the hard-hitting Jocko, began to treat his early 1930s fellow squadron commander more coolly.

Passions over unification flared so dramatically during the summer that Clark's great friend Radford as Deputy CNO (Air) had Jocko ordered to Washington to be his Assistant DCNO (Air) in September. Ziggy Sprague replaced him at Corpus Christi. Raddy and Clark also brought in former shipmates Rear Admirals Red Tomlinson, Artie Doyle, and Ernie Litch and Captain Raöul Waller "to find the right answer for unification." Jocko lost no time joining the fray. In October, at a luncheon of the Wings Club in New York, he envisioned atom-bomb-equipped long-range Navy patrol-bombers as well as (admittedly speculative) "submersible" aircraft carriers. (*New York Times,* 19 October 1946)

Clark accepted the idea of unification but only of the two traditional services with their own strong air arms, not a separate Air Force as a third. He expected Radford to work out the arrangement with AAF Major General Lauris Norstad, but Radford turned it over to Sherman—no longer

"Fuzz" to Clark. Sherman quickly concluded that any compromise had to include an independent Air Force as the third service.

Jocko discussed it with his friend from early flying days, Admiral Duke Ramsey, now Vice CNO, who said, "If two people are married and want a divorce, a third party should not intervene."

"But," Jocko countered, "what will this do to naval aviation?"

"Of course, it will not be helpful," Ramsey admitted.

"Then why should the Navy condone it?" Clark insisted. Even as an "interested party" to the divorce of the AAF from the Army, the Navy "is the one that suffers most and therefore has the right to oppose it."

Jocko was saddened to see Admirals Nimitz, Ramsey, and Tommy Sprague join Sherman in accepting a separate Air Force in opposition to Towers, Radford, Ziggy Sprague, Artie Doyle, Felix Stump, and himself. (*New York Times*, 26 January 1947) Raddy remained in the fight even after he transferred to command of the Second Task Fleet in the Atlantic in February 1947. And he reinforced Jocko's stature with a glowing fitness report:

> He has demonstrated . . . the same qualities of intelligence, leadership, initiative, and determination which made him one of our greatest fighting men during World War II. I selected him for my assistant and his performance of all assigned duties has been outstanding. He is qualified and recommended for duty as DCNO (Air) or a Fleet Commander. (17 February 1947)

Radford also hailed Clark as "one of the outstanding younger flag officers"—all of 53 years old to Radford's mere 50. In a sense they both *were* young, compared to Pete Mitscher, who died at 60 only two weeks before this fitness report, and Jack Towers, who retired at year's end at 62.

Clark was acting DCNO (Air) for two weeks until Wu Duncan succeeded to Radford's job. Jocko continued to lead the fight against unification. But in the final congressional hearings Congressman James W. Wadsworth "pinned me down by making me admit that a separate Air Force would strengthen America's air power in the overall defense picture."

Congressman W. Sterling Cole, long a Navy advocate, saw passage of the bill as inevitable and assembled Towers, Clark, Captain George Anderson, and others to draft a statement that Cole inserted into it: "The Navy shall have naval aviation and naval air transport necessary to naval operations." Unification became law in July 1947.

It immediately proved to be a less than perfect administrative arrangement. And, in the struggle over funding the new Air Force, generals and political supporters continued to denigrate the Navy (and its Marine Corps) as obsolete. Clark called a meeting of all officers on duty in the DCNO (Air) and Bureau of Aeronautics offices to encourage them to "develop a technique, a weapon, or a way to wage war on the seas that was our own" and that would require congressional funding.

Clark offered the idea of jet-propelled seaplanes capable of carrying atom bombs, flying between secluded harbors where large submarines could refuel them. Several such planes, P6M, were built a few years later but never caught on. Also, in September 1947 he flew to England to assist the British in changing their carrier landing procedures to conform to those of the U.S. Navy, so that planes of both navies could land on each other's carriers during joint operations.

Clark's professional activity included a full social life, given the fact that new wife Shannon loved to entertain and hobnob with politicians and admirals. She insisted they purchase and lavishly decorate a house in the exclusive Kenwood section of Washington's Maryland suburbs. Lauded in newspaper society pages as a major hostess of the capital social scene, Shannon was equally generous and caring with her stepdaughters. Her own son, a commercial airline pilot, visited regularly. So that Jocko's daughters could continue to see their mother and benefit from her artistic talents, he found housing for M.C. in the Washington area.

During the fall of 1947 Admiral Nimitz decided to step down as CNO in December, setting in motion an internal scramble for a successor. Forrestal, now Secretary of Defense, favored a naval aviator, the senior one being Duke Ramsey. Clark opposed Ramsey for having "sold out" to unification, while President Truman, advised by Admiral Leahy, preferred politically wise compromiser and nonaviator Admiral Louis Denfeld.

Clark figured the next best thing was to ensure that the Vice CNO be an aviator like the incumbent Ramsey. The logical choice was Radford, a friend of Denfeld's, though denigrated by Forrestal, Nimitz, and Sherman for his opposition to unification. So Jocko "sent an emissary" to Pearl Harbor to sound out Denfeld, then commanding the Pacific Fleet. Denfeld replied that, if appointed CNO, he would support naval aviation by naming Raddy as Vice Chief. That satisfied Jocko and the brown shoes. Denfeld said nothing until taking office on 15 December, whereupon he immediately demanded and got Radford as VCNO. This immensely pleased Raddy's supporters, recalled Jocko, "for now we had our brand of leadership for the Navy."

Also during the fall of 1947 Clark obtained Wu Duncan's approval to have Jack Towers and the General Board resurrect Pete Mitscher's idea of constructing one carrier capable of delivering the atomic bomb to targets inside the Soviet Union in order to keep pace with the Air Force's strategic bombers. The General Board agreed, as did Defense Secretary Forrestal, and design of the 65,000-ton supercarrier *United States* went forward. Development of the twin-engine AJ Savage heavy attack bomber was already proceeding. (Reynolds, *Admiral John H. Towers*, 543)

Meanwhile, Congress continued to cut the military, in spite of the Cold War, and included the closing of NAS Corpus Christi on the advice of the chief of BuAer, Rear Admiral Mel Pride. Clark opposed this measure virtually alone, encouraged by Senator Tom Connally and other members of the Texan congressional delegation that supported naval aviation. Worse, incumbent Vice CNO Ramsey informed Jocko that he planned to give Corpus to the Air Force, which already had two training bases in Texas. John L. Sullivan, Secretary of the Navy (now subordinate to the Secretary of Defense), ordered Jocko's boss Duncan to inspect Corpus Christi and make a recommendation.

Wu, never having even been to "Corpus," had Jocko brief him first. When he returned from there, Duncan and Sullivan were summoned to Senator Connally's office before the two men had even talked about Corpus. When the senator asked for their recommendations, Duncan replied that the Navy should retain the station at least for the time being. A surprised Sullivan blamed Clark for this change and ordered Duncan "to get rid of me," remembered Jocko. Wu defended the assessment as his own, endorsed by Radford when he reported as Vice CNO in January 1948. Under pressure from Sullivan, however, Duncan fell in line for closing Corpus.

Then Duncan suddenly fell ill, leaving Clark as acting DCNO (Air) late in the month until Vice Admiral John Dale Price could arrive to replace Duncan. Meanwhile, Assistant Secretary of the Navy (Air) John Nicholas Brown convened a meeting for the final decision on Corpus. Clark adroitly maneuvered Mel Pride into leaving his supporting staff of experts out of the meeting, which was attended only by CNO Denfeld, Radford, Pride, Clark, and Corpus's training director, Captain John B. Moss. Jocko had Jack Moss read aloud a one-page statement to retain Corpus, and it was immediately endorsed by Denfeld, Radford, and Clark (in that order). Pride, outnumbered, yielded, and the great Texas naval air training center was saved.

Wu Duncan's fitness report on Clark (13 February 1948) recognized the great respect that Jocko's colleagues had for him, "an officer of superior military characteristics and professional attainments. I have the highest regard for him. He is strong and aggressive, conscientious and thorough and possesses that sterling quality of loyalty to a high degree." This was obviously a word of wisdom aimed at those superiors who resented Clark's opposition to their points of view. Indeed, concluded Duncan, "his performance of duty has left nothing to be desired."

The superb BuAer chief, Mel Pride, though stung by his defeat, "took it in good grace" (Clark's words) simply because the intellectual Pride was that kind of person. Still having to economize, however, Pride decided to close one of Florida's two naval air stations. Because Pensacola as the traditional home of naval aviation was out of the question, it had to be Jacksonville. Clark, as virtual first exec at Jax, received a two-man Chamber of Commence delegation from that city to discuss the situation.

As they entered his office, Jocko recalled, "Suddenly—for once in my life—I had a flash of ingenuity." He remembered that, although Jax had opened as a training station in 1940, its original purpose had been envisioned as a fleet air base for deterring Nazi Germany from moving into South America. With the Soviets now threatening Western Europe and the eastern Mediterranean, Jacksonville could be turned into a fleet air base for aircraft carriers operating in the Atlantic. The only cost to the taxpayer would be dredging the Mayport basin to accommodate flattops.

Vice Admiral Price, who arrived as the new DCNO (Air) in February 1948, endorsed Clark's idea, followed by Radford and CNO Denfeld. Jax was saved, and Jacksonville-Mayport soon became the Atlantic Fleet's main carrier base.

As the end of Clark's tour of duty as acting DCNO (Air) neared, he took great satisfaction for having been instrumental in saving Corpus and Jax, getting Raddy appointed Vice CNO, and promoting the new supercarrier. The lost fight over unification was his one great disappointment.

Clark was gratified to learn that his former shipmates on the *Yorktown* (CV-10) were forming their own veterans' organization, the Yorktown Association. He attended its first reunion in New York City on 15 April 1948—the fifth anniversary of its commissioning. A week later he joined Admiral Nimitz, Eddie Ewen, and others enshrining the battleship *Texas* at Houston. The air show was provided by NAS Dallas's commander Captain Lefty Nation, Jocko's air group commander on the *Suwannee*. (*Houston Post*, 21 April 1948)

In May, Admirals Denfeld and Radford recommended Clark for promotion to vice admiral and as the relief for Gerry Bogan as Commander Air Force Atlantic Fleet (ComAirLant). Rear Admiral John Cassady was ordered to relieve Clark as ACNO (Air). But Navy Secretary Sullivan refused to approve his promotion. No matter how strongly Denfeld and Raddy argued with Sullivan, he would not forgive Jocko's disloyalty to him by having successfully opposed the closing of Corpus and Jacksonville.

Clark's only hope lay in what the Navy's climate of opinion expected to be the defeat of President Truman for reelection by New York Governor Thomas Dewey in November. With Truman out, Sullivan would have to leave too. So the CNO kept Bogan at his post until then, allowed Cassady to relieve Clark, and had Jocko assist Johnny Price by inspecting eastern seaboard naval air stations from Newfoundland to Panama.

But Truman surprisingly won reelection, and Clark "knew my fate was sealed." Sullivan immediately assigned Felix Stump to Bogan's job and promoted him to vice admiral. Clark in effect was passed over, usually the signal for a dead-end job followed by retirement. Indeed, Johnny Price, protecting his own position, did no favors for Clark in his fitness report (24 November 1948). He marked down Jocko for poor judgment, failing to understand and follow instructions, and inability to adapt to changing needs and conditions. He added a backhanded compliment: "R. Adm. Clark . . . has great tenacity and is unyielding in anything he thinks is right. He is a great fighting man."

Jocko, seeing his status in the Navy "at an all-time low," resolved to "rebuild my standing" by applying for sea duty, "always my cup of tea." It would also get him out of Washington, where Sullivan would surround himself with "yes" men. For similar reasons Forrest Sherman had wrangled command of the Navy's forces in the Mediterranean in June, and Radford soon managed to get command of the Pacific Fleet. This enabled Price to slip in as Vice CNO.

The sea duty Clark received was Carrier Division Four—virtually a parallel assignment with his last seagoing command in combat three years before. But there would be little if any shooting in this "Cold War." His command would divide its time between East Coast operations out of Norfolk and deployments with Sherman's Sixth Task Fleet in the Mediterranean. Time away from wife Shannon was a mixed blessing, as she was starting to suffer financial reverses, contributing to friction between them. He did, however, have her flown to the Med to join him in social affairs.

On 22 November 1948 Jocko relieved Rear Admiral Ralph Jennings on board the flagship *Philippine Sea* (CV-47) at Quonset Point, Rhode Island, the ship's home port. *Philippine Sea* was a two-year-old *Essex*-class carrier, and its captain was John L. Pratt, an old friend. The other carrier was the 45,000-ton *Midway* (CVB-41). The cardiv, normally based at Norfolk as part of the Second Task Fleet, prepared to deploy to the Mediterranean for four months, rotating with the other four carriers as part of the Atlantic Fleet. Because of numerous port visits to "show the flag," Jocko had an automobile brought aboard, along with a personal driver, Engineman Thomas Haley.

The new ComAirLant, Vice Admiral Felix Stump, wrote Clark's fitness report (6 April 1949) covering the three months beginning 3 December 1948: top marks across the board, plus the observation that "his present duties provide opportunity for further display of his colorful and effective leadership." This observation may well have been a reminder to Sixth Task Fleet commander Forrest Sherman, who was *not* a Clark admirer.

The two carriers formed the nucleus of Task Force 87, which made a stormy crossing to Gibraltar during January 1949. It operated out of the island of Malta in the central Med and from which Clark led it on port calls to southern European cities. As part of Sherman's Sixth Task Fleet (the word "task" was dropped a year later), TF 87 helped enforce the Truman Doctrine of deterring the spread of communism into war-torn Italy, France, and especially Greece. There communist guerrillas were fighting to overthrow the British-supported postwar royalist government.

Sherman directed Clark to continue to help British aircraft carriers convert to American carrier operating procedures as the U.S. Navy now became the senior partner in the Med. Jocko accomplished this by working closely with British Vice Admiral C. Douglas-Pennant and exchanging pilots and planes between his own carriers and the latter's flagship, light carrier *Triumph*. Together these allies conducted carrier and antisubmarine exercises. (One of the pilots on the *Philippine Sea*, incidentally, was Lieutenant (jg) "Wally" Schirra, a future astronaut.)

Jocko formed a friendship with, and great admiration for, the British cruiser commander Rear Admiral Lord Louis Mountbatten, who had reverted in rank from his wartime full admiralty in order to gain experience. Jocko hosted him and Lady Mountbatten on board the *Philippine Sea*.

When Task Force 87 put in at Athens, Clark met Lieutenant General James A. Van Fleet, the senior American military adviser helping the Greeks to eventually defeat the Soviet-backed rebels. While Clark was there, a U.S. Air Force brigadier general requested that Navy SB2C Helldivers be given the Greeks to help dislodge the guerrillas from their mountain positions. They arrived later and proved effective. Jocko received an official visit aboard his flagship from King Paul (in admiral's attire) and Queen Frederika of Greece, who both impressed him greatly.

As part of Forrest Sherman's anti-Soviet measures, TF 87 paid port calls to Augusta, Sicily, and Naples, Italy. Overflights of Italy and Turkey by the carriers' F4U Corsairs and SB2Cs were designed to encourage their confidence in protecting them against the Red menace. Once while being driven around Turkey Jocko was running late and told his driver Haley to speed up. Ere long, they rammed into another car, and along came the local police.

As Clark's operations officer Commander Tom Moorer remembered it, Jocko jumped out and speaking through an interpreter declared, "This is the worst driver I ever had. As soon as I get him back aboard ship, I'm going to fire him. I told him not to go so fast!" Haley looked on "a little hurt," but the ruse worked as the police let them go.

In fact, Clark depended so much on his driver that he kept driver and car with him the rest of his career. Haley did much more, answering to Jocko's every need. Often Clark—as throughout his career—could look fairly rumpled. Haley would say, "Admiral, you have to go back in the cabin and brush off your uniform and straighten your tie. You look like hell, Admiral!"

"Jocko *did* look like hell, too," recalled Moorer. "So Jock wouldn't say a word. He'd go back in and do what Haley told him to do." (Moorer Interview #30, 1592–93)

Jocko's handling of his two-carrier task force *appeared* to be casual, too, as he adroitly led it in much the same manner as he had his wartime four-carrier task group. In day-to-day operations during the war he had bypassed chief of staff Raöul Waller—concerned with overall administration—to work directly with operations officer Red Sharp. Here too he left routine ship movements to ops boss Moorer, who regarded Clark's policy as "just standing back and watching" the staff run things. It was

> my good fortune, because he allowed me to do everything. . . . That gave me an opportunity to gain a new kind of experience. I had been operations officer on the *Midway,* and every time you changed course you had to ask the captain's permission. . . . [Now,] I could change the course of 15 or 20 ships any time I pleased and ask no one's permission! (Interview #30, 1587)

Indeed, Jocko had so much faith in Moorer that he would even fall asleep and snore in his chair on the flag bridge—unfazed by messages constantly coming in through four separate speakers. Most of the traffic was routine, but the instant a question or something important came through he was awake and replied when necessary. Apparently, he had "a subconscious screening mechanism that permitted him to sift out important things," Moorer marveled. (Ibid., 1589)

On other occasions Jocko just moved to the operations room, sat in the leather lounge, and listened to a baseball game on the Armed Forces radio. This left Moorer to "run the outfit, which he was perfectly capable of doing at any time." (Robert W. McNitt Interview #4, 214) Or he just remained in his chair on the bridge and read a comic book from a stack of them kept fresh with new ones by his Marine orderly. (John W. Lee Jr. Interview #1, 116)

Something else that amazed Moorer was Clark's uncanny ability to always predict the weather correctly. As Jocko recalled, his current weather-guesser just told him whatever he wanted to hear (the guy was no Vonk!) "so

I learned to do it myself." Tom Moorer "didn't know whether his corns hurt or what, but ... he was always right." (Moorer Interview #30, 1594)

Clark's confidence, including his aerology, rankled his immediate superior, Admiral Sherman, who repeatedly annoyed Clark throughout this deployment. Jocko's flag secretary Lieutenant Charles Melhorn observed "no love between them at all" as Sherman "never, never lost an opportunity" to badger him. "Forrest Sherman was harassing Jocko all the time," Tom Moorer recalled. "They just didn't like each other at all." (Melhorn Interview, 135; Moorer Interview #30, 1587)

Clark told Melhorn that their differences had begun at the Academy when intellectual classmate Sherman had taken umbrage at "cowboy" Clark's hazing activities, which led to Clark's being turned back a year. Later, in the early 1930s, they had competed for awards as squadron commanders. Then during the war Sherman had lost his one carrier command, the first *Wasp* (CV-7), sunk off Guadalcanal, whereas Clark had excelled as Mitscher's top combat leader. The final blow to their relationship had been Jocko's blatant but abortive opposition to Sherman's plan for unification.

Sherman plagued Clark during flight operations by signaling the carriers to join up with the other ships soon after having sent the carriers off to conduct flight operations. Or he would change the base course "and head right for us" just as the carriers were in position to rejoin, causing Clark's ships to scatter. Then came the order: "Expedite join-up." (Moorer Interview #30, 1588) Once when the *Philippine Sea* was steaming downwind to recover planes, it still had a lone plane on deck. Sherman signaled by flag, "You are supposed to have a ready deck," that is, empty.

Reply: "Affirmative," meaning the flagship knew it and planned to remove the plane easily with a tractor.

Sherman: "What is that plane doing on the deck? How can you have a ready deck when you have a plane sitting in the arresting gear?" (Melhorn Interview, 136)

Another time Jocko was ashore at Cannes eating lunch with Tom Moorer when they received a message to report to Sherman's flagship, heavy cruiser *Des Moines*. "We dashed over there at full speed in the admiral's barge," thinking that secret orders had been received from Washington. But when they presented themselves all Sherman said was, "Jock, how are you going to get your car back aboard ship?"

That was all, a matter done routinely using a barge. Melhorn saw it as silly bickering (136); Moorer called it hazing (Interviews #6, 302; #30, 1588), perhaps a sly allusion to payback for Jocko's own Academy high jinks. Sherman's animus might well have been partly motivated by this intellectual loner's jealousy or hidden envy of the ebullient Indian.

Jocko got so angry at Fuzz's tormenting him that he would avoid the lee side of the ship so as not to see Sherman's flagship: "He couldn't stand to look at him." So from the starboard wing of the bridge Clark instructed Moorer, "Go over there and see what the old son of a bitch is signaling now." (Moorer Interview #30, 1588) (Clark was three years older!)

In April 1949, while the *Philippine Sea* was anchored a mile off Cannes on the Riviera, Clark received a letter from Herman Rosenblatt, now a practicing attorney in New York. He wanted to serve his annual two weeks' active duty as a Reserve lieutenant commander on the flagship. "By all means," replied Jocko, "come on back, and you'll just be my aide." When Herm arrived, Clark took him along to a reception ashore at Cannes that also was attended by Sherman. But when Jocko showed up, he now had three aides instead of the customary two that Sherman had. "There was hell to pay over that." (Melhorn Interview, 138)

At the same time, wife Shannon flew in to rub elbows with Europe's social elite on the Riviera. This included movie actress Rita Hayworth, whom Rosenblatt had helped get a divorce from actor-director Orson Welles the year before, freeing her to marry Prince Aly Khan of Pakistan. Still courting, Rita and Aly were vacationing at Cannes.

One thing on which Admiral Sherman insisted was the good behavior of all personnel ashore, essential to enhancing America's image in the Cold War. Clark took advantage of the vacationing celebrities to entertain them with a buffet supper aboard the *Philippine Sea* the evening of 29 April 1949. Sherman and several other admirals attended, forcing Jocko to stay on his best behavior.

The combination of such disparate personalities as admirals, royalty, millionaires, and the Hollywood set was accentuated by the presence of social butterfly and Texan Shannon Clark as official hostess, an obnoxious Herm Rosenblatt, and another former *Yorktown* shipmate—the humorous yet superb Commander Cooper Buck Bright, exec of the transport *Winston*, also at anchor.

Aly Khan, having served with the wartime AAF in North Africa, was fascinated by aircraft carriers and enjoyed talking with the admirals. Otherwise, it was a "stupid party," in Bright's opinion, with everyone just standing around chatting after dinner. "It doesn't have to be that way," thought this bald-headed master of grabass. He took aside the glamorous Rita, whom *Life* magazine had recently dubbed "the Love Goddess" for her recent steamy films *Gilda* and *Down to Earth*.

"When the admirals stop talking," Bright quietly suggested a comical charade to the gorgeous long-haired Hayworth: "I'll ask you, 'If you had met me before you met Aly Khan, and if I'd preferred marriage to you [instead of to my wife] what would your answer be?' And you say, 'I would select you over Aly Khan in a day.' And I'll say, 'Why would you do that?' And you say, 'Because you have more face to kiss.'" She agreed at once, and Coop remarked, "I think we can break the ice."

At the next break in the overall conversation, Coop, standing on the opposite side of the room from Hayworth, said loudly, "Rita!" All chatter stopped, especially since only the admirals were supposed to address the actress by her first name (and Bright thought too many admirals were present anyway). The two went into their routine. Rita, the consummate actress that she was, not only remembered her lines perfectly but gave them "the real play."

The place "went up in smoke," recalled Coop, with everyone laughing uproariously. When it died down, Jocko bellowed, "Goddam you, I'll bet he *paid* her to say that!" More laughter, whereupon Bright seized the moment. He said to Rita that during the war he had been "the Pacific Ocean Area Sex Typhoon," a boast that he, happily married, had used to rib the *Yorktown*'s horny pilots. (Reynolds, *Fighting Lady*, 24, 243–44) "And you are the 'goddess of love,' so let's have a photograph." As the two posed for the camera, Herm Rosenblatt "stuck his mug into it and ruined the picture!"

When the guests were descending the ladder to the gig to take them ashore, Bright stayed way in the background on the hangar deck. Suddenly, Aly Khan stopped and said, "Could we have Commander Bright come back with us?" So he did. The following night the famous couple took Bright and Clark—as the only admiral—to Monte Carlo. Coop stayed over a week, partying with them. Being no drinker, "I survived," Coop recalled. Rita and Aly were married a month later.

The entire dinner party doubtless cemented Forrest Sherman's enmity toward Clark. But it also rekindled Jocko's admiration for "Buck" (he called him by his middle name) Bright as a man and friend he could trust.

The individual he could not trust was Sherman. On 15 May, as Clark's task force left "the Med" to return home, Sherman wrote an unsatisfactory fitness report on his former classmate. He did praise Clark's handling of his carrier force, "well trained and brought to a high state of efficiency," and recommended that he retain the command.

But on the checklist of command "factors" Sherman gave him a damning average mark in both "exercising judgment" and maintaining discipline within his command. In several other categories he rated Clark only satisfactory—ability to command, carrying out responsibilities, understanding instructions and using offered suggestions, transmitting orders, working well with others, and adapting to changing conditions. Sherman gave him top marks in the eight remaining categories, including "bearing and dress"!

Brilliant though Sherman was, his reputation as a cold fish was amply demonstrated in Clark's case. (See Reynolds, "Forrest Percival Sherman")

Jocko delivered the *Philippine Sea* to the Boston Navy Yard for overhaul—and soon a new captain, none other than Raöul Waller. He established his flag ashore at Quonset Point and then reported to Atlantic Fleet headquarters at Norfolk. With Tom Moorer in tow, he visited Rear Admiral John Ballentine, who showed him the fitness report by Sherman.

"It was real funny," Moorer recalled. "Here was a fellow who had been through the whole war and had made quite a splash, and then he gets an unsatisfactory fitness report, just like some ensign." Jocko said simply, "Ha, ha, ha" and refused to sign it as required for any "unsat" report. "He couldn't have cared less," noted Moorer, who regarded the incident as "good training for a young commander—to watch some of these backs and forths. It helps to understand the problem better." (Moorer Interview #6, 203) Such an education helped Moorer eventually achieve the post of CNO.

The *Essex*-class carrier *Kearsarge* (CV-33) replaced the *Philippine Sea* in Jocko's carrier division for coastal operations out of Quonset. Its skipper was Curt Smiley, air group commander on the first *Yorktown* (CV-5) when Jocko had been exec. Clark occasionally shifted his flag to *Kearsarge*, where newer officers avoided him on the strength of his earlier reputation until they dealt with him firsthand. The assistant navigator, Lieutenant (jg) John W. Lee Jr., the regular Navy's first black officer, found Jocko just "laid back," as if he was finally "winding down." (Lee Interview #1, 117) His demeanor was likely due partly to his dim career prospects in the wake of the CNO's negative fitness report.

Jocko's immediate boss, Felix Stump, did not share Sherman's judgment. In his fitness report, covering March through August 1949, Felix gave Clark unanimously superlative marks (except for the usual slight markdown on "military bearing and dress"). Stump would never forget the long night of 4–5 December 1943 off Kwajalein when Jocko's *Yorktown* had stood by Felix's stricken *Lexington*. He added that Clark "continues to demonstrate the high qualities of aggressive leadership and sound judgment that have consistently marked his outstanding naval career."

In his personal life, Clark had tired of wife Shannon's continuous entertaining in their sumptuous suburban house. So she sold it and bought an apartment building at 2500 Massachusetts Avenue on Embassy Row in northwest Washington. They occupied the ground floor, where the children visited them when home from school, and rented out the upper floors.

The top floor was leased to the grandson of Spanish-American War hero Admiral George Dewey. One day Clark discovered that the man kept a live-in mistress there. That evening Jocko physically blocked the door to prevent her from reentering the apartment. When she tried to get by him, he kept his arms behind his back—to avoid a potential lawsuit for possibly striking her—and just butted her with his chest.

She did sue him. The court eventually ruled in his favor, but not before the story reached the national news. It turned out to be a Pyrrhic victory because of the heavy legal fees he had to pay. (Conversation with Clark; letter from daughter Mary Lou Clark in 2004) And it did not help his chances for promotion.

Neither did his involvement in a renewed imbroglio over unification. An exhausted Defense Secretary Forrestal had been forced to yield his job to pro–Air Force Louis Johnson, and then he committed suicide in May. Johnson cancelled construction of the supercarrier *United States* in favor of pushing the B-36 Air Force strategic bomber. This sparked the "revolt of the admirals" against this attack on naval aviation.

It was led partly by the outspoken Captain John G. Crommelin Jr., brother of the late Charlie and renowned pilot in his own right. CNO Denfeld and Vice Chief Price asked Clark to persuade Crommelin "to keep quiet." After many hours of conversation, Jocko got him to agree to stop making public statements.

The Navy launched a public relations campaign to promote carriers and involved its colorful Cherokee. A new historical but fictionalized motion picture, *Task Force,* portrayed the rise of carrier aviation since the 1920s. It starred Gary Cooper as a wartime skipper and was black-and-white to accommodate very early carrier footage, then shifted to color scenes lifted from *The Fighting Lady.* On 20 September 1949 Jocko provided the *Midway* for a special cruise out of New York; the movie was previewed on board and an air show observed by dignitaries. Jocko and four other admirals present were interviewed over three radio networks—NBC's was conducted by the "senior" Tex McCrary.

More dramatic was an "orientation" cruise for Secretary Johnson and the Joint Chiefs of Staff six days later. Felix Stump put Clark in charge of the demonstration as Commander Task Force 87 and accompanied him and the VIPs on board the *Franklin D. Roosevelt.* The Navy Department dramatically demonstrated its newest weapons. The *FDR,* sister ship *Midway,* antisub escort carrier *Mindoro,* two cruisers and a dozen tin cans stood out 60 miles from Hampton Roads on 26 September, while a double-rotored helicopter flew Johnson out to the *FDR.* Then fast McDonnell F2H Banshee jet fighters and rugged Douglas AD Skyraider bombers executed impressive mock attacks on the *Midway.*

*FDR's* AA gunners shot down a radio-controlled F6F Hellcat at 4,500 yards. *Mindoro's* planes tracked a submarine equipped with a German-derived snorkel underwater air-intake device, and several cans dropped depth charges at a safe distance. To demonstrate an atomic bomb delivery capability for large carrier-borne strike aircraft, each large carrier launched a Lockheed P2V Neptune land patrol plane using JATO (jet assisted take-off). One of them flew nonstop to San Diego via the Panama Canal and Corpus Christi—4,800 miles. The other took Johnson and selected VIPs back to Washington. (Hanson W. Baldwin in the *New York Times*, 27 September 1949)

Clark then proceeded north with his task force to Halifax, Nova Scotia, to help that city celebrate its 200th anniversary. The Atlantic Fleet commander, Admiral W. H. P. Blandy, who had also witnessed the carrier show, flew his flag in the cruiser *Newport News*. Jocko had pleased his superiors with his handling of the demonstration, although it failed to convince Secretary Johnson to revive the supercarrier construction. He continued to support the B-36 as the only viable strategic weapon.

Suddenly, on 3 October, John Crommelin broke his promise to Clark by going public in his attack on defense policy. He released a copy of a confidential letter Vice Admiral Bogan had written to Secretary of the Navy Francis P. Matthews. In it, Bogan complained about Johnson's bad treatment of the Navy, the limited funding, and resulting low morale. Crommelin called for congressional hearings.

Matthews, little more than a factotum for Johnson, had no recourse but to punish CNO Denfeld, as the man on top, and Crommelin with retirements. First, however, Carl Vinson and other congressmen immediately held hearings over the Navy's grievances. Admiral Radford flew in from Pearl Harbor to lead the attack. Sherman came from the Mediterranean but was talked out of testifying by Johnson and Matthews. The nation watched as naval aviators "revolted" against the Air Force's monopoly of the strategic bombing mission, even criticizing the B-36 as obsolete.

Clark elected to stay out of the fracas, allegedly because he regretted, without explaining his reasons, "that the B-36 was criticized." (Clark, "31-Knot Burke," 56) Given his reputation as a fighter, he certainly would have been a forceful and articulate spokesman. More than likely, however, he probably realized he would risk his career by becoming involved, and his champion Raddy likely counseled him accordingly.

Fortunately for Jocko, he did not testify. In the search for a new CNO, President Truman accepted Admiral Nimitz's recommendation of Forrest Sherman. Jocko's archenemy assumed the post on 2 November, and with the cool determination and great industry that made others fear him Sherman set about restoring Navy morale. He was aided by the plain fact, which few people realized at the time, that the "revolt of the admirals" hearings had won over Congress, which began to restore funding, although not at the expense of the Air Force. Sherman also maneuvered Gerry Bogan into retiring, a hint of what would have happened to Jocko had he participated. (Reynolds, "Forrest Percival Sherman," 213–17; conversation with Bogan; Barlow, *Revolt of the Admirals*)

In the meantime, on 13 October, Clark lost a "trusted, brilliant, and close friend." Herman Rosenblatt had shot himself, ostensibly by accident when cleaning a rifle. Former shipmates and others figured that this complex individual had committed suicide. In the postwar years Rosenblatt had been seen by those who knew him as pleasant enough yet as appearing to have psychological problems. (Conversations with actress Nina Foch and others) His will stipulated that he be cremated and requested that his ashes be "scattered at sea from one of my planes," said Clark.

If his death had not been a suicide, the accident seemed strange—that such a dynamic and talented individual who knew guns so well had wasted his life in this way. Indeed, the mystery is deepened by one account—virtually impossible to corroborate—that claimed that this brilliant Jewish combat veteran had fabricated the story of his death, moved to Europe, and had his face altered by plastic surgery. Assuming a new identity, he then allegedly dedicated the rest of his life to hunting down and eliminating former Nazis guilty of administering the Holocaust. (Conversations with Barney Rosson up until his death in 1986)

Clark took Rosenblatt's (apparent) ashes with him when he departed for the Arctic on 31 October as Commander Task Force 28. On 11 November, Armistice Day (of World War I), he held a memorial ceremony for Herman Rosenblatt on the *Midway*, ending with the ship's helicopter dropping the ashes at sea above the Arctic Circle.

The mission to the far north was to test the carriers in cold weather operations, anticipating any shooting war against the new Russian enemy. Second Fleet commander Duncan flew his flag in the *FDR*, Jocko his in the *Midway*, although Raöul Waller's *Philippine Sea* relieved the *Roosevelt* in the midst of three weeks of the worst weather Clark had ever encountered. On one occasion he marveled at Waller's ability to recover a full deckload of planes in a bitter 68-knot wind over the deck.

Another day a huge wave slammed a sailor on the destroyer *Power* into its depth-charge racks, apparently breaking his back. The skipper, Commander S. M. "Moe" Archer, recommended his ship take the man back to Norfolk for proper medical attention. Instead, Clark decided to take him aboard the *Midway* by high-line, in spite of the pitching seas. The transfer was accomplished safely for the man—but not his ship.

The tin can had gotten too close to the big carrier—perhaps 35 feet—and was being sucked in (the Bernoulli effect) for an inevitable collision with the carrier. The *Midway* "smashed the *Power*'s bridge flat with the first roll," hit the 40-mm guns amidships on the second, and threatened to strike and detonate the depth charges on deck on the next roll." But Captain Archer rang up "All ahead flank [speed]" and ripped his ship loose of the carrier.

Clark immediately radioed the CNO's office in Washington: "I ordered the ship alongside. I accept full responsibility for damage to the *Power*. We were trying to take care of an injured crewman," who, incidentally, did not have a broken back and recovered. "Old Jocko took it on his own shoulders," remembered Commander Robert W. McNitt of the *Midway*. (Interview #4, 229) In so doing, he saved Moe Archer's career. When Archer found out, he wrote to Clark, "If you ever need anyone to go through hell with you, I am your man!"

After the return to base at the end of November Clark encountered Cooper Bright in Times Square during a visit to New York on a rainy day. Well dressed as ever in civvies, Jocko was amazed to see "old Buck" in a crumpled raincoat. It was obvious to Bright that Clark thought he was broke, as if "I was on skid row," and asked Bright what he was doing.

"I'm working for Ralph Bunche at the UN," Bright replied. Bunche was the distinguished African-American diplomat laboring for a permanent peace settlement between the new nation of Israel and neighboring Transjordan (soon to become Jordan). Coop explained he was still on active duty while working at the UN. Jocko had "a heart and a lot of kindness" in Coop's view and generously invited "Buck" to join him at his Naval Academy reunion. Bright declined, gratefully, and chuckled over Clark's concern after they parted.

The chance meeting apparently motivated Clark to seek out Bright for advice over his future. He telephoned Buck to have lunch with him at a New York club. When they met, Jocko poured out his sorrows: Forrest Sherman had put him "in the doghouse" with a dead-end job—another Mediterranean deployment with his task force. He would obviously never be promoted. "The Navy is going down the hill. My career is ruined," he lamented and asked if Bright thought he should get out.

Bright regarded Clark's solicitation of his advice as a high honor—to be treated as a friend and even consulted by "the great Jocko!" But Coop responded in his gentle way, "No. Stay in. Something's going to happen. The country is in a mess. You've always had the breaks, even going into San Francisco [with the *Yorktown* in 1943] when somebody raised the antennas. By God, you drifted through instead of off" the bridge pilings.

As Coop continued to reminisce, he seemed to make an impression on his old boss. In addition to the admirals' "revolt" at home, Russia had exploded its first A-bomb and the Red Chinese had just driven the Nationalists off the mainland. And an anticommunist hysteria was growing within the United States. But the Berlin airlift had also saved that Soviet-blockaded city, and the North Atlantic Treaty Organization (NATO) had been created to deter the Russians in Western Europe. The Greeks had even defeated their communist guerrillas.

In fact, Clark's star was gradually starting to rise again. Second Fleet commander Duncan and ComAirLant Stump gave him superlative fitness reports for his performance over the autumn. And now old friend Ballentine became Sixth Fleet commander in the Mediterranean as vice admiral.

In mid-January 1950 TF 87 returned to the middle sea, Clark's flag in the *Midway*, its captain Wallace Beakley. Its duties were the same as the previous year, except that the Greek victory meant only policing the region to keep it stabilized as the Cold War deepened.

Jocko renewed his friendship with Lord Mountbatten, now vice admiral, who flew over by helicopter to witness air operations off the *Midway*. On one visit they had "an amusing discussion" about the flying saucers (unidentified flying objects) that were exciting public attention for the first time. "I maintained it was alcohol that made people say they saw flying saucers," said Clark, who later sent Mountbatten a newspaper limerick:

> There once was a man named McFisk
> Who thought he'd been hit by a flying disk,
> But on second thought
> It was only that last drink of whisk.

Replied the British admiral, "Next time I visit your flagship I'll come by flying saucer rather than helicopter."

Clark also renewed his acquaintance with Aly Khan and Rita Hayworth at Cannes and with whom he exchanged visits between the *Midway* and their chateau. Wife Shannon flew over again to act as official hostess, although their marriage was growing rockier.

On one occasion Aly and Rita attended a shipboard dance. Aly could not participate because his hip and leg were in a cast from a skiing accident in Switzerland. But every sailor wanted to dance with Rita, so many in fact that the dance committee decided only one of its members would have that privilege. Alas, Clark recalled, as soon as "she took the first step with him, the crew mobbed her. It is safe to say that in a space of about two minutes she danced with a hundred sailors."

The "real" Jocko Clark? This is how many officers and crewmen who caught his wrath viewed him. Photo taken on the flagship *Midway* en route to the Mediterranean, 12 January 1950. *U.S. Navy photo*

Jocko greets actress Rita Hayworth on board the *Midway* off Cannes in February 1950. He gives her his undivided attention! *U.S. Navy photo*

The year before, Clark had met Aly Khan's father Aga Khan III, spiritual leader of the Ismailite Muslims centered in India, Pakistan, and Africa. On the 1950 deployment, however, Jocko insisted on including him in a dinner visit aboard the flagship. Although the Aga Khan was a large man, his staff assured Clark's that "he was in excellent shape" to climb the ship's accommodation ladder, even "that he played golf every day." "What we didn't know," recalled flag secretary Charles Melhorn, was that "he did play golf every day—but only one hole!" He weighed some 300 pounds and was 72 years old.

At the dock Melhorn met the "cavalcade of Cadillacs" with the Aga Khan; his current (and fourth) wife, the young Begum Yvette; his previous wife, the Princess Andrée; and assorted staffers and bodyguards. Melhorn shuttled them out to the *Midway* in the admiral's barge and the captain's gig. When they got to the ship's ladder, however, not only could the old gentleman not make the strenuous climb but neither could his injured son Aly.

Jocko and skipper Beakley held a parley up on the quarterdeck and accepted a bosun's suggestion to hoist the entire barge and its passengers up to the flight deck by the ship's big aircraft crane. Jocko went down the ladder and boarded the barge to reassure and accompany his guests—the Aga Khan, the Begum, Aly Khan, and Rita. The crane lifted the barge all the way up to the boat cradle on the flight deck. Because the cradle was now suspended 20 feet above the deck, crewmen put a pallet and bosun's chair onto a forklift, which they raised to the level of the dangling barge.

The Aga Khan simply stepped from barge to bosun's chair, sat down, and was lowered to the flight deck. The forklift then trundled down the deck to the number one plane elevator—"the funniest picture I ever saw in my life," remembered ops officer Tom Moorer, "with the Aga Khan sitting up like he was on a throne." Then the elevator descended to the hangar deck, putting him right at the tomato juice being served before dinner. (Melhorn Interview, 138–42; Moorer Interview #30, 1590)

The meal was followed by a dance, during which Rita Hayworth had great fun with the sailors. The mayor of Cannes came aboard briefly to escort Clark and his guests ashore for a late dinner. With the clock ticking, Jocko remarked to wife Shannon, "It's time for us to go. We can't be late for the mayor's dinner."

"We can't go now," said Shannon. "Rita's with her public. She's having such a good time. We'll have to wait until she finishes."

Replied Jocko, "I want to tell you one thing. When we're ashore, you're the boss. When I'm aboard ship, I'm the boss. Goddammit, get your hat!" (Moorer Interview #30, 1591)

During March TF 87 visited Greece to help celebrate the victory over the communist guerrillas. Clark joined the king and queen in an impressive combined Roman Catholic and eastern Orthodox thanksgiving service in Athens. Moving to Naples, he was driven to Rome to attend Easter services at St. Peter's Cathedral; the serene beauty of the ceremony "touched me deeply."

Next day he had an audience with Pope Pius XII, arranged by old friend Monsignor Maurice Sheehy. For 35 minutes the strongly anticommunist Holy Father did most of the talking—in perfect English, one of his many languages—pumping Clark for information about the Greek victory. The Pope then presented the Oklahoma Episcopalian with a rosary that he blessed.

Clark brought his task force home from the Mediterranean during May 1950. John Ballentine lost no time in giving him unanimous superior marks on his fitness report that month because of his having handled his command "in an exemplary manner. He has been cheerful, efficient and cooperative at all times. Under his leadership, the *Midway* and attached Air Group developed into a fine fighting team. It was a pleasure to have Rear Admiral Clark in the Sixth Fleet."

One month later, on 25 June, communist North Korea, an ally of the Soviet Union, invaded pro–U.S. South Korea. President Truman and the United Nations rallied to the support of South Korea; despite this, most of the south was quickly overrun by the Reds. Jocko hastened to Washington to offer his services to the CNO, Forrest Sherman, whatever their differences.

"My specialty is combat," he told Sherman. "I want to get in the war." The CNO had obviously been considering his best available admirals for combat. He told Clark that he would be shore based first, in charge of the Navy's air bases on the California coast—a rear admiral's billet. If he measured up there, "I'll send you to war." The two men discussed this limited war—confined to the Korean peninsula—with Jocko asking Sherman if he thought the conflict would expand into a global war.

"By fighting in Korea," Sherman replied, "we may be fighting a little war to stop a big war."

Felix Stump reinforced Jocko's case by writing a fitness report of all perfect marks on 1 August, the date of Clark's detachment as ComCarDiv Four. He added:

> Clark's performance of duty has been of the highest order. His detachment from Air Force, Atlantic Fleet is a great loss to the Fleet. He is strongly recommended for higher rank in an important command at sea.... Especially qualified and recommended for sea duty in command of a position of great responsibility.

Any promotion would have to be to the next grade, vice admiral. Any seagoing vice admiral's billet "of great responsibility" would be a fleet command. If in a combat role, that could only mean Seventh Fleet—the naval force fighting the Korean War. Jocko's peers were all pulling for him to take the lead there in the same manner he had commanded in the war against Japan. To get the job, however, he had first to do everything right in the eyes of the CNO.

# TWENTY

# Korean Finale, 1950–1953

ON 14 AUGUST 1950, AS THE NAVY MOBILIZED FOR THE KOREAN War, Jocko Clark returned to North Island, San Diego, as Commander Naval Air Bases, 11th and 12th Naval Districts. His command embraced all naval air stations and auxiliary fields in California, Arizona, Nevada, and Utah. If his performance satisfied his superiors and CNO Sherman, he could be expected to command either the fast carrier Task Force 77 and/or the overall Seventh Fleet in Korean waters.

Like most Americans, Clark labored to understand the nature of this limited war and how to wage it. The North Korean army, backed by the Soviet Union, drove the American-supported South Korean army all the way from the 38th parallel treaty line to Pusan on the southern tip of the Korean peninsula. There the Seventh Fleet and its carriers helped the South Korean army hold on until September.

At that time the Seventh Fleet landed General Douglas MacArthur's American army at Inchon on the west coast near the 38th parallel in the enemy's rear. The North Korean army fled back to its homeland, then nearly out of it altogether as MacArthur pushed all the way to the Chinese Manchurian border at the Yalu River.

Then in November the massive Red Chinese army crossed the Yalu and drove MacArthur back into South Korea. The frustrated general publicly criticized President Truman's refusal to let him escalate the war with a counterattack into North Korea. Because this amounted to insubordination, he was relieved of command. His successor, General Matthew B. Ridgway, and Lieutenant General James Van Fleet, leading the Eighth Army, fought back to the 38th parallel by June 1951, at which time the diplomats accepted a stalemate there and initiated truce talks.

To keep a fresh supply of pilots available for the carriers Admiral Clark focused on training the Naval Reserve pilots being recalled to active duty after having been only "weekend warriors." The ultimate destination for most of them was the *Essex*-class flattops of Task Force 77 (the *Midway*-class carriers remained in the Atlantic, shoring up NATO). The major air stations under Clark's jurisdiction were located along the California coast—the 11th Naval District embracing San Diego to Santa Barbara, the 12th north of Santa Barbara through the San Francisco Bay Area.

Jocko plunged into his work with customary alacrity, distracted somewhat, however, by his deteriorating family situation. Wife Shannon and Jocko's attractive teenage daughters Mary Lou and Cathy came with him to North Island. But Shannon's financial resources steadily dwindled, which with other stresses led to heated arguments between them. The threat of an ugly divorce quickly reached Admiral Arthur Radford, the Pacific Fleet commander busy orchestrating the Navy's activities in the Korean War.

Raddy, anxious that Jocko eventually get command of the Seventh Fleet, was suitably alarmed. He immediately recalled Bob Reynolds to active duty, again to act as Jocko's flag lieutenant with one particular task—to keep Jocko and Shannon from divorcing, at least until he got his sea command. For many months Reynolds pleaded with them to desist—and they did. But matters worsened early in 1951 when Shannon lost her fortune.

Clark fulfilled his professional tasks so successfully that he received a superlative 4.0 in his 1950–51 fitness reports by his naval district superiors, Rear Admirals Wilder Baker as Com11 and Bertram J. Rodgers as Com12. Only slightly negative comments were made about his industry, initiative, and intelligence for the six months beginning 1 March 1951. His physical exams also noted a weight gain of 14 pounds between early 1950 and September 1951 to 196—the same weight he had had at the start of 1942. This was likely due to marital stress and added professional responsibilities.

In January 1951 the nation's concerns over the Soviet menace led to an additional appointment—as Commander Air Emergency Forces, Western Sea Frontier. The overall commander of West Coast defenses was Sixth Army commander Lieutenant General Albert C. Wedemeyer in San Francisco. Jocko, however, reported directly to Commander Western Sea Frontier, Vice Admiral George Murray and later J. L. Hall Jr. He met with Canadian counterparts in Vancouver to initiate a hemispheric defense system against a possible Soviet air attack. The eventual result was creation of the North American Air Defense (NORAD) in 1957.

The most instructive exercise to test continental defense was against a missile launched from a submarine. It was simulated by a Lockheed F-80

Shooting Star, the Air Force's first jet fighter, launched from land to fly over a sub near Santa Barbara Island and attack San Diego. To intercept it, Clark employed antisub hunter-killer carrier planes, land-based Navy patrol planes, Air Force planes, and Army radar.

Alas, like the kamikazes off Okinawa, the F-80 flew low to avoid the radar beams and suddenly appeared over San Diego. This vulnerability—hardly Clark's fault—led to major innovations. Two years later the first of several *Essex*-class carriers were designated as specialized antisubmarine carriers (CVS), the rest remaining as "attack" carriers (CVA). By the end of the decade, several CVS operated in specialized Navy hunter-killer groups, and the submarine-launched Polaris ballistic missile system joined the fleet.

Forrest Sherman, satisfied with Clark's performance, in June 1951 let him know that he was next in line to command the Seventh Fleet. Another aviator, Vice Admiral Harold M. "Beauty" Martin, had just gotten the job, meaning that Jocko still had to wait a few months. Unfortunately, one month later Admiral Sherman died of a heart attack during a diplomatic mission to Europe.

During the wrangle over who would be next CNO, Arthur Radford withheld his name in favor of remaining CinCPac and directing the fleet in the Korean War. To achieve ultimate victory, Raddy wanted to get Clark into action as soon as possible. He wrote Jocko a letter asking him whether he "would be willing to take a rear admiral combat job until a three-star job opened up."

Clark jumped at the possibility, hoping for command of Task Force 77, the fast carriers of the Seventh Fleet. In the meantime, a black shoe, Vice Admiral Bill Fechteler, became CNO, and Clark waited. Due for leave time, he took Shannon and his daughters on a camping trip to Yosemite, where he and his wife fought viciously. Then in September, he accepted an invitation from Owen Sowerwine to go hunting and fishing in Montana. Leaving Sowerwine's address and phone number with nearby Vice Admiral Tommy Sprague, ComAirPac, Clark departed for Kalispell with Bob Reynolds by car; Haley, his regular driver, and another enlisted man shared the driving.

From there Sowerwine-Zero and his brother drove them through the forest to the end of a road, where they mounted horses (recalling Jocko's youth) and rode 21 miles into the mountains to a campsite. Heavy rains turned to snow during the night and next day. Clark had no intention of joining the younger sportsmen in trekking through the snow in search of game, so he spent the day fishing. Unfortunately,

they got cut off by snowdrifts and had to remain in the woods all night.
At dusk a forest ranger appeared with the news that somebody wanted

to talk to me on the telephone. I accompanied the ranger to his station and found Tommy Sprague on the other end of the line in San Diego. "I'm sending a plane for you in the morning," he said. "You have immediate orders to go to Korea."

Next morning, 26 September, a small plane flew in to a nearby mountain airstrip, took Clark to Kalispell, where Sprague's Navy plane rushed him back to San Diego. He arrived to a headline saying, "Adm. 'Jocko' Clark Ordered on Korean Secret Mission." (*San Diego Union*, 27 September 1951) There he packed his bags and, the morning of 27 September, relinquished his two commands. Having sent his daughters to their schools in Texas near his kinfolk, he and Reynolds were flown straight to Pearl Harbor.

Admiral Radford was on hand when they landed and even placed a Hawaiian lei on Jock's shoulders. Another greeter was Raddy's new chief of staff, old comrade in arms Rear Admiral Sol Phillips.

Flag lieutenant Reynolds did not remain. Having fulfilled the task of keeping Shannon from divorcing Jocko and out of the news, he returned to teaching high school in Los Angeles. Shannon soon just walked away, and divorce followed. Her financial resources spent, she ended up joining the crusade of the African-American religious leader Father Divine (to Jocko's utter dismay).

As ComCarDiv Three, Clark became one of the rotating commanders of TF 77. It was the third time in his career that he led a fast carrier task group/force, and the second time in combat. From Hawaii he flew to Tokyo, headquarters for Vice Admiral C. Turner Joy, commanding Naval Forces Far East. Rear Admiral Ralph Ofstie, Joy's chief of staff, briefed him on a plan for another landing in the enemy's rear similar to the Inchon operation. The target was to be Kojo, just south of Wonsan Harbor on the east coast of North Korea. The goal was for the landing forces to turn south, attack the enemy rear, and link up with Van Fleet's Eighth Army.

That suited Clark, and he strongly advocated it. But soon General Omar Bradley, chairman of the Joint Chiefs of Staff, visited Van Fleet in Korea and scotched that or any plan that had the goal of taking more "of the enemy's real estate." Jocko regarded this statement as unusual, inasmuch as "the occupation of enemy territory had always been an obvious step toward a complete military victory." (Cagle and Manson, *Sea War in Korea*, 390–91)

Thus was Jocko rudely awakened to the hard reality of the different character of this war—limited objectives instead of a "win" psychology. His dislike for it was shared by all U.S. commanders, who longed to renew the offensive and drive the Communist North Koreans and their Red Chinese allies completely out of Korea.

Pacific Fleet commander in chief Admiral Arthur W. "Raddy" Radford (*left*) welcomes Clark with a Hawaiian lei and a combat command in the Korean War at Pearl Harbor, 27 September 1951. Bob Reynolds (*right*) had both men autograph the snapshot. *U.S. Navy photo*

On 1 October Clark flew to Korea and visited with Van Fleet. Two days later he was flown aboard the Task Force 77 flagship *Bon Homme Richard*, where he relieved Red Tomlinson as ComCarDiv Three and on the 7th replaced Jack Perry as task force commander. (Perry and Tomlinson had been successive captains of the *Belleau Wood* in Jocko's TG 58.1 in 1944–45, and the "Bonnie Dick" had joined his TG 38.1 during his final days attacking Japan.) The force included the usual cruisers, destroyers, and occasional battleship. "At last I was again in a war," Jocko told himself.

Tomlinson informed Jocko that he had issued an order forbidding sailors emergency leaves "except in very unusual cases" because he thought the privilege was being abused. Clark's first act was to cancel Tomlinson's order as contrary to Navy policy. Unfortunately, a sailor had already been denied emergency leave when his mother died, and the press spread the story, creating an outcry. The culprit was identified only as the unnamed TF

77 commander, as a result of which Clark received letters of outrage (one written on toilet paper!). Ere long, thankfully, the press absolved Clark of Tomlinson's blunder.

With the battle line in Korea basically static, TF 77 concentrated on interdicting enemy roads, railroads, and bridges. The day after Clark took command, 8 October, he launched daylong strikes from the *Bon Homme Richard* and *Essex* off the east coast of Korea. The planes hit transportation targets and antiaircraft positions around Hamhung. The third heavy carrier, *Antietam*, rotated with its sister ships over successive days, while planes from the Australian light carrier *Sydney* struck targets from the west side of Korea.

The carrier air groups represented the ideal combination of planes advocated by Clark during the last year of the Pacific war: three squadrons of fighter-bombers and one of attack planes. The former, equipped to carry rockets, light bombs, and/or napalm bombs, included the older propeller-driven F4U Corsair and jet-engined Grumman F9F Panther and McDonnell F2H Banshee. Neither jet, however, could match the enemy's Russian-built MIG-15 jet fighter, which had to be handled by the Air Force's F-86 Sabrejet.

Conversely, the Air Force, having emphasized strategic bombers, had no effective tactical bombers and depended largely on the Navy. The carriers' rugged prop-driven Douglas AD Skyraider did this job admirably. It embodied all the functions of the World War II divebombers and torpeckers and carried a heavier payload.

An immediate boon in identifying targets came at the suggestion of Lieutenant Commander James A. Scholes, Clark's flag lieutenant. This was JACK (Joint Advisory Commission Korea), which utilized radio-equipped undercover agents behind enemy lines. Clark and Scholes visited JACK headquarters at Pusan and worked out a system of targeting based on JACK agents' information and aerial photographs by carrier planes.

Several successful strikes culminated on the morning of 29 October when eight AD Skyraiders from the *Essex* surprised a secret meeting of enemy commissars at Kapsan near the Yalu River. Each "Spad" roared in over the mountains and dropped a 1,000-pound proximity-fused napalm bomb and several 250-pound general purpose bombs. Three of the big bombs hit directly on top of Red officials running for the air raid shelter. Then the ADs strafed the survivors with 20-mm incendiary and high-explosive machine gun fire. Finally, the buildings were flattened.

The final count by JACK agents was 144 party officials and 376 soldiers killed, many others wounded, all 12 buildings and 10 houses reduced to flaming rubble. No planes were lost. Sadly, the identity of what the Reds called the "butchers of Kapsan"—the JACK operatives—was discovered,

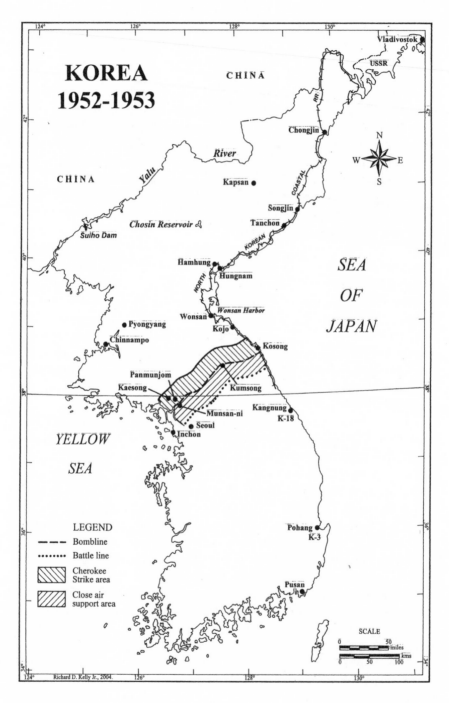

Korea in 1952–53

forcing them to terminate their work. (Cagle and Manson, *Sea War in Korea*, 248–51)

Meanwhile, Clark rotated the TF 77 command with Jack Perry 17 to 31 October, a common pattern in this unique war. Radford arrived on the 18th and instructed Jocko to assist the Air Force. Its generals hoped that carrier fighters could augment the F-86s in escorting the B-29s during daylight bombing raids over North Korea. Even though F9Fs and F2Hs had done it successfully in August, Clark doubted they would be equal to the task. But he flew to Seoul to discuss the idea with Major General Frank F. Earnest, commanding the Fifth Air Force.

During the course of their deliberations, enemy MIGs shot down five out of 11 B-29s on one mission. The Air Force immediately shifted its strategic bombing to nighttime, eliminating the need for fighter escorts. Strategic bombers—neither the B-29, much less the B-36—were not suitable in a limited war, especially over the mountainous terrain of Korea. What the United States needed were fewer advocates of strategic bombers and more aircraft carriers—symbolized respectively by the ouster of Louis Johnson as Secretary of Defense in September 1950 and the laying of the keel of the 59,000-ton carrier *Forrestal* (CV-59) in July 1952.

Clark, after duck hunting with Earnest near Seoul, visited General Van Fleet, then went on a jeep ride around Heartbreak Ridge with Major General Gerald C. Thomas. Thomas's First Marine Division had captured it two weeks earlier. In the front seat flag lieutenant Jim Scholes remarked to the Marine corporal at the wheel, "This is a pretty rough country to be fighting for."

"Sir," replied the gyrene, "we ain't fighting for that country; we're fighting for freedom."

"This one sentence," recalled Jocko, "told me all I needed to hear about the fighting men in Korea. They knew why they were there."

From a promontory overlooking the battle line, and then in a helicopter flying near it, Clark saw Marine Corps artillery, the 8-inch guns of heavy cruiser *Toledo* 12 miles offshore, and Navy and Marine aircraft all pummeling one enemy strongpoint—real teamwork.

Before returning to the task force, Clark visited truce negotiators Turner Joy and Rear Admiral Arleigh Burke, a former TF 58 colleague. They met at the headquarters tent of the U.S. delegation in an apple orchard at Munsan-ni just south of Panmunjom. Both men were pessimistic about achieving a peace settlement. Burke told Jocko the Reds were "crazy" thinking "they are going to walk away from here with everything. . . . They certainly haven't won a military victory, and as far as I am concerned they aren't going to be able to say so!" (Clark, "31-Knot Burke," 53)

Clark resumed command of TF 77 on 31 October, welcomed aboard visitors General Ridgway and Seventh Fleet commander Beauty Martin, and continued daily strikes off the east coast of North Korea. On the night of 21 November, a South Korean army corps ran out of ammunition while battling large enemy forces near Kojo. It radioed the fleet for help until reinforcements could arrive.

Clark detached heavy cruiser *Los Angeles* to bombard the enemy—after overriding his staff, who feared the absence of its AA guns during any enemy air attack on the carriers. How different from another November night eight years before off the Gilbert Islands when Japanese Kates had attacked for hours. (Cagle and Manson, *Sea War in Korea*, 329)

On the 29th, as Admiral Martin was presenting medals on the flagship's flight deck, G.Q. sounded. While the crew dispersed to battle stations, Martin and Clark raced up to the flag bridge. Two large blips on the radar screen were rapidly approaching from the north at 37,000 feet, 60 miles out—possibly bombers from Vladivostok in Russia. Jocko launched fighters, who made the intercept 30 miles away . . . of two Air Force B-47 bombers without IFF turned on. But the Soviet threat was constant.

At the completion of the awards ceremony, Jack Perry relieved Clark for the next rotation, and Jocko flew back to San Diego to await the *Bon Homme Richard*'s arrival there. He planned to return to Korea aboard the ship. But Admiral Radford had been successful in convincing the new Secretary of the Navy, Dan A. Kimball, to approve Clark's promotion to vice admiral. So he did not rejoin his carrier flagship.

Clark's orders were to relieve Beauty Martin as Commander Seventh Fleet, although the newspaper flap over emergency leaves caused a brief delay. Martin already had his orders, however, so the Navy sent an interim Seventh Fleet commander. This was black-shoe Vice Admiral Robert B. Briscoe, already earmarked to relieve Turner Joy in command of Naval Forces Far East. On 26 February Jocko handed over his carrier division to Rear Admiral Apollo Soucek, his former Anacostia test pilot. Tommy Sprague wrote Clark a one-line fitness report that said it all: "A great naval officer and an inspired leader of men."

Promotion to vice admiral officially came—finally—on 7 March 1952, after which Clark flew to Albuquerque for a quick but interesting course in atomic energy and its use in a general war. On the 25th, he relieved Vice Admiral "Rip" Struble as Commander First Fleet on board the *Bon Homme Richard* at San Diego. Like the Second Fleet on the East Coast, readying ships for deployment with the Sixth Fleet in the Med, the First Fleet did the same on the West Coast for Seventh Fleet vessels.

Jocko next headed to Washington to be briefed by CNO Fechteler, Vice CNO Wu Duncan, and John M. Allison, undersecretary of state for Far Eastern affairs. The latter explained President Truman's war aim of containing the fighting in the Korean peninsula, thereby avoiding a global war. He suggested that Nationalist Chinese Formosa (Taiwan) might be given up to the Red Chinese. Clark took issue with this idea, saying that Formosa was a vital link in America's defense perimeter from Japan to Australia.

Allison discussed the ongoing war in French Indochina, where the native Vietminh forces were trying to drive out their colonial masters. He surprised Jocko when he said that in the event of active American support for the French, the United States should capture Red Chinese Hainan Island in the South China Sea for airfields. Clark replied, "Why give up Formosa and then capture Hainan?" As it turned out, neither was ever tried.

Duncan informed Clark that General Mark W. Clark was about to replace General Ridgway as commander of U.S. and UN forces in Korea and had Jocko flown to Norfolk to meet him. The general, about to leave for Korea, remarked on certain generals there also named Clark; he thus welcomed Jocko to his "Clark Team." Jocko offered to become the "pick-and-shovel member." The two men got on famously, sharing the frustration that "fighting along a fixed battle line was like fighting with one hand tied behind our backs," yet they agreed to try "to win under the existing ground rules."

Clark flew back to San Diego, relinquished command of the First Fleet on 10 May, then flew to Pearl Harbor, where he reported to Radford. When he related Allison's idea of giving up Formosa, Radford reacted strongly and promised to charge Allison's mind—and did so.

On the 20th Clark relieved Admiral Briscoe as Seventh Fleet commander on board the flagship, battleship *Iowa*. This was the first time his flag had been raised over a gun ship instead of a carrier. As they shook hands, Briscoe remarked, "It's all yours, Jock, loaded and cocked." Two weeks later Briscoe relieved Joy as Far East naval commander.

Captain Tom Moorer, among Clark's fervent admirers, sent him a message from the naval ordnance test center in the California desert: "You're living proof: you can't keep a good man down." (Transcript #30, 1592) Captain George Anderson, about to get command of the *FDR*, recalled Jocko as "the type of man who put zip into the fleet," which he lost no time doing. Captain Truman Hedding, who had assisted Radford in getting Clark the job, recalled that it turned out as simply "a good thing" at that point in the Korean conflict.

The Seventh Fleet's area of responsibility ran from Hokkaido, Japan's northernmost island, to Singapore at the base of the Malay Peninsula—that is, America's western shield for containing the further expansion of Russian, Chinese, and North Korean communism. The three task forces were 77, the fast carriers; 95, blockading and escort forces; and 92, logistics. Clark inherited a staff of about 140 officers, headed initially by Captain C. Wade McClusky Jr., the hero of Midway for having led the divebombing attack that sank the Japanese carriers.

The first thing Clark did was to familiarize himself with all aspects of the fighting. The day after assuming command he visited Mark Clark at his Tokyo headquarters. The day after that he sailed for South Korea where he met Eighth Army commander Van Fleet, Fifth Air Force commander Lieutenant General Glenn O. Barcus, and the new truce talks negotiator at Munsan-ni, Lieutenant General William K. Harrison Jr. of the Army. At Van Fleet's invitation he then surveyed the entire battle front, where his host had him meet all the division commanders.

Clark also met South Korean president Syngman Rhee at the presidential palace in Seoul—the first of many visits—and Rhee later came to the flagship several times by helicopter. They even did some ocean fishing together. Rhee ruled with virtual dictatorial authority, which Clark did not admire, but they cooperated. Almost immediately, Jocko informed Admiral Briscoe that Rhee's excellent CNO, Vice Admiral Won Yil Sohn, was threatened by internal opposition. Briscoe had Sohn whisked off to Tokyo as an official guest until the crisis passed.

In early June Clark journeyed to Taipei, capital of Nationalist Chinese Formosa/Taiwan, where he met the head of state, Generalissimo Chiang Kai-shek. When Clark asked him if he would be willing to send some of his half-million troops to Korea, Chiang replied, "Yes, if you fight to win." But Clark knew Chiang could not get to mainland China except in U.S. amphibious craft, much less fight the millions of Red Chinese there. The United States refused to let him try to recross the Formosa Straits but had stationed naval and air forces on the island to help defend Formosa itself.

Chiang's generals and those of the U.S. 13th Air Force based there convinced him that any Communist Chinese bombing attack could be beaten back by Nationalist, U.S. Air Force, and Task Force 77 Navy planes. Clark declared the chances of a Red Chinese invasion of Formosa "remote." (*New York Times*, 9 June 1952)

But Korea was the main show, and Clark wanted to bomb North Korea's electric power complexes. The Joint Chiefs of Staff had left them alone in the event that a future Allied overland drive would need them. Because the Joint Chiefs had ruled out further ground offensives, Jocko brought the idea to Mark Clark. The general readily agreed and simply informed the Joint Chiefs that he was going to bomb the great Suiho Dam complex on the Yalu River in northwestern Korea—the fourth largest in the world. The Joint Chiefs could always reject the idea.

Jocko was at Admiral Briscoe's headquarters in Tokyo a few days later when a Joint Chiefs message arrived giving the Air Force permission for the bombing. Jocko remarked to Rear Admiral Freddie McMahon, Briscoe's chief of staff, "That's a job for the Navy," meaning pinpoint bombing by TF 77's AD Skyraiders—in daylight at that, unlike the B-29s now relegated to night bombing due to daytime enemy MIG interceptors. Indeed, MIG bases on the Chinese side of the Yalu posed a threat to any planes attacking in daylight.

Jocko offered General Barcus 36 Skyraiders to assist the Air Force planes in the raid. Barcus communicated with TF 77 commander Apollo Soucek, and they reduced the number of ADs to 20. Then Barcus radioed Jocko that he intended to cancel the mission as too risky. Jocko, who had just departed Tokyo for South Korea on the *Philippine Sea*, replied that he was on the way to Barcus to discuss it. When in range, Clark was catapulted from the carrier and flown to Air Force headquarters. (1956 Clark interview in Cagle and Manson, *Sea War in Korea*, 443–50)

He persuaded Barcus by outlining a plan: 36 ADs from three carriers would each carry three bombs totaling 5,000 pounds, escorted by 36 F9F Panther jet fighters, each with two 250-pound bombs. They would fly low across the Sea of Japan and the Korean peninsula to avoid radar beams and surprise Suiho before its MIG interceptors could scramble. Barcus liked the plan and added 84 F-86 Sabrejets to fly fighter cover over the target, followed by a second attack by 124 F-84 Thunderjets.

Everything worked perfectly. On 23 June Soucek launched his planes from the *Philippine Sea, Boxer,* and *Princeton,* leaving the "Bonnie Dick" to defend the task force—the first time TF 77 had four carriers on the line. The enemy was so surprised that not one MIG took off. Suiho's power plants and AA installations were pounded, and flak from the Chinese side of the river only damaged five planes. Simultaneously, and on the next day, Marine Corps planes joined others of the Air Force and Navy to knock out *all* power plants in North Korea, hitting Suiho again. Even the North Korean capital Pyongyang went dark. This was the first time in the war that all three air services operated together.

"My hat is off to the Navy," Barcus signaled Clark. "We must get together again sometime." Indeed they did and often, starting when *Bon Homme Richard* and *Princeton,* under rotating TF 77 Admiral Blackie Regan, joined a massive Air Force bombing of Pyongyang on 11 July. These operations initiated the "Air Task Group" concept in striking targets, and sometimes South Korean, British, and Australian planes were included.

South Korean president Syngman Rhee comes aboard the flagship *Iowa*, anchored off Pusan, for a luncheon with Clark on 8 July 1952, just after the Seventh Fleet's devastating carrier air strikes on North Korea's Suiho Dam complex. *U.S. Navy photo*

Jocko Clark, always the pragmatist, remained a team player in combat in order to get every job done expeditiously, pragmatically, and without regard to service loyalties or differences. Also, his reputation as a boisterous leader had preceded him, in spite of his markedly reduced bombast since the big war. And his voice call sign affirmed it.

The author of this radio signature is unknown—possibly Jocko chose it himself, for it was nothing less than "Jehovah." (He had indeed made it to the top.) At appropriate times when he needed to make an authoritative point to any unit or individual in the Seventh Fleet, he began his radio message: "This is Jehovah himself!" "It was," remembered John Lee, "a very appropriate call sign for the boss. Very, *very* appropriate." (Interview #1, 158)

In general, however, Jocko Clark "just hated sending messages," recalled Joshua W. Cooper, captain of the flagship *Iowa* from July 1952. To Clark, such radio traffic "was a fruitless business in the main. He usually preferred to tell people what he wanted" and leave it at that.

Cooper admired Clark's

> restless nature and his absolute addiction to getting where the action
> was or where he thought it might be. . . . We were fortunate in being
> shipmates because his presence guaranteed a full schedule all the time.
> Things were never dull. [He "never" interfered with me. Instead,] he
> would frequently come up and suggest that we shoot at this or at that
> target, and of course his suggestion was taken as a command. I can't
> think of any occasion when it was an injudicious one. (Interview #6,
> 333–35)

Because the war had become relatively static—no more amphibious operations or major changes in the battle line on land—Clark as Seventh Fleet commander could focus on his own particular expertise, carrier operations. But the fact that he utilized the Navy's four battleships as flagships and for coastal bombardment enabled him to participate closely in their movements—shelling enemy targets ashore and returning to Japanese "home" ports periodically to refuel and take on ammunition.

Jocko flew his flag in the *Iowa* until October 1952, when he shifted to the *Missouri*. Neither these nor any of his ships ever fired their AA batteries. The air spaces as well as open seas around the Korean peninsula were UN sanctuaries in this tightly contained limited war. Tit for tat, UN forces never violated Chinese or Russian air space or coastal waters.

But North Korean territory, air, and waters were fair game for UN forces, enabling the battleships and one or two escorts—backed by carrier planes— to move up and down the North Korean east coast bombarding the key ports of (south to north) Kosong near the battle line, Wonsan, Hungnam, Tanchon, Chongjin (close to the Soviet border), and points in between. Favorite pinpointed targets were railroad trains and tunnels and power stations.

Clark instituted economy measures. One was saving on expensive 16-inch battleship shells by carefully selecting key targets in lieu of blanket bombardments. Another saving on fuel was restricting all warships to an 18-knot speed between their bases in Japan and the combat zone.

Wonsan was unique in that Yodo and several smaller islets within the harbor had been seized and used by the Navy, which erected an emergency airstrip. Inasmuch as the fleet's use of Yodo rarely brought enemy counterfire—or if so, it was quickly silenced by ships' batteries—minesweepers kept Wonsan clear for the gun ships. On 23 September 1952 General Mark Clark and Bob Briscoe were Jocko's guests when the *Iowa's* 16-inchers blew up the ammunition stores of an enemy battery, completely neutralizing it. The next month Jocko commanded Joint Amphibious Task Force 7 in

Operation Decoy, a mock assault at Kojo, south of Wonsan. Carrier planes and gun ships pounded the place, while loaded transports went through all the motions short of an actual landing. (Cagle and Manson, *Sea War in Korea*, 391–96, 435)

In the middle of this exercise, obscured by rain and mist, Jocko needed the flagship's helicopter to go somewhere. As usual, men on the bridge saw him climb into the helo and could read the pilot's lips saying, in effect, "The weather is bad, Admiral, we shouldn't fly in this thing." But, against the din of the rotating prop, they saw him give a thumb's up, and the chopper—prone to breaking down and without good navigational aids—"reluctantly rose from the deck." By 2100 the admiral had not returned as scheduled, leading skipper Josh Cooper to consider reporting him missing—to the CNO, CinCPac, "and the world." Happily, soon "we heard this chug-chug of our antique helicopter coming out of the darkness"—disaster averted. (Cooper Interview #6, 335–37)

On 18 November 1952, returning to the *Kearsarge* from one of his trips to Seoul, Jocko was greeted by the superb TF 77 commander, Rear Admiral Robert F. Hickey. "I've got a MIG for you," he told Jocko, handing him a wooden model of the Russian-built MIG-15 fighter used by the enemy.

Earlier that afternoon, Hickey explained, with his carriers operating some 90 miles south of Vladivostok, several blips appeared on the radars—60 miles out and closing. Intercepted radio transmissions were in Russian. Hickey dispatched three F9Fs on CAP to intercept seven Soviet MIGs. In eight minutes they shot down one MIG and scored two probables.

One Russian pilot parachuted into the sea and obviously froze to death when task force destroyers failed to locate him. Clark awarded all three pilots medals for having successfully taken on a larger "enemy" force. (Cagle and Manson, *Sea War in Korea*, 469–75)

Ever the exacting leader, Clark knew his carrier admirals better than those of his gun ships, who therefore had to learn his modus operandi. When he himself was nearest the scene of some incident, he would scurry hence with the flagship and take charge. Once a small vessel struck a mine after evacuating agents near Chongjin Harbor. So he ran the *Iowa* up from Wonsan and took charge, removing the wounded. On another occasion, contrary to Clark's unannounced but well-known preference to run into Sasebo to take on 16-inch shells, cruiser division commander Rear Admiral Walter G. Schindler ordered the *Iowa* to remain at sea with TF 77 and rearm later. Jocko did not like this. But preferring a face-to-face exchange to a message countermanding Schindler's order, he went to the latter's flagship by helo "to unnegative the negative," as he told Captain Cooper. (Interview #6, 331–32, 334–35)

Vice Admiral Bob Briscoe (*center*) and General Mark Clark (*right*)—respective U.S. Navy and United Nations commanders in the Far East—autographed this photo of Seventh Fleet commander Jocko Clark while the *Iowa* was bombarding the North Korean coast from its anchorage in Wonsan Harbor. Both men admired his aggressive leadership during the final year of the war. *U.S. Navy photo*

A more serious event occurred on 18 January 1953 when Red Chinese AA batteries near Swatow shot down an Okinawa-based P2V Neptune on patrol over the Formosa Strait. A PBM Mariner amphibian landed, picked up the survivors, then crashed trying to take off after dark in heavy seas. A destroyer managed to rescue some of the men, and two British frigates from Hong Kong joined the five-ship search for the remaining 11 men the next day, dodging fire from shore batteries. They were never found.

When Clark learned this, he sent a "blistering" dispatch to CinCPac Radford, blaming the fleet air wing commander, Rear Admiral T. B. Williamson, thus ending his chances for anticipated further promotion. Clark did not even learn that the search had been unknowingly conducted in a Nationalist Chinese minefield. (Charles S. Minter Jr. Interview #5, 277–82)

Part of Clark's unique routine was hosting a constant flow of VIPs to witness the fleet's operations. The fact that this did not interfere with shipboard activity was due in no small part to Jocko being the gregarious person that he was and therefore "not one to avoid a task or to shorten it on account of a VIP." On the *Iowa* he was greatly assisted by its superb radio officer, Lieutenant Samuel P. Gravely, destined to become the first black admiral in the Navy.

Because Far East headquarters was located in Tokyo, six TBM Avengers had been converted into small transports for photographs, equipment, and selected VIPs between there and TF 77. The service became known as the "CODfish Airline" for Carrier On-board Delivery, an acronym that soon became standard. In March 1953 its base was shifted from Tokyo to coastal airfield K-3 in southeastern Korea to be closer to the fighting.

VIPs touring military forces in Korea, however, flew out to Clark's flagship or another battleship in one of its helicopters. This occurred almost daily—CNO Fechteler, CinCPac Radford, General Clark, a diplomat, a congressman, a newspaper editor, and so forth. By far the most popular VIP was Francis Cardinal Spellman, who said post-Christmas mass in the crew's compartment on the *Iowa*.

The routine was simple but impressive. The flagship headed into Wonsan Harbor where Clark and the VIP or two would witness the bombardment with its main and secondary batteries. Or they were flown by helo to Yodo or an adjacent islet to watch the battleship's shells pass overhead. The only enemy "reply" occurred during the visit of Assistant Secretary of the Navy (Air) John W. Floberg to Clark's flagship *New Jersey* the following April. Red artillery shells started to fall 2,000 yards from the ship, then "walked" closer until one exploded only 35 yards in front. The burst sprayed shrapnel on deck, hitting a Marine protected by a bulletproof vest.

The flagship rejoined the carriers during the night. After sunup a helo delivered them to a carrier to observe the pilots being briefed, launched, and later landed and debriefed. The VIP was thereupon returned by chopper to the shoreside airfield.

One particular VIP, the head of the Navy League, caused concern to the helo pilot, who informed Captain Cooper, "I've noticed our visitor is quite a heavy man, and the Admiral is no lightweight himself"—Clark's weight was in the process of rising from 196 to 212 pounds during his two-plus years with TF 77 and Seventh Fleet. The pilot feared that downdrafts in the area might cause the overloaded chopper to crash; he preferred to take one man at a time. Cooper interrupted Clark's luncheon and conveyed the pilot's fears.

At that, Jocko slapped his stomach and said, "Maybe I shouldn't have eaten that last piece of pie."

Whereupon the alarmed VIP remarked, "You know, I don't need to go at all!"

Jocko: "We'll go as planned." And they did, quite safely. Cooper, however, had to chuckle at the VIP's reluctance "to endure all of the hospitality that was thrust upon him." (Interview #6, 329–31, 338–41)

A different caliber of visitors during the spring of 1953 was a group of National War College students—bright Navy captains and Army and Air Force colonels earmarked for promotion. They were suitably impressed by all they saw and heard of Seventh Fleet activities, except for the words from Admiral Clark. As one of the naval officers recalled, "His part of the performance was talking in such a fashion that nobody understood what he was talking about!" (Edwin A. Hooper Interview #5, 234) But in a way, such double-talk took "talent" too.

An especially important VIP to Clark was his sister Lucy's son Bill Beatty, a recent Texas A&M Army ROTC graduate and second lieutenant with the 224th Infantry near Pusan. Early in June Beatty was ordered out of the field to report immediately and without explanation to General Van Fleet's headquarters at Seoul—300 miles away. Beatty was rushed hence as the only passenger on President Syngman Rhee's private train. "They even moved off other trains to let us by," he remembered. MPs met and escorted him to a private room at Van Fleet's headquarters, where they told him to wait.

Presently, Beatty's Uncle Joe appeared, had him wait even longer until a meeting ended, then took him to the helo pad for the flight out to the *Iowa*.

> Admiral Clark was in dress whites, and I was in combat fatigues with blood all over me from combat, and I had my basic load of ammunition and my M-1 carbine hanging on me. When we arrived aboard the *Iowa* the band was playing, and the sailors were standing at attention. Can you imagine what they were thinking as I was dirty, unkempt and out of actual combat.

Beatty's first shower in three months was followed by a nap in a VIP room and his first real meal in the same period—with Van Fleet and his staff, no less, the full VIP treatment. "A total surprise and a great two-day break," he recalled. "My Uncle Joe had put a tracer on me knowing where I was at all times."

Clark, though frustrated at not being able to conduct offensive operations, found a way to hurt the Communists sufficiently for them to desire an armistice. In September 1952, while flying over the front lines in a helicopter, he and First Marine Division commander Major General John T. Selden clearly saw the heavy concentration of the Marines' supplies in the rear—ammo dumps, medical units, truck parks, and housing for personnel. He realized that if the enemy had employed air power at the front, it could have devastated these vital rear areas.

Conversely, "I reasoned that the Reds too had many such exposed areas of supplies behind their own lines and that we should look into the possibilities of bombing such targets." Returning to the flagship, he had Jack Perry's carriers confirm his suspicions with aerial photographs (although matériel stored in tunnels or underground could not be hit). Jocko sent his operations officer, Commander Ray M. Pitts, ashore to interview the ground commanders, who confirmed the growing need for more close air support.

Clark and Pitts then flew to the TF 77 flagship *Kearsarge* and began planning with the task force commander, Admiral Hickey. General Clark and Admiral Briscoe came aboard the *Iowa* to discuss it with Jocko on 24 September. Pitts named the concept the "Cherokee Strikes" in honor of Jocko's Indian heritage. This differentiated it from the normal close air support operations of eight closely coordinated planes using light pinpoint attacks as far out as a designated "bombline" limit. Cherokee Strikes of up to 50 planes—escorted by flak-suppressing jets—would engage in heavy precision bombing of predesignated targets 20 to 30 miles beyond the bombline. (Cagle and Manson, *Sea War in Korea*, 460–69)

On 9 October the first Cherokee Strikes took the Reds by complete surprise. The smoke from the Navy's bomb blasts rose high enough for the U.S. troops to see and cheer. For many weeks the strikes intensified, severely punishing the enemy and raising American morale in the process. General Van Fleet praised their success, although Lieutenant General Otto P. Weyland, Far East Air Forces boss, complained that Fifth Air Force strike coordinators could not handle such large numbers of planes near the front lines.

Jocko met with both men on 17 November to resolve the difficulties. He pointed out to Weyland that the pre-briefed Cherokee Strikes needed no target control, but he offered to let the Air Force coordinate them and even to use Navy attack techniques. Then Van Fleet agreed to have the bombline moved up to within several hundred feet of his troops. This system worked so well through December that Van Fleet arranged to present the Army Commendation Medal to Clark for his "'Cherokee Strike' method of pre-briefed close air support attacks."

General Mark Clark was sufficiently impressed to say, "If I were to order my friend Jocko Clark to take his flagship"—the battleship *Missouri* since October 1952—"up the Yalu River, the answer would be, 'Aye, aye, sir!'"

Stories circulated about Jocko's audacity, in particular in dealing with Air Force generals and their strategic bombing mind-set. One account claimed that after listening to their complaints about these proposed strikes, Jocko had simply replied, "I think we've got to kill a lot of Chinamen, and I'm going back to the ship." Hence the Cherokee Strikes. (A. M. Pride Interview #4, 222–23)

Several casualties to friendly troops occurred due to navigational errors, forcing the Strikes to be somewhat curtailed during the first two months of 1953. But improved briefings and accuracy provided the remedy, and Clark's heavy attacks resumed with telling effect for the rest of the Korean War.

Jocko's success in dealing with the sister services was applauded in his fitness report. Admiral Briscoe (18 November 1952) praised him for having won "the full support of all field and air commanders, and I personally feel that the present close cooperation of the [armed] services in Korea is largely due to his personal efforts toward effecting real teamwork at the point of contact with the enemy." Radford seconded this in his fitness report (15 December 1952).

Clark's politics were died-in-the-wool Democratic, but he had high hopes for the Republican presidential candidate, General Dwight D. Eisenhower, who had promised that if elected he would go to Korea and end the war. Because this came from a military man, Jocko convinced himself that this would mean ultimate victory by shifting to the offensive. "Ike" won the election in November and next month headed for Korea as promised. On 4 December Admiral Radford accompanied him to Seoul.

Van Fleet invited Clark to be present at a dinner for Ike. At Bob Briscoe's suggestion, Jocko brought with him the three victorious fighter pilots, all lieutenants, who had beaten the MIGs. At about 1700, when everyone gathered in Van Fleet's private suite for cocktails, the host, a tee-totaler, said to Clark of his pilots, "I don't think we ought to expose these young men to all this drinking." (He had obviously never known naval flyboys!)

He suggested moving them into an anteroom to meet Ike there, whereupon Eisenhower suddenly appeared and said, "Bring those boys in here, and let's give them a drink!"

With Ike's son John, an Army major, pouring the drinks, the three tail-hookers described the dogfights, responding to many penetrating questions by the president-elect. "I could see a gleam in Radford's eye," recalled Jocko, "as the Navy stole the show." In walked ranking Air Force generals "Opie" Weyland and Glenn Barcus, who could say little.

Later Raddy met privately with Jocko and the three pilots. When he mildly criticized them for having become separated during the dogfight, thereby sacrificing mutual protection (as in the Thach weave), Jocko retorted to his old friend, "Everything was wrong but the score! *That* was in our favor!"

Next morning Eisenhower began an all-day tour of the front lines. The Air Force gave an unimpressive divebombing demonstration with each plane one at a time dropping a 500-pounder. Just as Ike was being conducted away from his observation post, recalled Clark,

> a Cherokee Strike came roaring in from the sea—12 Panther jets as flak-suppressors and 24 Skyraiders each carrying 5,000 pounds of bombs. The 36 planes dived in on the target, dropped their bombs, and were out again in less than 30 seconds. The whole earth erupted in the target area. Again the Navy had stolen the show.

The following day Eisenhower held a conference with all of the senior four- and three-star commanders and asked each one his views about the war. All wanted to put maximum pressure on North Korea to somehow win it. Clark, the most junior three-star, said simply, "Sir, let's get on with the war. Let's get the job done!" He received "a ripple of applause, but I could see the overall die was cast."

"The war in Korea goes on," Jocko replied to a Christmas card from veteran *Yorktown* torpecker pilot Joe Kristufek. "There isn't any way to end it except for a full offensive for ultimate victory, which I hope Eisenhower and the new administration will take steps to achieve." (Letter, 26 January 1953)

Clark wanted to drive all the way back to the Yalu River. He agreed with Raddy that if a permanent truce ended with a divided Korea, the Red Chinese would shift their military efforts to Indochina and help the Vietminh drive out the French (which was exactly what happened). He completely accepted General MacArthur's farewell speech to Congress in 1951, "There is no substitute for victory."

At the dinner following Ike's meetings at Seoul, Clark sat next to the designated Secretary of Defense, Charles E. Wilson, whose late brother he had known as mayor of Corpus Christi. Wilson asked at once, "How about Admiral Radford for the next Chairman of the Joint Chiefs of Staff?"

"You can never find a better man," replied Jocko. This only confirmed what Ike and his advisers had already concluded, as Wilson informed Clark over breakfast next morning. Clark also supported their preference for Secretary of the Navy, Texas governor Allan Shivers, but Shivers declined the offer.

Eisenhower returned home to take office in January 1953 and to consider use of the atomic bomb to force the Communists to agree to an armistice. Initially, the president ordered more divisions to Korea, and fresh commanders arrived to press the attack. Mark Clark and Jocko Clark remained at the head of UN forces and the Seventh Fleet respectively. On 7 February Van Fleet visited flagship *Missouri* to introduce Jocko to his relief as Eighth Army commander, Lieutenant General Maxwell D. Taylor. Lieutenant General Samuel E. Anderson took over the Fifth Air Force from Glenn Barcus.

Jocko inherited a diplomatic role over the winter. Early in 1952 President Rhee had established the "Rhee Line" around South Korea waters, behind which Red Chinese and Japanese fishermen were prohibited. The result had been that hundreds of Japanese—accustomed to free movement for their livelihood and ignorant of the dictum—had violated the line, which came to be known as the "Clark Line" for General Mark Clark. The Japanese at Sasebo, one of the Seventh Fleet's bases, protested to Jocko, especially when South Korean maritime police arrested and detained them. The Koreans hated the Japanese because of their long and brutal occupation of Korea (1910–45).

Mark Clark called upon Bob Briscoe and Jocko to resolve the festering problem. "That is not *my* line," he joked. "If it is to be called the 'Clark Line,' it should be called the '*Jocko* Clark Line.'" Mark Clark appointed the senior South Korean commander within TF 95 to negotiate with President Rhee along with task force commander Rear Admiral Clarence E. Olsen. The latter settled the matter by getting the Japanese captives returned and promising to educate them about the restricted waters. But no diplomatic avenue existed for dealing with Red Chinese captives in the hands of the South Koreans because their government was not recognized by the United States.

In Clark's fitness reports for the six months ending in February 1953, Briscoe lauded him not only for his tactical innovations but "in the equally important duties requiring contacts with other services and foreign officials . . . , exceptionally aggressive, a shrewd planner." (28 February 1953) Radford echoed Briscoe, praising his friend Jocko for never overlooking "an opportunity to damage the enemy. His personal and military character are excellent, and his integrity of purpose is of the highest order." (24 April 1953)

Task Force 77's initial part in the stepped up pressure on the enemy consisted of heavy two-day air strikes (9–10 February) against coastal supply and shipping centers between Songjin (now Kimchaek) and Chongjin—targets nearest the Soviet and Red Chinese borders. In early March planes from the three carriers destroyed parts of the hydroelectric plant at the Chosin Reservoir, and on the 19th they pounded the industrial part of Chongjin.

Lieutenant General Maxwell D. Taylor (*left*) is Vice Admiral Clark's guest on board the Seventh Fleet flagship *Missouri* early in 1953 on the eve of Taylor's promotion to full general in command of the Eighth Army in Korea. *U.S. Navy photo*

Cherokee Jocko participated in all of these operations on his flagship *Missouri,* whose skipper was Captain Warner R. Edsall. Sadly, while on the bridge 26 March, Edsall suffered a massive and fatal heart attack.

Two weeks later, 6 April, Clark shifted his flag to battleship *New Jersey* at Yokosuka, Japan. Its captain, Charles L. Melson, had some trepidation about Clark due to the legendary tales about him. They proved groundless: "I never dealt with a more pleasant [and interesting] individual . . . who never once corrected me or told me how to do anything. He said, 'Do this or do that,'" and that was it . . . , a very competent officer." (Quoted in Stillwell, *Battleship New Jersey,* 153)

Flagship and fast carriers pounded Chongjin on 13 April, the only danger being a mine that floated by the *New Jersey* until a rifleman on a tin can touched it off. TF 77 resumed its routine of day and night attacks on coastal targets, usually observed by the ubiquitous VIPs. The flagship's helo shuttled to and from a carrier as well as South Korean airstrips, such as coastal K-18 near Kangnung, for conferences. (The helo's nickname was "Jersey Bounce," a play on the title of a 1941 swing tune.)

On one occasion the fog was so thick that Jocko had to return from a tiny harbor in a small Coast Guard cutter that threaded its way back to the ship through a swarm of South Korean fishing boats. It was such a nerve-wracking ordeal that as Jocko finally set foot on the *New Jersey* he remarked, uncharacteristically, "Thank God, I'm back aboard again!" (Charles L. Melhorn Interview #4, 173–74)

Such breaking off of bombardments in order to run south for the "Jersey Bounce" to get in range for the admiral's helo trip ashore seemed to be a waste in the opinion of the battleship's assistant navigator, Ensign Rodion Cantacuzene, a fresh Annapolis grad. (June 1952) While bending over his charts one day, he complained out loud to the chief quartermaster, "I wonder who the goddam fool was that thought this up?"

Amid audible gasps by shipmates came a reply to the rhetorical question, "I was."

He turned to behold the gold-braided admiral. "Young man," said Clark, "why am I a goddammed fool?"

Cantacuzene explained the high fuel consumption during each run south and back, as well as the absence of the big guns for shore bombardments during the battleship's absence. Jocko calmly explained his reasons for these trips south, ending with a slight rebuke: "Son, do your course and keep your nose clean. And if you get promoted to vice admiral, you can do it your way. But in the meantime, we're going to do it *my* way." (The ensign did not make it; he retired in the rank of captain.)

Jocko had certainly mellowed, but this milder demeanor achieved the same result. The young shavetail replied meekly, "Yes, sir," and Clark exited, only to encounter an approaching Captain Melson. "Charlie," said Jocko, "I haven't been called a goddam fool in 15 years!" (Stillwell, *Battleship New Jersey* 156–57) (This was surely an offhand exaggeration. That would mean since 1938, leaving out his turbulent shipboard demeanor of the World War II years.)

That the enemy was hurting became evident when, on 26 April 1953, the Communists agreed to resume peace negotiations. But the U.S.–led United Nations forces kept up the pressure. Far East Air Force commander Weyland on 3 May listed 30 North Korean airfields to be henceforth kept neutralized. Six of these he assigned to the fast carriers. The enemy responded with ground attacks along the battle line and delayed resuming the truce talks until 4 June.

The carrier *Lake Champlain* arrived from the Atlantic Fleet to relieve the *Valley Forge* and join *Philippine Sea, Princeton,* and *Boxer* for two weeks of carrier as well as land-based aerial counterattacks, especially near the bombline. The Eighth Army requested 48 close air support strikes a day and more Cherokee Strikes than ever. Clark sounded his own battle cry (borrowing from Charles Weller's famous 1867 typewriting exercise), "Now is the time for naval aviators to come to the aid of the Eighth Army."

To ensure that the carrier planes were fully integrated into the Fifth Air Force's relentless air offensive, Jocko flew ashore to the Joint Operations Center (JOC) in Seoul. He informed General Anderson that his pilots would take their orders from the Air Force. To ensure it, he provided his operations officer as temporary planner at JOC, until Captain Roy C. Sempler arrived for full-time duty.

Clark also assigned two of his carrier squadron commanders to transmit target instructions to TF 77. From the JOC Lieutenant Commander Gerald E. "Jerry" Miller of *Princeton's* VF-153 and a fellow squadron commander selected the targets and radioed them to the fleet. They did this for three weeks, then rotated back to the carriers, a system that lasted until war's end. (Miller, "Korea—The Carrier War," in Wooldridge, *Into the Jet Age,* 159–64)

In late May, while fast carrier planes hammered away from the waters east of Korea, the *New Jersey* and one destroyer rounded the peninsula into the Yellow Sea to support British naval operations on the west side. They put into Inchon first for a major conference of Clark, Admiral Briscoe, and other senior commanders, who then joined President Rhee and his wife in a visit to the flagship.

The "Big Jay's" 16-inch guns pounded the Chinnampo area some 30 miles west of Pyongyang and within range of Red Chinese Manchurian-based planes (which did not attack). British cruiser *Newcastle* supported the flagship, while Royal Navy planes from light carrier *Ocean* spotted targets for the gunners. The *Ocean* had been kept isolated, striking targets in this remote area because British carrier planes had a fuel capacity of little more than an hour of flying time—a third of that of American carrier planes. (Miller in Wooldridge, *Into the Jet Age*, 163)

Jocko was ambivalent about Britain's role in the war: "Never could I understand how British soldiers could fight Red Chinese in Korea, while at the same time the British government recognized the Peiping government." (Clark, "31-Knot Burke," 23)

Although enemy troops remained well dug in, in mountain caves and valley ravines, they now began to come out during daylight hours in trucks and railroad trains in a new offensive that captured the Anchor Hill complex near the coast. These gains only made them more plentiful as targets for UN planes, which daily wreaked devastation—but also suffered up to 10 percent losses to flak. The *New Jersey* had difficulty seeing through fog to pinpoint shore targets, leading Clark to cancel any shooting without clear visibility as wasteful.

On 6 June Jocko ordered a maximum effort at the battle line. He put all of his propeller-driven planes—AD Skyraiders, F4U Corsairs—into close air support work. Their heavier payloads and longer loiter time over the target assured pinpoint accuracy and maximum punishment. He divided up his jets between Cherokee Strikes, interdiction of roads and rail lines, and reconnaissance.

Next day (6 June in the United States) Clark received a personal blow—a message informing him that his father had died at home in Chelsea, age 92 years and four days. The oldest child "Joe" could do nothing but wire condolences to sturdy mother Lillie Belle, who actively held the family together—including Joe's daughters—at age 80.

Despite deteriorating weather conditions, Clark's planes pounded enemy ground forces mercilessly in mid-June, especially to enable South Korean troops to recapture Anchor Hill. Both *New Jersey* and cruiser *St. Paul* bombarded the enemy position. Before the final assault on the hill on 15 June, Jocko boarded the "Jersey Bounce" to fly ashore to the South Korean command bunker to observe the assault. He was accompanied by cruiser division commander Rear Admiral Harry Sanders and his own operations officer, Captain Herschel House (who as a freshly minted ensign had been a spark plug of Jocko's baseball team on the old *Lexington* in 1931–33). The battleship's main batteries destroyed 44 bunkers before the hill finally fell, bringing praise from General Maxwell Taylor and the local Korean commander. (Cagle and Manson, *Sea War in Korea*, 482–84)

Next day, the 16th, Clark lunched with General Harrison, the head truce negotiator, who remarked, "Well, we're going to have an armistice. We just resolved the last issue this morning."

"I'll bet you don't," Jocko observed, convinced by the Anchor Hill battle that the Reds were not ready to stop fighting. Then, that very night, Syngman Rhee freed 27,000 North Korean prisoners who did not want to be repatriated. The enraged Reds again broke off negotiations, leading Jocko to chide Harrison at their next meeting, "I don't like to be in the position of saying 'I told you so.'"

Harrison laughed, "We have to keep talking." Jocko agreed with Rhee's action and disagreed when the Eisenhower administration publicly criticized the South Korean president for it. Shortly thereafter, one of Clark's captains encountered a diminutive Japanese hotel manager in Sasebo who observed, "Captain, Syngman Rhee is your friend. Why are you against him? We Japanese do not like Syngman Rhee, but we would like to see you stick by your friends."

Jocko recalled, "I felt that the little Japanese lady represented all of Asia, perhaps more than a billion people, who were looking to the United States for leadership and guidance."

Clark and the administration shared one ominous idea to save American lives and stop another possible Communist breakthrough into South Korea—potential use of the atomic bomb. Between March and May the president and his advisers actively discussed this alternative, and Clark hastened to Tokyo to plead with Mark Clark to have nuclear weapons "placed on board my carriers as a precautionary measure." The general agreed, obtained permission, and these first "special weapons" assigned to Navy ships were soon added to the Seventh Fleet's arsenal. (*Foreign Relations of the United States 1952–1954* [1984], summarized in the *New York Times*, 8 June 1984; Commander Seventh Fleet Action Report 1953)

At the opposite end of the weapons spectrum were the enemy's "Bed-Check Charlies"—slow, antiquated Russian training planes. Starting in May they flew low at night to drop small bombs as far south as Seoul. Their speed was much too slow for jets to engage them at night, and the air raid sirens they caused to sound rousted everybody out of bed, hence the nickname. Then, one of them chanced to hit and burn Air Force gasoline storage tanks at Inchon.

So on 25 June Jocko sent four prop-driven F4U-5N night fighters to General Sam Anderson, who assigned them to the First Marine Air Wing. Between the 29th and 17 July, Lieutenant Guy P. Bordelon shot down five Bed-Check Charlies, making him an ace—the Navy's first night ace ever and the only Navy ace during the Korean War. (Cagle and Manson, *Sea War in Korea*, 475–78)

Meanwhile, on 26 June, 15 divisions of the Communist army launched a massive assault on the battle line—the largest enemy offensive in two years—at Kumsong, some 50 miles west of the Sea of Japan coast. The Communist forces crushed the South Korean divisions there. General Taylor called in Air Force and carrier strikes while he shifted two U.S. divisions to stop the six-mile Red advance. For Clark, the massive drive was final proof that, despite all the air attacks on enemy supply lines and railroads, "the interdiction program was a failure." (Quoted in Cagle and Manson, *Sea War in Korea*, 270)

On 5 July Jocko initiated a timetable for each of his four carriers to operate every day all day long, and nine days later he assigned all their planes to close air support and Cherokee Strikes. This required constant nighttime underway replenishment, sometimes in the fog. Even Air Force planes now participated in Cherokee Strikes.

To ensure "more worthwhile targets," on 11 July Clark obtained General Taylor's permission to move the bombline from three miles out to within 1,000 meters of the front. This helped turn the tide. Taylor profusely thanked Sam Anderson and Jocko Clark for their planes' critical role in finally repulsing the enemy drive, "in spite of the most unfavorable flying weather" (Taylor dispatch, 23 July 1953).

On 14 July Admiral Radford wrote his last fitness report on his old friend. Jock had yet again lived up to Raddy's expectations:

> VADM CLARK's performance of duty in the combat area continues to be superior. An aggressive, competent leader who is continually alert for opportunities to damage the enemy. He has integrity of purpose to a high degree, and his personal and military character are above reproach.

Another long-time compatriot, Felix Stump, relieved Radford as CinC-Pac, and Raddy headed for Washington as the new chairman of the Joint Chiefs of Staff, the highest military office in the land.

"At last it looks as though I will be coming home soon," Clark wrote to his newly widowed mother on 20 July. "A relief has been ordered for me and although it will take a month or two, I will be there eventually." He poured out his "deepest gratitude" to her "for taking care of my girls," who were attending schools in the Southwest. He hoped that Mary Lou and Cathy would absorb "some of the courage and faith that you have and which you have given to all of us children. As I have told you before, I feel that all I have accomplished in life has been because of the faith which you inspired in me."

Then, his frustrations—to be shared by generations of Americans yet to face other limited conflicts much like the Korean War:

The war continues on. I believe the Reds are insincere in their negotiations and why our government is so naïve as to believe them is beyond me. Nobody has any business in a war unless they fight to win. It may be that the efforts of those who have sacrificed their lives on the battlefields of Korea will have been all in vain. I doubt very much if we will get a truce at all and if so it will be a defeat. But ultimately I am sure that the power of the country will, if necessary, be diverted along the right lines, and eventually our way of life will prevail.

The key to convincing the enemy to come to terms was increasing pressure over the ensuing week—indeed, the last week of the Korean War. In addition to relentless Cherokee Strikes and close air support at the battle line, on 23 July the fast carriers commenced five days of attacks on airfields in North Korea. On a single day they mounted a record 646 sorties. On the 24th Jocko went ashore to confer with General Max Taylor.

Once back on board the *New Jersey,* he received orders from General Clark on 26 July directing him to be present at the signing of the truce agreement the very next day. To make sure the Reds signed, throughout the 27th TF 77 planes conducted interdiction strikes against North Korean transportation networks—destroying highway bridges and railroad trains and bridges—and again pummeling airfields until the treaty took effect that night.

"Upon the occasion of an armistice in Korea this date," Clark announced to the men of the Seventh Fleet, "you have materially aided the cause of freedom by persuading the enemy that war is not in his interest. We pray that we have achieved a lasting peace. But we must remain ready and alert to meet any future threats to the security of the free world. I am proud of you. Well done to all hands."

That afternoon Jocko was greeted at Munsan-ni near Panmunjom by a smiling General Harrison, "Now whose turn is it to say, 'I told you so'?" The Communist leaders signed simultaneously at their headquarters at Kaesong north of the battle line. General Clark signed for the United Nations, flanked on his left by Bob Briscoe and Jocko Clark. The others at the table were Max Taylor of the Army and Opie Weyland and Sam Anderson of the Air Force.

Then General Clark observed, "This is not a moment for rejoicing. Rather, it is a moment of prayer that a way will be found for permanent peace."

At the date of this writing, over half a century later (2005), a permanent peace has yet to be found, with Communist North Korea as truculent as ever.

# TWENTY-ONE

## Postwarpaths, 1953–1971

THE STALEMATED CONCLUSION OF THE KOREAN WAR SATISFIED none of the U.S. commanders, Vice Admiral Jocko Clark among them. He believed that the Korean peninsula could have been reunified by another Inchon-style landing, perhaps at Kojo, and an overall drive all the way to the Yalu River. Indeed, he thought that an atomic bomb could have been dropped anywhere in North Korea during the war to convince the Red Chinese to withdraw. (Cagle and Manson, *Sea War in Korea*, 491)

The risk would have been a nuclear war with Joseph Stalin's Soviet Russia. In Clark's view, the "only man who can say if such actions would have expanded the war or not is Stalin—and he's dead." His death in March 1953 caused tension within the Kremlin over a successor, while the USSR was quickly developing a hydrogen bomb to match America's—whose first had been test exploded the year before.

By the end of 1953 JCS Chairman Radford and the Eisenhower administration considered the possible use of atomic weapons if the Red Chinese violated the armistice, even if it meant all-out war. (Documents reproduced in *New York Times*, 8 June 1984) To help deter this eventuality, Jocko Clark kept the Seventh Fleet—with A-bombs embarked—policing Asia's coastal waters from Japan to the South China Sea.

The Red Chinese, however, as expected, were shifting their main ground forces from North Korea to the border of French Indochina (Vietnam, Cambodia, Laos) to lend support to the Vietminh fighting for independence. Simultaneously, Clark had to prevent the Nationalist Chinese on Formosa/Taiwan from attempting to return to the mainland, which he announced as U.S. policy at a press conference when the flagship *New Jersey* visited British Hong Kong in August. (*New York Times*, 23 August 1953)

Clark showed the American flag there for a week, then moved on to Formosa, thence three Japanese ports, and finally Pusan, South Korea, in mid-September. (Stillwell, *Battleship New Jersey,* 161–63) Meanwhile, the four fast carriers of TF 77 continued to patrol both coasts of the Korean peninsula enforcing the truce.

Back in January, in Jocko's reply to former Yorktowner Joe Kristufek's letter, he had recalled "many memories of our service in the good ship *York-town,* which has been modernized and recommissioned recently [in fact, on 20 February 1953]. She will sail the seas again and some day I hope I can fly my flag in her."

Lo and behold, when the *New Jersey* returned to Yokosuka in September, the *Yorktown* was tied up at one of the piers, having just arrived. Jocko immediately informed its skipper, Captain Arnold W. McKechnie, of his desire to come aboard. The visit was quickly arranged, and McKechnie assembled a welcoming party to receive the staff car carrying Clark to the *Yorktown*'s pier.

Unfortunately—shades of Eleanor Roosevelt's visit to the ship nearly ten years to the day before—in the words of then Ensign and OOD Dan T. Englehardt, Clark "arrived via his barge at the starboard gangway ladder, and no one was there to render honors. The captain, executive officer, OOD, and sideboys ran across the hangar deck while the barge stood off." (Letter to author, 14 June 2004)

Jocko made his displeasure known but enjoyed the visit nevertheless, his three-star flag flying at the yardarm. Later, at sea, as *his* ship began its five-month deployment with TF 77, Clark landed aboard in the "Jersey Bounce" helo for a meeting with task force commander Bob Hickey.

Jocko's superiors had nothing but praise for his steady, outstanding performance. For the final five months of the Korean fighting, Bob Briscoe lauded his "professional know-how" in having provided the maximum striking power of the fleet at the battle line. (Fitness report, 31 August 1953) Felix Stump echoed such praise of "a superior fighting leader dedicated to the purpose of seeking out and destroying the enemies of the U.S." (25 September 1953)

On 5 October Clark received his last order from General Mark Clark— to report to his headquarters in Tokyo. There the senior member of the "Clark Team" presented Jocko with the Army Distinguished Service Medal. The general, embittered by the restraints that had prevented him from winning the war decisively, then returned home, retired, and proclaimed that the A-bomb should be used if the Reds broke the armistice.

Meanwhile, the war in Indochina was heating up, leading CinCPac Felix Stump to request reinforcements in the event that the United States

Always a sailor's admiral, Jocko messes with crewmen in their galley on his final visit to the *Yorktown* during the autumn of 1953. Ulcers long gone, he enjoyed a regular diet, ending his naval career at 185 pounds. *Photo from* On the Line, *the ship's 1953–54 cruise book*

did become involved there in addition to protecting South Korea. Clark's old friends Radford and Mick Carney, CNO since August, and the rest of the JCS approved it. They ordered the A-bomb–equipped First Fleet, with Vice Admiral Sol Phillips taking command in October, moved from California to the western Pacific.

Clark transferred his flag to the battleship *Wisconsin* in mid-October and on 8 November welcomed Carney aboard. Four days later Jocko celebrated his 60th birthday. By then, Vice Admiral Mel Pride was standing by to relieve him in command of the Seventh Fleet.

Jocko had always remembered Admiral Moffett's words, "When you leave, leave with all the flags flying and all the bands playing." That would not be Clark's case if, like most of his contemporaries (Phillips and Pride among them), he enjoyed his final two years on shore duty before reaching the maximum retirement age of 62. The notable exceptions were men who had emerged as Cold War managers and thinkers after World War II combat commands, namely Clark's classmates Felix Stump ('17) and Jerauld

Wright ('18), both younger than he and promoted to four-star rank. Stump commanded the Pacific Fleet for five years (1953–58), Wright the Atlantic Fleet for six (1954–60).

So Jocko decided to end his career while still at sea, with all the flourishes, after 40 years of naval service. On 1 December 1953, on the deck of the *Wisconsin* in Tokyo Bay, J. J. Clark read aloud his last orders to relinquish command—"with a lump in my throat"—and hauled down his flag. To it he added his fourth star—that of full admiral, awarded on the basis of his many combat awards (the so-called tombstone promotion).

A farewell message arrived from Mick Carney—the CNO for whom he had bought whiskey on the eve of his entry into the Naval Academy back in 1913:

> Your fearless and aggressive leadership in battle, and your unswerving adherence to the objective of victory, have engendered the confidence of your comrades in arms and will serve as an inspiration to future generations of Navy men. Well done. Repeat, well done.

Felix Stump gave Jocko all excellent marks on his final fitness report (17 December 1953), including—as a farewell gift—"military bearing and neatness of person and dress"! Stump hailed Clark's "superior leadership and ability in combat with the enemy" as "an inspiration to all personnel who served under your command." The Army's Distinguished Service Medal had justly recognized "his extraordinary contribution to the United Nations in Korea."

Several of America's lesser allies gave him honors: the (South) Korean Medal of Military Merit, Taiguk, with Silver Star; Mexico's Merito Naval Medal; and Peru's Flying Cross.

Henceforth, as with most military retirees, Clark's contact with the Navy would be vicarious. His most direct act to try to influence naval thinking was an article he wrote for *Flying* magazine, "31-Knot Burke." (January 1956, 22–23, 53–56) In it, he praised the 1955 appointment of Mitscher's wartime chief of staff as CNO. Based on his long association with the 53-year-old Arleigh Burke, Jocko hailed his having bypassed the rank of vice admiral, 92 more senior admirals, and seven Naval Academy classes (to '23, succeeding Carney of '16)—"an inspiring precedent for other younger officers." It meant that "merit alone" counted, instead of the plodding "seniority" or good-old-boy system of prewar years. *And,* the CNO need not be an aviator, given such wide experience with aviation as Burke had had.

Clark also took pride in the selection of key men he "helped" along the way to key appointments that he lived to see them attain: George Anderson as CNO succeeding Burke (1961), Roy Johnson becoming Commander Seventh Fleet (1964) and CinCPac (1965), and Tom Moorer also to Seventh Fleet (1962), CinCPac (1964), CinCLant (1965), CNO (1967), and Chairman of the JCS (1970).

The respect of all three of these officers and untold others for their mentor was reciprocal, although Jocko Clark represented the end of an era that had accepted hard-bitten admirals ("hard-bitten" according to *Webster's:* having a hard bite, steeled in battle, marked by severity of character, unyielding, rugged, harsh, rough or coarse in manner or appearance, tough-minded, hard-boiled, free of illusions, practical).

Raöul Waller told me, "I learned more under Jocko than any other officer under whom I served in my life." Yet postwar Rear Admiral Jig Dog Ramage took a minority, but occasionally shared, opposite view: "Jocko bordered on ridiculous. But that's why we have horse races." (Undated letter to author) (By contrast, Ramage, like many pilots, regarded John Crommelin of unification ill fame "as the greatest leader that I know"—in the air.)

George Anderson told me (in 1965), "There was no more dynamic a task force or cardiv commander in the Pacific Fleet during the war than Jocko Clark." Tom Moorer recalled in 1981, "I liked old Jocko," with whom "I went fishing, shooting, etc.," after Clark's retirement.

> He was a very good friend of mine. He was really a unique person. . . . They don't make characters like that anymore, because the system won't tolerate a person of individuality like that. Today, [such behavior] would immediately generate a letter from some sailor or from somebody who would send it back to the Pentagon, up to the Secretary of Defense, maybe over to the White House; a couple of articles in the *Washington Post;* and the fellow would be finished. But he did things like that every day. (Interview #30, 1589, 1591–92, 1594)

As Charles Melhorn put it, "They broke the mold when Admiral Clark retired; he is one of a kind." (Interview, 135)

After four decades of a secure livelihood within the Naval Service, Clark returned home—to Tulsa, Oklahoma—early in 1954 to live in an apartment on guaranteed Navy retirement pay plus free medical services at naval hospitals. But he was the proverbial duck out of water, unable to live comfortably on his fixed income, and still sending $100 a month alimony to first wife M.C. The state of Oklahoma had admitted him into its Hall of Fame in 1952, but that brought him no more income than did his naval reputation.

"Joe's" mother and brother Bill still looked after his daughters Mary Lou and Cathy, then in Texas schools, and he no longer had a wife. In need of supplementary income, sadly, he took a job selling used cars—but failed to make a single sale and gave up.

The problem of bachelorhood was soon remedied when he met and courted another thrice-married divorcee of substantial means. China Robbins Loring, 54, had two sons close in age to his daughters Mary Lou, 19, and Cathy, 18. She was the urbane sophisticate, he the Cherokee-weaned celebrity veteran. Jocko soon relocated to New York to be close to her and became an active member in the New York Yacht Club, New York Athletic Club, and Chevy Chase Club. Personal appearances included being a guest on the *Tex and Jinx* radio show on 19 July 1954; the host, Tex McCrary, was the older brother of his wartime staff officer.

Jocko and China were married at the Drake Hotel in Chicago in October 1954 and moved into a "country club" house in New York, with Clark acquiring an executive position—vice president of the Radio Receptor Company in New York. He soon moved, however, to Alaska Airlines as chairman of the board and then to Dominican Shipbuilding and Drydock Company. Joe's kinfolk found the new wife "real nice" when he brought her to the annual summer family reunions in Chelsea. (Conversation with sister Virginia Clark Easley)

Apparently the happiest of Clark's several marriages, this one was accompanied by family changes. Youngest daughter Cathy moved quickly into adulthood. She started by accepting her given first name in place of her middle name, Carol, which she had preferred as a child. Still beset by emotional and apparently drug-related physical problems, she married in 1956 at age 20 and soon had a baby daughter. Her problems worsened, divorce followed, and Jocko simply failed to cope with her difficulties or to help her—to the dismay of his other kinfolk.

Mother Lillie Belle died in May 1958 at age 85, whereupon her oldest daughters kept the spread-out family connected. The annual reunion was centered around the same family table, eventually enlarged to 17 leaves. Mary Lou, Jocko's older daughter, married in 1959 at age 24, and by 1963 she had two daughters of her own before divorcing. Clark loved them all but—having been "wedded to the sea"—lacked the interest or knowledge to give them advice or financial support. And he eventually cut off his monthly alimony payments to first wife M.C., whose maladies and addiction steadily worsened, and she lacked the means to challenge him.

Jocko instead became active in numerous patriotic and veterans organizations, notably a term as national commander, Naval Order of the United States, and one year as commander of the New York chapter of Military Order of the World Wars. A great raconteur possessed of a razor-sharp memory, he became a popular public speaker before these and other organizations, including the Boy Scouts and Sea Scouts. Once asked why he devoted so much time to such endeavors, he explained, "I'm paying back my debt to America." (Quoted in the *Chelsea Reporter*, 18 May 1972)

Between the speeches and the memories Clark conceived the idea—sometime during the mid-1950s—of writing an autobiography devoted exclusively to his outstanding naval career. To help him write it, he approached several authors, some of whom agreed to do it. But they never followed through. Apparently—as Raöul Waller guessed—they were waiting for him to die and then do a biography on their own. At this stage in Clark's life I became involved (see the preface). During my first visit with him in September 1959 I urged him to start committing his experiences to paper. "I will try," he said, "to jot down anything I can for future use." (Letter to me, 17 September 1959)

Columbia University soon initiated its oral history program and solicited Clark's participation. Enthused, in 1962 he gave them several interview sessions. Clark's reward was a copy of the complete 840-page transcript of his candid reminiscences. About 1965 the Naval Photographic Center in Washington interviewed him on camera and tape recorder for an unrealized motion picture (his words have finally been utilized, however, on the CD accompanying this book).

One month after my graduation from college I wrote to him about my interest in interviewing him about the wartime fast carriers before I headed off to graduate school at Duke University. He agreed in a card from the Bohemian Club in San Francisco (21 July 1961), where he was attending his first (invited) "annual summer encampment" of national leaders brainstorming major issues of the day.

He telephoned my Uncle Bob, and on 24 July we three met at my parents' home in San Gabriel, a suburb of Los Angeles, to discuss the war and his prospective autobiography. Apparently, whatever doubts he had about this unpublished graduate student becoming his "ghostwriter" were dispelled when he received the December 1961 issue of the *U.S. Naval Institute Proceedings*. It contained my very first published professional article—an account of the carrier *Saratoga*'s joint operations with the British Eastern Fleet in the Indian Ocean during the spring of 1944. And, it was based on interviews and correspondence with Air Group 12's wartime skipper, Rear Admiral J. C. "Jumpin' Joe" Clifton, and his pilots—the same type of sources I planned to utilize for Clark's book.

"Last night," he wrote in a Christmas card (15 December 1961), "I read your 'Sara in the East' with great interest. It is very well written and I am now certain that you can do a tip top job on my book." The same mail had brought him a note from me suggesting that we meet during the summer and get under way. He agreed, "I will be glad to work with you any way I can."

Alas, however, the heavy demands of graduate school prevented me from getting started on his book until after I received my doctorate. He accepted that but nevertheless invited me to be his guest for the Armed Forces Day parade in New York on 19 May 1962. I was able to squeeze it into my schedule and thereby got a heady dose of his "presence" in the New York social scene.

The stirring parade swung down Fifth Avenue, with Jocko riding near the head in "Car A." Afterward, we attended that evening's sumptuous black-tie banquet and ball of the Military Order of the World Wars at the Waldorf-Astoria Hotel. He introduced me as the collaborator "of my book" to Mayor Robert Wagner, General Leslie Groves of Manhattan Project atomic bomb fame, and other dignitaries. General Van Fleet was also present. Very heady stuff for me, yet I intended to keep my promise to collaborate.

But not all was well with Jocko. He had bought a home in suburban Pelham Manor, Westchester County, where I spent the weekend with him. We perused his private papers (mostly wartime action reports), and he spilled out much about his past marital woes. He did not discuss wife China, who I did not know was about to divorce him. Her two urbane sons had little regard for his Oklahoma demeanor (one of them sold this West Coast neophyte his tuxedo for the banquet—for 15 bucks!). And Jocko's girls had found their counterparts "pleasant but cold."

Indeed, China took me aside at one point while we three were in the city. In a threatening tone that left me—all of 22 years old—almost speechless, she said that I had better write a best seller because "he needs the money." She soon divorced him per a prenuptial agreement. It left him "heartbroken." (Conversations with Mary Lou Clark in 2003–4)

Typically, the aging warrior recovered. In the mid-1960s he became chairman of the board at Hegeman-Harris, a construction and investment firm in the city. He closely followed the ominous events shaking the nation and the world—the Cuban Missile Crisis, the assassination of President John F. Kennedy, and the escalation of America's involvement in Vietnam (the denouement from the 1954 fall of French Indochina to the Communist Vietminh). In order to get around the city by car, he arranged to have an inactive but very willing Naval Reserve lieutenant commander serve as his driver and personal aide—Walter F. J. Wemyss (pronounced "Weems"). And he met Olga.

Russian-born, Olga Evgenyevna Choubaroff was 65 when Clark turned 70 in late 1963. She had an exotic past. Like Jocko's wives Shannon and China, she had been married three times. Her first husband was an officer in the White Russian army with whom she had fled from the Red Army in 1920. After Jocko's death she claimed to have met Clark in Constantinople when he was on the *Brooks*—perhaps an apocryphal story. She was next married to the renowned Cuban world chess champion and diplomat José Raul Capablanca from 1938 until his death in 1942. Later she wed a much younger Olympic rower. Quite the aloof beauty in her day, the childless Olga proved as feisty and outspoken as Jocko. (Information from jacklummus.com)

Clark met her through the well-known former New York Congressman Hamilton Fish III, a widower who at the time was "dating" Olga's sister Marie C. Blackton. The two couples summered together in a beach house at Tom's River, New Jersey. Olga claimed she married Jocko in 1965 in the chapel at nearby NAS Lakehurst, but another source says it was 1967. I spent a research weekend with them and assorted relatives in July 1965, and they "acted" married. On that occasion Jocko, however, awkwardly whispered to me that Ham Fish and Marie were secretly married, perhaps intimating the same situation for himself and Olga to explain why the two otherwise "morally correct" couples were cohabiting.

The four were indeed strange bedfellows (pun unintended). Fish had valid military credentials, having led black companies of the famous 369th Infantry Regiment in the heaviest American fighting of World War I. (Harris, *Harlem's Hell Fighters*) He had become a civil rights advocate, unlike Clark. Politically, Fish had been an urbane FDR-hating, isolationist, conservative Republican as against the agrarian, FDR-admiring, internationalist lifelong Democrat Clark.

Hothead Olga—unlike her quiet sister Marie—profoundly embarrassed Jocko when during my visit she loudly proclaimed she was glad President Kennedy had been shot, saying, "He deserved it!" ("Don't listen to her," Jocko muttered to me.)

In 1967 Fish and Marie were openly married. The two couples purchased a Park Avenue upper-story two-apartment home connected by a hallway. The arrangement was altered only by Marie's death three years later.

This somewhat turbulent home life did not deter Jocko from pursuing his quest to write his memoirs. He hired a literary agency to find a publisher for the proposed autobiography.

He achieved success late in 1964, just as I was beginning my college teaching career at the Naval Academy in Annapolis. The contract was signed with the David McKay Company on 29 January 1965. Jocko received an advance of $4,000, and I got $2,000 as collaborator. The company's outspoken president, Kennett L. Rawson, and its sage executive editor, Howard S.

Cady, sufficiently liked the few writing samples that I had given them to regard me as "probably more qualified than anyone else to make it the book it should be." (Cady letter to me, 4 January 1965)

Jocko wanted to title the book simply that—"Jocko." Unfortunately, he was scooped by the well-known baseball umpire Jocko Conlan, whose memoirs (written with Robert Creamer) were entitled *Jocko* (1967). The working title was "Carrier Command," which evolved into *Carrier Admiral.*

I went to work on a rough draft immediately, utilizing the Columbia University transcript, Clark's action reports, and our conversations, and in late February Clark made the first of several visits to Annapolis to discuss our work. His desire to exploit the Academy's resources eventually caused problems for the administration, which could not deny his wishes for VIP treatment, as a four-star admiral, during each visit.

Ere long, as soon as he would appear, the word went out: "Get Reynolds!" (to take him off their backs). I soon received a firsthand sampling of how my Uncle Bob had felt as his wartime flag lieutenant.

That was tolerable, often even enjoyable, whereas Clark's penchant for rewriting every draft chapter that I sent him was decidedly not. Howard Cady observed that the admiral "wants to be as blunt and outspoken as he is" personally. Also, "his staccato prose" revealed a tendency "to be allergic to long sentences," and he is "unable to restrain himself from rewriting everything he sees." Ken Rawson also preferred my style to Jocko's and told him so. And Cady informed me of Clark's "comparing your style with that of [Winston] Churchill" (a backhanded compliment). In response to my expressions of frustration, Cady counseled me not to share my feelings with Jocko, lest he "feel you are trying to push him around." (Cady letters, 20, 23 April, 14 May, 6 August, 29 September 1965)

Whenever possible I interviewed Clark's close wartime associates; I enjoyed one unexpected, but particularly delightful, incident. On 4 May 1966—three weeks after a Jocko visit—the Academy superintendent, Rear Admiral Draper L. Kauffman, whose wartime leadership had been in underwater demolition ("frogman"), invited my wife and me as additional dinner guests with Admiral Radford and his wife Mariam. After the meal, the six of us got around to discussing Jocko, whereupon Mariam—a red-headed pistol of a gal—launched into a marvelously funny parody of Olga with her Russian accent: "Oh Jocko, oh Jocko, etc. . . ." I laughed uproariously at her vivid imitation (the two admirals were embarrassed).

Clark's continual changes to the manuscript—he would always rewrite my drafts, and I his—led the exasperated publisher to consider changing the book from an autobiography to a general account about "carrier warfare." But passions cooled, and Rawson spent late summer 1966 meeting with the

Admiral and fine-tuning the manuscript. In late August, Jocko, Bob, and I attended the *Yorktown* reunion at Long Beach. Only after that did I learn that Rawson was eliminating the chapters about the period before Clark had entered flight training in 1924, except for his earlier contacts with naval aviators. This (regrettable) change was made in order to seize the reader's attention at the outset. Also, the book had given Jocko's life new meaning, and he was trying to prolong its completion. But he had met his match in Rawson, who was determined to expedite its publication.

Simultaneously, Dwight Barnes had written a short general manuscript for publication called *Sea Power and Its Meaning*. Its publisher, Franklin Watts, asked Clark to add his name to it to enhance sales. Unfortunately, Jocko could not resist altering this manuscript too. So, he informed me, "as it turned out, I wrote a large part of and worked over all of the book, so I am in fact a co-author." (Letter, 6 October 1966) It appeared during the autumn.

In November, with *Carrier Admiral* going to press, Clark and his aide Wally Wemyss embarked on the carrier *Ticonderoga* in Hawaii for "Yankee Station," the Seventh Fleet's operating waters off the coast of Vietnam. They observed fast carrier operations in the war raging there, enabling Jocko to add brief reflections about the conflict to the last chapter. During his absence, the David McKay editors solicited Admiral Radford to provide a foreword for the book. I agreed to write a draft of it, to which Raddy affixed his name. Jocko thought it "excellent." (Letter, 16 February 1967— the first of most of his subsequent communications to me written with a thick blue felt-tip pen on both sides of a 4 x 6 note card having the crest of a four star admiral's flag.)

Clark could be a "stinker" when it suited him. On his own he sent an excerpt of the book (dealing with the Marianas Turkey Shoot) to be published in *American Heritage* (October 1967) without my name in the byline. He claimed that he *had* included my name, leaving the journal's editor Oliver Jensen the culprit, which may well have been true. (Letter, 12 October 1967)

Then, in the acknowledgments section of the book (in which he gave my middle initial as "E," incorrectly), Clark recognized my part as only having "rendered invaluable assistance to me in the writing of this book by assembling the subject matter and arranging it in chronological order."

Suffice it to say, in his shoes I would have been tempted to do the same thing. After all, he was the great war hero and I—even though a junior partner—a veritable nobody who only suffered a bruised ego from this slight.

Howard Cady had Clark autograph my copy of *Carrier Admiral,* hot off the press in early October 1967. Howard sent it to me with a covering letter on the 10th, noting "I am sure you will be pleased with what he has written."

6 October 1967

> To Dr. Clark G. Reynolds, my collaborator without whose untiring research and painstaking labor there never would have been a book. With high admiration and esteem from his friend, J. J. "Jocko" Clark

"It is lamentable," Cady continued, "he could not have been equally enthusiastic in the 'Acknowledgments' section." Indeed, Jocko's slighting of my role so irritated the soft-spoken Cady that he tried twice to convince Jocko to eliminate the paragraph from the acknowledgments section on the second printing, but, "he absolutely refuses to do so."

Cady wisely advised me not to "make an issue of it or, for that matter, to make an issue in connection with anything that has to do with Admiral Clark. Let it go"—which I did—"and don't worry about it"—which I didn't, and the bruise quickly healed. (Letter, 19 October 1967)

In fact, when the first bound copy reached Jocko's hands, one look at the dust jacket and binding revealed what was clearly intended to be a slap on Jocko's wrist by the editors for all the aggravation he had caused them—*and* a nice plum for me as well for having persevered. Neither Clark nor our editors ever said anything about this item to me: The contract stipulated that in the byline, my name was to appear under Clark's and at half the print size on the cover and binding, including the spine (which all library users see on the shelves). On the spine, above the title of the book, the name "CLARK" is placed, with "Reynolds" at half-size directly under CLARK. Voilà! "CLARK Reynolds"—as if *I* were the sole author.

Jocko must have been furious, hence his adamancy not to change the acknowledgment section. As for myself, I endeavored to keep the peace as collaborator by personally autographing an extra copy of the book to him as the true author. This delighted him. (Letter, Clark to Reynolds, 27 November 1967) Jocko held no grudges. Two years later (20 August 1969) he wrote to me, "My best to Howard Cady. I rate him very highly." And I did not forget Howard Cady's sage editorial work and was later pleased to work with him again on a book of my own at another publishing house. (*Command of the Sea: The History and Strategy of Maritime Empires*, William Morrow, 1974)

Jocko and I had an additional bond of sorts—the revision of my doctoral dissertation into book form as *The Fast Carriers: The Forging of an Air Navy*, in which he obviously figured as a key player. He provided a photograph of himself for it, but otherwise I had no reason to call upon him for this work. Its completion was already in sight by McGraw-Hill for one year hence—late 1968.

The publication of *Carrier Admiral* marked the opening gun of Clark's personal campaign to promote sales. The book's appearance at the start of the 1967 Christmas season helped. By mid-December he could write ecstatically, "It is going great—selling like hot cakes." (Letter, 11 December 1967) This he knew firsthand, by crossing the country to visit book stores, first in New York, then on to New Orleans, Houston, Dallas, Tulsa, San Francisco, and San Diego.

"So we have a best seller," he let me know, "but McKay's sales force is dragging their feet. . . . I have sold over 1,100 copies." This included several books he autographed and sent personally to many friends and former shipmates—with the $6.95 bill of sale (plus tax) enclosed. An obviously incredulous Admiral George Anderson—recently retired from a second career as ambassador to Portugal—did not reply immediately. When Jocko pressed him, Andy allowed that the book must have gotten lost in the mail. So Jocko sent him another one. (Clark letter to me, 6 January 1968)

Book reviews were generally favorable. The most extensive, thoughtful, and honest one was titled "Candid Jocko" by Walter Lord in the *New York Times Book Review*. (19 November 1967) Lord had written sea-oriented best sellers under Howard Cady's editorship—*A Night to Remember* about the *Titanic* and *Day of Infamy* on the Pearl Harbor attack. He roundly praised *Carrier Admiral*, except for Clark's almost "needless cruelty" describing Miles Browning, certain admirals, and the officers of the first *Yorktown*—as opposed to too much self-praise. Clark likely complained to Lord, who quickly sent him "a note . . . further praising my book." (Clark to me, 27 November 1967)

In *BookWorld*'s "Books They Liked Best" for the year 1967 (3 December), Samuel Eliot Morison, whose list consisted solely of autobiographies, ranked *Carrier Admiral* second, after military historian Basil Liddell Hart's *Memoirs* and ahead of diplomat George Kennan's *Memoirs 1925–1950* (a truly classic work). That was after Jocko had sent Morison his own autographed copy, to which the Harvard icon responded, "I . . . have no hesitation in saying that it is in every way the best U.S. admiral's autobiography that has come out of the war." (Morison to Clark, 25 October 1967) But Morison never said that in print.

(Collaborators are rarely mentioned in book reviews. Remarkably, I was: *Carrier Admiral* was "written in monotone by Clark G. Reynolds though in collaboration" with Clark [A. A. Hoehling, *Washington Star*, 12 November 1967]; "Professor Reynolds . . . gets an A-plus for his assist" in this "unique" military memoir [J. Frederick Doughty, *Baltimore Sun*, 3 December 1967]. I preferred the verdict of my graduate school mentor Theodore Ropp who informed questioners that the book "was more Jocko than Clark.")

Jocko pressed the U.S. Naval Institute to review his book in its *Proceedings,* through which word of it would reach the naval officer market. Its editors initially stalled but finally prevailed upon the president of the Naval War College, Vice Admiral John T. "Chick" Hayward, to write it. (Clark to me, 11 December 1967, 6 January 1968)

Hayward, a highly respected naval aviator with a doctorate in physics, had extensive experience both in patrol-bombers and carriers. He pulled no punches. In a three-page review, Hayward accused Clark—"a fighter, outspoken, and controversial"—of blurred vision through hindsight, virtual "self aggrandizement," and incorrect criticism of Halsey's conduct at Leyte Gulf. (*Proceedings,* June 1968, 119–21) This latter item was ironic, he thought, for at *that* time (late 1944) "I would have said that Jocko and Bull [Halsey] were very similar types."

Former *Langley* pilot Hayward agreed with Clark's discussion of early naval aviation but had to agree also with Lawrence Bell's 1941 joke about Jocko: "I've got it. Your halo is too tight!"

Needless to say, Clark was chagrined at this biting review, an advance copy of which the Naval Institute had sent him in May. He fired off a three-page typed letter to Hayward (6 May 1968) written with wit and candor: "Many thanks for the fine objective (?) review. It will sell a lot of books." Jocko answered Hayward's comments with brevity, point by point, including Chick's displeasure with his criticism of others:

> Actually, I think I let them down easy, and I do not have any malice towards any one of them. . . . I get quite a kick out of your clever quip on my "halo." All I can say is if anybody wants to wear a tight halo, let him match my combat score.

Clark sent me a copy of his letter (7 May 1968) with the suggestion that I discuss it with the Naval Institute's director, retired Commander R. T. E. Bowler Jr. "This is going to start a controversy as I do not intend to take it lying down," Jocko wrote. But it did not occur, because the only real incident had already taken place—between Jocko and Chick. "Bud" Bowler, whose office was in the building next to mine on the Naval Academy grounds, only chuckled over it (to me anyway).

In fact, Bowler had let me see Hayward's review in early April as a courtesy, and I had chosen not to alert Clark. But later that month I happened to attend a conference at the Naval War College. During the crowded cocktail hour after an afternoon session, I saw Admiral Hayward—a short man—walk unnoticed into the large room full of milling officers and academics. He headed to the bar. Knowing his reputation as a good-humored and fine fellow, I—all of 6 foot 3—sidled up behind him (he was not talking to anyone), leaned over, and said quietly, "Excuse me, Admiral Hayward, I'm Clark Reynolds."

"Oh Shit!" he bellowed—loud enough to quiet the entire room. Knowing from my name that I was Jocko's collaborator, Hayward was speechless for a moment. Then we both laughed and had a nice chat—to the bewilderment of all hands.

The reaction of the general naval community to the book was positive, one strong indication being a positive five-column book review in *Navy Times* by retired Captain W. W. Armstrong. (3 January 1968, p. 23) Privately, some naval officers responded to the book from a somewhat backhanded perspective. Vice Admiral Fred Pennoyer, a brown shoe, congratulated *me* for "an outstanding, grand job in the narration" of Jocko's book. (Letter, 28 January 1968) "Having known this *Cherokee* tiger most of my life as a close friend and shipmate, there is no question in my mind as to who did the actual writing."

Lloyd Mustin, a black-shoe vice admiral whose father Henry had been an aviation pioneer, found the book "a strange mixture of fact and fiction," sort of a "the war according to Jocko Clark." He regarded many of Clark's "assumptions and implications" as unjustified. A few were "some of the worst heresies that you sometimes hear uttered by the worst type of chip-on-the-shoulder aviator who thinks all the rest of the Navy is down on the aviators or something." For example, Clark's assertion that he had wanted to move his task group in behind the Japanese fleet after the Jimas raid on the eve of the Battle of the Philippine Sea in June 1944 "is pretty subjective nonsense on good old Jocko's part." (Interview #20 in 1973, 779)

Clark assembled a four-page 9 x 11 pamphlet of direct quotes from book reviews and personal letters to him praising his autobiography and his *Sea Power* book and sent it out. It even included an endorsement of *Carrier Admiral* by his own aide Wally Wemyss and a statement by syndicated columnist Bob Considine that "John Paul Jones never said anything more important" about navies than did Clark's *Sea Power*. The flier included an order form to be sent with a check to Clark's own business address.

Jocko's massive mailing out of this blurb was only part of his personal and frankly overpowering marketing offensive. He had an overcoat specially fitted with two pockets, each to hold a copy of *Carrier Admiral*. He would boldly and brazenly introduce himself to complete strangers—such as a fellow customer in line for a teller at a Manhattan bank—and say, "Hello, I'm Admiral Jocko Clark. Would you like to have an autographed copy of my book?"

When the polite victim mumbled anything remotely affirmative, he pulled out a copy, endorsed it with his blue felt-tipped pen to the person by name on the inside front cover, and asked for the $6.50. (Conversation with *Field and Stream* editor George Reiger, one such buyer)

Clark's worst gaffe (known to me) was taking two boxes full of his books aboard a destroyer serving as flagship for VIPs to witness yacht races at Newport, Rhode Island. Clark was so obnoxious peddling his book to other dignitaries on board that the tin can's skipper chased him off the bridge. In June 1968 he peddled the books while participating in a "brass hat huddle" on aviation training procedures at Corpus Christi. (*Corpus Christi Caller*, 14 July 1971)

Jocko even wanted *Carrier Admiral* made into a motion picture to enhance sales, but first he succumbed—as did I—to a will-o'-the-wisp promise of Eugene E. Wilson to involve both of us in a documentary/movie/ television history of "naval air and sea history." Wilson had left naval aviation as a commander in 1929 in order to build airplanes. He had risen to head of United Aircraft Corporation (later United Technologies) before retiring. Both Clark and I visited him separately on his yacht in West Palm Beach over 1967–68 to discuss the project, but it evaporated. Two years later Jocko convinced someone to write a movie script based on his book, but it never matured. (Letters to me, 14, 28 August 1970)

Admiral George Anderson commented on Jocko's "magnum opus" in a letter to me. (8 July 1968) Repeating what he had told me in 1965, Anderson expressed his regret that Clark

> did not see fit to have it written *after* he had gone to the Happy Hunting Ground—and by you rather than as an autobiography. Frankly, it has not gone over well within the Navy family, and his personal efforts to stimulate its sales have provided a broad basis for ridicule and snide comments which might otherwise have been avoided.

Even though the present biography had to wait another 40 years after Anderson's concerns in 1965, my treatment of Clark in *The Fast Carriers*— judging him most favorably in the context of his World War II peers— became known when my book appeared in print at the end of 1968. Anderson was immensely gratified with "your excellent book" as "an outstanding history." (Letter, 6 December 1968) He spent much of the Christmas season reading it in detail, only to be horrified—as was I—by the "grossly unfair" review of it in the *New York Times Book Review* (12 January 1969). The reviewer, Army historian Louis Morton, admired certain aspects of the book but concluded that the aircraft carrier's role in the Korean and

Vietnam wars had been performed "as well or better" by "land-based aviation and the obsolete battleship."

"The battleship is a dead duck," Jocko wrote me (14 January 1969),
acknowledging only that it had been requested by the Marines as useful near
the rugged coastal terrain and jungles of Vietnam. But carriers could do
such tasks even better and much more in "conventional as well as nuclear
wars." Recalling Walter Lord's generally favorable review of *Carrier Admiral* in the *Times*, Clark said that his book "has withstood the test of time
[one year], and I feel yours will too." After many positive reviews of the
book followed Morton's negative one, Jocko remarked that *The Fast Carriers* "should be a textbook for all students of naval aviation." (Letters to me,
3, 13 March 1969)

Although 10,000 copies of *Carrier Admiral* had been sold by the summer of 1969, it did not long survive him, ceasing publication in 1973. *The
Fast Carriers* survived its initial bashing by Morton who, remarkably, was
able to change his estimation of it in print. He gave it the ultimate accolade
for "real value as the definite account, based on primary sources . . . of the
bitter struggle between the well-entrenched battleship admirals and those
who led the fast carrier forces." (*American Historical Review*, December
1970, 2004–5) It too went out of print in 1973 but returned four years later
and has remained available down to the completion of this book (2005).

Clark had a bad fall walking on ice-covered pavement early in 1970—
"not recommended," he kidded his brother John. (Letter, 4 March 1970)
But the injury did not deter him from writing, now about contemporary
affairs. During the summer he added his name to that of his former fire
marshal on the *Yorktown*, Captain Barney Lally, as a "contributing editor"
(writer) of *Counterattack*, an anticommunist preparedness newsletter published in New York.

Though Clark "acknowledged that warfare is the most hideous operation
man can perform against man," remembered Vice Admiral Smoke Strean, a
fellow northeastern Oklahoma native (although not Native American), he
saw "a vast difference in going to war to enslave half of Europe and going to
war to prevent an aggressor from doing just that." An apolitical man,

> Jocko disapproved of the trend of modern education in training too
> many executives and opinion makers and not enough carpenters and
> artificers. He said there must be some dignity in working with one's
> hands since Jesus Christ worked with his. . . . He was no friend of . . .
> [anti-Vietnam War violent] leftists and radicals. He was a great patriot
> and he expected patriotism from all other Americans. (21 October
> 1974 speech)

The ongoing fight for freedom ended for Jocko's gallant "fighting lady" as she headed for the "mothball fleet." He journeyed to Boston with hundreds of his former shipmates for the final decommissioning of the *Yorktown* on 27 June 1970. Continuing her long service policing the western Pacific, she had been reclassified from attack carrier (CVA-10) to antisub carrier (CVS-10) in 1958 and had served as such in TF 77 during the Vietnam War, 1964–68, and thereafter in the Atlantic. She now joined the Reserve Fleet at Bayonne, New Jersey. As Smoke Strean, who had led TF 58's air attack on the Japanese fleet in the Philippine Sea, rose to give the farewell speech, he noticed that "sitting in the front row of the audience was Admiral Clark. She was still his ship." (Strean, Review of *The Fighting Lady, U.S. Naval Institute Proceedings,* July 1987, p. 125)

Two months after the ceremony (31 August 1970), I wrote to Jocko, strongly recommending that he make an effort to see the excellent motion picture *Patton,* which depicted General George S. Patton's role in the European theater of World War II: "George C. Scott portrayed a lot of Jocko in the role. In fact, you and Patton were probably very much alike in the field." (Coincidentally, when I was five I had seen the real Patton in person before I ever saw Jocko—in a June 1945 motorcade through San Gabriel, California, Patton's and my hometown.)

No sooner had Clark seen the film than he began to bill himself as the "Patton of the Pacific"—a moniker already claimed by Army General John R. Hodge for having led troops up to the corps level from Guadalcanal to Okinawa. Still, the title was picked up by the press for Jocko.

He was slowing down but not sufficiently to prevent him from "repaying my debt to America" in patriotic ways. On May Day 1971, while the large but sparsely observed Veterans of Foreign Wars parade moved down Fifth Avenue in the city, Jocko led a secondary VFW miniparade of Boy Scouts, Girl Scouts, and Little League baseball players on a seven-block march through the Bronx. They outnumbered by about one hundred persons the labor, radical, and Communist rally at Union Square. (*New York Times,* 2 May 1971)

Overall, the aged warrior had serious problems. His financial situation, book sales notwithstanding, had never improved beyond the edge of bankruptcy. His marriage to Olga had soured to the point that he contemplated divorce. His injured hip still pained him. And he contracted cancer, likely the result of his lifelong cigarette habit. It tired him sufficiently to check himself in to New York's St. Albans Naval Hospital on 5 June.

Jocko gradually realized the end might be at hand, and he regaled the hospital chaplain, Captain William R. Howard, with his wartime innovation of having placed two chaplains on his ship. Howard was impressed even more by Clark's belief "that the 'Divine Will' could not be neglected, ignored, or changed." (Howard to Clark's sister Mary, 8 October 1971)

Admiral Jocko Clark died at the hospital about sunrise (0700) on 13 July 1971, age 77—not old by Cherokee standards. He was buried with full military honors at Arlington National Cemetery near Washington on the afternoon of the 15th. The long list of honorary pallbearers was headed by Admiral Tom Moorer, chairman of the Joint Chiefs of Staff; Admiral Arthur Radford, former JCS chair; Admiral George Anderson, former Chief of Naval Operations; Vice Admiral Smoke Strean; and Rear Admiral Red Sharp. Many former shipmates from the *Yorktown* similarly paid their last respects to their skipper.

Daughter Mary Lou, having been shabbily treated by Olga, elected not to attend. Nor was she present at the burial of her mother M.C., who died alone the following February in New York City after suffering a broken hip injury. Neither Jocko nor M.C. had known of each other's ailments, or even of the other's presence in the same city. And both died virtually penniless. Jocko was buried beneath an engraved admiral's headstone at Arlington, M.C. in an unmarked pauper's grave.

The first posthumous honor given Clark was as the second inductee into the newly established Cherokee Hall of Fame at the tribal Tsa-La-Gi cultural center south of Tahlequah one year later. Unveiled before Oklahomans and former *Yorktown*ers on 20 May 1972 was an Oklahoma-granite and larger-than-life bust of Clark. Felix deWeldon, World War II naval aviation artist and a friend of Jocko's known for his famous Iwo Jima monument at Arlington, had sculpted it. Rear Admiral Raöul Waller gave the address. (*Cherokee Nation News*, 23 May 1972)

Two years later, the Eastern Band of Cherokees formally named two hitherto unnamed North Carolina peaks in the Great Smoky Mountains National Park for Clark and Confederate General Stand Watie. Smoke Strean spoke at the formal ceremony held at Cherokee, North Carolina, on 5 October 1974. Mt. Clark—elevation 3,854 feet—is located in the Smokemount quadrangle, Swain County, five miles north of Cherokee (35° 32' 50" N–80° 19' 30" W). (*Cherokee One-Feather*, 24 April 1974)

The greatest monument to Clark, however, was the Fighting Lady. In 1975 the state of South Carolina convinced the Navy to transfer the *Yorktown* from the mothball fleet to Charleston Harbor to become flagship of the Patriots Point Naval and Maritime Museum. The carrier was towed from Bayonne to Charleston in June and formally dedicated as a museum ship on 13 October, the 200th anniversary of the Navy. Museum and ship were opened to the public in January 1976—soon to be joined by other vessels. Jocko's ship had been saved for posterity.

A potential Clark legacy occurred in 1977 when a granddaughter by his daughter Cathy entered the Naval Academy from Oklahoma with the class of 1981. But she did not complete the course.

The U.S. Navy bestowed its supreme accolade on Clark by naming a new *Oliver Hazard Perry*-class guided missile frigate after him. On 24 March 1979, the 3,600-ton USS *Clark* (FFG-11) was launched at Bath Iron Works in Maine. Olga was the sponsor, and I was one of the speakers. (The ship served until decommissioned and transferred to the Polish navy in 2000.)

On 15 November 1984, Oklahoma dedicated the stretch of its state Highway 66 that runs through Clark's hometown of Chelsea (between Bushyhead and Whiteoak) as "Admiral Joe (Jocko) Clark Trailways" in "memory and honor" of him. It parallels the Will Rogers Turnpike.

A year later, 11 November 1985, Clark was inducted into the Oklahoma Air and Space Hall of Fame, followed in 1987 with admission into the Carrier Aviation Hall of Fame on board the *Yorktown*.

Steadily and brilliantly, Jocko Clark served his country, the Navy, and the cause of freedom in a superlative manner for 40 years and informally for another 18. In personal, family, and financial matters, however, success eluded him. Suffice to say, he was one of the few hard-hitting American "sea dog" admirals of the twentieth century—in fact, the last.

# Legacy

## *Policing the World, Round Three*

THE LONG SHADOW OF JOCKO CLARK STRETCHED INTO THE future as his fighting lady *Yorktown* stood out of Bayonne, New Jersey, in June 1975 against the backdrop of New York City's Twin Towers, home to the World Trade Center. The ship and Twin Towers were destined for immortality. Under tow, the *Yorktown* was bound for Charleston, South Carolina, to become a museum ship and help preserve the nation's naval heritage.

More than a quarter century later—on 9-11-01—Middle Eastern terrorists destroyed the Twin Towers. They employed kamikaze-style tactics using hijacked commercial airliners there and against the Pentagon in Washington. These attacks by tribal extremists were motivated by fear, ignorance, and thus hatred of the modern civilized world as defined by American hegemony (global leadership):

freedom of speech and assembly
freedom of religion(s)
free market middle-class capitalism
urban culture (cities)
international law and police forces

Jocko Clark had fought similar foes during his naval career. His formal training and skills focused on fighting *modern* Western-style high-technology enemies in the two world wars and the Cold War. The U.S.–led victories in all three had destroyed the dictatorial states and empires of imperial and Nazi Germany, Japan, and the Soviet Union (the latter in 1989–90 without a "hot" conflict).

But he had also learned *on the job* how to fight small-scale conflicts. These had been caused by the collapse of the sprawling authoritarian powers as the

The Fighting Lady *Yorktown* and the World Trade Center Towers. *Photo courtesy of Patriots Point Museum*

freed subject peoples strived to create their own nations after 1918, 1945, and 1990. The result each time has been ensuing political, economic, and social chaos—in Eastern Europe, the Middle East, East Asia, and Africa.

The United States rejected assuming a major role in rebuilding the post–World War I world. But—out of sheer necessity—it took the lead after World War II and again following the Cold War. Americans have had no choice, because freedom and democracy have always been incompatible with—and therefore a threat to—the other basic forms of government: tribal, feudal, monarchy, dictatorship. (See Reynolds, "Democracy versus the Other: Incompatibilities of the Modern World," 15–16)

The Cherokee were one tribal people who had realized that they must end their nomadic ways, become farmers, intermarry outside the tribe, and accept American values. Joe Clark's generation was the first to bear the full fruits of this assimilation and modernization. He himself remains the highest-ranking military officer in American history with strong Indian roots. The United States and the world have become the better for it.

The Fighting Lady and the Twin Towers—and the people who gave their lives there—symbolize the on-going struggle. Leaders like Jocko Clark have had much to teach and to inspire in those who value human freedom in the face of fierce resistance: "Watch for every angle, and fight for every inch."

# ACKNOWLEDGMENTS

THE CAREFUL EDITORIAL, BIBLIOGRAPHICAL, AND TYPING SKILLS and labors of my wife Constance Caine Reynolds made this book a reality. Admiral Clark's eldest daughter Mary Lou generously provided letters from her father to her mother, M.C., and other 1930s and 1940s correspondence of Jocko's as well as information about her family. Captain Gilbert P. Lauzon, USN (Ret.), tirelessly fulfilled his duties as my able research assistant, tracking down and resolving innumerable historical questions. Paul Stillwell of the U.S. Naval Institute provided the invaluable oral history transcripts of Clark's naval associates.

James W. Grimes meticulously and expertly transferred, edited, and improved the quality of my 25- to 40-year-old tape-recorded interviews and those of Clark by the Naval Photographic Center to create the CD that accompanies this book. My historian-daughter Colleen assisted my research on the early Cherokee. Fellow naval aviation historians Steve Ewing, John Lundstrom, and Barrett Tillman generously supplied historical items from their own research. Art Nicholson, who married into the Clark family, provided the spark that initiated the writing of this book.

No previous archive of J. J. Clark papers existed. The admiral kept copies of his action reports from the Yorktown, Task Group 58.1, and the Korean War period Seventh Fleet as well as his 1962 Columbia University Oral History transcript. Identical copies of these action reports are available at the Naval Historical Center, Washington Navy Yard, D.C., the staff of which—especially at the Navy Department Library—was immensely helpful. Clark's letters to first wife M.C. and others, as well as clippings, photographs, and miscellaneous items given me by Mary Lou Clark, have been deposited at the Naval Historical Center.

His widow, Olga, kept Clark's own copies of the above, plus artwork and personal memorabilia. She, however, secretly married a man some 30 years her junior, and they surreptitiously received the admiral's widow's pension until the ruse was uncovered during the mid-1980s. A lien was put on the admiral's items, which were then sold in an estate sale. Olga died in 1994 at 95. Jocko's younger daughter, Cathy, died four years later after a troubled life.

Betty Joe Clark Mayer, Jocko's niece and family archivist, generously provided most of the genealogical materials of the Clark and Berry families, including the information in the above paragraph. (Letters to me, 26 June, 3 November 2001, and telephone conversations) She donated numerous items about her uncle's life collected by her father John to Patriots Point Naval and Maritime Museum in Charleston, South Carolina. Many of them have been displayed there on board the *Yorktown*.

Although U.S. Navy photographers took most of the photographs in the book, curator E. L. Wimett of Patriots Point generously provided fresh prints from its collection for the present work.

Wearing Sioux Indian headress, Fleet Admiral William F. Leahy, chairman of the Joint Chiefs of Staff, and Rear Admiral Jocko Clark celebrate the end of World War II with the Sioux Nation at Yankton, South Dakota, 3 September 1945. *Clark Papers*

# BIBLIOGRAPHY

## DOCUMENTS

**I. Naval Historical Center, Washington Navy Yard, Washington, D.C.**

A. Admiral Joseph James Clark papers

Lucy J. Clark Beatty (sister), "The Clark Family History," manuscript, 1983

Betty Joe Clark Mayer (niece), Pedigree Chart (genealogy) of Clark and Berry families, 2002

J. J. Clark letters to M. C. Clark and relatives, 1932–42

Academy of St. Genevieve-of-the-Pines, Asheville, N.C., transcript of Mary Catherine Wilson (first wife)

Fitness Reports and Medical Records, J. J. Clark, 1919–1953 (originals at National Personnel Records Center, St. Louis)

Miscellaneous papers, clippings, and photographs, including the speech of Vice Admiral B. M. Strean, Cherokee, N.C., 5 October 1974

B. *Yorktown* (CV-10) Action Reports

6 September 1943, "Air Attack on Marcus Island on 31 August 1943"

3 September 1943, Commander Air Group Five

4, 22 September 1943, C. A. Pownall

10 October 1943, "Air Attack on Wake Island on 5 and 6 October 1943"

1 December 1943, "Operation GALVANIC, 19 November to 27 November 1943"

12 December 1943, "Post Galvanic Operation, Attacks on Kwajalein and Wotje Atolls, 4 December 1943"

4 February 1944, Commander Air Group Five, "Combat Report of Attack on Maloelap and Kwajalein Atolls, 29 January–3 February 1944"

C.  Other Reports

Commander Task Group 58.1 Action Report, 6 June to 27 June 1944
Court of Inquiry Proceedings, 4–5 June 1945 Typhoon

## II.  Library of Congress

A.  *Yorktown* log, April 1943–February 1944, June 1944
B.  Commander Carrier Division Five and Thirteen Action Reports, 1944–45
C.  Task force and task group commanders' and ships' logs, Battle of the
Philippine Sea, 20 June 1944: CTF 58, CTG 58.1, CTG 58.2, CTG 58.3,
*Hornet, Bataan, Lexington, Wasp, Essex, Bunker Hill, Belleau Wood,
Enterprise, Oakland, Boston, Reno, Santa Fe, Baltimore, Canberra, San Juan*
D.  CTF 58 Message File, 20 June 1944

## III.  Patriots Point Naval and Maritime Museum, Charleston, South Carolina

Miscellaneous plans of the day, photographs, letters, diaries, taped interviews,
general memorabilia

## DIARIES

Jesse G. Bradley Jr.
Joe E. Chambliss
Raymond F. Gard
John Gray
Harry W. Harrison
Oliver Jensen (private notes)
Charles D. Ridgway III
E. T. Stover, *The Saga of Smokey Stover: From His Diary* (Charleston, S.C.: Tradd
Street Press, 1978), edited by Clark G. Reynolds, and other diary entries sub-
sequently discovered.
C. Roger Van Buren
Alexander Wilding Jr. (copy deposited at the Buehler Library, National Museum of
Naval Aviation, Pensacola, Fla.)
George A. F. Wille

## INTERVIEWS

### I.  U.S. Naval Institute (transcripts), conducted during the 1970s and 1980s

| | |
|---|---|
| George W. Anderson Jr. | Joshua W. Cooper |
| Gerald F. Bogan | Ernest M. Eller |
| Arleigh A. Burke | Truman J. Hedding |

Edwin B. Hooper
Roy L. Johnson
Stephen Jurika Jr.
Cecil S. King
John W. Lee Jr.
Robert W. McNitt
Charles W. Melhorn
Charles L. Melson
Gerald E. Miller

Harold B. Miller
Charles S. Minter Jr.
Thomas H. Moorer
Lloyd M. Mustin
Charles A. Pownall
Alfred Melville Pride
Herbert D. Riley
Malcolm F. Schoeffel
Paul D. Stroop

**II. By Clark G. Reynolds (the author), conducted during the 1960s and 1970s**

Robert L. Alexander
George W. Anderson Jr.
Wallace M. Beakley
Robert W. Bender
Gerald F. Bogan
Henry E. Bolden
William B. Bowie
Cooper Buck Bright
James T. Bryan Jr.
Arleigh A. Burke
James W. Campbell
Joseph James Clark
Mary Lou Clark (daughter)
Charles Coburn
James W. Condit Jr.
Richard E. Drover
Virginia Clark Easley (sister)
Robert E. Eaton
Raymond F. Gard
William Griffin
Harry W. Harrison
Verne W. Harshman
Melvin C. Hoffman
Thomas P. Jeter
Ernest B. Kelly Jr.
George H. Klaus
Joseph R. Kristufek

George J. Largess
Ruth Hope Lessley (cousin)
Dwight Long
Frank J. Losey
Douglas A. McCrary
H. Shackleford Moore
James W. Morrison
Douglas Petty
James W. A. Pickard
Paul E. Pihl
Charles A. Pownall
Ronald Radke
Les Rector
Frank Robert Reynolds
Herbert D. Riley
Jesse Rodriguez
Bernard Rossen (né Rosen)
Raymond N. Sharp
Alexander A. Sims
Walter J. Spiess
Edgar E. Stebbins
Felix B. Stump
Daniel J. Sweeney
Joseph L. Tucker
James J. Vonk
Raymond R. Waller
Thomas Whitney

**III. By miscellaneous interviewers**

A. Columbia University: J. J. Clark (transcript), 1962

B. Naval Photographic Center: J. J. Clark, 1960s

  C.  John J. McClaire Jr.:
      C. H. Duerfeldt
      Evan E. Fickling
      Joseph T. Hazen
      Leonard T. Morse

  D.  Walter Muir Whitehill: Ernest J. King "Comments on Flag Officers," 1949 (Naval Historical Center transcript)

  E.  John B. Lundstrom: William N. Leonard

  F.  Warren R. Omark remarks at "The Marianas Turkey Shoot" Symposium (Clark G. Reynolds, moderator), Pensacola, Fla., 5 May 1994

  G.  Webley Edwards: John Raby ("World News Today" transcript, 12 September 1943)

## LETTERS (TO AUTHOR UNLESS OTHERWISE NOTED)

George W. Anderson Jr.
William D. Beatty (nephew)
Howard S. Cady
J. J. Clark, to M. C. Clark 1932–37; to sister Mary, 1940–41, 1945; to author, 1959, 1961–70; to Tex McCrary, 1970)
Robert E. Clements (to Barrett Tillman)
Roland H. Dale
Virginia Clark Easley (sister)
Dan T. Englehardt
E. E. Fickling
Raymond F. Gard (to his family)
Hugh H. Goodwin
John E. Greenbacker
Joseph W. Hachet (to his family)
Roy L. Johnson
Ernest B. Kelly Jr.
Ruth Hope Lessley (cousin)
Betty Joe (Clark) Mayer (niece)
James E. McCardell
John J. McClaire (regarding Miles Browning)
Marc A. Mitscher (to Admiral Nimitz, in Nimitz Personal Correspondence, Naval Historical Center)
Samuel Eliot Morison (to Clark)
Chester W. Nimitz (to Admiral Halsey, in Nimitz Personal Correspondence)
Frederick W. Pennoyer Jr.
John Raby
J. D. Ramage
H. E. Regan

F. Robert Reynolds (and to my parents)
James S. Russell
Raymond A. Spruance
E. E. Stebbins
Paul Stillwell
Barrett Tillman
Charles A. Turner
Alexander Wilding Jr.


## MOTION PICTURES AND TELEVISION SERIES

*The Fighting Lady.* Twentieth Century Fox, 1944.
*Task Force.* Warner Brothers, 1949.
*Victory at Sea* (television series). National Broadcasting Company, 1952.
*Wing and a Prayer.* Twentieth Century Fox, 1944.


## PUBLISHED SOURCES

Alexander, Jack. "They Sparked the Carrier Revolution," *Saturday Evening Post* 217, no. 2 (September 16, 1944): 9–11, 46–52.

Barlow, Jeffrey G. *The Revolt of the Admirals: The Fight for Naval Aviation, 1945–1950.* Washington, D.C.: Naval Historical Center, 1994.

Bogan, Gerald F. "Kamikazes, Typhoons, and the China Sea." In *Carrier Warfare in the Pacific,* edited by E. T. Wooldridge, 239–42.

Braisted, William R. "Mark Lambert Bristol: Naval Diplomat Extraordinary of the Battleship Age." In *Admirals of the New Steel Navy,* edited by James C. Bradford, 331–73. Annapolis: Naval Institute Press, 1990.

Bruce, Roy W., and Charles R. Leonard. *Crommelin's Thunderbirds: Air Group 12 Strikes the Heart of Japan.* Annapolis: Naval Institute Press, 1994.

Bryan, Joseph, III, and Philip Reed. *Mission Beyond Darkness.* New York: Duell, Sloan, and Pearce, 1945.

Buell, Harold L. "Death of a Captain [Browning]." *U.S. Naval Institute Proceedings* (February 1986): 92–96.

Buell, Thomas B. "Oral Histories Help Tell the Tale." *U.S. Naval Institute Proceedings* (July 1994): 44–48.

———. *The Quiet Warrior: A Biography of Admiral Raymond A. Spruance.* Boston: Little, Brown, 1974.

Burke, A. A. "The First Battle of the Philippine Sea: Decision Not to Force an Action on the Night of 18–19 June 1944." Informal typed reflections. Ann Arbor, Mich.: University Microfilms, n.d. [ca. 1945].

Cagle, Malcolm, and Frank Manson. *Sea War in Korea.* Annapolis: U.S. Naval Institute, 1957.

Calloway, Colin G. *First Peoples: A Documentary Survey of American Indian History.* Boston: Bedford/St. Martin's, 1999.

Clark, Gladys Engbrock. *The Family of William Andrew Clark and Wife, Lillie Belle Berry*. N.p.: Privately printed, 1985.

Clark, J. J. "The Marianas Turkey Shoot." *American Heritage* 18, no. 9 (October 1967): 26–29, 92–94.

Clark, J. J., with Clark G. Reynolds. *Carrier Admiral*. New York: David McKay, 1967.

———. "31-Knot Burke." *Flying* 58 (January 1956): 22–23, 53–56.

"Clark, Joseph James." *Current Biography 1954*.

Cressman, Robert. *That Gallant Ship: USS* Yorktown *(CV-5)*. Missoula, Mont.: Pictorial Histories, 1985.

Cunningham, Frank. *General Stand Watie's Confederate Indians*. Norman: University of Oklahoma Press, 1998 [1959].

Evans, David C., and Mark R. Peattie. *Kaigun: Strategy, Tactics, and Technology in the Imperial Japanese Navy, 1887–1941*. Annapolis: Naval Institute Press, 1997.

Ewing, Steve. *Reaper Leader: The Life of Jimmy Flatley*. Annapolis: Naval Institute Press, 2002.

Foley, Francis D. "Searching for Amelia." In *The Golden Age Remembered*, edited by Wooldridge, 203–19.

Frank, Pat, and Joseph D. Harrington. *Rendezvous at Midway*. New York: John Day, 1967.

Gamble, Bruce D. "First Mission Blues—The Story of Rear Admiral James W. Condit, USNR (Ret)." *Foundation*, pt. 1 (spring 2002), 22–31; pt. 2 (fall 2002), 9–19.

Gray, William P. "'Jocko' Clark." *Life* (January 22, 1945), 41–48.

Grossnick, Roy. *United States Naval Aviation, 1910–1995*. Washington, D.C.: Government Printing Office, 1997.

Harris, Stephen L. *Harlem's Hell Fighters: The African-American 369th Infantry in World War I*. Washington, D.C.: Brassey's, 2003.

Hayward, John T. Review of *Carrier Admiral*. *U.S. Naval Institute Proceedings* (June 1968): 119–21.

Jensen, Oliver. *Carrier War*. New York: Pocket Books, 1945.

Johnson, Roy L. "The *Hornet*, Jocko, and Typhoons." In *Carrier Warfare in the Pacific*, edited by Wooldridge, 243–46.

Ketchum, Richard M. *Will Rogers: His Life and Times*. New York: American Heritage, 1973.

King, Cecil S. "Reflections of a Patriot." In *Carrier Warfare in the Pacific*, edited by Wooldridge, 276–86.

King, Ernest J., and Walter Muir Whitehill. *Fleet Admiral King*. New York: W. W. Norton, 1952.

Lee, Fitzhugh. "First Cruise of the *Essex*." In *Carrier Warfare in the Pacific*, edited by Wooldridge, 106–14.

*Lucky Bag* (midshipman yearbook). Annapolis: United States Naval Academy, 1914, 1915, 1916, 1917, 1918, 1927, 1936.

Lundstrom, John B. *The First Team: Pacific Naval Air Combat from Pearl Harbor to Midway.* Annapolis: Naval Institute Press, 1984.

Markey, Morris. *Well Done! An Aircraft Carrier in Action.* New York: D. Appleton-Century, 1945.

Messimer, Dwight R. *No Margin for Error: The U.S. Navy's Transpacific Flight of 1925.* Annapolis: Naval Institute Press, 1981.

Moorer, Thomas H. "The End of an Era." In *The Golden Age Remembered,* edited by Wooldridge, 263–73.

Morton, Louis. Review of *The Fast Carriers. American Historical Review* (December 1970): 2004–5.

"Olga Choubaroff Clark." Available online jacklummus.com.

Reynolds, Clark G. *Admiral John H. Towers: The Struggle for Naval Air Supremacy.* Annapolis: Naval Institute Press, 1991.

———. "Democracy versus the Other: Incompatibilities of the Modern World." *Historically Speaking* 3, no. 4 (April 2002): 15–16.

———. *The Fast Carriers: The Forging of an Air Navy.* New York: McGraw-Hill, 1968; Annapolis: Naval Institute Press, 1992.

———. *The Fighting Lady: The New Yorktown in the Pacific War.* Missoula, Mont.: Pictorial Histories, 1986.

———. "Forrest Percival Sherman." In *The Chiefs of Naval Operations,* edited by Robert William Love Jr., 208–32, 411–15. Annapolis: Naval Institute Press, 1980.

———. *Navies in History.* Annapolis: Naval Institute Press, 1998.

———. "Submarine Attacks on the Pacific Coast, 1942." *Pacific Historical Review* 33, no. 2 (May 1964): 183–93.

———. "The Truth about Miles Browning." In *"A Glorious Page in Our History": The Battle of Midway,* edited by Robert J. Cressman et al., 214–16. Missoula, Mont.: Pictorial Histories, 1990.

———. "The U.S. Fleet-in-Being Strategy of 1942." *Journal of Military History* 58, no. 1 (January 1994): 103–18.

———. "William A. Moffett: Steward of the Air Revolution." In *Admirals of the New Steel Navy, 1880–1930,* edited by James C. Bradford, 374–92. Annapolis: Naval Institute Press, 1990.

Scarborough, William E. "Fighting Two—The Flying Chiefs, Part One, 1927–1941." *The Hook* 19, no. 2 (summer 1991): 16–35.

Small, William A. *The Johnnys, Jocko, Tiger and Me.* Privately published, 2004.

Stillwell, Paul. *Battleship New Jersey.* Annapolis: Naval Institute Press, 1986.

Strange, Hubert Ellis. *A Full Life: An Autobiography.* Hyattsville, Md.: privately published, 1980.

Strean, Bernard M. Review of *The Fighting Lady. U.S. Naval Institute Proceedings* (July 1987): 125.

Taussig, Betty Carney. *A Warrior for Freedom* [Robert B. Carney]. Manhattan, Kan.: Sunflower University Press, 1995.

Thach, J. S. "A Beautiful Silver Waterfall." In *Carrier Warfare in the Pacific*, edited by Wooldridge, 49–65.

Trimble, William F. *Admiral William A. Moffett: Architect of Naval Aviation*. Washington, D.C.: Smithsonian Institution Press, 1994.

van Deurs, George. *Anchors in the Sky: Spuds Ellyson, the First Naval Aviator*. San Raphael, Calif.: Presidio Press, 1978.

Wildenberg, Thomas. *All the Factors of Victory: Admiral Joseph Mason Reeves and the Origins of Carrier Airpower*. Washington, D.C.: Brassey's 2003.

Wooldridge, E. T., Jr., ed. *Carrier Warfare in the Pacific*. Washington, D.C.: Smithsonian Institution Press, 1993.

———. *The Golden Age Remembered*. Annapolis: Naval Institute Press, 1998.

———. *Into the Jet Age: Conflict and Change in Naval Aviation, 1945–1975*. Annapolis: Naval Institute Press, 1995.

## UNIQUE SOURCE

### "Change the Name of Arkansas"

During 1965–66, while teaching at the U.S. Naval Academy and writing Clark's book with him, I expressed frustration to a first class (senior) midshipman that nowhere could I find the words to this infamous and long-forgotten poem. He replied, "Leave it to me." A few days later he handed me a freshly written note containing the words.

He had ordered a plebe that he was "running" to obtain a copy. Because the poem had not been part of the hazing repertoire for many years, the plebe had sought out a retired alumnus in the Annapolis area who remembered and recited it to the plebe, who jotted it down. I believe this is its first appearance in print (but I claim no copyright!).

# INDEX

# ABOUT THE AUTHOR

CLARK G. REYNOLDS is a recognized authority on the fast carriers of World War II and of naval history in general. After collaborating on Jocko Clark's autobiography, he wrote *The Fast Carriers: The Forging of an Air Navy*, *The Fighting Lady*, and the biography *Admiral John H. Towers: The Struggle for Naval Air Supremacy*, for which he received the Samuel Eliot Morison Award from the Naval Order of the United States and the John Lyman Award from the North American Society for Oceanic History. The Naval Aviation Museum Foundation gave him the Admiral Arthur W. Radford Award for excellence in naval aviation history and literature.

The broader works of Dr. Reynolds include *History and the Sea, Command of the Sea: The History and Strategy of Maritime Empires*, *Navies in History*, and *Famous American Admirals*. He has taught at the U.S. Naval Academy, the University of Maine, the U.S. Merchant Marine Academy, and the College of Charleston, where he received the singular faculty distinguished teaching and research awards for 1999 and is now distinguished professor emeritus of history. His academic degrees are in history: B.A., University of California, Santa Barbara (1961) and M.A., Ph.D., Duke University (1963, 1964).

Dr. Reynolds lives with his wife and professional helpmate of more than forty years, Connie, in North Carolina. They have three children, one of whom is a budding historian in her own right.